THE CAMBRIDGE HISTORY OF MEDIEVAL PHILOSOPHY

The Cambridge History of Medieval Philosophy comprises over fifty specially commissioned essays by experts on the philosophy of this period. Starting in the late eighth century, with the renewal of learning some centuries after the fall of the Roman Empire, a sequence of chapters takes the reader through developments in many and varied fields, including logic and language, natural philosophy, ethics, metaphysics, and theology. Close attention is paid to the context of medieval philosophy, with discussions of the rise of the universities and developments in the cultural and linguistic spheres. A striking feature is the continuous coverage of Islamic, Jewish, and Christian material. There are useful biographies of the philosophers, and a comprehensive bibliography. The volumes illuminate a rich and remarkable period in the history of philosophy and will be the authoritative source on medieval philosophy for the next generation of scholars and students alike.

ROBERT PASNAU is Professor of Philosophy, University of Colorado, Boulder. His publications include *Theories of Cognition in the Later Middle Ages* (1997), *The Cambridge Translations of Medieval Philosophical Texts*, vol. III: *Mind and Knowledge* (2002), and *Thomas Aquinas on Human Nature: A Philosophical Study of Summa Theologiae, 1a 75–89* (2002).

The Cambridge History of
Medieval Philosophy

Volume I

EDITED BY
ROBERT PASNAU

ASSOCIATE EDITOR
CHRISTINA VAN DYKE

CAMBRIDGE
UNIVERSITY PRESS

CAMBRIDGE UNIVERSITY PRESS
Cambridge, New York, Melbourne, Madrid, Cape Town, Singapore, São Paulo,
Delhi, Dubai, Tokyo

Cambridge University Press
The Edinburgh Building, Cambridge CB2 8RU, UK

Published in the United States of America by Cambridge University Press, New York

www.cambridge.org
Information on this title: www.cambridge.org/9780521866729

© Cambridge University Press 2010

First published 2010

Printed in the United Kingdom at the University Press, Cambridge

A catalogue record for this publication is available from the British Library

Library of Congress Cataloguing in Publication data
The Cambridge history of medieval philosophy / Robert Pasnau, editor ; Christina Van Dyke,
associate editor.
p.   cm.
Includes bibliographical references and index.
ISBN 978-0-521-76216-8 (v. 1 : hardback) – ISBN 978-0-521-86672-9 (set : hardback)   1. Philosophy,
Medieval–History.   I. Pasnau, Robert.   II. Dyke, Christina van, 1972–   III. Title.
B721.C355   2009
189 – dc22   2009032501

Volume I ISBN 978-0-521-76216-8
Available only as a set: ISBN 978-0-521-86672-9 Hardback

CONTENTS

v

VI Ethics

PREFACE

The present pair of volumes succeeds, without superseding, *The Cambridge History of Later Medieval Philosophy*, published in 1982 by Norman Kretzmann, Anthony Kenny, Jan Pinborg, and Eleonore Stump. It is a considerable privilege to edit the successor to Kretzmann *et alii*, for that volume distils the work of a brilliant generation of scholars without whom our own scholarly careers would be almost inconceivable. These volumes are entirely new, but we expect their predecessor will remain valuable for many years to come, especially for its detailed treatment of medieval theories of logic and the philosophy of language.

The present volumes differ most notably from their predecessor in three ways: first, their scope extends not just to Christian but also to Islamic and Jewish thought; second, they cover not only the later Middle Ages but also earlier centuries; third, they address in some detail the entire spectrum of medieval thought, including philosophical theology.

Each chapter in these volumes stands on its own, but there are numerous points of contact between chapters, and we have liberally supplied cross-references. One could thus in principle begin reading anywhere and eventually, by following these links, make one's way through the whole. Readers will also want to consult the biographies of medieval authors, in Appendix C, for extensive information on the lives and work of the figures discussed in the chapters.

It would be difficult to exaggerate the challenge posed by editing this disparate material, and we are all too conscious of our limitations in this regard. Our primary debt of gratitude is, of course, to our international team of contributors, who generously set aside their own projects to work on this collaborative venture, submitted their chapters in an unusually timely fashion, and then responded graciously to the complex process of editing. We are also grateful to Hilary Gaskin at Cambridge University Press for her support of this venture. Christina Van Dyke's work on these volumes was underwritten in part by a year-long sabbatical from Calvin College, and by further support from the College of Arts and Sciences at the University of Colorado. Special thanks go to Peter Adamson and Dimitri Gutas for their extensive advice regarding Arabic material, and to Matthew Campono, an undergraduate at the University of Colorado at Boulder, who volunteered a great deal of his time to help with the biographical and bibliographical material.

CONTRIBUTORS

PETER ADAMSON
Department of Philosophy
King's College, London

JAN A. AERTSEN
Thomas-Institut
Universität zu Köln

ROGER ARIEW
Department of Philosophy
University of South Florida

E. JENNIFER ASHWORTH
Department of Philosophy, *emerita*
University of Waterloo

JOËL BIARD
Centre d'études supérieures de la
    Renaissance
Université François-Rabelais, Tours

ANTONY BLACK
School of Humanities, *emeritus*
University of Dundee

DEBORAH L. BLACK
Department of Philosophy
University of Toronto

JOHN BOLER
Department of Philosophy, *emeritus*
University of Washington

CHARLES BURNETT
Warburg Institute
University of London

ALESSANDRO D. CONTI
Dipartimento di Storia e
    Metodologie Comparate
Università degli Studi di L'Aquila

RICHARD CROSS
Department of Philosophy
University of Notre Dame

MICHAEL F. CUSATO OFM
Franciscan Institute
St. Bonaventure University

JOHN A. DEMETRACOPOULOS
Department of Education
University of Patras

G. R. EVANS
Faculty of History, *emerita*
University of Cambridge

HESTER GOODENOUGH GELBER
Department of Religious Studies
Stanford University

NADJA GERMANN
Department of Philosophy
Loyola University, Maryland

LENN E. GOODMAN
Department of Philosophy
Vanderbilt University

DIMITRI GUTAS
Department of Near Eastern
    Languages and Civilizations
Yale University

JOHN HALDANE
Philosophy Department
University of St. Andrews

DAG NIKOLAUS HASSE
Institut für Philosophie
Julius-Maximilians-Universität
    Würzburg

TOBIAS HOFFMANN
School of Philosophy
The Catholic University of
    America

KATERINA IERODIAKONOU
Department of Philosophy and
    History of Athens
University of Athens

BONNIE KENT
Department of Philosophy
University of California at Irvine

GYULA KLIMA
Department of Philosophy
Fordham University

SIMO KNUUTTILA
Department of Systematic Theology
University of Helsinki

TANELI KUKKONEN
Department of History and
    Ethnology
University of Jyväskylä

BRIAN LEFTOW
Oriel College
University of Oxford

DAVID LUSCOMBE
Department of History
University of Sheffield

WILLIAM E. MANN
Department of Philosophy
University of Vermont

JOHN MARENBON
Trinity College
University of Cambridge

STEVEN P. MARRONE
Department of History
Tufts University

CHRISTOPHER J. MARTIN
Department of Philosophy
University of Auckland

GARETH B. MATTHEWS
Department of Philosophy, *emeritus*
University of Massachusetts, Amherst

CARY J. NEDERMAN
Department of Political Science
Texas A&M University

TIMOTHY NOONE
School of Philosophy
The Catholic University of America

CALVIN G. NORMORE
Department of Philosophy
McGill University
University of California, Los Angeles

CLAUDE PANACCIO
Département de Philosophie
Université du Québec à Montréal

ROBERT PASNAU
Department of Philosophy
University of Colorado at Boulder

DOMINIK PERLER
Institut für Philosophie
Humboldt Universität

SARAH PESSIN
Department of Philosophy
University of Denver

JEAN PORTER
Department of Theology
University of Notre Dame

FRANÇOIS-XAVIER PUTALLAZ
Département de Philosophie
Université de Fribourg

STEPHEN READ
School of Philosophical and
    Anthropological Studies
University of St. Andrews

IRÈNE ROSIER-CATACH
Laboratoire d'Histoire des Théories
    Linguistiques
Centre National de la Recherche
    Scientifique, Paris

FREDERICK H. RUSSELL
Department of History
Rutgers University at Newark

A. MARK SMITH
Department of History
University of Missouri at Columbia

PAUL VINCENT SPADE
Department of Philosophy
Indiana University

M. W. F. STONE
Institute of Philosophy
Katholieke Universiteit Leuven

ELEONORE STUMP
Department of Philosophy
Saint Louis University

JOHANNES M. M. H. THIJSSEN
Faculteit der Filosofie
Radboud Universiteit Nijmegen

CECILIA TRIFOGLI
All Souls College
University of Oxford

MICHELE TRIZIO
Thomas-Institut
Universität zu Köln

CHRISTINA VAN DYKE
Department of Philosophy
Calvin College

THOMAS WILLIAMS
Department of Philosophy
University of South Florida

JOHN F. WIPPEL
School of Philosophy
The Catholic University of
    America

ROBERT WISNOVSKY
Institute of Islamic Studies
McGill University

REGA WOOD
Department of Philosophy
Stanford University

MIKKO YRJÖNSUURI
Department of Social Sciences and
    Philosophy
University of Jyväskylä

MAURO ZONTA
Dipartimento di Studi Filosofici ed
    Epistemologici
Università di Roma 'La Sapienza'

INTRODUCTION

ROBERT PASNAU

Medieval philosophy emerges after the decline of ancient Greece and Rome, when new cultures begin to produce works of philosophy that are at once inspired by that ancient legacy and yet responsive to new cultural and religious circumstances. There is now some consensus on when and where to place the beginnings of medieval philosophy, understood as a project of independent philosophical inquiry: it begins in Baghdad, in the middle of the eighth century, and in France, in the itinerant court of Charlemagne, in the last quarter of the eighth century.[1] It is less easy to say when medieval philosophy ends, because the methods and doctrines that are characteristic of the medieval period endure, and indeed remain dominant, into what is conventionally called the Renaissance. It is not until the seventeenth century, in Europe, that an indisputably new kind of philosophy becomes dominant.

The present volumes give an overview of the people and ideas that shape philosophy through these Middle Ages, from the eighth through the fourteenth century and beyond. One of the most compelling and challenging features of this era is its global reach. Whereas the study of ancient and modern philosophy confines itself mainly to work done within a homogeneous cultural sphere of at most a few hundred miles, the world of medieval philosophy runs from Oxford to Nishapur and from Fez to Prague, through Islamic, Jewish, and Christian thought, and correspondingly through Arabic, Hebrew, Latin, and Greek texts (to mention only the most prominent languages). It is the ambition of these volumes to provide a broad, integrated account of this material.

More than just the modern fancy for multiculturalism impels this holistic treatment of the field. Despite the vast distances and linguistic barriers, the

---

[1] For further discussion of the origins of medieval philosophy, see Chapters 1–2. Traditionally, Augustine (354–430) and Boethius (*ca.* 475–526) have been included in the medieval curriculum, but they are manifestly a part of the ancient world. This tradition stems in part from the former tendency of classicists to neglect late antiquity, and in part from the former tendency of medievalists to assimilate medieval philosophy with Christian philosophy. The philosophy of late antiquity is the subject of a forthcoming *Cambridge History*, edited by Lloyd Gerson.

various traditions surveyed in these volumes constitute a continuous and coherent body of thought, such that to study one without the others is liable to distort it.[2] The philosophical foundations of Thomas Aquinas's theology – to take the most prominent example – are inseparable from the thought of Avicenna and Averroes, while his understanding of God is deeply indebted to Moses Maimonides. Maimonides in turn is writing in Arabic, in the midst of the Islamic culture of North Africa, and his ideas are thoroughly grounded in that philosophical tradition. And while Arabic philosophy is foundational for these other traditions, its influence on the others is so pronounced and immediate that it can hardly be understood as a separate movement. Averroes's great commentaries on Aristotle – again to take just the most prominent example – would be translated into Latin and take their place at the core of the university curriculum at Paris and elsewhere within around fifty years of being written in 1180–90. The only justification for treating these traditions separately is that it is in truth desperately difficult for any one scholar to master so much disparate material.

Although written with an eye toward the future, the chapters that follow are necessarily constrained by the boundaries of our present knowledge. These boundaries, it must be said, do not extend very far. Indeed, another of the most compelling and challenging features of the medieval era is our remarkably poor understanding of it. Like soldiers making a stand against an onrushing enemy (to borrow a famous image from Aristotle), medievalists have banded together around a few authors and texts, leaving vast territory practically deserted. An immense amount of work has been done in the quarter century since the last *Cambridge History*. Yet even in these concentrated clusters of research, a great deal remains untouched. Much of the work of Thomas Aquinas – by far the most studied medieval author – still awaits a critical edition, or a translation into English, and sophisticated philosophical work has been done only on certain aspects of his thought. For other authors, even well-known Latin ones, the situation is vastly worse, and in Arabic it is worse still, given the many important texts that remain available only in manuscript. It is, moreover, not even clear that Aquinas deserves his status as the most important figure in the field. Our knowledge of other contenders for that title – such as Avicenna, Maimonides, Peter Abaelard, John Duns Scotus, William of Ockham, and John Buridan – remains too limited to judge the case fairly. With so much exploration still to be done, the medieval era stands as the Wild West of philosophy's history, suited for those who prefer the rugged frontier to a well-cultivated garden.[3]

---

[2] On the same principles, the volumes do not extend to contemporaneous but disconnected philosophical traditions such as that on the Indian subcontinent.

[3] A vivid sense of the field's lacunae, as well as its many recent achievements, can be acquired by reading through some of the biographies of medieval authors (Appendix C), with its long lists

In an attempt to conceive more clearly the ways in which medieval scholarship might develop in the twenty-first century, I invited five contributors representing a range of interests and perspectives to join me in composing a list of desiderata for research in the century to come. One immediately obvious feature of the lists is how very different they are. They differ with respect to periods and authors, focusing variously on Latin and Arabic texts, and earlier and later centuries. They also differ widely with respect to topics: some raise questions of metaphysics, others of language or ethics, while still others focus on the boundaries of philosophy's intersection with politics, medicine, and law. A still further difference is between those items focused on philosophical problems, as when Dominik Perler poses the question of why radical skepticism was not a medieval concern, and those focused on historical scholarship, as when Martin Stone presses the need for more critical editions. It should go without saying that these last two kinds of desiderata go hand in hand. The most important development for medieval philosophical scholarship in the last twenty-five years has been the Ockham critical edition, which precipitated much of the most sophisticated philosophical work of recent years. There is every reason to expect that further philological work in the editing and translating of texts will lead directly to still more progress of a philosophical sort. Here again, however, we see another challenging feature of the era: the importance of the sort of bedrock historical and philological research that in other historical periods has long since been brought to a very high standard. This is a challenge, but also a compelling feature of the period, because here one can make the sorts of fundamental historical contributions that in ancient philosophy, for instance, were made by famed scholars of previous centuries. It is crucial to the future of medieval philosophy that the broader philosophical community be brought to recognize the importance of such scholarly initiatives, even when they lack the sort of immediate philosophical payoff that the profession has now come to expect in other areas.

THIRTY DESIDERATA FOR RESEARCH ON MEDIEVAL PHILOSOPHY IN THE TWENTY-FIRST CENTURY

PETER ADAMSON

1. What impact did ideas and problems from Islamic speculative theology (*kalām*) have on the tradition of Greek-inspired philosophy (*falsafa*) in Arabic, for instance on thinkers such as Avicenna?

---

of works that remain both unedited and untranslated, alongside the many works that have been published since 1982.

2. What were the distinctive achievements of the Arabic logical tradition, especially in modal logic? What impact did these advances have on other areas of philosophy?
3. Many medieval philosophers did important work in the physical sciences, especially medicine. To what extent did their philosophical thought inform their scientific writing and vice versa?
4. Was the eleventh to the fourteenth century the "golden age of Arabic philosophy"?
5. In what way was practical (political and ethical) philosophy in Arabic – and in other traditions as well – dependent on theoretical philosophy (metaphysics, psychology, and epistemology)?

JOHN MARENBON

1. The Byzantine tradition of Aristotelian commentary.
2. The Avicennian tradition of philosophy in Islam, from *ca.* 1300 onwards.
3. Philosophy in the Latin West, 1200–1500, outside the universities.
4. The logico-theological schools of Paris in the period *ca.* 1150 – *ca.* 1200.
5. The scholastic tradition outside the Iberian peninsula, 1500–1700.

DOMINIK PERLER

1. Some ancient texts were available in translation (Plato's *Meno*, Sextus Empiricus's *Outlines of Skepticism*) but did not attract interest. Why?
2. Some intellectual centers and schools had extensive interchanges, whereas others had none. (For instance, William of Ockham and Meister Eckhart were contemporaries, but they do not seem to have been interested in each other.) Why?
3. All medieval philosophers agreed that we can have doubts about this or that example of knowledge, but never about the possibility of knowledge in general. Why?
4. Medieval philosophers had endless debates about the function of intellect and will or about the relationship between sensory and intellectual faculties, but they basically agreed that there are such things as faculties of the soul. Why did they not question the existence of faculties, as so many early modern philosophers did?
5. Was there any medieval philosopher who held that colors are not to be found in material objects but only in our mind? If not, why? Is this principle the decisive difference between medieval and early modern philosophy?

IRÈNE ROSIER-CATACH

1. The relationship between law and philosophy of language: for example, theories of lies, of falsity, and the semantics of interpretations. Also, interrelations between moral philosophy and law: for instance, the problem of intention.

2. Was there a political aspect, purpose, or background to philosophical controversies? Did philosophical and theological theories have political influence, were they themselves influenced by political problems, or were they totally speculative?

3. The development of speculative grammars in the thirteenth and fourteenth centuries, and the various forms of opposition to it. Very little is know about this. Texts should be edited, especially commentaries on Michel of Marbais and Thomas of Erfurt.

4. What was the relevance of the way in which university curricula and the faculties were organized on the development of philosophical doctrines?

5. Methodological reflections on the production of knowledge in the Middle Ages: especially how is one to read a *text*, knowing that very often we have it preserved in many versions, slightly or highly different from each other, sometimes in interpolated versions containing different strata of doctrines. In which way can we then talk of *the* position of an author? How are we to handle the anonymous production of texts that is so important in the arts faculty?

M.W. F. STONE

1. The full and synoptic study of medieval moral thought, which incorporates not just the obvious sources of medieval 'moral philosophy,' but also those areas of canon law, pastoral thought, and confessional writings where matters of ethical interest are discussed.

2. The systematic study of the fifteenth-century schools and the pluralism of late medieval philosophy. This will facilitate an improved understanding of the putative transition of 'medieval' to 'modern' philosophy, and the continuation of the scholastic tradition in the seventeenth and eighteenth centuries.

3. The completion of the *Opera omnia* of Henry of Ghent and Giles of Rome, and the start of new critical editions of Durand of Saint-Pourçain and Peter Auriol. Within twenty years Henry, Giles, Durand, and Auriol will become a part of the canon.

4. Integration of so-called 'philological' and 'philosophical' methods of interpretation, whereby philological/contextualist approaches are appropriated and then improved by means of firm and assured philosophical analysis.

5. A communal appreciation of the importance and intellectual worth of critical editions. A greater encouragement of younger scholars, especially in North America and the UK, to acquire the skills necessary to complete good editions of texts, and for members of the 'philosophical' community to see that such scholarly endeavors are indispensable to the good order of the subject of medieval philosophy.

ROBERT PASNAU

1. A clearer appreciation of the respects in which Thomas Aquinas is dependent on earlier Latin and Arabic thought, so that we can have a clearer appreciation of the respects in which he is original.

2. An intensive scholarly effort to grasp the brilliant philosophers of the mid-fourteenth century, especially John Buridan and Nicole Oresme.
3. A comprehensive dictionary of Latin philosophical terms.
4. The integration of research into Latin and Arabic sources, so that a continuous story can be told about what is, very nearly, a continuous philosophical tradition across three faiths.
5. A narrative for medieval philosophy that can be taught to undergraduates in a single term, and that would give the field a core curriculum of texts and philosophical problems analogous to those of the early modern era.

The wide range of suggestions for future research reveals still another challenging feature of medieval philosophy: the absence of any settled canon of texts and problems – especially in the English-speaking world. One hundred years ago, medieval scholarship rallied largely around the great theological *summae* of Thomas Aquinas and others. Within the last half century, considerable attention has been paid to scholastic logical texts, and to natural philosophy. Even within this limited domain there is little sense of a core curriculum, and moreover that domain is far too limited to do justice to the field. Each desiderata list makes its own suggestions about fruitful areas for further investigation. John Marenbon mentions, among other things, the severely neglected field of Byzantine philosophy. Peter Adamson wonders about Arabic logic. Irène Rosier-Catach asks about the relation between legal theory and the philosophy of language. As the field broadens in these and other directions, however, it will face the countervailing challenge of articulating a concise, compelling narrative for the period. Both the ancient and early modern periods have long since embraced such narratives, and the resulting clusters of texts and problems now form a part of what any philosopher must know. It is hardly an exaggeration to say that there is nothing from the medieval period, except perhaps Anselm's ontological argument and Aquinas's Five Ways, that has achieved this sort of canonical status. This is not because medieval philosophy is less worthy of study, but because scholars in the field have not yet found a unifying narrative that would engage the attention of a broader philosophical audience.

Whether the period deserves such attention depends entirely on the quality of its philosophical thought. One can hardly study the history of philosophy without being responsive to this concern. For as much as any historian should value historical scholarship for its own sake, as intrinsically worthwhile, the study of philosophy's history has special value because philosophical understanding is valuable, and is often best achieved by setting to one side the assumptions of one's own era and immersing oneself in the most brilliant work of earlier centuries. There is no point in simply insisting that medieval philosophy is worthwhile in this regard; one must show that it is, case by case. The chapters to come do just this across a wide range of areas. Most familiar is medieval work in philosophical theology, and in the development of an Aristotelian metaphysics and ethics. Even here, scholars have barely begun to convey the richness of the extant material. Yet as many of the following chapters show, medieval philosophy goes well beyond these relatively familiar areas, into logic and language, natural philosophy, cognitive theory and epistemology, moral psychology, and much more.

Ultimately, the status among today's philosophers of this or any historical period can be expressed as a function of two factors: the worth we place on the philosophical ideas of that period, as measured against the worth we place on our own contemporary ideas. In view of the second factor, this is not a good time for historical scholarship in any area of philosophy. We live in an era that – for reasons that are unclear – regards with great self-satisfaction its own philosophical accomplishments, to such a degree that it has little time for the ideas of previous generations. Still, to the extent there is room in the profession for historical inquiry at all, it is a good time to study the medieval era. Whereas fifty years ago one could hardly express interest in the topic without risking marginalization, the intervening years have seen a dramatic shift in the field's reputation. Although few philosophers know very much about medieval philosophy, it is now widely recognized as fertile ground for historical inquiry. There is, then, no longer any need for special pleading regarding the merits of medieval philosophy; that case has been made by the labors of prior generations. All that remains for us is to go out and do the work.

I

FUNDAMENTALS

I

ORIGINS IN BAGHDAD

DIMITRI GUTAS

THE END OF PHILOSOPHY IN LATE ANTIQUITY AND THE REMNANTS OF GREEK THOUGHT

Philosophy died a lingering death before Islam appeared. The long demise started arguably with the reign of Diocletian (284–305), as the social, demographic, administrative, and other changes that would eventually lead to the end of the ancient world first set in; in consequence of these changes, philosophy – as the living practice of rational thinking about human beings and the universe outside socially instilled and institutionally sanctioned mythologies and superstitions – was seen to represent attitudes and habits of mind little appreciated and even less tolerated.[1] After Justinian's 529 edict prohibiting pagans to teach, whatever was left of the much attenuated academic practice of philosophy limped on for another two or three generations until, as the current interpretation of the evidence has it, the last philosopher in Alexandria, Stephanus, was invited by the Emperor Heraclius to Constantinople around 610. And that is the last we hear for some time of philosophy *in Greek*, for in the ensuing two centuries – during, that is, the Iconoclastic controversy in Byzantium and the so-called "Dark Ages" – philosophical treatises were not even copied, let alone composed.[2] This situation continued until the Macedonian renaissance of the

---

[1] The story of the demise has not been told in the detail it deserves except, characteristically, in the work of Ramsay MacMullen who provides the social context and ample documentation. See in particular his *Christianity and Paganism in the Fourth to Eighth Centuries* (New Haven: Yale University Press, 1997) ch. 3, esp. pp. 83–92. Also useful for this discussion is his characterization of philosophy as thinking "along lines of reason, along lines of the likely," and as the "sceptical and empirical-thinking extreme" of "the spectrum of belief" (pp. 77 and 83); see p. 205 n. 27 for references to earlier treatments. More recently, MacMullen has revisited the same subject in *Voting about God in Early Church Councils* (New Haven, CT: Yale University Press, 2006) ch. 4. For the social transformations in late antiquity, see the work of John F. Haldon, and especially his *Byzantium in the Seventh Century: The Transformation of a Culture* (Cambridge: Cambridge University Press, 1990).

[2] Dimitri Gutas, "Geometry and the Rebirth of Philosophy in Arabic with al-Kindī," in R. Arnzen and J. Thielmann (eds.) *Words, Texts and Concepts Cruising the Mediterranean Sea* (Leuven: Peeters, 2004) pp. 195–6.

second half of the ninth century when there was, if not a resurrection of philosophy, at least renewed interest in philosophical literature apparently occasioned by the Graeco-Arabic translation movement in Baghdad.[3] The interest manifested itself in the transcription of philosophical writings in new manuscript copies – an activity to which we owe the very survival of many an ancient text – and in the production of some logical scholia by men like Photius and Arethas.

The emphasis on the language is intended to highlight the fact that philosophy in antiquity was done in Greek. After Alexander the Great and the spread of Hellenism throughout the Near East, it is in fact remarkable that although *participation* in philosophy became internationalized, its *expression* was not envisaged in anything but Greek. Even after the Hellenistic empire of Alexander's successors was supplanted by that of the Latin-speaking Romans, the usual linguistic development – the language of the empire imposing itself on *cultural* activities – did not take place, and even philosophers whose mother tongue was not Greek did philosophy not in Latin but in Greek. A pertinent case in point is that of Plotinus and Porphyry. Plotinus, who dominated ancient philosophical activity in Rome in the middle of the third century, was most probably a native speaker of Latin, while his most eminent student, Porphyry, was a native Aramaic speaker from Tyre on the eastern coast of the Mediterranean. Nevertheless, they both wrote their very influential philosophy in Greek; what is even more interesting, the rather sloppy Greek style of Plotinus (Longinus, the great literary critic, calls it "defective" [*diēmartēmena*])[4] was corrected by Porphyry in preparation for an edition of Plotinus's work. To be sure, there were attempts at translating the philosophy that was written in Greek into other languages – the presumed intention being to implant it in the cultures of the target languages – but such attempts, in the end, did not produce the intended results. Two great contemporary scholars at the antipodes of the cultural spread of Hellenism, Boethius in Rome (d. 525) and Sergius of Rēšʿaynā in northern Mesopotamia (d. 536), conceived of the grand idea of translating all of Aristotle into Latin and Syriac respectively.[5] The conception is to their credit as individual thinkers for their noble intentions; their failure indicates that the receiving cultures in which they worked had not developed the need for this enterprise. Philosophy in Latin was to develop, even if on some of the foundations laid by Boethius, much later,[6] while in Syriac it reached its highest point with BarHebraeus in

---

[3] Dimitri Gutas, *Greek Thought, Arabic Culture* (London: Routledge, 1998) pp. 175–86.

[4] Porphyry, *Life of Plotinus*, par. 19 (lines 21 and 27).

[5] See Henri Hugonnard-Roche, "Aux origines de l'exégèse orientale de la logique d'Aristote: Sergius de Rēšʿaina († 536), médecin et philosophe," *Journal Asiatique* 277 (1989) p. 12.

[6] And under the incentive, it appears, provided by the existence of Arabic philosophy even before the Arabic–Latin translations; but see below, Chapter 2.

the thirteenth century only after it had developed in Arabic and was translated from it.[7] The rebirth of philosophy in Arabic in the first third of the ninth century has to be seen against this background in order for its revolutionary character to be fully realized.

If living philosophy was dead in Greek and had, furthermore, failed to be transplanted and to acquire an independent status in other languages, what survived were its physical remains in the form of manuscripts and libraries,[8] as well as certain – much reduced, enfeebled, and diluted – *philosophical curricula* and *theological applications*, primarily of logical studies, in various schools and communities throughout the area that was to come under Muslim rule and be politically reunited for the first time since Alexander the Great. The following are some specific developments in the various communities in late antiquity that were to provide the necessary, but clearly not sufficient, conditions within which a philosophical tradition was later to be resuscitated, in Arabic.

In Greek, the most significant area to which these curricula were reduced was the rudiments of Aristotelian logic. It is possible, for instance, to discern a major structural change in the medical curriculum in Alexandria toward the end of the sixth century, perhaps as a reaction to the decline of philosophical instruction in that last remaining center of Greek philosophical studies. Some medical professors, whose names are given in the Arabic sources as Gessios, Anqīlāʾus (?), Marinos, and Stephanus of Alexandria (perhaps the same individual mentioned above, offering a last service to philosophy before he left for Constantinople), decided to organize and simplify the medical curriculum. They restricted the number of medical books for study, and they added logic to the curriculum in a formal way, bringing the total number of books a medical student had to study to twenty-four. Logic may have been studied in association with medical studies earlier: Galen's devotion to logic is well known and two at least of his most popular works that were included in this new curriculum – *Ars medica* and *Methodus medendi* – start with significant sections on logical procedures in therapeutic methods. What this new Alexandrian curriculum appears to have done is to have formally included as part of medical studies specific books on logic, namely the first four works in Aristotle's Organon: the *Categories*, *De interpretatione*, *Prior* and *Posterior Analytics*. The medical books consisted, in turn, of four books by Hippocrates (*Aphorisms*, *Prognosticon*, *Acute Diseases*, and *Airs, Waters, Places*), and abridged versions and summaries of sixteen Galenic

---

[7] Gutas, "Geometry and the Rebirth of Philosophy," p. 196; but also see John Watt, "Syriac Translators and Greek Philosophy in Early Abbasid Iraq," *Journal of the Canadian Society for Syriac Studies* 4 (2004) p. 15.

[8] See now the collection of articles in Cristina D'Ancona (ed.) *The Libraries of the Neoplatonists* (Leiden: Brill 2007).

books, collectively known as the *Summaria Alexandrinorum*. Accounts of this new curriculum, like the texts of Galen's summaries, have not survived in Greek, but they are prominent in Arabic medical and bibliographic literature that is amply corroborated by the scattered indications that have survived.[9] How far beyond the Islamic conquest of Alexandria (in 642) this instruction continued in Greek is not known, nor is there any evidence that this curriculum was transplanted to another city within the new and much reduced borders of the Byzantine Empire. Nevertheless, this is the only indication we have even of any kind of philosophical *instruction* in Greek; active philosophizing had ceased to exist.[10]

The theological applications of philosophy in Greek patristic literature, by contrast, were many and longevous, though clearly harnessed to their theological, apologetic, and polemical goals rather than free philosophical discourse. To the extent, however, that the patristic authors had been exposed to Greek philosophy, they could be expected to be knowledgeable about individual philosophers and the main philosophical currents. The sixth-century theologian John of Scythopolis in Palestine, for example, wrote the first known commentary on the writings of pseudo-Dionysius, in which he incorporated apparently extensive quotations from, and paraphrases of, passages in the *Enneads*. The pseudo-Dionysian work, *On the Divine Names*, was translated again into Syriac by Phokas ibn Sarjīs some time in the early eighth century, this time together with scholia by John. In this way some Plotinian material became available in Syriac translation, for we have no information that the *Enneads* as such was ever translated into Syriac.[11] This casts an interesting light on the selective Arabic translation of *Enneads* IV–VI a century later by Ibn Nāʿima al-Ḥimṣī; if none of the Plotinian texts known to have been quoted by John reappears in the extant Arabic Plotinus, it gives some indication of the intellectual milieu in which the Arabic Plotiniana may have their roots.[12]

In Syriac Christianity, as in Greek, there is a similar development of a logical curriculum, except that it was rather shorter: the books studied and commented

---

[9] Dimitri Gutas, "The 'Alexandria to Baghdad' Complex of Narratives: A Contribution to the Study of Philosophical and Medical Historiography among the Arabs," *Documenti e studi sulla tradizione filosofica medievale* 10 (1999) pp. 169–74; Mossman Rouché, "Did Medical Students Study Philosophy in Alexandria?" *Bulletin of the Institute of Classical Studies* 43 (1999) 153–69.

[10] For a sample of elementary logical schoolbooks in circulation at this time see Mossman Rouché, "Byzantine Philosophical Texts of the Seventh Century," *Jahrbuch der Österreichischen Byzantinistik* 23 (1974) 61–76.

[11] Sebastian Brock, "A Syriac Intermediary for the Arabic Theology of Aristotle? In Search of a Chimera," in D'Ancona, *The Libraries of the Neoplatonists*, pp. 293–306.

[12] See Brock, "Chimera," and Richard M. Frank, "The Use of the Enneads by John of Scythopolis," *Le Muséon* 100 (1987) 101–8. This and other papers by Frank are reprinted in *Islamic Mysticism, Theology, and Philosophy: Texts and Studies on the Development of Kalam*, ed. D. Gutas (Aldershot: Ashgate, 2005).

upon were Porphyry's *Isagoge* and Aristotle's *Categories, De interpretatione,* and *Prior Analytics* – but only as far as Book I, Chapter 7, omitting the section on modal logic and the rest of the treatise. The reasons for this are not yet clear; it has been suggested that in Syriac there developed – or was adapted – an understanding of modality based on logical matter, and hence there was no interest in Aristotle's modal logic based on logical form.[13] The rest of the Aristotelian Organon appears to have been hardly studied, if at all. There are references to Syriac translations of the *Posterior Analytics, Topics,* and *Sophistics* by Athanasius of Balad (d. 686), done before the Graeco-Arabic translation movement, but it seems hardly likely that they amounted to much or were conducive to further study; the Baghdad Aristotelians in the tenth century, who had access to these versions, uniformly condemned them as hopelessly inaccurate.[14] Similarly there are no Syriac commentaries attested for these later treatises of the Organon before the beginnings of Arabic philosophy. Awareness among Syriac scholars of these works and their tradition certainly existed, but their study, let alone creative thinking about the issues discussed in them, was not part of the procedures in the Syriac schools.[15] What was, was the application of certain logical categories and an occasional biblical thesis (like the question of the creation of the universe) to theological training and analysis, and more importantly, to theological disputations and inter-faith debates.[16]

Some of these debates took place within the borders of the Persian Sasanian Empire (226–642), between representatives of the Nestorian community and Zoroastrians. It is evident that classical learning had also permeated Middle Persian literature (though perhaps not to the same extent as it did Syriac), mainly through translations, but also through osmosis and interpersonal contact.

---

[13] Henri Hugonnard-Roche, *La logique d'Aristote du grec au syriaque* (Paris: Vrin, 2004) p. 273.

[14] Ibn Suwār, for example, writes in a note in the Paris ms. of the Arabic Organon (Bibliothèque Nationale Ar. 2346) that Athanasius understood nothing of the *Sophistics*; see Khalil Georr, *Les Catégories d'Aristote dans leurs versions syro-arabes* (Beirut: Institut français de Damas, 1948) pp. 198–9.

[15] For a list of Syriac translations and commentaries of the Organon see Sebastian Brock, "The Syriac Commentary Tradition," in C. Burnett (ed.) *Glosses and Commentaries on Aristotelian Logical Texts* (London: Warburg Institute, 1993) 3–18. Watt, "Syriac Translators," collects all the available evidence to present a more favorable picture of Syriac involvement with the Aristotelian logical tradition than the one presented here, but the knowledge *about* this tradition that he documents to have been possessed by Syriac scholars does not amount to an active engagement with the problems it discusses. See the summary account by Hans Daiber, "Die Aristotelesrezeption in der syrischen Literatur," in D. Kuhn and H. Stahl (eds.) *Die Gegenwart des Altertums* (Heidelberg: Edition Forum, 2001) 327–45.

[16] This is revealed by some recent and very welcome studies that provide concrete evidence for the structure of theological education and religious disputation in the Syriac schools just before and after the Islamic conquests. See Adam Becker, *Fear of God and the Beginning of Wisdom: The School of Nisibis and Christian Scholastic Culture in Late Antique Mesopotamia* (Philadelphia: University of Pennsylvania Press, 2006) esp. ch. 7, and Joel Walker, *Legend of Mar Qardagh: Narrative and Christian Heroism in Late Antique Iraq* (Berkeley: University of California Press, 2006) pt. 2, ch. 3.

The Sasanian rulers actively endorsed a translation culture that viewed the transferral of Greek texts and ideas into Middle Persian as the "restitution" of an Iranian heritage that was allegedly pilfered by the Greeks after the campaigns of Alexander the Great.[17] It was this cultural context, and the atmosphere of open debate fostered most energetically by Chosroes I Anushirwan (ruled 531–78), that must have prompted the Greek philosophers to seek refuge in his court after Justinian's 529 edict prohibited them from teaching. And yet, though there is evidence for the translation of a number of non-philosophical Greek books into Middle Persian, and of the integration in its literature of a certain amount of knowledge and some use of philosophical material for distinctly non-philosophical purposes, there are no indications that any philosophical literature as such developed in it.[18]

The most important philosopher of the pre-Islamic period known to have come from Sasanian Iran, Paul the Persian, wrote treatises on logic dedicated to Chosroes. Although there are some references to his having written in Middle Persian, the fact remains that his works are extant in Syriac and that he was widely familiar with Syriac logical literature.[19] In general, then, and given the extensive presence of Nestorian Christians in the Sasanian Empire, there does not seem to have existed in it, as far as a philosophical curriculum and its application are concerned, anything drastically different from what is found among Syriac Christians. Finally, in connection with the Greek philosophers in the court of Chosroes, it should also be mentioned that upon their return from Persia they did not move to Ḥarrān (Carrhae) in upper Mesopotamia. The Syriac-speaking population of that city remained obstinately pagan until the eleventh century; they clearly had knowledge of and access to philosophical material, which they happily shared with their Muslim overlords when a demand for it had been generated under the early Abbasids, but there is absolutely no evidence either that they developed a philosophical tradition among themselves

---

[17] Gutas, *Greek Thought*, pp. 34–45, with belated acknowledgment to Shaul Shaked, "Paymān: An Iranian Idea in Contact with Greek Thought and Islam," in *Transition Periods in Iranian History* (Paris: Association pour l'Avancement des Études Iraniennes, 1987) p. 217 and n. 2.

[18] Most accounts of philosophical activity in Sasanian Iran concentrate on Chosroes – see, e.g., Michel Tardieu, "Chosroès," in *Dictionnaire des Philosophes Antiques* (Paris: CNRS Éditions, 1994) II: 309–18, and Joel Walker, "The Limits of Late Antiquity: Philosophy between Rome and Iran," *The Ancient World* 33 (2002) 45–69 – though this culture of translation and openness to Greek learning was apparently characteristic, to a greater or lesser extent, of the entire Sasanian dynasty. For references to the philosophical material in Middle Persian, and a model analysis of the way in which some philosophical ideas were integrated into Persian literature, see Shaked, "Paymān," p. 217 nn. 1 and 2.

[19] Dimitri Gutas, "Paul the Persian on the Classification of the Parts of Aristotle's Philosophy: A Milestone between Alexandria and Baġdād," *Der Islam* 60 (1983) 231–67; Hugonnard-Roche, *Logique d'Aristote*, pp. 233–5; Javier Teixidor, *Aristote en Syriaque* (Paris: CNRS Éditions, 2003).

or that they ran a philosophical academic institution (a Platonic "Academy") gratefully attended by the disappointed Greek philosophers upon their return from Persia.[20]

Other languages that were culturally significant during the period in question and were influenced by Hellenism include Armenian and Georgian. The latter may be discounted insofar as a philosophical literature in translation developed much later than the period from the seventh through ninth centuries with which we are concerned.[21] In the case of Armenian, although it is true that there exist some few translations of Aristotle (*Categories* and *De interpretatione*), Plato (five dialogues), and Porphyry (*Isagoge*), these translations – even if it is accepted that they were made in the course of the seventh century, which is disputed – did not give rise to what may be called a philosophical literature, much less a philosophical movement; it appears that they are to be classed along with the similar productions in Syriac of a philosophical curriculum.[22]

TRANSLATION AND THE RISE OF ARABIC PHILOSOPHICAL LITERATURE

After the advent of Islam, the resurrection of philosophy as Arabic philosophy is intimately connected with the Graeco-Arabic translation movement that started in Baghdad shortly after its foundation in 762 and lasted through the end of the tenth century. This translation movement, during the course of which almost all non-literary and non-historical secular Greek works on science and philosophy were translated upon demand into Arabic, was introduced by the caliphs and the ruling elite of the newly established Arab Abbasid dynasty (750–1258) as an ideological response to pressing political and social problems. Once thus introduced and sponsored from the top, the translation movement found

---

[20] Tardieu's deplorable thesis to this effect has been most recently defended by I. Hadot, "Dans quel lieu le néoplatonicien Simplicius a-t-il fondé son école de mathématiques, et où a pu avoir lieu son entretien avec un manichéen?," *International Journal of the Platonic Tradition* 1 (2007) 42–107. For a refutation, see Concetta Luna's review of Rainer Thiel, *Simplikios und das Ende der neuplatonischen Schule in Athen*, in *Mnemosyne* 54 (2001) 482–504, and Edward Watts, "Justinian, Malalas, and the End of Athenian Philosophical Teaching in A.D. 529," *Journal of Roman Studies* 94 (2004) 168–82, and "Where to Live the Philosophical Life in the Sixth Century? Damascius, Simplicius, and the Return from Persia," *Greek, Roman, and Byzantine Studies* 45 (2005) 285–315.

[21] Cf. Michel van Esbroeck, "La version géorgienne de deux commentaires d'Ammonius fils d'Hermias," in G. Fiaccadori (ed.) *Autori classici in lingue del vicino e medio oriente* (Rome: Istituto poligrafico e Zecca dello Stato, Libreria dello Stato, 1990) 55–64.

[22] See Abraham Terian, "The Hellenizing School: Its Time, Place, and Scope of Activities Reconsidered," in N. Garsoian *et al.* (eds.) *East of Byzantium: Syria and Armenia in the Formative Period* (Washington, DC: Dumbarton Oaks, 1980) 175–86, and Constantine Zuckerman, "A Repertory of Published Armenian Translations of Classical Texts," in Fiaccadori, *Autori classici*, esp. pp. 428, 436–8. I am indebted to Kevin van Bladel for a fruitful discussion of the issues raised in this section.

further support from below in the incipient scientific tradition in Arabic, which
was developing at the hands of scholars and scientists actively recruited to the
capital by the same elite who were commissioning the translations. The dialectic
between the translation activity on the one hand and scientific thinking and
research on the other was responsible for the amazingly rapid development
of the sciences in Arabic in the second half of the eighth century and their
establishment as a major cultural force in early Abbasid society.[23]

The beginnings of Arabic philosophical literature can be described as taking
place in two stages. The first occurs from roughly the middle of the eighth
century until the appearance of al-Kindī in the first third of the ninth century.
It is characterized by the continuation of the engagement with the remnants of
philosophy in Greek, Syriac, and Middle Persian that have just been reviewed,
though in Arabic this time – by the study, that is, of the logical curriculum
and the application of philosophical ideas to theological concerns of the time;
it is represented by some philosophical texts that appeared in Arabic, in the
course of the translation movement, to serve non-philosophical purposes. The
second stage begins with al-Kindī and represents a resurrection of philosophy
as a discipline in its own right, independent of theological or other concerns.

The first Arabic philosophical text that is extant from the preliminary stage
is an abridged and interpolated paraphrase of the beginning of the logical
curriculum, covering Porphyry's *Isagoge*, the *Categories*, *De interpretatione*, and
Prior Analytics up to I.7.[24] An ancient colophon preserved in the manuscript
transmission of the work ascribes its "translation" to either the famous *littérateur*,
courtier, and translator from Middle Persian, Ibn al-Muqaffaʿ (d. 756) or his son
(d. *ca.* 760), thus dating it to the very beginning of the Graeco-Arabic translation
movement. Although on linguistic and other grounds it may seem unlikely that
either the father or the son would have produced such a text, it is not far-
fetched or indeed surprising that Ibn al-Muqaffaʿ the father, in particular, was
associated in some capacity with the project. Intellectual life in the caliphal
court just before and after the Abbasid revolution (750), during which time
Ibn al-Muqaffaʿ was active, revolved around questions of what we would now
call rationalism – that is, questions of verifiability of information beyond the
claims of revealed religions which necessarily, and notoriously, contradicted
each other. This attitude may hearken back to Sasanian times and indeed to the
court of Chosroes, as mentioned above, during whose reign such attitudes are

---

[23] See the detailed discussion of the Graeco-Arabic translation movement in Gutas, *Greek Thought*.

[24] In addition to the edition by M. T. Daneshpajuh, see Giuseppe Furlani, "Di una presunte versione
araba di alcuni scritti di Porfirio e di Aristotele," *Rendiconti della R. Accademia Nazionale dei Lincei*
6.2 (1926) 205–13.

attested both in the works of Paul the Persian and in the introduction to the Middle Persian version of the Indian fable book and mirror for princes, *Kalīla wa-Dimna*. Ibn al-Muqaffaʿ, with his translation of the *Kalīla wa-Dimna* and its introduction into Arabic,[25] and in view of its manifestly enthusiastic reception in early Abbasid society, may also have been reflecting this rationalistic attitude in wider intellectual circles. In this context, his affiliation with the project of the production in Arabic of these texts from the Organon – perhaps as editor, given his mastery of Arabic style – is easily understandable.[26]

The occasion which prompted the production of this work is not known, but it clearly must reflect some attempt to put into Arabic the main texts of the logical curriculum then available, for the Arabic text intends to present precisely what that curriculum studied: Porphyry's *Isagoge* and the first four treatises of the Organon. In this regard, the text belongs to the Greek, rather than the Syriac, tradition of this curriculum, as described above. However, despite the author's express statement in the text to present all four books, in effect the text breaks off after *Prior Analytics* I.7, thus following Syriac practice.[27] How these two traditions became entangled in this case is not known. The nature of the texts selected for presentation shows that there were no philosophical intentions behind the choice: texts of this nature were routinely read in schools as part of the curriculum, and had no aspirations to philosophical profundity. One may guess that the commissioning of this work must have come from a wish to have in Arabic what students were reading in the Christian schools as part of their general education,[28] and that somehow this wish was related to the social developments at the very beginning of the Abbasid dynasty – or perhaps, more specifically, to the increased interest in the theological implications of the grammar of statements, the structure and logic of language, and consequent meaning, issues manifestly treated in the first works of the Organon.[29]

---

[25] See Paul Kraus, "Zu Ibn al-Muqaffaʿ," *Rivista degli Studi Orientali* 14 (1934) 1–20; Francesco Gabrieli, "L'opera di Ibn al-Muqaffaʿ," *Rivista degli Studi Orientali* 13 (1931–2) pp. 201–5.

[26] See in general Josef van Ess, *Theologie und Gesellschaft im 2. und 3. Jahrhundert Hidschra: Eine Geschichte des religiosen denkens im fruhen Islam* (Berlin: De Gruyter, 1991–7) II: 22–36; Cornelia Schöck, "Aussagenquantifizierung und –modalisierung in der frühen islamischen Theologie," in D. Perler and U. Rudolph (eds.) *Logik und Theologie* (Leiden: Brill, 2005) 19–43; Michael Cooperson, "Ibn al-Muqaffaʿ," in O. Leaman (ed.) *The Biographical Encyclopaedia of Islamic Philosophy* (London: Thoemmes, 2006) I: 280–6, who also discusses the issue of the authorship of the logic version.

[27] Gutas, "Alexandria to Baghdad," pp. 183–4.

[28] The Muslims appear to have been very much aware of the existence (and usefulness) of this curriculum in Syriac among the Christians: al-Kindī expressly refers to it in his polemic against the doctrine of the Trinity; see Peter Adamson, *Al-Kindī* (Oxford: Oxford University Press, 2006) p. 41.

[29] See Gérard Troupeau, "La logique d'Ibn al-Muqaffaʿ et les origines de la grammaire arabe," *Arabica* 28 (1981) 242–50; Rafael Talmon, "Naẓra ǧadīda fī qaḍiyyat aqsām al-kalām: dirāsa ḥawl kitāb Ibn

Other more easily identifiable social, political, and ideological concerns also played a role during this first stage of the appearance of philosophical texts and arguments in Arabic. Certainly the most significant of them was the development of Islamic theology and the intense debate among the various groups and individuals about its eventual orientation. It is generally acknowledged that the first discussions of a theological nature among Muslims were the result of political and social developments during the first century of Islam, before the beginning of the translation movement. At the center of discussion were the questions of legitimacy of succession to the caliphate, the relationship of leadership to faith, and the concomitant problem of unbelief when that relationship was considered by some factions as inadequate. The conflicting views that were expressed on these controversial issues eventually gave rise to theological positions, or to a theology of controversy (*Kontroverstheologie*), as termed by Josef van Ess, which constituted part of the political discourse of the nascent Muslim society.[30] Right after the turn of the first Islamic century and just before the Abbasid revolution (*ca.* 720s), however, a new, cosmological element was introduced into theological discussions – in particular, atomism – apparently through the Manichean sects.[31] The need for a cosmology other than atomism occasioned the translation of Aristotle's *Physics* by the end of the eighth century, a work that was repeatedly to be re-translated (or revised).[32] Also related to such theological disputes is the appearance, in the first half of the eighth century and before the beginning of the translation movement, of certain Plotinian ideas in the theology of Jahm Ibn Ṣafwān (d. 746), ideas that, in this case, appear to have traveled without written translations.[33]

Another aspect of theological discussions that played a role in philosophical arguments is apologetics – that is, Muslim disputations with non-Muslims, a practice directly affiliated with inter-faith debates in both Greek and Syriac in pre-Islamic times. The need for Muslims, as newcomers to the genre, to understand better the rules of dialectical argumentation prompted the caliph al-Mahdī (ruled 775–85) to commission a translation of the best handbook on the subject – Aristotle's *Topics* – from the Nestorian Patriarch Timothy I, whom he debated; thus, there appeared what was to be the first of three Arabic

---

al-Muqaffaʿ fī l-manṭiq," *al-Karmil* 12 (1991) 43–67; and esp. Schöck, *Koranexegese, Grammatik und Logik. Zum Verhältnis von arabischer und aristotelischer Urteils-, Konsequenz- und Schlusslehre* (Leiden: Brill, 2006) ch. 7.

[30] Van Ess, *Theologie und Gesellschaft*, I: 48; Gutas, *Greek Thought*, p. 70.

[31] Especially the Bardesanites; see van Ess, *Theologie und Gesellschaft*, I: 418ff.; Alnoor Dhanani, *The Physical Theory of Kalām* (Leiden: Brill, 1994) pp. 182–6.

[32] Gutas, *Greek Thought*, pp. 69–74.

[33] Richard M. Frank, "The Neoplatonism of Ǧahm ibn Ṣafwān," *Le Muséon* 78 (1965) 395–424.

translations of this Aristotelian treatise.[34] Such debates continued unabated in the following centuries.[35]

In all these discussions, the philosophical arguments and texts whose translation was sought were geared to the service of other concerns, primarily political and theological. There was no question of an interest in philosophy as such. With al-Kindī at the beginning of the ninth century, however, there is a qualitative change in the approach to these subjects, and philosophy is introduced as an intellectual discipline independent of religion and other ideological currents.

AL-KINDĪ AND THE REBIRTH OF PHILOSOPHY

Al-Kindī (*ca.* 800 – *ca.* 870), the first to develop philosophical thought as such in Arabic, was a polymath in the translated sciences and very much a product of his age. Like other scientists of his time, he gathered around him a wide circle of individuals capable of advising him on various issues and translating the relevant texts. He commissioned translations of scientific subjects and he himself wrote on all the sciences: astrology, astronomy, arithmetic, geometry, music, and medicine – he even has a treatise on swords.[36] This broad and synoptic view of all sciences, along with the spirit of encyclopedism fostered by the translation movement for the half century before his time, led him to an overarching vision of the unity and interrelatedness of all knowledge. At the same time, and as a result of this view, he developed a unitary epistemological approach – namely, that of mathematics. His goal became to approach mathematical accuracy in his argumentation; influenced by both Ptolemy and Euclid, he held mathematical or geometrical proof to be of the highest order. In the introduction of the *Almagest*, Ptolemy says the following about scientific method:

From all this we concluded that the first two divisions of theoretical philosophy should rather be called guesswork than knowledge, theology because of its completely invisible and ungraspable nature, physics because of the unstable and unclear nature of the matter; hence there is no hope that philosophers will ever be agreed about them; and that only mathematics can provide sure and unshakable knowledge to its devotees, provided one approaches it rigorously. For its kind of proof proceeds by indisputable methods, namely arithmetic and geometry (tr. Toomer, p. 6).[37]

---

[34] Gutas, *Greek Thought*, pp. 61–9; Watt, "Syriac Translators," pp. 17–19, with references to recent literature.

[35] See in general Sidney Griffith, *The Church in the Shadow of the Mosque* (Princeton, NJ: Princeton University Press, 2008) esp. ch. 4.

[36] Recently edited and translated with commentary and related texts by R. G. Hoyland and B. Gilmour, *Medieval Islamic Swords and Swordmaking* (Cambridge: Gibb Memorial Trust, 2006).

[37] This assessment of the relative epistemological value of the objects of physics, mathematics, and metaphysics became the standard view (directly borrowed from Ptolemy?) in the prolegomena

Al-Kindī echoed this understanding in his paraphrase of the *Almagest* where
he spoke about the "true methods of mathematics that are manifested by geometrical and arithmetical proofs, which contain no doubt at all" (*Ṣināʿa*, ed.
Aḥmad, p. 127). In his philosophical writings he regularly employed certain
proofs where his method is clearly derived from the *Elements* of Euclid,[38] and
he maintained that a prerequisite for the study of Aristotle's philosophy, even
of logic, was mathematics. In this he was clearly influenced by Proclus's *Elements of Theology*, a partial translation of which he commissioned. Proclus thus
appears to be the link that connects al-Kindī's mathematical (indeed, geometrical) epistemology with philosophy. Proclus's work, with its geometrical mode
of argumentation, was living proof for al-Kindī that abstract problems, such as
those debated by the theologians of his time – Muslims and non-Muslims alike –
could be resolved through philosophical discourse which transcends religious
sectarianism and proceeds on the basis of a geometrical methodology acceptable
to all, just like the rest of the sciences. Al-Kindī's coming to philosophy was
therefore secondary and the result of his earlier preoccupations with science and
scientific method; it was not primary.

Once introduced to philosophy in this fashion by Proclus – and, hence, to the
possibility that theological questions can be treated with an amount of certainty
equal to that in the mathematical sciences – al-Kindī tried to gain access to
this methodologically rigorous discipline. Accordingly he commissioned, and
then corrected and edited, translations of Greek metaphysical texts, foremost
among which are the selections from Plotinus (*Enneads* IV–VI) and Proclus
(*Elements of Theology*) in Arabic known respectively as the *Theology of Aristotle*
and *The Pure Good* (*Liber de causis* in the medieval Latin translation), as well as
Aristotle's *Metaphysics*. Al-Kindī and the circle of scholars he gathered around
him further commissioned translations of other Greek works, both philosophical
and scientific; a full list of what is now known would include, in addition to the
works already mentioned, pseudo-Ammonius's *De placitis philosophorum*, Euclid's
Elements and Proclus's commentary on it (at least the first book), Proclus's
Elements of Physics, Nicomachus of Gerasa's *Introduction to Arithmetic* and *Great
Book on Music*, Aristotle's *De caelo*, *Meteorology*, *De animalibus*, *De anima*, *Parva
naturalia*, and *Prior Analytics*, Alexander of Aphrodisias's *Questions*, and possibly

---

to philosophy by late antique philosophers like David and Elias, who, however, true to their
Aristotelian tradition, championed logic, not mathematics, as the method leading to certainty (see
the translation and discussion of their relevant passages in Gutas, "Paul the Persian," pp. 247–9).
Al-Kindī, though he may have known about their works, does not appear to be directly indebted
to them.
[38] Roshdi Rashed, "Al-Kindī's Commentary on Archimedes' 'The Measurement of the Circle',"
Arabic Sciences and Philosophy 3 (1993) 7–12; Gerhard Endress, "Mathematics and Philosophy in
Medieval Islam," in J. P. Hogendijk and A. I. Sabra (eds.) *The Enterprise of Science in Islam* (Cambridge:
Cambridge University Press, 2003), pp. 127–31; Adamson, *Al-Kindī*, p. 36 and ch. 7.

Porphyry's *De anima*.[39] Al-Kindī appears to have paid significant attention also to Platonic texts, especially to the Socratic dialogues, echoes of which we can still find in some of the surviving titles and fragments of his works.[40] This is as it should be, given his encyclopedic interests; nevertheless, the core of his philosophical enterprise was centered in the geometrical approach to the solution of all problems associated with metaphysics and cosmology.

This focus explains the fragmentary nature of the translations from Proclus and Plotinus that he commissioned, just as it explains his philosophical eclecticism: he was interested primarily in the question of the One or God as the first principle and in all the issues – methodological, metaphysical, cosmological – related to that concept; he was, accordingly, fashioning his own approach from the *disjecta membra* of Greek philosophy available in the written (but not living) tradition. This is why his philosophical thinking does not belong to a school tradition, why it does not rest on preexisting translations of Greek philosophical works, and why it is an original creation, in Arabic, of the intellectualism of early Abbasid society.[41]

Al-Kindī's work revived philosophy as living practice and introduced it in the new social environment of Abbasid Baghdad by making it relevant to its intellectual concerns and widely acceptable as the indispensable means for critical and rigorous thinking based on reason, not authority. The resurrection of philosophy in Arabic in the early ninth century was a revolutionary event, as mentioned above, because up to that point anybody doing philosophy creatively in multicultural post-classical antiquity – regardless of linguistic or ethnic background – did it in Greek, while all the other philosophical activities were derivative from, and dependent upon, the main philosophizing going on simultaneously in Greek. When Arabic philosophy emerged with al-Kindī, however, the situation was completely different: it was from the very beginning independent, it chose its own paths, and it had no contemporary and living Greek philosophy either to imitate or seek inspiration from. Arabic philosophy engaged in the same enterprise Greek philosophy did before its gradual demise, but this time in its own language: Arabic philosophy internationalized Greek philosophy, and through its success it demonstrated to world culture that philosophy is a supranational enterprise. This, it seems, is what makes the transplantation and development of philosophy in other languages and cultures throughout the Middle Ages historically possible and intelligible.

---

[39] Gerhard Endress, "Building the Library of Arabic Philosophy: Platonism and Aristotelianism in the Sources of al-Kindī," in D'Ancona, *The Libraries of the Neoplatonists*, pp. 335–50.

[40] Dimitri Gutas, "Plato's *Symposion* in the Arabic Tradition," *Oriens* 31 (1988) 36–60, and Endress, "Building the Library," pp. 332–3.

[41] For the argument and details see Gutas, "Geometry and the Rebirth of Philosophy."

Arabic philosophy was also revolutionary in another way. Although Greek philosophy in its declining stages in late antiquity may be thought to have yielded to Christianity, and indeed in many ways imitated it, Arabic philosophy developed in a social context in which a dominant monotheistic religion was the ideology par excellence. Because of this, Arabic philosophy developed as a discipline not in *opposition* or *subordination* to religion, but *independent from* religion – indeed from all religions – and was considered intellectually superior to religion in its subject and method. Arabic philosophy developed, then, not as an *ancilla theologiae* but as a system of thought and a theoretical discipline that transcends all others and rationally explains all reality, including religion.

A SECOND BEGINNING

Colossal as al-Kindī's achievement (and that of the society which fostered it) was, the practice of his immediate line of successors – notably al-Sarakhsī, Abū Zayd al-Balkhī, and al-ʿĀmirī – slowly evaporated into apologetics. The cause of philosophy was taken up by a new generation of thinkers, however, who reintroduced it, as it were, to Baghdad, benefiting from the fact that it had won a permanent place in the intellectual environment there through the efforts of al-Kindī and his circle.

In ways that have not yet been properly understood, philosophy had a second beginning in Abbasid society by the end of the ninth century after the death of al-Kindī, clearly in response to additional demand, but this time in a largely Aristotelian vein. The protagonist in this case was the Nestorian Christian Abū Bishr Mattā ibn Yūnus, who came from Dayr Qunnā on the Tigris south of Baghdad. His Aristotelianism, which can be surmised to have been based on the philosophical curriculum known, if not actually practiced, at the monastery at Dayr Qunnā, can be traced directly to the Alexandrian commentators of late antiquity and reaches beyond them to Alexander of Aphrodisias and Themistius.[42]

The philosophical curriculum introduced by Mattā and the line of Baghdad Aristotelians that he established followed the classification of the sciences current in Alexandria in late antiquity, a classification that had developed from that of Aristotle's works.[43] Aristotle's Organon, including the *Rhetoric* and *Poetics*,

---

[42] Gerhard Endress, "Mattā b. Yūnus," in H. A. R. Gibb (ed.) *The Encyclopaedia of Islam*, 2nd edn (Leiden: Brill, 1960–97) VI: 844–6.

[43] Gutas, "Paul the Persian," esp. pp. 240–6, and 261–6. For a detailed treatment of the classification of the parts of philosophy (or of all the sciences) in late antiquity and early Islam, a subject of singular significance in the formation and transmission of philosophical curricula and education, see Christel Hein, *Definition und Einteilung der Philosophie von der spätantiken Einleitungsliteratur zur arabischen Enzyklopädie* (Frankfurt: Lang, 1985).

and prefaced by Porphyry's *Isagoge*, constituted the canonical nine books of logic, the instrument of philosophy. Philosophy proper was then divided into theoretical and practical components; theoretical philosophy was further subdivided into physics, mathematics, and metaphysics, and practical philosophy into ethics, economics (household management), and politics. This entire curriculum, including all the extant works of Aristotle, was translated into Arabic, in some instances by the Baghdad Aristotelians themselves. The corpus of Aristotle's writings (with the exception of the *Politics*, which was apparently made available only in excerpts at various intervals, the *Eudemian Ethics* and some of the lesser zoological treatises), together with the complete range of commentaries from Alexander of Aphrodisias onwards, was established as the Arabic curriculum of school textbooks in logic, physics, metaphysics, and ethics by Mattā Ibn Yūnus, who also provided the guidelines of a method for their study.

His colleague al-Fārābī, al-Fārābī's student Yaḥyā ibn ʿAdī, and the wide circle of disciples of the latter, prominent among whom were Abū Sulaymān al-Sijistānī, ʿĪsā ibn Zurʿa, al-Ḥasan ibn Suwār, ʿAlī ibn al-Samḥ, and Abū al-Faraj ibn al-Ṭayyib, engaged in rigorous textual analysis and philosophical interpretation of Aristotle's works, as well as composing commentaries and independent monographs on all branches of philosophy.

The significance of the Baghdad Aristotelians lies not only in their cultivation and dissemination of a rigorous Aristotelianism but also – and perhaps more importantly – in their development of a scholarly and philological approach to the study of the translated texts in the Aristotelian tradition. In their efforts to understand the meaning of these texts precisely, they frequently prepared new translations of the key texts, compared and collated earlier Syriac and Arabic translations, and lavishly annotated the school textbooks of their tradition.[44] They established Aristotelianism as the dominant philosophical current in Baghdad and, by extension, throughout the Islamic world. Their teachings traveled to Islamic Spain, where they formed the foundation of philosophical activity generally, and in particular the twelfth-century philosophy of Averroes. In the East, Avicenna effected in the eleventh century a grand philosophical synthesis of both preceding lines of philosophy, al-Kindī's and al-Fārābī's; though he benefited from the texts of the Baghdad Aristotelians, he also criticized them severely for their pedantry and lack of philosophical insight. His philosophy, which quickly dominated intellectual life in the Islamic world, put an end to the independent existence of their line by the end of the eleventh century.

---

[44] To their diligence we owe the survival of the most important (and, for some treatises, the only extant) manuscript of the Arabic Aristotelian Organon (Paris, Bibliothèque Nationale Ar. 2356) and the *Physics* (Leiden, Warner 583).

2

THE EMERGENCE OF MEDIEVAL
LATIN PHILOSOPHY

JOHN MARENBON

Many scholars are tempted to speak not of an emergence, but a rebirth or reawakening of thought in the Middle Ages, as if the ideas of antiquity had simply been put on hold for a while and then resumed. The image is, however, not just clichéd, but also misleading. We awake refreshed, perhaps, but not fundamentally changed or reinvented. After two and a half centuries, from *ca.* 525 to *ca.* 775, when there seems to have been no philosophizing, Latin Europe did not simply reassume, a little bleary eyed, its former philosophical existence. Indeed, it is even uncertain what that former existence would have been. Late ancient philosophy as practiced in the great Platonic schools of Athens and Alexandria? No; its links with medieval Latin thought, as opposed to Byzantine and Islamic thought, were partial and indirect. Ancient Latin philosophy? But that was hardly a tradition, just a handful of books and authors. Instead of envisaging a reawakening, then, it is more profitable to picture the emergence of a set of cultural circumstances utterly different from those of the ancient world, even once it had been christianized, and then to see in what way people began philosophizing within them. This is the aim of the first two parts of this chapter: the first outlines the places, institutional and intellectual, where philosophy took place from the late eighth to the twelfth century; the second looks at the ways in which thinkers thought philosophically within them – both externally, through written forms, and internally, through forms of argument. In the much briefer third part, I try to justify some of my choices – the way I have identified philosophy, and my marking out *ca.* 780 – *ca.* 1200 (for short: 'the early Middle Ages') as a discrete period in Latin philosophy.

PLACES FOR PHILOSOPHY: THE INSTITUTIONAL SETTINGS

Philosophizing in medieval Latin Europe began in the eighth century, in the royal court of Charlemagne, then moved in the later ninth century to the great monasteries, such as St. Amand and Corbie in northern France, Fleury and

Tours on the Loire, Reichenau in Germany, Bobbio in northern Italy, and St. Gallen in present-day Switzerland. It began to flourish, from the late tenth century, in urban cathedral schools with such figures as Gerbert at Rheims, Fulbert at Chartres, Anselm of Laon at the cathedral school there, and William of Champeaux at Paris. From the 1120s, Paris became the preeminent center.[1] In order to see why the differences between these institutional settings are important for the historian of philosophy, let us look a little more closely at the first and the last of them.

Charlemagne was intimately involved in the new interest in philosophy in his court. One of the earliest, in-part philosophical texts was issued as if it were by Charlemagne himself, no less: the *Work of King Charles against the Synod* (known also as the *Libri Carolini*) – the Latin response to the Greek position on image worship.[2] Charlemagne's leading court intellectual, Alcuin, depicts the king as his pupil, being instructed in logic and rhetoric in two of Alcuin's didactic dialogues. One of these, *On Dialectic*, is the first medieval logical textbook. Of course, Charlemagne's authorship and participation in classroom instruction represent not realities, but an ideology: that of royal approval for logic especially, both as a tool for understanding Christian doctrine and as a weapon in religious controversy. Charlemagne's grandson, Charles the Bald, went further in providing a congenial atmosphere for philosophy. The leading philosopher of this period was John Scottus Eriugena, and he not only taught at the court but was also protected by his royal patron when his critics accused him of heresy.[3] Culturally, Charles the Bald emulated Byzantium; it is no accident that his court philosopher learned Greek and translated and assimilated the Greek Christian Platonists.

Paris became the center for twelfth-century philosophy because of the decision to allow any qualified master to set up a school there, on payment of a fee

[1] For a general account see Émile Lesne, *Histoire de la propriété ecclésiastique en France*, vol. V: *Les écoles de la fin du VIIIe siècle à la fin du XIIe* (Lille: Facultés catholiques, 1940).

[2] In fact, the author is Theodulf of Orleans. On the philosophical material here, see John Marenbon, "Alcuin, the Council of Frankfurt, and the Beginnings of Medieval Philosophy," in R. Berndt (ed.) *Das Frankfurter Konzil von 794: Kristallisationspunkt karolingischer Kultur* (Mainz: Selbstverlag der Gesellschaft für Mittelrheinische Kirchengeschichte, 1997) II: 603–15; Ann Freeman's introduction to her edition of Theodulf's *Libri Carolini*, printed in the original English version in Ann Freeman, *Theodulf of Orléans: Charlemagne's Spokesman Against the Second Council of Nicaea* (Aldershot: Ashgate, 2003); and, most trustworthy, Eva Bohn, "Candidus and the Continuity of Carolingian Intellectual Life after Alcuin" (Ph.D. dissertation: University of Cambridge, 2004).

[3] See John Marenbon "Carolingian Thought," in R. McKitterick (ed.) *Carolingian Culture: Emulation and Innovation* (Cambridge: Cambridge University Press, 1984), and "John Scottus and Carolingian Theology: from the *De praedestinatione*, its Background and its Critics, to the *Periphyseon*," in M. Gibson and J. Nelson (eds.) *Charles the Bald: Court and Kingdom*, 2nd edn (Aldershot: Variorum, 1990) 303–25.

to the cathedral authorities.[4] By the 1130s, as John of Salisbury's account of his education there shows (*Metalogicon* II.10), the student could choose among a great variety of masters – rather than being constrained to a single one, however illustrious – and the work of each teacher was stimulated by contact and competition with the others. Outstanding thinkers of the 1130s and 40s, such as Peter Abaelard, Alberic of Paris, and Gilbert of Poitiers explicitly or implicitly adapt and criticize the others' logical and metaphysical ideas. In the second half of the century, distinct schools form, each following one of these masters' teachings, and defending them against the attacks of rival schools. Often – as is very strikingly the case with the Porretans (followers of Gilbert) – these schools develop and refine the theories they have inherited.[5] These ways of doing philosophy could not have grown up in the disparate, geographically isolated schools of the previous century.

PLACES FOR PHILOSOPHY: THE INTELLECTUAL SETTINGS

Although various activities were described as "philosophy" in the early Middle Ages, none corresponds directly to what we mean today by doing philosophy. This is true in various ways, as we shall see, but one way in which it manifests itself vividly is in the absence of any distinct intellectual context for the subject: philosophizing happened only because other activities offered the occasion or the stimulation for it. What were these activities? They appeared most prominently in the course of studying the standard curriculum of the seven liberal arts (especially logic), in religious controversy, and in trying to systematize theology.

Philosophy and the seven liberal arts

Late ancient authors, from Augustine onwards, began to formulate their educational scheme in terms of seven liberal (as opposed to merely practical) arts,

---

[4] A good account of the factors that made Paris preeminent is given in Richard Southern, *Scholastic Humanism and the Unification of Europe*, vol I: *Foundations* (Oxford: Oxford University Press, 1995) pp. 163–233. Southern's disparagement of Chartres as an intellectual center is controversial, but probably broadly correct: see N. M. Häring, "Chartres and Paris Revisited," in J. R. O'Donnell (ed.) *Essays in Honour of Anton Charles Pegis* (Toronto: Pontifical Institute of Medieval Studies, 1974) 268–329 for a pro-Chartrian view, and Thomas Ricklin, "Chartres (École de)," in Gauvard *et al.* (eds.) *Dictionnaire du moyen âge* (Paris: Quadrige/Presses Universitaires de France, 2002) 269–71, for an intelligent, balanced assessment. For the beginnings of the importance of Paris, shortly after 1100, see Irène Rosier-Catach (ed.) *Les Glosulae super Priscianum, Guillaume de Champeaux, Abelard: Arts du langage et théologie aux confins des XIe/XIIe siècles* (Turnhout: Brepols, forthcoming).
[5] See the special issue on nominalism of *Vivarium* 30 (1992), ed. W. Courtenay, especially Sten Ebbesen, "What Must One Have an Opinion About," 62–79, and Yukio Iwakuma and Sten Ebbesen, "Logico-Theological Schools from the Second Half of the 12th Century: A List of Sources," 173–210.

which came to be divided into the linguistic arts of the trivium (grammar, logic, and rhetoric) and the mathematical arts of the quadrivium (arithmetic, geometry, astronomy, and music). For example, Martianus Capella's *On the Marriage of Philology and Mercury*, a fifth-century encyclopedic work that was much studied from the ninth to the twelfth century, dedicates a book to each art. Logic above all – but also grammar and, to an extent, rhetoric – offered early medieval writers occasions to explore philosophical questions.[6]

The earliest medieval logical curriculum, studied from the time of Alcuin's *On Dialectic* (late 780s?) until the late tenth century, was based mainly on the accounts of logic in the encyclopedias of Cassiodorus, Isidore of Seville and Martianus Capella, together with Apuleius's *Periermenias* (an account of basic Aristotelian syllogistic) and the *Ten Categories*, a paraphrase-commentary of Aristotle's *Categories*. The last of these was written in the circle of Themistius, but attributed in the Middle Ages to Augustine. This misattribution points to one of the reasons why logic had such a large place in early medieval education: it was seen as indispensable in theological discussion, both because it provided a way of posing fundamental questions about God and his relation to his creation, and because it furnished a formidable argumentative weapon in controversy. In this first phase of medieval logic, its study was philosophical not so much because it involved a grasp of concepts and problems about argumentation – that would come a little later – but because its theological use provoked wider questions. For example, the question of whether God fits into any of the ten Aristotelian categories provided thinkers from Alcuin to John Scottus Eriugena and his followers the chance to reflect both on some basic metaphysics and on the adequacy of language to its subject matter.[7]

By the eleventh century, the logical curriculum was organized around Boethius's translations of Aristotle's *Categories* and Porphyry's *Isagoge* (an introduction to the *Categories*), studied with the help of Boethius's commentaries, along with Boethius's textbooks on categorical and hypothetical syllogisms and topical argument. Unlike the earlier curriculum, these works could, and did, give medieval readers a firm grasp of many areas of ancient logic. For instance, starting from an analysis of hypothetical syllogisms (those in which one of the premises is a compound proposition), Abaelard's *Dialectica* (probably *ca.* 1107–15) is able to explore in unparalleled depth the relationship between truth in

[6] See Günter Glauche, *Schullektüre im Mittelalter: Entstehung und Wandlungen des Lektürekanons bis 1200 nach den Quellen dargestellt* (Munich: Arbeo-Gesellschaft, 1970); William Stahl and Richard Johnson, *Martianus Capella and the Seven Liberal Arts* (New York: Columbia University Press, 1971); Ilsetraut Hadot, *Arts libéraux et philosophie dans la pensée antique* (Paris: Études Augustiniennes, 1984).

[7] See John Marenbon, *From the Circle of Alcuin to the School of Auxerre* (Cambridge: Cambridge University Press, 1981), and "The Latin Tradition of Logic to 1100," in D. M. Gabbay and J. Woods (eds.) *Handbook to the History of Logic*, vol. II (Amsterdam: North-Holland, 2008), 1–63, 65–81.

conditionals and validity in argument (see Chapter 10).[8] There are enough
unresolved metaphysical problems in the *Categories* and the *Isagoge* (a brilliantly
unsuccessful attempt to defuse these problems) to make a logic curriculum based
on these works a path to questions in metaphysics and the philosophy of mind.
Similarly, the *De interpretatione*, as presented by Boethius's long commentary
(heavily based on Porphyry's lost work), opens up the philosophy of language.[9]

In addition to logic, grammar also provided opportunities for philosophizing,
in two distinct ways (see Chapter 15). First, the textbook for the advanced study
of grammar was the *Institutions*, written by Priscian in the early sixth century.
Priscian was influenced by Stoic linguistic theory and, though most of the
work is about the particularities of Latin, some passages raise issues in semantics
that were taken up by medieval readers, especially by eleventh- and twelfth-
century readers familiar with the Aristotelian semantics of *De interpretatione*.
Second, ancient Latin texts were studied as part of grammar. They included not
only poetry (Virgil, Ovid, Lucan), but also a quartet of philosophical works:
Plato's *Timaeus* in Calcidius's partial translation, along with his commentary;
Martianus Capella's *On the Marriage of Philology and Mercury*, which prefaces its
encyclopedic treatment of the liberal arts with an allegorical account of an ascent
by learning to heaven; Macrobius's commentary on *The Dream of Scipio* (the last
book of Cicero's *Republic*), which combines astronomy, political philosophy, and
an account of some Platonic doctrines; and Boethius's *Consolation of Philosophy* –
the work of a Christian written, however, without recourse to revelation and as a
philosophical argument, drawing on Stoic ethics and Neoplatonic epistemology
and metaphysics. These works all had to be glossed and commented on, forcing
their readers to grapple both with the philosophical issues they raised and with
the often difficult negotiation between the positions such authorities proposed,
on the one hand, and the doctrines of Christianity on the other.[10]

As for rhetoric, although it did not yet link up with political philosophy as it would in the later Middle Ages, it did stimulate the study of
ethics. For, at the end of the most popular rhetorical textbook – Cicero's *De*

---

[8] See Christopher J. Martin, "Embarrassing Arguments and Surprising Conclusions in the Develop-
ment of Theories of the Conditional in the Twelfth Century," in J. Jolivet and A. de Libera (eds.)
Gilbert de Poitiers et ses contemporains (Naples: Bibliopolis, 1987) 377–401; "Logic," in J. Brower
and K. Guilfoy (eds.) *The Cambridge Companion to Abelard* (Cambridge: Cambridge University
Press, 2004) 158–99; Ian Wilks, "Peter Abelard and his Contemporaries," in Gabbay and Woods,
Handbook to the History of Logic, II: 83–105.

[9] See Margaret Cameron, "Boethius on Utterances, Understanding, and Reality" in J. Marenbon
(ed.) *The Cambridge Companion to Boethius* (Cambridge: Cambridge University Press, 2009) 85–104.

[10] See Édouard Jeauneau, "L'héritage de la philosophie antique durant le haut Moyen Âge," *Settimane
di studio del Centro italiano di studi sull'alto medioevo* 22 (1975) 17–54; see also William of Conches's
Glosae super Boetium, one of the most important twelfth-century commentaries on Boethius's
Consolation, with an extensive discussion of methods of interpretation in Lodi Nauta's introduction.

inventione – there is a brief discussion of the virtues and their divisions. This discussion proved far more influential than its size would suggest. Alcuin's dialogue, the earliest medieval rhetorical textbook, is called *On Rhetoric and the Virtues*; Abaelard would later refer to *De inventione* as "the treatise on ethics" and twist Cicero's unpondered classifications into something thoughtful and thought-provoking.[11]

Philosophy and religious controversy

By the eighth century, Christian doctrine in the Latin church was rich in positions that were formulated in highly philosophical vocabulary, often borrowed from the ancient schools, and yet at the same time either underdetermined or implicitly contradictory. Not surprisingly, their interpretation led to controversies, and these controversies occasioned philosophical debate. Two striking examples are the dispute over predestination in the ninth century, and that over the Eucharist in the eleventh.

The terms for the medieval debate on predestination were set by Augustine. He had tried throughout his life to reconcile two conflicting ideas: first, that humans must have freedom of choice in order to be moral agents; second, that God owes nothing to humans because, after the Fall, all humans stand to be damned unless God rescues them, something he would not do because they deserve it but because he graciously so chooses. Augustine's later work stresses the second of these requirements, and in the mid-ninth century Gottschalk of Orbais brought out its full force by insisting that there is a dual predestination, either to salvation or to damnation. Worried by the social implications of a teaching that seemed to offer no scope to the individual's efforts in gaining salvation, some of the leading Carolingian churchmen reacted by claiming that there is no predestination to hell but only to heaven – a position only superficially less deterministic than Gottschalk's, since anyone *not* predestined to heaven would in fact be damned. John Scottus, asked to intervene, was led to a bold analysis of free will and law in his *De praedestinatione*. His position, radical in its insistence against the grain of Augustinian Christianity on real human

---

[11] See Karin Fredborg, "The Commentaries on Cicero's *De Inventione* and *Rhetorica ad Herennium* by William of Champeaux," *Cahiers de l'Institut du Moyen Age Grec et Latin* 17 (1976) 1–39; "Abelard on Rhetoric," in C. J. Mews *et al.* (eds.) *Rhetoric and Renewal in the Latin West 1100–1540: Essays in Honour of John O. Ward* (Leiden; Brill, 2003) 55–80; V. Cox and J. Ward (eds.) *The Rhetoric of Cicero in its Medieval and Early Renaissance Commentary Tradition* (Leiden: Brill 2006). On Abaelard's use of the *De inventione*, see Gabriella d'Anna, "Abelardo e Cicerone," *Studi Medievali* (3a series) 10 (1969) 333–419, and John Marenbon, *The Philosophy of Peter Abelard* (Cambridge: Cambridge University Press, 1997) pp. 283–7.

freedom and responsibility, in its turn provoked some intelligent philosophical discussion from his opponents (see Chapter 29).[12]

The problem of the Eucharist came into prominence two centuries later, when Berengar of Tours attacked the orthodox views of Lanfranc, according to which the bread and wine in the Eucharist is really transformed into the body and blood of Christ. According to Berengar, this doctrine is doomed to incoherence given an Aristotelian analysis of substance and accident. In Berengar's view, accidents are individuated by the substances in which they inhere, so that the individual accidental properties of the bread and wine could not inhere in some other substance. Through the course of this debate, Berengar and his contemporaries were forced to interpret and discuss the metaphysics implicit in the *Categories*, choosing one reading among the various possible ones.[13]

Philosophy and systematic theology

From the late eleventh century onwards, thinkers tried to systematize the teaching of Christian doctrine. One method looked to scriptural exegesis and treatises of canon law and sought to draw together the material they provided so as to offer a coherent, orderly whole, in which points of contention – often suggested originally by apparently contradictory texts from the Bible or the Church Fathers – could be not merely presented, but argued through and resolved. Originated by Anselm of Laon and William of Champeaux at the turn of the twelfth century, this method was developed by Abaelard and Hugh of St. Victor, in their different ways, from both of whom Peter Lombard borrowed in his *Sentences* (*ca.* 1155). Although Peter Lombard is a far less philosophically minded author than the thirteenth- and fourteenth-century theologians who used the *Sentences* as their textbook, his work is full of philosophical problems, some of which are more fully treated both by Abaelard and by some of the later twelfth-century theologians: for instance, the problem of whether divine prescience is compatible with human freedom, or whether God could act differently from the way in which he does in fact act.[14]

---

[12] See Marenbon, "John Scottus and Carolingian Theology," and the bibliography there.

[13] See Toivo Holopainen, *Dialectic and Theology in the Eleventh Century* (Leiden: Brill, 1996) pp. 44–118; John Marenbon, "Les Catégories au début du moyen âge," in O. Bruun and L. Corti (eds.) *Les* Catégories *et leur histoire* (Paris: Vrin, 2005) pp. 232–7; see also Irène Rosier-Catach, *La parole efficace: signe, rituel, sacré* (Paris: Seuil, 2004) pp. 355–63.

[14] Cf. A. M. Landgraf, *Introduction à l'histoire de la littérature théologique de la scolastique naissante*, tr. A. M. Landry and L.-B. Geiger (Montréal: Institut d'études médiévales, 1973); Philipp Rosemann, *Peter Lombard* (Oxford: Oxford University Press, 2004). For texts, see Anselm of Laon and William of Champeaux in Odon Lottin, *Psychologie et morale aux XIIe et XIII siècles* (Gembloux: Duculot,

The other method was invented by Gilbert of Poitiers on the basis of Boethius's short theological treatises, which themselves use Aristotelian logic and physics to refute heretical doctrines and had been an intellectual influence since the ninth century. Gilbert's systematization involves a theory of the different roles of different disciplines and their principles in gaining different sorts of knowledge; on this basis, he suggests a method of coming to an understanding of some of the most mysterious Christian doctrines, such as God's triunity. Gilbert was also led to elaborate one of the most ambitious metaphysical schemes of the period, partly in order to show the limits of its application to God. His followers explored his line of thought critically and with even more sophistication.[15]

WAYS OF PHILOSOPHIZING: THE WRITTEN FORMS

The *quaestiones* characteristic of thirteenth- and fourteenth-century scholastic thought are not found in the early Middle Ages. One does, however, find a form of writing that looks nearly as strange to our modern eyes: the method of assembling or paraphrasing existing writings by authorities of the past. This was Alcuin's regular method; few of his words, and fewer of his ideas, are his own. But even the philosopher of the period most famed for his originality, Peter Abaelard, produced a work, *Sic et non* ("Yes and No"), that apart from its preface consists of quotations, mostly from the Church Fathers. As we shall see, however, this method should not be thought unphilosophical.

The practice of commentary is central to how philosophy was taught and ideas were developed from mid-antiquity until the seventeenth century. In the ninth, tenth, and eleventh centuries, the schoolmasters' work of commentary tended to be preserved as glosses in the margins and between the lines of manuscripts. These glosses often belonged to anonymous "Gloss Traditions" – that is to say, a slightly different selection of the same glosses (with small variations) appears in a number of manuscripts. Sometimes there is more than one Gloss Tradition to a particular work, and sometimes the traditions are intermixed in a single manuscript; many manuscripts contain a few glosses not found elsewhere. In the twelfth century, Gloss Traditions tend to be replaced by continuous commentaries: Abaelard commented on the logic of Aristotle, Porphyry, and Boethius; William of Conches commented on Priscian, Macrobius, Boethius's *Consolation*, and the *Timaeus*; Gilbert of Poitiers commented on Boethius's theological treatises. These commentaries, written by known, single writers,

---

1948–60) vol. V; Hugh of St. Victor's *De sacramentis*, his theological *summa*; and Peter Abaelard, *Opera theologica* vol. III.
[15] Lauge Nielsen, *Theology and Philosophy in the Twelfth Century* (Leiden: Brill, 1982).

are the exception, however, and even they may be less unified texts than they seem. Most early medieval Latin commentaries – including a good hundred on logical texts – are anonymous; they are sometimes made up of different layers of composition, probably by different teachers; in some cases, they are students' transcripts of what they heard, perhaps at the lectures of a number of different masters.[16]

Not many early medieval philosophical works are written simply as independent treatises. There are, indeed, the treatises on logic (*De dialectica*) by Garland of Besançon (*ca.* 1100/20?), Abaelard, and William of Lucca (late twelfth century), as well as William of Conches's *Philosophia mundi* (*ca.* 1125), a survey mainly of natural science, and some of Anselm's works, such as his work on the "concord" of free will and divine prescience. Occasional treatises, such as those written for a controversy (John Scottus's treatise *De praedestinatione*, for instance, and Lanfranc's and Berengar's treatises on the Eucharist) are more common.

The dialogue was a widely used form for setting out theological and philosophical ideas. Alcuin, following earlier medieval didactic traditions, used a pupil–teacher dialogue for his treatises on the arts of the trivium. Anselm liked to write in a dialogue form heavily influenced by Augustine's early philosophical dialogues. Eriugena cast his vast *Periphyseon* (all five books of it) in the form of a dialogue between a teacher and pupil, but he used this format creatively – sometimes allowing the pupil to misunderstand or argue badly, and to be corrected by the teacher, sometimes, by contrast, putting into the pupil's mouth bold ideas that he perhaps wanted to suggest only tentatively. In Anselm's *De grammatico* and Adelard of Bath's *Natural Questions*, the pupils are portrayed as querulous or even aggressive.[17] More ambitious literary forms were also used, especially in the twelfth century. Abaelard's *Collationes* is a dream-vision dialogue between a Jew (whose way of life in twelfth-century Christendom is vividly sketched), a Philosopher – who is like an ancient Greek or Roman thinker brought back to life – and a Christian. In his *Cosmographia*, Bernard Silvestris retells in prose and verse the story of how the world and humans were created, drawing on and implicitly commenting on the *Timaeus*. In *The Plaint of Nature* (1160/70), Alan of Lille copies the form of Boethius's *Consolation*, and by echoing and contrasting with this model, enriches the meaning of his own discourse.

---

[16] Editing and study of this material should thus not be undertaken, as sometimes happens, according to the scholarly model of a literary text as a finished work by one author. For a survey of the genres of glosses and commentaries in the logical tradition, see the introduction to John Marenbon, "Medieval Latin Commentaries and Glosses on Aristotelian Logical Texts, Before c. 1150 A.D.," in C. Burnett (ed.) *Glosses and Commentaries on Aristotelian Logical Texts: The Syriac, Arabic and Medieval Latin Traditions* (London: Warburg Institute, 1993) 77–127.

[17] See Klaus Jacobi, *Gespräche lesen: philosophische Dialoge im Mittelalter* (Tübingen: Narr, 1999).

WAYS OF PHILOSOPHIZING: FORMS OF ARGUMENT

Within these various different types of writing, philosophical argument was conducted in a number of different ways – affected, though not determined, by the written form (and, in some cases, the type of oral teaching that lay behind it) and by the broader setting, physical and intellectual. Here are six types of argument that were used in the early Middle Ages: all of them are philosophical in a broad and useful sense of the word, although the first two types are especially close to the ways in which analytical philosophers are now taught to argue.

1. Conceptual analysis. The conceptual adequacy of the stages of an argument are defended or attacked. In his *Proslogion* ch. 2 argument for the existence of God, for instance, Anselm claims that the Fool who denies the existence of God will mentally grasp the meaning of 'that-than-which-nothing-greater-can-be-thought.' The first critic of his argument, Gaunilo, rejects this claim, however (sec. 4). One can grasp the meaning of an expression by having in mind the thing to which it refers, but whether that-than-which-nothing-greater-can-be-thought exists is the question at issue. Alternatively, one can understand an expression that refers to something that might not or does not exist if one is familiar with the genus or species of the thing (thus, I understand 'the man sitting in my room hates Anselm,' although no one is in fact sitting in my room), but that-than-which-nothing-greater-can-be-thought belongs to no genus or species we know. The term 'that-than-which-nothing-greater-can-be-thought' therefore generates almost nothing in the way of a meaning. Anselm replies (sec. 8) that that-than-which-nothing-greater-can-be-thought must have every attribute that it is better to have than not to have; by thinking through these attributes we can give the term a meaning.[18]

2. Argument through disambiguation. An apparent problem is resolved by pointing out hidden ambiguities in the way it is stated. In his *Dialectica*, for instance, Abaelard considers an argument designed to show that the contingency of future events is incompatible with the claim that, being omniscient, God foresees the future. The argument claims that, since:

1. If (a) something happens otherwise than God has foreseen, then (b) God is mistaken, and there is a logical principle:

P. If the antecedent of a conditional is possible, so is the consequent; it follows that:

2. If (a) it is possible that something happens otherwise than God has foreseen, then (b) it is possible that God is mistaken.

---

[18] For a discussion of these passages, see John Marenbon, "Anselm Rewrites his Argument: *Proslogion* 2 and the *Response* to Gaunilo," in J. Hamesse and O. Weijers (eds.) *Écriture et réécriture des textes philosophiques médiévaux* (Turnhout: Brepols, 2006) 347–65.

According to Abaelard, the antecedent (2a) consists of a subject ('that some-thing happens'), a predicate ('it is possible'), and a qualification ('otherwise than God has foreseen'). His way of showing that future contingent events are not precluded by this argument depends on showing that (2a) is ambiguous: it has different meanings depending on how it is analyzed:

understood one way, [2] is false (that is, when its antecedent is true), and in another way, it is true (when the antecedent itself is false). The antecedent is true when understood thus: when 'otherwise than God has foreseen' is the qualification of the predicate, i.e. of 'possible,' in this way — 'for the thing to happen is possible-other-than-God-has-foreseen,' in that it has the power of happening otherwise. But if the qualification is placed on the subject, which is 'happen,' in such way as for it to say 'for-a-thing-to-happen-otherwise-than-God-has-foreseen (all of this) is possible' the antecedent is false and cannot be proven. For what this proposition says is altogether impossible: 'for-a-thing-to-happen-otherwise-than-God-has-foreseen,' which as a whole is the subject, and 'possible' as the predicate without qualification, just as the following is impossible: 'a thing happens otherwise than it happens." (*Dialectica*, ed. de Rijk, p. 218)

But, Abaelard continues, what Principle P establishes is that a true non-modal conditional remains true if 'is possible' is predicated of the whole antecedent and of the whole consequent. On the second reading of (2) — 'If for-a-thing-to-happen-otherwise-than-God-has-foreseen is possible, then it is possible that God is mistaken' — Principle P is indeed applied to (1), because the whole antecedent as well as the whole consequent is said to be possible — and so the whole conditional is true. But since the antecedent (2a) on that second reading is false, the truth of the consequent (2b) is not demonstrated. In contrast, the first reading — 'If for the thing to happen is possible-other-than-God-has-foreseen, then it is possible that God is mistaken' — has a true antecedent, but the conditional itself is false.[19]

3. *Argument through juxtaposition.* When texts from the past are selected and juxtaposed in certain ways, the choice and arrangement can serve to make a philosophical point. This was Alcuin's method, and Abaelard's in *Sic et non*. Abbo of Fleury, an underrated logician of the late tenth century, also worked this way, combining material from Boethius's newly discovered *De hypotheticis syllogismis* with an account of the Stoic modes of the syllogism, which — by contrast with Boethius's presentation — are genuinely propositional logic.[20]

---

[19] For a detailed discussion of this argument and its influence, see John Marenbon, *Le temps, la prescience et les futurs contingents de Boèce à Thomas d'Aquin* (Paris: Vrin, 2005). Note that the existing editions of the *Dialectica* emend this passage so as to destroy its sense.

[20] This point is brought out in Franz Schupp's notes and introduction to Abbo's *De syllogismis hypotheticis.*

4. Argument through interpretation. In the *Timaeus*, Plato talks of a World Soul. In his commentaries, William of Conches at first accepts the identification of this World Soul with the Holy Spirit of Christian doctrine; later, he distances himself from the idea and eventually gives it up.[21] A number of philosophical and some pragmatic non-philosophical issues (such as ecclesiastical criticism and fear of punishment) are bound up with both this interpretation and its abandonment. If Plato grasped Christian truths, how? If not, how should his thought be regarded? On what principles do we select from what ancient science teaches? What is the place for non-literal modes of expression in philosophical writing, and what are the criteria for interpreting them? Argument through interpretation goes on in logical commentaries as well. Apparent contradictions between Boethius and Aristotle, for instance, lead medieval readers to posit new theories that are found in neither.

5. Imaginative argument. Bernard Silvestris's *Cosmographia* is a retelling of the Platonic creation story; his *Mathematicus* is a story that takes up elements of the Oedipus legend and its questioning about fatalism. Abaelard muses, in prose and poetry, about Jephthah, the Old Testament king who found that a vow he had taken bound him to sacrifice his daughter.[22] Abaelard uses the story to explore moral dilemmas more fully and openly than in his more theoretical ethical writings.

6. Opening a conceptual space. In his *Periphyseon* (ed. Jeauneau, II: 597AB), Eriugena argues that, contrary to the accepted view, the Aristotelian categories do not include everything, because "no one of those who correctly philosophize doubts that possible things and impossible things should be counted in the number of things." Although Eriugena refers to Aristotle's *De interpretatione*, what he is saying is strikingly un-Aristotelian, because for Aristotle – who accepts the Principle of Plenitude (that all genuine possibilities are realized at some point in time) – merely possible things have no ontological standing. In a way that he probably did not notice fully himself, Eriugena thus opens the conceptual space in which would develop tentatively in the eleventh and twelfth centuries, and then explicitly with John Duns Scotus at the end of the thirteenth, a non-Aristotelian theory of modality that leads to Leibniz's possible worlds.[23] It is the setting – not merely theological, but one strongly influenced by Greek negative theology – that explains how he was able to do so.

---

[21] The texts are well set out in the text and apparatus of William's *Glosae super Platonem*, ed. Jeauneau, p. 124.

[22] See Marenbon, *Philosophy of Peter Abelard*, pp. 319–20 (with references to the various texts).

[23] For the background to medieval modal theory, see Simo Knuuttila, *Modalities in Medieval Philosophy* (London: Routledge, 1993).

METHODOLOGY AND EARLY MEDIEVAL PHILOSOPHY:
TWO EXPLANATIONS AND A CHALLENGE

The phrase 'early medieval philosophy' calls for some explanation, which it is easier to give now than it would have been at the start. How can we distinguish philosophy from non-philosophy during this time? Also, granted that 'early medieval' is taken to stand for *ca.* 780–1200, what justification is there for treating it as a separate period in Latin philosophy, distinct from a later 'scholastic' period?

Although early medieval writers used the term 'philosophy' in various ways, what they most often included under it is either too wide (all theoretical learning) or too narrow (non-Christian learning and speculation) to yield what a reader of a history of philosophy today might reasonably expect. As the section above on the intellectual setting of philosophy indicates, we must thus search out philosophizing in various different educational and ecclesiastical contexts. We can recognize it as such because the questions raised and the methods used to explore them have a broad similarity with those used today, although there is no clear boundary line and it would be wrong, in thinking about the methods used by philosophers today, to restrict ourselves to those used in analytical philosophy departments.

The reason for regarding the early medieval period as a unit is that, before and after it, the range of sources (as outlined above) is very different; both the institutional and intellectual places for philosophizing become, in the main, radically simplified, and the universities and the arts and theology courses within them become standardized (see Chapter 4). The forms of philosophical writing change, mainly to reflect university teaching, and for the most part the methods of philosophizing become restricted to the first three classified above.

By arguing in this way for a periodization within medieval philosophy, I am suggesting the need for a way of envisaging the material that complements the arrangement by topics, in which the contours of different periods in different geographical and cultural settings are allowed to play in counterpoint to the analysis of arguments. This and the other introductory chapters may seem to be an historical aperitif, before the serious philosophical banquet. I think of my piece, however, rather as a preparatory shot of something stronger, to steel the reader's resolve to read what follows both with *and* against the analytical grain, along with some hints, for one period and cultural setting, of how to start doing so.

3

BYZANTIUM

KATERINA IERODIAKONOU

PHILOSOPHY IN BYZANTIUM

The Greek-speaking scholars of Byzantium – the eastern part of the Roman Empire, which was not devastated in the fifth century by barbarian invasions – have often been praised for their diligence in copying a great number of ancient philosophical texts, thus making an invaluable contribution towards the preservation and transmission of these texts for the generations to come. It is more often than not overlooked, however, that in Byzantium the works of ancient philosophers were arduously copied in order to be closely studied, commented on, and otherwise used for educational purposes. There is ample evidence that, at least from the ninth century to the fall of Constantinople in 1453, the Byzantines seriously engaged in a fervent dialogue with the different ancient philosophical traditions. This dialogue resulted in the composition of many philosophical works that belong to various genres of philosophical writing, including paraphrases, extended commentaries, commentaries in question-and-answer form, small handbooks, treatises on specific topics (sometimes in dialogue form), and letters and orations with philosophical content.[1]

Though philosophy in Byzantium was undoubtedly influenced by ancient Greek philosophical doctrines – which, after all, provided the Byzantines with

---

[1] For a general survey of the philosophical production in Byzantium, though somewhat outdated, see Basil Tatakis, *La philosophie Byzantine* (Paris: Presses Universitaires de France, 1949), tr. N. Moutafakis, *Byzantine Philosophy* (Indianapolis: Hackett, 2003). See also Klaus Oehler, *Antike Philosophie und byzantinisches Mittelalter* (Munich: Beck, 1969); Paul Lemerle, *Le premier humanisme byzantin* (Paris: Presses Universitaires de France, 1971); Gerhard Podskalsky, *Theologie und Philosophie in Byzanz* (Munich: Beck, 1977); Herbert Hunger, "Philosophie," in *Die hochsprachliche profane Literatur den Byzantiner* (Munich: Beck, 1978) I: 3–62; Alain de Libera, *La philosophie médiévale* (Paris: Presses Universitaires de France, 1993) pp. 9–51; Michel Cacouros, "De la pensée grecque à la pensée Byzantine," in J.-F. Mattéi (ed.) *Encyclopédie philosophique universelle* (Paris: Presses Universitaires de France, 1998) IV: 1362–84. For a detailed bibliography of works on Byzantine philosophy, see Linos Benakis, "Bibliographie internationale sur la philosophie Byzantine (1949–1990)," in *Bibliographie Byzantine publié à l'occasion du XVIIIe Congrès Internationale d'Études Byzantines* (Athens: Comité hellénique des études byzantines, 1991) 319–77.

both a well-articulated theoretical framework and a sophisticated philosophical language – its character could not but also be influenced by the Christian faith in which the Byzantine thinkers were deeply immersed. For they read and criticized the ancient philosophical texts in the light of their Christian beliefs and with the purpose of either rejecting pagan views or trying to incorporate them into their Christian outlook. Indeed, the connection between Byzantine philosophical works and theology is admittedly so strong that in recent years it has constituted the basis for seriously questioning the autonomy of Byzantine philosophy.[2] Even if the Byzantine thinkers often were concerned with problems that arose in the context of a Christian theological tradition, however, and even if their theological preoccupations were sometimes at the forefront of their philosophical writings, there are still abundant cases in which the Byzantines discussed genuine philosophical questions that intrigued them for their own sake – that is, questions that could or would be of interest to every philosopher, irrespective of her or his religious dogma.

In addition, some Byzantine philosophers, notably John Italos in the eleventh century, were not in favor of the view that philosophy should be treated as the handmaiden of theology. Italos rather followed the ancient philosophers in thinking that it is theology that constitutes part of philosophy, since philosophy is supposed to culminate in the attempt to understand the first principle of everything. In the same spirit, many Byzantine philosophers repeatedly advocated the adoption of a rational approach to central theological issues, even issues that concerned some of the most fundamental Christian beliefs, in opposition to those who proclaimed that Christians should rely merely on God's grace and divine revelation. From the ninth century on, Photios, Michael Psellos, John Italos, Eustratios of Nicaea, and Barlaam the Calabrian, to name but a few, strongly supported the systematic use of logic in the defense as well as in the demonstration of Christian dogmas against pagans and heretics. Others, however, including Nikephoros Gregoras and Gregory Palamas, were adamant in their claim that logical studies are useless for acquiring knowledge of God and his attributes.

The philosophical topics that the Byzantines raised and discussed in their writings vary tremendously and cover virtually all areas of philosophy.[3] They

---

[2] See Linos Benakis, "Die theoretische und praktische Autonomie der Philosophie als Fachdisziplin in Byzanz," in M. Asztalos *et al.* (eds.) *Knowledge and the Sciences in Medieval Philosophy* (Helsinki: Yliopistopaino, 1990) I: 223–7.

[3] For recent volumes of collected papers in which different topics of Byzantine philosophy are systematically discussed, see Katerina Ierodiakonou (ed.) *Byzantine Philosophy and its Ancient Sources* (Oxford: Oxford University Press, 2002); Michel Cacouros and Marie-Hélène Congourdeau, *Philosophie et sciences à Byzance de 1204 à 1453* (Leuven: Peeters, 2006).

commented on every treatise of Aristotle's Organon; they wrote logical text-books in which they summarized the main elements not only of Aristotelian but also of Stoic logic; they dealt with specific logical issues such as whether we should regard the two Basils (Basil the Elder and Basil the Great) as homonyms or synonyms, and whether logic should be treated as an instrument or a part of philosophy.[4] They were intrigued by all subjects in natural philosophy, and wrote cosmological and astronomical treatises on the origin of the world and the cosmic order.[5] They were interested in the relation between the soul and the body, in the problem of evil, and in human free will. They commented on Aristotle's ethical writings and repeatedly discussed the necessary require-ments for a good life.[6] Moreover, their writings are full of remarks on questions concerning epistemology and the skeptical challenge to knowledge, as well as on aesthetics and the interpretation of holy icons, and political philosophy and the possibility of a just state.[7]

In discussing these philosophical problems, the Byzantine thinkers exhibit different degrees of originality; sometimes they diverge considerably from the ancient philosophers with whom they disagree, sometimes they add a new argument to support an already established theory, and sometimes they simply try to appropriate an ancient view by introducing a novel example. It should be underlined, though, that originality was not what they aspired to; in this, they followed the commentators of late antiquity. On the other hand, the eclecti-cism that characterizes Byzantine philosophical works neither reduces them to mere compilations of ancient doctrines nor excludes the possibility of independent thinking, especially since there was the need to reconcile the Christian viewpoint with the ancient philosophical traditions. On such occasions, the Byzantines' aim surely was to present a Christian understanding of the world; if this understanding could be helped by the ancients' knowledge, they were

---

[4] See Michel Cacouros, "Recherches sur le commentaire inédit de Théodore Prodrome aux *Analytiques postérieurs*, livre II d'Aristote," *Atti della Accademia Pontaniana* n.s. 38 (1990) 313–38; Katerina Ierodiakonou, "The Byzantine Reception of Aristotle's *Categories*," *Synthesis Philosophica* 39 (2005) 7–31.

[5] Cf. Börje Bydén, *Theodore Metochites' Stoicheiosis astronomike and the Study of Natural Philosophy and Mathematics in Early Palaiologan Byzantium* (Gothenburg: Acta Universitatis Gothoburgensis, 2003).

[6] See H. P. F. Mercken, "The Greek Commentators on Aristotle's *Ethics*," in R. Sorabji (ed.) *Aristotle Transformed: The Ancient Commentators and their Influence* (London: Duckworth, 1990) 407–43; Katerina Ierodiakonou, "Byzantine Commentators on the Epistemic Status of Ethics," in P. Adamson *et al.* (eds.) *Philosophy, Science, and Exegesis in Greek, Arabic, and Latin Commentaries* (London: Institute of Classical Studies, 2004) 221–38.

[7] See John Demetrakopoulos, "Nicholas Cabasilas' *Quaestio de rationis valore*: An anti-Palamite Defense of Secular Wisdom," *Byzantina* 19 (1998) 53–93; Karin Hult's edition and translation of Theodore Metochites's *Semeioseis gnomikai* 1–26 and 71; Charles Barber, "Living Painting, or the Limits of Pointing? Glancing at Icons with Michael Psellos," in C. Barber and D. Jenkins (eds.) *Reading Michael Psellos* (Leiden: Brill, 2006) 117–30.

happy to appropriate this knowledge, though sometimes it proved hard to bring together worldviews that otherwise were perceived as opposing each other, as for instance the Aristotelian view of the eternity of the world and the Christian notion of creation (see Chapter 17).

The above general remarks on Byzantine philosophy cover such a long period and so many different thinkers, however, that they can present only a rudimentary and simplified picture of a section in the history of philosophy for which a lot of basic work still needs to be done.[8] Most of the relevant texts are still unpublished or are available in old (and often quite imperfect) editions; only when these texts are finally available in critical editions and carefully studied as serious philosophical works can the different styles, interests, views, and approaches of their authors emerge fully and be properly assessed. In the meantime, it is reasonable to avoid hasty categorizations of the Byzantine thinkers as either Platonists or Aristotelians – a distinction that, after all, became important only towards the end of Byzantium, notably in the fervent fifteenth-century controversy between George Gemistos Plethon and George Scholarios – Gennadios II.[9] The following examination of the Byzantines' views concerning the issue of universals will show that such categorizations can be misleading. At the same time, inquiry into these views will provide a better understanding of how the Byzantines reasoned on such central philosophical issues and of how they diverged from the previous tradition in subtle and interesting ways.

A CASE STUDY: THE THEORY OF UNIVERSALS

As with most issues, it has been widely supposed that Byzantine philosophers followed the Neoplatonic commentators of late antiquity with respect to their position on universals. Linos Benakis, for instance, has suggested that the attempt of the Neoplatonist commentators to reconcile the doctrines of Plato and Aristotle on the issue of universals was closely followed in Byzantium by prominent thinkers like Photios, John Italos, Eustratios of Nicaea, Nikephoros Blemmydes, Nikephoros Choumnos, George Scholarios – Gennadios II, and Bessarion.[10] More specifically, Benakis has suggested that the Byzantine philosophers, as

---

[8] See Michele Trizio, "Byzantine Philosophy as a Contemporary Historiographical Project," *Recherches de théologie et philosophie médiévales* 74 (2007) 247–94; Georgi Kapriev, "The Modern Study of Byzantine Philosophy," *Bulletin de philosophie médiévale* 48 (2006) 3–13.

[9] See George Karamanolis, "Plethon and Scholarios on Aristotle," in K. Ierodiakonou (ed.) *Byzantine Philosophy and its Ancient Sources* (Oxford: Oxford University Press, 2002) 253–82.

[10] Linos Benakis, "The Problem of General Concepts in Neoplatonism and Byzantine Thought," in D. J. O'Meara (ed.) *Neoplatonism and Christian Thought* (Albany: State University of New York Press, 1982) esp. pp. 75–86 and 248–9.

a rule, adopted the Neoplatonist commentators' three ways of understanding genera and species terms as referring to:

(i) the universals before the many particulars (*pro tōn pollōn*), which are generally identified with the Platonic Ideas;
(ii) the universals in the particulars (*en tois pollois*), which are supposed to correspond to Aristotle's immanent forms; and
(iii) the universals after the particulars (*epi tois pollois / meta tous pollous*), which are concepts or thoughts.

These three types of universals are the ones first introduced by the fifth-century Neoplatonist Ammonius in his commentary on Porphyry's *Isagoge*; they also are discussed in Elias's and David's commentary on the same work, in Olympiodorus's *Prolegomena*, and in Philoponus's commentary on Aristotle's *Categories*.[11] Indeed, after Porphyry's well-known presentation of the problem of universals at the start of the *Isagoge*, every ancient commentator writing either on this work or on Aristotle's *Categories* tried to give an account of the issue.

Systematic study of the relevant texts does not, however, seem unqualifiedly to support the claim that the Byzantines adhered to the theory propounded by the Neoplatonist commentators on the subject of universals. Rather, it suggests that they diverged from this tradition at certain points – points which, although they at first may seem marginal and obscure, nevertheless reveal a somewhat different approach to the problem of universals. In this way, a close examination of their specific views on universals serves as a useful illustration of general trends in Byzantine philosophy.

It is helpful here to sketch briefly what Ammonius has to say about the three types of universals – so that his account may serve as the standard presentation of the Neoplatonists' position to which the Byzantines' views can be compared. In his commentary on Porphyry's *Isagoge* (*Comm. in Arist. Graeca* IV.3: 41), Ammonius asks us to imagine a ring with a seal that portrays, for instance, Achilles, which we then press into different pieces of wax. Someone who later enters the room and observes the imprints on the different pieces of wax will soon come to realize that they all share common characteristics, and that they are all made by one and the same seal; these common characteristics will subsequently be retained in the observer's mind. According to Ammonius, the seal on the ring represents the universal before the many particulars, the imprint on the different pieces of wax represents the universal in the particulars, and

---

[11] Ammonius, *In Porphyr.* (*Comm. in Arist. Graeca* IV.3: 39–42, 68–9, 104–5); Elias, *In Porphyr.* (*Comm. in Arist. Graeca* XVIII.1: 45–8); David, *In Porphyr.* (*Comm. in Arist. Graeca* XVIII.2: 113–16); Olympiodorus, *Prolegomena* (*Comm. in Arist. Graeca* XII.1: 19); Philoponus, *In Categorias* (*Comm. in Arist. Graeca* XIII.1: 9).

the common characteristics as the observer mentally retains them represent the universal after the particulars.

Ammonius proceeds (41–2) to apply this three-fold distinction to the case of the universal human being. The Demiurge, he says, possesses in his mind the idea of the universal human being, which serves as the archetypical paradigm when he creates the different particular humans, just as the seal on the ring serves as the Achilles paradigm for the various wax imprints. This and other ideas possessed by the Demiurge are the universals before the many particulars. They are intelligible substances that constitute the causes of perceptible individuals but are separated from them, and they are identified with the Platonic Ideas in the *Timaeus*. The universal human being is also understood as the form of human being, which is on Ammonius's view both inseparable from and the same in every single human being, just as the imprints of the same seal are both inseparable from and the same in the different pieces of wax. These forms are the universals in the particulars; they are inseparable from perceptible individuals, and they represent the one in the many in the sense of Aristotle's notion of immanent forms. Finally, after observing many different human beings, we can formulate in our mind the concept of the universal human being, derived from the common characteristics shared by all the individual human beings we have observed, just as the common characteristics of the imprints on the different pieces of wax lead us to form a concept of the seal. These are the universals after the particulars, which are thoughts or concepts (*ennoēmatika*: p. 69.1, 4, 6) formed posterior to ("later born than") perception of the individuals (*husterogenē*: pp. 41.20, 42.13, 69.1), and acquired by our mind by the abstraction of their common characteristics.

With Ammonius's understanding of the three types of universals in the background, it is now time to look more closely at what the Byzantine thinkers say on the same topic. Arethas of Caesarea discusses the same three ways of understanding genera and species terms in his *Scholia* (*ca.* 900) on Porphyry's *Isagoge* (secs. 21, 23, 52); they are also hinted at in Photios's ninth-century treatise *Various Questions for Discussion on Amphilochia* (q. 77), as well as in Michael Psellos's eleventh-century paraphrase of Aristotle's *De interpretatione* (ed. 1503, p. 10). It is Psellos's student John Italos, however, who seems to have thought at greatest length about the problem of universals; in particular, he repeatedly discusses the issue in his eleventh-century *Quaestiones quodlibetales*, a collection of ninety-three answers to philosophical questions posed to him by his students.[12]

---

[12] For a more detailed account of Italos's views on universals, see Katerina Ierodiakonou, "John Italos on Universals," *Documenti e studi sulla tradizione filosofica medievale* 18 (2007) 231–47.

In Question 5, for instance, Italos talks about the same three types of universals in the same order, but a certain detail of his account proves distinctive. Like Ammonius, Italos regards the universals before the many particulars as the causes and paradigms of perceptible individuals; as such, these universals cannot properly be predicated of the particulars, are separate from them, and exist in God's mind. In this way, Italos both follows Ammonius and perfectly accommodates the requirements of Christian dogma (ed. Joannou, p. 7). He then goes on, however, to present the universals in the particulars and the universals after the particulars in a manner different from Ammonius's account. Italos claims (ibid., p. 8) that both the universals in the particulars and the universals after the particulars differ from the universals before the particulars, because they are later born than the perceptible individuals, can be predicated of them, are inseparable from them, and are acquired by our mind by abstraction. Moreover, it is exactly the way in which they are acquired by our mind through abstraction that makes the universals in the particulars differ from the universals after the particulars: the universals in the particulars, according to Italos, are not predicated of many particulars, but only of the one particular from which they are inseparable. Thus he refers to the universal animal, which he regards as one of the universals in the particulars; when it is predicated of Socrates, it cannot be predicated of anything else, such as Plato. On the other hand, the universals after the particulars are predicated of many particulars, and it is one and the same universal that is predicated both of all the particulars together and of every single one of them separately.

What is the significance of this detail? Does it mean that Italos understands the universals in the particulars as referring to forms that are particular? In other words, does it mean that he interprets Aristotle's immanent forms as particular rather than universal? The pedigree of such an interpretation is not negligible; both Proclus and his teacher Syrianus[13] viewed the immanent forms as particular, without implying in any way that they disagreed with Aristotle on this point. In addition, although Ammonius is not clear on this subject – and, hence, his illustration of the imprint on the different pieces of wax may be taken to suggest that the imprint is one and the same in all cases – there is no reason to believe that he was not here in agreement with these other Neoplatonists. Although this, of course, does not mean that such an interpretation of Aristotle's theory is correct, it is reasonable to think that, by Italos's time, treating Aristotle's immanent forms as particular was an acceptable, if not standard, interpretation.

---

[13] See Proclus, *Elements of Theology* (ed. Dodds, pp. 23, 24, 116); Syrianus, *In Metaphys.* (*Comm. in Arist. Graeca* VI.1: 83). For the lack of agreement between Plotinus and Proclus on this topic, see A. C. Lloyd, "Neoplatonic Logic and Aristotelian Logic," *Phronesis* 1 (1955–6) pp. 62–3.

Most importantly, though, the point on which Italos seems to differ from Ammonius's account of the three types of universals is that he considers not only the universals after the particulars but also the universals in the particulars to be acquired by our mind through abstraction. For Italos seems to hold not only that the universals after the particulars are acquired by our mind through abstraction of the common characteristics of perceptible individuals – just as in Ammonius's commentary – but also that the universals in the particulars are acquired by our mind through abstraction of the particular form from the matter involved in each particular. Therefore, for Italos, the universals in the particulars do not represent the one in the many, in the sense of Aristotle's notion of immanent forms, as they do for Ammonius.

But if both the universals after the particulars and the universals in the particulars are acquired by our mind by abstraction, does this mean that, for Italos, they are not beings (onta)? Italos addresses this question often, and in great detail, in his Quaestiones, objecting strongly to the view that they are not. In Question 58, for instance, he presents a series of arguments in support of Antisthenes's position that genera and species are not beings.[14] All the arguments that support Antisthenes's position are meant to demonstrate that the universals are neither corporeal nor incorporeal – and, hence, that they are not beings, since beings have to be either corporeal or incorporeal. According to one of these arguments, for example, universals are not incorporeal because, if they were, the subjects they are predicates of would be incorporeal too, which is absurd; for instance, if we say that Socrates is a human being, and that the universal human being is incorporeal, then Socrates would be incorporeal too, which is absurd. On the other hand, universals also are not corporeal because, if they were, they would be perishable, since bodies are perishable; but since universals are not perishable, they cannot be corporeal (ed. Joannou, p. 79). Therefore universals are neither corporeal nor incorporeal, and hence they are not beings; rather, they are bare concepts stripped of every reality and existing only in thought.

To rebut this argument, Italos takes the position that universals are incorporeal, and he argues that they can be so without their subjects being incorporeal too; so, for instance, the genus substance is incorporeal, although it is predicated also of subjects that are corporeal (ibid., q. 3, p. 4). Italos further offers a whole series of arguments to support his own thesis. Before doing so, however, he stresses, again in Question 3 and in Question 8, that it is important to draw

---

[14] Given that Antisthenes's text is no longer extant, the source of these arguments is a puzzle: it could be that Italos copied them from ancient sources still available in his time, or it could be that he himself constructed them for dialectical purposes – that is, in order subsequently to refute them and thus strengthen his own rival position.

what he takes to be Aristotle's distinction between two senses of something's being incorporeal:

(i) Something can be incorporeal *per se*, truly, and strictly speaking. For instance, the soul, demons, the first cause, and the highest genera are all incorporeal in a strict sense, because they do not need a body for subsisting.

(ii) Something can be incorporeal *per accidens* and by abstraction. For instance, time, space, line, surface, and body are all incorporeal in a weak sense, because they depend on a body for subsisting.

Thus, according to Italos's interpretation of Aristotle, universals are incorporeal in the second, weaker sense: they are not strictly speaking incorporeal but depend on a body for subsisting. This is the sense that Italos himself adopts in his understanding of universals as incorporeal. For both in Question 3 (ibid., p. 4) and in Question 4 (p. 6), Italos explains that universals are incorporeal *per accidens* and not *per se*, because they are incorporeal insofar as they are in the human soul, while at the same time they are corporeal by participation (*kata metheksin*) insofar as they subsist in the particulars. The universals that he has in mind in such contexts are obviously the universals in the particulars and the universals after the particulars.

If, however, universals are indeed incorporeal beings, then is there a special sense in which they are said to be beings? In Questions 3, 6, 19, and 31, Italos makes use of a distinction that is a commonplace in Platonic texts from Plotinus to Simplicius, but that seems to have even earlier origins: namely, the distinction between something subsisting and something depending on mere thought.[15] According to Italos, things that do not subsist (*anupostata*) but depend on mere thought are not beings. As for things that subsist, he distinguishes between two different kinds of beings (see q. 52, p. 71): those that subsist *per se*, which he calls "subsistences" (*hupostaseis*), and those that subsist in something else (*enupostata*). Subsistences are prior by perception, they are particulars, and they are for the most part bodies; in contrast, beings that subsist in something else are prior by belief and knowledge, they are incorporeal, they are predicates shared by many things, and they are thoughts (*noēmata/dianoēmata*). Italos's terminology here clearly shows the influence of the Christian Fathers – in particular, John of Damascus, whose *Dialectica* draws just this distinction between subsistences, things that subsist in something else, and things that do not subsist (§10/30; §26/43; §28/45; §29/46).

According to Italos, therefore, both subsistences and beings that subsist in something else are beings, and thus they do not depend on mere thought. Italos

---

[15] See Jonathan Barnes's commentary to his translation of Porphyry's *Isagoge*, p. 41.

distinguishes these two kinds of beings both from the standard examples of things that do not subsist, such as goat-stags and centaurs, and from his own examples of many-eyed human beings and four-headed horses; all these are, as he explicitly says (q. 3, p. 4), nothing but fabrications of the human mind and products of our imagination (*phantasmata*). On the other hand, there is also an important difference between subsistences and beings that subsist in something else. Although the first subsist *per se*, the latter are thoughts that subsist in something else. Hence, Italos's position on the three types of universals could be summarized as follows: All three are incorporeal beings, but the universals before the many particulars are subsistences, whereas the universals in the particulars and the universals after the particulars are beings that subsist in something else.

Italos's student Eustratios of Nicaea seems to follow his teacher on this issue both in his commentaries on Aristotle's works and in his theological treatises. For, on Eustratios's view, too, the distinction that matters for these issues is that between the universals that are the paradigms of perceptual individuals and exist in God's mind, and the universals that are later born than the perceptual individuals and that subsist in them.[16]

Neither Italos nor Eustratios, therefore, seems to try to reconcile Plato's and Aristotle's views on universals in the way the Neoplatonists did. Rather, they disagree with both ancient philosophers; they understand the Platonic ideas as God's thoughts, and they conceive of Aristotle's immanent forms both as inseparable from perceptible individuals and as existing in the human mind. Still, although on their view only God and the perceptible individuals exist in the strong sense as subsistences, they also want to stress that all types of universals are beings. They may be beings in a different sense from these subsistences, but they all are beings and not constructions of our mind devoid of reality.[17]

Many more Byzantine philosophers discussed the issue of universals, especially during the fourteenth and fifteenth centuries. To present them as following the Neoplatonist commentators on this subject before closely studying their (sometimes unedited) works, it seems, would not do them justice. In addition, Italos's

---

[16] For a more detailed study of Eustratios's account of universals, see Katerina Ierodiakonou, "Metaphysics in the Byzantine Tradition: Eustratios of Nicaea on Universals," *Quaestio* 5 (2005) 67–82.

[17] For this reason, I think it is misleading to label them as "nominalists," as A. C. Lloyd does in *The Anatomy of Neoplatonism* (Oxford: Oxford University Press, 1990) pp. 70–5, where he also describes the view as "conceptualist". Benakis, in contrast, has labelled the Neoplatonist and Byzantine account as "conceptual" or "moderate realism" (see note 10). On the alleged nominalism of John Italos and Eustratios of Nicaea, in particular, see Tatakis, *La philosophie Byzantine*, pp. 170–1; Périclès-Pierre Joannou, *Christliche Metaphysik in Byzanz: Die Illuminationslehre des Michael Psellos und Johannes Italos* (Ettal: Buch-Kunstverlag, 1956) pp. 140–6; "Die Definition des Seins bei Eustratios von Nikaia: Die Universalienlehre in der Byzantinischen Theologie im IX Jh.," *Byzantinische Zeitschrift* 47 (1954) 358–68; "Der Nominalismus und die menshliche Psychologie Christi: Das Semeioma gegen Eustratios von Nikaia," *Byzantinische Zeitschrift* 47 (1954) 369–78.

case demonstrates that there may be subtle but important details in Byzantine views that should be taken into consideration when trying to reconstruct their reasoning. This holds, of course, not just for the problem of universals, but for all philosophical issues that occupied them. Such a reconstruction, attentive to crucial detail, should be a prerequisite before one ventures to grasp the theological implications of Byzantine philosophy – or before one undertakes a comparison with the relevant and more thoroughly studied Western texts.

4

THE RISE OF THE UNIVERSITIES

STEVEN P. MARRONE

The culture of the learned elite in the Latin world bordering on the Mediterranean and stretching north into Europe underwent a profound transformation
between the eleventh and the thirteenth centuries. Although the traditions of
the immediately preceding period were never completely submerged, speculative and literary activity from the twelfth and thirteenth centuries on began
to generate a kind of work that speaks to us with a philosophical immediacy
that almost nothing from the seventh through eleventh centuries can presume
to do. As with any cultural process, the roots of the change reached back deep
in time, and in its entirety it extended to all areas of society, economic and
political as well as literary and intellectual. It is no accident that the twelfth
century has been characterized by Western medievalists as a period of "renaissance," while the origins of "Europe" as we think of it, and as it has
exercised power in the modern world, have increasingly been pushed back
to that era.

In a guide to medieval philosophy there is no need to engage this historical
phenomenon in all its breadth or to speculate very deeply on its causation.[1]
Reduced to the scope of medieval intellectual history, our concern is with
the emergence of "scholasticism" in its strictest sense – or, as the title of this
chapter suggests, with the appearance of a cultural sphere linked to the universities. Despite the fact that either orientation – broadly cultural or narrowly
intellectual – must necessarily go seriously astray about the place it assigns the
history of Arabic culture or of Byzantine Greek culture (see Chapters 1 and 3),
the perspective they both provide gives us an entrée to a cultural shift of dramatic
proportions.

---

[1] For those with an ear to the sometimes controversial terminology of Max Weber, what we are talking
about is the beginning of the "rationalization" of "the West." See Max Weber, *The Theory of Social
and Economic Organization*, tr. A. M. Henderson and T. Parsons (New York: Oxford University
Press, 1947) pp. 115–18 and 120–3.

SIGNS OF THE NEW INTELLECTUAL CLIMATE

So long as we resist allotting them a special causal status, three cultural events of more than a century long can stand as indicators of the intellectual transformation we should have in mind. They are a wave of translations into Latin of writings in Arabic, Greek, and Hebrew, a rapid evolution of educational institutions and the consequent proliferation of new institutional forms, and the construction of a social context, at once economic and political, that fostered what can only be called an incipient "professionalism." Of course all three did play a formative role in the shaping of high medieval scholastic culture, but standard accounts habitually distort their importance by extracting them from the web of social factors at work in so complex a cultural change.[2] Each was in truth as much effect as cause.

Translations into Latin

The rash of translations that began in the twelfth century has usually attracted the primary interest of intellectual historians because it so readily suggests a transfer of philosophical capital, inherited from Greek antiquity by medieval Arabs and Jews, to the Latin cultural coffers of the high Middle Ages. In addition to downplaying the fact that mere translation without interpretation, assimilation, and then development would almost surely have had little historical impact, the focus on translation obscures the important causal lesson that unless a need or desire had already been cultivated by preceding cultural evolution, no translating would have occurred. Still, a look at what was translated and when can serve as a useful barometer of intellectual interest and alteration. (See Appendix B for further details.)

For the study of logic, the medieval Latin tradition up through the early twelfth century was confined to a textual foundation later referred to as the *ars vetus* or *logica vetus* (old logic), consisting of Aristotle's *Categories* and *De interpretatione*, the Greek Neoplatonist Porphyry's *Isagoge* or *Introduction*, commentaries on them all by the sixth-century Roman Boethius, and a few further compendia, most notably again from Boethius's pen. Considerable technical sophistication was possible starting from this base alone, as is evident from Chapter 2's discussion of Anselm, Peter Abaelard, and others from the later eleventh century

---

[2] Classic examples are David Knowles, *The Evolution of Medieval Thought* (New York: Vintage Books, 1962) pp. 151–205; Gordon Leff, *Medieval Thought St Augustine to Ockham* (Baltimore, MD: Penguin, 1958) pp. 168–82; and Étienne Gilson, *History of Christian Philosophy in the Middle Ages* (New York: Random House, 1955) pp. 235–50.

on. But beginning in Abaelard's own day a number of new works were either brought back into circulation after centuries of dusty neglect or made available for the first time in Latin, and the field of logic accordingly expanded beyond anything seen even in the ancient world. Aristotle's *Prior Analytics*, *Topics*, and *Sophistical Refutations*, long available in Boethius's translation, began actually to be read in the twelfth century, while sometime prior to 1150 James of Venice translated the remaining piece of Aristotle's Organon, the *Posterior Analytics*. These four, making up the *logica nova* (new logic), took decades to digest, with the first written commentary on the *Posterior Analytics*, by Robert Grosseteste, dating from around 1228. But as the subjects with which they were concerned took central stage, the range of logical speculation dramatically enlarged and its novelty rapidly intensified. Beginning with syllogistic and theory of demonstration, already by the mid-thirteenth century an elaborate modal logic was being fashioned accompanied by investigation into the properties of terms, to be supplemented in the fourteenth century by a whirlwind of activity on questions of invention, logical puzzles about sophisms and insoluble arguments, elaborate inferential exercises such as those called "obligations," and renewed attention to the rules of inference or "consequence" (see Chapters 10–14).[3]

Keeping to Aristotle alone, equally destabilizing advances were made in natural philosophy. Prior to the twelfth century, not a single one of Aristotle's natural works was available in Latin. Again, before 1150 James of Venice translated both the *Physics* and *De anima*, with other versions soon in circulation, followed late in the twelfth and anew in the thirteenth century by translations of *De caelo*, *De generatione et corruptione*, the *Meteorology* and eventually the rest of the *libri naturales*. By the end of the thirteenth century, all of Aristotle's philosophy of nature was at hand, the subjects he treated beginning to evolve into fields of investigation on their own. It is important to remember, however, that Aristotle did not come to Latin readers without introduction. His writings were accompanied by, indeed initially interpreted in light of, a much larger corpus of works in Arabic reaching far beyond the authentic Aristotle. Most important of these initially was the massive *Book of Healing* (*Al-Shifā'*) of the eleventh-century Persian Avicenna, the parts of which labeled in Latin as *De anima* and *De generatione* having been translated in the second half of the twelfth century. Although the *Shifā'* was not a commentary, its structure paralleled that of the Aristotelian corpus, and so it could be used as a guide to the Philosopher himself. Soon, however, Latin readers had access to proper commentaries, in the form of the equally influential and even more massive works of the twelfth-century Spaniard

---

[3] Still the best introduction is Jan Pinborg, *Logik und Semantik im Mittelalter: ein Überblick* (Stuttgart: Frommann-Holzboog, 1972).

Averroes. His commentaries began to be turned into Latin in the early thirteenth century, with Michael Scot's translations of the long commentaries on the *Physics* and *De anima* probably being read in Paris already by 1225.[4]

Even this only scratches the surface. Perhaps of greatest weight for philosophy from a modern perspective was the translation of Aristotle's *Metaphysics*, partially accomplished already by the late twelfth century and then fully in several versions in the thirteenth. Here, too, Arabic writings established the context of interpretation, with Avicenna's *Metaphysics* (again from the *Shifā'*) preparing the way for Aristotle's, and Averroes's *Great Commentary* once more following and providing a standard gloss. Not far behind were the *Nicomachean Ethics*, first completely rendered in Latin by Robert Grosseteste in the 1240s, and the *Politics*, put into Latin by William of Moerbeke in the second half of the thirteenth century. It can almost be said that these latter two translations coincided with a virtual reinvention of both ethics and the study of politics in the Latin Middle Ages, though in either case Arabic thinkers had anticipated the change by at least two hundred years. Moreover, focusing just on Aristotle and Aristotelian commentaries scarcely conveys the scale of the influx of new texts, carrying with them whole new ways of thinking and mountains of unfamiliar data and ideas. Translations from the Greek Neoplatonic and late Peripatetic tradition continue throughout the thirteenth century, not to speak of a flood of original works on philosophy as well as what we would call natural science from Arabic and Hebrew well into the fourteenth. The enormity of the debt in the theory of science alone is apparent when we consider that Euclid's *Elements* and Ptolemy's *Almagest* were first read by Latin thinkers – in translation by way of Arabic exemplars – only in the twelfth century.[5]

New educational institutions

If the story of translations conveys an idea of the revolution in subject matter and forms of learning from the eleventh to the thirteenth centuries – practically the emergence of philosophy in something like the sense we mean today – the second of the cultural events mentioned above helps us understand how such

---

[4] On Aristotle translations, consult L. Minio-Paluello, *Opuscula: The Latin Aristotle* (Amsterdam: Hakkert, 1972); and Bernard G. Dod, "Aristoteles Latinus," in N. Kretzmann *et al.* (eds.) *The Cambridge History of Later Medieval Philosophy* (Cambridge: Cambridge University Press, 1982) 45–79. The crucial articles on Avicenna and Averroes are still M.-T. d'Alverny, "Notes sur les traductions médiévales des œuvres philosophiques d'Avicenne," *Archives d'histoire doctrinale et littéraire du moyen age* 19 (1952) 337–58, and R. A. Gauthier, "Notes sur les débuts (1225–1240) du premier 'averroïsme'," *Revue des sciences philosophiques et théologiques* 66 (1982) 322–73.

[5] An excellent synopsis of the whole range of translations is Fernand van Steenberghen, *La philosophie au XIIIe siècle*, 2nd edn (Louvain-la-Neuve: Institut supérieur de philosophie, 1991) ch. 3.

a transmutation was sustained. Until the late eleventh century, the monastery was the near exclusive locus for training in Latin letters and for acquiring familiarity with even the rudiments of the classical traditions of thought (see Chapter 5). For centuries, however, the education of monks had been ordered more toward producing performers of the liturgy than either thinkers or, if we anticipate a more mystical bent, adepts at meditation. As for the late antique obligation of bishops to provide the clergy attached to their cathedral church with opportunities for further learning in Latin literature (typically including the Bible, exegetical texts, and bits of ancient rhetoric and encyclopedic lore), that had long since fallen into decay. The exceptions, as at Rheims in the tenth century under the scholar–bishop Gerbert, later Pope Sylvester II, stand out by their isolation.

It was thus a phenomenon of vast importance when towards the end of the eleventh century and through the beginning of the twelfth an entirely new array of educational institutions sprang up, first in France and then throughout northwestern Europe. Most significant in the long run was a proliferation of episcopal sees where teachers were brought in and paid to offer courses – open not just to the resident clergy – that went beyond simple grammar, composition, and elementary rhetoric. These so-called cathedral schools at times took on a permanence and complexity of organization that made them hubs of intellectual activity in the novel disciplines described above – logic, in particular, and natural philosophy. A few even attracted students from far away, intensifying excitement at these schools and greatly spreading their fame. Among such, Paris excelled in prestige and size already by the second and third decades of the twelfth century. The masters huddled around the cathedral of Notre Dame constituted an educational resource unimaginable in Europe just a few centuries before.

As developments at Paris reveal, the cathedral schools were soon joined by other institutional types competing for students in a fast-growing market. An enterprising scholar like Abaelard, lured to Paris by its cathedral school, might set himself up on his own to give lessons in advanced subjects to students willing to pay to sit at the feet of so renowned a master. Abaelard experimented with such ad hoc educational establishments often in his early career – first at Mount St. Geneviève across the Seine from the cathedral, then at two royal domains, Melun and Corbeil. The fact that such irregular institutions could survive indicates the changing climate for intellectual pursuits. Even some monasteries got into the business of higher studies, particularly where the spillover from cathedral schools presented an opportunity. Abaelard's sometime nemesis, William of Champeaux, quit the cathedral school of Notre Dame once

Abaelard had established a presence there, only to take up residence at the monastery of St. Victor, not far from Mount St. Geneviève. Assured a sustenance from his monastic calling, he there founded a school renowned for the rest of the century.[6]

By the middle of the twelfth century, the concentration of educational activities at a place like Paris reached the point where central coordination became a necessity. Consolidation was gradual, proceeding by fits and starts, but before century's end there had arisen at least in practice a network of masters and students gathering the earlier enterprises – cathedral school, ad hoc establishments, students at the monastery door – under an institutional umbrella that was to underwrite the scholarship we associate with the high and late Middle Ages and to characterize higher education as it has spread from Europe throughout the modern world. Most basically, this new instrument of knowledge production was a corporation of masters who could act together financially and at law, and whose incorporation allowed them to systematize all instructional procedures within the limits of, for instance, a city's walls. By the early fourteenth century, such an institution was habitually referred to as an *universitas*, a Latin synonym for the modern word 'corporation.' At Paris, the earliest extant document registering its existence is a royal charter of 1200, confirming the corporate rights and privileges of the masters. It was in effect a guild of teachers, monopolizing higher education within the precincts of the city.

Emergence of professionalism

Of course, just as the emergence of universities helps explain the expansion of subjects and sources for inquiry represented by the new translations, so the universities would be incomprehensible outside a context of still wider social innovation. Here it suffices to glance at the third of the cultural events listed above – increasing professionalism in society's upper ranks. Before the twelfth century, the business of ruling, acquiring, producing, even healing in medieval Europe required little in the way of specialized training. Growing up in the environment where such work was done provided experience enough, and the right background made it entirely possible to engage in several such areas of activity over the course of one's maturity. After all, in feudal society the

---

[6] On all these early twelfth-century developments, see Stephen C. Ferruolo, *The Origins of the University: The Schools of Paris and their Critics 1100–1215* (Stanford, CA: Stanford University Press, 1985); and Richard Southern, *Scholastic Humanism and the Unification of Europe*, vol. I: *Foundations* (Oxford: Oxford University Press, 1995).

landlord was typically also local ruler and usually the manager of a considerable agricultural estate. After the twelfth century, each one of these pursuits had its specialists. Social institutions such as governments, houses of commerce, even urban hospitals had arisen, where if those in charge were not formally trained, they had to surround themselves with technical experts who were.

A single example suggests how, and why, this was so. In England, already by the eleventh century government was as centrally oriented as anywhere in Europe. Still, most of the activity that governing entailed was transacted locally, usually under the supervision of the lower aristocracy, and almost completely by means of the spoken word. By the mid-1200s, all that had changed. Royal authority had become a prime mover, royal courts the common site for transaction, royal agents required for even mundane operations, and written documents everywhere instrumental. The wrenching nature of the change is apparent in a controversial episode involving King Edward I. In 1279, Edward sent commissioners into each English county in order to compile a written survey of all tenements and proprietary holdings throughout the realm. Shortly thereafter, the king's justiciars initiated a decade-long campaign of bringing suit in royal court against lords and magnates claiming to exercise any of the many privileges or franchises at the heart of aristocratic governance. In technical terms such proceedings were designated *quo warranto*, asking by what warrant the privilege was held.[7] Beyond the novelty of so global an assault on noble prerogatives, particularly disruptive about the king's proceeding was that his courts would no longer accept as "warrant" testimony regarding customs or oral accounts of events long past, but instead only written documents appropriately authenticated to certify their legal worth.

The English aristocracy reacted with such outrage that in 1290 the king, by way of compromise, fixed Richard I's accession in 1189 as the date before which claims to privilege would not require written documentation. In the long run, of course, this compromise mattered less and less. By 1300, in England, it was increasingly the case that an assertion of privilege, ownership, or special dispensation – down to the level of manorial serfs – could be effectively exercised only on the basis of written title. Making that possible, of course, demanded an army of lawyers and notaries understanding the law, fluent in its technical language, and producing the writs themselves. From a land of legal amateurs in 1100, England had become by 1300 a nation dependent on professional legists. Faced with so imposing a model, the monarchies and emerging principalities

---

[7] A fascinating examination of Edward's *quo warranto* proceedings and their cultural import can be found in M. T. Clanchy, *From Memory to Written Record*, 2nd edn (London: Blackwell, 1993) pp. 2–6 and 35–43.

on the continent made sure not to be left far behind. Moreover, what was true of law rapidly became true of administration, true of healing and, at least to a modest degree, true of business as well. It became true of teaching just as it did of delineating religious orthodoxy. To enter into society as a lawyer, a physician, a magistrate, a royal clerk, a tax collector, a professor, or a theologian meant spending years in training, formally acquiring the habits of mind necessary to be awarded the proper authority. In what was an increasingly "rationalized" world, all such tasks were delivered into the hands of professionals. And universities provided the setting par excellence where professional training was done and from which certification was procured. They had become a cultural sine qua non.

THE UNIVERSITY CURRICULUM

As indicated above, these universities – the delivery systems whereby a more complicated education was afforded to a larger number of people at the upper levels of society than ever before – originated in the narrowest sense as corporations with specific legal privileges and obligations. For the most part, the corporation comprised the collected masters at a particular locale, though in Italy it was occasionally the student body that received incorporation. Earliest to achieve such status were the clusters of schools at Paris, Oxford, and Bologna, all operating in the requisite manner before 1200.

Several other competitors arose in the thirteenth century at Padua, Naples, Montpellier, Toulouse, Salamanca, and Cambridge. Another designation for such an entity was *studium generale*, a general center of learning. To count as a *studium generale* an educational establishment had to contain more than one faculty of study attracting students from far and wide and possessing adequate standing to guarantee its graduates the privilege of teaching at any other such school. Over the course of the thirteenth century the mendicant friars – Dominicans and Franciscans – established in a few cities like Cologne and Florence centers of study more or less meeting these requirements and thus regarded as functionally equivalent to those on the preceding short list. In the fourteenth century formal universities were set up in German-speaking regions – the first so-called German university was constituted at Prague in 1348. By the end of the fifteenth century universities were to be found all over Europe.[8]

---

[8] A compact history of the universities is Olaf Pedersen, *The First Universities: Studium Generale and the Origins of University Education in Europe* (Cambridge: Cambridge University Press, 1997). Fundamental for Oxford is J. I. Catto (ed.) *The History of the University of Oxford*, vol. I: *The*

Operations at each were determined by a division into the faculties of learning alluded to above. Most basic was the faculty of arts, offering instruction to those entering the university at the primary level. Starting with a reinforcement of the knowledge of Latin construction and composition obtained in grammar school, the arts masters quickly turned their attention to providing the grounding in Latin literature, natural philosophy, and – most importantly – logic that would qualify a person as *litteratus* or literate, and so suitable for employment as administrator or clerk in this increasingly professionalized society. Responsible for the equivalent of the modern undergraduate education, the arts faculty was present at every university, usually dominating the governing apparatus and enrolling far and away the largest number of students.

Once they mastered the arts, some students set their sights on a career in one of the technical professions requiring yet further training and study. For them arose faculties in the so-called higher disciplines, corresponding loosely with graduate education in the modern world. Most widespread were the faculties of law, which in medieval Europe were divided between those devoted to civil law, built on the foundations of Roman jurisprudence, and those concerned with the canon law of the church, also drawing on Roman models. The mushrooming demand for experts in legal counsel and documentation ensured a ready supply of graduates of the arts to enroll under either of the two sorts of law faculty for certification in those specialized fields. Medicine, too – at least the medical expertise increasingly demanded by wealthy elites in cities and at ruling courts – called for a professionalized corps of physicians with formal instruction beyond the arts. In Italy especially, where classical traditions of learned medicine had never fully disappeared, but also in southern France, universities had from the earliest days included a cohort of professors who eventually constituted independent faculties of medicine. Finally, the institutional church began to make its own professional demands. Beyond the canon law required for ecclesiastical courts, a need arose for the technical interpretation of doctrine – in other words, for theology. In the first half of the thirteenth century, faculties of theology quickly distinguished themselves as most prestigious of all in advanced studies, most spectacularly at Paris but also at Oxford and eventually at a few other institutions as well.

Within each faculty, it was the professors who established the curriculum, fixing the subject matter, required texts, and sequence of courses. Foundational

Early Oxford Schools (Oxford: Oxford University Press, 1984); J. I. Catto and Ralph Evans (eds.) vol. II: *The Late Middle Ages* (Oxford: Oxford University Press, 1993). The classic general reference is Hastings Rashdall, *The Universities of Europe in the Middle Ages*, rev. edn by F. M. Powicke and A. B. Emden (Oxford: Clarendon Press, 1936).

for any literate career and all higher study, the curriculum in arts set the tone for intellectual endeavor throughout the period. Here is where to look first for the educational correlatives to much of what we would consider medieval philosophizing.[9] Foremost came training in what was referred to since antiquity as the trivium, the triad of arts concerned specifically with language. At the outset stood grammar, which aimed both at polishing grammar-school studies and at imparting the theory found in the classical texts of Donatus and Priscian (see Chapter 15). From here, the way proceeded fast to logic, the heart and soul of the arts in the Middle Ages. Formal training focused on the logic of Aristotle, both old and new, though students were expected to keep abreast of advances beyond Aristotle in the so-called "logic of the moderns" (*logica modernorum*). Rhetoric was squeezed in at the margins, sometimes just on feast days when other classes were suspended. In the late 1100s, students passed beyond these linguistic arts on to the ancient "group of four" or quadrivium, of which geometry, by way of Euclid, and music, by way of Boethius, received the greater emphasis, with only modest time allocated to arithmetic and astronomy.

By the turn of the thirteenth century, Aristotle's writings on natural philosophy, and subsequently metaphysics, posed a serious challenge to this classical Latin conception of the arts curriculum. Authorities, both bishops' officials and some professors instigated primarily by the theologians, at first resisted incorporating Aristotle's broader corpus into the course of study, fearing that his philosophy of nature in particular would endanger Christian belief. In Paris, where opposition was strongest, prohibitions in 1210 and 1215 formally excluded from the curriculum Aristotle's natural works and commentaries on them from the Arabic tradition, most probably those of Avicenna. Yet a papal proclamation of 1231 suggests that already by then the prohibition was wearing thin, and a curricular statute of the arts faculty in 1255 shows that by mid-century the Aristotelianizers had won the day. From then until the end of the Middle Ages, Aristotle's *libri naturales* and the *Metaphysics*, as well as the *Ethics*, came at all universities to dominate the arts curriculum outside of logic.

Teaching progressed by way of lectures on the foundational texts, supplemented by classroom and sometimes public disputation on theoretical problems or issues of interpretation and elaboration. Though the precise terms varied according to time and place, in all cases students began by attending lectures for a few years, then added the obligation to take part in the public disputations, and finally moved to "determination," when as bachelors of arts they would

---

[9] A good survey of current knowledge of the curriculum at Paris and Oxford is provided by Olga Weijers and Louis Holtz (eds.) *L'enseignement des disciplines à la Faculté des arts, Paris et Oxford, XIIIe–XVe siècles: actes du colloque international* (Turnhout: Brepols, 1997).

themselves lecture on the base texts in submagisterial or "cursory" classes. After as many as seven or eight years altogether, the successful candidate would be granted official license to teach, shortly thereafter commencing, or "incepting" on, a teaching stint as full-fledged master of arts. A similar system was adopted in the faculty of theology, which provided, we moderns must never forget, perhaps even more than arts, the central locus for the philosophical thinking surveyed in this book. There the base texts were the Bible and a twelfth-century course book on the major issues of Christian doctrine, Peter Lombard's *Book of Sentences*. Again, following several years spent auditing magisterial lectures on both, students began to participate in disputations and then advanced as bachelors to lecturing "cursorily" themselves – at Paris, for two years on the Bible and then another one or two on the *Sentences*. At the end came licensing, succeeded – if and when an opening was available – by inception and a few years (or sometimes much longer) teaching as master of theology.

TYPES OF PHILOSOPHICAL WRITING AND
OCCASIONS FOR PHILOSOPHIZING

When university masters lectured on a text, they proceeded section by section, stopping after each to comment on its meaning, both in the literal sense and in more general terms. The whole procedure was technically designated a *lectio* or reading. When, instead, they engaged in *disputationes*, an *aporia* or *quaestio* was introduced for debate. Under the master's supervision, contrary arguments were then presented by an opponent and a respondent, often followed by more freewheeling discussion but always by a formal determination or resolution of the issue (typically by the master himself) and then by answers to initial arguments still left unresolved.[10]

Loosely paralleling these two instructional methods were the two main literary genres, both probably originating as records of what had taken place in class but turning increasingly over the years into artificial pieces executed privately by the master. Linked to the readings of texts were commentaries, the most philosophically substantive being those on Lombard's *Sentences* (among theologians) and on the works of Aristotle (among both arts masters and sometimes theologians). Associated with disputations were collections of redacted, sometimes considerably revised *quaestiones disputatae*, or disputed questions. The

---

[10] For a survey of the evolving form of the disputation, both as a classroom exercise and as a literary genre, see Olga Weijers, *La "disputatio" à la Faculté des arts de Paris (1200–1350 environ). Esquisse d'une typologie* (Brepols: Turnhout, 1995) and *La "disputatio" dans les Facultés des arts au moyen âge* (Brepols: Turnhout, 2002).

latter could range from an investigation inspired by a particular Aristotelian text to a wide-ranging overview or *summa*, spanning an entire area or field. Less prominent was a third genre, consisting of the *tractatus* or treatise on a particular subject or theme – for example, Thomas Aquinas's *On Being and Essence* – and also handbooks for a specific discipline, such as Peter of Spain's *Summulae logicales*. These circulated widely in the arts.

Of course it is taken as given here that the venue for philosophical thinking and writing, during most of the Latin Middle Ages, was the university. Beginning in the fourteenth century, laymen outside the walls of academe – Dante Alighieri is a case in point – increasingly intruded on the proceedings. So far as the university was concerned, however, the preeminent locus of activity was, by profession, within the faculty of arts, even if much of what we would consider philosophical speculation was a product of the three higher faculties as well. Current scholarship is only just beginning to mine works in law and medicine for the sometimes surprising yield of medieval philosophy to be found there. More customary has been the attention of historians of philosophy to scholastic theological writings. Much of what is covered in the chapters that follow will be taken from the literary legacy of bachelors and masters in theology. Perhaps a final reflection is warranted on why this is the case.

Simply put, the fact is that practicing theologians throughout the high medieval period regularly concerned themselves with philosophy as we conceive it and composed what we recognize as philosophical works. Aquinas, for instance, produced most of his commentaries on the logical and natural works of Aristotle, as well as on the *Metaphysics*, while he was a master of theology, often long after his earliest professorship in the faculty of theology at Paris. Perhaps more importantly, Thomas the theologian continued to tackle issues of sometimes exclusively philosophical import, making room for them extensively in his theological writings. It is no accident that his *Commentary on the Sentences* and *Summa theologiae* figure prominently in discussions of medieval philosophy.

There is a reason why this was so. Scholastic theologians saw their primary task as explicating their beliefs. But for them, especially in the Latin thirteenth and early fourteenth centuries, thinking about religious truth was not to be kept separate from understanding the rest of the world. If the clarification of doctrine was to aspire to anything like Aristotle's standards for certain knowledge or science (see Chapter 26), it would have to turn to natural reason and philosophy for much of both its content and its argumentation. Indeed, if theology were to maintain its prestige among its sister faculties at the university, it would have to be especially scrupulous about its arguments and careful to show how their conclusions were consistent with knowledge in other fields. No wonder theologians spent so much time philosophizing. And no surprise that they were punctilious in distinguishing between appeals made solely to reason and those drawing upon revelation vouchsafed by faith. In such an intellectual atmosphere, philosophy might well find a home in the work of a theologian. And theological writings might easily be read and appreciated for their philosophical worth, without sacrificing even the most rigorous division between reason and revelation.

5

MONKS AND FRIARS

DAVID LUSCOMBE

Most medieval Christian philosophers were clerics and priests, who staffed the schools (and later the universities) in towns and cathedral cities. Many of these were also monks and friars. Monks contributed to philosophy in the cloisters of their monasteries and in universities, and friars also contributed both in the schools or *studia* of their orders and within universities.

MONKS

The transformation of the Roman Empire, particularly between the fifth and sixth century, was accompanied by educational initiatives on the part of bishoprics and monasteries. Between 397 and 421, Augustine of Hippo outlined a program in his treatise *On Christian Doctrine* for communicating Christian doctrine into which was integrated the study of profane authors and ancient culture.[1] Influential works were produced in Italy (by Boethius, Cassiodorus, and Pope Gregory the Great) and in Spain (by Isidore of Seville), which enabled active centers of culture in the West as far away as Anglo-Saxon England to counteract the stagnation of imperial decline.

The task of the monk was to escape from this world in order to find God. What place Benedict of Nursia (d. *ca.* 550), the father of Western monasticism, allowed for scholarly studies by the monks who followed his *Rule* is not clear, although *lectio divina* was an obligation that required literacy, books, meditation, and thought. Cassiodorus (d. *ca.* 580), on the other hand, provided a library in his monastery in Calabria in southwest Italy, called the *Vivarium* or "fish pond," from which ancient and Christian books were disseminated throughout Europe – to Northumbria, for example, and to the court of Charlemagne and to Isidore's Seville. Cassiodorus divided his *Institutions* into two books: *Divine* and *Human*. The first was devoted to the Bible, and the second to the seven liberal arts that provided the introduction for philosophical studies to be integrated

---

[1] See Henri I. Marrou, *Saint Augustin et la fin de la culture antique* (Paris: E. de Boccard, 1938–49).

into the study of Christian doctrine, following the example of Augustine. In this way, a new culture was being born in princely courts, episcopal centers, and monasteries that could withstand decay – one that tied together the legacy of the ancient study of the arts and of philosophy with a Christian education.[2]

Monasteries and nunneries in medieval Europe were numerous. Some ran schools for boys or girls, while others were also important centers of scholarship and of book production: Corbie in Saxony, for instance, in the ninth century, or Malmesbury in Wiltshire in the twelfth. The survival within early medieval Western Europe of the literature – and therefore also the thought – of antiquity, both classical and Christian, is (to put it conservatively) largely due to the dedication of monasteries in the Carolingian epoch to the collection and the copying of texts.[3] Studious monks engaged in the study of the Bible and the writings of the Fathers, both Western and Eastern, who had interpreted and expounded the sacred text, such as Origen, Basil, Ambrose, Augustine, Jerome, Leo, and Gregory. *Theoria* for such monks meant prayer and contemplation in anticipation of celestial beatitude, while *philosophia* meant living wisely, not so much in accordance with the wisdom of this world as with that of Christ and with that of the next world (see Chapter 33). Its pursuit, however, also involved the study of grammar and of pagan literature. The Carolingian kings of Francia valued the education given in monasteries and in other church schools, and Alcuin of York – who developed the practice of using the tools of logic when inquiring into Christian doctrine – taught a generation of new monastic leaders, first at the Carolingian court and later as abbot from 796 to 804 at St. Martin's at Tours.[4]

In Carolingian education, scholarship and speculation about both secular and divine wisdom and learning were fused – and generated controversy. The foremost disputants in vigorous debates about the soul, the Eucharist, predestination and human free will, the nature and person of Christ, and icons all included monks as well as secular clergy, whose attitudes to learning and whose

---

[2] See Jacques Fontaine, "Education and Learning," in P. Fouracre (ed.) *The New Cambridge Medieval History*, vol. I: *c.500–c.700* (Cambridge: Cambridge University Press, 2005) 735–59; Jacques Fontaine, *Isidore de Séville et la culture classique dans l'Espagne wisigothique* (Paris: Études Augustiniennes, 1984); John Contreni, "The Carolingian Renaissance: Education and Literary Culture," in R. McKitterick (ed.) *The New Cambridge Medieval History*, vol. II: *c.700–c.900* (Cambridge: Cambridge University Press, 1991) 709–57.

[3] See Pierre Riché, *Education and Culture in the Barbarian West, Sixth through Eighth Centuries*, tr. J. J. Contreni (Columbia: University of South Carolina Press, 1976); Claudio Leonardi, "Intellectual Life," in T. Reuter (ed.) *The New Cambridge Medieval History*, vol. III: *c.900–c.1024* (Cambridge: Cambridge University Press, 1999) 186–211.

[4] See John Marenbon, *From the Circle of Alcuin to the School of Auxerre: Logic, Theology and Philosophy in the Early Middle Ages* (Cambridge: Cambridge University Press, 1981).

functions were not always much different.[5] Contributions to new learning were also provided by monks such as Hilduin of St. Denis, who in the ninth century first translated the writings of pseudo-Dionysius from Greek into Latin (although this translation was quickly supplanted by a new translation by John Scottus Eriugena, the philosopher and scholar at the court of King Charles the Bald).

In the eleventh century, Anselm – monk and later prior and abbot of Bec in Normandy and, from 1093, Lanfranc's successor as archbishop of Canterbury – owed much to Lanfranc's mastery of the application of grammar and dialectic to the study of theological questions. Like his teacher, Anselm had traveled far, from Italy to Normandy, in search of a cloistered setting in which he could study and pray. Arriving at Bec around 1059, he soon produced distinctive, original, and carefully articulated works of prayer that led into deeply philosophical meditations. Anselm seems to begin with truths provided by scriptural revelation and to proceed to formulate deductions according to the rules of logic. But his work was also guided by conversations (*colloquia*) he had within the monastery of Bec with his monastic companions. Anselm was a fascinating speaker, fond of using analogies and images to illustrate his inquiries, but he was also deeply introspective in meditation and in pursuit of arguments that drew their strength from reason alone.

Peter Abaelard, usually portrayed as an aggressive teacher of logic in schools in and around Paris and as a champion of the use of dialectic in the field of theology, before being brought down as a heretic by Bernard, abbot of Clairvaux (the foremost Cistercian monk of the day), was also himself for over twenty years a monk, as well as an abbot who came to show a (perhaps still underestimated) dedication to the promotion of monastic ideals in the study of philosophy. In the years before his entry into monastic life, Abaelard took philosophy to mean the study of dialectic above all other branches of philosophy (*Historia calamitatum*, ed. Monfrin, lines 25–6, 78, 226). Admittedly his entry into monastic life – following a violent attack upon his person which resulted in his castration and his separation from his wife Héloïse – was not entirely voluntary, but he thereafter advocated the teaching of the arts as a hook or a bait to lead students to the study of true philosophy that is found in sacred books, thus following the example of Origen, whom Abaelard regarded as the greatest of Christian philosophers (ibid., 663–89).

---

[5] See David Ganz, "Theology and the Organisation of Thought," in R. McKitterick (ed.) *The New Cambridge Medieval History*, vol. II: *c.700–c.900* (Cambridge: Cambridge University Press, 1995) 758–85; David Luscombe, "Hrabanus Maurus and the Predestination Controversy," in F. J. Felten and B. Nichtweiss (eds.) *Hrabanus Maurus. Gelehrter, Abt von Fulda und Erzbischof von Mainz* (Mainz: Publ. Bistum Mainz, 2006) 141–58.

Such a close convergence between dialectic and theology was, however, unusual, not least in monastic circles. Abaelard's condemnation for heresy at an ecclesiastical council held at Sens in 1141 was driven by monks such as Bernard of Clairvaux, who also sought the condemnation of the teaching of Gilbert of Poitiers in 1148.[6] Perceived antitheses between the meditation sought in the monastic cloister and disputations fought in the schools – between Christian reflection, pagan philosophy, and scholarly exercises – underlay such clashes.

Indeed, these disputes were fueled in part by competition to lay claim to the true meaning of philosophy. For many monks, as for some of the Greek Fathers of the church, philosophy was a way of living the monastic life wisely in imitation of Christ, in accordance with reason and after having renounced the world. Benedictine monastic meditation was, understandably, centered on the discipline of the inner self in the presence of God and according to the teaching of Scripture. The truest philosopher in this sense was Jesus Christ.[7] But the ancient philosophers of Greece and Rome were also held in high esteem, whatever limitations were heaped upon them. "Spoiling the Egyptians," it was often said, "served to enrich the Hebrews" – in other words, pagan philosophy could be put to good use by Christians. Abaelard, for instance, taught that among the Hebrews (such as the disciples of Elisha, the Essenes, and the Nazarenes) and the gentiles (such as Diogenes), as well as among the early Christians (such as John the Baptist and the Desert Fathers), there had always been people who lived chaste, contemplative lives separated from the world, seeking the truth about God while living a life of virtue. Abaelard claimed that a monastic instinct was universal, by which he meant the linking of the solitary life with prayer and the study and practice of philosophy.[8] Guided by Jerome, whose *Adversus Jovinianum* provided arguments for proclaiming that chastity and good philosophy were interdependent qualities,[9] Abaelard also saw models of monastic life in the lives of the ancient philosophers, and even their statesmen.

---

[6] See John of Salisbury, *Historia pontificalis* (ed. Chibnall, pp. 15–41).

[7] Cf. Jean Leclercq, "Pour l'histoire de l'expression 'philosophie chrétienne'," *Mélanges de sciences religieuses* 9 (1952) 221–6; *L'amour des lettres et le désir de Dieu: initiation aux auteurs monastiques du moyen âge* (Paris: Cerf, 1957) pp. 99–100, and Henri Rochais, "*Ipsa philosophia Christus*," *Mediaeval Studies* 13 (1951) 244–7.

[8] When abbot of the monastery of St. Gildas in Brittany, Abaelard invoked, in a *Sermon* on John the Baptist, the Old Testament examples of Elijah and Elisha who lived in solitude, of John "who philosophized with the angels in the hermitage," and of Paul, Anthony, Hilarion, and Macharius, early Christian monks who were models of the monastic life which is the "Christian philosophy." Abaelard, *Sermon* 33 (*Patr. lat.* 178: 585). See Jean Leclercq, "*Ad ipsam sophiam Christum*: Das monastische Zeugnis Abaelards," in F. Hoffmann *et al.* (eds.) *Sapienter ordinare: Festgabe für Erich Kleineidam* (Leipzig: Benno, 1969) 179–98; Jean Leclercq, "'Ad ipsam sophiam Christum': Le témoignage monastique d'Abélard," *Revue d'ascétique et de mystique* 46 (1970) 161–81.

[9] See Philippe Delhaye, "Le dossier anti-matrimonial de l'*Adversus Jovinianum* et son influence sur quelques écrits latins du XIIe siècle," *Mediaeval Studies* 13 (1951) p. 71.

His insights are best presented in the second book of his *Theologia christiana*, where he explores the themes that, in his view, the ancients best exemplified: *contemptus mundi*, love of solitude, manual work, continence, temperance – and the study of letters. The truth of pagan philosophical teachings was the fruit of their perfect living (*Opera theol.* II: I.56–115).[10]

Many schools were run by canons who belonged to cathedral chapters or to lesser collegiate churches. Here the liberal arts were taught and boys were often prepared for the priesthood. A notable example around the year 1000 is the cathedral school of Chartres under Fulbert, and later, in the early twelfth century, under master Bernard of Chartres. New orders of regular canons – canons who lived under a rule, usually the one attributed to Augustine – sometimes also provided education and spectacularly so in the twelfth century at the abbey of St. Victor near Paris under Hugh, whose highly influential teaching and writing covered a very wide field. His *De sacramentis*, on the sacraments of the Christian faith, presents a sweeping view of the history of salvation from the work of Creation to the work of Restoration. His *Didascalicon*, perhaps the most important guide to the arts written in the twelfth century, seeks to show how the study of four branches of philosophy (theoretical, practical, mechanical, and logical) can restore the divine likeness within human nature.

FRIARS, THEIR *STUDIA*, AND UNIVERSITIES

Universities, which provided an arts curriculum, as well as supporting within a *studium generale* other faculties that might include theology, law, or medicine, began to take hold from the late twelfth and early thirteenth centuries when and where masters were incorporated (see Chapter 4). These developments were partly driven by secular and regular clergy – that is, by priests or canons who, in addition to teaching the arts, theology, or canon law, had been ordained to perform such tasks as preaching, while living either singly or within communities that observed a rule – but independent practitioners of medicine and civil law also taught and mentored pupils, and their incorporation in universities is not to be left out of account. Indeed, in some places their search for a more vocational education may have been the main driver of change.

In addition to students who learned the arts and studied the higher disciplines of theology, law, or medicine, there arrived, from the early thirteenth century

---

[10] See also *Theologia "Scholarium"* (*Opera theol.* III: I.96–176). In his *Historia calamitatum* Abaelard reports Héloïse saying to him that all the world's peoples – Gentiles and Jews as well as Christians – have included some who sought a life of virtue in detachment from the world (ed. Monfrin, lines 482 ff.).

onward, students who belonged to orders of mendicant friars, especially the Franciscan order of Friars Minor (the Greyfriars) founded in 1209 by Francis of Assisi (1181/2–1226), and the Dominican Order of Preachers (the Blackfriars) founded by Dominic (*ca.* 1172–1221), which took definite shape in 1220, as well as the Carmelite and Augustinian (or Austin) friars. The mendicant orders dedicated themselves, under the special care of the papacy, to the ideals of poverty and humility for the sake of following the example of Christ (see Chapter 42), and also (unlike monks, generally speaking) to the tasks of preaching and teaching to public audiences outside their convents, and typically within cities and towns. They often enjoyed great success, and ran their own schools.

According to his biographer, Thomas of Celano, Francis was not a highly educated man, and he once said that educated men should forsake all their learning along with their other possessions: "learning robs many people of their gentle characters" (*Vita secunda*, par. 194). There were reservations within the Franciscan order about learning and study – there always had been some such reservations within religious communities – but there was a need for training in order to preach. According to his companions, Francis "venerated most warmly those who were wise in religion." He was happy for learned but prayerful men to enter his order. As his Testament reads, "We ought to honor all theologians and ministers of the divine word."[11] An early example was the Portuguese Antony of Padua (*ca.* 1195–1231), who became an Augustinian canon and studied theology at Lisbon and then Coimbra. In 1220 he joined the Franciscans, becoming, with the approval of Francis, the first lector in theology and also famous as a preacher. At Paris Alexander of Hales, a master who joined the Franciscan order in 1236, lent his weight to the emergence of the Franciscan *studium* there as well as to the use of the *Sentences* of Peter Lombard in preference to the Bible as the basic text for the teaching of theology. His students included John of La Rochelle, Odo Rigaldus, William of Middleton, and, above all, Bonaventure, who, when they became masters in Paris, showed the way to developing the teaching of theology in a systematic and comprehensive manner with the support of a detailed command of philosophical materials.

Long years of study were a necessary preparation for the Dominicans, who were especially committed to preaching. Dominic developed a style of itinerant, mendicant preaching against dissenting Albigensian communities in the south of France. Having established a permanent community for his mission at Toulouse, he gained recognition between 1216 and 1218 from Pope Honorius III for his new religious order, the Order of Preachers. A training in preaching was already

---

[11] Ed. R. B. Brooke, *Scripta Leonis, Rufini et Angeli sociorum S. Francisci* (Oxford: Clarendon Press, 1970) p. 70.

important for clergy in cathedral schools; training for pastoral duties became more important for students, seculars and mendicants alike, with the arrival of the mendicant friars. The mendicants in their priories established independent schools for the education of their own number and of others also. In the case of the Dominican order, founded to preach the faith and to combat heresies, every convent was required to have a *lector* or teacher who had himself studied theology for four years.[12] And in some places *studia generalia*, which drew students of the order from all parts, promoted advanced study and research. Moreover, Dominic dispersed his earliest companions to university cities.

In Paris, Oxford, Cambridge, and elsewhere, as well as in Toulouse, mendicant *studia generalia* were implanted within university towns, but sometimes, as in Cologne, Erfurt, and Prague, the establishment of mendicant *studia generalia* preceded that of universities. Moreover, in many important universities, including Oxford, the teaching of theology was at times dominated by mendicant friars.[13] In some southern universities (such as Montpellier and Bologna), where there was for a long period no faculty of theology, mendicant *studia* had a monopoly in the teaching of theology.[14] On the other hand, although the Carmelite *studium* in Oxford in the early fourteenth century was highly active, the Carmelite order's *studium generale* for England was located in London from 1294. According to some scholars, William of Ockham, a student and a teacher at Oxford between 1307/8 and 1320, was in residence at the London Greyfriars between 1320 and 1324, together with Walter Chatton and Adam Wodeham, a period when he produced much of his philosophical and theological work.[15]

When located in university towns, the mendicants were closely linked with university activities, with mendicant teachers also occupying university chairs, non-mendicant students attending lectures given by mendicant masters, and some non-mendicant masters lecturing to mendicant students in their *studia*. It

[12] See Marian Mulchahey, *"First the Bow is Bent in Study . . .": Dominican Education before 1350* (Toronto: Pontifical Institute of Mediaeval Studies, 1998). Also William Hinnebusch, *The History of the Dominican Order* (State Island, NY: Alba House 1966–73) vol. II.
[13] At Oxford the Dominicans and the Franciscans established *studia* in 1229–30. Carmelites arrived there in 1256 and Augustinian friars in 1266–7. Especially important studies relating to Oxford are those of J. I. Catto, "Theology and Theologians 1220–1320," in J. I. Catto (ed.) *The History of the University of Oxford*, vol. I: *The Early Oxford Schools* (Oxford: Oxford University Press, 1984) 471–517, and William Courtenay, *Schools and Scholars in Fourteenth-Century England* (Princeton: Princeton University Press, 1987).
[14] For Bologna see Hastings Rashdall, *The Universities of Europe in the Middle Ages*, rev. edn by F. M. Powicke and A. B. Emden (Oxford: Clarendon Press, 1936) I: 253.
[15] See William J. Courtenay, "The Academic and Intellectual Worlds of Ockham," in P. V. Spade (ed.) *The Cambridge Companion to Ockham* (Cambridge: Cambridge University Press, 1999) p. 23 with note, but for doubts about the London connection see Rondo Keele, "Oxford *Quodlibeta* from Ockham to Holcot," in C. Schabel (ed.) *Theological Quodlibeta in the Middle Ages: The Fourteenth Century* (Leiden: Brill, 2007) pp. 654–9.

was not until 1247, for instance, that the Franciscan *studium* at Oxford acquired a Franciscan, as distinct from a secular, master. Robert Grosseteste, who was not a friar, taught in the Franciscan *studium* there until 1235 and was succeeded by three other secular masters. At Paris as well, the first teacher of theology in the Dominican *studium* was a secular master, John of St. Albans, who was succeeded *ca.* 1225 by another secular, John of St. Giles. Some secular masters, such as John of St. Giles, Alexander of Hales, and Robert Bacon, later became friars and thereby brought the mendicant houses into closer association with their universities; in the 1240s and 1250s the friars established themselves in Oxford as teachers of theology: Richard Rufus of Cornwall, Thomas of York, Henry Wodstone, John of Wales, Thomas Docking, Adam Marsh, and Roger Bacon as Friars Minor; Richard Fishacre, Simon of Hinton, and Robert Kilwardby as Dominicans. Some of these had studied or taught at Paris and were also to return to Paris.

Although Augustinian friars were largely Italian, they and the other three major mendicant orders were 'international.' Their leading teachers and scholars had a European status that was reinforced both by their mobility and by their migrations around different centers of study. Links, for example, between the courses taught by friars such as Richard Rufus and John Duns Scotus when in Paris and when in Oxford are well attested. By 1250 or so, the friars were predominant among masters of theology in these two universities; the quality of their teaching was very high and their *studia* seem to have been well organized. The religious orders also did well in promoting contacts and exchanges, with students and teachers being sent from England or Italy or Germany to France and in other directions as well. Two notable examples are the Franciscan Scotus, who taught in Oxford, Cambridge, Paris, and Cologne, and the Dominican Meister Eckhart, who was sent from the Dominican convent in Erfurt to study in Paris (where he also later taught), but who was active as well within his order in Thuringia, Saxony, Strasbourg, and Cologne.

Despite these facts, most universities were principally the preserve of secular masters and secular students; friars, and to a lesser extent monks, were an additional presence. Benedictine and Cistercian monks, often rooted in the countryside, risked being left behind by the rise of university centers in cities and by the appearance of the orders of mendicant friars. At times from the mid-thirteenth to the fifteenth century, relations were very strained between the mendicant orders and the secular masters within some universities, notably Paris.[16] The causes of disputes varied: there were concerns over privileges,

---

[16] For Paris see especially Michel-Marie Dufeil, *Guillaume de Saint-Amour et la polémique universitaire parisienne 1250–59* (Paris: Picard, 1972), and also Rashdall, *Universities* I: 370–97. For Oxford

over competition for the recruitment of students to courses given within the universities and of novices within the *studia* run by the friars, over the content of the teaching given, and also over the apocalyptic prophecies and teachings of the twelfth-century monk Joachim of Fiore and the issue of apostolic poverty that the friars especially supported (see Chapter 42).

One source of tension, at least in Oxford and Paris, was that secular theologians gained their degrees in theology after studying philosophy, whereas the mendicants were not allowed to study in the arts faculty but lectured on the *Sentences* and the Bible without graduating in arts. A further difficulty was that the mendicant friars, often operating outside of the traditional parochial and diocesan structures but directly subject to the pope, encountered opposition from those who defended a church hierarchy that was rooted in parishes, monasteries, and bishoprics. When they asked for licenses to undertake some of the functions of parish priests, such as hearing confessions, mendicant friars were seen by many secular clerics as intruders into a church that derived its proper form from a vision of the primitive church, in which the apostles and disciples were seen to be forerunners of the bishops and their clergy. In response, some apologists for the friars argued that church hierarchy rightly evolves over time; the earlier institutional hierarchy (notably, bishops and parish priests) was now accompanied by a "contemplative" hierarchy in which those who professed a purer life (such as Francis) had become preeminent over office-holding clergy. These debates in turn acquired a cosmic dimension when visions of the right structure for the church on earth were adjusted to suit visions of the heavenly or angelic hierarchy.[17]

THE UNIVERSITIES AND THE MONASTIC ORDERS

Important as the mendicant orders were in the development of university life and learning, monks contributed as well. Although outnumbered and overshadowed by friars – in the promotion of philosophical debate, they scarcely mattered – in their search for a university education for themselves monks founded colleges and *studia* in Paris, Oxford, and elsewhere. At Oxford they studied mainly

see Michael Sheehan, "The Religious Orders 1220–1370," in Catto, *The Early Oxford Schools*, pp. 204–8, and also Rashdall, *Universities* III: 70–4.

[17] See Yves Congar, "Aspects ecclésiologiques de la querelle entre mendicants et séculiers dans la seconde moitié du XIIIe siècle et le début du XIVe siècle," *Archives d'histoire doctrinale et littéraire du moyen âge* 28 (1961) 35–151; David Luscombe, "The *Lex divinitatis* in the Bull *Unam Sanctam* of Pope Boniface VIII," in C. Brooke *et al.* (eds.) *Church and Government in the Middle Ages* (Cambridge: Cambridge University Press, 1976) 205–21; David Luscombe, "The Hierarchies in the Writings of Alan of Lille, William of Auvergne and St Bonaventure," in I. Iribarren and M. Lenz (eds.) *Angels in Medieval Philosophical Enquiry* (Aldershot: Ashgate, 2008) 15–28.

theology. They were not dominant as teachers, although John Uthred of Boldon, a notable preacher and controversialist, was a distinguished exception. In the thirteenth century monks had not had the rush of recruits that the mendicant friars experienced. Still, in Paris a college was founded in 1246 for students of the Cistercian order (the white monks), and in 1292 the general chapter of the order at Cîteaux ordained that every abbey with more than twenty Cistercian monks had to send one monk to a university. In Oxford, the Cistercians had already established a *studium*, perhaps in 1282. Benedictine (or black) monks also established colleges there, including Gloucester College in 1283, Durham College in 1286, and Canterbury Hall in 1361.[18] In 1336, constitutions of Pope Benedict XII laid a requirement on all monasteries to send suitable monks to study at universities.

EMERGING DIFFERENCES BETWEEN THE MENDICANT ORDERS

After the condemnation of 1277 (see Chapter 8), some (although by no means all) Franciscan and Dominican students developed pronounced differences over the correct use of philosophy, especially with respect to Aristotelian philosophy, the distinction between essence and existence (see Chapter 45), and the unity and plurality of forms (see Chapter 46). In 1286, for instance, John Pecham – who became lector to the Franciscans in Oxford after teaching theology in Paris, and who had a notable career as provincial of the order, as a teacher of theology in the papal court, and finally as archbishop of Canterbury – condemned as heretical the teaching of Thomas Aquinas on the unity of the substantial form (the rational soul) in human beings. Franciscan friars in England who studied Aquinas's *Summa theologiae* were required from 1282 on to use a *Correctorium* of his teaching provided by William de la Mare, to which there were five replies from Dominican critics, including Thomas of Sutton and Robert Orford, who called William's work a *Corruptorium*.

The differences that emerged between the mendicant orders generated various *viae* – a *via beati Thomae*, a *via domini Alberti*, etc. – but masters within each of the orders were not in perfect agreement either. For example, Aquinas, who had already come under attack from other Dominican masters between 1269 and 1270 over his view of the unity of the form that holds together the intellective and moral powers of a human being, was further condemned on this issue at Oxford in 1277 by Kilwardby, the Dominican archbishop of Canterbury.[19] On

---

[18] Rashdall, *Universities* III: 185–91.
[19] See D. A. Callus, *The Condemnation of St Thomas at Oxford* (London: Blackfriars Publications, 1955).

the other hand, a series of chapter meetings of the Dominican order defended the study of Aquinas's thought. As well as being controversial, early Thomism was dynamic and creative, and mounted robust attacks against the threats facing it successively from the teachings of Henry of Ghent, John Duns Scotus, and Peter Auriol.

Albertism, the *via Alberti*, is often seen as a movement among followers of Albert the Great who turned against the teachings of Aquinas and who promoted the Neoplatonic tradition found, for example, in the *Liber de causis*, in Solomon ibn Gabirol, and in pseudo-Dionysius. This opposition was much more marked in fifteenth-century Cologne than in other parts of Europe, where it is more difficult to discern; in Cologne, the claims of the Albertists to be the true followers of Aristotle, as well as their differences with the followers of Aquinas, are perhaps best illustrated by Heymeric de Campo in his *Problemata inter Albertum Magnum et Sanctum Thomam*. The Albertists were also inspired by the works of the Dominicans Ulrich of Strasbourg, who had been a fellow student of Thomas but scarcely knew his work, and Dietrich of Freiberg, who was sharply anti-Thomist.[20] The Albertists were not all friars, however: one of Ulrich's most careful readers was Denys, the Carthusian monk of Roermond who had become a master of arts at Cologne in 1424[21] and whose writings were themselves widely read. They tended to reject the Thomist distinction between *esse* and *essentia*. They were also anti-nominalist: one of Heymeric's teachers was the Parisian master John of Nova Domus, whose critique of nominalism, the *via moderna*, is contained in his *De universali reali* (see Chapters 48–9).

The bold innovations – the "English philosophy" – that penetrated Paris and other places in the early fourteenth century were especially due to two Franciscans, Scotus and Ockham. Scotus's attack on "necessitarianism" or determinism was supported by Ockham, his fellow Franciscan, who also sought to free God from all limitations, be they essences, causes, universals, or Ideas. In the early fourteenth century there was also considerable tension between the members of the mendicant orders and others about the relationship between grace, free will, and predestination. Robert Holcot, for instance, a Dominican friar and also a pupil of Ockham, gave attention to humanity's partnership with God, whereas Thomas Bradwardine complains in *The Case of God Against the Pelagians* that, when he had studied philosophy at Oxford, "what he heard day in, day out,

---

[20] See Maarten Hoenen and Alain de Libera (eds.) *Albertus Magnus und der Albertismus: Deutsche philosophische Kultur des Mittelalters* (Leiden: Brill, 1995); Gilles-Gérard Meersseman, *Geschichte des Albertismus* (Paris: Haloua, 1933–5).

[21] See Alessandro Palazzo, "Ulrich of Strasbourg and Denys the Carthusian," *Bulletin de philosophie médiévale* 46 (2004) 61–113.

was that we are the masters of our own free acts, that ours is the choice to act well or badly, to have virtues or sins."[22]

The sharpening in the early fourteenth century of differences between schools of thought – Dominican friars, for example, mostly proving to be followers of Thomas Aquinas and Franciscan friars becoming committed to support of the teaching of Scotus – led to a deepening conservatism. Dominican and Franciscan friars tended to follow the traditions of their own orders, and at chapter meetings Dominicans strove to promote the teachings of Aquinas. Although his teachings had been put under a shadow in 1277, Aquinas was canonized as a saint in 1323; in 1325 the current bishop of Paris, Stephen Bourret, reversed the condemnation of 1277 insofar as it affected St. Thomas.[23] Durand of St. Pourçain, a Dominican master in Paris in the early fourteenth century, had his teaching examined by a commission of fellow Dominican friars, led by Hervaeus Natalis, and was censured for departing from Aquinas's teachings in numerous ways. Criticism of Thomist and Aristotelian thought was a feature of much philosophical and theological inquiry in the fourteenth century. Peter of Ailly, a prominent nominalist and chancellor of the University of Paris in 1389, warned the faculty of theology against the method of Aquinas that resulted in interpretations of the articles of faith that were predetermined by philosophical doctrines.[24]

Such sharp differences also had soft edges. It would be misleading to think of Dominican friars as Thomists and Franciscan friars uniformly as Scotists. The lines of division between the mendicant orders were not so hard. The teaching of Scotus on the univocity of being (see Chapter 54) was sharply criticized, or at least received in a guarded way, by such fellow Franciscan friars as Richard of Conington, Robert Cowton, Peter Auriol, Nicholas of Lyra, and Ockham. Scotus's teaching on common natures (see Chapter 47) was also criticized by fellow Franciscans such as Auriol and Ockham, who claimed instead that all that the human mind knows is the individual. After the 1320s, distinctive schools of thought were marked by their absence in the two English universities;[25] the ascendancy of the Franciscans and Dominicans had begun to weaken.

---

[22] Cited in Gordon Leff, *Bradwardine and the Pelagians: A Study of his "De Causa Dei" and its Opponents* (Cambridge: Cambridge University Press, 1957) p. 14.

[23] See Henri Denifle and Émile Chatelain (eds.) *Chartularium Universitatis Parisiensis* (Paris: Delalain, 1889–97) II: n. 838. (See also Chapter 8.)

[24] Peter of Ailly, *Consistorio per eundem contra M. Joannem de Montesano*, in C. Duplessis d'Argentré (ed.) *Collectio judiciorum de novis erroribus* (Paris: apud A. Cailleau, 1728–36) I. 2: 69–74.

[25] Courtenay, *Schools and Scholars*, pp. 190–2.

Ockham's nominalism did not establish firm roots even in Franciscan soil in the fourteenth century. It was influential insofar as it led many to question whether cognition requires species to act as intermediaries between a knowing subject and a known object, but Ockham's theory of knowledge, like Scotus's views on being, was largely rejected in England by such scholars as Walter Chatton and Adam Wodeham, both Franciscans, and by Robert Holcot, a Dominican. Ockham left no school: thirteenth-century views favoring cognition through species proved tenacious in his century, and nominalism enjoyed no triumph.

Furthermore, the divisions between realists and nominalists (see Chapters 47–8) cut across the distinctions between the various religious orders. The *via antiqua* was adopted by followers of Albert and Aquinas, whereas the *via moderna* was adopted by, among others, the majority of scholars in the University of Cologne in the fifteenth century. The "new" or "modern" way was associated with nominalism, and Ockham was its standard bearer, but realists tended to be associated with Scotus as well as with Aquinas.

In the fifteenth century each *via* could be followed in different ways: at Pavia, for example, there was one chair of theology for a Dominican follower of Thomas Aquinas and another for a Franciscan follower of Scotus, who was also regarded as a realist. There was also a widespread Thomist revival: in some Dominican convents, the *Summa theologiae* of Aquinas replaced Lombard's *Sentences* as the basis of teaching theology. Lorenzo Valla, no friend of scholasticism as such, nor a friar, celebrated the feast of St. Thomas by pronouncing in the church of Santa Sabina in Rome an *Encomium Sancti Thomae de Aquino*, published in 1457: Thomas, he proclaimed, was one of the authorities in the Christian tradition of theology that included Augustine and Anselm. The young Martin Luther, on the other hand, who entered the order of Augustinian friars (or hermits) at Erfurt in 1505, attended the University of Wittenberg in 1508, where he at first accepted a theology of justification derived from the nominalists.

6

PLATONISM

JAN A. AERTSEN

In 1939 Raymond Klibansky published a programmatic essay entitled *The Continuity of the Platonic Tradition during the Middle Ages*, in which he presented a new project: the *Corpus Platonicum Medii Aevi*, meant as a counterpart of the *Aristoteles Latinus*. The term "continuity" in the title of the essay had a polemical intent: the principal aim of the planned collection of texts was, as it is stated in the Preface, "to reveal a neglected link" in the history of thought. In the study of medieval philosophy there existed a strong tendency to regard this period as an era dominated by Aristotelianism; it was not until the Renaissance that Plato would have been rediscovered.[1] Against this prejudice Klibansky's essay pointed to the continuity of the Platonic tradition throughout the Middle Ages. Medieval Platonism originated from two sources, a *direct* tradition, based on translations of Plato's own works, and an *indirect* one through the intermediary of authors who transmitted essential doctrines of Platonism in their own accounts.[2] This chapter will be focusing on the Latin Plato – a clear restriction, because, as Klibansky stresses, a full understanding of the role of Platonism in the Middle Ages has to take the Arabic tradition into account.[3]

---

[1] How strong this tendency still is was shown by *The Cambridge History of Later Medieval Philosophy* (N. Kretzmann *et al.* [eds.] [Cambridge: Cambridge University Press, 1982]), which has a section on "Aristotle in the Middle Ages" (pp. 45–98), but which completely ignores medieval Platonism.

[2] Raymond Klibansky, *The Continuity of the Platonic Tradition during the Middle Ages. Outlines of a Corpus Platonicum Medii Aevi* (London: Warburg Institute, 1939). Fifty years after Klibansky's essay, Carlos Steel took stock of the study of Platonism in the Middle Ages in his article "Plato Latinus (1939–1989)," in J. Hamesse and M. Fattori (eds.) *Rencontres de cultures dans la philosophie médiévale: traductions et traducteurs de l'Antiquité tardive au XIVe siècle* (Louvain-la-Neuve: Publication de l'Institut d'études médiévales, 1990) 301–16.

[3] There does not exist a comprehensive study on Plato's reception in Arabic thought. A classical survey of Plato Arabus remains Franz Rosenthal, "On the Knowledge of Plato's Philosophy in the Islamic World," *Islamic Culture* 14 (1940) 387–422, plus addenda in *Islamic Culture* 15 (1941) 396–8 (reprinted in Rosenthal, *Greek Philosophy in the Arab World* [Aldershot: Ashgate, 1990]). For the Arabic–Latin transmission of Plato, see Dag Hasse, "Plato arabico-latinus: Philosophy – Wisdom Literature – Occult Sciences," in S. Gersh and M. J. F. M. Hoenen (eds.) *The Platonic Tradition in the Middle Ages: A Doxographic Approach* (Berlin: De Gruyter 2002) 31–65.

PLATO LATINUS

Boethius, one of the "founders of the Middle Ages," saw it as his mission to make the treasures of philosophy accessible to the West. He tried to realize Cicero's exhortation to transfer philosophy from the Greek to the Latin world and formulated to that end an ambitious program: he wanted to translate the complete works of Plato and Aristotle into Latin and to show the fundamental accordance between the two philosophers by commentaries on their works.[4] But Boethius could only realize a fraction of this project, namely, translations of and commentaries on Aristotle's logical works. During the entire Middle Ages the direct knowledge of Plato remained rather restricted. In contrast to the Arabic-speaking world, the Latin West had no access, for instance, to the *Republic* and the *Laws*. Given the limited number of Latin texts available, the *Plato Latinus* cannot be seen as a real counterpart of the *Aristoteles Latinus*.

Up until the end of the fifteenth century, only four dialogues were translated into Latin: (i) the *Meno*, translated by Henry Aristippus in the twelfth century; (ii) the *Phaedo*, by the same translator; (iii) the *Parmenides* in the partial thirteenth-century translation of William of Moerbeke (note that the Latin *Parmenides* is not a translation of the dialogue, but a reconstruction on the basis of the lemmata, found in the commentary of Proclus, which ends with the first hypothesis); and (iv) the *Timaeus* in the partial translation – only the first part (17a–53b) was known – and commentary of Calcidius (fourth century).[5]

Among these works, only the *Timaeus* exerted a real influence on medieval philosophy, as the large number of extant manuscripts confirms. Platonism in the Middle Ages coincides to a large extent with the history of this dialogue. The *Timaeus* clearly exemplifies the continuity of the Platonic tradition from late antiquity to the Renaissance.[6] The principal medieval commentaries on this writing were composed by masters of the school of Chartres in the twelfth century, Bernard of Chartres and William of Conches. It was in the twelfth century that the Platonic influence reached its peak; Plato was called the *maximus philosophorum* (Abaelard) and the *princeps philosophorum* (John of Salisbury).

The study of the *Timaeus* in the twelfth century provided the materials for developing a rational account of the physical world, that is, for a natural science

---

[4] Boethius formulates his program in his second commentary on the *De interpretatione* (ed. Meiser, II: 79). He refers to Cicero's exhortation in his commentary on Cicero's *Topics* (*Patr. Lat.* 64: 1152b).

[5] All published by the Warburg Institute in the series *Plato Latinus*, under Klibansky's general editorship.

[6] See Thomas Leinkauf and Carlos Steel (eds.) *Platons* Timaios *als Grundtext der Kosmologie in Spätantike, Mittelalter und Renaissance* (Leuven: Leuven University Press, 2005). See in particular in this volume the paper by Andreas Speer, "*Lectio physica*: Anmerkungen zur *Timaios*-Rezeption im Mittelalter," 213–34.

and cosmology. In contrast to the symbolic interpretation of the world in the early Middle Ages, which tended to reduce phenomena to a direct manifestation of the divine will, the dialogue's main task is to explain natural phenomena by reducing them to their ultimate natural causes, in accordance with Plato's search for the "legitimate cause and reason" (*Timaeus* 28a). Another Platonic feature of natural science in the twelfth century is the fundamental role of mathematics in the account of the order of sensible things. The commentaries in the school of Chartres establish the conformity of the philosophical teachings of the *Timaeus* on the origin and structure of the universe with the biblical narrative on the creation of the world in Genesis. Plato's divine Craftsman or Demiurge (*Opifex*), who constructed this world, was identified with the biblical creator.[7]

The Platonic science of nature was supplanted by Aristotle's physics in the thirteenth century. The turn from Plato to Aristotle, who became "The Philosopher" in this century, is one of the most remarkable developments in medieval philosophy. The change cannot be understood merely as the result of external factors, such as the texts becoming available in translation. The essential reason must rather be sought in a fundamental reorientation in intellectual life toward a new model of scientific rationality, which was better met by Aristotelianism.[8]

PROCLUS LATINUS

The information medieval thinkers had on Plato's philosophy was much more comprehensive than one would possibly expect on the basis of the few translations in the *Plato Latinus*. This fact can be accounted for by the indirect tradition, which was the most important source for the knowledge of Platonism in the Middle Ages. An example of this transmission is Boethius, who was not able to realize his translation project, but whose main work, *The Consolation of Philosophy*, impressively expressed the Platonic ideal of philosophy. Besides Boethius, the great exponents of Latin Platonism were Augustine (especially through his reports of Platonism in *The City of God*) and Macrobius in his commentary on the "Dream of Scipio" (*Somnium Scipionis*).[9] An important channel of Platonic doctrines from the Greek tradition was the *Corpus dionysiacum*. Thomas Aquinas observes that its author, who claims to be the Dionysius (the Areopagite) mentioned in the Acts of the Apostles (17:34), follows "the Platonic way of thought,"

---

[7] See Tulio Gregory, "The Platonic Inheritance," in P. Dronke (ed.) *A History of Twelfth-Century Western Philosophy* (Cambridge: Cambridge University Press, 1988) 54–80.

[8] George Wieland, "Plato or Aristotle: A Real Alternative in Medieval Philosophy?," in J. Wippel (ed.) *Studies in Medieval Philosophy* (Washington: Catholic University of America Press, 1987) 63–83.

[9] See the rich documentation in Stephen Gersh, *Middle Platonism and Neoplatonism: The Latin Tradition* (Notre Dame, IN: University of Notre Dame Press, 1986).

and modern scholarship has established Dionysius's dependency on the thought of Proclus (d. 485).[10] The various channels transmitted Platonic doctrines with accents of their own, so that one could speak of medieval "Platonisms" in the plural, by distinguishing a strand going back to Augustine and another deriving from pseudo-Dionysius.[11]

From the end of the thirteenth century an immediate knowledge of Proclus, the philosopher who gave Platonism a systematic form, was possible through the Latin translation of some of his works. The most important text is the *Elementatio theologica*, the translation of which William of Moerbeke completed in 1268. We want to focus on the *Proclus Latinus*, since this translation had several effects on medieval philosophy.

First, it modified the thirteenth-century view of Aristotelianism. Thanks to the translation of Proclus, Thomas Aquinas discovered the Platonic character and the true paternity of the anonymous *Liber de causis*. This "Book of the Causes" was part of the curriculum in the arts faculty in Paris and was regarded as the necessary completion of Aristotle's *Metaphysics*. But in the prologue to his commentary (*ca.* 1271–2), Aquinas points out for the first time that "this book is an excerpt from the *Elementatio theologica* of Proclus."

Second, the Latin translation of Proclus made it possible to note certain differences between Plato's teaching and Proclus's Neoplatonism – a recognition that is quite exceptional in the Middle Ages. This insight was expressed by Henry Bate of Malines, who composed at the end of the thirteenth century a monumental encyclopedia *Speculum divinorum et quorundam naturalium*. Part XI of it is devoted to the "Platonic philosophy," in which he quotes nearly the entire text of Proclus's *Elementatio*. Henry observes that, following Plato, Platonists like Proclus distinguish many modes of participation. But he notices that he has never found in the "books of Plato that have been transmitted to us hitherto" any such complex theory. He refers to passages in the *Timaeus*, the *Meno*, and the *Phaedo*, and concludes his survey of Platonic texts with the observation: "Perhaps there is more to be found about participation in the *Parmenides* of Plato, a book that is not yet generally known among us; that is what I heard a short time ago from the translator of that book, who promised to send it to me, but his death prevented it" (XI.12, ed. Boese, pp. 42–4). The death to which reference is

---

[10] See Aquinas, *Quaest. de malo* (ed. Leonine vol. XXIII) 1.2c, and H. D. Saffrey, "Nouveau liens objectifs entre le pseudo-Denys et Proclus," in *Recherches sur le Néoplatonisme après Plotin* (Paris: Vrin, 1990) 227–48.

[11] For the expression "Platonisms" in the plural, see M.-D. Chenu, *La théologie au douzième siècle* (Paris: Vrin, 1966) pp. 108–41. See also Josef Koch, "Augustinischer und Dionysischer Neuplatonismus und das Mittelalter," in W. Beierwaltes (ed.) *Platonismus in der Philosophie des Mittelalters* (Darmstadt: Wissenschaftliche Buchgesellschaft, 1969) 317–42.

made is that of the famous translator William of Moerbeke in 1286. Henry is obviously frustrated by his limited access to authentic Platonic texts. The dream of a complete translation of Plato's works was not realized until Marsilio Ficino's efforts during the Renaissance (1484).

Third, a remarkable manifestation of the superiority of Platonism over and against Aristotelianism is to be found in the voluminous commentary on the *Elementatio theologica* of Proclus, which was written by Berthold of Moosburg, Eckhart's successor as head of the *studium generale* of the Dominicans in Cologne, sometime between 1327 and his death in 1361.[12] This work – the only commentary on Proclus known from the Middle Ages – shows the vitality of the Platonic tradition after the reception of Aristotle, for, as we shall see, the commentator fully identifies himself with the philosophical project he is commenting upon.

A feature of Berthold's *Expositio* is that it does not make any attempt to harmonize Platonism and Aristotelianism according to the program formulated by Boethius of a fundamental "concordance" between the two protagonists of ancient philosophy: *Plato et Aristoteles . . . non concordant*. In the *praeambulum* of his Commentary, Berthold opposes "Platonic science," which is concerned with the divine things, to "the Peripatetic metaphysics," which deals with being insofar as it is being. He argues that the Platonic position is superior to the Aristotelian *habitus* of metaphysical wisdom and is therefore called a "superwisdom" (*supersapientia*), since it deals not only with the principles of being, but also with principles that are above being (*super entia*), such as the first good. The commentator clearly identifies himself with this more eminent position by speaking of "our (*nostra*) superwisdom" (praeamb. C, ed. Pagnoni-Sturlese *et al.*, I: 65–6, 68).

Berthold's criticism of Aristotle's ontological conception of metaphysics is specified in the commentary itself, which is carefully constructed: it discusses first what is presupposed (*suppositum*) by Proclus's propositions, and explains then the meaning of the *propositum* itself. In this analysis, Berthold appeals again and again to the different philosophical positions of "Plato" and "Aristotle." A telling example is his account of the *suppositum* of the eleventh proposition ("All beings proceed from a single first cause"), in which he observes that Aristotle and Plato held different views of being, the one, and the good.

Typical of Aristotle's position is the transcendental way of thought, which is characterized by three claims. (i) He posits some *communia*, which he calls *transcendentia*, because they surpass the single categories and "run through all of them." Among these transcendentals are *being*, *one*, *good*, *true*, *thing*, and *what* (*quid*) or *something* (*aliquid*). They are the same in reference and convertible with

---

[12] On Berthold, see Alain de Libera, *Introduction à la mystique rhénane d'Albert le Grand à Maître Eckhart* (Paris: OEIL, 1984) pp. 317–442.

each other, but conceptually different. (ii) Among the common notions, *being* is first. It is the most formal of all concepts, by which each thing is distinguished from nothing or non-being. The most remarkable feature of Berthold's account is the conclusion that (iii) the transcendentals do not have extramental reality. This idea seems to be the consequence of the kind of generalness that applies to *being*. The commonness of *being* is a commonness of abstraction, realized by the intellect, which effects universality in things. "Hence *ens* does not have being in natural reality, but only in the soul" (prop. 11A, I: 185–6).

Berthold contrasts Plato's view of being and good with Aristotle's teaching. Plato denies all three elements of the Aristotelian position, claiming that (i) there is no convertibility between *being* and *good*; (ii) *being* is not the first among the *communia*; and (iii) *being* and *good*, taken in their generalness, also exist in reality. The last difference is decisive and can be accounted for by the kind of universality on which Plato bases his position. He does not understand the generalness of being and good in the sense of a "logical" or "predicative" universality, according to which the more universal something is, the more potential it is. He takes their generalness rather in the sense of a "theological" universality or a universality of "separation," according to which the more universal something is, the more actual or active it is. The consequence of the Platonic view is that *being* and *good* are really and conceptually distinct from one another, since the good, as the most universal cause of things, is prior, more universal, and more absolute than being. Berthold substantiates the primacy of the good by referring to Dionysius the Areopagite, whose *On the Divine Names* places the name 'good' before 'being' (ibid., I: 186–7).[13]

To sum up, Berthold understands Platonism and Aristotelianism as opposed structures of thought, as two competing archetypes of philosophy, which are mutually exclusive. The "Plato" and "Aristotle" of whom Berthold speaks are patently medieval transformations of the two protagonists of ancient philosophy. Berthold's "Plato" is in fact "a person with a double face": it is Proclus–Dionysius.[14] His "Aristotle" has also undergone a medieval metamorphosis, insofar as in the Greek philosopher there is certainly no *system* of the transcendentals; the development of a systematic theory was an original achievement of thirteenth-century philosophy. Berthold's commentary testifies to a Platonic reaction against the transcendental way of thought that dominated medieval philosophy after 1250.[15]

---

[13] See *Expositio* prop. 1A (I: 73–4), where Berthold already introduces the opposition between *universalitas praedicationis* and *universalitas separationis*, between *universale logicum* and *universale theologicum*.

[14] See de Libera, *Introduction à la mystique rhénane*, pp. 388–9.

[15] See Jan Aertsen, "Ontology and Henology in Medieval Philosophy (Thomas Aquinas, Master Eckhart and Berthold of Moosburg)," in E. Bos and P. Meyer (eds.) *On Proclus and his Influence in Medieval Philosophy* (Leiden: Brill, 1992) 120–40.

THE "PLATONIST" THOMAS AQUINAS

An author who is a telling example of the considerable indirect knowledge of Platonic thought is Aquinas. Although Plato's *Timaeus* was the only dialogue he knew, he gives evidence of a clear insight into the basic doctrines of Platonism.[16] In the twentieth-century interpretation of Aquinas's thought it was initially common to describe its distinctive character as "Christian Aristotelianism." The rediscovery of the "Platonist" Thomas began in the 1950s with two studies that recognized the fundamental importance of the Platonic concept of "participation" for Aquinas's metaphysics – a notion that Aristotle had sharply criticized. Since then several studies have shown that central elements of his conception of being are traceable to the thought of Plotinus, Proclus, and pseudo-Dionysius.[17]

Aquinas presents an evaluation of the Platonic approach in the prologue of his commentary on pseudo-Dionysius's *De divinis nominibus*. He mentions some reasons why Dionysius's writings are difficult to read. The principal difficulty is that the Areopagite employs the manner of speaking of the Platonists, a manner that has fallen into disuse among modern thinkers (*apud modernos*), that is, among those who are trained in Aristotelian conceptuality. Thomas proceeds to sketch the Platonist approach to reality that underlies their way of speaking.

The Platonists want to reduce all that is composed and material to simple and "abstract" principles (*abstracta*). "Abstract" has no cognitive meaning here, but an ontological meaning: the term means *separated from matter*. Thus the Platonists posit the existence of separate Forms of natural things: for example, Human-Being-in-itself. A concrete individual is not a human being by its essence, but by participation in that separate Human Being. This is called "human being *per se*," because it is identical with the human nature or species. The Platonists apply this "abstract" approach not only to the species of natural things but also to that which is most common, namely, *good, one,* and *being*. They hold that there is a first, which is the essence of goodness, of unity, and of being – a principle that we, Aquinas adds, call "God." The other things are called "good", "one" and "being" because of their derivation from the first principle. Therefore the Platonists called the first principle "the Good itself," "the Good *per se*," or "the goodness of all good things" (*In De divinis nominibus*, prologue).

---

[16] See Cristina d'Ancona, "Historiographie du platonisme médiéval: le cas de saint Thomas," in S.-T. Bonino (ed.) *Saint Thomas au XXe siècle* (Paris: Éditions Saint-Paul, 1994) 198–217.

[17] See Cornelio Fabro, *Participation et causalité selon S. Thomas d'Aquin* (Louvain: Publications Universitaires, 1961); Louis-Bertrand Geiger, *La participation dans la philosophie de S. Thomas d'Aquin* (Paris: Vrin, 1942); Robert Henle, *Saint Thomas and Platonism: A Study of Plato and Platonici Texts in the Writings of Saint Thomas* (The Hague: Nijhoff, 1956); Klaus Kremer, *Die neuplatonische Seinsphilosophie und ihre Wirkung auf Thomas von Aquin* (Leiden: Brill, 1966); Wayne Hankey, "Aquinas and the Platonists," in Gersh and Hoenen, *The Platonic Tradition in the Middle Ages*, 279–324.

In the next part of the prologue, Aquinas rejects the first application of the Platonic method: there are no separate, subsisting Forms of natural things. But with regard to the first principle of things, he recognizes the legitimacy of the Platonist's reduction. In this respect their opinion is "the truest" and "in agreement with Christian faith." Therefore Dionysius called God sometimes "the Good itself," "the supergood," or "the goodness of every good" (ibid.).

Aquinas's evaluation of Platonism is mixed. As negative he assesses, like most medieval authors, its conception of the nature of things, subscribing to Aristotle's critique of the doctrine of Forms. The essence or nature of a thing is not a subsisting Form separated from it. The Platonic isomorphism between our abstract mode of knowing and the mode of being of things is a criticism that recurs again and again in Aquinas's writings. He values positively, on the other hand, the Platonic view of the relation of things to the first principle. This principle is transcendent and is the essence of goodness and being. Other things stand in a relation of participation to the first principle. Their being has been derived from the first, divine being. Thomas advances no argument for the validity of the Platonic method of reduction, but this can lie in nothing else than its application to the *maxime communia*, that is, to the transcendental notions. The Platonic approach is valid, insofar as the first principle, God, is regarded as the universal cause of things; he is the cause of what is most common. In this manner, Aquinas succeeds in showing the complementarity of the Dionysian–Platonic approach and the Aristotelian way of thought.

QUAESTIO DE IDEIS

Through all ages the doctrine of the Ideas has been seen as the core of Platonism. In the Middle Ages, there was with respect to this doctrine also a direct and an indirect tradition. The Latin translation of the *Timaeus* provided an immediate access to Plato's teaching; an important secondary source was Augustine's short treatise *Quaestio de ideis*. Without knowledge of the Ideas, he states, nobody can be wise (*sapiens*). Augustine takes the Ideas to be the primordial forms, the permanent *rationes* of things, which themselves are not formed and therefore are eternally present in the divine mind. What is subject to coming-to-be and to passing-away, that is, the whole sensible world, is formed according to the Ideas. For Augustine it is evident that the exemplar according to which everything is created is not something outside the divine mind. Such an opinion would be a "sacrilege" (*De diversis quaest. 83*, q. 46).[18]

---

[18] See Martin Grabmann, "Des heiligen Augustinus Quaestio De ideis (*De diversis quaestionibus* LXXXIII, qu. 46) in ihrer inhaltlichen Bedeutung und mittelalterlichen Weiterwirkung," in *Mittelalterliches Geistesleben* (Munich: Hueber, 1936) II: 25–34.

The reception of Aristotle in the thirteenth century, however, confronted the medieval reader with a severe criticism of the doctrine of Ideas. In Books VII and XIII of his *Metaphysics*, the Philosopher argues that Plato's hypothesis of the Ideas is fully superfluous. The Ideas are necessary neither for the knowledge of things nor for their being. *Homo generat hominem*: the begetter suffices for the coming-to-be of things (VII.7, 1034a2–9). In his *Nicomachean Ethics* (I. 4), Aristotle presents a radical critique of Plato's Idea of the Good: such an Idea is theoretically impossible and practically irrelevant. These criticisms led to discussions that reflect the entire range of medieval attitudes toward Plato.

Aquinas endorses Aristotle's objections to Plato's Ideas, taken as the Forms of the natural things, which exist apart from those things. But he does not think Aristotle's criticisms apply to Augustine's version of the doctrine of Forms and accepts the necessity of the Ideas in the divine mind for our understanding of the world as creation: "Since the world was not made by chance, but by God acting by his intellect . . . there must exist in the divine mind a form to the likeness of which the world was made. And in this the notion of an Idea consists" (*Summa theol.* 1a 15.1c). When, on the one hand, Plato is rejected with the help of Aristotle, and, on the other, he is supported with the help of Augustine, it is not surprising that Ferrarius the Catalan, probably a student of Aquinas, could raise the question (*ca.* 1276) of "whether the Ideas that theologians posit in God are identical with the Platonic ideas."[19]

An example of a thinker who attempts to show, according to the program formulated by Boethius, the real concordance between Plato and Aristotle is Henry Bate. Part VII of his *Speculum* is entirely devoted to a defense of the Platonic doctrine of Ideas against the objections of Aristotle in the *Metaphysics*. There does not exist a deep opposition between the two philosophers, since the Philosopher's criticism concerns only the "surface" of Plato's language. When Aristotle, for instance, remarked that "the begetter suffices," he did not intend to deny the existence of the Ideas, but only refused to take them as entities entirely separated from the sensible substances, as some Platonists did (VII.1, ed. Steel and van de Vyver, pp. 100–2).[20]

Other authors severely criticize Aristotle's criticism of Platonism: he proves to be "the worst metaphysician."[21] According to Bonaventure, the "true"

---

[19] *Quodlibet* q. 1: "Utrum idee quae theologi ponunt esse in Deo sint eedem cum ideis quae Platonici posuerunt" (Paris, Arsenal 379, ff. 225r–33v).

[20] See Carlos Steel, "Das neue Interesse für den Platonismus am Ende des 13. Jahrhunderts," in T. Kobusch and B. Mojsisch (eds.) *Platon in der abendländischen Geistesgeschichte: Neue Forschungen zum Platonismus* (Darmstadt: Wissenschaftliche Buchgesellschaft, 1997) 120–33.

[21] The expression is used by the Scotist Francis of Meyronnes (*ca.* 1320) in his discussion of Plato's doctrine of the Ideas (*Sent.* I.47.3 (ed. 1520, f. 134rbF).

metaphysician studies the exemplary cause of being. Aristotle had secluded himself from this center of metaphysics, because he had cursed (*exsecratur*) Plato's Ideas. Consequently he fell into several errors: he ignored the exemplary cause of things and denied divine providence (*Collationes in Hexaemeron* VI.2–4).

Because of a particularity in the reception of Aristotle's *Ethics*, the medieval commentators were familiar with the commentary of a marked critic of Aristotle. Robert Grosseteste, who first published a complete translation of the *Nicomachean Ethics* into Latin (1246–7), at the same time translated a corpus of Greek commentaries on this work. Part of this corpus was a commentary on the first book composed by the eleventh-century Byzantine scholar Eustratios of Nicaea, and containing a critique of Aristotle's critique that was clearly inspired by Neoplatonism. According to Eustratios, Aristotle fundamentally misunderstood Plato's Idea of the Good, whose commonness is not the univocal commonness of a genus but is based on the universal causality of the Good.[22]

In his Commentary on the *Ethics* (1250), Albert the Great, when discussing Aristotle's critique of Plato's Idea of the Good, refers to the "Commentator," that is, to Eustratios. He concludes that Aristotle's arguments against Plato are only compelling when one takes the Idea of the Good as the form of a genus. When, however, one understands, along with the Commentator, the Idea in the sense of the exemplary cause of all good things, it is clear that Aristotle's arguments are "useless" (*nihil valent*) (*Super Ethicam* I.6 n. 30). In this respect, Plato, not Aristotle, has it right.

---

[22] *In Ethicam Nicomacheam* I.6, in Robert Grosseteste (tr.) *The Greek Commentaries on the Nicomachean Ethics of Aristotle* (Leiden: Brill, 1973) I: 76–7. See Kimon Giocarinis, "Eustratios of Nicaea's Defence of the Doctrine of Ideas," in *Franciscan Studies* 24 (1964) 159–204.

7

AUGUSTINIANISM

GARETH B. MATTHEWS

St. Augustine, bishop of Hippo, was both a theologian of great influence and a philosopher of remarkable originality. He helped shape Christian orthodoxy by identifying the Christian heresies of Pelagianism, Manicheanism, and Donatism, the first two of which have special philosophical interest. Pelagianism, as captured by the maxim philosophers associate with Kant, 'Ought implies can,' stakes out a plausible limit on moral responsibility. Augustine's idea that human beings are obligated to obey the moral law despite the fact that, after the fall of Adam, they have been in a state of depravity in which they can do no good apart from the grace of God, poses a direct challenge to this plausible limit on moral responsibility (see Chapter 29). Augustine also sought to refute Manicheanism, according to which there is a cosmic principle of evil and darkness coeval with the principle of goodness and light. In responding to this attractive way of thinking about the origin of evil in the world, Augustine came up with several responses to the problem of evil, responses that directly influenced medieval discussions of the topic.

In writing no fewer than five detailed commentaries on the creation story in the biblical book of Genesis, Augustine did perhaps as much as any philosopher has done to try to make sense of the idea that God created the world out of nothing. Indeed, in the thirteenth-century debate on whether the world is eternal Augustine's view of *ex nihilo* creation became the antipode to the Aristotelian view that the world had no beginning (see Chapter 17).

This chapter focuses on several features of Augustine's philosophical thinking that prove especially important for later thought: (i) his first-person point of view, (ii) his doctrine of illumination, (iii) his ideas about the relationship between faith and reason, (iv) his argument for the existence of God, (v) his discussions of God's nature, (vi) his attempts to solve the problem of evil, (vii) his discussion of the problem of God's foreknowledge and human free will, (viii) his psychological voluntarism, and (ix) his internalism in ethics.

THE FIRST-PERSON POINT OF VIEW

Perhaps the single most striking feature of Augustine's philosophical thinking is that it often takes an explicitly first-person point of view.[1] One of his early works, *Soliloquies*, is written entirely in the first person. Augustine admits in that work to having coined the word 'soliloquies' (*soliloquia*) for use when "we are talking to ourselves alone" (II.7.14). His inner conversation partner is "Reason." Among Augustine's other works, his *Confessions*, written in the form of a prayer, is also notable for taking a first-person point of view.

Augustine seems to be the first philosopher to have thought that 'I exist' can be used to state a philosophically important truth. For him the knowledge claim that each of us can make by saying "I know that I exist" is the first and best response to the threat of global skepticism posed by the Academics: "I have no fear of the arguments of the Academics. They say, 'Suppose you are mistaken?' I reply, 'If I am mistaken, I exist.' A non-existent being cannot be mistaken; therefore I must exist, if I am mistaken" (*City of God* XI.26). Among later philosophers it is perhaps Descartes who makes the most use of the first-person point of view. Notably, Descartes, in his Second Meditation, offers 'I exist' as the foundation stone for his rational reconstruction of knowledge. But various medieval philosophers also recognize the philosophical importance of 'I exist.' Thus Gaunilo, in his reply "On Behalf of the Fool" to Anselm's ontological argument, makes use of Augustine's idea of the special status of 'I exist' to challenge Anselm. In *Proslogion* 3, Anselm had claimed that something than which nothing greater can be conceived (that is, God) cannot be conceived not to exist. The implication might seem to be that God alone cannot be conceived not to exist. Gaunilo responds:

Furthermore, I know with absolute certainty that I myself exist, but nonetheless I also know that I can fail to exist. But I understand beyond all doubt that the supreme being that exists, namely God, both exists and cannot fail to exist. Now I do not know whether I can think I do not exist even while I know with absolute certainty that I do exist. But if I can, why can I not do the same for anything else that I know with the same certainty? And if I cannot, it is not God alone who cannot be thought not to exist.

(tr. Williams, pp. 125–6)

The dilemma Gaunilo here offers Anselm is clever. Augustine's response to skepticism (namely, I cannot be mistaken in thinking that I exist) seems to leave us no alternative but to agree that God is not the only being who cannot be conceived not to exist.

---

[1] See Gareth Matthews, *Thought's Ego in Augustine and Descartes* (Ithaca, NY: Cornell University Press, 1992) and *Augustine* (Oxford: Blackwell, 2005) ch. 1.

The "Flying Man" argument of Avicenna also seems remarkably Augustinian in making one's knowledge of one's own existence philosophically basic.
According to this argument one is to think of oneself as suspended in a void
without any sensory or other somatic input: even in this circumstance, Avicenna
claims, one would know that one exists (see Chapter 23).[2] Avicenna then goes
on to draw conclusions about the nature of the immaterial soul in the fashion
of Book 10 of Augustine's *On the Trinity*. Avicenna's thought, however, could
not have been inspired by his having actually read Augustine.[3] Thus we have
here a parallel development in philosophy that underlines the significance of
Augustine's thinking without being derived from it.

ILLUMINATION

Augustine's doctrine of illumination first appears in his early dialogue, *The
Teacher* (*De magistro*):

Indeed, when we are concerned with things that we perceive with the mind, that is, by
the intellect and reason, they are said to be things that we see immediately in that inner
light of truth by which he himself who is called the inner man is illuminated, and from
which he takes pleasure (12.40).

In this dialogue Augustine tries to convince us that, to learn what a head
covering is, we must first use our senses. But, as we know from earlier examples
in the dialogue, seeing one, or even several, instances of such a thing will not
guarantee that we have grasped exactly what a head covering is. It is only by
the inner light of reason and truth that we will come to know that.

The idea that knowing eternal truths is a result of an inner illumination is
Platonic in origin. But, whereas Plato in *Republic* VI says that this illumination
is an "offspring" of the Form of the Good (508b), Augustine makes God its
source. Thus when, in *De Trinitate* XII, Augustine rejects the Platonic idea of
"recollecting" the Forms from the soul's previous life, he adds this:

But we ought rather to believe that the nature of the intellectual mind is so formed as
to see those things which, according to the disposition of the Creator, are subjoined to
intelligible things in the natural order, in a sort of incorporeal light of its own kind, as
the eye of the flesh sees the things that lie about it in this corporeal light.

(XII.15.24)

---

[2] For a full discussion of Avicenna's argument, see Deborah L. Black, "Avicenna on Self-Awareness
and Knowing that One Knows," in S. Rahman (ed.) *Arabic Logic, Epistemology and Metaphysics*,
(Dordrecht: Springer, 2008) 63–87.
[3] Richard Sorabji suggests a common Neoplatonic source: see *Self: Ancient and Modern Insights about
Individuality, Life, and Death* (Chicago: University of Chicago Press, 2006) ch. 12.

The generally recognized rival to divine illumination is the Aristotelian idea of abstraction, which struggles with the question of how we ever learn to abstract red, crimson, round, and ball – as well as an indefinitely large number of other universals – from our sample red ball. Augustinian illumination was supposed by generations of medieval philosophers, all the way through the thirteenth century, to supply a better answer (see Chapters 26–7). However, Augustinians in the thirteenth century also began to modify and adapt Augustine's teaching on illumination. Thus, for example, Bonaventure, although he speaks of illumination as a heavenly light "that gives infallibility to the knower," also allows for degrees of illumination (*Quaest. de scientia Christi* q. 4), and Henry of Ghent gradually develops a significantly Aristotelianized version of the idea of divine illumination.[4]

FAITH AND REASON

In the dialogue *On Free Choice of the Will* Augustine asks his interlocutor, Evodius, whether he is certain that God exists. Evodius replies that he accepts God's existence by faith, not by reason. Augustine then asks Evodius what he would say to an atheist. Evodius responds that he would appeal to the evidence of Scripture. When Augustine asks what room is left for philosophical investigation, Evodius replies that we want to know and understand what we believe (II.2.5.16); Augustine compliments Evodius and quotes Isaiah 7:9, which in his "Old Latin" translation reads: *Nisi credideritis, non intellegetis* ("Unless you have believed, you will not understand").

The idea that we should believe in order to understand is an Augustinian theme. In *Tractate* 29 on the Gospel of John, for example, Augustine writes: "If you have not understood, I say, 'Believe!' For understanding is the reward of faith." He adds: "Therefore, do not seek to understand that you may believe, but believe that you may understand." This ordering of faith and reason has profound implications for natural theology. So, for instance, even an argument for the existence of God should not be undertaken from a position of presumed neutrality. An opposed view is taken by Thomas Aquinas when he distinguishes between the articles of faith and the preambles to the articles. According to Aquinas, the preambles, including the conclusion that God exists, can be known simply by natural reason, without any presumption of faith (*Summa theol.* 1a 2.2 ad 1).

---

[4] The complex and intricate details of how Augustinian and Aristotelian epistemologies competed with each other and transformed each other in the thirteenth century are well presented in Steven Marrone, *The Light of Thy Countenance: Science and Knowledge of God in the Thirteenth Century* (Leiden: Brill, 2001).

Anselm is most explicit in accepting Augustine's admonition to believe that we may understand. He first thought of calling his *Proslogion*, in which he argues for the existence and nature of God, "Faith in Search of Understanding" (*Fides quaerens intellectum*). It remained a motto for that work (see Chapter 51).

GOD'S EXISTENCE

Augustine is hardly the first philosopher to have proposed an argument for the existence of God. Moreover, he himself suggests more than one line of reasoning for the conclusion that God exists. But his most systematic attempt to prove the existence of God is to be found in Book II of *On Free Choice of the Will*. The argument there is not one that has become particularly important in the philosophy of religion. But it is remarkable in being, like Anselm's much more impressive and influential argument in his *Proslogion*, a purely a priori bit of reasoning. Like Anselm's argument, it begins with a definition of 'God,' which we can render this way:

x is God $=_{df}$ x is superior to the human mind (or rational soul) and nothing is superior to x.

Augustine then goes on to argue that Truth is superior to the human mind. So either Truth itself is God, or something superior to Truth is God. In any case, God exists.

The idea that Truth is superior to the human mind may strike us as rather strange. Augustine's notion seems to be that Truth sits in judgment on our thinking and what passes judgment on x must be superior to x. The idea that Truth might be God is also rather peculiar. For Augustine, however, the saying of Jesus, "I am the way, and the truth, and the light" (John 14:6), mitigates against its oddity.

THE NATURE OF GOD

The definition of 'God' above marks supremacy as the prime feature of God's nature. Augustine elaborates on this point in *On Christian Doctrine*: "For when the one God of gods is thought of, even by those who recognize, invoke, and worship other gods, either in Heaven or on earth, he is thought of in such a way that the thought seeks to attain something than which there is nothing better or more sublime" (I.7.7).

Modern readers may be reminded of Anselm's formula for God: "something than which nothing greater can be conceived." Even closer to Anselm is this characterization of God in the *Confessions*: "Nor could there have been or be any soul capable of conceiving that which is better than you, who are the supreme and highest good" (VII.4.6).

Augustine, like Anselm after him, uses his general characterization of God to pick out the divine attributes. Thus the next sentence in the *Confessions* after the one above is this: "Since it is most true and certain that the incorruptible is superior to the corruptible . . . had it been the case that you [O God] are not incorruptible I could in thought have attained something better than my God." On this basis Augustine claims that God is incorruptible, all-powerful and all-knowing.

Although Augustine's treatment of the various divine attributes sets the stage for later medieval discussions of God's nature (see Chapter 54), it is, first and foremost, Augustine's idea of divine simplicity that most influenced later philosophical theologians. Here is the classical statement of that doctrine in Augustine's work, *De Trinitate*:

> But God is not great by a greatness that is not that which he himself is – as if God were, so to speak, a partaker in greatness when he is great. For in that case greatness would be greater than God. But there cannot be anything greater than God. Therefore, he is great by that greatness that is identical with himself . . . Let the same also be said of the goodness, the eternity, the omnipotence of God, in fact of all those attributes that can be predicated of God.
>
> (V.10.11)

The doctrine of divine simplicity is important in much of medieval philosophical theology. Thus Aquinas, for example, says that perfections cannot be predicated univocally of God and creatures because, whereas perfections in human beings are distinct from each other and from that being's essence, such is not the case with God, who is perfectly simple (*Summa theol.* 1a 13.5). The doctrine that God is perfectly simple remains a topic of discussion and controversy even today.[5]

THE PROBLEM OF EVIL

In addition to offering rational support for faith in God, Augustine also confronted the biggest threat to faith in a Being whose attributes include omnipotence and omnibenevolence, namely, the problem of evil (see Chapter 56). Indeed, the problem of evil occupied Augustine throughout most of his adult life. The obvious presence of evil in the world was part of what first attracted

[5] See, e.g., William Mann, "Divine Simplicity," *Religious Studies* 18 (1982) 451–71; Alvin Plantinga, *Does God Have a Nature?* (Milwaukee, WI: Marquette University Press, 1980); Eleonore Stump and Norman Kretzmann, "Absolute Simplicity," *Faith and Philosophy* 2 (1985) 353–91.

him to Manicheanism, with its idea of a cosmic force of evil co-equal with the cosmic force of good.

Long after Augustine had rejected Manicheanism and become a Christian, he still thought the Platonic idea, that it is matter that is evil, worth mentioning and rejecting: "Is it that the matter from which he made things was somehow evil? He gave it form and order, but did he leave in it an element that he could not transform into good? If so, why? Was he powerless to turn and transform all matter so that no evil remained, even though God is omnipotent?" (*Confessions* VII.5.7). If, however, God is perfectly good and God is the cause of everything besides himself, how could it be that God is not the cause of evil?

One of Augustine's responses to this question is to invoke the Neoplatonic thought that evil is "non-being," that is, a lack, or privation. As Augustine writes in *Enchiridion* ch. 12, "All things that exist, therefore, seeing that the Creator of them all is supremely good, are themselves good. But because they are not, like their Creator, supremely and unchangeably good, their good may be diminished and increased." Thus, in making something distinct from Himself, God made limited beings. But their limitations and their susceptibility to corruption are not anything substantial; they are limitations of something in itself good.

The idea of evil as a privation is echoed by other medieval philosophers. It appears, for example, in Anselm's *De casu diaboli* ch. 10; and Aquinas writes that "the absence of good, taken in a privative sense, is evil" (*Summa theol.* 1a 48.2). Augustine, however, sometimes expresses dissatisfaction with the privation solution to the problem of evil. Thus the continuation of *Confessions* VII.5.7 goes this way:

Or does [evil] not have any being? [But] why should we fear and avoid what has no being? If our fear is vain, it is certain that fear itself is evil, and that the heart is groundlessly disturbed and tortured. And this evil is the worse for the fact that it has no being to be afraid of. Yet we still fear.

The form of the problem of evil most discussed in recent philosophy is this: how can we consistently maintain that God is all-powerful as well as all-good and yet also admit that there is evil? This form of the problem is to be found in Augustine, too. Here is a statement of it from *Confessions* VII:

Here is God and see what God has created. God is good and is most mightily and incomparably superior to these things. But, being God, he created good creatures. See how God surrounds and fills them. Then where and whence is evil? How did it creep in? What is its root and what is its seed? Or does it not have any being?

(VII.5.7)

Perhaps Augustine's primary response to the problem in all its various forms is to say that sin, and hence evil, arises from the will, and indeed from a will that is free. An important good, he supposes, would be missing from creation if there were no free agents. Evil is thus the price of the great good of free agency: "Just as a stray horse is better than a stone which is not astray, since the stone does not have its own motion or perception, so the creature who sins of his own free will is more excellent than the creature who does not sin because he has no free will" (*On Free Choice of the Will* III.5.15.57).

In Book I of *On Free Choice of the Will* Evodius had asked why God could not have given us free will the way he gave us justice. Justice cannot be used to do unjust things. Why, Evodius had wanted to know, could God not have given us free will in such a way that we could not use it to do evil?

Evodius's question is echoed in recent philosophy by J. L. Mackie: "If God has made men such that in their free choices they sometimes prefer what is good and sometimes what is evil, why could he not have made men such that they always freely choose the good?"[6] Alvin Plantinga has argued, in response to Mackie, that it is at least logically possible that even an omnipotent being could not create free agents who never sin. In Plantinga's memorable phrase, it is logically possible that each human being with free will whom God could have created suffers from "transworld depravity."[7]

In the last book of the *City of God*, however, Augustine explains that God will, in fact, give the blessed in heaven the perfect freedom of the will that includes an inability to sin. Earthly human beings have a freedom of the will that includes the ability to sin as well as the ability not to sin. But the perfect freedom the blessed will receive in heaven includes only the ability not to sin.

Evodius's question, echoed sixteen centuries later by Mackie, now becomes more urgent. Why would God not have given Adam and all his descendants the perfect freedom Augustine says he will give the blessed in heaven? Augustine's answer in *City of God* XXII.30 is that the blessed will attain their perfect freedom only by partaking of God's own nature. Some merit would have been lost, Augustine reasons, if some human beings who could have chosen otherwise had not, with the grace of God, chosen not to sin.

GOD'S FOREKNOWLEDGE AND HUMAN FREE WILL

The chief threat to human freedom that Augustine confronts is not determinism, but rather God's foreknowledge, which suggests a kind of fatalism. Augustine

---

[6] J. L. Mackie, "Evil and Omnipotence," *Mind* 64 (1955) p. 209.
[7] Alvin Plantinga, *The Nature of Necessity* (Oxford: Oxford University Press, 1974) pp. 49–53.

frames the problem of God's foreknowledge and human free will for all later Western philosophy. The problem is this: if God is truly omniscient and so fore-knows everything that is going to happen, how is it possible for human agents to do anything of their own free will? Although Augustine states the problem in its most influential form, and indeed offers some of the most promising responses to it, the problem was not entirely original to him. As he himself makes clear in *City of God* V.9, he took the threat foreknowledge poses for free will from Cicero's *On Divination*. It is not, however, Cicero that subsequent philosophers have turned to in their discussions of this problem, but rather Augustine, whose *On Free Choice of the Will* offers at least three promising solutions and suggests a fourth.

Foreknowledge as a guarantee of freedom

This solution attempts to turn the problem into its own solution. We cannot will, Augustine writes, what is not in our power to will. So what we will is in our power to will, and, "since it is in our power, it is free in us" (III.3.8.33). If God foreknows everything, he foreknows that we will will certain things, that it will be in our power to do so, and that our power to will these things will be free in us. In this way God's foreknowledge guarantees our freedom. Anselm echoes this point when he insists that God can foreknow that it is without necessity that one is going to sin (*De concordia* I.1).

God's foreknowledge of his own free actions

Augustine's interlocutor, Evodius, points out that "God foresees with certainty what he will do" (III.3.6.23). Augustine then points out that the very same reasoning that leads us to suppose that God's foreknowledge threatens human freedom should lead us to conclude that it would also threaten God's freedom. But God is perfectly free. Thus, there must be something wrong with the reasoning that leads us to conclude that God's foreknowledge threatens human freedom.

God is not in time, but rather is eternal

As Evodius remarks, nothing ever happens, or comes to pass, within God (III.3.6.24). If there is no "beforehand" with God, then there is no foreknowl-edge either. This solution is perhaps less promising than the previous two, however, since God's knowledge from all eternity of what one will do seems no less a threat to freedom of the will than foreknowledge.

The modal solution

Augustine comes tantalizingly close to distinguishing between the necessity of the conditional ('Necessarily, if God foreknows that Adam will sin, then Adam will sin') and the necessity of the consequent ('If God foreknows that Adam will sin, then it is by necessity that Adam will sin'). Thus, for example, he writes: "Your foreknowledge that a man will sin does not of itself necessitate the sin" (III.4.9.39). But later philosophers, beginning with Boethius, make this distinction explicit. Aquinas, for example, uses the later medieval distinction between necessity *de re* and necessity *de dicto* to explain why arguments like this one are fallacious:

(1) Necessarily, if God foreknows that Adam will sin, Adam will sin.
(2) God foreknows that Adam will sin.
    Therefore,
(3) Adam will necessarily sin.
    The necessity in (1) is *de dicto*; that in (3) is *de re*. All that follows validly from (1) and (2) is
(4) Adam will sin.[8]

PSYCHOLOGICAL VOLUNTARISM

When Augustine introduces the will into Western thought, the question of how it might be related to other human faculties, in particular, the intellect, becomes a major philosophical issue. According to Augustine himself, the will has a remarkable independence, since, as he writes in the *City of God* XII.6, it has no efficient cause outside itself. Yet Augustine also seems to think that the intellect and the will are yoked together through the virtual unity of memory, understanding, and will, which, he writes, are "not three minds, but one mind" (*De Trinitate* X.11.18).

Aquinas gives the Augustinian balance between reason and will an important structure when he writes that intellect moves the will as an end and that the will moves the intellect as an agent (*Summa theol.* 1a 82.4). But Aquinas also appears to recognize cases of *intellectual determinism* when he writes that "if the will be offered an object which is good universally and from every point of view, the will tends to it of necessity, if it wills anything at all, since it cannot will the opposite" (ibid., 1a2ae 10.2c). The possibility of such intellectual determinism seems to be excluded by John Duns Scotus when he writes that "nothing other than the will is the total cause of volition in the will" (*Additiones magnae*

---

[8] See Boethius, *Consolation of Philosophy* V.6; Thomas Aquinas, *Summa theol.* 1a 4.13 ad 3.

II.25.1 n. 22, ed. Wadding VI: 888).[9] Scotus thus counts as a psychological voluntarist. In this he echoes Augustine (see Chapter 30).

One difficulty with psychological voluntarism is the threat that the will, apart from the intellect, will be simply 'blind,' and so unable to make any genuine choice among the alternatives that the intellect presents to it. Scotus tries to avoid this difficulty by attributing a cognitive or rational aspect to the will. He speaks of there always being indistinct and imperfect intellections besides the entirely distinct and perfect ones. It may happen that the will takes pleasure in one of these indistinct or imperfect ones so that by taking pleasure in that particular intellection, the will "strengthens and intends it, whereas the intellection that is nilled, or in which the intellect takes no pleasure, is weakened and dismissed" (*Ordinatio* II.42.3).[10]

Augustine's solution to such problems seems to be much simpler. Even though his admonition, "If you have not understood, I say 'Believe!'" (as quoted earlier) apparently gives the will an edge over the intellect in matters of belief, his trinitarian conception of the mind as memory, understanding, and will in Book X of *De Trinitate* requires that there also be an essential unity in that psychological trinity, a unity that mirrors, even if only very imperfectly, the unity of the divine Trinity.

ETHICS

Augustine follows Ambrose in adding the four cardinal virtues of Greek antiquity – courage, temperance, wisdom (or prudence), and justice – to the Christian virtues of faith, hope, and love (or charity) that Paul recognizes in II Corinthians 13. Later medieval philosophers, such as Aquinas, followed him in accepting this list (see Chapter 36).

Perhaps Augustine's most distinctive contribution to ethics, however, arises from his commentary on this saying of Jesus: "You have heard that it was said, 'You shall not commit adultery.' But I say to you that everyone who looks at a woman lustfully has already committed adultery with her in his heart" (Matthew 5:27–8). Augustine's discussion of this verse in his *Commentary on the Lord's Sermon on the Mount* puts forward what William Mann has called, quite

---

[9] The views of Scotus on human freedom are much more complex than this single quotation might suggest. See, e.g., William Frank, "Duns Scotus on Autonomous Freedom and Divine Co-Causality," *Medieval Philosophy and Theology* 2 (1992) 142–64.

[10] For translation see, *Duns Scotus on the Will and Morality*, tr. A. Wolter (Washington: Catholic University of America Press, 1986) pp. 173–5.

appropriately, Augustine's "inner-life ethics."[11] Central to Augustine's thinking here is his account of what he takes to be a complete sin. According to this account, the components of a complete sin are these: (1) suggestion, (2) pleasure, and (3) consent. Here is the way he explains these components:

> The suggestion is made either through the memory or through the bodily senses – when we are seeing or hearing or smelling or tasting or touching something. If we take pleasure in the enjoyment of this [suggestion], it must be repressed if the pleasure is sinful. For example, if the craving of the palate is aroused at the sight of viands while we are observing the law of fasting, it arises only through pleasure; we do not consent to it, we repress by the law of reason, to which it is subject. But, if consent is given, then a sin is fully committed in the heart, and it is known to God, even though it be not made known to men, through the medium of any act.
>
> Therefore, as I was beginning to say, these three successive stages may be likened to the action that is described in Genesis [3]. For the suggestion, as well as a kind of persuasion, is made as though by a serpent; the pleasure is in the carnal desire, as though in Eve; and the consent is in the reason, as though in the man [Adam]. And if a man passes through these three stages, he is, as it were, cast out from Paradise; that is to say, he is expelled from the most blessed light of justice and is cast unto death. And this is most strictly in accordance with justice, for persuasion is not compulsion.
>
> (I.12.24; tr. Kavanagh, pp. 53–4)

Augustine is not explicit about whether the first component by itself, that is, the mere suggestion of doing something illicit, counts as a sin, or whether it is only the first component plus the second, that is, pleasure in the thought of performing an illicit act, that counts as a sin. What we do learn is that nothing is a *complete* sin without all three components. But the most startling claim Augustine makes is that these three components together constitute a complete sin, whether or not the action suggested and consented to is ever carried out (see also Chapter 37).

The influence of Augustine's inner-life ethics on later thought is nowhere more direct or profound than it is on the ethics of Peter Abaelard. According to Abaelard's *Ethics, or Know Thyself*, one sins by showing contempt for the creator, God. And one does that by consenting to violate one of God's laws. Abaelard gives the example, which he takes from Augustine's *On Free Choice of the Will* I.4.25, of a servant who kills his master, not because the servant actually wants to kill his master, but because he wants to save his own life and believes that to do so he must kill the master. Abaelard rejects what we might call a Principle of the Transitivity of Desire (that is, one wants what one believes to be the

---

[11] "Inner-Life Ethics," in G. Matthews (ed.) *The Augustinian Tradition* (Berkeley: University of California Press, 1998) 140–65.

consequences of what one wants), but accepts a Principle of the Transitivity of Consent (that is, one consents to what one believes to be the consequences of what one consents to). Thus, Abaelard can allow that the servant does not want to kill his master, even though the servant believes that killing his master will be a consequence of his defending himself. Nevertheless, on Abaelard's view, the servant indirectly consents to the killing, and, since killing violates God's command not to kill, he sins. As William Mann points out, although Abaelard makes use of Augustine's example from his *On Free Choice of the Will*, he does not follow Augustine's analysis of the case; instead, he uses and develops Augustine's account of sin in his *Commentary on the Sermon on the Mount* to handle the case of the servant's homicide.[12]

Abaelard insists that success in carrying out a sinful act that one has consented to adds nothing to one's sin. At the same time, he also thinks that an action that would otherwise be sinful is not a sin if it is done under compulsion or through ignorance. It is the consent that is the sin. In all this he is remarkably Augustinian.[13]

---

[12] William Mann, "Ethics," in J. Brower and K. Guilfoy (eds.) *The Cambridge Companion to Abelard* (Cambridge: Cambridge University Press, 2004) 279–304.

[13] For a fuller account of Augustine's ethics, see Bonnie Kent, "Augustine's Ethics," in N. Kretzmann and E. Stump (eds.) *The Cambridge Companion to Augustine* (Cambridge: Cambridge University Press, 2001) 205–33.

8

CENSORSHIP*

FRANÇOIS-XAVIER PUTALLAZ

INTRODUCTION

A great many medieval thinkers were involved in the process of censure, either as defendants or as members of an inquiry commission. Often nothing came of the process beyond suspicions or denunciations; other times judicial procedures were initiated; sometimes these led to drastic disciplinary measures.

It is very tempting to judge the Middle Ages in light of these practices of information control and to draw the conclusion that freedom of thought was systematically restricted. Another temptation – more subtle – is to reconstruct the history of ideas from these condemnations. Judicial procedures usually entailed a list being made of very short, allegedly erroneous propositions taken from the work of one or more authors: 13 condemned by the bishop of Paris in 1270, and 219 more in 1277; 22 against Peter of John Olivi in 1283; 51 against William of Ockham in 1326, to mention but a few. It is thus very appealing to any historian to cling to these collections of articles in order to reconstruct, by antithesis, an author's thought, thereby dispensing with the detailed reading of an all too vast body of work. This is one of the reasons why contemporary historiography has focused on the phenomenon of medieval censorship, uncritically adopting the hermeneutical principle that has been widely accepted since Ernest Renan, according to whom "every condemnation in ecclesiastical history rests on a professed error."[1] Reality, however, is more complex.

In order to understand this, it is useful to begin with the famous condemnation of 1277, whose long list of condemned theses targets the arts masters at the University of Paris, but without mentioning any specific names. The range of philosophical theses touched on in this condemnation is vast, and united only by the fact that every thesis is said to stand in real or apparent opposition to the Christian truth. This is arguably the most important censure of the Middle

---

* Translated from the French by Amandine Catala.
[1] Ernest Renan, *Averroès et l'averroïsme* (Paris: Calmann-Lévy, 1949), p. 211. Cf. Alain de Libera, *Penser au Moyen Âge* (Paris: Seuil, 1991).

Ages, and indeed is paradigmatic of the great medieval condemnations. Still, it is important to underscore the great diversity of realities that fall under the general label of 'censure,' and to take care that presenting doctrinal history through examples in this way should not interfere with the broadening of the cultural field – including, for instance, a deeper understanding of the pressures connected with Islam that were exerted on various thinkers. In this chapter, however, such broadening will be limited to Latin examples in the thirteenth and fourteenth centuries, while making no claims about the modes of censorship experienced outside the Latin West.[2]

THE CONDEMNATION OF MARCH 7, 1277

Reactions against the censure

In 1308, John of Pouilly testified: "That is what I wanted to say in the hall of the bishop, but I could not do so, because I was prevented from it." In those solemn circumstances, a venerable master stood up, reducing John to silence. The latter remembers: "Oh, Blessed God! I saw there was no one in Paris to dare hold this conception that I deem true; God knows the reason why, and I know it too."[3] It is the noxious effect of the 1277 condemnations that John of Pouilly is complaining of, thirty years after the fact. Moving back closer to the event, we find the testimony of James of Douai, master in the faculty of arts at Paris *ca.* 1275. He too attacks the pernicious influence of the censors: "Though philosophy is the great perfection of man, philosophers are oppressed nowadays . . . And the fact that philosophers are thus oppressed keeps many from practicing philosophy."[4]

The most famous reaction comes from Godfrey of Fontaines, master of theology in Paris. Long after the death of Stephen Tempier, the censor–bishop responsible for the 1277 condemnations, Godfrey is asked in a quodlibetal question in 1291 "Whether a master in theology should contradict an article of the

---

[2] Among Islamic authors, al-Ghazālī notoriously concluded his *Incoherence of the Incoherence* by issuing a *fatwā* decreeing that anyone who teaches one of these three claims – that the world is eternal; that God knows only universals; and that the soul does not return to its body after death – is an apostate from Islam, deserving of death (see Chapter 50). See Frank Griffel, *Apostasie und Toleranz im Islam: die Entwicklung zu al-Gazālīs Urteil gegen die Philosophen und die Reaktionen der Philosophen* (Leiden: Brill, 2000). Averroes is perhaps the best-known case where such pressure was brought to bear, although he was ultimately rehabilitated after a period in exile. See, e.g., Roger Arnaldez, *Averroes: A Rationalist in Islam,* tr. D. Streight (Notre Dame, IN: University of Notre Dame Press, 2000).

[3] John of Pouilly, *Quodlibet* II.13 (Paris Bibl. Nat. lat. 15372, f. 58r).

[4] See the discussion in Luca Bianchi, *Censure et liberté intellectuelle à l'Université de Paris (XIIIe–XIVe siècles)* (Paris: Les Belles Lettres, 1999) pp. 73–6.

bishop if he believes that the opposite proposition is true" (*Quodlibet* VII.18 [ed. *Phil. Belges* III: 402]). Either the master in theology is going to lie, which is detrimental to his mission, or he incurs a sentence of excommunication. Godfrey's response is nuanced: if the thesis in question touches upon salvation, the master should say what he believes, whatever the threat; if, on the contrary, the issue is ancillary, the master should of course not teach error, but it is still safer to refrain from telling the truth. If, however, the thesis in question can be proved, then the bishop's condemnation "constitutes an error, because it prevents the search for and knowledge of the truth." In this case, one should insist that the new prelate should "lift the condemnation and excommunication," whose continuation:

is harmful to the perfection of intellect, since people cannot freely search for the truths that are a great perfection for their intellect. And, moreover, what a scandal for non-believers as well as many of the faithful are the ignorance and simplicity of these prelates who hold as erroneous and contrary to faith that which is incompatible neither with faith nor with morals!

(ibid., III: 403–4)

According to Godfrey, the articles condemned in 1277 hinder scientific progress, create scandal in the academic world, and are harmful to the irreplaceable doctrine of Thomas Aquinas.

Aquinas and the condemnation

It was indeed common to think that Thomas's views were a target of the censure. Thomas did not belong to the faculty of arts – which was the only faculty implicated by the condemnation – but several contemporaries suggest that he was, nevertheless, a target. Indeed, the Dominican John of Naples felt compelled to write a defense of Thomas, showing that the incriminated articles do not touch his teachings. And on February 14, 1325, two years after the canonization of St. Thomas, the bishop of Paris, Stephen Bourret, lifted the sentence of excommunication weighing on those articles that touched (or seemed to touch) upon Thomas's thought.[5]

Some modern historians have also thought that Thomas was the main target of the condemnation, under the cover of a criticism of the arts masters. Fernand van Steenberghen, however, notes that Thomas's two most controversial

---

[5] The symbolic date of March 7, the third anniversary of the death of Thomas of Aquinas, bolsters this interpretation. John of Naples's defense is in the form of a question "Whether it can be permitted in Paris to teach the teachings of Brother Thomas with respect to all of his conclusions" (ed. Jellouschek).

theses – the unicity of substantial form and the impossibility of matter's existing without form (see Chapter 46) – are not listed in the 219 Parisian propositions; the authority of Thomas, he argues, would have protected him from attack.[6] Robert Wielockx agrees that Thomas was not a target of the 1277 condemnation, but for a different reason: he believes that, besides the great condemnation targeting the arts masters, Bishop Tempier initiated two other actions, one against Giles of Rome (which interrupted Giles's career) and another against Thomas, which did not go through because of the influence of certain cardinals at the papal court.[7] More recently, however, Johannes Thijssen has shown the low probability of a distinct trial against Thomas. Thijssen's thesis is that Tempier initiated a total of two actions: one, anonymous, on March 7, and another against Giles of Rome, which included certain Thomistic doctrines.[8]

Between these two divergent interpretations – one treating Aquinas as an explicit target of the condemnation of 1277, the other not regarding him as a target of that particular condemnation at all – there remains the view that has been common since the ground-breaking works of Roland Hissette: namely, that Thomas was indirectly targeted by the censure, which contains some fifty-three articles that one might see as having a basis in Thomas's work.[9] John Wippel, who characterizes as purely verbal the distinction between a "direct" or "indirect" target, thinks that the censors had to have known whether a certain thesis was also held by Thomas.[10]

One reason for this diversity of opinions is that it is not always easy to distinguish the views of different authors in the condemned propositions. A recent study has shown that the author principally targeted by thirty such articles, the arts master Siger of Brabant, was using a method that would nowadays be

---

[6] Fernand van Steenberghen, *Maître Siger de Brabant* (Louvain: Publications universitaires, 1977) pp. 147–8.

[7] See Giles of Rome, *Apologia*, ed. Wielockx, pp. 75–120, 215–24; Robert Wielockx, "Autour du procès de Thomas d'Aquin," in A. Zimmermann (ed.) *Thomas von Aquin: Werk und Wirkung im Licht neuerer Forschungen* (Berlin: De Gruyter, 1988) 413–38.

[8] Johannes M. M. H. Thijssen, *Censure and Heresy at the University of Paris, 1200–1400* (Philadelphia: University of Pennsylvania Press, 1998) pp. 54–6. According to Thijssen, the second action did not result in a formal condemnation of Giles, precisely because of the resemblance of his doctrines to those of Thomas. Rather than face a condemnation for heresy, Giles suffered a mere disciplinary measure, which would be lifted in 1285, when he was finally accepted as a master of theology.

[9] Roland Hissette, *Enquête sur les 219 articles condamnés à Paris le 7 mars 1277* (Louvain: Publications universitaires, 1977). Jürgen Miethke, "Papst, Ortsbischof und Universität in den Pariser Theologenprozessen des 13. Jahrhunderts," in A. Zimmermann (ed.) *Die Auseinandersetzungen an der Pariser Universität im XIII. Jahrhundert* (Berlin: De Gruyter, 1976) 52–94.

[10] John P. Wippel, "Thomas Aquinas and the Condemnation of 1277," *The Modern Schoolman* 72 (1995) 233–72. See also John P. Wippel, "The Parisian Condemnations of 1270 and 1277," in J. Gracia and T. Noone (eds.) *A Companion to Philosophy in the Middle Ages* (Oxford: Blackwell, 2003) 65–73.

characterized as plagiarism: Siger uses phrases taken directly from Thomas's texts, silent borrowings that touch upon central themes, but whose original meaning Siger transforms by giving them an exclusively philosophical flavor.[11] For example, article 98 (198) condemns the idea that "in the order of efficient causes, the secondary cause exercises an activity that it does not receive from the first cause." This has to do with a doctrine that Siger defends explicitly in Question 2 of his *Quaestiones super librum de causis*, where he denies all direct intervention in the universe on the part of the first cause, on the grounds that this would undermine secondary causes. To explain this, however, he appeals to an argument that Aquinas had developed in his theology of the Eucharist in order to explain the separability of accidents during the miracle of transubstantiation. Thus one sees how Thomas's texts are transformed.

The history of the censure

How did such measures arise? In Paris, the emergence of Aristotelianism had inspired distrust for many years, and there was no lack of prohibitions. In 1210, Archbishop Peter of Corbeil convened a council that, upon threat of excommunication, banned the teaching in Paris of Aristotle's books on natural philosophy.[12] On April 13, 1231, Pope Gregory IX reiterated these bans, demanding that the speculative books of Aristotle not be used before being examined by a commission responsible for expurgating them of any "suspicion of heresy."[13] These measures did not, however, hinder the rise of Aristotelianism. Although the University of Paris had forbidden the teaching of Aristotle's main books since 1210, their efforts had no effect in the long run. On March 19, 1255, the Paris faculty of arts officially included the full range of Aristotle's works in the catalogue of texts required for teaching.

Within this same faculty, however, various philosophers adopted theses that seemed to stand in direct opposition to the Christian faith. According to Bonaventure in 1267, the main such errors concerned the eternity of the world, the unicity of intellect within all human beings, and astral determinism – all theses that are linked to Averroes's interpretation of Aristotle, and that, he says, make the cross of Christ vain. According to Bonaventure, it is not philosophy

---

[11] Ruedi Imbach, "Notule sur le commentaire du 'Liber de causis' de Siger de Brabant et ses rapports avec Thomas d'Aquin," *Freiburger Zeitschrift für Philosophie und Theologie* 43 (1996) 304–23; François-Xavier Putallaz and Ruedi Imbach, *Profession, philosophe: Siger de Brabant* (Paris: Cerf, 1997) pp. 162–8.

[12] Henri Denifle and Émile Chatelain (eds.) *Chartularium Universitatis Parisiensis* (Paris: Delalain, 1889–97) I: 70.

[13] Ibid., I: 138.

itself that is at issue, but rather the pretension of those who want to turn it into a self-sufficient type of knowledge, "instead of seeing in it a way toward other types of knowledge." When philosophy is viewed as self-sufficient, "the one who wants to remain in it falls into darkness" (*Collationes de septem donis Spiritus sancti* IV.2 [*Opera* V: 476]).

In 1270, the response to suspect theses propagated in the faculty of arts took various forms. Aquinas's *De unitate intellectus* refutes in detail Siger of Brabant's Averroistic theory of the intellect (see Chapter 23). Others respond more brutally, not by engaging their opponents philosophically but by compiling diffuse lists of errors. The *De erroribus philosophorum*, traditionally ascribed to Giles of Rome, denounces various theses of Aristotle, Averroes, Avicenna, al-Ghazālī, and al-Kindī. On December 10, Tempier, already the bishop of Paris, condemns thirteen propositions and threatens to excommunicate anyone who supports them. The condemned theses are all said to stand in real or apparent opposition to the Christian truth.

It does not seem that this measure had the effect hoped for, however, for the bishop reiterated his condemnation on March 7, 1277 – now with 219 proposi-tions. The prologue describes several trustworthy persons as having informed the ecclesial authority of certain masters of arts who have exceeded the limits of their faculty by encroaching upon theology. These masters have allegedly dared to spread "abhorrent errors" in their schools without refuting them, claiming that there are things that are "true according to philosophy, but not according to the catholic faith, as if there were two opposite truths."[14]

This condemnation has been the object of many studies,[15] but some novel elements deserve to be underlined.[16] First, it is an anonymous condemnation: the persons being targeted are not designated. This is unusual: normally, a list of censored propositions is imputed to named suspects, who are ordered to appear. Moreover, it seems that cases not resolved by the competent authority (for example, the university) would ordinarily be transferred to the court of the bishop; yet here it is the bishop who is initiating the process. To understand this, we should pay more attention to the role played by the pontifical legate Simon de Brion, the future Pope Martin IV: might it have been under his influence that the various censures were brought forward? Shortly after his death in 1285, the turmoil over these censures ends. It is also likely that the January 18, 1277 letter of Pope John XXI – concerned with the propagation of certain ideas at

---

[14] Ed. David Piché, *La condamnation parisienne de 1277* (Paris: Vrin, 1999) p. 75.

[15] In addition to the works cited already, see Kurt Flasch, *Aufklärung im Mittelalter? Die Verurteilung von 1277* (Mainz: Dieterich, 1989); J. Aertsen et al. (eds.) *Nach der Verurteilung von 1277: Philosophie und Theologie an der Universität von Paris im letzten Viertel des 13. Jahrhunderts* (Berlin: De Gruyter, 2001).

[16] Thijssen, *Censure*, pp. 43–8.

the faculty of arts – played a role in the origin of the condemnation. This is especially so since a few months later a new letter from the pope, dated April 18, 1277, demands an investigation focused on the theologians. Finally, it is possible that the three arts masters, including Siger of Brabant, who were cited to appear before the Inquisitor Simon du Val on November 23, 1276, were acquitted at that appearance. This would explain why their names could not appear in the condemnation of 1277, since the procedures mandated that no one could be prosecuted twice for the same crime.

A TYPOLOGY OF CENSORSHIP

Forms of condemnation

It is useful to begin with 1277, since it is the most famous condemnation, but it certainly was not the only one; as mentioned above, there were many, and of many different forms. Here I will set aside censorship within Jewish and Islamic circles, and within the Christian context I will deal only briefly with extra-academic condemnations, including those that were prior to the creation of the universities. Of these, Abaelard's trial is particularly well known. Around 1138, William of St. Thierry was offended by his reading of Abaelard's *Theology*, and alerted Bernard of Clairvaux: "Once more Peter Abaelard teaches new things, and his books go beyond the seas and the Alps . . . He produces in the divine Scripture what he used to produce in dialectic, inventions that are his own."[17] Abaelard is rebuked both for his originality and for his rationalistic tendencies with respect to church dogma. Bernard of Clairvaux subsequently writes a *Treatise against Various Erroneous Articles of Peter Abaelard*. As for Abaelard, he is asked to defend his doctrine personally, against Bernard, at the Council of Sens, on June 2 and 3, 1140. But the debate is biased, the Abaelardian theses having been judged beforehand. Unable or unwilling to explain himself, Abaelard turns to Rome. This backfires, for in July 1240 a pontifical decree condemns him and reduces him to silence, as though he were a heretic. At this point Abaelard gives up the fight and asks Peter the Venerable of Cluny for shelter.

Can we say that Abaelard was "censored"? What is the meaning of this term in the Middle Ages? First, there exist ecclesiastical censures, which deprive people of certain spiritual goods: a "suspension" deprives clerics of one or more of their roles as priest; an "interdict" applies to a whole community; and "excommunication" expels one from the community of believers. Such

---

[17] Jean Jolivet, *Abélard, ou la philosophie dans le langage* (Paris: Seghers, 1969) pp. 35–6.

ecclesiastical censures concern the church, and should not be confused with academic censures, even though the latter can lead to the former. On the academic side, there is the "prohibition," which is a ban often limited to a place and a time, forbidding the propagation of certain ideas viewed as heterodox, dangerous, or objects of scandal. The "condemnation," valid by contrast in any place and for an unlimited period of time, targets theses that explicitly contradict the teaching of the church. But these distinctions are not rigid, and there are exceptions, such as the "condemnation" of 1277, which seems to have applied only in Paris.

In general, although here too the vocabulary is not strictly fixed in the Middle Ages, one can distinguish between error and heresy. There is an *error* when a thesis is false or erroneous – that is, when a thesis is *intellectually* incompatible with orthodoxy, whatever the subjective intention of the author might be. By contrast, *heresy* entails both the explicit will to defend a thesis contradicting the faith, and persistence in one's error.[18] Some heresies consisted in popular movements that were hostile to ecclesiastical authority, such as the Cathar heresy; in the academic field, on the other hand, the term 'heresy' was often used with a certain semantic plasticity, in order to stigmatize an assertion thought to be erroneous. For example, in his *Summa quaestionum super sententias*, the Franciscan Peter of John Olivi had the imprudence to characterize as "heretical" a common thesis, defended even by Aquinas.[19] An inquiry commission would later rebuke Olivi for this use of the term.[20] His remark was indeed likely to offend, since by calling this thesis "heretical" he was attacking not only the Dominican Aquinas, but also William de la Mare – a Franciscan himself, regent master in theology in Paris around 1274–5, and author of the *Correctorium fratris Thomae* (see below). William had become one of the most important characters of the Franciscan order, so to proclaim loud and clear that one of his theses was heretical was to look for trouble. At the same time, this shows how unprincipled the usage of this term sometimes was.

The vocabulary of censure was itself not univocal. In the strict sense, as noted above, a *heretic* (*hereticus*) is a person who voluntarily persists in a position contrary to the faith (*pertinax*). The word 'heresy,' however, has come to designate a proposition that stands in direct opposition to revealed truth or established

---

[18] On the term "heresy," see W. Lourdaux and D. Verhelst, *The Concept of Heresy in the Middle Ages (11th–13th c.)* (Leuven: Leuven University Press, 1976).

[19] *Summa* I.6 (Vat. Borgh. 322, f. 174vb; Borgh. 328, f. 159rb). See Putallaz, "Les idées divines dans la censure: le cas Olivi (1248–1298)," *Revue thomiste* 103 (2003) 411–34.

[20] Ed. G. Fussenegger, "'Littera septem sigillorum' contra doctrinam Petri Ioannis Olivi edita," *Archivum Franciscanum Historicum* 47 (1954) n. 5, p. 51; cf. Damascus Laberge (ed.) "Responsio quam fecit Petrus [Ioannis] ad litteram magistrorum, praesentatam sibi in Avinione," *Archivum Franciscanum Historicum* 28 (1935) n. 4, p. 127.

dogma.[21] If a proposition contradicts a positive theological conclusion that follows from a premise of the faith, then it is declared *erroneous* (*erronea*), as opposed to a *false* proposition, which merely contradicts the truth. The characterization *temerarious* (*temeraria*) applies to any opinion standing in opposition to common opinion, without being founded on robust reasons. Finally, a thesis is *dangerous to the faith* (*fide periculosa*) if it leads to noxious consequences that are likely to contradict a truth of the faith. In his 1285 response to the Parisian commission that was censoring him, Olivi refers to the panoply of judgments that this commission has attached to some excerpts from his work: "Some passages were judged false, others heretical, others dubious in the context of the faith, others dangerous for our order, others filled with ignorance, others established in a presumptuous manner, others were simply crossed off or marked with an X."[22]

Objects of censorship

Luca Bianchi[23] has presented a useful typology of censorship, showing that condemnations could target different objects:

BOOKS Either they were burnt, as were the notebooks of David of Dinant (1210), the *Periphyseon* of John Scottus Eriugena (1225), the *De periculis* of William of St. Amour (1259), and the *Exigit ordo* and the *Letters to Bernard* of Nicholas of Autrecourt (1346); or they were prohibited, as were alchemy books and the *Defensor pacis* of Marsilius of Padua (1327); or their use in education was limited – by making lists of condemned articles, for example, or by erasing certain passages. Books were purged, cut, censored. Finally, there was a form of advanced censorship, which amounted to a kind of preventive control, in the manner of today's *nihil obstat*.

IDEAS Most often, it was the freedom of teaching that was limited, by prohibiting certain courses on delicate matters: this was the case in 1210 for Aristotle's natural philosophy, for example, and in 1339 for the views of Ockham. Alternatively, there were doctrinal censures, where certain ideas were reproved by characterizing the errors as dangerous, temerarious, or contrary to faith: the condemnation of 1277 is of that type. Finally, in some cases a certain doctrine was imposed upon an author: this was the case for Durand of St. Pourçain, who was forced to rewrite his *Sentences* commentary.

---

[21] See Thijssen, *Censure*, pp. 2–5.   [22] Laberge, "Responsio," p. 132.
[23] See Bianchi, *Censure*, pp. 21–52.

PERSONS At times sanctions – such as prison or exile – were taken against
individual persons, as in the case of William of St. Amour in 1259. Pressure was
also exerted, and sometimes intimidation. There were, to be sure, few very harsh
punishments, but the sentences inflicted varied greatly. Despite the common
stereotype, extreme measures against heretics were no more common during
the Middle Ages than during antiquity (think of Socrates) or the Renaissance
(think of Giordano Bruno). To be sure, there were a few notable cases – as when
the corpse of Amalric of Bene was exhumed and some of his partisans were
condemned to be burned alive – but these were exceptions.[24] Most sentences
consisted in a public retraction of the suspect theses.

PROCEDURES As Thijssen has shown,[25] disciplinary procedures could consist of
five steps:

1. Most cases were initiated by *denunciations* to a competent authority (see below).
   These authorities thus had a reactive function: they rarely took the initiative themselves. Denunciations almost always stemmed from suspect teachings or the dissemination of ideas thought to be dangerous.
2. Once a denunciation has been made, the competent authority begins a *preliminary
   inquiry*, which consists, on the one hand, of judging whether the incriminated
   ideas are erroneous and, on the other hand, of identifying the suspects who are
   propagating them. Witnesses are called to testify, documents are seized, personal
   notes are demanded, and, as in Olivi's case, a *rotulus* is made that consists of verbatim
   quotations from the suspect's works. A list is thus crafted of articles deemed heretical,
   false, erroneous, or simply presumptuous.
3. The suspect is then *summoned to appear*. If he does not, he is judged by default
   and often excommunicated, since – not having appeared – he is persisting in
   error. The accused might defend themselves with a panoply of tactics. They might
   maintain, for instance, that they never defended the propositions they are accused
   of holding, that the propositions were taken out of context to alter their meaning,
   or (as Durand of St. Pourçain claimed) that the suspect propositions were private
   opinions, never publicly taught.[26] Alternatively, they might insist that they merely
   "recited" the opinions – that is, stated them without endorsing them – or they
   might complain that no one has ever asked them what they really meant, as when
   Olivi asserts that his intentions were different.[27] Finally, like Meister Eckhart, they
   might simply object that there is nothing they can do if readers are unable to
   understand.[28]

---

[24] See Denifle and Chatelain, *Chartularium*, I: 70–2. On the thirteenth century as compared to other
eras, see Yves Dossat, *Les crises de l'inquisition toulousaine au XIIIᵉ siècle, 1233–1273* (Bordeaux: Bière,
1959) pp. 266–7.
[25] See Thijssen, *Censure*, pp. 19–39.   [26] Ibid., p. 29.
[27] Laberge, "Responsio," p. 133. Olivi also distinguishes between reciting and endorsing (ibid.,
pp. 128–30).
[28] Eckhart of Hochheim, *Eine lateinische Rechtfertigungsschrift des Meister Eckhart*, ed. A. Daniels
(Münster: Aschendorff, 1923) p. 65. See Heinrich Stirnimann and Ruedi Imbach, *Eckhardus*

4. There then ensues *the sentence*, and its enactment. Pure and simple acquittal was very rare; at a minimum, the suspect was compelled to retract the erroneous theses publicly. Many authors anticipated such judgments with a *revocatio conditionalis* as follows: "If I have said something false against faith or morals, I revoke it in advance in obedience to the church." After the sentence follows the condemnation and the subsequent handing over to the secular authorities if the defendant has not retracted, as in the case of William of St. Amour, who was exiled from Paris in 1259.[29]

5. Finally, it was always possible to *appeal* to the pontifical court, but such a process was costly in terms of both time and money.

The authorities who could be asked to initiate such a procedure were numerous. It could, for example, be the head of a religious order, as it was in the case of Olivi (who had to sign the *Letter of Seven Seals*, which ordered him to retract a series of twenty-two theses taken from his works).[30] Olivi, in fact, complained about the procedure. Other disciplinary authorities included members of academic institutions, most often the chancellor, surrounded by a group of masters in theology. If the case were not settled at that level, the file could then be transferred to the bishop or the pope, the only two courts having the power of jurisdiction in "criminal" cases – that is, cases leading to a penalty such as excommunication.

Places other than Paris also saw censures, as in the case of the following three censures that specifically targeted Aquinas. First, on March 18, 1277, the Dominican archbishop of Canterbury, Robert Kilwardby, condemned thirty propositions, including several concerning Aquinas's doctrine of the unity of substantial forms. Second, representing a different sort of censure, the Franciscan William de la Mare crafted a *Correctorium* of Aquinas's work. This was adopted by the general chapter of the Franciscans meeting in Strasbourg in May 1282, which authorized "the diffusion of the *Summa* only under the condition that it be put in the hands of particularly intelligent readers, and that it be presented with the declarations of brother William de la Mare." Finally, on October 29, 1284, the new archbishop of Canterbury, the Franciscan John Pecham, gave a speech before the members of the University of Oxford that reprised the theses condemned seven years earlier. As reported, "he even specifically insisted on one of these doctrines that in his opinion was particularly noxious, the one that claims there is in a human being but one form."[31]

Theutonicus, homo doctus et sanctus: Nachweise und Berichte zum Prozeß gegen Meister Eckhart (Freiburg: Universitätsverlag, 1992).

[29] See Michel-Marie Dufeil, *Guillaume de Saint-Amour et la polémique universitaire parisienne, 1250–1259* (Paris: Picard, 1972).

[30] Ed. Fussenegger, "Littera"; see David Burr, *The Persecution of Peter Olivi* (Philadelphia, PA: American Philosophical Society, 1976).

[31] See François-Xavier Putallaz, *Figures franciscaines, de Bonaventure à Duns Scot* (Paris: Cerf, 1997) pp. 43–6.

ANTI-OCKHAMIST MEASURES

As we have seen, there were a great number and variety of condemnations. Although the focus has been on the 1277 condemnation, we could have singled out the famous condemnation of Autrecourt (1346),[32] or that of John of Monzon, who fled in 1387 after the faculty of theology prohibited the support of fourteen of his theses on the Immaculate Conception, and the censure commission appointed by Clement VII forbade any relations with him, even drinking and eating.[33] Before closing, however, we will consider still another – one that is particularly important for the history of medieval philosophy.

In his *Dialogus*, crafted after he had fled the pontifical court of Avignon to take refuge in Munich with the Emperor Ludwig of Bavaria, William of Ockham presents a set of conclusions in favor of the freedom of thought. According to him, no one should condemn ideas, at least not those philosophical ideas that do not touch upon theology and that have never been formally condemned, "because in these areas, everyone should be free to say freely whatever he pleases" (I.2.24).[34]

This is not the first time one finds an author claiming the right to a freedom of thought that he himself was deprived of. Ockham was the object of a lengthy trial in Avignon, and his teachings were eventually the target of decrees issued by the faculty of arts in Paris between 1339 and 1341.

During the trial (on May 12, 1325), when King Edward II writes to John Lutterell in Avignon, asking him to come back to England as soon as possible, Pope John XXII himself responds to the king, asking him to excuse the prolonged stay of Lutterell at the court, for he has to remain longer in order to "pursue before the pope his own cause against a pestilent doctrine."[35] It is clear that this *doctrina pestifera* is Ockham's. But why does it deserve such a harsh critique? If one looks at the list of the fifty-one articles ultimately incriminated by the inquiry commission, one notices that it has undergone a modification since the first inventory made by Lutterell himself. It is not the philosophical theses that are targeted. Indeed, these theses are only of secondary importance;

---

[32] Zénon Kaluza, *Nicolas d'Autrecourt. Ami de la vérité* (Paris: Académie des inscriptions et belles-lettres, 1995).

[33] Denifle and Chatelain, *Chartularium*, III: 511. See Peter of Ailly, *Tractatus ex parte universitatis studii Parisiensi pro causa fidei, contra quemdam fratrem Johannem de Motesono Ordinis Praedicatorum*, in C. Duplessis d'Argentré (ed.) *Collectio judiciorum de novis erroribus* (Paris: apud A. Cailleau, 1728–36) I.2: 87–8.

[34] Ockham here explicitly targets Robert Kilwardby, but also indirectly the condemnations by Stephen Tempier, and the one that affected Olivi. This second part seems to be a later text inserted in the *Dialogus* after 1331–2.

[35] Ed. A. Pelzer, "Les 51 articles de Guillaume Occam censurés, en Avignon, en 1326," *Revue d'histoire ecclésiastique* 18 (1922) 246–7.

the commission did not think that the heart of Ockhamism lay in its philosophical structure.[36] What was at stake lay elsewhere – in Ockham's impact on theology, especially what might be called his "Pelagianism." Ockham thought that the habit of charity is not indispensable for a meritorious act, and that God can embrace any good act of the human will produced by our natural capacities alone. It is essentially because of the Pelagian naturalism entailed by Ockham's thought that his teachings are characterized as "pestilent."

The trial went on and on. Ockham stayed at the Franciscan convent of Avignon from 1324 until he fled on May 26, 1328, when, with the general minister of the Franciscan Order Michael of Cesena and three other coreligionists, he joined the worst enemy of the papacy, the Emperor Ludwig of Bavaria. Ockham died at the court of the emperor, most likely in 1347.

The year before, in a letter of May 20, 1346, the new pope, Clement VI, reminded the members of the faculty of arts in Paris to avoid novelties and to stick with Aristotle's text and with ancient commentators. What are these novelties? To be sure, they included Ockhamism. As of 1341, members of the faculty had to formally swear "to observe the statutes issued by the faculty of arts against the science of Ockham and by no means to support that science and any like it, but only the science of Aristotle and his commentator Averroes, and other ancient commentators and interpreters of Aristotle, except in cases that run counter to the faith."[37] Members of the English nation at the university also had to abjure the activities of the *secta occamica*.[38] These two oaths echoed two statutes issued in 1339 and 1340 that were aimed, if not directly against Ockham's ideas, then at least against their propagation.

A great deal of patient effort has been spent untangling this complicated case.[39] The statute of September 25, 1339, for instance, sought to bring a halt to the normal practice of various members of the faculty by prohibiting the public or private teaching of Ockham's doctrines, but this was probably not a doctrinal condemnation; most likely, it was only to prevent the use of texts from Ockham that had not previously been examined by a commission of experts and that were, thus, not clear of all suspicion. This statute cleverly appears to

[36] See Josef Koch, "Neue Aktenstücke zu dem gegen Wilhelm Ockham in Avignon geführten Prozess," in *Kleine Schriften* (Rome: Edizioni di Storia e Letteratura, 1973) II: 347.

[37] Denifle and Chatelain, *Chartularium*, II: 680.

[38] Zénon Kaluza, "Les sciences et leurs langages: Note sur le statut du 29 décembre 1340 et le prétentdu statut perdu contre Ockham," in L. Bianchi (ed.) *Filosfia e teologia nel trecento. Studi in ricordo di Eugenio Randi* (Louvain-la-Neuve: Fédération internationale des instituts d'études médiévales, 1994) 197–258, esp. pp. 216–77.

[39] Besides Thijssen, Kaluza, and Bianchi, one can mention the numerous studies by William Courtenay, including "The Registers of the University of Paris and the Statutes Against the 'Scientia Occamica'," *Vivarium* 29 (1991) 13–49.

be a purely administrative act: extra-curricular courses are forbidden (that is, public lectures on Ockham's works or private courses on his logic), as well as citation of his work.

As for the real reasons behind this measure, they still remain unclear today. Most likely, in addition to the philosophical problem of Ockham's reduction of Aristotle's ten categories to two (see Chapter 48), and his critique of the notion of time, it is Ockham's interpretive method – his hermeneutics – that does not respect the traditional interpretations of the authorities. Does terminist logic, applied to Aristotle's texts, not make the intention of the reader prevail over the intention of the author? It is thus possible that this new hermeneutics was viewed as threatening the survival of Aristotelianism, which until then was seen as a body of scientific doctrines, with nothing metaphorical about it.

This perceived threat is also one of the possible motivations behind the second statute, issued on December 29, 1340, which is one of the real puzzles of Ockham studies. Without citing any specific propositions, this statute sets the tone for curricular lectures on the Aristotelian corpus. Since it is the "errors of the Ockhamists" that are targeted here, the statute can be read as warning against a series of themes originating in Ockham, as manifested in arts masters who were making a reprehensible use of them. As Luca Bianchi puts it, they are probably "protocols of philosophical exegesis founded on just those forms of propositional analysis that were prohibited by the faculty of arts."[40]

The first article, for example, which may have originated with John Buridan, forbids arts masters to "declare absolutely false a well known proposition of an author whose work they are teaching, if they deem that this author, by establishing this proposition, meant something true." In other words, it is forbidden to stick to the letter of a text and to reject it on that basis, without paying attention to the author's intention. Ironically, the censors were prohibiting precisely that which had been the leitmotiv of prior censures: namely, to take the author's actual intention into account to a lesser degree than the objective force of a thesis as interpreted in concrete terms.

The 1340 statute is probably the second phase of the same crisis that brought about the 1339 statute. At a time when, for political reasons, Ockham was at best unwelcome, the arts masters decided to get rid of his growing influence, which threatened to disrupt a long tradition of philosophical interpretation of Aristotle. The task of policing educational practices meant that, in order to defend the traditional Aristotle, the Ockhamist reading of it had to be proscribed.[41] However, with Ockhamism still spreading in Paris and throughout the rest of Europe during the second half of the fourteenth century, these

---

[40] Bianchi, *Censure*, p. 147.   [41] For this interpretation, see ibid, pp. 157–62.

prohibitions do not seem to have exerted a decisive influence on the movement of ideas, except perhaps insofar as Ockham became viewed not as an Aristotelian but as an alternative to Aristotelianism, all the way into the seventeenth century. This is by no means the least influence that such a censure might have.

CONCLUSION

This last observation raises the difficult problem of what influence condemnations have. Neither a secondary phenomenon nor a central event in themselves (Duhem), the condemnations perhaps bear witness to the irrepressible emergence of the autonomy of thought (Flasch, de Libera, Bianchi).[42] At the same time, it is also possible that medieval thinkers (in contrast to our own modern sensibilities) never interpreted freedom of thought as if it were a goal in itself; and that instead they saw free discussion as always in service to the truth. This balance, of course, was unstable. The historian who wants to avoid projecting onto the Middle Ages our strong convictions regarding freedom of thought will find an interesting articulation of this mindset in Godfrey of Fontaines:

> Sometimes a question is so unsettled, its truth being uncertain, that one can have different opinions about it, without danger for faith or morals, and without rashly defending one or the other side. In that case, to impose an obligation or restraint that compels people to steadfastly stick to one of these opinions is to impede knowledge of the truth. For it is thanks to the diverse opinions that cultured and learned men hold concerning such questions, through various discussions taking one side or the other so as to find the truth, that that truth is best discovered... Consequently, to impede this method of investigating and establishing the truth is evidently to impede the progress of those who study and seek to know the truth.
>
> (*Quodlibet* XII.5 [ed. *Phil. Belges* V: 101])

Here, freedom of debate is the indispensable prerequisite for the search for truth; nevertheless, the truth itself retains priority.

---

[42] See Pierre Duhem, *Le système du monde: histoire des doctrines cosmologiques de Platon à Copernic* (Paris: Hermann, 1913–59); Flasch, *Aufklärung im Mittelalter?*; de Libera, *Penser au Moyen Âge*; Bianchi, *Censure.*

9

MODERNITY

ROGER ARIEW

There is very little content to the concept of modernity except as a term of contrast with antiquity and the Middle Ages, and what is signified as "modern" changes, depending upon the specific contrast one wishes to make. Historians often use the term to designate nineteenth-century phenomena such as the industrial revolution, the rise of capitalism, the institution of representative democracy, and urbanization. In philosophy, "modernity" is usually taken to refer to the period that discarded medieval or scholastic philosophy, beginning roughly in the sixteenth century and encompassing such intellectual movements as the Renaissance, the Reformation, and the Counter-Reformation, continuing in the seventeenth with what is called the Age of Reason (early modern philosophy), and culminating in the eighteenth with the Enlightenment.

THE *COGITO* AND MODERNITY

Of course, all of the terms above are imprecise and disputed, but few will disagree that the work of René Descartes typifies early modern philosophy and sets the agenda for the philosophers who came after him. So the question of philosophical modernity – namely, how best to describe the reasons for the rise of modern philosophy and the waning of scholasticism – may be resolved by determining the break one wishes to depict between the work of Descartes and that of the scholastics.

Numerous elements in Descartes's *Meditations* have been considered modern and contrasted with scholastic philosophy; these have included his use of radical skepticism and his appeal to the first-person perspective – that is, the *cogito* – as the first principle of knowledge. These modern elements are sometimes contrasted with what is thought to be a residual scholastic element in Descartes's thought, namely his use of a causal principle to prove the existence of God.[1] Of

---

[1] See, for example, Martial Gueroult, *Descartes' Philosophy Interpreted According to the Order of Reasons*, tr. R. Ariew *et al.* (Minneapolis: University of Minnesota Press, 1984–85) II: 255–60, as against I: 128–33.

course, many moderns such as Baruch Spinoza were neither skeptical nor committed to the first-person perspective; in addition, these elements were not unknown in medieval philosophy. Nicholas of Autrecourt, for example, took skepticism most seriously (see Chapter 28). Thomas Hobbes, in his Objections to the *Meditations*, even chided Descartes for bringing up stale old skeptical arguments: "since it is commonly observed that there is a difficulty in distinguishing waking from dreams, I would have preferred the author, so very distinguished in the realm of new speculations, not to have published these old things" (ed. Adam and Tannery, VII: 171).[2] Moreover, the *cogito* can be found before Descartes and, in particular, in several of Augustine's works. When Descartes published the *Discourse on Method* (1637) containing his argument, a number of people informed him of this fact. Descartes responded to one of them as follows:

You have obliged me by bringing to my notice the passage of St. Augustine that bears some relation to my "I think, therefore I am." Today I have been to read it at the library of this city, and I do indeed find that he makes use of it to prove the certainty of our being, and then to show that there is in us a kind of image of the Trinity, in that we exist, we know that we exist, and we love this being and the knowledge that is in us. On the other hand, I use it to make it known that this *I* who is thinking is an *immaterial substance*, and has nothing in it that is corporeal. These are two very different things. It is something so simple and natural in itself to infer that one exists from the fact that one is doubting, that it might have come from anybody's pen. But I am still glad to have come together with St. Augustine, if only to shut the mouths of the little minds who have tried to quibble with that principle.

(ed. Adam and Tannery, III: 247–8)

Descartes here sketches what he thinks is a significant contrast between his *cogito* and Augustine's. According to Descartes, he, unlike Augustine, uses the *cogito* to argue that the self is an immaterial substance and that thus it is immortal.[3]

One can dispute whether Descartes's claimed contrast with Augustine is accurate.[4] There are, however, other precedents for Descartes's *cogito* that seem

---

[2] Some propose that a major shift occurred in skepticism itself, between ancient and modern skepticism, a thesis that was even held during the seventeenth century (see Pierre Bayle's *Dictionary*, "Pyrrho," note B). But again, not all moderns took skepticism seriously. Even Cartesians in the seventeenth century rejected, reinterpreted, or severely limited Descartes's method of doubt; see Tad Schmaltz, *Radical Cartesians* (Cambridge: Cambridge University Press, 2002); or Roger Ariew "Cartesian Empiricism," *Revue roumaine de philosophie* 50 (2006) 71–85. In any case, when one sees a genuinely skeptical modern philosopher such as David Hume, his skepticism is Ciceronian and practiced in opposition to Descartes's "antecedent" skepticism. See Hume's *Enquiry conc. Human Understanding*, sec. 12, "Of the Academical or Sceptical Philosophy."

[3] For the intellectual relations between Augustine and Descartes, see Stephen Menn, *Descartes and Augustine* (Cambridge: Cambridge University Press, 1998), and Gareth Matthews, *Thought's Ego in Augustine and Descartes* (Ithaca, NY: Cornell University Press, 1992).

[4] Blaise Pascal thought that the differences between Augustine's and Descartes's *cogito* were so significant that Descartes could be claimed its "true author," even if he had learned it by reading

to use the argument in the same way Descartes claims he does, and these
may even shed light on Descartes's intentions. One can, for instance, find
something akin to the Cartesian line of reasoning in the treatise by Jean de
Silhon entitled *L'immortalité de l'âme*. Silhon, a religious apologist, was a friend
and correspondent of Descartes. *L'immortalité de l'âme* was published in 1634,
before the *Meditations* and *Discourse on Method*. In it, the existence of God,
supreme cause of our being, is unfolded from the *cogito*, knowledge of self,
which is taken to trump the possibility that the senses are deceiving us or that
we are dreaming:

Every man who has the use of judgment and reason can know *that he is*, that is, that he has
being. This knowledge is so infallible that, even though all the operations of the external
senses might in themselves be deceptive, or even though we cannot distinguish between
them and those of an impaired imagination, nor wholly assure ourselves whether we
are awake or asleep, or whether what we are seeing is the truth or illusion and pretense,
it is impossible that a man who has the power, as some have, to enter into himself,
and to make the judgment *that he is*, should be deceived in this judgment, and *should
not be*. . . Now this judgment that a man makes, *that he is*, is not a frivolous piece of
knowledge, or an impertinent reflection. He can rise from there to the first and original
source of his being, and to the knowledge of God himself. He can draw from it the
demonstration of the existence of a divinity . . . He can draw from it the first movements
toward religion and the seed of this virtue that inclines us to submit ourselves to God,
as to the first cause, and to the supreme principle of our being.[5]

The reason why Silhon's line of reasoning might be relevant to considerations
about modernity is that the above passage occurs in his Second Discourse, entitled: "That It Is Necessary to Show God Exists before Proving the Immortality
of the Soul. Refutation of Pyrrhonism and of the Arguments That Montaigne
Brings Forth to Establish It." Thus Silhon makes use of a *cogito* as the basis for
an argument for God's existence and for the immortality of our souls in order
to refute the skepticism of Michel de Montaigne. Silhon issues a Counter-
Reformation response to the Catholic brand of skepticism to which Montaigne
and his close follower Pierre Charron were appealing, itself a Renaissance-
inspired Catholic Counter-Reformation move; as Charron said, "an academic
or a Pyrrhonist will never be a heretic: the two things are opposites" (ibid.,

Augustine: "For I know what difference there is between writing a word by chance, without making a longer and more extended reflection on it, and perceiving in this word an admirable series of
consequences that prove the distinction between material and spiritual natures, and making of it a
firm principle, supporting an entire physics, as Descartes claimed to do" (*Œuvres*, p. 358).
[5] Tr. Ariew *et al.*, *Cambridge Texts in Context: Descartes' Meditations* (Cambridge: Cambridge University
Press, 1998), pp. 199–200.

p. 62).[6] The modernity of the *cogito* as first principle of knowledge derived through a skeptical method is challenged when one sees a *cogito* used as a response to Montaigne's and Charron's brand of skepticism, a *cogito* that does not really stop to discover the self as subjective, but immediately goes on to find God and establish religion. This *cogito* is the seventeenth-century version of the Augustinian *cogito*; at the very least, it shows that one can hold a *cogito* not for modern reasons, as a phenomenologist, let us say, but for reasons rooted in issues germane to seventeenth-century thought and attempting to defend the status quo.

Silhon was not the only thinker within Descartes's circle who made use of a *cogito* to prove the immortality of the soul. Marin Mersenne, Descartes's principal correspondent, referred to two such works in a letter written in 1635 to the Leyden Protestant professor of theology André Rivet: "we have recently published two books on the immortality of the soul, one a large quarto in French, the other an elegant octavo in Latin" (ed. de Waad *et al.*, V: 80). The two books published on the immortality of the soul in 1634–5 were the French quarto by Silhon and a Latin octavo by the Jesuit Antoine Sirmond, entitled *De immortalitate animae demonstratio physica et Aristotelica*. In another letter to Rivet in 1638, Mersenne objected to his correspondent's position by claiming that "there is a difficulty with thinking that the soul or human understanding has some operation that is independent of the senses, if one holds Aristotle's axiom *nothing is in the intellect without being prior in sense*." To emphasize the difficulty, Mersenne added that several of his people – that is, French thinkers from his circle – "have recently written a small number of books to prove the immortality of the soul on the grounds that it has operations that do not at all depend on the senses" (ibid., VII: 24). Clearly in 1638, Mersenne was thinking of Silhon and Sirmond, as well, perhaps, of the Descartes of the *Discourse*.

It is not clear whether Mersenne meant to include Descartes with these other figures, as engaged in a common project, but Sirmond's line of reasoning resembles not just Silhon's but also Descartes's. His intent (as he claims in his title and specifies in his subtitle: *Adversus Pomponatium et asseclas*) was to demonstrate the immortality of the soul against the interpretations of Aristotle by Pietro Pomponazzi and his followers, using arguments based on Aristotelian principles. As an Aristotelian, Sirmond granted that if our soul had an operation proper to itself, that is, independent of the body, it would be able to survive the body; now, the action of the understanding would be the soul's proper operation, which it could do without the body, as long as it did not require phantasms to do so. If, as Pomponazzi thought, phantasms were necessary for the

---

[6] For background on the use of skepticism by Montaigne and Charron as a response to the intellectual crisis of the Reformation, see Richard Popkin, *The History of Scepticism: From Savonarola to Bayle* rev. edn (Oxford: Oxford University Press, 2003).

soul to think, then the soul would have no operation of its own independent of the body. So the issue revolved around whether some sort of impressed species was necessary for the perception of external objects. Sirmond argued that the soul could use intentional species, lacking anything better, but he also argued that there is no need for an intermediary such as an intelligible object in the case of the soul's knowledge of itself, in which intellect and intelligible object are conjoined (French ed. 1637, p. 193). Thus, he judged that "our soul can know itself without the impression of any species" (ibid., p. 169).[7] And, of course, Sirmond also judged, as did Silhon and Mersenne, that "the mind that can operate without body can also subsist by itself. The human mind can accomplish the former. Therefore, it can accomplish the latter... Therefore it is immortal" (ibid., pp. 56–60). Unlike Descartes and Silhon, Sirmond did not use his *cogito* to answer any skeptical challenge. Like them, he used it to prove the immortality of the soul, but – again unlike them – he did so within a self-consciously Aristotelian framework.

We seem to be seeing similar views that can be described in dissimilar ways. Descartes's attempt to answer the skeptic by establishing that he exists as a thinking thing is often considered emblematic of modern philosophy, even though the line of argument continues in an effort to prove the existence of God and immortality of the soul from these foundations. Silhon's similar endeavor to answer the skeptic by proving his own existence, continuing with the existence of God and immortality of the soul, cannot be thought of as a progressive move, being clearly rooted within a Renaissance perspective, in the debates between Reformation and Counter-Reformation positions. Finally, Sirmond's attempt to show that the soul knows itself without the intermediary of the senses, and thus is immortal, is issued in an Aristotelian context, in continuity with scholastic philosophy. As a result, it does not look as if this set of doctrines can constitute the contrast between medieval and modern philosophy.

CARTESIANS AND ARISTOTELIANS

It should not be too surprising if the difference between modern and scholastic philosophy cannot be located in a specific set of doctrines. To do so, we would have to contrast, let us say, the views of Cartesians against those of the

---

[7] Sirmond extends this ability of the soul to know itself without intermediary to the separated soul and to angels: "the separated soul... knows itself without any means other than itself. And it is not difficult to believe that angels who have a more penetrating eye, similarly see in their own nature, without any other aid or impression of species, not only themselves, but many other things" (ibid., p. 193). For more on Sirmond and Silhon, see Léon Blanchet, *Les antécédents historiques du "Je pense, donc je suis"* (Paris: Alcan, 1920) pp. 126–38.

Aristotelians. But either group may be difficult to delineate in that manner. Take for example, "Aristotelian." In the seventeenth century we find the case of Jean-Cécile Frey, who was associated with the University of Paris from 1607 to his death in 1631. As was usual then, he lectured on the four parts of philosophy: logic and ethics the first year; physics and metaphysics the second. Among Frey's lectures is a small treatise called *Cribrum philosophorum qui Aristotelem superiore et hac aetate oppugnarunt* ("A Sieve for Philosophers Who Oppose Aristotle Both in Earlier Times and in Our Own"), a straightforward defense of Aristotle against those who have challenged his doctrines. In his preface Frey writes: "My intention here is to shake the principal anti-Aristotelian doctrines of the principal authors (collected here into this little bundle, as it were) through a sieve of dialectical truth" (*Opuscula*, p. 29). The work that follows is a diatribe against his contemporaries and those of the previous generation who had the temerity to challenge the philosophy of Aristotle. Frey is eager to defend The Philosopher against every attack and every perceived slight. This may strike one as odd, however, particularly since, like all seventeenth-century scholastics, Frey himself departs from properly Aristotelian doctrines in his own teaching. Thus we have a situation in which the same doctrine can be designated as anti-Aristotelian or as Aristotelian depending upon the context in which it is pronounced.

Such dual perspectives can be seen everywhere. Théophraste Bouju, for instance, a contemporary of Frey, wrote a textbook, *Corps de toute la philosophie* (1614), whose subtitle announced: "All of it by demonstration and Aristotle's authority, with explanations of his doctrine by Aristotle himself." Despite the subtitle, Bouju denied in his textbook that there is a sphere of fire and an absolute division between the sublunary and superlunary world. These, most would agree, were important Aristotelian doctrines; dispensing with them requires Bouju to rework substantially the Aristotelian theory of the four elements, of natural and violent motion, and of the heterogeneity of the sublunary and superlunary world (along Stoic lines) – doctrines that happened to be among those most contested by anti-Aristotelians. For the schoolmen, departures from properly Aristotelian doctrines were generally presented as elaborations of his intentions; outside the schools they were often cited as objections to them. Thus, the terms 'Aristotelian' and 'anti-Aristotelian' seem to depend upon the contexts in which they are uttered. Similar things can be said about 'Cartesian.' As a result, it becomes difficult to specify a set of philosophical doctrines that identifies Aristotelians versus Cartesians – and more so for scholastics versus moderns.

Still, there are clear indications that significant changes were taking place. One sees the multiplication of titles, such as Frey's *Cribrum* or Pierre Gassendi's

Exercitationes paradoxicae adversus Aristoteleos (*Unorthodox Essays Against the Aris-totelians*, 1624), together with the rhetoric of "new philosophers," or ancients versus moderns, accepted even by scholastics. For example, the Oratorian[8] Jean Baptiste de la Grange wrote *Les principes de la philosophie contre les nou-veaux philosophes, Descartes, Rohault, Regius, Gassendi, le P. Maignan, etc.* Authors of seventeenth-century scholastic textbooks, such as the Dominican Antoine Goudin and the Franciscan Claude Frassen, felt the need to discuss critically Descartes's philosophy, alongside that of their respective heroes, Thomas Aquinas and John Duns Scotus. Descartes himself saw himself in opposition to the Aris-totelians and at times considered himself at war with Jesuits and other scholastics; as he said to Mersenne, "these six Meditations contain all the foundations of my physics. But please do not tell others, for that might make it harder for sup-porters of Aristotle to approve them. I hope that readers will gradually get used to my principles, and recognize their truth, before they notice that they destroy those of Aristotle" (ed. Adam and Tannery, III: 298). There were even thinkers who set out to mitigate the differences between the ancients and the moderns. René le Bossu published *Parallèle des principes de la Physique d'Aristote et de celle de René Des Cartes* (1674). As he saw the situation, Aristotle had been teaching beginners, and so started with what was obvious to everyone, the sensible things around us, for example, and asked what they were made of. Descartes, at a more advanced stage of science, considered the matter common to everything, which is extended substance, and claimed that every particular is given a form by the way that general matter is shaped. Their principles are therefore not so opposite to one another.

More importantly, one also sees political and ecclesiastical condemnations, consisting in institutional attacks on the moderns and a corresponding support for the scholastics. In 1663 the Catholic church put Descartes's works on the *Index of Prohibited Books*. Shortly thereafter, in 1671, the archbishop of Paris issued a verbal decree from King Louis XIV directed initially at the University of Paris, but immediately extended to the whole kingdom: "The King exhorts you, sirs, to bring it about that no other doctrine than the one set forth by the rules and statutes of the University is taught in the Universities and put into theses. He leaves you to your prudent and wise conduct to take the necessary course of action." The reason for the decree was a possibility of "confusion in the explanation of our mysteries." The decree mentions "certain opinions the

---

[8] The Oratory of France was founded in 1611 by Pierre de Bérulle. Given that the most famous Oratorian, Nicolas Malebranche, was also a noted Cartesian, Oratorians are often thought to be followers of Descartes. This is not an altogether accurate view; for the relationship between Carte-sianism and the Oratory, see Roger Ariew, "Oratorians and the Teaching of Cartesian Philosophy in Seventeenth-Century France," *History of Universities* 17 (2001–2) 47–80.

faculty of theology once censored," a reference to a condemnation of fourteen anti-Aristotelian propositions in 1624, when the Sorbonne had censored various opinions disseminated by some alchemists. The faculty objected to their philosophical claims, which attacked "peripatetic dogma," and asserted that "the prime matter of the Peripatetics is fictitious" and "their substantial forms are absurdly defended." The faculty also censored the claim rejecting that "physical alterations happen through the introduction or destruction of an accidental entity," because, the Sorbonne said, it attacked the "holy sacrament of the Eucharist." The king's 1671 exhortation recalled the subsequent *arrêt* issued by the Court du Parlement in the earlier incident, which prohibited "all persons, under pain of death, from either holding or teaching any maxims against the ancient authors approved by the doctors of the Faculty of Theology." Although anti-scholasticism comes in countless forms during the seventeenth century, Cartesianism was clearly the "other doctrine" against which the 1671 decree was directed, even if Louis did not directly mention it, since Cartesianism dominated the discussion in Paris during the latter part of the century. In any case, he clarified his intent as early as 1675, specifically naming those who "taught the opinions and thoughts of Descartes" as ones who "might bring disorder to our Kingdom." The Sun King ordered that they "be prevented from continuing their lessons in any way whatsoever."[9]

There is a first-hand account of the subsequent events at the college of Angers in the *Journal* kept by François Babin, doctor of the faculty of theology, who was horrified by the attitudes of the Cartesians:

Young people are no longer taught anything other than to rid themselves of their childhood prejudices and to doubt all things – including whether they themselves exist in the world. They are taught that the soul is a substance whose essence is always to think something; that children think from the time they are in their mothers' bellies . . . It is no longer fashionable to believe that fire is hot, that marble is hard, that animate bodies sense pain. These truths are too ancient for those who love novelty. Some of them assert that animals are only machines and puppets without motion, without life, and without sensation; that there are no substantial forms other than the rational soul.

(ed. 1679, p. 2)

---

[9] On the 1671 decree, see Jean-Baptiste Duhamel, *Philosophia universalis* (ed. 1705, V: 18). For the 1624 condemnation of atomism, see Jean de Launoy, *De varia Aristotelis fortuna* (ed. 1656, 128–9, 132), and Charles Duplessis d'Argentré, *Collectio judiciorum de novis erroribus* (ed. 1736, II: 147). Louis XIV's 1675 restatement is described in François Babin's *Journal* (ed. 1679, p. 6). For more on the events in 1624, see Daniel Garber, "Defending Aristotle/Defending Society in Early 17th C Paris," in C. Zittel and W. Detel (eds.) *Wissensideale und Wissenskulturen in der frühen Neuzeit* (Berlin: Akademie Verlag, 2002) 135–60.

It is clear that, for Babin, something had gone terribly wrong. He continued his observations, moving from pedagogical and epistemic to metaphysical and theological problems, and ultimately to political ones:

The Cartesians assert that accidents are not really distinct from substance; that it would be well to guard oneself from attributing some knowledge or certainty to the testimony of our senses . . . They make the essence of all bodies consist in local extension, without worrying that Christ's body does not better accommodate their principles and our mysteries; they teach that something does not stop being true in philosophy even though faith and the Catholic religion teach us the contrary – as if the Christian and the philosopher could have been two distinct things. Their boldness is so criminal that it attacks God's power, enclosing him within the limits and the sphere of things he has made, as if creating from nothing would have exhausted his omnipotence. Their doctrine is yet more harmful to sovereigns and monarchs, and tends toward the reversal of the political and civil state.

(ibid.)

According to Babin, the Cartesians were so out of control that, far from heeding the king's edict, they were making a mockery of it. They wrote satirical verses and issued their own decree: if the king and his henchmen were going to condemn Cartesianism, the Cartesians in turn were going to condemn the authorities to their fate for having supported Aristotle.

The Cartesians' satire traveled even to Angers. Babin reproduced the verses and prefaced a version of the satirical decree with the following comment:

We produce this piece here to show that the innovators use all their wit and industry in order to evade and translate into ridicule the powers that fight against them; and that they do not fail to use mockery, caricatures, or jokes to validate their decried opinions, wishing by that means to dazzle the common minds by the effect of a false light and to persuade the rabble that reason, truth, knowledge, and good sense are theirs alone.

(ibid., p. 18)

In their "*arrêt burlesque*" the Cartesians mandated that Aristotle be reestablished "in the full and peaceful possession of the schools" and commanded "that he always be taught and followed by the regents, masters, and professors of the schools – without, however, their being required to read him, or to know his opinions" (ibid., p. 19). They similarly ordered the heart to remain the principle of the nerves and the blood to stop circulating. They even reestablished the good reputation of the Scotistic *haecceities* and other formalities. In fact, other than protecting Aristotle from the examination of Reason, the Cartesians, in their burlesque, seemed most eager to prevent Reason from defaming and from banishing from the schools the "formalities, materialities, entities, identities, virtualities, *haecceities*, petreities, polycarpeties, and all the other children of the defunct master of the Schools, John Scotus, their father." If the court did not act, they suggested, this "would bring about a great prejudice and cause a complete subversion of the Scholastic philosophy which derives all its substance from them" (ibid., p. 19). The Cartesians' *arrêt* "banishes Reason to perpetuity from the schools of the aforementioned University, prohibits it from entering there, from troubling or bothering the aforementioned Aristotle" (ibid., p. 18).

Of course, the authorities at Angers prevailed. They submitted some professors' writings to examination and found that the authors were teaching the prohibited propositions. Consequently, Fathers Fromentier and Cyprien Villecroze of the Oratory were censured; Fathers Bernard Lamy and his successor, Vincent Pélaut, were ultimately prohibited from teaching and exiled from Angers (ibid., pp. 35–45). The censors of Angers identified a number of Oratorian theses as Cartesian; for example, they objected to Fromentier's teaching that real accidents are not to be distinguished from substances and to his explanation of the Eucharist without having recourse to real accidents. They also complained about the doctrine of the indefiniteness of the universe and of Cartesian doubt, against which they asserted: "To say that we must doubt all things is a principle that tends toward atheism and upsets the foundations of the highest of mysteries . . . It manifestly entails atheism or at least the heresy of the Manicheans, who accepted a good and an evil principle for all creatures" (ibid., pp. 40–1). And they objected to both Fromentier's doctrine about the immateriality and immortality of animal souls and Descartes's animal-machines as originating from the same impoverished ontology. In the case of Lamy, the censors protested against numerous propositions identified as Cartesian. Two of these concerned problems previously raised against Fromentier about the explanation of the Eucharist. However, with Lamy, instead of just complaining about real accidents, they objected to the definition of extension as the essence of body and the rejection of substantial forms. They also derided Lamy's acceptance of the *cogito*, his assertion that children think in their mother's womb and that sensations such as pain are experienced in the soul, not in the body. Apart from their critique of skepticism and of the *cogito*, for the authorities of Angers to be a Cartesian was mostly equated with two things: first, with the acceptance of a mechanistic or corpuscularian philosophy of bodies, entailing the denial of real qualities and substantial forms together with the rejection of formal and final causation; second, with dualism, requiring the clean separation of soul as immaterial thinking substance and body as material extended substance.[10] These

---

[10] For questions about mechanism and forms, see Roger Ariew, *Descartes and the Last Scholastics* (Ithaca, NY: Cornell University Press, 1999), Dennis Des Chene, *Physiologia: Philosophy of Nature in Descartes and the Aristotelians* (Ithaca, NY: Cornell University Press, 1995), and Robert Pasnau,

metaphysical theses were thought to have significant negative consequences for Catholicism. Most interesting as well is the rhetoric of the episode, the sense of incomprehension on both sides: the mockery of the Cartesians, the indignation of the journal writer, and so forth. The positions are so polarized that the situation looks like what Thomas Kuhn would have signaled as a paradigm shift.

VARIETIES OF ARISTOTELIANISM

Despite such clashes, the elements considered modern by both the Cartesians and the scholastics were not really so modern. William of Ockham and others might have agreed that final causes need not be invoked in the explanation of natural phenomena.[11] In any case, notable moderns, such as G. W. Leibniz and Robert Boyle, reintroduced formal and final causes,[12] and there were plenty of corpuscularian scholastics in the seventeenth century (at the very least, Fromentier, as above, the Minim Emmanuel Maignan and the Jesuit Honoré Fabri). A significant variation in late Aristotelian matter theory was the theory of *minima naturalia,* generally discussed in the context of rarefaction and condensation, or change of quantity. Although Aristotle was strongly anti-atomist, thinking that the continuum could be divided indefinitely, he also uttered the seemingly innocuous proposition that "neither flesh, bone, nor any such thing can be of indefinite size in the direction either of the greater or of the less" (*Physics* I.4). This comment took off on its own, and by the seventeenth century the resulting doctrine entailed that there are intrinsic limits of greatness and smallness for every sort of living thing. For example, some argued that since every natural body has an actually determined substantial form, every natural body must have a determinate assortment of accidents and its quantity must be limited to some particular range. Moreover, they asserted limits even for the four basic elements (earth, air, fire, water), which have no intrinsically determinate magnitude; the elements might be augmented indefinitely, if there were matter enough, and their division can be continued indefinitely. They

---

"Form, Substance, and Mechanism," *Philosophical Review* 113 (2004) 31–88, among others. More generally, for an account of the relation between Descartes's philosophy and science, see Daniel Garber, *Descartes' Metaphysical Physics* (Chicago: University of Chicago Press, 1992) and *Descartes Embodied* (Cambridge: Cambridge University Press, 2001).

[11] For Ockham, see *Quodlibet* IV.1. Also see Marilyn McCord Adams, *William Ockham* (Notre Dame, IN: University of Notre Dame Press, 1987) chs. 18 and 22, esp. pp. 975–9.

[12] For Boyle, see *A Disquisition about the Final Causes of Natural Things* (1688), in *Works* vol. IX; for Leibniz, *Discourse on Metaphysics* (1686) sec. 18–21 etc. in *Philosophical Essays* 35–68. Christia Mercer, *Leibniz's Metaphysics: Its Origins and Development* (Cambridge: Cambridge University Press, 2001) traces Leibniz's early and continued commitment to final and formal causes.

do have an extrinsic limitation, however, with respect to prime matter: there may not be enough prime matter to sustain a form and the amount of prime matter is finite. Moreover, they cannot be indefinitely condensed or rarefied – that is, they cannot have their quantity diminished or augmented indefinitely – without being corrupted. For example, earth cannot become as rarefied as fire, and fire cannot become as condensed as earth. When air is condensed beyond a certain point, it becomes water, and water overly rarefied becomes air. Thus, for a late scholastic, rarefaction and condensation could result in generation and corruption under appropriate circumstances. There is, then, a natural minimum of any given element, which is to say that late scholasticism could countenance a kind of atomism. This doctrine of a natural minimum became a bridge between Aristotelian and alchemical theories of matter.

Daniel Sennert, professor of medicine at Wittenberg, provides a good example of a corpuscularian alchemist working within scholastic tradition.[13] In a discourse on "Atoms and Mixtures," originally published in his *Hypomnemata physica* of 1636, Sennert develops the notion that the matter constituting bodies is composed of particles that can be divided again into their original minimal form. Like other chemists, he uses chemical operations to argue that there are atoms in nature. "And although those Atomes be so exceedingly small; yet the essential forms of things remain in them entire, as was lately said, and experience it self does witness" (*Thirteen Books* XI.1 [ed. 1659, pp. 453–4]). Sennert's atoms are of two kinds. First are those from which all things are made, that is, the four Aristotelian elements, each with its own form. They are the smallest things in nature. Sennert argues that the particles of fire are the smallest atoms, that they are "more subtile than the atomes of earth," and "that they diffuse not themselves beyond their Natural bounds" (ibid., p. 454). He constructs an argument on analogy with light, which he claims has a *minimum naturale*: "though there is not a smallest in quantity, yet Light hath a smallest in Nature, that is to say, so smal a Light that it cannot be smaller without perishing. After which manner there are also the smallest among Natural Bodies; which if they be any more divided they lose their form and essence" (ibid.). Sennert even argues that this view is consistent with the division of the continuum to infinity:

Now those disputes against Atomes concerning the infinite division of that which is continued of indivisible Lines, are disputed not from Natural but Mathematical Principles. For the question is not here . . . whether a thing continued to be perpetually

---

[13] William Newman, *Atoms and Alchemy: Chymistry and the Experimental Origins of the Scientific Revolution* (Chicago: University of Chicago Press, 2006), is an excellent exposition of early modern alchemy centered around Sennert and his influence on Boyle.

divisible Mathematically? but, whether or no Nature in her Generation and resolution of Bodies does not stop at some smallest Bodies, than which there are not, nor can be any smaller.

(ibid.)

The second atoms, which Sennert specifically identifies with the principles of the chemists – such as quicksilver, vitriol, sulfur, and salt – are the first mixtures, or second-order corpuscles composed out of the atomic elements. These are rarely divided, but other compound bodies normally resolve into them. "For there are (in the second place) Atomes of another kind besides the Elementary (which if any man wil term first mixt bodies, he may do so as he please) into which as similar parts other compounds are resolved" (ibid., p. 451). Sennert's hierarchy of particles enables him to recover the alchemical tradition as a middle-level theory within a broadly Aristotelian framework of the four elements differentiated at the basic level by their natures. This provides just one example of how the connection between the philosophers we consider modern and the onset of modern science is not as straightforward as one might think.

The rise of modern philosophy and the waning of medieval philosophy cannot be accounted for by pointing to a new doctrine or set of doctrines. Perhaps one can say that some doctrines that were once on the periphery coalesced at the center; one can also point to many social and institutional changes, together with the growing tendency to philosophize in the vernacular and the beginnings of scientific societies outside the schools. Early modern figures such as Descartes began to construct systems they considered to be in opposition to those of the scholastics, and the scholastics often accepted the characterization of that opposition, further polarizing the situation. In the second generation, such philosophers as Leibniz and Malebranche saw themselves as philosophizing with both scholastic and Cartesian doctrines among their options, together with other possibilities such as Gassendi's neo-Epicureanism. Ultimately, in the third or fourth generation, philosophy was done in the background of debates between rationalists and empiricists, with Descartes, Locke, and Hume in mind. By the time Immanuel Kant referred to "school metaphysics," the scholastic philosophy he was thinking of was not that of the medieval period, but of Christian Wolff.

II

LOGIC AND LANGUAGE

10

THE DEVELOPMENT OF LOGIC IN THE
TWELFTH CENTURY

CHRISTOPHER J. MARTIN

The twelfth century was one of the most important and exciting periods in the history of logic. At the start of the century, the production of elementary glosses on ancient texts gave way to a sophisticated commentary literature in which writers developed and debated their own theories concerning what we would now classify as ontology and philosophical logic. Most famous today are the disputes over the status of universals; the present chapter, however, focuses on the less well-known – but, I believe, more important – work done on theories of meaning, modality, and the relation of logical consequence. Many of the works that have survived from the twelfth century are anonymous, but fortunately at least some of those by Peter Abaelard do bear his name: in particular his survey of logic, the *Dialectica* (probably written around 1112) and a set of commentaries on the books of the *logica vetus* known as the *Logica "Ingredientibus"* (probably written between 1115 and 1120). Abaelard is the outstanding logician of this period and is, indeed, one of the greatest of all logicians.[1] His work in these areas fundamentally shaped later development in logic; what follows is essentially an account of his views and of the problems to which they gave rise.

To grasp the importance and originality of Abaelard's work, it is first necessary to understand in some detail the character of the semantical and logical theories that Boethius bequeathed to the Middle Ages. These were transmitted in his translations of both Porphyry's *Isagoge* and Aristotle's *Categories* and *De interpretatione*, together with his own *Introductio ad syllogismos categoricos* and *De syllogismo categorico* (which together paraphrase *Prior Analytics* I.1–7), his treatises *De hypotheticis syllogismis*, *De differentiis topicis*, and *De divisione*, and his commentaries on the *Categories*, as well as on the *Isagoge* and *De interpretatione*, both of which he commented on twice. This small collection of works, later referred to as the *ars vetus* or the *logica vetus* (the Old Logic), would determine the structure

---

[1] For a more extensive discussion of Abaelard's revolution in logic, see Christopher J. Martin, "Logic," in J. Brower and K. Guilfoy (eds.) *The Cambridge Companion to Abelard* (Cambridge: Cambridge University Press, 2004) 158–99.

and aims of logic, or dialectic, at the beginning of the twelfth century. Abaelard's monumental achievement was to transform Boethius's confused and sometimes incoherent material into a unified logical theory.

THE MEANING OF NAMES: IMPOSITION AND ESSENCE

Twelfth-century theories of the meaning of names – and, indeed, all such theories developed in the Middle Ages – take as their starting point Aristotle's remarks in the first three chapters of *De interpretatione* and Boethius's extensive commentary on them. For both Aristotle and Boethius, the meaning of a name is an understanding (*intellectus*) – that is, an affection of the soul (*passio animae*) – that in the mind of a speaker prompts an utterance of the name and that, in turn, is constituted as an understanding in the mind of a listener who hears the utterance. Aristotle postulated a natural relationship of likeness between understandings and things in the world. Boethius explained this relation in terms of a simple but influential theory of form-transference: the sensible forms of extramental individuals are transferred to the mind through the sense organs and reproduced there as images of their sources. The form that constitutes an individual as the kind of thing that it is is separated out by the mind from the other forms to yield the understanding of the thing's species. (Unfortunately for the history of semantics, in his longer commentary on *De interpretatione* 1 [ed. Meiser, pp. 27–8], Boethius complicated this account by translating a cryptic aside from *De anima* III.8, and so bequeathed to his early twelfth-century successors Aristotle's authority for the highly problematic claim that every understanding requires a co-present image.)

Names, both spoken and (by extension) written, are causally but conventionally associated with understandings. This association is established and maintained by acts of *imposition* – that is, the initial baptism and later ostension of individuals with their proper names and of paradigms of natural kinds with their specific and generic names. A name primarily signifies the understanding with which it is associated by this process and secondarily signifies the things in the world of which that understanding is a likeness (ibid., pp. 33–4). The understandings signified by common names are the same for all speakers of a given language. Those signified by proper names differ, however, in that corresponding to the different descriptions that may be given of the named individuals, different collections of accidental forms distinguish one individual from another at different times (ibid., ch. 7, pp. 136–7). The understandings signified by natural kind terms such as 'human being' or 'stone' – unlike those signified by descriptions or propositions – are said to be simple since no mental act of composition is involved in obtaining them. Nevertheless, according

to Boethius, these understandings possess a conceptual structure corresponding to the definition of the kind in question; this allows him to say that, in
understanding *human being*, we understand *mortal rational animal* (ibid., ch. 2,
p. 74).

Abaelard agrees with Boethius's general picture of the relationship between
names, understandings, and things, and he develops this basic account into a
sophisticated theory of signification and reference in which proper and general
names both function in the same way. He rejects the naïve form-transference
model of understanding, however, in favor of a combination of an act-object and
adverbial theory. On this approach, understanding is not invariably mediated
through an image; rather, the understanding signified by a name is a mental act
of attending to an object *as* something – the adverbial component of the theory.[2]
The object may be either an extramental individual – Socrates, for example, if he
is standing in front of me when I hear the name 'Socrates' – or a mental image,
if an appropriate extramental object is not present. Abaelard further maintains
that since everything that exists is individual, the understanding associated with
a species name has as its object a *confused* image resembling equally all and only
the individual members of that species. His theory of understanding does not,
however, really need such an image, since it makes no distinction between the
mental operation of understanding a general name and that of recognizing an
individual as a member of a particular kind. For the latter, what is necessary
is that the extramental individual be attended to as belonging to the kind in
question. We may thus, Abaelard says, attend to a particular piece of oak either
as oak, as wood, or as body (*Logica "Ingredientibus,"* p. 329).

Abaelard apparently assumes that our recognition of the kinds into which the
world is divided is entirely unproblematic. When the impositor (and so in the
first place Adam) introduces a new general name, he intends that it shall apply
to all and only individuals of the kind to which the paradigm example belongs.
His audience associates the new name with an understanding that attends to
either an individual or an image, *as* (or *as of*) an individual of that kind. We
thus recognize stones as stones, according to Abaelard, and we understand what
a speaker is talking about when he uses the name 'stone' (*Logica "Nostrorum
petitioni sociorum,"* ed. Geyer, p. 567).

Abaelard is an essentialist, though he does not use the term 'essence' but
rather 'nature' for the set of features that constitute something as a member of
a species. Natures are expressed by definitions, which must be determined by
the investigations of the natural scientist (*physicus*),[3] since without them we do

---

[2] See, e.g., *Logica "Ingredientibus,"* ed. Geyer, p. 322; *De intellectibus*, ed. Morin, nn. 28, 62 sq.
[3] See *Dialectica*, ed. de Rijk, pp. 286–7.

not in general know the definitions even of the natural kinds that we are easily able to identify: "we all know in our ordinary use of language which things are called 'stones.' What the proper *differentiae* of stone are, however, or what the properties of this species are, we are still not able, I believe, to assign with a word with which the definition or description of stone might be completed" (*Collationes*, ed. Orlandi and Marenbon, p. 207).

Although in introducing the word 'stone' the impositor is ignorant of the nature of stones, its meaning is nevertheless, as he intends it to be, precisely that of the definition that completely expresses the nature of stones. That is to say, the understanding signified by 'stone' *contains* everything contained in the not yet, and perhaps never, formulated definition. The understanding signified by the term is, however, *simple*, whereas that signified by the definition is composite. In understanding the name we attend to precisely what we would attend to in understanding the definition if we knew it. The only difference is that in the first case we understand the components all together and all at once, whereas in the second case we understand them separately and in succession (*Logica "Ingredientibus,"* p. 325).

Abaelard differs from Boethius in treating proper names in the same way that he treats natural kind terms. Whereas Boethius had taken differences between individuals to require different proper names to signify their different sets of accidents, Abaelard takes 'Socrates' to signify only what 'human being' signifies. He defends this view on the grounds that Socrates's accidental features change over time, and that Socrates might have an identical twin brother.[4]

Abaelard's essentialism and his theory of imposition entail that natural kind and proper names rigidly designate the kinds and the individuals on which they are imposed. His account of signification and understanding guarantees both that the understanding signified by a natural kind term contains everything contained in the compound understanding that is signified by its definition, and that a proper name signifies everything contained in the understanding signified by the corresponding species name, even though someone using the terms may well not know what this is. Propositions such as 'If something's a human being, then it's rational' and 'If something's Socrates, then it's an animal' are thus, on Abaelard's account, what we would now call analytic a posteriori truths.

THE DISCOVERY OF PROPOSITIONALITY

If one had to choose a single passage to illustrate the true greatness of Abaelard as a philosophical logician, it might be this:

[4] *Logica "Nostrorum Petitioni Sociorum,"* p. 547; *Logica "Ingredientibus,"* p. 142.

Since [Boethius] concedes that 'If it's day, then it's light' is a single proposition in which different propositions are reduced to a single sense by the preposed conjunction, I do not understand why 'Apollo is a prophet and Jupiter thunders' cannot be called a single proposition, just like 'When Apollo is a prophet, Jupiter thunders.' Whence each of them may have a single proposition [that is its negation and] with which it divides [truth and falsity]. So that just as we say 'It's not the case that if it's day, then it's light,' we may also say 'It's not the case [both] that Apollo is a prophet and Jupiter thunders.'

(Logica "Ingredientibus," p. 380)

As well as maintaining that the copulative conjunction 'and' does not form a single proposition from the two given propositions, Boethius rejects the Stoic practice of preposing a negative particle to a proposition. Instead, he insists that it must be applied directly to the verb. Neither he nor the commentary tradition to which he belongs had any notion at all of a propositional operation in the modern sense, and so recognized nothing corresponding to a modern propositional logic.[5] From the sources available to us it seems that Abaelard was the first in the Middle Ages fully to understand propositionality as we do and the first to deploy this understanding in the formulation of the principles of propositional logic.

Believing that Frege discovered it, Peter Geach honors as the *Frege Point* the distinction between propositional content and the force with which that content is employed. It is this distinction that must be drawn if propositional contents are to be manipulated with propositional operations.[6] A propositional operation is a function that takes any propositional content and transforms it into a new propositional content. The assertion 'Socrates is sitting,' for example, and the command 'Be seated, Socrates!' have the same propositional content – *that Socrates is sitting.* The operation of truth functional propositional negation transforms this into the content *it is not the case that Socrates is sitting,* which is true if the original is false and false if the original is true. This content may then be asserted with 'Socrates is not sitting' or commanded with 'Do not sit, Socrates!'

Although he lacks a terminology adequate to formulate this point generally, Abaelard clearly makes this very distinction between force and content. He maintains, for example, that the very same understanding is signified by an utterance of the assertion 'I hope that the king will come,' and an utterance of the wish 'Would that the king will come.' He believes that the difference in the force of utterances is indicated either by their different grammatical moods or

---

[5] See Christopher J. Martin, "The Logic of Negation in Boethius," *Phronesis* 36 (1991) 277–304.
[6] Peter Geach, "Assertion," *Philosophical Review* 69 (1960) 221–5.

by the occurrence in them of markers such as adverbs (*Logica "Ingredientibus,"* p. 374).

Abaelard refers to the operation of propositional negation as what he calls *extinctive* or *destructive* negation, distinguishing it from the predicate negation found in the works of Aristotle and Boethius, which he calls *separative* or *remotive* negation. Extinctive negation is what we would classify as a truth-functional operation that, applied to any propositional content, forms another that is false if the original is true and true if the original is false, independently of whether or not the extension of the subject term is empty. Such negation may be iterated without limit. Separative negation, on the other hand, applies only to categorical propositional contents and cannot be iterated. In the standard case, according to Abaelard, the truth of an affirmative categorical 'S is P' requires that the extension of 'S' is not empty. The separative negation 'S is not P' is then true just in case the extension of 'S' is not empty and 'S is P' is false (*Dialectica*, pp. 173–84).

Abaelard can thus distinguish the extinctive negation of any simple categorical as its contradictory from the separative negation as its contrary. Relying on both this and the distinction between propositional content and the force with which that content is employed, he is able to reinterpret Aristotle's claims about the relations between general categorical propositions in terms of a genuinely propositional logic.

In addition, contrary to Boethius's insistence that his own expression 'Some S is not P' (corresponding to the formulation 'P does not inhere in some S' employed by Aristotle in the *Prior Analytics*) has the same meaning as the expression 'Not every S is P' (given by Aristotle as the contradictory opposite of 'Every S is P' in *De interpretatione* 7), Abaelard finds here the distinction between predicate and propositional negation and constructs a rectangle of opposition rather than the Aristotelian square (*Logica "Ingredientibus,"* pp. 408–11), as shown in Fig 10.1.

Like propositional negation, copulative conjunction is for Abaelard a purely extensional operation; the conjunction 'P and Q' is true just in case each of 'P' and 'Q' is true. The logical operations of disjunction and conditionalization on the other hand, as we will see below, are highly non-extensional.

Abaelard's *Dialectica* distinguishes the syntactic constructions (*constructiones*) employed in making modal claims from the sense (*sensus*) of these constructions.[7]

---

[7] Although Abaelard certainly knew something of at least the first few chapters of the *Prior Analytics* (part of the *logica nova* that would become fully available only later in the century), his complex and sophisticated treatment of the logic of modal terms seems to be based only on the discussion of the interaction of negation and modality in Chapters 12 and 13 of *De interpretatione*.

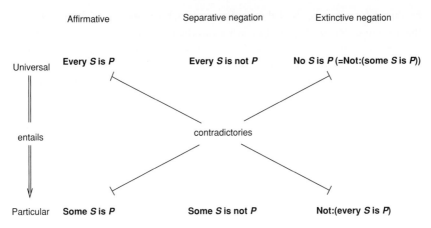

Fig. 10.1 Rectangle of opposition.

With respect to syntax, the subject and predicate are determined by the rules of grammar. With respect to sense, however, the mode is an adverbial operator modifying the connection of the predicate to the subject in the corresponding simple categorical. Thus, both 'Socrates is necessarily human' (using an adverbial mode to modify the predicate) and 'Socrates being human is necessary' (using a nominal mode as the predicate) are, according to Abaelard, used to make precisely the same modal claim. Yet only the first shows properly in its construction that what is intended is a claim about the connection between the grammatical and logical subject 'Socrates' and the grammatical and logical predicate 'human.' Although the second has the same logical subject and predicate, its grammatical subject is 'being human' and its grammatical predicate 'necessary.'

Hence, according to Abaelard, modal claims are properly understood as claims about things (*de rebus*), and their equivalence or otherwise is determined by considering the sense of modal sentences rather than their grammatical construction (*Dialectica*, pp. 191–210). Adopting this procedure for resolving their meanings, he works out the relations of equipollence (that is, identity of truth value) that hold between the modal propositions derived from simple categoricals of different quantity and quality. Indeed, Abaelard goes on to develop the first medieval account of the modal syllogism (and one quite unlike Aristotle's, of which he had no knowledge). He notes that corresponding to every mood and figure of Aristotle's categorical syllogism there is a mixed modal syllogism – that is, a syllogism in which either one of the premises or else the conclusion is non-modal. On Abaelard's *de rebus* account of modality, a syllogism may have two modal premises only if the predicate of each premise is modalized. But in that case in order for there to be a syllogism the predicates must be the same and the middle term of an argument in the second figure, the conclusion of which is non-modal. In the first and third figures the major premise may be modal, but the minor must then be categorical and the conclusion modal. In contrast to Aristotle, there are thus for Abaelard no completely modal syllogisms (that is, syllogisms of which both of the premises and the conclusion are modal), since on the *de rebus* account of modality the corresponding arguments would lack a middle term, and so not be syllogisms (ibid., pp. 245–8).

In the *Dialectica*, Abaelard contrasts his *de rebus* theory of modals with the theory of one of his teachers (whom he does not further identify). According to this theory, a grammatical construction with a nominal mode does in fact properly represent the logical structure of the claim being made; the claim made by 'Socrates being human is necessary,' for example, is that the propositional content of the corresponding simple categorical is a necessary truth. We thus have clearly formulated by the second decade of the twelfth century the distinction between the *de re* and *de sensu* accounts of modality. The latter, however, construes modalities as predicates of propositional contents, and there is no suggestion that modality is a propositional operator. In the *Dialectica* Abaelard rejects the *de sensu* reading as not properly modal, and he argues at length that its proponents do not properly understand what it commits them to in terms of the truth or falsity and the convertibility of propositions containing nominal modes (ibid., p. 195).

In the *Logica "Ingredientibus*," Abaelard again distinguishes between the grammatical construction and the sense of modal propositions. He adds, however, that he has now seen Aristotle's *Sophistical Refutations* (part of the *logica nova*), and he proceeds to identify the distinction made there between the divided (*per divisionem*) and composite (*per compositionem*) readings of modal propositions with his own distinction between what are today called *de re* and *de sensu* claims. He then acknowledges that some modal claims are irreducibly impersonal and so not resolvable into equivalent *de rebus* claims (pp. 195–8). In addition to establishing which propositions are equipollent, he shows how to work out, for all the various quantities and qualities they might have, which *de rebus*/divided modal claims follow from which other ones and which of them are contradictories, contraries, and subcontraries. He also begins to investigate the logical relations between *de rebus*/divided and *de sensu*/composite modal claims (pp. 198–203). It would be well over a hundred years before there was a comparable attempt to develop a theory of modal propositions.[8]

---

[8] See Henrik Lagerlund, *Modal Syllogistic in the Middle Ages* (Leiden: Brill, 2000).

ARGUMENTATION AND CONDITIONAL PROPOSITIONS

Although Boethius's treatise *De hypotheticis syllogismis* offers an account of the logic of conditional and disjunctive sentences, it played no role in the development of logic after the middle of the twelfth century – apparently as a result of Abaelard's criticisms. Because he lacks an understanding of propositionality, Boethius has no way to formulate the rules for the manipulation of conditionals generally by saying, as we do, that, if 'p' and 'q' and 'r' are any propositional contents, no matter how complex, then the following are all valid arguments: 'If p, then q, p; therefore q' (*modus ponens*); 'If p, then q, not:q; therefore not:p' (*modus tollens*); and 'If p, then q, if q, then r; therefore if p, then r' (*perfect hypothetical syllogism*). Rather, Boethius lists all the possible forms of simple conditionals with a simple categorical affirmation as antecedent and consequent, and he states *modus ponens* and *modus tollens* separately for each case. He does the same for composite conditionals with one of the antecedent and consequent a simple categorical and the other a simple conditional, and likewise for conditionals with both antecedent and consequent a simple conditional. For all forms of the simple conditional he also gives the appropriate perfect hypothetical syllogism. And that is all as far as inferences with conditionals are concerned. In addition, Boethius imposes some very curious constraints on compound conditional premises, which perhaps reflect an ancient attempt to connect hypothetical and categorical syllogistic, but which have some strange consequences. For example, the conditionalized contraposition 'If (if p, then q), then (if not:q, then not:p)' is unacceptable, since a necessary condition for the truth of such a conditional, according to Boethius, is that there is an appropriate connection between the antecedent and consequent conditionals, and for this to be so both conditionals must be false. This, however, contradicts his own proof of *modus tollens* in which he argues that 'if p, then q' is true 'not:p' follows from 'not:q' (*De hypotheticis syll.*, pp. 354–80).

Boethius stipulates that a necessary condition for the truth of a simple conditional is that the truth of the antecedent is inseparable from that of the consequent – that is, it is not possible for the antecedent to be true and the consequent false at the same time. He does not explicitly indicate whether this is also sufficient, but he does distinguish between conditionals in a way that suggests it is not. The distinction, which will be standard in medieval logic until William of Ockham, is that between conditionals such as 'If fire is hot, then the heavens are spherical,' which hold accidentally, and those such as 'If something is a human, then it is an animal,' which express a natural consequence (*consequentia*) in which there is an explanatory connection between antecedent and consequent (ibid., pp. 218–20). A disjunction, according to Boethius, is equivalent to a conditional that has the opposite of the first disjunct as its antecedent and the second disjunct as its consequent. Since he also holds that as a matter of fact the only conditionals of the form 'If it's not:A, then it's B' that are true are those in which 'A' and 'B' are simple terms immediately opposed to one another (and so exclusive and exhaustive of the domain to which they apply), the same holds for 'It's A or it's B,' for example 'It's sick or it's well' with respect to animals (ibid., p. 234). Disjunctions containing negative terms, like the corresponding conditionals, hold for terms that are exhaustive but not necessarily exclusive.[9]

Boethius classifies a conditional as affirmative or negative depending only on whether its consequent is affirmative or negative (ibid., p. 252). Despite repeatedly giving examples that show that he does not accept the principle of conditional excluded middle for an affirmative and the corresponding negative conditional – that is, that 'If it's A, then it's B' and 'If it's A, then it's not B' are contradictory – his treatment of the hypothetical syllogism appears to commit him to just this. The problem arises because Boethius has no operation of negation to apply to the whole of a conditional proposition and so no way of distinguishing its negation from the negative conditional corresponding to a given affirmative. As a result, he claims as valid the arguments 'If it's A, then (if it's B, then it's C), but if it's B, then it's not C; therefore it's not A' and 'If (if it's A, then it's not B), then it's C, but it's not C; therefore if it's A, then it's B' (ibid., pp. 285, 298).

Aristotle's logic also lacks propositional negation and includes a principle for argumentation that reflects this, which would prove fundamental for twelfth-century logic. In Boethius's obscure report, the principle appears as follows: "It is not necessary that the same is when the same both is and is not – as when A is, if for this reason it is necessary that B is, if the same A is not, it is not necessary that B is, that is, that it is because A is not" (ibid., p. 222). This principle is harmless if it is read as insisting that 'if something's A, then it's B' and 'if something's not A, then it's B' cannot both be true where 'A' and 'B' are general names and the predications are contingent. It becomes extremely dangerous, however, as we will see, when it is interpreted as maintaining – as it is by Abaelard – that 'if A, then B' and 'if not:A, then B' cannot both be true where 'A' and 'B' are propositions of any degree of complexity.

Abaelard tries extremely hard to make some sense of Boethius's account of the hypothetical syllogism; even he can do nothing with it, though, since it is not a logic of compound propositions. In the end he replaces the various figures with the schema for *modus ponens*, *modus tollens*, and perfect hypothetical syllogism, and he converts Boethius's term negations into propositional negations. These

[9] See Martin, "The Logic of Negation."

are applied to the entire conditional in instances of *modus tollens* where the antecedent is itself a conditional. Disjunction likewise combines propositions of any complexity, with 'either *p* or *q*' equivalent to 'if not *p*, then *q*' (*Dialectica*, pp. 469–532).

Unlike Boethius's treatment of hypothetical syllogisms, the account of topical inference he sketched in *De differentiis topicis* remained important throughout the Middle Ages. Indeed, perhaps the most characteristic feature of twelfth-century logical commentaries is their analysis of arguments in terms of the topical warrant involved. An argument might, for example, rely on a property of definitions, and so hold 'from definition,' or it might rely on an appeal to authority, and so hold 'from authority.' According to Boethius, following Cicero, topical differences (*loci differentiae*) are that from which we draw *argumenta*; they are the reasons that settle questions one way or the other, which we express in arguments. Boethius claims that these *loci* are employed with syllogisms, and he does indeed give some examples of their use to 'justify' inferences that have the form of an Aristotelian categorical syllogism. More often, however, his examples are of *loci* used to warrant enthymematic inferences and to furnish a direct proof of conditional propositions.

Each topical difference is associated with a collection of undemonstrable self-evident principles, known as *maximal propositions*, which state the logical properties of that difference. According to Boethius, these are what do the work in topical arguments. For example, the conditional 'If the world is ruled by providence, then humans are ruled by providence' is proved from the premise that humans are part of the world, appealing to the *locus* 'from an integral whole' and the maximal proposition 'what holds of a whole holds of its parts' (*De topicis differentiis*, pp. 32–3 [1188C]).

Abaelard's development of Boethius's treatments of conditional propositions and the topics into a unified treatment of inference is one of the most remarkable achievements in the history of logic. He connects them by insisting that our only source for true conditionals are certain *loci differentiae* and their maximal propositions. Abaelard is perfectly clear that some arguments and the corresponding conditionals are valid and true simply in virtue of their form. Moreover, he introduces for the first time the modern definition of validity in terms of substitutability (*Dialectica*, p. 255). Categorical syllogisms from Aristotle's three figures, as well as certain syllogisms not mentioned by Aristotle, hold for all uniform substitutions of terms, while *modus ponens*, *modus tollens*, and perfect hypothetical syllogisms hold for all uniform substitutions of propositional contents. Arguments and the corresponding conditionals that satisfy the substitutability criterion and have a canonical form are classified by Abaelard as *perfect entailments* (*inferentiae*). Such entailments are distinguished from *imperfect entailments* (that is, enthymemes and the corresponding conditionals), which hold only for substitutions of terms that stand in particular relationships (ibid., p. 253). These relationships are some of those that are catalogued by the topical differences. Thus, the relationship of species to genus, according to Abaelard, is such that any substitution for 'human' and 'animal' in the conditional 'If Socrates is human, then Socrates is an animal' results in a true conditional if the first of the new terms is related to the second as species to genus. So, for example, 'If Socrates is a pearl, then Socrates is a stone' holds in virtue of the maximal proposition 'Of whatever the species is predicated the genus is predicated' (ibid., p. 310).

Contrary to Boethius, Abaelard insists that since syllogisms are perfect entailments, they do not require the support of a locus. This claim was controversial in the middle of the twelfth century and identified as one of a number of characteristic doctrines of the school associated with Abaelard and known as the Nominales. Abaelard sets out to establish in his *Dialectica* just which *loci* warrant imperfect entailments. Contrary to some of his contemporaries, he insists that not all can do this, since not all can provide the appropriately necessary connection between terms. For such a connection Abaelard requires not simply inseparability – the usual modern criterion for validity, according to which it is impossible for the first term to apply but not the second – but also that there be a relevant connection in the form of a meaning relation between them. In order for a conditional proposition to be true, the sense, or understanding, of the antecedent must contain that of the consequent; the conditional and the corresponding enthymeme are then imperfect entailments (p. 253). Abaelard distinguishes, however, between true conditionals and valid enthymemes. All that he requires of valid arguments is that a false conclusion never follow from true premises, which is the case if the inseparability condition alone is met. Since the truth of a conditional also requires relevance, he denies that an argument is valid if and only if the corresponding conditional is true; thus, he rejects what we now call the Deduction Principle.

For a conditional to be true, Abaelard requires that the sense or understanding of the antecedent must contain that of the consequent. This formalizes Boethius's notion of natural consequence by connecting it to a distinction, which Boethius takes from Porphyry, between features included in the definition of a natural kind and features that belong accidentally but inseparably to individuals of that kind. These latter inseparable accidents are such that, although their bearer cannot possibly exist without them, it is possible to think of that thing without thinking of those accidents. Porphyry's example, repeated throughout the Middle Ages, is the blackness of a crow; another is the ability of human beings to laugh. For Abaelard, the conditional 'If something is human, then it is able to laugh' is thus false, even though we can always validly argue from something's being human to its being able to laugh. The original imposition of the term 'human' guarantees that its sense (that is, the understanding constituted in the mind of someone hearing it) includes being mortal, rational, and an animal – but not being able to laugh. Hence, the conditional 'If something is human, then it is an animal' is true, even though those using the term 'human' perhaps do not realize this.

Abaelard recognizes, and is apparently the first medieval logician to do so, that if satisfaction of the inseparability condition alone were required for the truth of a conditional, then any conditional with an impossible antecedent would be true; his example is 'If Socrates is a stone, then Socrates is an ass' (ibid., p. 285). He does not, however, state the principle that anything follows from an impossibility (*ex impossibili quidlibet*), since this is not true of his own definition of consequence. Just how he does understand consequence is revealed in the arguments that he employs to show that certain of the *loci* do not warrant true conditionals. In particular, the *locus* from opposites – that is, exclusive but not exhaustive terms – would, if accepted, warrant conditionals of the form 'If Socrates is human, then Socrates is not an ass,' while the locus from immediates – that is, exclusive and exhaustive terms – would warrant 'If Socrates is not sick, then Socrates is well.'

Abaelard holds that both of these conditionals are false, as indeed are all conditionals in which the antecedent and the consequent are of different quality (that is, one negative and the other affirmative). This follows because he accepts the propositional version of the principle that Boethius reports from Aristotle and holds himself – namely, that no pair of propositions of the form 'not:$p \rightarrow q$,' '$p \rightarrow q$' nor any pair of the form '$p \rightarrow$ not:q,' '$p \rightarrow q$,' can both be true (ibid., pp. 290–2). These results follow from his accepting as fundamental for the logic of the conditional that no conditionals of the form 'not:$p \rightarrow p$' or '$p \rightarrow$ not:p' are true. (In the twentieth century, logics based on these principles have been called *connexive logics*.)

It is easy to see how the Nominales' thesis that an affirmation does not entail a negation follows, if one also accepts, as Abaelard does, the principles of conditional simplification ($p\&q \rightarrow p$, $p\&q \rightarrow q$), contraposition (($p \rightarrow q$) |– (not:$q \rightarrow$ not:p)), and perfect hypothetical syllogism:

1. $p \rightarrow$ not:q	Hypothesis
2. $(p \& q) \rightarrow q$	Simplification
3. $(p \& q) \rightarrow p$	Simplification
4. not:$q \rightarrow$ not:$(p \& q)$	2., Contraposition
5. $(p \& q) \rightarrow$ not:q	3., 1., Transitivity
6. $(p \& q) \rightarrow$ not:$(p \& q)$	5., 4., Transitivity

The conclusion (6) is of the forbidden form, and so the hypothesis (1) must be rejected. Likewise, by a similar argument, any conditional with a negative antecedent and an affirmative consequent must also be rejected. Similar arguments justify Abaelard's rejection of the principles of double negation '$p \rightarrow$ not:not:p' and 'not:not:$p \rightarrow p$.'

Abaelard's arguments are extraordinarily impressive, but his genius was also his downfall. Although Aristotle's principle is reasonable enough for simple terms and contingent predication, as mentioned above, Abaelard applies it to propositions of any degree of complexity – and in this form it is incompatible with the principle of simplification. This was noticed by Alberic of Paris (most likely in the 1130s), who proceeded to demolish Abaelard's logical project with a simple argument. For Abaelard, 'If something's human then it's an animal' is a paradigmatically true conditional. Yet, Alberic argues as follows:[10]

1. If (Socrates is human and not an animal), then Socrates is not an animal [Simplification]
2. If (Socrates is human and not an animal), then Socrates is human [Simplification]
3. If Socrates is human, then Socrates is an animal [Accepted by Abaelard]
4. If Socrates is not an animal, then Socrates is not human [3., Contraposition]
5. If Socrates is not human, then it is not the case that (Socrates is human and not an animal) [2., Contraposition]
6. If (Socrates is human and not an animal), then it is not the case that (Socrates is human and not an animal) [1., 4., 5., Transitivity]

One contemporary source tells us that Abaelard simply conceded this argument and so, in effect, conceded that his logic collapsed in inconsistency. Whatever his response, Alberic's discovery provoked a crisis in logic in the middle of the twelfth century. At this time a number of schools of philosophy flourished in Paris, each associated with a particular master. Manifestos for a number of these schools have survived, in which their logical principles are set out in detail. Each school had its own solution to Alberic's problem. The Nominales seem to have proposed an account of the interaction of negation and copulative conjunction for which simplification does not hold when the conjuncts are of different quality. The Porretani, followers of Gilbert of Poitiers, rejected conditional simplification, like modern connexivists, insisting that both conjuncts in a copulative antecedent must play a role in the inference to the consequent. The most curious solution was that of the Melidunenses, the followers of Robert of Melun, who denied that any conditional with a false antecedent is true, since 'nothing follows from the false.'

Final victory in this debate, however, went to the Parvipontani, the followers of Adam of Balsham (or Adam Parvipontanus, "Of the Little Bridge"), who

---

[10] Reported in the *Introductiones Montanae Minores*, ed. L. M. de Rijk, *Logica modernorum* (Assen: Van Gorcum, 1962–7) II.2: 65–6.

simply accepted that the inseparability condition is both necessary and sufficient for the truth of a conditional and the validity of an argument with the corollaries that anything follows from an impossibility, and that a necessity follows from anything. John of Salisbury, writing in 1159, tells us that a former student of his, William of Soissons, went on to study with Adam of Balsham and was responsible for the discovery of a "machine" (that is, an argument) for proving that from one impossibility all impossibilities follow – something that John says he himself could not be compelled to accept (*Metalogicon* II.10). A few decades later, however, towards the end of the twelfth century, Alexander Neckham observes that it surprises him that anyone denies that everything follows from an impossibility, and he provides us with the argument to prove that this is so for contradictory opposites:

Is it not the case that if Socrates is a human and Socrates is not a human, then Socrates is a human? But if Socrates is a human, then Socrates is a human or a stone; therefore, if Socrates is a human and Socrates is not a human, Socrates is a human or a stone. But if Socrates is a human and Socrates is not a human, then Socrates is not a human; therefore if Socrates is a human and Socrates is not a human, then Socrates is a stone. With a similar argument it can be proved that if Socrates is a human and Socrates is not a human, then Socrates is a nanny goat ... Do you not see, therefore, how from the impossibility that Socrates is a human and Socrates is not a human, there follows anything?

(De naturis rerum, ed. Wright, pp. 288–9)

This would prove to be the standard position on inference for the rest of the Middle Ages. For the truth of a conditional and the validity of an argument, all that is required is that it not be possible for the antecedent to be true and the consequent false at the same time. For the truth of a disjunction, all that is required is simply that one of the disjuncts be true. This is just what is required in twentieth-century modal logic to construct the famous *Lewis Argument*, showing that anything follows from a contradiction. As we have seen, this was part of logic from the twelfth century on.[11]

OBLIGATIONES

Though later logicians agreed that the inseparability of the truth of the consequent from that of the antecedent is necessary and sufficient for there to be a relation of consequence, they continued to distinguish between accidental and natural consequences in the way that Abaelard had until the beginning of the

[11] See Christopher J. Martin, "William's Machine," *Journal of Philosophy* 83 (1986) 564–72.

fourteenth century (see Chapter 13). Natural consequence adds to inseparability the requirement of relevance, and such consequences were employed in arguing about what follows from hypotheses acknowledged to be impossible. According to Boethius in *De hypotheticis syllogismis,* we are allowed to posit such hypotheses, and we may reason coherently about them. (An example is found in his treatise *Quomodo substantiae* where he supposes that God does not exist and explores the question of whether and how beings would be good in such an impossible situation.)

The second half of the twelfth century saw the regimentation of the rules for exploring an impossible hypothesis, the so-called *positio impossibilis.* These, along with the rules for reasoning under a false but possibly true hypothesis, the *positio falsa,* form part of the discipline of constrained argumentation known as *obligationes,* or the *ars obligatoria.* In these procedures, an opponent asks a respondent to accept that some hypothesis, the *positum,* is true. If he does, the opponent goes on to propose a series of claims to which the respondent must reply consistently with the *positum* and all of his earlier responses. If a given proposal neither follows from nor is inconsistent with the set of earlier responses, the respondent should grant it if it is in fact true and deny it if it is false. The role of the respondent is to preserve the consistency of his answers; he fails if he contradicts himself.

In *positio impossibilis,* the respondent cannot allow an appeal to the principle that anything follows from an impossibility but rather must concede only proposals that follow from what has gone before in a natural consequence. Just what counts as a natural consequence will thus determine what holds under an impossible hypothesis. In one of the earliest treatises on *positio impossibilis,* the *Tractatus Emmeranus,*[12] the relevant connection of containment required for such consequence is said to preclude consequences with an affirmative antecedent and a negative consequent. The treatise thus seems to come from Nominales or from the time when their logic was still well known, so not much later than the third quarter of the twelfth century. *Positio impossibilis* was employed in the thirteenth century in the solution of theological problems involving impossible hypothesis, but its use became controversial in the fourteenth century and eventually it disappeared from the logic textbooks.

From the same period as the *Tractatus Emmeranus* we have a related text, the *Obligationes Parisiensis,*[13] in which we find, perhaps for the first time, a version

---

[12] See de L. M. Rijk, "Some Thirteenth Century Tracts on the Game of Obligation I," *Vivarium* 12 (1974) 94–123.

[13] See L. M. de Rijk, "Some Thirteenth Century Tracts on the Game of Obligation II," *Vivarium* 13 (1975) 22–54.

of one of the glories of medieval logic: the discussion of the insoluble sentence 'this sentence is false.' The treatise explores the strategy of leading a respondent to contradict himself in a *positio falsa* by constructing a *positum* that is (or may become during the time that he is obligated to respond consistently) equivalent to 'the *positum* is false.' Once the *positum* becomes equivalent to 'the *positum* is false,' the respondent is bound to concede both that the *positum* is true (because he is obligated to this), and that the *positum* is false (because the *positum* says of itself that it is false and has been conceded to be true). The skill of the opponent lies in concealing the self-referential consequences of his *positum* by asking the respondent, for example, to admit as a *positum* that the *positum* is inconsistent with his being a human. Since this is certainly possible, it should be admitted by the respondent. The treatise then demonstrates in an argument of many steps that the respondent may be led to contradict himself, but we are told eventually that the proper response to the sophism is that at a crucial point the respondent should refuse the opponent's proposal and reply rather that he is simply babbling. This is referred to as "*cassatio*," the earliest of many solutions to the problem of insolubilia.[14]

The theory of argument and the conditional was developed to a very high degree of sophistication by the second half of the twelfth century. It remained essentially unchanged until Ockham's rejection of John Duns Scotus's metaphysics compelled him to construct a quite new account of consequence. Scotus holds, in effect, that items are formally but not existentially distinct if they are accidentally but not naturally inseparable. That is, since being able to laugh follows from being human in an accidental but not a natural consequence, there is a formal distinction between them. In order to do away with such arguments for the formal distinction, Ockham introduces a new definition of consequence that requires only inseparability but that excludes the trivial cases that hold merely in virtue of having an impossible antecedent or a necessary consequent. Such trivial consequences he classifies as *material* while all others are *formal* (see Chapter 13). After Ockham there is no mention of natural consequences nor any mention in the logic textbooks of impossible *positio*.[15]

[14] See Christopher Martin, "Obligations and Liars," in M. Yrjönsuuri (ed.) *Medieval Formal Logic: Consequences, Obligations, Insolubles* (Dordrecht: Reidel, 2001) 63–94.
[15] See Christopher Martin, "Formal Consequence in Scotus and Ockham: Towards an Account of Scotus' Logic," in O. Boulnois *et al.* (eds.) *Duns Scot à Paris 1302–2002* (Turnout: Brepols, 2005) 117–50.

TERMINIST LOGIC

E. JENNIFER ASHWORTH

Terminist logic is a specifically medieval development.[1] It is named from its focus on terms as the basic unit of logical analysis, and so it includes both supposition theory, together with its ramifications,[2] and the treatment of syncategorematic terms. It also includes other areas of investigation not directly linked with Aristotelian texts, notably obligations, consequences, and insolubles (see Chapters 10, 13, and 14).

Logic was at the heart of the arts curriculum, for it provided the techniques of analysis and much of the vocabulary found in philosophical, scientific, and theological writing. Moreover, it trained students for participation in the disputations that were a central feature of medieval instruction, and whose structure, with arguments for and against a thesis, followed by a resolution, is reflected in many written works. This practical application affected the way in which logic developed. While medieval thinkers had a clear idea of argumentation as involving formal structures, they were not interested in the development of formal systems, and they did not see logic as in any way akin to mathematics.

---

[1] Most of the literature dealing with terminist logic is in the form of articles and book chapters. Two bibliographical guides are E. J. Ashworth, *The Tradition of Medieval Logic and Speculative Grammar from Anselm to the End of the Seventeenth Century. A Bibliography from 1836 Onwards* (Toronto: Pontifical Institute of Mediaeval Studies, 1978), and Fabienne Pironet, *The Tradition of Medieval Logic and Speculative Grammar from Anselm to the End of the Seventeenth Century. A Bibliography (1977–1994)* (Turnhout: Brepols, 1997). The classic source of material is L. M. de Rijk, *Logica modernorum: A Contribution to the History of Early Terminist Logic* (Assen: Van Gorcum, 1962–7) vol. I: *On the Twelfth-Century Theories of Fallacy*, and vol. II: *The Origin and Early Development of the Theory of Supposition*. Translations of various texts are found in N. Kretzmann and E. Stump (eds.) *The Cambridge Translations of Medieval Philosophical Texts*, vol. 1: *Logic and the Philosophy of Language* (Cambridge: Cambridge University Press, 1988). Useful discussions are provided by P. Osmund Lewry, "Grammar, Logic and Rhetoric 1220–1320," in J. Catto (ed.) *The History of the University of Oxford*, vol. I: *The Early Oxford Schools* (Oxford: Clarendon Press 1984) 401–33, and by Norman Kretzmann *et al.* (eds.) *The Cambridge History of Later Medieval Philosophy: From the Rediscovery of Aristotle to the Disintegration of Scholasticism. 1100–1600* (Cambridge: Cambridge University Press, 1982).

[2] Not all of these ramifications will be discussed below. I shall omit the discussions of non-referring terms and of relations.

Logic involved the study of natural language, albeit a natural language (Latin) that was often regimented to make formal points, and it had a straightforwardly cognitive orientation. The purpose of logic was to separate the true from the false by means of argument, and to lead from known premises to a previously unknown conclusion. In this process, the avoidance of error was crucial, so there was a heavy emphasis on the making of distinctions and on the detection of fallacies. The procedures involved often have the appearance of being ad hoc, and modern attempts to draw precise parallels between medieval theories as a whole and the results of contemporary symbolic logic are generally doomed to failure, even though there are many fruitful partial correlations.

The core of the logic curriculum was provided by the works of Aristotle with supplements from Boethius, Porphyry, and the anonymous author of the *Liber sex principiorum* (about the last six categories), once attributed to Gilbert of Poitiers. The *logica vetus*, or Old Logic, included Porphyry's *Isagoge*, Aristotle's *Categories* and *De interpretatione*, and the *Liber sex principiorum*. During the twelfth century the *logica nova*, or New Logic, was rediscovered. It included the rest of the Organon, namely Aristotle's *Topics*, *Sophistical Refutations*, *Prior Analytics* and *Posterior Analytics*. Boethius's discussion of Topics, or ways of finding material for arguments, was also part of the curriculum, though in the fourteenth century his *De differentiis topicis* was largely replaced by the account of Topics given by Peter of Spain in his *Tractatus*. Together these works provided a basis for the study of types of predication, the analysis of simple categorical propositions and their relations of inference and equivalence, the analysis of modal propositions, categorical and modal syllogisms, fallacies, dialectical Topics, and scientific reasoning as captured in the demonstrative syllogism. The texts were lectured on and were the subject of detailed commentaries. Nonetheless, a need was felt for simplified introductions to the material and for the discussion of issues that were at best only hinted at by Aristotle.

NEW DEVELOPMENTS

The new developments of the late twelfth and thirteenth centuries were presented via new techniques and new genres of writing. The new techniques grew out of late twelfth-century use of *instantiae* or counterexamples, and they involved the use of *sophismata* or puzzle-cases intended to draw attention to difficulties and weaknesses in logical definitions and rules (see Chapter 14). The new texts fell into two groups: the *summulae* or general introductions, and shorter texts devoted to single issues. These writings are referred to in various ways. De Rijk has popularized a late fifteenth-century use of the phrase *logica modernorum* (the logic of the moderns) as a label for the *summulae* and for individual works on supposition theory and related issues. The latter are often called *parva logicalia* (the 'little logicals'), and sometimes the *parva logicalia* are also taken to include the texts on consequences, insolubles, and obligations.[3]

Important *summulae* were written in the fourteenth century by William of Ockham, John Buridan and Albert of Saxony (see Chapter 12), but here I shall focus on six of the extant thirteenth-century *summulae*, three associated with Oxford and three associated with continental Europe. The earliest English text chosen is the anonymous *Logica "Cum sit nostra,"* so called after its opening words, which may have been written in the late twelfth or the early thirteenth century, and which was still being used in one form or another at Oxford at the end of the thirteenth century.[4] It was followed by the *Introductiones in logicam* of William of Sherwood, written in the late 1230s or 1240s, and the *Summulae dialectices* of the Franciscan Roger Bacon, written around 1250. The most prominent continental work is the highly successful *Tractatus*, also called *Summulae logicales*, by Peter of Spain, probably written in the south of France or northern Spain between 1230 and 1245. Peter of Spain used to be identified with the Portuguese scholar who became Pope John XXI, but recent research has concluded that he was a Spanish Dominican, though attempts to identify him more precisely have so far failed.[5] The slightly later *Summe Metenses* has been identified as the work of Nicholas of Paris, and dates from 1240–50. Finally, there is the *Logica* of Lambert, probably begun in the 1250s and probably issued in its final form between 1263 and 1265. The author is often taken to be the Dominican Lambert of Auxerre, but could well be his contemporary, Lambert of Lagny. All these uncertainties of authorship and dating make it somewhat difficult to trace lines of influence, but with respect to content we can be clear. All the *summulae* contain material explaining elements of the Aristotelian curriculum, though the *Logica "Cum sit nostra"* and William of Sherwood omit the categories and none takes up demonstrative logic, the subject of the *Posterior Analytics*. In addition, they all contain the material about supposition and related topics that will be discussed in the last sections of this chapter.

Supposition theory focused on the nouns and adjectives that function as subjects and predicates of propositions, and these categorematic terms were contrasted with the syncategorematic terms that exercise some logical function

---

[3] For a discussion of this vocabulary, see Neal Gilbert, "Ockham, Wyclif, and the 'Via Moderna'," *Miscellanea Mediaevalia* 9 (1974) pp. 111–15, and H. A. G. Braakhuis, "School Philosophy and Philosophical Schools: The Semantic-Ontological Views in the Cologne Commentaries on Peter of Spain, and the 'Wegestreit'," *Miscellanea Mediaevalia* 20 (1989) esp. pp. 1–2 and 6.

[4] For an edition (excluding the final tract) see de Rijk, *Logica modernorum* II.2: 413–51.

[5] See Angel d'Ors, "Petrus Hispanus O.P., Auctor Summularum," *Vivarium* 35 (1997) 21–71, 39 (2001) 209–54, 41 (2003) 249–303.

within propositions. Syncategorematic terms included logical connectives such as 'and' and 'if-then,' quantifiers such as 'all' and 'some,' and negations such as 'none' and 'not,' but they also included the verbs 'begins' and 'ceases' because their implicit reference to past and future times affected the validity of inferences. One can argue 'I see Plato, therefore I see a man' but not 'I begin to see Plato, therefore I begin to see a man,' for I may have been looking at Socrates before I began to look at Plato. From the late twelfth century on, first in England and then on the continent, short texts were devoted to syncategorematic terms. The *Syncategoremata Monacensia* is a very early English text, and later texts were written by Peter of Spain, William of Sherwood, Nicholas of Paris, and Henry of Ghent.[6] These texts did not stand alone, in that they were closely associated with treatises on sophismata, on *abstractiones*, and on *distinctiones*, in all of which difficulties were solved by appeal to logical rules and distinctions relating to syncategorematic terms (see Chapter 14).

The discussion of *syncategoremata* was not entirely distinct from the discussion of categorematic terms. Some terms such as 'infinite' could be construed either categorematically or syncategorematically. For instance, in the invalid inference 'infinite is number, therefore < a > number is infinite,' the antecedent is taken syncategorematically, to show that one can keep adding to the number series, while the consequent indicates (falsely, according to medieval logicians) that there is a number which is actually infinite. Moreover, as we shall see, parts of supposition theory depend on the presence of syncategorematic terms. This gave rise to some differences of opinion. Thus in the first half of the thirteenth century the word '*omnis*' ('all' or 'every') was discussed, along with many other distributive terms, in the tracts on distribution associated with supposition theory in the *summulae* of Peter of Spain, Nicholas of Paris, and Lambert, but did not appear in the treatises on *syncategoremata* by Peter of Spain and Nicholas of Paris. However, it was discussed in the treatises on *syncategoremata* by the Englishmen William of Sherwood and Robert Bacon (not to be confused with Roger Bacon).[7] Moreover, a section on distribution is absent from William's *Introductiones*, and also from the *Logica "Cum sit nostra"* and the *Sumulae dialectices* of Roger Bacon.

Treatises on *syncategoremata* were most prominent in the thirteenth century, but they did not altogether disappear in the fourteenth century. For instance, the late fourteenth-century English logician Richard Lavenham wrote one.

[6] For translations of *Syncategoremata Monacensia* and material from Nicholas of Paris, see Kretzmann and Stump, *Cambridge Translations*, vol. I.

[7] See H. A. G. Braakhuis, "English Tracts on Syncategorematic Terms from Robert Bacon to Walter Burley," in H. A. G. Braakhuis *et al.* (eds.) *English Logic and Semantics from the End of the Twelfth Century to the Time of Ockham and Burleigh* (Nijmegen: Ingenium Publishers, 1981) pp. 138–40.

However, two other forms of writing come to the fore in the fourteenth century. First, there are a lot of short treatises on particular syncategorematic terms, including 'begins' and 'ceases' (*incipit* and *desinit*), and terms with the power of producing purely confused supposition (see below). Second, and most important, are the treatises on the proofs of terms (or proofs of propositions), whose best-known example is the *Speculum puerorum* of Richard Billingham, an Oxford author of the mid-fourteenth century. In this context, a proof seems to be a method of clarifying a sentence containing a particular sort of term, or of showing how one might justify that sentence. There were three groups of terms. Resoluble terms are those whose presence calls for explanation or clarification through ostensive reference, as captured in an expository syllogism (that is, one with singular terms). Thus 'A man runs' is resolved into the expository syllogism 'This runs; and this is a man; therefore a man runs.' Exponible terms are those whose presence calls for exposition of the sentence in terms of a set of equivalent sentences. For instance, the sentence 'Only a man is running,' which contains the exclusive term 'only,' is expounded as 'A man is running and nothing other than a man is running.' Other exponible terms are exceptives, such as 'except,' reduplicatives, such as 'inasmuch as,' 'begins' and 'ceases,' 'infinite,' and so on. In fact, they are the very terms figured prominently in treatises on *syncategoremata*. Finally, there are 'official' or 'officiable' terms (*officiales*, *officiabiles*), so called because they performed a function (*officium*). They included any term that governed a whole sentence or that treated a whole sentence as modifiable, such as modal terms ('necessarily', 'possibly'), and such terms as 'know,' 'believe,' 'promise,' 'desire,' and 'owe.' Analysis of sentences containing such terms shows why they are referentially opaque when taken in the compounded sense. Treatises on proofs of terms were very popular into the late fourteenth and fifteenth century, but by the late fourteenth century they were joined by treatises which dealt with exponible terms alone, including one by Peter of Ailly and another falsely attributed to Peter of Spain.[8]

SIGNIFICATION

In order to understand supposition theory and its ramifications, we first have to consider the central semantic notion of signification. As Paul Spade has pointed out, we must not confuse signification, when presented as what Spade calls "a

---

[8] For more discussion of all this material, see E. J. Ashworth and Paul Spade, "Logic in Late Medieval Oxford," in J. I. Catto and R. Evans (eds.) *The History of the University of Oxford*, vol. II: *Late Medieval Oxford* (Oxford: Clarendon Press, 1992) 35–64.

psychologico-causal property of terms," with meaning.[9] The meaning of a term is not an entity to which the term is related in some way, but one can say that an utterance signifies or makes known an entity, whether conceptual or real, universal or particular. Moreover, meaning is not transitive, but signification is. Lambert wrote: "An utterance that is a sign of a sign – i.e., of a concept – will be a sign of the thing signified – i.e., of the thing; it is, however, a sign of the concept directly but a sign of the thing indirectly."[10] This is not to deny that medieval thinkers had a general notion of meaning. They did talk about sense (*sensus*), about the thought or content (*sententia*) of a phrase, and about the force of a word (*vis verbi*), and they often used the word *significatio* itself along with its cognates quite widely.

If we take signification in a narrow sense, as a technical notion, we find that there were two not entirely compatible approaches, each based on a sentence from Aristotle, and each emphasizing the role of concepts, whether the hearer's or the speaker's. According to the first approach, based on *De interpretatione* 16b19–21, to signify is to generate or establish an understanding. This definition places emphasis on the hearer, whereas the second approach ties the significative power of an utterance to its making known the speaker's concepts. The crucial text is *De interpretatione* 16a3–4, read as saying "Spoken words are signs of concepts." Aristotle, as interpreted by medieval commentators, had gone on to say that concepts were similitudes or signs of things (*De interpretatione* 16a6–8), and this raised the question of what is meant by 'thing.' In other words, what is it that we understand when an utterance such as 'man' or 'animal' establishes an understanding? The usual assumption in the thirteenth century was that the understanding is of some kind of universal, an essence or common nature, and when logicians asked whether spoken words primarily signified concepts or things, the issue was whether concepts or common natures should be taken as the primary significates of an utterance. Whatever the final view adopted, individual objects were not themselves direct or primary significates. Indeed, Lambert makes it clear that a term such as 'man' signifies humanity, but supposits for Plato and Socrates (ed. Alessio, p. 206).

The terms of the debate were to change completely in the fourteenth century, first with the insistence of Scotus, like others before him, that individuals can be grasped by the intellect, but more especially with the reappearance of nominalism, the doctrine that all that exists are individual things, and that only concepts can be common or universal (see Chapters 12 and 48). The question

---

[9] Paul Spade, "The Semantics of Terms," in Kretzmann *et al.*, *The Cambridge History of Later Medieval Philosophy*, p. 188.
[10] Tr. Kretzmann and Stump, in *Cambridge Translations*, vol. I, p. 105; ed. Alessio, p. 206.

whether words primarily signify concepts or things was now construed as the question: does a word signify an individual thing in the world directly, or does it signify first the concept that is a necessary condition for signification? Even so, both nominalists and realists could agree that when we say 'Some men are running,' we are talking about individual men and their actions rather than about concepts or about universal natures.

SUPPOSITION THEORY

The roots of supposition theory can be found in grammar and in logic, particularly in reaction to the absorption of Aristotle's *Sophistical Refutations* and the general problem of fallacies, and perhaps also in theology, though here there is not sufficient evidence to determine how far logicians and theologians interacted, or who influenced whom. It is certainly the case that theologians felt a need to determine types of reference, particularly in the area of Trinitarian doctrine, where distinctions have to be made between the Godhead or essence, the three Persons, and the Notions, that is, those relations such as paternity and sonship which constitute the three Persons. The theologian Stephen Langton, probably writing before 1207, asserted that there were three modes of supposition, essential, personal, and notional (*De persona*, ed. Bieniak, p. 99), and William of Auxerre made the same claim in his *Summa aurea*, adding that the first two modes are natural, in that they also apply to created things (ed. Ribaillier *et al.*, I: 113–14). Later, Aquinas uses various elements of supposition theory in his discussion of the Trinity in his *Summa theologiae*.[11]

The vocabulary of supposition theory seems to be first found in the grammarians. Peter Helias, the twelfth-century commentator on Priscian, used the term *suppositum* semantically, to indicate the bearer of a form or property,[12] but shortly afterwards, from the 1260s onward, grammarians also used the notion purely syntactically. The verb *supponere* meant "to put as a subject term," and it was contrasted with *apponere*, "to put as a predicate term."[13] The terminology made its way into logical treatises, and both uses are needed to make sense of thirteenth-century discussions, particularly of the questions whether

---

[11] See, e.g., *Summa theol.* 1a q. 39. The reference to natural supposition in 1a 39.5c should not be taken as a reference to natural supposition in the logicians' sense to be discussed below.

[12] See, e.g., Peter Helias, *Summa super Priscianum*, ed. Reilly, p. 891. For discussion, see Sten Ebbesen, "Early Supposition Theory (12th–13th Century)," *Histoire Epistémologie Langage* 3 (1981) 35–48. Cf. Aquinas, *Summa theol.* 3a 2.3c on why "this man" is called a *suppositum*.

[13] See C. H. Kneepkens, "'Suppositio' and 'supponere' in 12th-Century Grammar," in J. Jolivet and A. de Libera (eds.) *Gilbert de Poitiers et ses contemporains: aux origines de la Logica modernorum* (Naples: Bibliopolis, 1987) 325–51. The passage about *supponere* and *apponere* frequently attributed to Peter Helias is a later interpolation (ed. Reilly, p. 448, apparatus).

supposition is only a property of substantival nouns, and whether supposition is only a property of grammatical subjects.

In logical treatises, the notion of *suppositio* was joined with the notions of *copulatio* and *appellatio*, and all three terms were used in various ways. The *Logica "Cum sit nostra"* starts by defining supposition in terms of signification: it is the designation or signification of a substantival term. It occurs only when something is put under an *appositum* or predicate, and so it is also described as the signification of a term that can be a subject (*sermonis subicibilis significatio*). In turn, *appellatio* is the time-free signification of a predicable term, and also what a common term has when compared to its inferiors. *Copulatio* is properly speaking the property of a verb, since it is the time-bound signification of a predicable term, and verbs are characterized by containing reference to time.[14] William of Sherwood has a somewhat different approach. Supposition is a property of substantival terms, but in actual supposition it characterizes subjects. If one considers habitual supposition, a term's aptitude for supposition, then supposition is the signification of something as subsistent, and can belong to both subjects and predicates. *Copulatio* is a property of adjectives and participles as well as of verbs, and *appellatio* belongs to terms referring to present existents (*Introductiones*, ed. Brands and Kann, pp. 132–4, 154–6). Peter of Spain and Lambert are clear that supposition is not a type of signification, but rather a property of signifying terms. For them, supposition is the acceptance of a substantival term for something, so it is not necessarily propositional and it can belong to both subjects and predicates; *copulatio* is the acceptance of an adjectival term for something; and appellation is the acceptance of a term for existent things.[15] Yet other uses of the three notions can be found, but in what follows I shall ignore these refinements, and speak as if supposition is a general property of subjects and predicates, nouns and adjectives. And since this broad usage becomes quite standard, leaving little room for *copulatio* or appellation in the sense just specified, I will likewise set aside these latter two notions.

SUPPOSITION THEORY AND TYPES OF REFERENCE

One can think of supposition theory as a theory of reference, but it is not a theory in the sense of an explanation of how it is that a linguistic expression designates one or more particular things in the world. Instead, supposition

---

[14] *Logica "Cum sit nostra"* in de Rijk, *Logica modernorum* II.2: 446–51.
[15] Peter of Spain, *Tractatus*, ed. de Rijk, pp. 80, 197; Lambert, *Logica*, ed. Alessio, pp. 206–7, 211. Lambert recognizes a wider sense of supposition that includes adjectives (p. 207), and he also recognizes the grammatical sense of appellation by which a common term appellates its inferiors.

theory is concerned with establishing what type of thing a term can refer to, given the predicate it is associated with, and what range of things it can extend over, given the presence or absence of ampliative and restrictive terms. These terms have the function of extending or limiting the range of reference. Thus 'can' is an ampliative term in the sentence 'A man can run,' since it extends the reference of 'man' to future men, and 'white' is a restrictive term when it appears in the subject phrase 'white men,' since it limits the reference of 'men' to a subgroup.

Supposition was normally divided into material, simple, and personal supposition. A term has material supposition when it is associated with such predicates as 'has three letters' and 'is a noun.'[16] These predicates have in common that they mention some feature of a term or its equiforms without using it in accordance with its specific signification. However, it is a mistake to think that material supposition was the medieval way of talking about modern quotation devices, though the not infrequent use of the French word 'li' (or 'ly') to indicate material supposition looks very like such a device. A term with material supposition was an ordinary significative term in a special sentential context; it was not a new term formed by producing the name of a name, as in ' "Dog" is the name of a dog.' Nor did every logician recognize material supposition explicitly. Both Roger Bacon and Lambert included it under simple supposition,[17] and both the *Logica* "*Cum sit nostra*" and Peter of Spain omitted it.

Simple supposition occurs when a name is taken for its significate, as in 'Man is a species.' One problem here was ontological. For nominalists, nothing could refer to a common nature, since common natures did not exist (see Chapter 12), and so some other account had to be found. Another problem has to do with the reference of terms in such sentences as 'Man is the worthiest creature among creatures' and 'Pepper is sold here and at Rome.' William of Sherwood distinguished three kinds of simple supposition (*Introductiones*, pp. 140–2). In 'Man is a species,' there is no reference to individuals; in 'Man is the worthiest creature among creatures,' the inclusion of individuals is indicated by the recommended addition of the phrase 'insofar as man' to the subject; and in 'Pepper is sold here and in Rome,' a vague or indeterminate relation of the significate to individuals is indicated, given that some peppercorns are sold here and some other peppercorns are sold in Rome. A third problem is found in Peter of Spain, who assigned simple supposition to the predicates of universal affirmative propositions (*Tractatus*, pp. 81, 83–8). This made sense

[16] For full discussion, see Claude Panaccio and Ernesto Perini-Santos, "Guillaume d'Ockham et la *suppositio materialis*," *Vivarium* 42 (2004) 202–24.
[17] Roger Bacon, *Summulae* II (ed. de Libera, p. 266); Lambert, *Logica*, p. 209.

insofar as a categorical proposition ascribes a property or form to a subject, but was unhelpful when accounting for the validity of such inferences as 'All A is B, therefore some B is A,' where the second occurrence of B must have personal supposition. Here it is relevant to note that medieval logicians did not regard inherence and identity accounts of propositional truth as mutually exclusive.[18] Indeed, they go together. Something is identical to an animal only if it has a certain substantial form, and something is identical to a white thing only if it has a certain quality (see also Chapter 12).

This brings us to personal supposition, whereby terms are taken to refer to individuals, as in 'Some man is running.' Peter of Spain and Lambert distinguished accidental personal supposition, in which the range of reference was restricted by the propositional context, from natural supposition, which allowed a term to have pre-propositional reference to all its referents, past, present, and future.[19] Nor did natural supposition belong only to terms standing alone, for John le Page, writing *ca.* 1235, said, like Buridan in the fourteenth century, that terms had natural supposition in universal necessary truths.[20] English logicians in the thirteenth century did not allow natural supposition. For them, all supposition was contextual, and the notion of ampliation had to be used when the subject of a proposition was to extend beyond present existent things. Moreover, they saw present-tense verbs as non-restrictive, while the Parisians saw them as restrictive. That being said, there was general agreement about types of restriction and ampliation. As we have already seen, the verb 'can' ampliates the range of reference, while the addition of an adjective, as in 'A white man runs,' restricts the range of reference. However, logicians explicitly denied that the predicate had a restrictive role.[21] In 'A man is white,' the range of reference is all men, not just white men.

TYPES OF PERSONAL SUPPOSITION

The doctrines of ampliation and restriction were not sufficient to answer such questions as why it is impossible to infer 'There is a head that everyone has' from 'Everyone has a head,' or 'There is a horse that I promise to you' from

---

[18] See John Malcolm, "A Reconsideration of the Identity and Inherence Theories of the Copula," *Journal of the History of Philosophy* 17 (1979) 383–400.

[19] Peter of Spain, *Tractatus*, p. 81; Lambert, *Logica*, p. 208.

[20] See Alain de Libera, "Supposition naturelle et appellation: aspects de la sémantique parisienne au XIIIe siècle," *Histoire Epistémologie Langage* 3 (1981) 63–77, and "La littérature des *Sophismata* dans la tradition terministe parisienne de la seconde moitié du XIIIe siècle," in M. Asztalos (ed.) *The Editing of Theological and Philosophical Texts from the Middle Ages* (Stockholm: Almqvist and Wiksell International, 1986) 213–44.

[21] Peter of Spain, *Tractatus*, p. 201; Lambert, *Logica*, p. 217; Bacon, *Summulae* II, pp. 280–2.

'I promise you a horse,' or 'Every donkey belonging to some man is running' from 'Every man has a donkey which is running.' In order to deal with these and other problems, personal supposition was divided into three types, discrete, determinate, and confused (a word that indicates plurality), and rules were provided to govern inferences involving these types.

Of the three standard types of personal supposition, discrete is the simplest. A term such as 'Socrates' or 'this man' has discrete supposition since it supposits for just one individual. A term has determinate supposition when it supposits for many things but its truth requires reference to just one individual, no matter who, while leaving open the possibility that more individuals are involved. The propositions 'A man is running' (*homo currit*) and 'Some man is running' (*aliquis homo currit*) are true if at least one man, no matter who, is running, and Roger Bacon remarked that a term with determinate supposition supposits for an individual in a disjunctive manner (*sub disiunctione*) (*Summulae* II, p. 274). It is important to emphasize the phrase "no matter who," since a distinction was made between sentences related to their non-linguistic context and sentences not so related. According to Peter of Spain, Nicholas of Paris and Lambert, if I say *Rex venit* ('< A > king is coming'), common usage indicates that reference should be restricted to the local ruler.[22] However, logicians did not usually conceive of context so broadly, but were generally concerned only with the intra-propositional relations of terms.

Confused supposition differs from determinate supposition with respect to truth conditions, and it is further divided into two subtypes, confused and distributive supposition and merely confused supposition. Leaving aside the problem of common nouns with only one referent, such as 'sun' and 'phoenix' (to use medieval examples), standard common nouns extend over a plurality of things, and the truth of many propositions requires reference to more than one member of that plurality. In some cases, truth requires exhaustive reference. Thus, 'Every A is B' is true only if every single individual A is a B, and the truth of 'No A is B' requires both that every single A will fail to be a B and that every single B will fail to be an A. Hence the subjects of universal affirmative propositions were said to have confused and distributive supposition, as were the subjects and predicates of universal negative propositions. This kind of supposition allowed for descent to individuals. For instance, from 'All men are animals' one can infer that Socrates is an animal, and more generally one can infer that this man is an animal and the other man is an animal, and so on (*et sic*

---

[22] Peter of Spain, *Tractatus*, pp. 207–8; Nicholas of Paris (ed. de Rijk, *Logica modernorum* II.1: 463); Lambert, *Logica*, pp. 226–7.

de singulis).[23] Such descent could be impeded by other syncategorematic terms. For instance, one cannot argue from 'Only every A is B' to 'Only this A is B.'

Merely confused supposition was introduced to deal with the case in which reference is made to more than one member of a plurality without being exhaustive.[24] Consider the predicate of the universal affirmative proposition, 'All men are animals.' For this proposition to be true, each man must be identical to some animal or other, and a plurality of animals must be involved, since we will not want to say that every man is identical to one and the same animal. Nonetheless, even when each man has been identified with some distinct animal, all the non-human animals will be left over, and no descent to a conjunction or disjunction of sentences about individual animals is possible.

Originally, the notion of descent to individuals had been introduced in relation to confused and distributive supposition in order to further clarify what inferences were possible. During the fourteenth century, the notion of descent was applied to determinate and merely confused supposition as well, and gave rise to elaborate accounts of how propositions with quantified terms related both to conjunctions or disjunctions of propositions with individual terms and to propositions with disjoint terms (as in 'Socrates is this animal or that animal or the other animal').[25] Another later development was the recognition of propositions with conjoint terms as a tool for analyzing a fourth type of non-discrete supposition, called collective supposition.[26] This type applied to 'apostles' in 'All the apostles were twelve,' an example used in the thirteenth century to distinguish between collective and distributive senses of *omnis*.[27]

THE FATE OF TERMINIST LOGIC

Terminist logic as described above was dominant for most of the thirteenth century, and it continued to be prevalent in Oxford into the fourteenth century, though without any notable new developments. However, during the last decades of the thirteenth century and the beginning of the fourteenth century,

---

[23] See, e.g., *Logica "Cum sit nostra"* in De Rijk, *Logica modernorum* II.2: 447; Bacon, *Summulae* II, p. 267.

[24] Lambert writes "in connection with such supposition a common term is not interpreted for all its supposita" (tr. Kretzmann and Stump, p. 112; ed. Alessio, p. 211).

[25] See Paul Spade, "The Logic of the Categorical: The Medieval Theory of Descent and Ascent," in N. Kretzmann (ed.) *Meaning and Inference in Medieval Philosophy* (Dordrecht: Kluwer, 1988) 187–224.

[26] See Stephen Read, "Thomas of Cleves and Collective Supposition," *Vivarium* 29 (1991) 50–84.

[27] Peter of Spain, *Tractatus*, p. 210; Lambert, *Logica*, pp. 231–2. (The example is further discussed in Chapter 14.)

modist logic predominated in Paris, Erfurt, and Bologna (see Chapter 15), and it was only with the work of Ockham and Buridan that there was a general revival of supposition theory. The late fifteenth and early sixteenth centuries saw a number of interesting developments,[28] and, despite the attacks of the humanists, some elements of supposition theory persisted into the seventeenth century.

[28] See E. J. Ashworth, *Studies in Post-Medieval Semantics* (London: Variorum Reprints, 1985).

NOMINALIST SEMANTICS

GYULA KLIMA

OCKHAM'S SEMANTIC INNOVATIONS

The most significant development in the history of late medieval philosophy and theology was the emergence of late medieval nominalism, eventually culminating in the quasi-institutional separation of the realist "old way" (*via antiqua*) and the nominalist "modern way" (*via moderna*).[1] This chapter will confine itself to analyzing the fundamental changes in semantic theory initiated by William of Ockham, and brought to fruition by John Buridan. In order to be able to see the significance of these conceptual changes against the background of the older theory, the discussion begins with a brief sketch of those common characteristics of the "old semantics" that Ockham abandoned. After presenting Ockham's main reasons for breaking with the older model and sketching his alternative ideas, the discussion proceeds to a more detailed analysis of Buridan's radically new approach to constructing semantic theory.

The term 'realism' in connection with medieval philosophy is generally used to indicate a metaphysical position concerning universals, namely, the assumption of the existence of some abstract, universal entities expressed by our universal terms, such as 'man' or 'animal.'[2] But medieval realism as a semantic conception is more than just a theory of universals; it is rather a comprehensive conception of the relationships between language, thought, and reality. The easiest way to introduce the basic ideas of this conception is through the analysis of a simple example. Consider the proposition 'Every man is an animal.' When I refer to the sentence enclosed in quotation marks as a proposition, I use the term 'proposition' in the medieval sense, meaning the token-inscription

---

[1] For a detailed historical discussion of the late medieval separation of the *via antiqua* and the *via moderna*, see W. L. Moore, "Via Moderna," in J. Strayer (ed.) *Dictionary of Middle Ages* (New York: Scribner, 1989) XII: 406–9.

[2] For some of the historical and theoretical problems involved in this somewhat simplistic characterization, see Gyula Klima, "Nominalism," in E. K. Brown (ed.) *Elsevier's Encyclopedia of Language and Linguistics* (Elsevier: Oxford, 2006) VII: 648–52, and "The Medieval Problem of Universals," in E. Zalta (ed.) *The Stanford Encyclopedia of Philosophy* (http://plato.stanford.edu, Winter 2004).

between the quotes. But of course this inscription and its significative parts are meaningful to us only because reading it produces some understanding in our minds. The inscription 'biltrix' or the corresponding utterance is meaningless to us precisely because we literally have *no idea* what, if anything, someone writing or uttering it would mean by it. The understanding generated by the entire proposition in our minds is a complete thought, a "mental proposition," whereas the simpler acts of understanding corresponding to the meaningful units making up the proposition are the *concepts* making up the thought. The subject and predicate terms of this proposition are its categorematic terms, constituting the matter of the proposition, and the rest are its syncategorematic terms, determining its form (in this case, its being a universal, affirmative, categorical proposition).[3] The semantic properties of these terms are primarily determined by the concepts they immediately signify in the mind. Thus, the written term 'every' is syncategorematic, because it signifies a syncategorematic concept in the mind, whereas the subject and predicate terms are categorematic, because they signify categorematic concepts. (On categorematic and syncategorematic terms, see Chapter 11.)

The categorematic terms of this proposition are *common* terms (as opposed to *singular* terms, such as proper nouns). A categorematic term is common if it can be predicated of several things without equivocation – that is, by signifying the same concept in the mind. Clearly, if the proper name 'John' can be truly predicated of several individuals, then this is due to the fact that the name is used once according to the concept whereby we conceive of an individual named 'John,' and then again according to another concept, whereby we conceive of another individual, who also happens to be named 'John.' Hence the need to number the names of all the popes and kings named 'John,' where the numbering clearly indicates the equivocation. By contrast, we can truly predicate the term 'man' of all these individuals without any change of meaning – that is, according to the same concept – and as a result there is no need for numbering. But if there is no single individual that this term is the name of, then on account of what does it apply universally to all the individuals it is true of? This is one way of putting the *semantic* problem of universals. The typical medieval (moderate) realist answer is most succinctly stated by Thomas Aquinas – although he himself is relying heavily on the work of earlier scholars (see Chapter 11). Commenting on Aristotle's conception of the "semantic triangle" of words, concepts, and things (*De interpretatione* 1), he writes:

[3] For a detailed discussion of the distinction, see Gyula Klima, "Syncategoremata," in Brown, *Elsevier's Encyclopedia of Language and Linguistics* XII: 353–6.

names, verbs, and speech signify . . . conceptions of the intellect immediately, according to the teaching of Aristotle. They cannot immediately signify things, as is clear from their mode of signifying, for the name 'man' signifies human nature in abstraction from singulars; hence it is impossible that it immediately signify a singular man. The Platonists for this reason held that it signified the separated idea of man. But because in Aristotle's teaching man in the abstract does not really subsist, but is only in the mind, it was necessary for Aristotle to say that "vocal sounds signify the conceptions of the intellect immediately and things by means of them."

(*In De interp.* I.2 n. 5)[4]

Accordingly, the semantic function of common terms is determined by the representative function of the universal concepts they signify. This representative function, in turn, is due to the activity of the abstractive mind, which forms these concepts by abstracting the individualized natures of individual things from their individuating conditions. Thus, common terms are truly predicable of those things that actually have the natures or forms represented by the concepts they signify in the mind. Accordingly, common terms have a twofold signification: they *immediately signify* the concepts of the mind to which they are subordinated, and which therefore render them meaningful, but they *ultimately signify* the individualized natures or forms of the things represented by these concepts in an abstract, universal manner.

Besides their signification, these terms also have a referring function (*supposition*) determined not only by their signification, but also by their propositional context. Thus, the subject term of our sample proposition, 'Every man is an animal' (namely, 'man'), obviously has the function of standing for (*supponere pro*) individual humans, the things that actually have the nature represented by the corresponding concept. But in the proposition 'Man is a species' the same term *with the same signification* would have to stand for something else. Indeed, according to Peter of Spain, the term 'man' in this proposition would have to stand for the same thing that it would stand for in any affirmative proposition in which it is the predicate (as in 'Socrates is a man') – namely, human nature conceived in a universal manner.[5] But what ultimately makes the predicate

---

4 The same conception is also very clearly expressed at length in Lambert's *Logica* (*Summa Lamberti*), tr. N. Kretzmann and E. Stump, in *The Cambridge Translations of Medieval Philosophical Texts*, vol. I (Cambridge: Cambridge University Press, 1988) pp. 104–10. For the same type of reasoning concerning the signification of common terms, as used by Walter Burley against Ockham, see his *On the Purity of the Art of Logic* sec. 33 (tr. Spade, pp. 87–8).

5 Interestingly, Aquinas would disagree with Peter on this point. He argues that 'man' as a predicate term must stand for human nature according to its absolute consideration, which he would not identify with human nature insofar as it is a species. But this issue should not detain us in this context. For details, see Gyula Klima, " 'Socrates est species': Logic, Metaphysics and Psychology in St. Thomas Aquinas' Treatment of a Paralogism," in K. Jacobi (ed.) *Argumentationstheorie: Scholastische Forschungen zu den logischen und semantischen Regeln korrekten Folgerns* (Leiden: Brill, 1993)

'man' true of Socrates in 'Socrates is a man' is the actual existence (*esse*) of the humanity of Socrates, signified by the copula. Thus, the copula on this conception is not a mere syntactical marker of the composition of subject and predicate; it also has a significative function: signifying the individualized acts of existence of the ultimate *significata* of the predicate in the *supposita* of the subject. Moreover, according to Peter, not only the copula but also the other syncategorematic terms of a proposition have such a significative function: they signify certain ways of being (*modi essendi*) of the things signified by the categorematic terms.[6] The combination of the *significata* and *supposita* of categorematic and syncategorematic terms in turn yields the *significatum* of the whole proposition, the existence of which renders the proposition true. This is how these authors would interpret the Aristotelian dictum that "a sentence is true according as the thing [signified by the sentence] is or is not."[7] However, this "thing" is not on a par with ordinary things. It is, rather, a *being of reason* (*ens rationis*), on a par with abstract universals, relations of reason, negations, and privations – an object of thought, having some foundation in reality.[8]

Thus, summarizing the *via antiqua* analysis of the proposition 'Every man is an animal,' we can say the following: this written proposition is true if and only if the corresponding mental proposition is true, which in turn is true if and only if its *significatum*, the corresponding "real proposition" – which would be variously called *enuntiabile*, *dictum*, or *complexe significabile* – exists (see Chapter 26). But the existence of these quasi-entities is conditioned on the way things are in real existence. In particular, since our sample proposition is a universal affirmative, it is true if and only if all the corresponding singular propositions are jointly true, which in turn are true if and only if there are human beings (individuals informed by individualized instances of the human nature that is signified by the subject), each of whom is actually informed by animality, the nature signified by the predicate.

489–504, and "The Medieval Problem of Universals," in Zalta, *The Stanford Encyclopedia of Philosophy* (http://plato.stanford.edu, Fall 2000) esp. sec. 7.

[6] For a more detailed account of Peter of Spain's conception of syncategoremata, see Gyula Klima, "Peter of Spain, the Author of the *Summulae*," in J. Gracia and T. Noone (eds.) *Blackwell's Companion to Philosophy in the Middle Ages* (Oxford: Blackwell, 2003) 526–31, and de Rijk and Spruyt's excellent bilingual edition of his *Syncategoremata*.

[7] See Cajetan (Thomas de Vio), *In Praedicamenta*, ed. Laurent, p. 87: "And note that Aristotle's maxim posited here, 'A sentence is true according as the thing is or is not' [*Cat*. 4b8], is to be understood not of the thing that is the subject or the predicate of this sentence, but of the thing that is signified by the whole sentence – e.g., when it is said 'a man is white,' this is true not because a man or a white thing is, but because a man's being white is, for this is what is signified by this sentence."

[8] For a discussion of how this semantic conception *necessitates* positing such quasi-entities, see Gyula Klima, "The Changing Role of *Entia Rationis* in Medieval Philosophy: A Comparative Study with a Reconstruction," *Synthese* 96 (1993) 25–59.

As can be seen, on this conception truth and existence are closely intertwined notions. The truth of a proposition primarily requires the (quasi-)existence of the corresponding complex state of affairs, which in turn requires the existence of a whole array of entities (and quasi-entities) as the various semantic values of the components of the proposition. The payoff of this complex semantic picture is a very simple, uniform theory of truth ("a proposition is true if and only if what it signifies exists," disregarding complications with self-referential propositions), as opposed to the clause-by-clause specification of different types of truth-conditions for different types of propositions found in nominalist or in contemporary semantics – but apparently at the expense of an "overpopulated" ontology containing various layers of entities: substances, their accidents and/or their privations, underpinning the existence of the *significata* of propositions. This, however, is precisely the price a nominalist like Ockham is not willing to pay.

Extravagance in ontology is one of Ockham's major complaints against "the moderns," as he is wont to refer to representatives of the older realist theory. The main root of their errors, according to Ockham, was "multiplying beings according to the multiplicity of terms . . . which is erroneous and leads far away from the truth" (*Summa logicae* I.51 [*Opera phil.* I: 171]). To be sure, Ockham's charge that the older conception is committed to a "Porphyrian forest" in its ontology – that is, a system of categories having a distinct *Porphyrian tree* of essential predicables in each Aristotelian category – is not entirely justified, for his realist predecessors did have their own metaphysical strategies of reducing the ontological commitment of their semantics.[9] It is at least true, though, that their semantics, involving so many different types of semantic values for all kinds of terms (categorematic as well as syncategorematic) and propositions, sets up a whole array of metaphysical problems concerning the nature and conditions of identity and distinctness of these semantic values, many of which Ockham regards as easily avoidable in a different semantic framework.

Ockham's arguments against the older framework, therefore, can be sorted into those that directly attack some of the (perceived) ontological commitments of that theory as leading to some patent absurdity, and those that are designed to show that such commitments are easily avoidable if one has the right semantic theory. He uses the first type of argument when he argues against the perceived commitment of the older theory to ten distinct classes of entities in the ten Aristotelian categories. The existence of such distinct entities, he charges, leads

---

[9] For a detailed discussion of this issue, see Gyula Klima, "Ockham's Semantics and Ontology of the Categories," in P. V. Spade (ed.) *The Cambridge Companion to Ockham* (Cambridge: Cambridge University Press, 1999) 118–42.

to various logical or physical absurdities. For example, a logical absurdity would be that one thing could be equal to another on account of an entity from the category of Relation – equality – inhering in it, even if it does not have the same quantity as another thing. Conversely, one thing might be unequal to another for lack of this inherent equality-thing, even if they are of the same quantity. A physical absurdity would be that the movement of a donkey here on earth would have to cause an infinity of position-things or distance-things (from the categories of either Position or Where) in the fixed stars as their relative position and distance to the donkey changes with its movement (see *Summa logicae* I.50).

Another example of this sort of argumentation is the array of arguments Ockham uses against Scotus's conception of universals and individuation, which also illustrates the fact that what bothers Ockham in the older theory is not only the extent of its ontological commitment, but also the obscurity of the distinctions on which it relies. For instance, Ockham treats as absurd Scotus's claim that the common nature of a thing is *formally* but not *really* distinct from the individual difference that individuates it. Ockham insists to the contrary that if there is any distinction in things outside the mind, then that distinction must be a real distinction. He offers this argument: clearly, a common nature is not formally distinct from itself (as nothing differs from itself in any way outside the mind); but it is formally distinct from the individual difference (according to Scotus); therefore, the common nature is not the same as – that is, it is really distinct from – the individual difference, which contradicts Scotus's original claim (ibid., I.16 [I: 54]).

The real strength and novelty of Ockham's approach, however, lies not in these destructive arguments (which, after all, might be handled in the older framework), but rather in presenting a viable alternative that need not entail either the ontological commitments or the obscurities of the earlier theory. Thus, wielding his famous Razor,[10] Ockham and his followers are entitled to get rid of both, even without having to argue against them any further.

In fact, this was precisely the kind of argumentation (coming from his confrère, Walter Chatton) that convinced Ockham himself to abandon his early view of universal concepts, according to which the concepts expressed by our common terms are universal objects of thought (that is, mere beings of reason, *entia rationis*), the so-called *ficta*.[11] The important feature of that argumentation from our point of view is its pointing out that whatever

---

[10] Ockham's Razor, often quoted in the form "entities are not to be multiplied without necessity," clearly licenses the elimination of unwanted entities, even if no patent absurdity follows from their assumption. It is enough to present a viable alternative theory that can do without them.
[11] Cf. Rondo Keele, "Walter Chatton," in Zalta, *The Stanford Encyclopedia of Philosophy* (http://plato.stanford.edu, Fall 2006). For an excellent, detailed discussion of Ockham's theory of concepts in general, see Claude Panaccio, *Ockham on Concepts* (Aldershot: Ashgate, 2004).

semantic features of common terms Ockham's *ficta* were posited to explain can equally well be explained by the properties of the corresponding mental acts. After all, the universal signification of our common terms is due to the universal representation of the concepts to which they are subordinated. But such universal representation does not require any universal objects. For a universal representation does not have to represent *a universal thing* (whether as an object in reality or as an object in the mind); rather it has to represent several individuals indifferently, *in a universal manner*. However, this function can be carried out by a concept, which for Ockham is just the mental act itself, representing several individuals indifferently at once. Hence there is no need to posit ontologically dubious *ficta* as intermediary objects between mental acts and their ultimate, individual objects.

Abandoning *ficta* naturally leads to abandoning the entire distinct realm of beings of reason (*entia rationis*) demanded by the older conception. Thus, once *ficta* are eliminated, beings of reason for Ockham are not distinct from real beings in the two really distinct categories he allows, namely, substance and quality: a being of reason is either a real quality inhering in reason (that is, a concept, which is a mental act), or something outside the mind that is denominated with the further connotation of some quality inhering in reason (in the way that money is just a piece of paper, which can be denoted as 'money' only by connoting people's mental acts whereby they are willing to accept it as legal tender).[12] This move, together with reducing the number of distinct categories of real entities to two, certainly did provide Ockham with the type of "desert landscape" a nominalist likes to see in his ontology. But this strategy inevitably raises a number of issues about the viability of this semantic theory: in particular, how is it possible to provide a sufficiently fine-grained semantics for our language, given the apparent dearth of distinct semantic values in this parsimonious nominalist ontology? Taking his cue from Ockham, it was John Buridan who first provided a comprehensive, detailed answer to this question, in his massive *Summulae de dialectica*, and so in what follows it will be helpful to consider his account together with Ockham's.

BURIDAN'S NOMINALIST SEMANTICS

The signification and supposition of terms

Ockham and Buridan subscribe to the idea of the Aristotelian "semantic triangle" just as much as their predecessors did: the terms (both categorematic and

---

[12] For a detailed discussion, contrasting Ockham's conception with Aquinas's, see Klima, "The Changing Role of *Entia Rationis*."

syncategorematic) of the proposition 'Every man is an animal' are meaningful on account of being subordinated to concepts of the human mind, whereby we conceive of things outside the mind. However, the two share a radically different conception of what these concepts are and how they function semantically – that is, how these concepts map our words onto a parsimoniously conceived nominalist ontology.

In the first place, the signification of the categorematic terms of our sample proposition is determined by the concepts whereby we conceive indifferently all human beings and whereby we conceive indifferently all animals, whether they are present to us or not (that is, whether they are past, present, future, or merely possible). Thus, these terms are construed as signifying precisely these individuals, and not some common nature existing individualized, but represented in an abstract manner by the corresponding concept. Since such a concept represents the individuals themselves indifferently, the corresponding term signifies the same in the same way. To be sure, the same individuals can be represented in a number of different ways, in terms of different concepts: thus, human beings can be conceived not only absolutely, but also in relation to other things, say, as children or parents, or as predator or prey. This is the basis for the nominalist distinction between *absolute* and *connotative* (or in Buridan's terminology, *appellative*) concepts and the corresponding terms. Connotative terms, besides indifferently signifying certain things, also connote others. The term 'parent,' for instance, signifies parents but connotes their children. However, it is important to note that the class of connotative terms is broader than that of relative terms. There are a number of syntactically monadic terms (say, 'predator') that nominalists would classify as connotative, because they are subordinated to complex connotative concepts (say, the concept explicated by the phrase 'animal preying on other animals'). Thus, the deceptive syntactic simplicity of such connotative terms hides a conceptual complexity, which can be revealed by providing their nominal definitions – that is, complex phrases whose syntactical structure matches the compositional structure of the complex concepts to which these terms are subordinated.[13]

The significance of this point should be clear once we realize how nominal definitions can serve to eliminate unwanted ontological commitment in the Aristotelian categories. In the first place, relative concepts and terms obviously need not carry the kind of ontological commitment they appear to have in

---

[13] For a discussion of the idea of conceptual composition and the mere *semantic* complexity of complex concepts that is compatible with their ontological simplicity, see the introduction to my translation of the *Summulae*, pp. xxxvii–xliv. For the same ideas in Ockham, and an account of the controversial issue of whether he admitted simple connotative concepts, see Panaccio, *Ockham on Concepts*, esp. ch. 4.

the older framework. For instance, the relative term 'father' in the nominalist framework is not construed as signifying some inherent "relation-thing" in a man somehow joining him to a child; rather, it merely signifies the man in relation to the child on account of the man's being conceived as the progenitor of the child.[14] Monadic terms in other accidental categories that may appear to signify inherent accident-things may also be interpreted as being subordinated to complex connotative concepts. This method of elimination by definition can easily get rid of the older framework's apparent need for a "Porphyrian forest."

Thus, as far as their signification is concerned, common categorematic terms in the nominalist framework need not carry commitment either to ten classes of obscure quasi-entities (universal thought-objects or less-than-numerically-one common natures and their like) or to several other classes of spooky inherent entities (such as the when-ness of temporal things);[15] the signification of any such categorematic term may be construed either as the indifferent absolute signification of ordinary entities, or as the indifferent signification-plus-connotation of the same, on account of the corresponding absolute or connotative concepts. But those concepts form just another set of ordinary entities: real inherent qualities of individual minds, which Ockham and Buridan never wanted to eliminate from their ontology.[16] Indeed, the same goes for syncategorematic concepts: they are also inherent qualities of the mind, which however do not represent anything in themselves, but rather have the function of modifying the representative function of categorematic concepts by joining them in complex concepts, such as mental propositions expressed by spoken and written propositions, or the complex concepts expressible by complex spoken or written terms.

Therefore, admitting the immediate *significata* of our terms commits us merely to individual qualities inhering in singular minds. Acknowledging the ultimate *significata* of the same commits us only to entities in the permitted categories (namely, Substance, Quality, and – for Buridan but not Ockham – Quantity), for the ultimate *significata* of terms pertaining to the other *logical* categories will be construed as entities in the same *ontological* categories, the terms variously

---

[14] For a detailed discussion of the example with diagrams comparing the nominalist and realist conceptions, see again my introduction to the *Summulae*, pp. l–lx.

[15] This was actually posited by Ockham's staunch opponent, pseudo-Campsall, in his aptly titled work, *The Very Useful Realist Logic against Ockham of Campsall the Englishman*, 38.12.

[16] In principle, however, as far as their semantics is concerned, Ockham and Buridan could have eliminated quality as a distinct category. See the excellent discussion in Marilyn McCord Adams, *William Ockham* (Notre Dame, IN: University of Notre Dame Press, 1987) I: 277–85. See also Gyula Klima, "Buridan's Logic and the Ontology of Modes," in S. Ebbesen and R. Friedman (eds.) *Medieval Analyses in Language and Cognition* (Copenhagen: Royal Danish Academy of Sciences and Letters, 1999) 473–95.

connoting further entities in those same categories. Furthermore, since the *supposita* of these terms in various propositional contexts are either their ultimate *significata* (when these terms stand in *personal supposition*), or their immediate *significata* (when they stand in *simple supposition*), or themselves or similar token-terms (when they stand in *material supposition*), the supposition of terms does not have to commit us to any other entities either.[17]

The semantics of propositions

Given the semantic properties they attribute to categorematic terms, Ockham and Buridan adopt a new theory of the copula, which historians of medieval logic usually refer to as the "identity theory," as opposed to the earlier "inherence theory."[18] According to the identity theory, the function of the affirmative copula is *not* that of asserting the existence of the *significatum* of the whole proposition (which in turn is grounded in the actual existence of the ultimate *significata* of the predicate in the *supposita* of the subject), but rather asserting the identity of the *supposita* of the subject with the *supposita* of the predicate. Therefore, the copula will not signify existence at all, although the identity of the relevant *supposita* will still *require* the existence of those *supposita*; so affirmative propositions will still have existential import in this framework.[19]

From the semantic point of view, what is more important is that the identity theory leads to a theory of truth that is radically different from that of the older semantics. Since the function of the affirmative copula is that of asserting the co-supposition of the categorematic terms of propositions, the truth conditions of propositions need not be construed in terms of the existence/actuality of

---

[17] Buridan actually lumps together material and simple supposition under the heading of material supposition, in contrast to personal supposition. But this is just a matter of terminology, as he notes in *Summulae* IV.3.2.

[18] To be sure, the identity theory had been around in the earlier framework as well, as a compatible *complement* to the inherence theory. Aquinas, for instance, allows both analyses, although he regards the inherence analysis as "more appropriate" (*magis propria*), and in the case of adjectival predicates the only acceptable one, e.g., in *Sent.* III.5.3.3 *expositio* and *Summa theol.* 1a 39.6 ad 2. But the nominalists use the identity analysis to the *exclusion* of the inherence analysis, to eliminate its (perceived) ontological commitments in their *semantic* theory, even if they admit really inherent qualities in their ontology. Thus, they would allow that 'Socrates is white' is true just in case whiteness inheres in Socrates, but in their view the *semantic function* of the predicate is *not* to signify this inherent whiteness, and the function of the copula is *not* to assert its existence: the function of the predicate is to signify white things connoting their whiteness, and the function of the copula is to assert the identity of such a thing with Socrates.

[19] For more on this issue, including the complications concerning *natural supposition* and *ampliative contexts* that cancel out this existential import, see Gyula Klima, "Existence and Reference in Medieval Logic," in A. Hieke and E. Morscher (eds.) *New Essays in Free Logic* (Dordrecht: Kluwer, 2001) 197–226, and Terence Parsons, "The Traditional Square of Opposition," in Zalta, *The Stanford Encyclopedia of Philosophy* (http://plato.stanford.edu, winter 2006).

their *significata*, but rather in terms of the co-supposition of their terms. This will lead to the abandonment of the "neat" Aristotelian definition of truth for all types of propositions, but this precisely is the price a nominalist is willing to pay. Thus, instead of having to deal with a dubious ontology of the *significata* of propositions, Buridan will opt for a clause-by-clause statement of the truth conditions of different types of proposition one by one, based on their syntactical structure. To be sure, in the "conservative" spirit of medieval philosophy, he also preserves the Aristotelian formula, but merely as a somewhat improper abbreviation of what he really means by it. As he says:

> But in the end we should note – since we can use names by convention (*ad placitum*), and many people commonly use this way of putting the matter – that with respect to every true proposition we say 'It is so,' and with respect to every false one we say 'It is not so,' and I do not intend to eliminate this way of speaking. But for the sake of brevity I may use it, often intending by it not what it signifies on account of its primary imposition, but the diverse causes of truth and falsity assigned above for diverse propositions.
>
> (*Summulae* IX [*Sophismata*] ch. 2 concl. 14)

So, truth for Buridan is no longer tied to the existence of the *significata* of propositions, such as the *complexe significabilia* that Gregory of Rimini posited in the 1340s.[20] Therefore, he does not need such *significata* for specifying the truth conditions of propositions at all.

Buridan still needs an account of propositional signification for other purposes, however, such as accounting for the semantics of sentential nominalizations (accusative with infinitive or gerundive constructions, or what we call "that-clauses"). Intuitively, these would seem to have the function of referring to what the corresponding propositions signify. (For example, 'Socrates to be wise,' 'Socrates's being wise,' or 'that Socrates is wise' as the direct object of 'Socrates desires' would seem to have the function of referring to what the proposition 'Socrates is wise' signifies.) However, since Buridan is absolutely not willing to buy into a dubious ontology of *complexe significabilia*, he has to bite the bullet and provide a semantic account of propositions and the corresponding nominalizations according to which propositions do not signify anything over and above what their categorematic terms signify. Thus, he claims that the contradictory propositions 'God is God' and 'God is not God,' as well as the simple term 'God,' signify one and the same thing, namely, God. However, this does not render them synonymous, for although they signify the same ultimately (*ad extra*), they clearly signify different concepts in the mind (*apud mentem*),

---

[20] See Gregory of Rimini, *Sent.* 1.1, and the discussion in Gabriel Nuchelmans, *Theories of the Proposition: Ancient and Medieval Conceptions of the Bearers of Truth and Falsity* (Amsterdam: North-Holland, 1973) pp. 227–37. (See also Chapter 26.)

whereby the mind conceives of the same absolutely simple thing in different ways, in a simple or a complex fashion.

Sentential nominalizations, however, need not always stand for what the corresponding propositions ultimately signify. Functioning just as any other complex categorematic term does, these nominalizations may also be taken materially or personally. Suppositing materially, they stand for the corresponding token-propositions, as in 'Every that no man runs is possible.'[21] But Buridan realizes that sentential nominalizations sometimes cannot be interpreted this way. For example, when we truly say 'To cut is to act,' this cannot be interpreted as making the claim that a proposition 'Someone is cutting' is identical with a proposition 'Someone is acting,' for that interpretation is obviously false. Therefore, Buridan says that when the nominalization stands in personal supposition, it stands for those *significata* of the terms of the corresponding proposition of which they are jointly true, provided the proposition is true; otherwise it stands for nothing. Clearly, this is a good solution for the foregoing example, for then the sentence 'To cut is to act' is true because someone cutting is indeed identical with someone acting, which is to say that its terms co-supposit. It is not clear, though, how this type of solution would work for other types of propositions (negatives, and so forth). Buridan simply does not say. This is a characteristic feature of nominalism: it usually stays programmatic. But Buridan took this program farther than anyone before or even after him.

Validity under semantic closure

Buridan does work out another issue that Ockham did not have much to say about – namely, a general nominalist account of logical validity in semantically closed natural languages. Since nominalists have to treat items of the languages they work with (conventional written or spoken languages as well as mental language) as a part of their ontology, where these items have to be identified with individual substances or their individual quantities or qualities, the definition of a valid consequence (inference), as Buridan argues, will have to take into account both the contingent existence of these items, and the possibility of using these items to refer to themselves or other tokens of the same type (yielding what Alfred Tarski called "semantic closure").[22] Buridan deploys an impressive array

---

[21] See *Summulae* I.8.9.3 (tr. Klima, p. 93), where Buridan interprets this sentence as saying: "Every proposition like 'no man runs' is possible."

[22] For more on this issue, see Gyula Klima, "Consequences of a Closed, Token-Based Semantics: The Case of John Buridan," *History and Philosophy of Logic* 25 (2004) 95–110; Catarina Dutilh Novaes, "Buridan's *consequentia*: Consequence and Inference within a Token-based Semantics," *History and Philosophy of Logic* 26 (2005) 277–97.

of arguments to show that logical validity in his framework cannot be defined in terms of truth, but rather in terms of the correspondence conditions of propositions in different possible situations. Take, for instance, the proposition 'No proposition is negative' (which is just this token-inscription that may or may not exist here and now). This, being a negative proposition itself, cannot be true in any situation in which it exists. However, the proposition clearly corresponds to a possible situation in which no negative proposition exists. So, it corresponds to a situation in which it is not true, and thus correspondence is not the same as truth. Such considerations quite naturally lead to a peculiar semantic construction in which the correspondence conditions of a proposition may diverge from its truth conditions, and in which it is the former, rather than the latter, that will have to figure in the definition of validity. This is also the core of Buridan's solution of the Liar paradox.[23] Buridan's discussion of the issue is rather difficult, but exhibits an absolutely relentless consistency in pursuing the nominalist project to its utmost consequences.

CONCLUSION

No doubt this relentless consistency was one of the features of Buridan's philosophy that earned him universal respect both in his lifetime and in the following two centuries, when his works became required reading in the curricula of many of the newly established universities from Poland to Scotland. Indeed, because of Buridan's role in developing a nominalist semantics, the impact of his ideas can hardly be overestimated. To be sure, Ockham was more controversial, especially for his theological and metaphysical views, and so may have been cited more often in disputations of that sort. Moreover, those who belonged to Buridan's immediate or wider circle (such influential authors as Albert of Saxony, Nicole Oresme, Themon Judaeus and Marsilius of Inghen, and probably large numbers of unidentified, less famous figures) may not have been strictly speaking his students and followers.[24] But it was Buridan's careful attention to theoretical detail, coupled with his prudent practical judgment and pedagogical skill, that in his hands could turn Ockham's innovations into relatively uncontroversial, viable textbook material, capable of laying the foundations of a new, paradigmatically

---

[23] See Stephen Read, "The Liar Paradox from John Buridan back to Thomas Bradwardine," *Vivarium* 40 (2002) 189–218, and the classic treatments by Spade, Hughes, Scott, Moody, and Prior cited in Read's paper. A detailed analysis of Buridan's solution, along with its consequences concerning his construal of validity, can be found in ch. 10 of my *John Buridan* (Oxford: Oxford University Press, 2009).

[24] For an excellent analysis and re-evaluation of the relationships among these authors see J. M. M. H. Thijssen, "The Buridan School Reassessed: Buridan and Albert of Saxony," *Vivarium*, 42 (2004) 18–42.

different conception of the relationships between language, thought and reality. And this is what renders the emergence of nominalist semantics the most significant development of late medieval philosophy. In the subsequent two centuries, the new theoretical conflicts that inevitably arose between practitioners of the nominalist "modern way" (*via moderna*) and those of the realist "old way" (*via antiqua*) were different in kind from the theoretical conflicts between members within each camp. Conflicts of this kind, to use Wittgenstein's happy analogy, are no longer about who wins the game, but rather about whose game everybody ought to play. The emerging situation, therefore, is most aptly described by the succinct term of German historiography: *Wegestreit*, "the quarrel of the ways."[25] As a result, those in the middle of it all, university professors and administrators, faced a radically new situation that had to be handled both in theoretical and practical, institutional terms – not unlike the situation of the recent conflict between the analytic and continental *viae* in contemporary philosophy.

---

[25] Indeed, no wonder this situation directly had an impact on the emergence of "the battle of the faiths," *Glaubenskampf,* in the age of the Protestant Reformation. See Heiko Oberman, *Werden und Wertung der Reformation: Vom Wegestreit zum Glaubenskampf* (Tübingen: Mohr, 1977).

13

INFERENCES

STEPHEN READ

Much of the recent attention of historians of medieval logic has focused on medieval semantics. Just as prominent in medieval logical treatises, however, is the topic of inference, and a great deal of sophisticated work was done in this area, particularly by the fourteenth-century Latin authors on which this chapter will concentrate.

KINDS OF INFERENCE

Inferences are the building blocks of scholastic thought, and it is scarcely possible to read a paragraph of later medieval philosophy without encountering the terminology in which inferences are couched. Indeed, nothing is more familiar from scholastic texts than phrases such as this: *Patet consequentia, antecedens est verum, ergo et consequens* ('The inference is seen to hold, the premise is true, so the conclusion is true too'). The term *consequentia* translates most readily as 'inference,' but what counts as an inference, to say nothing of what counts as a *valid* inference, is a thorny question. Even as good a logician as John Buridan may describe a *consequentia* as a molecular proposition (*propositio hypothetica*): "Now an inference is a molecular proposition, for it is composed from several propositions conjoined by the expression 'if' or by the expression 'therefore' or something similar" (*Tract. de consequentiis* I.3, ed. Hubien, p. 21). Yet when one argues: 'This is false, Socrates utters it, so it follows that Socrates utters a falsehood,' there is no conditional in this inference (*consequentia*), but two premises (*antecedentia*) and a conclusion (*consequens*). The same is true of syllogistic inference,[1] in which there are two premises and a conclusion. It is an inference, not a conditional proposition. Inferences can have one, two, or more premises. Let us look first at syllogisms.

A proper syllogism has two premises, a major and a minor, where the major premise, containing the major term of the argument, is simply the first premise.

---

[1] So called in Buridan, *Tract. de consequentiis* III.1, p. 79.

(The stock definition of the major term as the predicate of the conclusion does not come until the sixteenth century.) The middle term of a syllogism is the one that appears in each premise but not in the conclusion. An enthymeme is a one-premise argument that can be turned into a syllogism by adding an extra premise, called a "middle" (*medium*), inasmuch as it shares a middle term with the other premise. Aristotle's *Prior Analytics* had described this basic structure and then worked out the valid forms of the syllogism. The medievals followed Aristotle in distinguishing three figures: figure one, where the middle term is subject of one premise and predicate of the other; figure two, where the middle term is predicate of both premises; and figure three, where the middle term is subject in both premises. Each of the constituent propositions is of four forms: A-form, universal affirmative; E-form, universal negative; I-form, particular affirmative; and O-form, particular negative. Each affirmative proposition entails that its subject is non-empty, whereas each negative proposition is true if its subject is empty. This ensures that A- and O-propositions, and E- and I-propositions, are mutually contradictory (forming the Square of Opposition), and that universal propositions entail the corresponding particular propositions.[2] Aristotle showed how to reduce the validity of any valid assertoric (non-modal) syllogism to that of four basic forms in the first figure:

Barbara	*Celarent*	*Darii*	*Ferio*
All B is C	No B is C	All B is C	No B is C
All A is B	All A is B	Some A is B	Some A is B
So all A is C	So no A is C	So some A is C	So not all A is C

The fanciful names are a medieval mnemonic device, one for each of the nineteen valid forms, the vowels describing the structure of the syllogism, the consonants the reduction procedure.[3]

The medievals introduced many and varied divisions of *consequentiae*. One such division was between formal and material inference (*consequentia formalis* and *materialis*). However, 'formal' and 'material' should not always be taken in their modern connotation. In John Buridan and the Parisian tradition, a formal inference was indeed one that held solely in virtue of its form, whereas a material inference held in virtue of its descriptive terms.[4] However, the English tradition, continued in Italy, drew this distinction within the class of formal inferences, contrasting *purely* formal inference (*formalis de forma*) with

---

[2] For this reason, the O-form is better represented as 'Not all S is P' than as 'Some S is not P.'
[3] See, e.g., Buridan, *Summulae de dialectica* tr. 5 (On Syllogisms) ch. 2.
[4] See, e.g., Buridan, *Tract. de consequentiis* I.4, p. 22: "A formal inference is one that holds for all terms retaining the same form ... but a material inference is where not every proposition of the same form is valid ... e.g., 'A man runs, so an animal runs'."

materially formal inference (*formalis de materia*),[5] the latter of which might, in contemporary terms, be described as analytically valid.[6] Robert Fland wrote (around the mid-fourteenth century):

General rules are given in order to appreciate when an inference is formally valid. The first is this: where the conclusion is formally understood in the premises. For example, this inference is formally valid: 'There is a man, so there is an animal' because the conclusion 'animal' is formally understood in the premise, namely, 'man.'

(*Consequentiae*, ed. Spade sec. 1)

In William of Ockham and the English tradition, material inference comprised just instances of the paradoxical principles *ex impossibili (sequitur) quodlibet* (from the impossible anything follows: e.g., 'if a man is an ass, there is no God') and *necessarium (sequitur) ad quodlibet* (the necessary follows from anything: e.g., 'if a man runs, there is a God').[7] All other inferences were formal.

Ockham explains the difference between formal and material inference with reference to intrinsic and extrinsic middles. An intrinsic middle is one composed of terms appearing in the inference; an extrinsic middle is a general principle not specific to the terms of the inference; e.g., "from an exclusive proposition [e.g., 'Only *A* is *B*'] to a universal proposition with the terms transposed [namely 'All *B* is *A*'] is a valid inference" (*Summa logicae* III-3 ch. 1). However, this distinction cuts across the formal/material one. Formal inference is accordingly two-fold, Ockham says: some inferences hold by reason of an extrinsic middle describing the form of the proposition, whereas others hold by virtue of an intrinsic middle, like the example from Fland above, where 'Man is an animal' serves as the tacit middle.

The formal/material division, in its various construals, seems towards the end of the thirteenth century to have replaced an earlier division between natural (or essential) and accidental inference (see Chapter 10). The idea of formal inference has been said to appear for the first time in Simon of Faversham at the end of the thirteenth century, and to be consolidated by Ockham in the early fourteenth century.[8] It was around this time that the nature of inference was recognized as a topic worthy of separate treatment, leading in turn to the emergence of distinct and separate treatises on inference. This is not to deny, of course, that inference was always central to all logical discussion. Indeed,

---

[5] See e.g., Paul of Venice, *Logica Parva*, tr. Perreiah, p. 168.

[6] As noted by Paul Spade, "Five Logical Tracts by Richard Lavenham," in J. O'Donnell (ed.) *Essays in Honour of Anton Charles Pegis* (Toronto: Pontifical Institute of Mediaeval Studies, 1974) p. 78.

[7] On the Latin tags, see, e.g., Ockham, *Summa logicae* III-3.38 (*Opera phil.* I: 730–1 n. 4).

[8] Christopher J. Martin, "Formal Consequence in Scotus and Ockham: Towards an Account of Scotus' Logic," in O. Boulnois *et al.* (eds.) *Duns Scot à Paris 1302–2002* (Turnhout: Brepols, 2004) pp. 135, 145.

inference played not only a central theoretical role but also a central practical role in the medieval curriculum through the method of disputations – and in particular through obligational disputations, which came to fruition at the start of the fourteenth century (see Chapter 10).[9]

A further common division was that between an absolute inference (*consequentia simplex*) and a matter-of-fact inference (*consequentia ut nunc*). In an absolute inference, the premises can never be true without the truth of the conclusion. In contrast, a matter-of-fact or *ut nunc* inference (sometimes also translated 'as-of-now') can have true premises and a false conclusion at some time, but not at present.[10] Walter Burley gives as an example:

Every man is running
So Socrates is running.

This inference is valid *ut nunc* only while Socrates (exists and) is a man.[11] Buridan's example of an inference valid *ut nunc* is more intriguing (slightly adapted):

A white cardinal has been elected pope
So a deceitful man (*homo falsus*) has been elected pope.

This inference is valid *ut nunc* on the assumption that at the time Buridan wrote his *Tractatus de consequentiis* he did not think well of the newly elected pope, Jacques Fournier, a member of the Cistercian order of "white monks," and a fierce opponent of fourteenth-century innovations in logic even before his election as Benedict XII.[12] Material inference *ut nunc* can be reduced to formal inference in Buridan's sense, to hold solely in virtue of its form, by the addition of a contingently true premise; absolute material inferences reduce to formal inferences by adding a necessarily true premise.[13]

Inference *ut nunc* was a contentious issue. For example, in a treatise on inference of unknown authorship, the notion is dismissed repeatedly: "There is no such thing as *ut nunc* inference." One argument given runs as follows: Suppose,

---

[9] The inference rules of obligations are a topic in themselves, too large to be treated here. See, e.g., Paul Spade, "Medieval Theories of *Obligationes*," in E. Zalta (ed.) *Stanford Encyclopedia of Philosophy* (http://plato.stanford.edu), and Mikko Yrjönsuuri, "Duties, Rules and Interpretations in Obligational Disputations," in Yrjönsuuri, *Medieval Formal Logic* (Dordrecht: Kluwer, 2001) 3–34.

[10] The distinction between truth *simpliciter* and *ut nunc* derives from the standard Latin translation by Boethius of *Prior Analytics* 34b6–8.

[11] Burley, *Purity of the Art of Logic*, ed. Boehner, pp. 61, 199; tr. Spade, pp. 3, 146. Ockham, *Summa logicae* III-3.1 (I: 587), has the same example with 'animal' for 'man.'

[12] See Buridan, *Tract. de consequentiis* I 4, p. 23; cf. Hubien's Introduction, p. 9.

[13] See, e.g., Ockham, *Summa logicae* III-3.2 (I: 591).

for instance, that only an ass is running. Then from 'Every man is running' we can infer 'Every man is an ass' *ut nunc*, by a syllogism in Barbara: 'Everything running is an ass, every man is running, so every man is an ass.' The premise of the enthymeme is possible and the conclusion impossible. But this violates Aristotle's definition of the possible in the *Prior Analytics* (32a19–20) as "that which is not necessary but, being assumed, results in nothing impossible." So, the author concludes, the very notion of *ut nunc* inference must be rejected.[14] One manuscript attributes this treatise to Thomas Bradwardine, but this seems unlikely. For in his treatise on *Insolubilia*, Bradwardine dismissed this argument, responding that Aristotle's definition was given with respect to absolute inference, not inference as a matter of fact: "This inference really is valid *ut nunc*, for *ut nunc* the conclusion is understood (*intelligitur*) in the premise" (*Insolubilia*, ad 6.5.4).

THE GROUNDS OF INFERENCE

Bradwardine's term *intelligitur* ('is understood in') has been described as psychological or epistemic, and identified as a peculiarly English phenomenon, though mostly in English authors of the latter half of the fourteenth century – Henry Hopton, Richard Billingham, Robert Fland, Ralph Strode, Richard Lavenham, and the *Logica Oxoniensis*.[15] This psychologistic interpretation is sometimes attributed to fifteenth-century Italian commentators on Strode: Alexander Sermoneta, for instance, proposed four ways to interpret *intelligitur*, preferring the fourth: "when it is impossible to imagine *B* or its significate to [hold] and not *A* or its significate without the implication of a contradiction resulting from both taken together."[16] But this kind of account of inference runs throughout the medieval history of inference, from Peter Abaelard in the early twelfth century right through to the sixteenth.[17] Nor is it peculiarly English. For example, it is found in Robert Kilwardby and Simon of Faversham, both representing Parisian doctrine in the thirteenth century. In Kilwardby, for instance, natural

---

[14] Edited in N. J. Green-Pedersen, "Bradwardine (?) on Ockham's Doctrine of Consequences: An Edition," *Cahiers de l'Institut Grec et Latin du Moyen Age* 42 (1982) secs. 6–8, p. 93.

[15] See, e.g., E. J. Ashworth and Paul Spade, "Logic in Late Medieval Oxford," in J. Catto and T. Evans (eds.) *The History of the University of Oxford*, vol. II: *Late Medieval Oxford* (Oxford: Clarendon Press, 1992) n. 15.

[16] See Calvin Normore, "The Necessity in Deduction: Cartesian Inference and its Medieval Background," *Synthese* 96 (1993) p. 450.

[17] See, e.g., Ivan Boh, "Consequences," in N. Kretzmann *et al.*, *The Cambridge History of Later Medieval Philosophy* (Cambridge: Cambridge University Press, 1982) pp. 305–6; E. J. Ashworth, *Language and Logic in the Post-Medieval Period* (Dordrecht: Reidel, 1974) p. 130.

and essential inference is marked by the conclusion's being understood in the premises.[18]

There is, however, no reason to import a psychologistic interpretation onto this talk of understanding. For what is understood by a proposition is what it signifies: as Ralph Strode put it (*ca.* 1360), a formal inference obtains "when, if the way in which facts are adequately signified by the antecedent is understood, the way in which they are adequately signified by the consequent is also understood. For instance, if anyone understands that you are a man, he will understand also that you are an animal" (*Tract. de consequentiis*, tr. Seaton, 1.1.03). Indeed, Bradwardine's notorious second postulate of his *Insolubilia* turns the criterion on its head, appealing to what follows from a proposition as an account of what it signifies: "Every proposition signifies either absolutely or *ut nunc* whatever follows from it absolutely or *ut nunc*" (6.3). The proposition signifies its consequences since these are understood in what is signified by the original proposition from which they are inferred.

Christopher J. Martin has suggested that the formula was intended to narrow the simple modal requirement that it be impossible for the premises to be true and the conclusion false.[19] The simple modal formula justifies the spread law *ex impossibili quodlibet* (from an impossibility anything follows), but (to take a common medieval example) clearly 'The stick is in the corner' is in no way to be "understood" in some arbitrary impossibility with which it shares no terms. Moreover, the principle seems to support Aristotle's requirement in the *Prior Analytics* (57b1–16) that no proposition may be inferred from its contradictory, or from contradictories. Abaelard agreed: "the truth of one of two propositions that divide truth [e.g., *p* and 'not-*p*'] does not require the truth of the other but rather expels and extinguishes it" (*Dialectica*, ed. de Rijk, p. 290). Hence inference *ex impossibili quodlibet* must be rejected, since if everything followed from an impossibility, its contradictory opposite would also follow.

Aristotle's scruples against such inferences were undermined, however, by an argument devised by William of Soissons and his teacher Adam of Balsham.[20]

---

[18] Kilwardby, *In Analytica Priora*: "For only in natural inferences is it necessary that the conclusion is really understood in the premises; in accidental inferences it is not necessary"; cited in Ivo Thomas, "Maxims in Kilwardby," *Dominican Studies* 7 (1954) p. 139. Kilwardby takes accidental inferences to be the paradoxical *ex impossibili quodlibet* and *necessarium ad quodlibet*, where premise and conclusion can be mutually irrelevant. See also Simon of Faversham, *Quaest. super libro* [sic] *elenchorum*, ed. Ebbesen *et al.*, p. 71: "It must be said that for a valid inference more is required than that the conclusion is included in the premise, namely, that in understanding the premise the conclusion is necessarily understood."

[19] See Christopher J. Martin, "William's Machine," *Journal of Philosophy* 83 (1986) p. 567.

[20] Identified by Martin as "William's machine," this argument was rediscovered in the twentieth century by C. I. Lewis and C. H. Langford in their *Symbolic Logic* (New York: The Century Co., 1932) p. 250.

For '*p* and not-*p*' entails not only 'not both *p* and not-*p*' (its contradictory opposite) but any proposition whatever. From '*p* and not-*p*' we may infer both *p* and 'not-*p*,' and from *p* we may infer '*p* or *q*'; finally, from '*p* or *q*' and 'not-*p*' we may infer *q*; so from first to last (*a primo ad ultimum*), from '*p* and not-*p*' we may infer *q*. Hence anything whatever follows from a formal contradiction, including its contradictory opposite, which is a necessary truth. (See Chapter 10 for further discussion.)

Other fourteenth-century authors retained the modal formula ('It is impossible that...') but chose not to express it in terms of truth because of a pregnant sophism famously found in the writings of John Buridan. Consider the following argument:

Every proposition is affirmative
So no proposition is negative.

The conclusion cannot be true, for it is itself a negative proposition, and so falsifies itself. But the premise can be true, so it seems that the premise can be true when the conclusion is not (for instance, if there are no negative propositions). Yet the argument is valid, being an enthymeme in Celarent with the suppressed premise, 'No affirmative is negative.' Dropping talk of truth, Buridan revised the modal criterion to read: "if it is impossible that things are as the premise signifies without their being as the conclusion signifies" (*Tract. de consequentiis* I.3).[21]

The need to replace talk of truth with talk of signification had been appreciated a generation before Buridan by Bradwardine. Suppose, he writes, that nothing is being referred to, and consider this argument:

Nothing is being referred to
So this is not being referred to,

where 'this' refers, say, to Socrates. The argument has the (valid) form of a universal instantiation. Yet the premise is true, by hypothesis, and the conclusion is false since 'this' refers to Socrates. But that reasoning is sophistical, Bradwardine observes. The premise was true when it was uttered, according to the hypothesis; the conclusion is false only because the situation changes when Socrates is referred to. 'This is not referred to' can never be true, any more than can 'No proposition is negative,' but it is still possible that Socrates is not referred to and that there be no negative propositions. So "a proposition is not possible

---

[21] See also Buridan, *Summulae de dialectica* tr. IX [*Sophismata*] ch. 8, tr. Klima, pp. 955–6. Note, however, that for Buridan the phrase 'as...signifies' is shorthand for a complicated condition in terms of supposition (ibid., ch. 2, pp. 849–59).

or impossible according to whether it can or cannot be true, but on account of whether things can or cannot be as is signified by it" (*Insolubilia* 11.6). We need to distinguish the question whether the circumstance described by a proposition could or could not obtain from the question whether the proposition could or could not be true.[22]

This raises an important point about the general rules of inference. The above inference from Bradwardine appears to be an instance of universal instantiation, but in fact it is not a correct instance. Even the Law of Identity, to infer p from p, can be undermined if p can change its signification between premise and conclusion. This is the basis of one of Roger Swineshead's iconoclastic theses from the 1330s, that a formally valid argument can have a true premise and a false conclusion (*Insolubilia*, ed. Spade, p. 189). Let A denote the conclusion of the following argument:

A is false
So A is false.

A, in addition to denoting the argument's conclusion, is also an example of the Liar paradox, which Swineshead thought falsified itself, and so was false. Hence the premise is true (A is false), but the conclusion is false (it is A). In fact, Bradwardine had anticipated and refuted this suggestion ten years earlier on the grounds that it is a fallacy of the relative and the absolute (*secundum quid et simpliciter*). According to Bradwardine, the conclusion signifies not only that it is false, but also that it is true, as a consequence of his second postulate, mentioned earlier ('Every proposition signifies whatever follows from it absolutely or *ut nunc*'). The argument is subtle, but the upshot is that "inferring the conclusion [A] absolutely according to the whole of what it signifies is to proceed from the premise *secundum quid* [A is false] to *simpliciter* [A is false and true]" (*Insolubilia* 7.11.2).

MODAL AND EPISTEMIC INFERENCE

Aristotle states the basic closure principles of alethic modal logic in his *Prior Analytics* (34a22–4): "If then, for example, one should indicate the premises by A and the conclusion by B it would not only result that if A is necessary B is necessary, but also that if A is possible, B is possible." That is, from $\Box(A \rightarrow B)$ we may infer $\Box A \rightarrow \Box B$ and $\Diamond A \rightarrow \Diamond B$, where '$\Box$' denotes necessity and

[22] Arthur Prior picked up the distinction between being possible and possibly being true in his article "The Possibly-True and the Possible," *Mind* 78 (1969) 481–92.

'◊' possibility. He adds the characteristic thesis of necessity, $\Box A \rightarrow A$, at *De interpretatione* 23a21: "that which is of necessity is actual," and the thesis relating necessity and possibility, $\sim\!\Diamond A \leftrightarrow \Box\sim\!A$: "when it is impossible that a thing should be, it is necessary ... that it should not be" and vice versa (22b5–6). Aristotle uses the closure principles to show that universal and particular modal propositions convert in the same way as do non-modal propositions; for instance, 'All *A* is necessarily *B*' converts simply to 'Some *B* is necessarily *A*' (25a33). However, this seems to require that we interpret 'All *A* is necessarily *B*' in the compounded sense, that is, *de dicto*.

The distinction between compounded and divided senses derives from Chapter 4 of Aristotle's *De sophisticis elenchis*, where he describes the fallacy of amphiboly – that is, of confusion over grammatical construction. For example, he notes, 'A man can walk while sitting' is true in the divided sense ('When he is sitting, it is possible that he walk' is true) but not in the compounded sense ('It is possible that a man walk at the same time as sit' is false). Here, the false proposition attributes possibility to the *dictum* 'that a man walk and sit,' so it is false *de dicto*; the true proposition predicates possibly walking of a sitting man, so it is true *de re*. The *de re/de dicto* distinction is a special case of, but narrower than, the divided/compounded one. For example, 'I believe *p* but not-*p*' has both compounded ('I believe both *p* and not-*p*') and divided ('Not-*p* but I believe *p*') senses, but it is not ambiguous *de re/de dicto*.

As applied to modal propositions, the compounded/divided distinction was the basis of a long-running puzzle for the ancients as well as the medievals concerning Aristotle's theory of the modal syllogism. Since 'All *A* is *B*' entails 'Some *B* is *A*,' 'Necessarily, all *A* is *B*' (*de dicto*) entails 'Necessarily, some *B* is *A*' by the closure principle: $\Box(p \rightarrow q) \rightarrow (\Box p \rightarrow \Box q)$ (with 'All *A* is *B*' for '*p*' and 'Some *B* is *A*' for '*q*'). Thus, it seems that Aristotle must take such modal assumptions in the compounded sense, *de dicto*. In *Prior Analytics* I.9, however, Aristotle accepts the validity of the modal version of Barbara with necessary major premise and non-modal minor (1), while rejecting the corresponding form with necessary minor premise and non-modal major (2):

(1) All *B* is necessarily *C*   (2) All *B* is *C*
      All *A* is *B*   All *A* is necessarily *B*
      So all *A* is necessarily *C*   So all *A* is necessarily *C*

For, although all animals move (All *B* is *C*), and all men are necessarily animals (All *A* is necessarily *B*), no men necessarily move (30a31). Yet, syllogism (1) can be similarly invalidated if the modal premise is taken *de dicto*. For example, although it is necessary that every *B* is *B* (*de dicto*), it does not follow that if all *A* is *B*, necessarily all *A* is *B*, even *de dicto*. Hence, one might conjecture that Aristotle took the major premise in syllogism (1) *de re*, for so taken, in the divided sense, the predicate is 'necessarily *C*,' and (1) is then an instance of non-modal Barbara. Thus we find Ockham, for instance, noting that in the first figure "from a necessary major taken in the divided sense and a non-modal minor, a necessary conclusion always follows in the divided sense but not in the compounded sense" (*Summa logicae* III-1.30 [I: 440]).

Ockham's view was a common one – but it leaves a puzzle, since it seems to attribute a confusion to Aristotle, taking modal premises in the compounded sense in Chapter 3 of the *Prior Analytics* but in the divided sense in Chapter 9.[23] In addition, although medieval thinkers generally accepted Aristotle's verdict on modal Barbara, they nonetheless differed in other cases. Indeed, John Buridan did not accept Aristotle's verdict even in this case. He interpreted the subject of a divided modal proposition as having its range extended ("ampliated") from the actual to the possible: "In all divided modals, of necessity and of possibility, the subject is ampliated to supposit for those that can be unless that ampliation is prevented by adding the phrase 'that is' to the subject" (*Tract. de consequentiis* IV.1, p. 111). Thus 'All *A* is necessarily *B*' is read as saying that everything that is or may be *A* is necessarily *B*. The modal syllogisms above consequently commit the fallacy of four terms – that is, one of the terms is equivocal, standing for '*B*' in one premise, and 'what is or may be *B*' in the other. (On supposition and ampliation, see Chapter 11.)

Why does Buridan interpret the modal premise in this way? The analogy with tensed propositions is instructive. Consider first, 'Not all *A* was *B*.' Reflection shows that this is true if something that is *A* wasn't *B*, or if something that was *A* wasn't *B*. Medieval authors further added that, being negative, the proposition is also true if nothing is *A*, in order to preserve the relations of the Square of Opposition, as noted earlier. By analogy, the modal O-proposition, 'Not all *A* might be *B*' is true if nothing is *A* or something that is or might be *A* might not be *B*. Consequently, its contradictory, the modal A-proposition, 'Every *A* is necessarily *B*,' is true if something is *A* and everything which is or might be *A* must be *B*. However, although the divided modal versions of Barbara and Celarent fail, the divided modal versions of Darii and Ferio, with particular minor premises, are valid by Buridan's lights (as they were by Aristotle's). Buridan wrote: "The sixteenth conclusion: from a major premise of necessity and an assertoric minor premise, there is always a valid syllogism

---

[23] For an account which avoids attributing such an error to Aristotle, see Nicholas Rescher, "A New Approach to Aristotle's Apodeictic Syllogisms," in N. Rescher (ed.) *Studies in Modality* (Oxford: Blackwell, 1974) pp. 3–15.

in the first figure to a particular conclusion of necessity, but not a universal one" (ibid., IV.2, p. 124). For example, given that necessarily every *B* is *C*, not everything that is or might be *A* must be *C* if every *A* is in fact *B*, for if it were not *A* it might not be *B*; but if some *A* is *B*, something that is or might be *A* is *B*, and so must be *C*, validating the divided mixed necessity version of Darii with assertoric minor premise.

Finally, let us turn to inferences in what is often called "epistemic logic," which despite the name includes propositions not only about knowledge, such as '*a* knows that *p*' (which we may symbolize as K_ap), but also about belief, '*a* believes that *p*' (B_ap), desire, understanding, doubt, obligation, permission, and all so-called propositional attitudes. The first question to ask about each of these operators is whether they are closed under consequence, or better, under what form of inference they are closed. (Knowledge, for instance, is closed under consequence if knowing that *p* entails knowing every consequence of *p*.) Ralph Strode gives this as his thirteenth rule: "if the premise is known, the conclusion is known" (*Tract. de consequentiis* 1.1.06). This has been understood as the implausible claim that knowledge is closed under consequence *tout court*.[24] But Strode's proof of this rule reads: "The premise is known by you, from which it follows that you know things to be as it principally signifies, and as it principally signifies, you know it to signify. Moreover, you know this conclusion to follow from that premise, so you know it to signify as the conclusion signifies" (ibid., 1.2.31). This makes it clear that Strode's rule is intended to be the more modest $K_a(p \rightarrow q)$, $K_ap => K_aq$, that knowledge is closed under *known* consequence.

Although it is plausible that knowledge is closed under known consequence, such closure is implausible for other attitudes. Walter Burley has an amusing example. Clearly, if I am stuck in the mud with £100, I am stuck in the mud, and I know that this follows. But though I might want to be stuck in the mud with £100 (if that is the best way to obtain it), I might nonetheless not want to be stuck in the mud.[25] Amusing, yes; convincing, no. It is reminiscent of counterexamples to Strengthening the Antecedent (that, assuming that if *p* then *q*, it follows that if *p* and *r* then *q*), on the ground that if, say, I put milk in my tea, I will like it, but if I put milk and diesel oil in my tea, I will not. Yet if the latter conditional is indeed true, then the former is false (absent an exceptive clause, 'milk and nothing else'). So, too, for Burley's £100. If I do want the £100, then (again, given that this is the best way to obtain it) I will have to

---

[24] See Ivan Boh, *Epistemic Logic in the Later Middle Ages* (London: Routledge, 1993) p. 96 and, following him, Simo Knuuttila, *Modalities in Medieval Philosophy* (London: Routledge, 1993) p. 177. Both attribute this claim to Strode, although Boh half-realizes the mistake on the very next page.

[25] *Purity of the Art of Logic*, ed. Boehner, p. 87 (cf. p. 206); tr. Spade, p. 175 (cf. p. 10).

want to be stuck in the mud (with the £100). A better example is perhaps that given by Roger Roseth (and others):[26] in order to repent, I must be guilty of sin (and know that I am guilty of sin). But though I may wish to repent, and indeed ought to wish it, it does not follow that I wish to be guilty of sin, nor ought I to wish it.

[26] See Knuuttila, *Modalities in Medieval Philosophy*, p. 195.

14

SOPHISMATA

PAUL VINCENT SPADE

The medieval sophismata literature is a genre of academic argument that began to take shape by the early twelfth century, grew in importance in the thirteenth and fourteenth centuries, and lasted to the end of the Middle Ages. This chapter offers only the briefest overview of that literature. Although some overall patterns can be discerned, the boundaries of the genre are ill-defined and seem to have been so even in the Middle Ages. Still, it is clear that sophisms were the occasion for drawing many subtle distinctions and pursuing theoretical issues in a variety of fields.

BACKGROUND

Sophismata is the plural of the Greek singular noun *sophisma*. Originally, the words did not have the derogatory sense of the modern English 'sophism' or 'sophistry.' Instead they referred to whatever a *sophistēs* or "sophist" produced. A "sophist" was anyone who dealt in "wisdom" (*sophia*) in a very broad sense of the term. The word was applied, for example, to Homer and to the Seven Sages of ancient Greece. By the time of Socrates, however, 'sophist' had come to be used especially to refer to those who used debate and rhetoric to defend their views and who offered to train others in these skills. Because they accepted payment for their services, and because some of them employed their skill to pursue unjust cases in courts of law, the term acquired the connotation of someone who uses ambiguous, deceitful and fallacious reasoning to argue a point. Plato's hostility to the sophists is well known, and indeed he is probably the one most responsible for the disparaging connotations 'sophist' and related words commonly have today.[1]

---

[1] The best discussion of the early Greek sophists remains G. B. Kerferd, *The Sophistic Movement* (Cambridge: Cambridge University Press, 1981).

Sophisma and _sophismata_ were taken over intact into classical Latin, where they were usually but not always used in the negative or pejorative sense.[2] Augustine, for instance, continues this usage when he writes: "For there are many things called sophisms, false conclusions of reasoning, and many of them so imitate true conclusions that they deceive not only slow people but even clever ones who are paying less diligent attention" (_De doctrina christiana_ II.31.48). By at least the middle of the twelfth century, however, the words are found with increasing frequency in Latin with no sense of disapproval at all. Instead, they are used quite neutrally to refer to the discussion of certain kinds of puzzling sentences, or to the sentences themselves so discussed, often quite artificial ones.[3] Because this neutral, non-disparaging medieval sense is at variance with modern English usage, some scholars prefer to keep the original _sophisma_ and _sophismata_ as terms of art rather than to translate them.[4] I shall not strictly observe this scruple here, but it is this medieval, non-pejorative sense of 'sophism' that is the focus of the present chapter.

A medieval sophism, then, is not just a piece of idle "sophistry" or argumentative fallaciousness, even if that meaning was never entirely lost.[5] Instead, it involves a kind of "problem-sentence," a sentence for which one can give more or less plausible and persuasive arguments on both sides, both pro and con. Such sentences served as vehicles for illustrating logical rules and distinctions or other theoretical points.

It is tempting to suppose that the emergence of the sophismata literature in the twelfth century, and particularly the use of the terminology of "sophisms"

---

[2] E.g., Cicero, _Academica Priora_ II.24.75, who explains "for that is what [Stilpo, Diodorus and Alexinus] call fallacious little conclusions"; Seneca, _Epist._ 45.8 and 111.1; Aulus Gellius, _Noctes Atticae_ 18.13.2. In all these places, the sense is quite scornful. But Seneca, _Epist._ 87.38, and Gellius, _Noctes Atticae_ 18.2.10, can be read without any negative connotations at all.

[3] For the early sophismata literature, see Martin Grabmann, _Die Sophismataliteratur des 12. und 13. Jahrhunderts mit Textausgabe eines Sophisma des Boethius von Dacien_ (Münster: Aschendorff, 1940); L. M. de Rijk, _Logica modernorum: A Contribution to the History of Early Terminist Logic_ (Assen: Van Gorcum, 1962–7). It is sometimes said that the word 'sophism' in the medieval literature did _not_ refer to reasoning or arguments: see, e.g., Norman Kretzmann, "Socrates Is Whiter than Plato Begins to be White," _Noûs_ 11 (1977) p. 12 n. 9; Fabienne Pironet, "Sophismata," in E. Zalta (ed.) _The Stanford Encyclopedia of Philosophy_ (http://plato.stanford.edu, spring 2006) sec. 2.1. But this needs to be qualified. Many sophism sentences are stated as inferences or "consequences" (e.g., John Buridan, _Sophismata_ VIII.1–3). But it remains true that the term 'sophism' was not used to refer to reasoning _about_ the sophism sentence, whether that sophism sentence is stated as a consequence or not.

[4] Kretzmann, "Socrates Is Whiter," p. 12 n. 9; Pironet, "Sophismata," sec. 1; cf. Stephen Read, _Sophisms in Medieval Logic and Grammar: Acts of the Ninth European Symposium for Medieval Logic and Semantics_ (Dordrecht: Kluwer, 1993) p. xii.

[5] E.g., Robert Holcot, _Sent._ 1.1 dub. 1, arg. 4, refers to someone who, knowing no better, assents to the conclusion of a "sophism" against an article of faith. Here the word refers simply to a fallacious argument with a false conclusion.

itself, had something to do with the circulation of the newly available translation of Aristotle's *Sophistic Refutations*.[6] The temporal coincidence is certainly there, but one should not make too much of it. For while it is true that the *Sophistic Refutations* prompted intense new interest in fallacies and in the kinds of distinctions frequently drawn in the sophismata literature, and while the study of that work contributed greatly to the newly developing theories of "properties of terms" that were among the most characteristic features of medieval logic (see Chapter 11),[7] it is also true that Aristotle's little treatise simply does not read like a medieval discussion of "sophisms." Unlike Aristotle's text, medieval sophismata proceed according to a stylized "question" format for disputation – the roots of which go back much earlier than the widespread availability of the *Sophistic Refutations* in Latin in the early twelfth century.[8] Although no one knows its precise origins, a prominent early example of this "question" format can be found in Boethius's famous early sixth-century discussion of the problem of universals in his *Second Commentary on Porphyry's Isagoge*.[9]

THE FORMAT AND PURPOSE OF MEDIEVAL SOPHISMS

As mentioned, sophism sentences admit of plausible arguments both for and against. The typical format begins by stating the sophism sentence and presenting these arguments pro and con. Often several arguments are given on each side, and they can come from a variety of sources, depending on the context – logic, grammatical theory, philosophy of nature, appeal to authoritative sources, and so on.

After reviewing the preliminary arguments, the author gives his own view of the matter. This is where the main theoretical work of the discussion gets done. The author may draw distinctions, present theoretical points, stipulate rules for disambiguating sentences, and so forth, but ultimately delivers a kind of "verdict" between the opposing sides. Then, in the last part of the format (sometimes omitted), he explains what he takes to be wrong with the arguments presented for the losing side.[10]

---

[6] On this translation, see Bernard Dod, "Aristoteles Latinus," in N. Kretzmann *et al.* (eds.) *The Cambridge History of Later Medieval Philosophy* (Cambridge: Cambridge University Press 1982) pp. 46, 53–5.

[7] De Rijk, *Logica modernorum*.

[8] Anthony Kenny and Jan Pinborg, "Medieval Philosophical Literature," in Kretzmann *et al.*, *Cambridge History of Later Medieval Philosophy*, pp. 24–5.

[9] Ed. Brandt, pp. 159–67. Translated in P. V. Spade, *Five Texts on the Mediaeval Problem of Universals: Porphyry, Boethius, Abelard, Duns Scotus, Ockham* (Indianapolis: Hackett, 1994) pp. 20–5.

[10] Variations on this format are common. John Buridan, for example, often presents a group of several sophisms at once, giving the arguments pro and con for each one individually, then explaining

This account is correct as far as it goes, but it is too broad. As it stands, it describes no more than the "question" format widely used in a variety of medieval academic contexts, by no means just in sophisms. It would fit, for example, any of the articles in Thomas Aquinas's *Summa theologiae* or his disputed questions on various topics. Yet none of those were called "sophisms."

Still, if the above account of sophisms is too broad, it is exasperatingly difficult to come up with a better one. In the end, the term seems simply not to have been used in any very precise sense, and the distinction between sophisms and other types of medieval "questions" is not a sharp one. Nevertheless, there are some additional factors to consider.

First, in the classic question format (as found in Aquinas and a great many other authors), the issue was framed in the form of a yes/no question, typically introduced by "whether." Sophism sentences, on the other hand, were more commonly given as statements, not as questions. Compare Aquinas, *Summa theol.* 1a 7.3, "Whether an actually infinite magnitude can exist," with Buridan's declarative sophism, "Nobody lies" (*Sophismata* I soph. 6). But this syntactical fine point was not universally observed.[11]

Second, and perhaps more striking, there is a difference of focus and purpose. With the question format generally, the interest is usually in whether the answer to the question is yes or no. With sophisms, it is otherwise. There the point is often not the truth or falsity of the sophism sentence as stated, but something else entirely. When Aquinas, for instance, asks "Whether an actually infinite magnitude can exist," his purpose is to settle exactly that. (He says no.) Even when the question is hardly controversial for him and we know very well what his answer is going to be – as when he asks (*Summa theol.* 1a 2.3) "whether God exists" and presents his famous "five ways" in reply – the focus of his discussion is still on the question as asked.

By contrast, in Buridan's sophism "Nobody lies," the center of attention is not really on whether people lie. In fact, the discussion *assumes* that the

the theoretical considerations that will provide the materials for solving all of them, and only then responding to the sophisms one by one. See, e.g., Buridan, *Sophismata* I, where he rehearses the preliminary arguments for no fewer than six sophisms dealing with the significations of terms and sentences, before presenting his own theory in eleven "conclusions" and finally returning to respond to the six sophisms in sequence.

[11] See James Weisheipl, "Curriculum of the Faculty of Arts at Oxford in the Early Fourteenth Century," *Mediaeval Studies* 26 (1964) pp. 177f. Again, Roger Bacon's *Summa de sophismatibus et distinctionibus* (ed. Steele et al., fasc. 14) proceeds mainly in terms of yes/no questions. On the other hand, Bacon himself does not call his questions sophisms, and perhaps the only reason to think they are is the *title* of the work. Grabmann, *Sophismataliteratur*, p. vii, denies they are "eigentliche sophismata," but does not say why. He is certainly willing to describe other collections of yes/no questions as sophismata (see, e.g., pp. 25–6).

sentence is false and that people do lie. Rather than giving an argument for this, Buridan says simply, "The opposite [of the sophism sentence] is obvious." Instead, the point of the discussion is to examine the theoretical notion, which Buridan accepts, that spoken language expresses thought, and that every spoken sentence corresponds to a semantically equivalent mental sentence. (How can this be so if lying is saying the *opposite* of what we think? This is the nub of the sophism.)

The argumentative role of medieval sophisms was thus often very much like that of Bertrand Russell's 'The present king of France is bald' or Frege's 'The morning star is the evening star.'[12] The real interest in Russell's and Frege's sentences does not of course lie in the condition of the royal head or in the planet Venus. In each case, there is a substantive philosophical point to be made, and the quoted sentence is merely the vehicle chosen for making it. So, too, with medieval sophisms. There is always a theoretical matter underlying their discussion, even if it is far removed from the truth or falsity of the sophism sentence itself. If one does not realize what it is, the sophisms can appear utterly inane. Thus William Heytesbury's *Sophismata asinina* consists of several sophisms, stated in the form of arguments or "consequences," each of which concludes that you are an ass!

Third, many researchers have pointed out the prominent role of sophisms according to the statutes for the arts curriculum at medieval universities. Indeed, Fabienne Pironet says, "I believe it is no exaggeration to say that *sophismata* in the Faculty of Arts were as important as Biblical exegesis in the Faculty of Theology."[13] In fact, however, the actual term 'sophism,' in the neutral and non-pejorative sense that concerns us in this chapter, tended to be confined to certain fields of study in the arts faculty: grammar, logic (including parts of what we would today call philosophy of language), and the more "mathematical" aspects of natural philosophy (continua, infinity, change). It would be hard, for instance, to find a medieval sophism the point of which was to address questions of moral psychology, freedom of the will, the matter/form distinction, or the four Aristotelian causes, even though these too were topics discussed in the faculty of arts. This is not to say such issues were not frequently treated in the two-sided "pro and con" manner, but only that such treatments were not called "sophisms." It is sometimes said that sophisms can be found in theology, a separate academic faculty altogether, but a careful reading of the texts cited

---

[12] Cf. Kretzmann, "Socrates Is Whiter," p. 6.
[13] Pironet, "Sophismata" sec. 3. See also Edith Sylla, "Oxford Calculators," in Kretzmann *et al.*, *The Cambridge History of Later Medieval Philosophy*, pp. 540–63; Weisheipl, "Curriculum," pp. 177–81.

in support of this claim suggests that the actual term is rare there, and when it does occur, it is only in the negative sense of a fallacious argument with a false conclusion.[14]

SOPHISMS AND RELATED GENRES

Sophisms cannot be sharply distinguished from other formats and styles of discussion in the Middle Ages. Still, we find the word starting to be used with some frequency as early as Adam of Balsham's *Ars disserendi* (1132), mainly as a way of describing fallacies of ambiguity (both equivocation and amphiboly).[15]

Likewise, by the early twelfth century medieval authors were interested in a related issue, the logical function of what Priscian the grammarian (*fl.* 500) had called *syncategoremata* (*Institutiones grammaticae* II.15). These were said to be expressions that cannot stand alone as the subject or predicate of a sentence, but "co-signify" together with words that can do that, which came to be called *categoremata* (see Chapter 12). This way of drawing the distinction would suggest that, in terms of modern formal semantics, the role of *categoremata* in a language is fixed by its models, whereas the role of *syncategoremata* is fixed by its valuation rules. *Syncategoremata* would thus be what we call "logical particles."

While this will work to a first approximation, in fact the situation is more complicated. Medieval authors sometimes distinguished between a categorematic and a syncategorematic *use* of a single expression. Thus Socrates is not his foot or his ear; rather, Socrates is the *whole* Socrates, nothing less. In that case 'whole' just means "entire" and is said to be used categorematically (even though, note, it is not here used by itself as the subject or predicate). On the other hand, Socrates's foot is less than (smaller than) Socrates, and likewise his ear, and so on for all Socrates's physical parts. Thus the *whole* Socrates (that is, every part taken individually) is less than Socrates. In this case, 'whole' is said to be used syncategorematically.[16]

Such expressions provide ample opportunity for ambiguity and puzzling arguments. In the thirteenth century, they were discussed in often loosely structured *De syncategorematibus* treatises, such as those by William of Sherwood and Peter

---

[14] See Holcot, *Sent.* 1.1 dub. 1, arg. 4. For the finding of sophisms in theology, see Simo Knuuttila, "Trinitarian Sophisms in Robert Holcot's Theology," in Read, *Sophisms in Medieval Logic and Grammar*, pp. 348–56.

[15] See Lorenzo Minio-Paluello, "The *'Ars disserendi'* of Adam of Balsham 'Parvipontanus'," *Mediaeval and Renaissance Studies* 3 (1954) 116–69, and de Rijk, *Logica modernorum* I: 62–81.

[16] See William of Sherwood, *Syncategoremata* (ed. O'Donnell, p. 54; tr. Kretzmann, pp. 40–1). The example is a common one.

of Spain. Gradually, however, much of this material came to be absorbed into the more stylized sophism format.[17]

Certain kinds of sophisms (namely, semantic paradoxes like the Liar) were discussed under the heading "insolubles." Others appeared in treatises called *Distinctiones* or *Abstractiones*, or in more comprehensive treatments of logic in general. The variations seem endless.[18]

Sometimes sophisms were discussed in treatises on *exponibilia* and solved by appeal to the theory of "exposition," a method of something like "contextual definition" that became increasingly important in the later Middle Ages.[19] Exponible sentences were said to be sentences that are categorical in their explicit form, but that implicitly require a molecular or "hypothetical" analysis (Ockham, *Summa logicae* II.11; Burley, *On the Purity of the Art of Logic* sec. 500). Thus Walter Burley remarks in the early fourteenth century that 'Whatever man runs is moved' can be expounded either as the conditional 'If some man runs, he is moved' or else as a universally quantified sentence with a relative clause modifying the subject: 'Every man who runs is moved' (*Purity*, sec. 372). To use a more complicated example, Burley says the "reduplicative" sentence 'An isosceles insofar as it is a triangle has three angles equal to two right angles' is expounded by a total of five sentences, all of which are required for its truth: (i) 'An isosceles has three angles'; (ii) 'An isosceles is a triangle'; (iii) 'Every triangle has three angles'; (iv) 'If an isosceles is a triangle, it has three angles, etc.'; and (v) '*Because* an isosceles is a triangle, therefore it has three angles, etc.'[20]

Throughout the twelfth century, we find increasing use of the terminology of sophisms, although few (if any) instances that fully exhibit all the characteristics

---

[17] See H. A. G. Braakhuis, *Die 13de Eeuwse Tractaten over Syncategorematische Termen* (Meppel: Krips Repro, 1979); Norman Kretzmann, "Syncategoremata, Exponibilia, Sophismata," in Kretzmann et al., *The Cambridge History of Later Medieval Philosophy*, 211–45; Pironet, "Sophismata," sec. 4.

[18] See P. V. Spade, "Insolubles," in Zalta, *The Stanford Encyclopedia of Philosophy* (http://plato.stanford. edu, fall 2005). For *distinctiones*, see L. M. de Rijk, *Some Earlier Parisian Tracts on Distinctiones Sophismatum* (Nijmegen: Ingenium, 1988). Other variations are mentioned below.

[19] Mikko Yrjönsuuri, "*Expositio* as a Method of Solving Sophisms," in Read, *Sophisms in Medieval Logic and Grammar*, 202–16. On the theory of exposition, see P. V. Spade, "Ockham, Adams and Connotation: A Critical Notice of Marilyn Adams, *William Ockham*," *Philosophical Review* 99 (1990) pp. 608–12. The theory of "exponibles" had been established by the middle of the thirteenth century, but grew to enormous importance from the mid-fourteenth century on. See E. J. Ashworth and P. V. Spade, "Logic in Late Medieval Oxford" in J. I. Catto and R. Evans (eds.) *The History of the University of Oxford*, vol. II: *Late Medieval Oxford* (Oxford: Clarendon Press, 1992) pp. 43–4.

[20] Burley, *Purity*, sec. 950. It is not clear why all five "exponents" need to be listed separately, since they are not independent of one another. (Thus (i) follows from (ii) and (iii), or from (ii) and (iv).) The most extensive account of the history of the theory of reduplication is Allan Bäck, *On Reduplication: Logical Theories of Qualification* (Leiden: Brill, 1996).

described above.[21] Even a text as late as Roger Bacon's *Summa de sophis-matibus et distinctionibus* (1240s) does not quite fit. Nevertheless, a relatively "pure" form of the genre may be found in Richard the Sophister's *Abstractiones* (1230s or 1240s), containing over three hundred sophisms.[22] By the early four-teenth century, sophismata are quite common. Good examples may be found in Richard Kilvington's *Sophismata* (early 1320s), Ockham's *Summa logicae* (*ca.* 1323), Burley's *Purity* (the longer treatise from 1325–8, the shorter treatise from before that), William Heytesbury's *Sophismata* (1330s) and *Rules for Solv-ing Sophisms* (1335), John Buridan's *Sophismata* (= Tract 9 of his *Summulae de dialectica*, probably 1320s–40s), Albert of Saxony's huge *Sophismata* (1351–62), and Paul of Venice's *Sophismata aurea* (*ca.* 1399).

Each of these works is demonstrably important and influential on subsequent discussions of the topics they treat. Yet none of them can be said to be important for shaping the sophismata literature itself. Indeed, it would be hard to find any one work that can be said to have done that. Perhaps it is this very "decentral-ized" nature of the sophismata literature that makes it so hard to define.

EXAMPLES OF SOPHISMS

It was stated above that a theoretical point always underlies the discussion of sophisms, no matter how silly they might otherwise appear. Frequently the point is merely to alert us to kinds of semantic ambiguity, as in the use of 'whole' as described above, or in the distinction between the collective and the distributive use of quantifiers.[23] Thus 'All the apostles are twelve' is true if 'all' is taken collectively, since altogether there are twelve apostles, but is false if 'all' is taken distributively, since none of them is twelve but rather each of them is one. (Peter is one, James is another one, and so on.) Hence one cannot argue: "All the apostles are twelve; Peter and James are apostles; therefore, Peter and James are twelve." Both readings are generally allowed, as long as one does not confuse them.[24]

---

[21] Except for Adam of Balsham's *Ars disserendi*, all of this literature seems to be anonymous. Much of it is surveyed in Grabmann, *Sophismatenliteratur* and de Rijk, *Logica modernorum*.

[22] See Paul Streveler, "Richard the Sophister," in Zalta, *The Stanford Encyclopedia of Philosophy* (http://plato.stanford.edu, spring 2005). For Bacon, see n. 11 above.

[23] The latter is one version of the medieval distinction between the "composed" and the "divided" senses. See Georgette Sinkler, "Medieval Theories of Composition and Division" (Ph.D. disserta-tion, Cornell University, 1985).

[24] The sophism is a common one, found from the very beginning of the literature. See de Rijk, *Logica modernorum*, I: index, 647, II.1: 487, II.2: index, 855. Where both readings are allowed, the last part of the sophism format – the replies to arguments for the losing side – is omitted, since of course there *is* no losing side.

In other cases, the ambiguity is one of scope. Thus 'All men are asses or men and asses are asses' (Albert of Saxony, *Sophismata*, soph. 11) can be read with either the 'or' or the 'and' as having the greater scope. In the former sense, it is a false disjunction the second disjunct of which has a compound subject ('men and asses'). In the latter, it is a true conjunction the first conjunct of which has a disjoint predicate ('asses or men'). Again, both readings are allowed.[25]

It is noteworthy that sophisms based on ambiguity rarely if ever involve straightforward *lexical* ambiguity, whereby for example the English 'bank' can mean either a kind of financial institution or the side of a river. Rather they concern structural or semantic ambiguity at the level of an entire sentence.

In some cases, the sophism sentence may be initially ambiguous enough to provide plausible arguments for both sides, but the discussion of the sophism legislates in favor of one reading to the exclusion of the others. In effect, the sophism is used to illustrate and recommend a particular way of regimenting language. Thus, Heytesbury maintains that the sentence *Infinita sunt finita*[26] is true because *infinita* is not being used there categorematically (*Sophismata* 18, ed. 1494, f. 130va). If it were, the sentence would mean either "The infinites are finite" (reading *infinita* as the subject) or "Infinite are the finites" (that is, "The finites are infinite" – reading *infinita* as the predicate), and both of those are false. (Not a single infinite is finite; on the contrary, each of them is infinite. Likewise, not a single finite [thing] is infinite; rather, each of them is finite.) Instead, Heytesbury maintains, the word *infinita* is being used in the sentence "syncategorematically." In effect, it encodes a recipe for unpacking the sentence's truth conditions on the basis of what its categorematic term *finita* signifies (namely, all finite things); roughly, the sentence means that no matter how many such things you pick, you could have picked twice as many more, three times as many more, and so on without limit. And that is true. (Analogously, when we say a process "goes on to infinity," we do not mean it ends at infinity; instead, we mean it does not end at all.)[27]

Heytesbury adopts this reading because, he claims, "according to the usual way of speaking" (although individual users may disregard this if they insist), if

---

[25] Note that 'and' and 'or' are allowed both as sentential connectives (yielding a complex proposition as the result) and as *term* connectives (yielding a complex *term* as the result).

[26] The sentence cannot be translated into English without disambiguating it and losing the point of the discussion. For an analysis of the sophism, see Edith Sylla, "William Heytesbury on the Sophism '*Infinita sunt finita*'," in J. P. Beckmann and W. Kluxen (eds.) *Sprache und Erkenntnis im Mittelalter* (Berlin: De Gruyter, 1981) II: 628–36.

[27] Other authors too had discussed categorematic and syncategorematic uses of 'infinite.' E.g., William of Sherwood, *Syncategoremata*, ed. O'Donnell, pp. 54–5; tr. Kretzmann, pp. 41–3.

'infinite' occurs on the subject side of a sentence (that is, before the copula) and if certain other conditions are met, then it is to be read syncategorematically; otherwise it is to be read categorematically.

It is doubtful whether this peculiar stipulation really conforms to the "usual way of speaking" at all. But note that it is a stipulation involving word order. Indeed, many authors appealed to artificial and arbitrary word order conventions in treating sophisms. One common device was to read the logical scope of certain words as always extending to the *right* of their occurrence in a sentence, not to the left. Walter Burley for instance held this explicitly for negation (*Purity*, sec. 59), and other authors adopted the convention in other contexts. It may be seen operating, for instance, in Albert of Saxony's rules for supposition in his *Perutilis logica*.[28] The fact that in modern quantification theory, as taught in elementary logic classes, quantifiers later in a sentence are taken as falling within the scope of those earlier in the sentence can be viewed as a descendant of this medieval convention. Burley, for example, solves a number of sophisms on exactly this basis (*Purity*, secs. 138–64). The convention is so familiar to us nowadays that it is worth emphasizing it is not the only one possible. (Consider, for example, "reverse Polish notation.") In fact, it is not even an especially "natural" convention, or else it would be much easier than it is to teach students how to translate from ordinary language into logical notation.

Sentences such as 'All men are asses or men and asses are asses' or *Infinita sunt finita* would be puzzling in any context. Sometimes, however, sophisms concern sentences that are not initially problematic at all, but become so in special contexts. Consider 'Socrates is saying a falsehood.' By itself there is nothing difficult about it in any way. Yet if Socrates himself makes that statement, and if it is the only thing he says, it becomes a version of the Liar paradox.[29] Sophisms, therefore, are often accompanied by a little story or "case" (*casus*) to set the context and motivate the opposing arguments.

In still other cases, sophism sentences are used as occasions not only to discuss ambiguity or to regiment language, but also to discuss larger theoretical issues, sometimes quite removed from language. Thus, the fourteenth-century Richard Kilvington devotes much of his *Sophismata* to problems reminiscent of Zeno's paradox, arising over continua, change, and motion.

---

[28] Albert of Saxony, *Perutilis logica*, ed. 1522, ff. 12vb–13rb. A discussion and partial translation of these rules may be found in Philotheus Boehner, *Medieval Logic: An Outline of its Development from 1250–c. 1400* (Manchester: Manchester University Press, 1952) pp. 103–14.

[29] Indeed, this formulation of the paradox became a standard one in the medieval literature on insolubles (e.g., Buridan, *Sophismata* II.6). See P. V. Spade, *The Mediaeval Liar: A Catalogue of the Insolubilia-Literature* (Toronto: Pontifical Institute of Mediaeval Studies, 1975).

Other popular topics include the intricacies of promising and debt.[30] Suppose I say: "I promise you a horse," in return for some service you have done me. Certainly I am under your debt and now owe you a horse. Yet there is no particular horse you can demand of me in repayment. No matter which horse you pick, I did not promise you *that* horse. Neither did I promise you a general or universal horse (if there even is such a thing) or "horsiness" (equinity). The issue here is partly semantic (what does 'horse' refer to in "I promise you a horse"?) and partly metaphysical (what *is* there to be referred to?).

Again, there are many sophisms involving modality, or epistemic and doxastic matters. Some of them merely concern what we nowadays call "quantifying into opaque contexts," such as Buridan's example: 'You know that the coins in my pocket are even in number,' given that there are exactly two coins in my pocket and you know two is an even number (*Sophismata* IV.10). These sophisms are interesting enough, but there are others that raise more unfamiliar issues.

Consider, for example, the sentence 'Socrates knows the sentence written on the wall to be doubtful to him' (Buridan, *Sophismata* VIII.13). This is one of those sophisms that require a story or case to set the context. Here the case stipulates that the sentence is the only one written on a certain wall, that Socrates sees it, does in fact doubt it (does not know whether it is true or false), and furthermore even *knows* that he doubts it. Is it then true or false?

It is hard at first to see the force of this sophism. Although Buridan's own presentation is extremely subtle, we might put the matter like this: Buridan posits that Socrates is "most wise," so that he can reason the case through. To begin with, then, Socrates does not know whether the puzzling sentence on the wall is true or false, any more than you or I do. He realizes this, however, and therefore doubts the sentence. Furthermore, being wise enough to follow this reasoning, he *knows* that he doubts the sentence (as in fact is stated by the case). But that means the sentence is true. Again, Socrates follows this too and so *knows* the sentence is true. But if he knows it is true, he does not doubt it after all, which (given what the sentence claims) means it is false. Once again, Socrates follows all this, ends up not knowing what to do, and so quite properly doubts the sentence. Realizing this, Socrates *knows* he doubts the sentence – and around we go.[31]

---

[30] See Gyula Klima, "'*Debeo tibi equum*': A Reconstruction of the Theoretical Framework of Buridan's Treatment of the Sophisma," in Read, *Sophisms in Medieval Logic and Grammar*, 333–47. Many authors had something to say about such sophisms; Klima cites much of the relevant literature.

[31] This sophism is insightfully discussed in Tyler Burge, "Buridan and Epistemic Paradox," *Philosophical Studies* 34 (1978) 21–35.

15

GRAMMAR

IRÈNE ROSIER-CATACH

According to the medieval division of the sciences, grammar is one of the three arts of the trivium, along with logic and rhetoric. In its most theoretical form, however, the development of medieval grammar is closely connected to the development of logic;[1] in contrast, grammar as a didactic discipline, aimed at teaching Latin, is linked to other genres, such as the "poetic arts," lexicography, and studies of the classics. Our knowledge of theoretical grammar, which is the object of the present study, has increased tremendously over the past twenty-five years as new editions have become available. As this chapter demonstrates, the major contribution of the *modistae* of the late thirteenth century – the group most closely associated with the development of theoretical grammar – is now understood as part of a broader and more diversified picture, which shows the interplay of grammar with logic, philosophy, and theology.

EARLY TWELFTH CENTURY

Recent studies have investigated the degree of continuity in the linguistic arts between the early and later Middle Ages. John Scottus Eriugena's recently edited commentary on Priscian shows that sophisticated discussions can be found in the Carolingian period of important issues such as the corporeal or incorporeal nature of an utterance (is it, for example, a substance [the Stoics and Priscian], or a quantity [Aristotle]?) and the meaning of the categorical notions of substance, quality, action, or time (as they occur in the definition of the parts of speech).[2] The interplay between grammar and dialectic was

---

[1] Sten Ebbesen and Irène Rosier-Catach, "Le *trivium* à la Faculté des arts," in L. Holtz and O. Weijers (eds.) *L'enseignement des disciplines à la Faculté des Arts (Paris et Oxford, XIIIe – XVe siècles)* (Turnhout: Brepols, 1997) 98–128.

[2] For the text, see Anneli Luhtala, "Early Medieval Commentary on Priscian's *Institutiones Grammaticae*," *Cahiers de l'Institut du Moyen Age Grec et Latin* 71 (2000) 115–88. See also "Glosses Based on Eriugena's Priscian Commentary," *Miscellanea Bibliothecae Apostolicae Vaticanae* 7 (2000) 199–213 and Paul Edward Dutton and Anneli Luhtala, "Eriugena in Priscianum," *Mediaeval Studies* 56 (1994) 153–63.

already present in Alcuin's *Dialogus*, and the use of Porphyry and of Aristotle's *Categories* and *De interpretatione* to rethink the definitions inherited from Donatus and Priscian is even more evident in Peter of Pisa and Sedulius Scottus.[3] The interplay between grammar and theology also became an important component of the medieval discussions of language, as seen in the ninth-century works of Gottschalk of Orbais on the Trinity,[4] and in the linguistic arguments used by Lanfranc of Bec and Berengar of Tours in their controversy over the Eucharistic conversion.[5]

At the turn of the eleventh into the twelfth century, Priscian's *Institutiones grammaticae* and Boethius's logical translations and commentaries – although hardly read in the earlier period – began to be studied in the same schools, and often by the same masters.[6] In spite of some shared interests, such as the problem of universals or the doctrine of categories, these commentaries show no sign of continuity with earlier Carolingian ones.[7] Particularly important for grammar are the *Glosulae in Priscianum*, which consist of two anonymous commentaries from the early twelfth century on Priscian's *Institutiones*, one on Priscian major (i.e. books I–XVI), and the other on Priscian minor (books XVII–XVIII on syntax), both extant in several versions.[8] The analyses developed by the *Glosulae*

---

[3] Louis Holtz, "La grammaire carolingienne," in S. Auroux (ed.) *Histoire des idées linguistiques*, vol. II: *Le développement de la grammaire occidentale* (Liège: Mardaga, 1992) 96–106; Vivien Law, "La grammaire latine," in Auroux, *Histoire des idées linguistiques*, II: 83–95; Vivien Law (ed.) *History of Linguistic Thought: The History of Linguistics in Europe, from Plato to 1600* (Cambridge: Cambridge University Press, 2003) chs. 6 and 7; *Grammar and Grammarians in the Early Middle Ages* (London: Longman, 1997); Edoardo Vineis, "La linguistica medievale: Linguistica e grammatica," in G. Lepschy (ed.) *Storia della linguistica* (Bologna: Il Mulino, 1990) II: 11–101; C. H. Kneepkens, "The Priscianic Tradition," in S. Ebbesen (ed.) *Sprachtheorien in Spätantike und Mittelalter* (Tübingen: Narr, 1995) 239–64.

[4] Jean Jolivet, *Godescalc d'Orbais et la trinité* (Paris: Vrin, 1958).

[5] Jean de Montclos, *Lanfranc et Bérenger. La controverse eucharistique du XIe siècle* (Louvain: Université catholique, 1971); Toivo Holopainen, *Dialectic and Theology in the Eleventh Century* (Leiden: Brill, 1996); Irène Rosier-Catach, *La parole efficace: signe, rituel, sacré* (Paris: Seuil, 2004) ch. 5.1.

[6] See the report of William of Conches, as quoted in Édouard Jeauneau, "Deux rédactions des gloses de Guillaume de Conches sur Priscien," *Recherches de théologie ancienne et médiévale* 27 (1960) p. 238.

[7] See John Marenbon, *From the Circle of Alcuin to the School of Auxerre: Logic, Theology and Philosophy in the Early Middle Ages* (Cambridge: Cambridge University Press, 1981).

[8] There exists a 1488 edition of the *Glosulae* on Priscian maior that needs to be checked against manuscripts. (The commentary on Priscian minor in that incunable edition is not the *Glosulae*.) A critical edition of the *Glosulae* is currently in preparation by A. Grondeux, K. M. Fredborg, E. Lorenzetti, and myself. For the moment, only extracts have been published in various studies, and from various manuscripts. See R. W. Hunt, "Studies on Priscian in the Eleventh and Twelfth Centuries: I. Petrus Helias and his Predecessors," *Medieval and Renaissance Studies* 1 (1941–3) 194–231; Margaret Gibson, "The Early Scholastic Glosule to Priscian, *Institutiones Grammaticae*: The Text and its Influence." *Studi Medievali* 1 (1979) 35–54; L. M. de Rijk, *Logica modernorum: A Contribution to the History of Early Terminist Logic* (Assen: Van Gorcum, 1962–7); K. M. Fredborg, "Tractatus Glosarum Prisciani in ms. Vat. lat. 1486," *Cahiers de l'Institut du Moyen Age Grec et Latin* 21 (1977) 27–44; C. H. Kneepkens, "Master Guido and his View on Government: On Twelfth-Century

were influential, and widely used by Peter Abaelard. They were responsible for important innovations; their originality lay in the interplay between grammar and logic, which can be seen in their analysis of syncategorematic terms, of the substantive verb (including the first use of the word *copula*), of predication (with the introduction of the distinction between inherence and identity), and of paronyms. Priscian's definition of the noun as signifying "substance with quality"[9] served as the occasion for commentators developing a realist conception of universals, akin to William of Champeaux's "material essence realism." Indeed, inspired by certain passages from Priscian (such as XVII.144), this realism even took on a Platonic tone, with universals signifying ideas in God's mind.[10] Interestingly, this discussion of universals — clearly influenced by Boethius's commentary on the *Isagoge* — developed semantic consequences that led to the influential distinction between signification (*significatio*) and denotation (*nominatio, appellatio*): on this view, the name 'human being' *names* individual human beings but *signifies* a common and universal quality shared by all members of the human species.[11] The *Glosulae* also initiated discussions of reference (*nominatio,*

Linguistic Thought," *Vivarium* 16 (1978) 108–41; Irène Rosier-Catach, "The *Glosulae in Priscianum* and its Tradition," in N. McLelland and A. Linn (eds.) *Papers in Memory of Vivien Law* (Münster: Nodus, 2004) 81–99.
    Although William of Champeaux, Abaelard's master, is not the author of the *Glosulae*, William certainly used them to lecture on Priscian. In the *Notae Dunelmenses*, a set of notes on Priscian, William's opinions (quoted as master G.'s) and the *Glosulae's* are opposed to one another. For the evidence, see Hunt, "Studies I," as well as Anne Grondeux and Irène Rosier-Catach, "Synthèse grammaticale," in Rosier-Catach (ed.) *Les Glosulae super Priscianum, Guillaume de Champeaux, Abelard: Arts du langage et théologie aux confins des XIe/XIIe siècles* (Turnhout: Brepols, forthcoming). On William more generally, see Constant Mews, "Logica in the Service of Philosophy: William of Champeaux and his Influence," in R. Berndt (ed.) *Schrift, Schreiber, Schenker: Studien zur Abtei Sankt Viktor zu Paris und zu den Viktorinern* (Berlin: Akademie Verlag, 2005) 61–101. An edition of the *Notae Dunelmenses* is being prepared by Franck Cinato, Anne Grondeux and myself.
  [9] The "substance" is the referent, the thing, to which is attributed a "quality," that is, a determination of some kind. For instance, on a Platonizing interpretation 'human being' means a thing that has the common quality 'humanity,' whereas 'Plato' means the same thing but with the singular quality 'Platonity.'
  [10] See de Rijk, *Logica* II.1, ch. 2; Fredborg, "Tractatus Glosarum Prisciani"; Constant Mews, "Nominalism and Theology before Abaelard: New Light on Roscelin of Compiègne," *Vivarium* 30 (1992) 4–33; Irène Rosier-Catach, "Abélard et les grammairiens: sur la définition du verbe et la notion d'inhérence," in P. Lardet (ed.) *La tradition vive: mélanges d'histoire des textes en l'honneur de Louis Holtz* (Turnhout: Brepols, 2003) 143–59; Irène Rosier-Catach, "Abélard et les grammairiens: sur le verbe substantif et la prédication," *Vivarium* 41 (2003) 176–248; Irène Rosier-Catach, "Priscien, Boèce, les *Glosulae in Priscianum*, Abélard: les enjeux des discussions autour de la notion de consignification," *Histoire Epistémologie Langage* 25 (2003) 55–84.
  [11] Rosier-Catach, "Les *Glosulae in Priscianum*"; William of Conches took over this distinction; see the text edited by K. M. Fredborg, "Some Notes on the Grammar of William of Conches," *Cahiers de l'Institut du Moyen Age Grec et Latin* 37 (1980) pp. 29 ff., and "Speculative Grammar," in P. Dronke (ed.) *A History of Twelfth-Century Western Philosophy* (Cambridge: Cambridge University Press, 1988) pp. 182–6.

which was to become *suppositio*) and coreference (*relatio*),[12] concepts that were
also to play a major role in terminist logic (see Chapter 11). It is clear that these
issues were the subject of lively discussion in the schools, because related topics
arise in contemporary logical commentaries, especially those on the *Categories*
and *De interpretatione*.

The *Glosulae in Priscianum maiorem* had a wide circulation, and were edited
as a marginal commentary in the earliest incunabula edition of Priscian (Venice
1488).[13] The text was used by William of Conches in his commentaries on
Priscian,[14] and by Peter Helias in his *Summa super Priscianum*. Peter's *Summa*,
which was also revised, became very popular.[15] Like the *Glosulae*, the *Summa*
uses ontology to build semantics; Peter explains, for instance, that it is because
"substance [with the meaning of what stands under: *sub-stans*] unifies all other
things, as far as it conjoins accidents, that the verb 'to be' has a copulative
function" (ed. Reilly, p. 201).[16]

There was also some interplay between grammarians and theologians commenting on Boethius's theological *Opuscula*, such as Gilbert of Poitiers and
Thierry of Chartres. Gilbert of Poitiers also uses Priscian's definition of the
noun, but in a new way. He equates the "substance" meaning of the noun with
the Boethian *id quod est* (that which is), and its "quality" meaning with the *id quo
est* (that by which the *quod est* is). He also explains that, in a given proposition,

---

[12] See de Rijk, *Logica* II.1, ch. 16; C. H. Kneepkens, "*Mulier quae Damnavit Salvavit:* A Note of the Early
Development of the Relatio Simplex," *Vivarium* 14 (1976) 1–25; C. H. Kneepkens, "The *Relatio
simplex* in the Grammatical Tracts of the Late Twelfth and Early Thirteenth Century," *Vivarium*
15 (1977) 1–30; C. H. Kneepkens, " 'Suppositio' and 'supponere' in 12th-Century Grammar,"
in J. Jolivet and A. de Libera (eds.) *Gilbert de Poitiers et ses contemporains: aux origines de la Logica
Modernorum* (Naples: Bibliopolis) 324–51.

[13] For other editions, see Margaret Gibson, "The Collected Works on Priscian: The Printed Editions
1470–1859" *Studi Medievali* 18 (1979) 249–60.

[14] See Jeauneau, "Deux rédactions"; Fredborg, "The Dependence of Petrus Helias' *Summa super
Priscianum* on William of Conches' *Glose super Priscianum*," *Cahiers de l'Institut du Moyen Age Grec et
Latin* 11 (1973) 1–57.

[15] Some thirty-one manuscripts have survived on Priscian major. The part on Priscian minor is
preserved in only five manuscripts, and was soon supplanted by another tract, called after its incipit
"*Absoluta cuiuslibet*" of a Peter of Spain (Petrus Hispanus, often referred to with the initials P. H.,
which entails confusion with Peter Helias), preserved in fifteen manuscripts, and circulated in a
short and a long version, the long ones presenting various interpolations, some of which date
from the end of the thirteenth century. It has been edited by C. H. Kneepkens, *Het Iudicium
Constructionis* (Nijmegen: Ingenium, 1987); see R. W. Hunt, "*Absoluta*: The *Summa* of Petrus
Hispanus on Priscianus minor," *Historiographia Linguistica* 2 (1975) 1–23; C. H. Kneepkens, "The
Absoluta cuiuslibet attributed to P. H.," in I. Angelelli and P. Pérez-Ilzarbe (eds.) *Medieval and
Renaissance Logic in Spain* (Hildesheim: Olms, 2000) 373–403.

[16] See C. H. Kneepkens, "Grammar and Semantics in the Twelfth Century: Petrus Helias and Gilbert
de la Porrée on the Substantive Verb," in M. Kardaun and J. Spruyt (eds.) *The Winged Chariot:
Collected Essays on Plato and Platonism in Honour of L. M. de Rijk* (Leiden: Brill, 2000) esp. pp. 253–5.

only one of these two meanings is operative: in the subject position the noun
signifies only substance (that is, it has a denotative meaning), whereas in a predicate position it signifies only the quality – an opinion that was considered typical
of the so-called Porretan school that Gilbert founded and which produced logical and grammatical texts.[17] On this analysis, the noun signifies not substance
with quality, as Priscian claimed, but substance *and* quality. Likewise, Gilbert
seems to have insisted on the difference between the *officium supponendi* and the
officium apponendi of the noun,[18] distinguishing three types of verbs (substantive,
vocative, adjective) according to the nature of the attributes (*apposita*).[19] This
contextual semantics would play an important role in the theologians' analysis
of propositions, especially in Trinitarian contexts.[20] In addition, the problem,
already present in the *Glosulae*, of whether Priscian's definition of the verb as
signifying action and passion applies to the substantive verb, and whether it
applies when used to talk about God and creatures, became a major issue in
twelfth-century theology.[21]

THE SECOND HALF OF THE TWELFTH CENTURY

Just as there were various schools in logic,[22] so there were different grammar schools. Apart from the Porretans we can name the schools of William
of Conches, Ralph of Beauvais, Robert of Paris, and Robert Blund, among
others. Whereas semantics formed the major focus of the discussion in the first
half of the twelfth century,[23] in interrelation with developments in dialectic,

---

[17] See the *Dialogus Eberardi et Ratii* (*ca.* 1193) (ed. Häring); the *Compendium logicae porretanum*
(ed. Ebbesen *et al.*); and the *Grammatica porretana* (ed. Fredborg and Kneepkens). See also the
Anonymus Leidensis discussed in K. M. Fredborg, "The Priscian Commentary from the Second Half
of the Twelfth Century: Ms Leiden BPL 154," *Histoire Epistémologie Langage* 12 (1990) 53–68. The
anonymous *Glosa "Promisimus"* (last quarter of twelfth century) oppose Priscian and the Porretan –
see the text in R. W. Hunt, "Studies on Priscian in the Twelfth Century: II. The School of Ralph
of Beauvais," *Mediaeval and Renaissance Studies* 2 (1950) p. 89. For Boethius's distinction between *id
quod est* and *id quo est*, see John Marenbon, *Boethius* (Oxford: Oxford University Press, 2003) ch. 5.
[18] *Grammatica porretana,* pp. 34–5; see Kneepkens, "Suppositio."
[19] *Grammatica porretana,* pp. 62–3. On the syntactic consequences of this doctrine, as far as the analysis
of transitivity is concerned, see again Kneepkens, "Grammar and Semantics," pp. 268–71.
[20] Luisa Valente, " 'Talia sunt subiecta qualia praedicata permittunt': Le principe de l'approche con-
textuelle et sa genèse dans la théologie du XIIe siècle," in J. Biard and I. Rosier-Catach (eds.) *La
tradition médiévale des catégories (XII e–XV e siècle)* (Louvain, Peeters, 2003) 289–311.
[21] Luisa Valente, *Logique et théologie: Les écoles parisiennes entre 1150 et 1220* (Paris: Vrin, 2008).
[22] Yukio Iwakuma and Sten Ebbesen, "Logico-Theological Schools from the Second Half of the
Twelfth Century: A List of Sources," *Vivarium* 30 (1992) 173–210.
[23] For instance, the *Glosulae* were interested in determining whether a property was a "real" or a
"vocal" one, distinguishing thus between *persona realis* and *persona vocalis*, and in the same way
for categories of mode, number, etc. William of Conches, followed by Peter Helias, classified the
accidents into purely formal properties (like conjugation of verbs) and "secondary significations."

syntax becomes of major interest among grammarians in the second half of the century.[24] One important discussion concerns the relation between the meaning of the word and its function (*officium, vis*).[25] The pronoun, for instance, does not have the same meaning as a proper noun (since the noun signifies substance with quality, whereas the pronoun signifies a "pure substance"), but it can have the *function* of the noun. This distinction between meaning and function was also raised for the consignificative parts of speech, or *syncategoremata* (see Chapter 11), leading to Abaelard's interesting solution (which explicitly contradicted the *Glosulae*) that these words do not have meaning, but contribute to the meaning of the sentence as acts of the mind.[26] The same distinction was at stake in discussions about the substantive verb – the disputed question in this case revolving around whether it had a meaning or only a function, and if it had the same meaning (often interpreted as existential import) both when used as a verb and when used as a copula.[27]

The important contribution to syntax realized by the grammarians of this period can be illustrated by four issues. The first is the notion of government (*regimen*), which integrates semantic and syntactic considerations. According to this notion, the relations between the words in a construction can be seen as semantic relations of "determination" (a notion borrowed from Boethius's *De divisione* and which also appears in logic), since an adjectival determination can imply a referential restriction, as in 'white man.'[28] But these relations can also be seen from a morpho-syntactical perspective, where grammatical cases play an important role: verbs are distinguished according to the "oblique cases" (*obliqui*) they can govern, parts of speech are described according to their property of being governed or not, and the government of each case (that is, the different constructions in which the name having such a case can enter) is carefully listed.

[24] Among the most important works are these *Summae*: Robert of Paris (ed. Kneepkens, *Het Iudicium*, vol. II); Huguccio of Pisa, *Summa* (discussed in ibid., vol. I: 141–2, 648–50); Robert Blund, *Summa de grammatica* (ed. ibid., vol. III); Peter of Spain, *Summa "Absoluta cuiuslibet"* (ed. Kneepkens, *Het Iudicium*). For Ralph of Beauvais, see the *Glose super Donatum*. The anonymous *Glosa "Promisimus"* is full of interesting references to the masters of its time. See also Hunt, "Studies II."

[25] '*Vis*' was a somewhat ambiguous term, since it can designate the semantic property of a word's intrinsic "force" taken in isolation, for instance when the substantive verb is defined as having a verbal meaning or force (*vis verbi*) and a substantive meaning or force (*vis substantivi*); but it can also designate the function that the semantic property allows the word to have in a particular context. See Fredborg, "The Dependence of Petrus Helias," pp. 22–7 (focusing on William of Conches); "Speculative Grammar," pp. 188–9.

[26] Abaelard, *Logica "Ingredientibus"* [*super Periherm.*], ed. Geyer, pp. 339–40.

[27] See Rosier-Catach, "Priscien, Boèce," and Klaus Jacobi, "Peter Abelard's Investigations into the Meaning and Function of the Speech Sign 'Est'," in S. Knuutila and J. Hintikka (eds.) *The Logic of Being* (Dordrecht: Reidel, 1986) 145–80.

[28] Kneepkens, "Master Guido"; Fredborg, "Speculative Grammar," pp. 192–4; A. de Libera and I. Rosier, "La pensée linguistique médiévale," in Auroux, *Histoire des idées linguistiques,* II: 115–86.

These last three applications of the government relation form the core of the syntactic part of didactic grammars, which were composed during this period and commented on until the end of the Middle Ages. It became clear that government and determination were not always parallel, and could even run in opposite directions; the distinction was important, nevertheless, since it helped widen syntax, extending it beyond the bare morphological relations involving cases.[29]

The second major issue in syntax, closely connected to the first one, was transitivity. (This had been thoroughly analyzed from as far back as the discussion in Priscian minor.) The major options were a dyadic analysis of construction and transitivity (which considered, for instance, the noun–verb relation or the verb–oblique relation), or a sentential analysis of transitivity, which involved the idea of referential identity or difference. On this latter account, the construction 'I eat an apple' is transitive because of the difference of reference between 'I' and 'apple.' (An awkward consequence of this theory is that 'I see myself' cannot be analyzed as transitive, because of referential identity, in spite of the accusative case of the object.)

The third issue was the elaboration of the functional notion of subject and predicate, resting on a distinction between the grammatical *suppositum* and *appositum* and the logical *subiectum* and *praedicatum*. There was a clear awareness, in grammar as in logic, that the grammatical subject (*suppositum*) was not necessarily the logical subject, or subject of discourse (*suppositum locutioni*). The distinction between categories and functions was important since it provided the possibility of building a real syntax that was based on rules and was not mere morphology.[30]

This leads to the last issue: completeness and correctness. The important advance here came from the thought given to the relations between correctness (grammaticality), completeness, and well-formedness (semanticity) – the question being whether a sentence had to be well formed to be understandable or not. This question, important for figurative and non-standard discourse, becomes a major issue in the next century, as we will see below.[31]

---

[29] The thirteenth-century notion of "dependency," subsuming determination and government, derives from this important move. See Michael Covington, *Syntactic Theory in the High Middle Ages: Modistic Models of Sentence Structure* (Cambridge: Cambridge University Press, 1984); Louis G. Kelly, *The Mirror of Grammar: Theology, Philosophy, and the Modistae* (Amsterdam: Benjamins, 2002) ch. 6.

[30] Kneepkens, "Suppositio"; L. M. de Rijk, "Each Man's Ass is not Everybody's Ass: On an Important Item in Thirteenth-Century Semantics," *Historiographia Linguistica* 7 (1980) 221–30.

[31] See also Ebbesen, "The Present King of France wears Hypothetical Shoes with Categorical Laces: Twelfth-Century Writers on Well-Formedness," *Medioevo* 7 (1981) 91–113.

THE THIRTEENTH CENTURY: THE RISE
OF SPECULATIVE GRAMMAR

Contrary to the way in which it is sometimes presented, speculative grammar did not emerge from nowhere, and it was not an absolutely new start in linguistic theory. Recent work has shown some continuity between syntactical tracts and the university grammars, and has also demonstrated that the didactic grammars of the turn of the twelfth and thirteenth century were not totally separated from the new orientations that grammar develops with the rise of the universities.

The thirteenth century began with the production of two influential "verse grammars" (grammars written in verse) – the *Grecismus* of Evrard of Béthune, and the *Doctrinale* of Alexander of Villa Dei – to which we can add the slightly later grammatical works written by John of Garland. Composed in the pre-university period, their primary purpose was didactic; nevertheless, the division between didactic and theoretical grammar cannot be seen as an absolute one, for at least two reasons. First, although John of Garland used to be seen as representative of the camp of the *auctores* (that is, the classical authors) against the philosophical or dialectical tendencies emerging in the Parisian grammatical schools (due to his strong criticism in the *Morale scholarium*), recent studies have shown that he also contributed to theoretical grammar. Indeed, he formed a link between the twelfth-century *Summa "Absoluta"* of Peter of Spain and Robert Kilwardby and Roger Bacon, who were, like him, English masters teaching in Paris in the faculty of arts in the 1240s, and who were influential representatives of the first period of speculative grammar (see below).[32] Second, the verse grammars always circulated with commentaries, which show similarities with the works produced in the arts faculties and which follow their developments. The *Glosa* on Evrard of Béthune's *Grecismus*, for instance, shows three layers: one connected to the teaching of John of Garland, another preserving a doctrine close to the mid-thirteenth-century teaching of Robert Kilwardby and Roger Bacon, and a third late thirteenth-century layer which adds material borrowed from the *modistae*. Furthermore, the various prologues that accompany the verse grammars are very close to the introductions to philosophy that began university courses in the faculty of arts.[33]

[32] See Anne Grondeux and Elsa Marguin, "L'œuvre grammaticale de Jean de Garlande (*ca.* 1195–1272?), auteur, réviseur et glosateur: Un bilan," *Histoire Epistémologie Langage* 21 (1999) 133–63.
[33] Anne Grondeux, *Le Graecismus d'Evrard de Béthune à travers ses gloses: entre grammaire positive et grammaire spéculative du XIIIe au XIVe siècle* (Brepols: Turnhout, 2000).

In considering the thirteenth century, then, it is no longer possible to focus exclusively on the *modistae* from the 1270s, such as Boethius of Dacia and Martin of Dacia, characterizing all other works as "pre-modistic" in view of a yet imperfect development of some key features of modistic doctrine, such as the notion of *modus significandi*. Recent editions and studies – not only on Robert Kilwardby, whose teaching in Paris in the 1240s had a considerable influence, but also of anonymous texts of various genres, glosses on didactic verse grammars, commentaries, treatises, and *summae* of sophisms – present a new picture of the development of thirteenth-century university grammar.[34]

For this reason, the remainder of this section offers a "modulary" presentation, organized by questions rather than by author. (See the appendix to this chapter for a guide to the texts that have been preserved.)[35] This approach helps show the continuity throughout the century as well as the divergences between the *modistae* and other grammatical approaches. The main characteristic of the *modistae* is their attempt to build a scientific grammar grounded in philosophical claims in epistemology, psychology, and ontology, together with their search for coherence between those claims and their theory of language.[36] The *modistae* cannot simply be equated with speculative grammarians, who include not only the *modistae*, but also earlier and later university masters who share the same conception of grammar as a science. Although some conceptions of the pre-modist speculative grammarians were taken over and developed by the *modistae*, others were strongly rejected. In particular, the salient feature that distinguishes "intentionalists" from the *modistae* is their divergent views on congruity and completeness.

---

[34] On the university literary genres for grammar, and the curriculum, see Ebbesen and Rosier-Catach, "Le *trivium* à la Faculté des arts." The students were to be lectured on Priscian (minor and major), on the pseudo-Priscian *De accentu*, and on the so-called *Barbarismus*, the third part of Donatus's *Ars maior* which was meant to supply Priscian with a theory of figurative speech. Moreover they had to attend to *disputationes*, both in schools and in "extraordinary" ceremonies; see I. Rosier-Catach, "Les sophismes grammaticaux au XIIIe siècle," *Medioevo* 17 (1991) 175–230.

[35] See I. Rosier-Catach, "Modisme, pré-modisme, proto-modisme, vers une définition modulaire," in S. Ebbesen and R. L. Friedman (eds.) *Medieval Analyses in Language and Cognition* (Copenhagen: Royal Academy, 1999) 45–81, for a fuller exposition of the same matter (with relevant texts). I do not consider here all the "modules" but the ones I consider most important.

[36] See Pinborg, *Die Entwicklung*; J. Pinborg, "Speculative Grammar," in N. Kretzmann *et al.* (eds.) *The Cambridge History of Later Medieval Philosophy* (Cambridge: Cambridge University Press, 1982) 254–69; J. Pinborg, *Medieval Semantics* (London: Variorum, 1984); G. L. Bursill-Hall, *Speculative Grammars of the Middle Ages: The Doctrine of partes orationis of the Modistae* (The Hague: Mouton, 1971); I. Rosier-Catach, "La grammaire dans le 'Guide de l'étudiant'," in C. Lafleur and J. Carrier (eds.) *L'enseignement de la philosophie au XIIIe siècle: Autour du "Guide de l'étudiant" du ms. Ripoll 109* (Turnhout: Brepols, 1997) 255–79; Marmo, *Semiotica*.

Grammar as a science

University teaching constitutes a new paradigm because of the requirements that it imposed on the disciplines to meet the Aristotelian criteria for a science (see Chapter 26). These requirements were discussed in the "divisions of the sciences" that flourished in the early years of the university.[37] The relevant questions – including "Is grammar a science?," "Is grammar prior to logic?," and "Is grammar a practical or a speculative science?" – formed the prologues of the modistic treatises, but they were already present in earlier texts, such as the prologues of the verse grammars,[38] John of Garland's *Clavis compendii*, commentaries on Priscian such as Kilwardby's and Nicholas of Paris's, or again in the student's guide preserved in a Ripoll manuscript.[39]

The demonstration of the scientific nature of grammar called for a distinction between what is variable, contingent, and accidental in language (and, thus, not liable to scientific analysis) and what is necessary and universal, that is, "the same for all." Borrowing from Dominicus Gundisalvi's influential *De divisione philosophiae*, a distinction was introduced between "positive grammar" and "regular grammar" to separate what belongs to *imposition* (and thus to the various languages) and what can be described with general rules (ed. Baur, pp. 45–6).[40] The basic idea is to identify something universal in language, so that different languages differ merely through accidental vocal features. Jordanus, for instance, explains (*ca.* 1240) that "the way words are ordered according to the conformity of their accidents is the same in all languages" (*Notulae*, ed. Sirridge, p. 5); pseudo-Kilwardby holds that "the signs taken in their universal nature abstracted from particular signs" are the subject of grammar as a science (ed. Fredborg *et al.*, p. 8); and, according to Boethius of Dacia, there is one grammar in all languages (*Quaest. super Priscianum maiorem* q. 2). The late medieval commentary on the *Flores grammatice* explains that this "regular

[37] Claude Lafleur, *Quatre introductions à la philosophie au XIIIe siècle* (Paris: Vrin, 1988), and Lafleur and Carrier, *L'enseignement de la philosophie au XIIIe siècle*, among other studies.

[38] Anne Grondeux, "Prologue, *prohemium*, glose du *prohemium* dans les manuscrits du Graecismus d'Evrard de Béthune," *Les prologues médiévaux* (Brepols: Turnhout, 2000) 323–44, and *Le Graecismus*, ch. 2.

[39] Lafleur, *L'enseignement*; Rosier-Catach, "La grammaire dans le 'Guide' "; Mary Sirridge, "Robert Kilwardby as 'Scientific Grammarian'," *Histoire Epistémologie Langage* 10 (1990) 7–28; Alessio, "Il commento"; C. H. Kneepkens, "The Tradition of Universal and Speculative Grammar in the Late Middle Ages," in C. Codoñer Merino *et al.* (eds.) *El Brocense y la Humanidades en el siglo XVI* (Salamanca: Ediciones Universidad, 2003) pp. 35–6.

[40] Twelfth-century grammarians distinguished differently between the *species* of the art of grammar, which are the various languages, and the grammar that can be found in each of them; see K. M. Fredborg, "Universal Grammar According to some Twelfth c. Grammarians," *Historiographia Linguistica* 7 (1980) 69–83.

grammar" is what is called "speculative grammar," "because it speculates about the principles, rules and conclusions of the grammatical science," whereas "positive grammar, which teaches the significates of the terms . . . is not a science."[41] In short, words have modes of signifying that correspond to modes of being and that can be constructed according to general rules. This is a general feature of all languages and is thus the object of scientific grammar. Grammar is both universal and "speculative" – a characterization justified either in a derived sense, by the fact that it is "useful for the knowledge of speculative sciences" (Boethius of Dacia), or intrinsically, because its goal is to obtain knowledge about language (Radulphus Brito).

Modi significandi

The notion of "mode of signifying" has a twofold origin, in Priscian's idea that the different word-classes should be distinguished by their "property of signification" (reformulated by the *Glosulae* as "mode of signifying"), and in the Aristotelian idea (transmitted through Boethius) of "consignification." This second idea, which was extended to all the grammatical accidents later called "consignificata" (because they were signified along with, *cum*, the lexical significate, *significata*), also helped to distinguish between signification properly speaking (lexical meaning) and consignification (grammatical meaning). So, for instance, the noun 'year' signifies time whereas a verb *consignifies* time because it has the grammatical accident of tense.

A word such as 'human being' was taken to have three kinds of properties: (1) its lexical meaning (rational mortal animal), which was often called "special signification" (*significatio specialis*); (2) its grammatical meaning or "general signification" (*significatio generalis*), which could be either (a) an essential property, such as being a noun or (b) a specific property, such as being a common or substantive noun; and (3) accidental properties, such as being masculine, singular, or nominative. For a time, there was a difference of terminology between Parisian masters such as Nicholas of Paris or John le Page and the English masters teaching in Paris such as Robert Kilwardby, who used the notion of "mode of signifying" in a more systematic way.[42] After a period where both systems were used in a somewhat confused way (as in Gosvin of Marbais's *Tractatus de constructione*) the English system was adopted and developed by the *modistae*. The

---

[41] Ed. in Rosier, "Modisme, pré-modisme," p. 51.
[42] See P. O. Lewry, "Robert Kilwardby's Writings on the Logica Vetus" (D.Phil. thesis: Oxford University, 1978) pp. 376–84; Kneepkens, "*Significatio generalis* and *significatio specialis*," in Ebbesen and Friedman, *Medieval Analyses in Language and Cognition*, 17–43; Grondeux and Rosier-Catach, in *Robertus Anglicus, Sophistria*, pp. 57–62.

whole of grammar was then unified through its principles, the *modi significandi*, which corresponded to all the grammatical features of a word, as distinct from its lexical meaning.

The speculative grammarians also took over an old idea, already found in the twelfth century, that words belonging to different word-classes can signify the same "thing" in different modes (for instance, 'white,' 'whiten,' 'whiteness'). Their favorite example was the notion of *pain*, which could be thought of, and thus signified, as a noun (*dolor*), a verb (*doleo*), a participle (*dolens*), an adverb (*dolenter*), or an interjection (*heu!*).[43] Analysis of interjections gave rise to a popular discussion, especially among English authors, of the distinction between the natural and the conventional way of expressing emotions – that is, between the "affective" and "conceptual" modes.[44] Likewise, a movement could be signified either by the name *motus*, and so as a substance, or by the verb *moveo*, and so as an action.[45] Authors writing in the 1270s, or thereabouts, devised a theory of imposition to explain this principle of independence between lexical and grammatical meaning. Matthew of Bologna talked about a double "imposition," and the *modistae* talked about a double "articulation" – an idea initially borrowed from Porphyry's commentary on the *Categories*, as transmitted by Boethius.[46] For Matthew, the *vox* is first imposed on its significate (usually, a thing in the world). With this lexical meaning in place, the significative vocal sound is then imposed on its general mode of signifying (turning the word into a part of speech of some kind, such as a noun, then into a species of this part of speech, such as an adjective or a substantive) and then on the accidental modes of signifying (giving the noun its accidents like case, gender, etc.). The *modistae* added the Aristotelian distinction between matter and form: through the first articulation, the vocal matter is associated with a form that is its signification (or *ratio significandi*), thus producing a *dictio*; then, through the second articulation, the *dictio* as matter is associated with various forms that are the modes of signifying (or *rationes consignificandi*), thus producing a *constructibile* – that is, a complete linguistic item.[47]

The *modistae* devised a complex system to explain the relationship between language, thought, and things, inspired by Avicenna's theory of common

---

[43] See, inter alia, Michael of Marbais, *Summa*, ed. Kelly, p. 13.

[44] See I. Rosier-Catach, *La parole comme acte: sur la grammaire et la sémantique au XIIIe siècle* (Paris: Vrin, 1994) chs. 2 and 5.

[45] See Kilwardby, *Super Priscianum minorem*, in Pinborg, *Die Entwicklung*, p. 48.

[46] Boethius, *In Categorias* (ed. *Patr. Lat.* 64: 159b) distinguished the imposition of nouns on things and the imposition of nouns (such as "*nomen*" and "*verbum*") on those first nouns.

[47] Note that the *dictio* is a linguistic item having only lexical meaning, and as such is an abstraction, not a real item. Pinborg, "Speculative Grammar," p. 257, compares it to Lyon's *lexeme*, and Marmo (*Semiotica*, ch. 3) to Hjelmslev's *sign function*.

natures. If the significate of a word corresponds to the thing itself, the modes of signifying (*modi significandi*) correspond to the modes of being (*modi essendi*) through modes of understanding (*modi intelligendi*). The fact that the modes of signifying have a real foundation in modes of being was the guarantee needed for the discipline to be a science, since this ensured that its principles were not mere fictions. Unlike Matthew of Bologna, then, who claims that the first and the second imposition were voluntary and independent from each other – and, thus, that a thing could become the significate of a word belonging to any part of speech – some *modistae*, such as Boethius of Dacia, secure a real, non-subjective foundation for all the modes, stating that "imposition is not purely dependent on our will." Once a significate has been chosen in the first imposition, the real thing corresponding to it "regulates" the imposition of the modes in the second imposition; so, for instance, the fact that 'Socrates' refers to an individual implies the choice of the proper noun to signify it (*Modi significandi* [*Opera* I: 40]).[48]

In addition to the requirement that a scientific grammar be grounded in reality, there was another requirement, going in the opposite direction: to prove the independence of the sphere of grammar and language from reality. For this purpose, stress was put on the intermediate level of the *modi intelligendi*: the intellect was free to think and to signify a thing in a different way from how it really existed, although the mode of signifying had to have *some* corresponding mode of being. For instance, privative nouns ('nothing,' 'blindness'), to which no real thing corresponds, derive the mode of permanence that makes them substantive nouns from the property of some other things, such as substances, that really have this permanence. Likewise, the fact that the feminine gender of 'deity' has an origin in a real property of passivity does not imply that the thing signified as God *has* this property, but only that human beings *thought* about God as if God were passive (as moved by their prayers, for instance).[49] There is also a theological history to the notion of *modus significandi*, developing from the early thirteenth century, and partly from the same sources, where the central problem is God's ineffable nature in contrast to the imperfect human modes through which that nature can be thought and signified.[50]

---

[48] See Roberto Lambertini, "*Sicut tabernarius vinum significat per circulum*: Directions in Contemporary Interpretations of the Modistae," in U. Eco and C. Marmo (eds.) *On the Medieval Theories of Signs* (Amsterdam: John Benjamins, 1989) pp. 118–19.

[49] See Marmo, *Semiotica*, ch. 4.

[50] See Gregory Rocca, "The Distinction between *res significata* and *modus significandi* in Aquinas' Theological Epistemology," *The Thomist* 55 (1990) 173–97; I. Rosier-Catach, "*Res significata* et *modus significandi*: Les implications d'une distinction médiévale," in S. Ebbesen (ed.) *Sprachtheorien in Spätantike und Mittelalter* (Tübingen: Narr, 1995) 135–68; Thierry-Dominique Humbrecht, *Théologie négative et noms divins chez saint Thomas d'Aquin* (Paris, Vrin, 2005).

Syntax and semantics

The partial or total independence of the significate from the grammatical features of a word effectively proved the independence of syntax from semantics. This independence was expressed through the "causal definition" (sometimes attributed to the *modistae*, but in fact commonly accepted by earlier authors such as Robert Kilwardby or Roger Bacon) of what a grammatical construction is: "Construction is the union of the *constructibilia* from their modes of signifying, caused to express a concept of the mind." This definition implies that the rules for construction and correctness are stated as rules of correspondence between modes: for instance, in a subject–predicate construction, the subject has such and such modes of signifying (being a noun, substantive, in the nominative case, etc.), corresponding to such and such modes of signifying of the verb (being a verb, personal, with an active mode, etc.). The correctness of the construction could then be automatically derived; if any one of these modes was missing, then the construction was automatically declared incorrect.

For the *modistae*, the independence of syntax from semantics was grounded in the Aristotelian potency–act distinction. The modes of signifying were the features of a word that gave it the *potency* to *act* or have a function (*officium*) in a given construction. This implied that a word should have all the required properties *before* entering in a construction, and that it should not get any new property by its occurring in a given construction. This conception had numerous consequences in both grammar and logic. One concerned the theory of the syncategorematic constituents, where discussion arose over whether such constituents have a significate distinct from their general mode of signifying and from their function (*officium*). Some authors, such as Gentilis da Cingulo, held that the significate and mode of signifying were identical; others, such as Martin of Dacia, held that the significate is identical with the accidental mode.[51] Michael of Marbais, in contrast, wanted to apply modistic principles in a strict way: every word should first have a significate and then some mode of signifying distinct from it, and its function was the "effect" of the modes of signifying.[52] A second important consequence was the "semantic irrelevance of the context." All the properties are attributed to a term at the moment of imposition, and they constitute the "essence" of the term. This means that they cannot be suppressed

---

[51] See Marmo, *Semiotica*, pp. 225ff. for the discussion of this problem; see also Lambertini, "*Sicut tabernarius.*"

[52] Michael of Marbais, *Summa*, ed. Kelly, pp. 122–4: "and thus in the indeclinable parts the significate and the mode of signifying differ in an essential way" and "the way in which they differ . . . is a great difficulty and an object of disagreement among our doctors of grammar."

or modified, and none can be gained through a particular use.[53] Thus grammar has a strong coherence: all the grammatical features required by the rules of syntax have to be given to the word through imposition and thus are defined in the first part of grammar, called "etymology"; the rules of construction are, in turn, described in the part of grammar called "syntax" (*diasynthetica*), stated as rules of dependency, which require only the features defined in the "etymology" part of grammar; finally, the rules for congruity depend only on the correct application of the rules of syntax. In Chomskian terms, the system is one of "internal adequacy" – that is, an adequacy defined according to the linguistic rules – and not of "external adequacy," which would depend on the context and particular use. As far as logic is concerned, this conception was the opposite of the "contextual approach" characteristic of terminist logic (see Chapter 11), and this had important consequences for the analysis of reference and equivocity.[54]

Congruity and intention

The major consequence of the radical division between lexical and grammatical properties was, for the *modistae*, that semantics did not have to interfere with syntax (for instance, the phrase 'a categorical hat' is for them just as correct, grammatically speaking, as 'a black hat') and that grammaticality was the condition for semanticity. This was not, however, a universally accepted position; as a matter of fact, the *modistae* developed this strict position against some earlier or contemporary grammarians who held that a sentence could be declared correct even though it contained some deviations from the accepted rules.

The thirteenth century had inherited two contrasting doctrines on congruity. On the one hand, Peter Helias accepted the division between grammatical or vocal correctness (*secundum vocem*) and semantic correctness (*secundum sensum*): 'categorical hat' was acceptable on the first ground but not on the second.[55] On the other hand, the late twelfth-century grammarian Peter of Spain placed

---

[53] This principle does not contradict the possibility of an *a posteriori* discovery of the modes of signifying: from the presence of a given word in a construction, one can deduce that it has this property. But the property did belong to it before it was used in this construction. See Pinborg, "Speculative Grammar," p. 261.

[54] See the important studies on the logic of the *modistae* – a topic that I cannot consider here – esp. Pinborg, *Medieval Semantics*; Ebbesen, "Can Equivocation Be Eliminated?," *Studia Mediewistyczne* 18 (1977) 103–24; Ebbesen, "The Dead Man is Alive," *Synthese* 40 (1979) 43–70; Marmo, *Semiotica*, ch. 5; Costantino Marmo, "A Pragmatic Approach to Language in Modism," in S. Ebbesen (ed.) *Sprachtheorien in Spätantike und Mittelalter* (Tübingen: Narr, 1995) 169–83; Costantino Marmo, "The Semantics of the Modistae," in Ebbesen and Friedman, *Medieval Analyses in Language and Cognition,* 83–104.

[55] Ebbesen, "The Present King."

semantic congruity first, putting much weight on Priscian's *dictum* that "all construction should be referred to the intellection of the utterance."[56] Although vocal congruity is taught first to children, it is not sufficient in itself: "mere vocal congruity does not make a construction (for example, 'a stone does not like its son'), if no intellection is grasped by the hearer from the vocal expression."[57] Peter of Spain's interpretation was very influential and was, in fact, copied by John of Garland.[58] Talking about elliptic expressions used in Scripture, John explains that the omission of the verb gives rise to an expression with an affective import; he further comments that "an imperfect construction has a stronger intention in the mind of the hearer than a perfect one." So, for instance, the interjection *Heu!* conveys a stronger intention than 'I suffer' (*ego doleo*). It was probably from John that this conception reached his fellow Englishmen Robert Kilwardby and Roger Bacon.[59] They claimed that the most correct sentence is not necessarily the one that is grammatically correct, but is rather the one that fits most adequately with the "intention of the speaker" (*intentio proferentis*).[60] This principle was meant to apply both to elliptic and incomplete constructions and to figurative ones: both types were incorrect "absolutely" (*simpliciter*) but could be accepted for certain purposes (*secundum quid*).[61]

On this view, then, there seem to be two levels of grammatical congruity: a first, which depends on the application of the standard rules; and a second, where these rules are not respected, but where there is an "excusatory reason" not to respect them that justifies deviation from the rules.[62] This excusatory reason came in two parts, explaining both the reason why the deviation is possible and the reason why the deviation is necessary. For instance, in the figurative

---

[56] *Institutiones grammaticae* XVII.187 (ed. Hertz, p. 201). On this dictum, see Mary Sirridge, "*Institutiones Grammaticae* XVII, 187: Three Reactions," in I. Rosier (ed.) *L'héritage des grammairiens latins de l'antiquité aux lumières* (Louvain: Peeters, 1988) 171–81.

[57] *Summa,* ed. Kneepkens, in *Het Iudicium* pp. 1–2; see Hunt, "Absoluta"; C. H. Kneepkens, "Roger Bacon on the Double *Intellectus*: A Note on the Development of the Theory of *Congruitas* and *Perfectio* in the First Half of the Thirteenth Century," in P. O. Lewry (ed.) *The Rise of British Logic* (Toronto: Pontifical Institute of Mediaeval Studies, 1985) 115–43; Kneepkens, "The *Absoluta*."

[58] See the gloss on John of Garland's *Ars lectoria ecclesie* (ed. Marguin-Hamon, p. 291); see also Garland's *Clavis Compendii,* verses 1770–81.

[59] The elliptic constructions taken from Scriptures and liturgy (such as *Ite missa est*) given in John's gloss on his own text are very close to the ones later analyzed in Roger Bacon's *Summa grammatica,* ed. Steele *et al.*, XV: 183–4; cf. John of Garland, *Ars lectoria ecclesie* (ed. Marguin-Hamon, p. 294).

[60] Robert Kilwardby, *Commentum super Priscianum minorem,* ed. Kneepkens, "Roger Bacon," p. 138, and Roger Bacon, *Summa grammatica,* ed. Steele, *et al.* XV: 15.

[61] The analysis is grounded on different oppositions, partly coinciding, qualifying congruity and completeness: *secundum vocem / secundum sensum; ad sensum / ad intellectum; secundum intellectum primum / secundum intellectum secundum*; see Rosier-Catach, "O magister," and *La parole comme acte,* ch. 1.

[62] Interestingly, this double reason was introduced in the second layer of the glosses on the *Grecismus,* as much as in the *Admirantes* gloss on the *Doctrinale*; see Grondeux, *Le Graecismus.*

Turba ruunt ("the crowd [singular] rush [plural]"), there is an incongruity of number. The first excusatory reason, of a linguistic nature, is the semantic plural meaning of the grammatically singular noun 'crowd'; the second reason, of an extralinguistic nature, is the necessity to use the deviant expression because of the speaker's intention to insist on the multitude composing the crowd. Because of these linguistic and extralinguistic reasons, the hearer can reconstruct the meaning that was intended by the speaker;[63] thus, the sentence is incongruous absolutely speaking (*simpliciter*) but not *secundum quid* – that is, according to the intended meaning.

This is a very powerful doctrine, but it seems to run against the principle that semantics and extralinguistic considerations should not interfere with grammar as such. The most refined expositors of this doctrine, such as Robertus Anglicus, Gosvin of Marbais, Magister Johannes (who wrote the *summa* "*Sicut dicit Remigius*"), and the anonymous author of the sophism "O Magister," devised a very complete system, including both sentences that are "vocally correct" (called *ad sensum* because in these cases the senses could grasp the linguistic marks) and those that are "intellectually correct" (called *ad intellectum* because the sensible information is misleading and seemingly unacceptable and, thus, there is the need of an intellectual interpretation to reconstruct the structure and form of the sentence). Among those are sentences we would call performative, such as *bene!*, addressed at someone beating a child (!), which means "go on beating him." Because the beating is already in progress, existing as an "exercised act" (*actus exercitus*), there is no need for it to be signified by a verb as a "signified act" (*actus significatus*). In the same way, the expression *Aqua!* – uttered to ask someone to get water when a fire is discovered – is perfectly understandable as having the meaning of a complete sentence, and moreover conveys in a better way the panic of the utterer. In the analysis of these and other examples, there was a clear awareness that utterances used to perform speech acts did not have the same properties as non-performative ones.

Thirteenth-century grammar can no longer be simply divided between "modists" and "pre-modists." Early university grammarians of the thirteenth century – often of English origin such as Kilwardby – developed some points of doctrine that were further elaborated by the *modistae*. This is especially true for the doctrine of *modi significandi*, and for their application of Aristotelian

---

[63] Mary Sirridge, "Robert Kilwardby: Figurative Constructions and the Limits of Grammar," in G. L. Bursill-Hall (ed.) *De ortu grammaticae* (Amsterdam: Benjamins, 1990) 321–37; Anne Grondeux, "*Turba ruunt* (Ov. 'Her.' I, 88?): Histoire d'un exemple grammatical," *Archivum Latinitatis Medii Aevi* 61 (2003) 175–222.

notions, taken from Aristotle's *Physics*, regarding the requirements on grammar to count as a science.[64] Other claims, however, regarding grammaticality, semanticity, and speech acts, were opposed by the first *modistae*.[65] This "intentionalist" approach to language is found in numerous sophismata collections, treatises, and commentaries on the versified grammars. Despite the initial opposition, later *modistae* seem to have taken a more conciliatory attitude toward this approach, and moreover some of the views held by the intentionalists are found in still later texts.

DEVELOPMENTS AFTER 1300

The philosophical principles defined by the *modistae* became the target of strong criticism from the beginning of the fourteenth century onwards. The claim that a word became significant and consignificant through some "superadded *ratio*" was rejected: "The vocal sound is only significative and consignificative because the speaker wants it and uses it to signify," says John Aurifaber, an art master at Erfurt in the 1330s.[66] Construction and congruency depend on use, and there is no need to find "causes" to explain them. The "destruction" of modism went along with the elaboration of a conceptualist grammar, based on the theory of mental language and the subordination of vocal language to it. Pseudo-Peter of Ailly, for instance, claims (*ca.* 1400) that government, congruity, and construction operate at the level of mental language, with mental concepts being composed to form mental sentences.[67] Such a mentalist approach is also found in the *Quaestiones* commentary on the second part of Alexander of Villa Dei's *Doctrinale*, written in the Netherlands in the last decades of the fourteenth century: "Even if there did not exist any vocal or written utterances, there would still be . . . some grammatical government in the mind, and thus a science of this mental government." An extreme consequence of the displacement of congruity at the mental level was the claim that at the written or oral level a sentence like *hominem currit* ('a human being runs,' with 'human being' in

---

[64] The use made by the *modistae* of Aristotle's *Physics*, for a new analysis of cases, transitivity, and dependency relations, was well described by Louis Kelly in his introduction to pseudo-Albert the Great's *Quaestiones*, and in "La Physique d'Aristote et la phrase simple dans les traités de grammaire spéculative," in A. Joly and J. Stefanini (eds.) *La grammaire spéculative: des Modistes aux Idéologues* (Lille: Presses Universitaires, 1977) 105–24. This began, however, in the earlier generation (see Grondeux and Rosier-Catach, *The Sophistria*, pp. 62–7). It again seems to have been introduced by English authors, and is already in John of Garland – we should remember that the *libri naturales* could not be taught in Paris in the first half of the thirteenth century.

[65] See, for instance, Gentilis da Cingulo, as quoted in Rosier-Catach, *La parole comme acte*, p. 237 n. 4; compare Martin of Dacia, *Modi significandi*, pp. 112–15. See Grondeux, "*Turba ruunt*."

[66] *Determinatio de modis significandi*, ed. Pinborg, *Entwicklung* p. 218.

[67] *Destructiones modorum significandi*, ed. Kaczmarek, pp. 58–63.

the improper accusative case) was just as acceptable as *homo currit* (with 'human being' in the proper nominative). The congruence of a vocal sentence was deemed accidental, being subordinated to the intrinsic congruence of the mental sentence (*oratio mentalis*).[68] The grammar of mental language is universal, but its study belongs to the logician, whereas the grammars of particular languages are the task of the grammarian. The *modistae*'s claim that grammar deserved to be called a science, which was based on the idea that universality belonged to the realm of language just as to the realm of reason, was thus challenged in a way that left no recourse other than either to retreat to a more elementary position in the disciplines or to adopt the mentalist approach adopted by the logicians.

Modistic grammars nevertheless continued to be written at the end of the fourteenth and into the fifteenth century, both in Paris and also in Germany and central Europe. With the revival of realism, the *via moderna* was challenged by followers of the *via antiqua,* who held modistic positions.[69] Among them, the Albertists John of Nova Domus wrote the *Commentum aureum*[70] and (pseudo-)Johannes Versor composed an elementary commentary on *Donatus minor,*[71] while, interestingly, Erhard Knab von Zwiefalten explicitly rejected the modist positions adopted in his first *Donatus* commentary to then adopt the "*via modernorum.*"[72] The opposition between *moderni* and *antiqui*, grounded on different presuppositions about metaphysics and language – especially the relation between vocal and mental language – had important consequences

---

[68] Texts quoted in C. H. Kneepkens, "Erfurt, Ampl. Q.70A: A Quaestiones-Commentary on the Second Part of Alexander de Villa Dei's *Doctrinale* by Marsilius of Inghen? An Explorative Note on a Specimen of Conceptualist Grammar," *Vivarium* 28 (1990) pp. 36–7, 53–4; "On the Notion of *Constructio* in Conceptualist Grammar: Quaestio XXXV of the *Doctrinale*-Commentary Preserved in Erfurt, Amplon. Q. 70A and attributed to a Master Marcilius," in H. A. G. Braakhuis and M. J. F. M. Hoenen (eds.) *Marsilius of Inghen* (Nijmegen: Ingenium, 1992) pp. 166–7; E. P. Bos, "An Anonymous Commentary on the Second Part of Alexander de Villa Dei's *Doctrinale* (circa 1400)," in M. C. Pacheco and J. F. Meirinhos (eds.) *Intellect et imagination dans la philosophie médiévale* (Turnhout: Brepols, 2006) 1743–56.

[69] See Pinborg, *Die Entwicklung*, p. 224; Alfonso Maierù, "La linguistica medievale: filosofia del linguaggio," in G. Lepschy (ed.) *Storia della linguistica* (Bologna: Mulino, 1990) p. 134. See also Kaczmarek's edition of the *Destructiones* and the works of Kneepkens cited in the previous note, along with C. H. Kneepkens, "Some Notes on the Revival of Modistic Linguistics in the Fifteenth Century: Ps.-Johannes Versor and William Zenders of Weert," in R. Friedman and S. Ebbesen (eds.) *John Buridan and Beyond 1300–1700* (Copenhagen: Royal Danish Academy of Sciences and Letters, 2004) 69–119.

[70] Zénon Kaluza, *Les querelles doctrinales à Paris: nominalistes et réalistes aux confins du XIVe et du XVe siècles* (Bergamo: Lubrina, 1988).

[71] Kneepkens, "The Tradition," pp. 49–52, and "Some Notes on the Revival."

[72] Ludger Kaczmarek, "Erhard Knab von Zwiefalten († 1480): *Improbatio modorum significandi*. Edition nach den Handschriften," in K. D. Dutz (ed.) *Individuation, Sympnoia panta, Harmonia, Emanation. Festgabe H. Schepers* (Münster: Nodus, 2000) 109–55; Kneepkens, "The Tradition," pp. 52–3.

for how grammar was understood among late scholastic authors (see Chapter 12).[73]

Throughout the Middle Ages, the claims made by authors of theoretical grammars depend not just on how they construe narrow linguistic issues, but also on how they understand a wide range of issues in metaphysics, epistemology, and psychology. A realist or a nominalist conception of universals, for instance, conditioned the definition of the noun and the analysis of predication, whereas one or another theory of relation influenced views of construction. Likewise, an approach focused on actual communication and understanding (and not only on the universality of the rules) allowed stress to be put either on context and use or on the stability of the linguistic code, and so either on the importance of the speaker's intention and will, or on the law of conventionality.

APPENDIX: THIRTEENTH-CENTURY UNIVERSITY GRAMMAR TEXTS

Texts that have been preserved from the thirteenth century fall into the following groups:

- *summae* of sophisms (Roger Bacon, *Summa Grammatica* [ed. Steele *et al.*, fasc. 15]; Robertus Anglicus, *Sophistria*);
- isolated long sophisms (Peter of Auvergne and Boethius of Dacia, in S. Ebbesen and I. Rosier-Catach, "Petrus de Alvernia + Boethius de Dacia: Syllogizantem ponendum est terminos," *Cahiers de l'Institut du Moyen Age Grec et Latin* 75 [2004] 161–218; Nicholas of Normandy, *Albus musicus est*; Walter of Ailly, "Un sophisme grammatical"). See also Christine Brousseau-Beuermann, "Le sophisme anonyme 'Amatus sum vel fui' du codex Parisinus BN lat. 16135," *Cahiers de l'Institut du Moyen Age Grec et Latin* 61 (1991) 147–83, and I. Rosier-Catach, "O Magister...: Grammaticalité et intelligibilité selon un sophisme du XIIIe siècle," *Cahiers de l'Institut du Moyen Age Grec et Latin* 56 (1988) 1–102;
- treatises (pseudo-Grosseteste and Gosvin of Marbais);
- commentaries on the *De accentu* (Kilwardby, *Notulae de accentibus*), on the *Barbarismus* (Kilwardby, *In Donati artem maiorem*), and on Priscian Maior and Minor.

The edited (or partly edited) non-modistic commentaries are pseudo-Kilwardby, *On Priscian Maior*; Jordanus, *Notulae super Priscianum Minorem* (for authorship of the latter, see René Gauthier, "Notes sur les débuts (1225–1240) du

---

[73] On the problem of the subject of a sentence, for example, see Gerhard of Zutphen's *Glosa notabilis* on the *Doctrinale* and William Zenders of Weert's commentary on the *Doctrinale*, studied in Kneepkens, "The Tradition," pp. 53–6; see also C. H. Kneepkens, "The *Via antiqua* and the *Via moderna* in Grammar: The Late Medieval Discussions on the Subject of the Sentence," in A. Maierù and L. Valente (eds.) *Medieval Theories on Assertive and Non-Assertive Language* (Florence: Olschki, 2004) 219–44, and "Some Notes on the Revival."

premier 'averroïsme'," *Revue des sciences philosophiques et théologiques* 66 (1982) 367–73).

The edited modistic grammars are the following: Matthew of Bologna, *Quaest. super modos significandi*; Boethius of Dacia, *Modi significandi*; Martin of Dacia, *Modi significandi*; Simon of Dacia, *Quaest. super secundo minoris voluminis Prisciani*; Gentilis da Cingulo, *Quaest. super Priscianum Minorem*; John of Dacia, *Summa gramatica*; Michael of Marbais, *Summa de modis significandi*; Radulphus Brito, *Quaestiones super Priscianum minorem*; Thomas of Erfurt, *Grammatica speculativa*; Siger of Courtrai, *Summa modorum significandi*; pseudo-Albert, *Quaestiones alterti de modis significandi*.

See also the extracts of anonymous texts in various studies, especially in Jan Pinborg, *Die Entwicklung der Sprachtheorie im Mittelalter* (Münster: Aschendorff, 1967); Costantino Marmo, *La semiotica e linguaggio nella Scolastica: Parigi, Bologna, Erfurt 1270–1330. La semiotica dei Modisti* (Rome: Istituto Storico Italiano per il Medio Evo, 1994); Gian Carlo Alessio, "Il commento di Gentile da Cingoli a Martino di Dacia," in D. Buzzetti *et al.* (eds.) *L'insegnamento della logica a Bologna nel XIV secolo* (Bologna: Istituto per la Storia dell'Università, 1992) 4–71.

Numerous grammatical texts are still unedited; see the useful *Census of Medieval Latin Grammatical Manuscripts* (Stuttgart: Frommann-Holzboog, 1981) by G. Bursill-Hall and the list in Pinborg, *Die Entwicklung*, pp. 309–44. For the *modistae*, Marmo's *Semiotica* is still the fullest existing study; see also Kelly, *The Mirror of Grammar*. Useful bio-bibliographies are given in Harro Stammerjohann and Sylvain Auroux (eds.) *Lexicon grammaticorum* (Tübingen: Niemeyer, 1996), of which a second edition is forthcoming.

III

NATURAL PHILOSOPHY

16

NATURAL PHILOSOPHY IN EARLIER
LATIN THOUGHT

NADJA GERMANN

WAS THERE A PHYSICS BEFORE THE *PHYSICS*?[1]

Was there anything like physics before the reception of the Aristotelian *libri naturales*? This question raises the problem of what kinds of discussions can be classified as "physical." Modern scholars have commonly held that the beginnings of a scientific interest in natural phenomena among medieval authors appear only in the early twelfth century. The main characteristic of this development is said to be a shift of interest and consequently of method: whereas medieval scholars had previously interpreted nature symbolically, in correspondence with the practices of biblical exegesis, they henceforth focused on the inherent structure of physical reality, which they intended to understand and explain as such, which is to say *secundum naturam* or *physicam*.[2]

While this approach to earlier medieval science has the advantage of having drawn scholarly interest toward the twelfth century, its weakness consists in its general neglect and global condemnation of the earlier stages of Latin thought.[3] For it suggests that an interest in natural phenomena as such can hardly be discovered prior to the twelfth century, which would imply the (more or less complete) absence of natural philosophy during this time. However, if one takes the trouble to investigate the available sources, the actual situation turns out to be much more complicated and interesting. First, the sources on which early medieval authors draw already attest to the presence of a notion of *physica*. Macrobius's *Saturnalia*, for instance, expressly mentions natural philosophy

---

[1] Unless otherwise indicated, the terms 'natural philosophy' and 'physics' are used interchangeably throughout.

[2] The framework for this interpretation was first set out by Marie-Dominique Chenu, who in this connection coined the notion of "the discovery of nature" in the twelfth century. See "La découverte de la nature," in Chenu, *La théologie au douzième siècle* (Paris: Vrin, 1957) pp. 21–30. It is still along these lines that more recent studies conduct their own investigations; see, for example, Andreas Speer, *Die entdeckte Natur. Untersuchungen zu Begründungsversuchen einer scientia naturalis im 12. Jahrhundert* (Leiden: Brill, 1995).

[3] See Chenu, *La théologie*, who discusses developments during the twelfth century, but does not provide a closer analysis of the preceding period.

(*physica*), which for him "deals with the divine bodies either of the heaven or of the stars." Certainly, he allows that it has further sub-parts. These parts, however, particularly medicine, are disqualified as "dregs" (*faex*) since they consider "earthly and worldly bodies."[4] Given the importance of authors such as Macrobius – both for the concept of science underlying their writings and for the actual content of their views – one might suppose not only that their early medieval successors had a notion of physics but also that they identified it primarily with astronomy and only subsequently with other fields.

These considerations lead, second, to the early medieval sources themselves. Here it is important to note that indeed there is a wealth of astronomical material that must carefully be distinguished from the so-called "symbolical" sources.[5] Although early Latin astronomy still needs thorough treatment, some important work has already been done. Bruce Eastwood, for instance, in his studies on planetary astronomy between the ninth and eleventh centuries, was able to show that scholars in this period were deeply interested in penetrating astronomical phenomena on both a conceptual and a "geometrical" level. They not only tried to understand peculiarities such as the retrogradation of planets or the occurrence of eclipses – assisted by the available late ancient handbooks – but also developed their own graphic devices in order to reconstruct qualitatively the movements of the celestial bodies in relation to each other.[6] Furthermore, it is worth noting that the authors themselves attest to a consciousness of what they are doing: they point out, for example, that the object of their considerations is "nature" (*natura*) and that their inquiry is conducted "according to nature" (*secundum naturam*).[7]

Against this background, it appears to be appropriate to interpret these astronomical sources as instances of early Latin natural philosophy. This concentration on astronomy ceases only at the beginning of the twelfth century, when

---

[4] Macrobius, *Saturnalia* 7.15, 14 (ed. Willis, p. 454). The identification of natural philosophy with astronomy in early medieval thought was already observed by Brian Lawn, *The Salernitan Questions. An Introduction to the History of Medieval and Renaissance Problem Literature* (Oxford: Clarendon Press, 1963) pp. 3–4.

[5] It is difficult to decide which sources Speer, for instance, has in mind when he contrasts the "awakening" physical interest (*Die entdeckte Natur*, p. 11) with a prevailing symbolism (p. 1), since he does not give a single example of the latter throughout his programmatic "Accessus" (pp. 1–17).

[6] See the handy collection of papers re-edited in Bruce S. Eastwood, *The Revival of Planetary Astronomy in Carolingian and Post-Carolingian Europe* (Aldershot: Ashgate, 2002).

[7] Although the term *physica* is already attested earlier (see, for example, Helperic of Auxerre, *Liber de computo* ii [*Patr. Lat.* 137, col. 23]: *physica signorum ratio*), it becomes increasingly popular during the second half of the eleventh and the first half of the twelfth century, when it starts replacing *natura* (see, for instance, Garland the Computist, who changes between the two notions, *De computo* ii, "*Prologus*" (Paris BN lat. 15118, f. 39r): "aliqua ante nos quod sciamus a nemine pertractata de scola phisice eruta calculamus"; ibid.: " Hic vero compotus dumtaxat naturalem explanare intendimus"; ibid. ii.14 (f. 46v): "His ad inuentionem deliquit luminum amborum necessario in difficultate phisica prelibatis").

Adelard of Bath's *Questions on Natural Science* appears on the scene. Henceforth, an increasing interest in the hitherto rather neglected phenomena that Macrobius rejected as "earthly and worldly" becomes visible. This results in what can be characterized as a turn from celestial physics, focusing on the study of the heavens, to terrestrial physics, dedicated to a study of earthly phenomena. Furthermore, natural philosophy begins to be considered as a scientific branch of its own right – a development well attested by the discussions concerning the division of the sciences that spread throughout the twelfth century.[8] Although physics continues to include astronomical phenomena (despite its emancipation from astronomy proper, which is subsumed under the mathematical sciences) and hence can be addressed as cosmology, the main focus shifts toward sub-lunar phenomena, ranging from biology through medicine to "physics" in a sense that is closer to the modern notion.

These observations have important consequences for the study of natural philosophy in earlier medieval thought. If we understand 'earlier medieval' as the period between the Roman Empire and the thirteenth-century reception of the Aristotelian *libri naturales*, then our subject requires a treatment not just of twelfth-century thought, but also of the central aspects of earlier discussions. This chapter will accordingly concentrate on two issues: (1) the late ancient heritage of natural philosophy within the realm of astronomy; (2) the "sub-lunar turn": natural questions and the search for the elements and principles of the physical cosmos.

NATURAL PHILOSOPHY WITHIN THE REALM OF ASTRONOMY

It is important to note that the majority of the scientific material here in question belongs to two chief traditions. On the one hand it derives from late ancient compendia such as the aforementioned *Saturnalia* of Macrobius,[9] which cover a variety of scientific branches and from which medieval scribes extracted select passages (if not the entire text), as well as figures or tables. On the other hand – and this has often been neglected or misjudged – it draws from computistical literature, which is concerned with determining the correct Easter date. According to late ancient regulations, this date must be established in relation to the courses of both the moon and the sun, and so this literature puts particular weight on lunar and solar astronomy. (The most

---

[8] See, for example, Hugh of St. Victor, *Didascalicon de studio legendi* 2 (ed. Buttimer, pp. 23–47); physics, to him, "considers by means of a thorough investigation the causes of things in their effects and the effects from their causes" (ibid., p. 34).

[9] Further examples are the *Commentaries on the Dream of Scipio* by the same author, Martianus Capella's *On the Marriage of Mercury and Philology*, and Pliny the Elder's *Natural History*.

important text in this connection is the Venerable Bede's *On the Structure of Time*.[10]) From approximately the ninth century onwards, these two traditions fused and developed into a wide-ranging kind of scientific literature, which spread considerably after the late tenth century.[11] Accordingly, in order to depict the most important developments within the field of natural philosophy before the "sub-lunar turn," we will focus upon the period stretching from the late tenth to the late eleventh century.

Early medieval scholars defend a geocentric worldview, which they owe to late ancient authors such as Macrobius and Pliny.[12] The most detailed body of knowledge addresses the movements of the sun and the moon – a peculiarity owing to the impact of the computistical literature mentioned above. In addition to this body of knowledge, the medievals inherited a bundle of questions already discussed in late ancient literature, concerning, for instance, the seemingly irregular movements of the planets and the obliquity of the paths of the planets with respect to the ecliptic. Such questions, and the geometrical analyses that were offered, clearly transcend the "classical" *computus* and must hence be addressed as an independent astronomical interest.[13]

Against this background, the question arises of the character of the medieval occupation with this type of natural phenomenon. Take, for example, a problem that appears to gain increasing interest during the eleventh century, namely, that of lunar and solar eclipses. Interestingly, whereas this phenomenon as such is well known already in late ancient literature, as are explanations for its occurrence, it is Hermann of Reichenau who first raised the question of when precisely eclipses happen. In his *Prognostics of Solar and Lunar Eclipses* (1049), Hermann develops a full-fledged theory for predicting lunar and solar eclipses on the basis of the cosmological knowledge available at his time.[14] Several peculiarities merit attention in this connection. First there is the kind of question asked: in contrast

---

[10] This is a more apt rendering of *De temporum ratione* than the title of the published English translation, *The Reckoning of Time* (tr. Wallis), which is misleading. Another important source for later authors is Helperic of Auxerre's *Liber de computo* (ca. 900).

[11] See, e.g., Bede's *On the Structure of Time*, with approximately 250 extant manuscripts. For the so-called scientific manuscripts (their contents as well as their spread), see Faith Wallis, "The Church, the World and the Time. Prolegomena to a History of the Medieval 'Computus'," in M.-C. Deprez-Masson (ed.) *Normes et pouvoirs à la fin du moyen âge* (Montréal: Ceres, 1990) 15–29.

[12] That is, they conceive of the world as a globe with the earth surrounded by the spheres of the planets and fixed stars. It is well known that each planet (including, on medieval terminology, the sun and the moon) has its own track through the zodiac and that some of them seem to have irregular movements (stops, loops, retrogradation).

[13] Eastwood's work has drawn attention to this point, and has highlighted the geometrical character of these analyses of astronomical phenomena.

[14] Hermann of Reichenau, *Prognostica de defectu solis et lunae*, ed. N. Germann in *De temporum ratione. Quadrivium und Gotteserkenntnis am Beispiel Abbos von Fleury und Hermanns von Reichenau* (Leiden: Brill 2006) pp. 341–50; for a discussion see ibid., pp. 219–32.

to the late ancient and earlier medieval tradition, it concerns the *quantitative* elaboration of an existing description of a natural phenomenon.[15] This kind of interest throughout the period under discussion is further corroborated in other works by Hermann as well as by other authors. Thus, in his *On the Structure of the Sphere* (978), Abbo of Fleury tries to develop a method to calculate the position of the planets in relation to the zodiac,[16] while pseudo-Columbanus in his *On the Leap of the Moon* (probably late tenth century) detects that the duration of a synodical lunar month (that is, the period stretching from one new moon to the next) must differ from the commonly accepted 29.5 days, and he attempts to determine it more precisely.[17] Hermann himself addresses this same problem. He furthermore argues that the same inaccuracy obtains with regard to further natural phenomena, such as the sidereal lunar month (that is, the period stretching from one lunar transition through a certain zodiacal sign to the next), and he tries to find solutions.[18] In this, he finds a successor in Garland the Computist, who – just like Hermann in his *Prognostics* – develops a theory for predicting lunar and solar eclipses.[19]

A second peculiarity of the sources under consideration concerns the method and argumentation employed: unlike earlier figures, Hermann, in his theory of eclipses, proceeds by means of mathematics (arithmetic), taking certain positions of his cosmological background knowledge as starting points. For example, one essential precondition for an eclipse to take place is that the moon crosses the ecliptic at this very moment. Hence the question arises of how to determine this date. Hermann's argumentation runs as follows: since he presupposes the uniformity of the lunar course (which would mean that the moon crosses the ecliptic always at the same two points, that is, in the same zodiacal signs), the feature relevant for his question is the sidereal month. Accordingly, he maintains that the period between two passages of the ecliptic by the moon corresponds to half a sidereal month. In order now to determine the lunar transitions he

---

[15] Apparently, Eastwood does not notice this transition to a quantitative occupation with astronomical issues well before the twelfth century; see his "Invention and Reform in Latin Planetary Astronomy," in M. W. Herren *et al.* (eds.) *Latin Culture in the Eleventh Century. Proceedings of the Third International Conference on Medieval Latin Studies* (Turnhout: Brepols, 2002) I: 264–97, here pp. 290–1.

[16] Abbo of Fleury, *De ratione spere*, ed. R. B. Thomson in "Two Astronomical Tractates of Abbo of Fleury," in J. D. North and J. J. Roche (eds.) *The Light of Nature. Essays in the History and Philosophy of Science Presented to A.C. Crombie* (Dordrecht: Nijhoff, 1985) 113–33; for a discussion see David Juste, "Neither Observation nor Astronomical Tables. An Alternative Way of Computing the Planetary Longitudes in the Early Western Middle Ages," in C. Burnett *et al.* (eds.) *Studies in the History of the Exact Sciences in Honour of David Pingree* (Leiden: Brill, 2004) 181–222, here pp. 195–200.

[17] Pseudo-Columbanus, *De saltu lunae*, ed. in Columban, *Opera* (ed. Walker, pp. 212–15).

[18] Hermann of Reichenau, *Abbreviatio compoti cuiusdam idiotae*, ed. Germann in *De temporum ratione*, pp. 314–40; for a discussion see ibid., pp. 199–219.

[19] Garland the Computist, *De computo* xiii–xiv.

simply must multiply the period between two intersections. Similarly, to correlate mathematically these events with the relative position of the sun (which must be either in opposition to or conjunction with the moon), he applies the method of the smallest common multiple of the two relevant time spans.[20] The only further information required is an empirically attested eclipse. With these data in hand, Hermann is in a position to begin his calculations and identify dates of future eclipses.[21]

Another noteworthy feature of texts such as Hermann's consists in the indications they provide concerning the authors' own notion of the subject they are dealing with, as well as of their own approach. Accordingly, the astronomical phenomena have an underlying "natural structure" (*ratio naturalis*) that can be both explained (qualitatively) and translated into rules (*regulae*). Consequently, anybody who wishes to investigate the "causes and reasons" (*causae ac rationes*) of these rules must be acquainted with this natural structure beforehand. It is notable that the relationship between these rules and the corresponding natural structure is characterized in terms of "truth"; thus, the natural structure is "the truth" in relation to which the accuracy of the rules must be evaluated (particularly *Abbreviatio* xi; ed. Germann, p. 320). It is by virtue of this criterion (conformity with the truth – that is, the natural structure) that different approaches are distinguished. Hence, for example, in the realm of lunar and solar astronomy – which is to say, in the *computus* – both Hermann and Garland clearly distinguish between the "ancient" or "ecclesiastical" authority on the one hand, and "nature" and "reason" (*ratio*) on the other. Notably, both of them leave no doubt whatsoever regarding their own sympathy: they proceed *secundum naturam* – that is, they rework existing yet inaccurate rules and calculations and develop new ones (concerning future eclipses, for example).[22]

Furthermore, this approach "in accordance with nature" is closely linked with reference to observation. Thus, for example, it is because of a discrepancy

---

[20] Interestingly, in order to accomplish his calculations, Hermann does not use the common Roman fractions, but rather invents fractional arithmetics. This is picked up by Garland.

[21] Hermann's theory, sadly, does not work, since the lunar course, contrary to his presupposition, is irregular, and hence the relevant feature in order to determine eclipses is not the sidereal but the draconic month (in combination with the so-called cycle of Saros).

[22] For a similar conception see also Abbo of Fleury; cf. Nadja Germann, "Zwischen *veritas naturae* und *fides historiae*. Zeit und Dauer bei Abbo von Fleury," in A. Speer (ed.) *Das Sein der Dauer* (*Miscellanea Mediaevalia* xxiv) (Berlin: De Gruyter, 2008) 171–95. For Garland the Computist see his distinction between a type of consideration *secundum naturam* or *physicam* and another "according to tradition" (*De computo* ii, "*Prologus*" [f. 39r]). For an analysis of Hermann's subtle polemic against mere reliance upon authorities, see Arno Borst, "Ein Forschungsbericht Hermanns des Lahmen," in *Deutsches Archiv* 40 (1984) 379–477, here pp. 418–21. This peculiarity must be emphasized in contrast to the global judgments (Chenu, Speer) mentioned at the beginning of this article. To them, this kind of rationality can be observed only since the twelfth century.

between the calculated position of the moon and the observable one that Hermann draws the conclusion that, in order to integrate the relevant figures into his reworkings of the *computus*, he must first re-determine them (ibid. xxvii, p. 327). The importance of this feature – that is, the observability of the difference between rule and nature – becomes obvious if we take into account the frequency with which this shortcoming is deplored, as well as the polemical force with which it is put forth. Accordingly, it is most surprising to find out that the observations Hermann and his contemporaries refer to are obviously *not* the result of their own empirical activities. As closer inspection reveals, they are based on the data transmitted by their sources. Thus, the above-cited discrepancy between the observable and the calculated position of the moon is taken from Bede. Similarly, Hermann's claim that everybody "except for the insane" agrees that "each lunar month has the same (*aequalis*) length" (ibid. xxv, p. 327) clearly attests that he did not rely upon his own observations; otherwise, he would have noticed the irregularities of the lunar course.[23] Consequently, the most important features of this approach to astronomical problems belong rather to the conceptual level: the discussed reasonings attest a high esteem toward natural phenomena and their underlying structure. Even more, this natural structure is considered to be the measure ("the truth") in relation to which transmitted rules and data must be evaluated.

With respect to the first stage of early medieval natural philosophy, therefore, we can summarize that there is an apparent interest in natural phenomena in the field of astronomy, an interest that is directed toward a more accurate (and this is to say a quantitative) determination of (existing) physical explanations. Moreover, scholars such as those evoked above attest a clear consciousness that the method they apply is a peculiar one: in analyzing natural phenomena to the best of their scientific knowledge, in identifying the figures relevant in order to develop a solution for the concerned problem, and in calculating the required dates, they proceed *secundum naturam* or *physicam*, in contrast to a procedure merely according with tradition or ecclesiastical practices. With this background we can now pass on to the second stage, terrestrial physics.

NATURAL QUESTIONS AND THE SEARCH FOR ELEMENTS AND PRINCIPLES

The turn to sub-lunar physics can best be connected with the early twelfth-century *Questions on Natural Science* of Adelard of Bath. These questions are

---

[23] Certainly, there are exceptions to this rule: the eclipses Hermann refers to in order to check his theory are indeed instances of observation.

not only the first evidence for this shift, but they are distinguished by two characteristics that are also pertinent to the majority of related texts of this second stage of natural philosophy: first, by the tradition to which they inhere, the genre of question literature; second, by the integration of newly received sources, particularly from southern Italy. It is worth noting that there had already been collections of natural questions available north of the Alps since the times of Charlemagne.[24] However, it is during this period that they are taken up with sudden interest and supplemented by new material. Both the former and the newly arrived sources center around medical, botanical, biological, and meteorological problems. Whereas the old collections can be traced back, for instance, to the combined pseudo-Aristotelian and pseudo-Alexandrian *Problemata*,[25] the new sources give access to formerly unavailable texts such as Nemesius's *Premnon physicon* (later rendered as *De natura hominis*) and the *Pantegni*, a Latin reworking by Constantine the African of 'Alī ibn al-'Abbās al-Majūsī's *Complete Book of the Medical Art*.

In comparison to the astronomical literature just described, the most significant difference concerns the nature of the questions put and solutions sought. In contrast to our aforementioned authors, twelfth-century scholars such as Adelard and William of Conches, to name but two, are interested in explanations for natural phenomena based on the inherent "reasons" (*causae*) for certain phenomena. This interest already becomes apparent from a glance at the table of contents in Adelard's *Questions*. The first chapter asks for the "reason why plants grow without a seed being sown beforehand," and the fourth raises the question of why they do not grow in the same way from water, air, or fire as they do from earth.[26] That this kind of question envisages a *qualitative* penetration of natural phenomena rather than a quantitative determination is furthermore corroborated by the answers given.

In order to reply to the first question (why "plants are born from the earth" [*Questions*, ed. Burnett et al., p. 93]), for instance, Adelard explains that everything that exists consists of ultimate elements (earth, water, air, and fire), each of which possesses particular properties. Although he sticks to the traditional

---

[24] This is lucidly described in Lawn, *Salernitan Questions*, pp. 1–15.

[25] The pseudo-Aristotelian and pseudo-Alexandrian problems were available in the Latin West in the so-called *Vetustissima translatio*; for this (and further sources) see, in addition to Lawn, *Salernitan Questions*, pp. 20–5; Charles Burnett's introduction to Adelard's *Conversations*, p. xxiii; and Charles Burnett, "Physics before the *Physics*. Early Translations from Arabic of Texts Concerning Nature in MSS British Library, Additional 22719 and Cotton Galba E IV," *Medioevo* 27 (2002) 53–109, here pp. 53–80. (See also Appendices B.1–2.)

[26] Adelard, *Questions on Natural Science* (ed. Burnett, p. 86); more than half of the questions ask for reasons, using the formulas "Qua ratione . . .", "Quare . . ." or "Ut quid . . .".

number of four elements and their common names,[27] and ascribes to them the traditional pair of qualities,[28] he emphasizes that what is usually called earth (but, according to Adelard, should better be referred to as "earthy matter") is a certain mixture of these elements in which the element earth is prevalent. "Thus, since in that earthy matter . . . these four causes are present, from them a certain composed thing necessarily arises, which is largely earthy, a little watery, less airy, and least of all fiery" (p. 93). What arises, in short, is a plant. Here, and in other cases, it is by reference to this microstructure of reality, which is to say to its inherent "causes" (*causae*), that Adelard tackles such problems. It may be worth noting that he is the first scholar in the early Middle Ages who – prior to the reception of Aristotle – defends this distinction between the elements proper and the mixts composed of them – a theory that became notorious throughout the later Middle Ages.

Adelard's "new" tendency to fall back on an element theory is also shared by other scholars of the same period, including first and foremost William of Conches. His *Dragmaticon* (*ca.* 1147–9), for example, develops a full-fledged theory of elements,[29] the most interesting feature of which is its corpuscular understanding of elements. In this connection, William maintains that his corporeal elements make up real bodies that have "a boundary and an end"; nonetheless he defends the infinite number of these smallest, indivisible particles within one body. He resolves the seeming incongruence of these positions by virtue of a distinction: "things are said to be infinite in number not because there is no limit to their number, but because it is virtually impossible for us to ascertain their actual number" (*Dragmaticon* I.6.4). Accordingly, 'infinity' does not mean an actual infinity but rather uncountability in practice. Similarly, William evades the problem of how elements can be at the same time corporeal and indivisible by holding that 'body,' when applied to elements, is a metaphorical term; the term applies to the elements inasmuch as they are the *principles* of bodies. Hence the elements, although in this sense corporeal, do not have three

[27] In antiquity there are of course concurring models, sometimes postulating only one ultimate element (Thales, for example, ascribes to water this founding position), sometimes even five (Aristotle, for example, postulates ether as a fifth element).

[28] These qualities are also the traditional ones, already introduced in antiquity, namely dryness, moistness, coldness, and heat. Each element, according to this scheme, possesses one of the two contrary types of qualities; thus earth is dry and cold, water is cold and moist, air is moist and hot, and fire is hot and dry.

[29] Regarding the importance of this theory it is worth noting that William introduces the elements at the end of the first book (ch. 6) and dedicates the entire second book to their discussion. It is furthermore on this basis that he explains the coming into being of the universe (beginning with the heavens and continuing through meteorology to the earth and its inhabitants). A similar order underlies his earlier *Philosophia*.

dimensions (*Dragmaticon* I.6.12–13). These discussions and their like foreshadow not only the importance that theories of elemental compositions were to have during the later Middle Ages, but also some of the crucial problems at stake then, such as how to explain the composition of a continuum out of atoms, or how to account for the obvious difference of qualities between different kinds of things, given that they all consist of the same four kinds of elements with precisely four kinds of elementary qualities (see Chapter 18).

Another important difference between this new sub-lunar physics and earlier literature concerns the general subject matter under consideration. Both Adelard and William deal with reality in the broadest sense: their explanations cover questions ranging from the smallest parts of the cosmos (the elements) to its most universal composition (spheres of the heavens). Interestingly, those questions dealing with astronomical issues – such as the movements of the planets and stars or eclipses – merely summarize well-known positions from both the late ancient and the early medieval computistical literature. Thus William takes into account neither the eleventh century's tendency to deal quantitatively with astronomical phenomena, nor his predecessors' critique of the older tradition. This is particularly apparent if we regard William's report concerning the moon: according to him, it "moves through the entire Zodiac in twenty-seven days and eight hours," while "the real lunation lasts twenty-nine days and twelve hours – that is, half a natural day."[30] Obviously, he is unaware of the discussions and specifications of the past century.

The situation, however, is utterly different with respect to William's investigation of the cosmos's microstructure. Certainly, the questions he raises derive from more or less the same sources as those of Adelard (as well as from Adelard himself);[31] similarly, neither his nor Adelard's answers come completely out of the blue. Nonetheless, they reveal the originality and scientific autonomy of their authors. This becomes apparent if we return to their element theories: although their most important sources in this field, Nemesius and the *Pantegni*, fall back on elements understood as the smallest parts of any existing body, neither of those sources develops a corpuscular theory of the kind most elaborately put forth by William in his *Dragmaticon*.

---

[30] *Dragmaticon* IV.14.1 (tr. Ronca *et al.*, pp. 83–4). This becomes even worse when he continues and claims that "the computists do not usually count anything less than one day" (p. 84), completely ignoring the developments by scholars such as pseudo-Columbanus, Hermann of Reichenau, and others.

[31] As for William's sources, see Lawn, *Salernitan Questions*, pp. 50–6; for the *Dragmaticon* see Ronca's "Introduction" to his edition (pp. xxiv–xxxi); in contrast to Adelard, William obviously draws on the *Pantegni*.

Accordingly, we may conclude that astronomy, insofar as it still belongs to natural philosophy, is degraded to a rather marginal existence, providing general cosmological background knowledge but not constituting a proper field of research. By contrast, theories concerning the structure and immanent causes of natural processes gain interest and are considerably elaborated. Moreover, it is in this connection that methodological considerations like those discussed earlier again come to the fore: just like Hermann or Garland, Adelard and William justify their method as "according to nature" or "to reason," and oppose it to blind reliance upon authority.[32]

A further distinctive feature of the period, related to this growing interest in naturalistic physical explanations, is an increasing concern for the first principles of the physical world. This can be characterized as the most fundamental sort of physical inquiry, grounding the search for the qualitative and causal explanations of reality discussed before. This focus, already present in William's work, is particularly notable in *On the Works of the Six Days* (*ca.* 1130–40) of Thierry of Chartres.[33] The first part of this treatise is explicitly dedicated to an explanation of Genesis "according to physics" (*secundum physicam*). To Thierry, the first principles are the four ultimate causes: the efficient cause, God; the formal cause, God's wisdom or Christ; the final cause, God's benignity or the Holy Spirit; and the material cause, the four elements. The "necessity" for such a cooperation of causes in generating the cosmos, he continues, results from the mutability and fallenness of worldly substances, which requires one originator and the imposition of a rational order (*Works* sec. 2, ed. Häring, *Commentaries*, pp. 555–6).

Although Thierry is not explicit on this point, from what follows it becomes clear that he conceives of creation as one single act effecting the coming into being of primordial matter; however, it must be part of this first and single act that the constituting parts of matter, namely the elements, were each endowed with a particular "nature" (*natura*). Notably, Thierry describes the further developments – the formation of the heavens, the coming into being of the stars and planets, and so forth – as a gradual process resulting from the natures of the aforementioned elements.[34] Hence it was by virtue of these "seminal causes"

---

[32] This subject has found considerable scholarly interest; see particularly Speer, *Die entdeckte Natur*, pp. 36–43 (on Adelard) and 130–9 (on William).

[33] For a discussion see Speer, *Die entdeckte Natur*, pp. 222–88; regarding *On the Works of the Six Days* see particularly pp. 232–52. See also Peter Dronke, "Thierry of Chartres," in Dronke (ed.) *A History of Twelfth-Century Western Philosophy* (Cambridge: Cambridge University Press, 1988) 358–85, here pp. 374–82.

[34] This resembles the gradual coming into being and structuring of reality William depicts in both his *Philosophia* and *Dragmaticon*.

(*seminales causae*) that, once matter was there, the universe evolved into the state we perceive today.[35]

It is obvious that this kind of reasoning somehow replies to element theories such as those developed by Adelard and William, since it provides the grounding principles of physical explanations presupposing the existence of "necessary" effects inherent in the nature of things. The particular "nature" of each element consists – as we can now conclude – precisely of its pair of qualities by means of which it contributes to the composition of new things, or resolves and transforms existing ones. Although today we might dismiss this as metaphysical speculation, Thierry and his contemporaries obviously regard it as a substantial part of natural philosophy itself. This interest in the metaphysical foundation of the proposed physical theories is as original an interest as the one concerning the microstructure of reality, which might be regarded as the effect of the seminal causes.

A final comment concerns the empirical character of the second stage of early Latin natural philosophy. It has frequently been claimed that the questions Adelard or William raise result from everyday observations, and that the answers they propose refer to an actual empirical approach. An often-quoted example for this claim is Adelard's localization of the different mental faculties in the brain. In order to corroborate his solution, he refers to injuries of certain parts of a person's head that were accompanied by disabilities of particular mental faculties. From this observation he concludes that these are the parts where the respective faculties are localized. However, in this case, as in many other instances, the related observation turns out to be extracted from the sources he used (in this case, Nemesius). Despite both the superficial appearance of an empirical orientation and the actual interest in the "mechanisms" of natural processes, it must therefore be concluded that earlier medieval physics – even during this second stage – is theoretical rather than empirical. It proceeds by means of applying presupposed principles and tends to quote transmitted examples instead of relying on personal observation. Yet this work still stands out – and this is true for both stages discussed in this chapter – for its scientific curiosity and originality of thought, as well as for the critical distance from authority exhibited by all the authors discussed.

In many respects, therefore, earlier Latin thought foreshadows the kind of natural philosophy that emerged with the recovery of Aristotle. Many of the core questions would remain important, such as the element theory; similarly, the qualitative approach of the second stage would continue in the

---

[35] For the entire process see *Works* sec. 5–17 (ed. Häring, pp. 557–62); for the seminal causes, which God inserted into the elements, see ibid. sec. 17 (p. 562).

thirteenth century and beyond. Nonetheless, central aspects underwent considerable change – first and foremost the chief object of investigation. In accordance with Aristotle's *Physics*, questions regarding change (*motus*) and, accordingly, the main principles of change – matter, form, and privation – come to the fore (see Chapters 19–20). Moreover, natural philosophy becomes integrated into the curriculum of the universities. As a result, not only does its conceptual place become fixed within the canon of the sciences, but so do its methods, procedures, and literary forms. This, however, must be the object of an independent investigation.

17

CREATION AND CAUSATION

TANELI KUKKONEN

Medieval thinkers regarded it as a foundational tenet of faith that the world had come to be through divine agency. The three monotheist Scriptures testify to this in clear terms, and each of the attendant theologies also came to regard it as important that God be recognized as creator. But how is God's creative act to be understood? Is it entirely *sui generis*, or does it correspond to some recognized category of change, either straightforwardly or by analogy? Are the facts of creation and its salient characteristics susceptible to rational analysis and demonstration, or do they fall outside those phenomena that it is the business of philosophy to investigate? And what might the connection, or lack thereof, tell us about either creation or causation?

After lengthy deliberations, and not without dissent, Christian orthodoxy settled on the world's having been created *ex nihilo* in a limited past.[1] At the same time, medieval philosophers also inherited the dominant philosophical view that the sensible world has always existed, a sempiternal beneficiary of an eternal agency. The compatibility of these two positions was considered problematic early on, and gave rise to an extensive debate over the eternity of the world. Because eternity was closely linked with self-sufficiency in the philosophical tradition, the idea that there might be other eternal principles besides God prompted questions about the necessity and contingency of the current world order and the different ways in which causal dependency might be construed. The majority of the developments occurred under *falsafa* (Arabic Aristotelianism), which will accordingly be given precedence in what follows.

PLATONIC BEGINNINGS

Despite the centrality of Aristotle for the tradition as a whole, early medieval cos-mological speculation is best viewed as a series of attempted mediations between

---

[1] Gerhard May, *Schöpfung aus dem Nichts: Die Entstehung der Lehre von der Creatio ex nihilo* (Berlin: De Gruyter, 1978).

Scripture and the theoretical considerations introduced by Plato's *Timaeus*. The latter tells the "likely story" (*eikos mythos*) of the Demiurge, a divine craftsman of sorts, and his attempts to bring about a sensible world containing as much goodliness and order as it can. Because Plato was the foremost philosophical authority throughout the final phase of antiquity, and because Judaism and Christianity first encountered the Greek philosophical tradition through Philo and the *sophia* tradition, monotheist writers soon became privy to the numerous debates that sprang up among the Platonists regarding the principles the dialogue evokes.[2]

Agreement was reached relatively soon with regard to the eternal model to which the Demiurge is said to look when fashioning the sensible universe. This was equated with the contents of the divine mind.[3] But did the Demiurge's actions have an origin in time, as the Greek term *gegonen* ("it began to be") implied? And if so, were they preceded by a receptacle (*Timaeus* 49a) and disorderly motion (52d–53c) of some kind? When John Scottus Eriugena talks about the "appearance of the non-apparent, manifestation of the hidden, formation of the formless, measuring of the incommensurable" (*Periphyseon* III.4), what is that non-apparent, formless, incommensurable on which God operates?[4] A subsistent principle would imply something coeternal with God: the twelfth-century Latin interpreters of Plato, working from Calcidius's translation of the receptacle as *silva*, consequently expended considerable energy coming up with a satisfactory account of this primordial stuff.[5] Furthermore, the divine essence was customarily thought to be too exalted to be restricted to any particular form, just as it stands above any material limitations. If this is so, and if like produces like while nothing comes from nothing – as two venerable principles would have it – then how is it that a universe is formed out of two amorphous principles?[6]

The most radical response to these questions was staked out by David of Dinant in the early thirteenth century: since God created the world out of

---

[2] See Matthias Baltes, *Die Weltentstehung des platonischen Timaios nach den Antiken interpreten* (Leiden: Brill, 1976–8).

[3] See Vivian Boland, *Ideas in God According to Saint Thomas Aquinas: Sources and Synthesis* (Leiden: Brill, 1996).

[4] Similarly Bernard Silvestris, *Cosmographia* XIII.1, who adds to the list the "setting of limits to the interminable." All these are standard Neoplatonic formulations.

[5] In early Islamic speculation a parallel discussion took place regarding the expressions *min lā shayy'* and *lā min shayy'*, "out of no thing" and "not out of a thing"; see Harry Wolfson, *The Philosophy of the Kalam* (Cambridge, MA: Harvard University Press, 1976) pp. 359–72.

[6] See, e.g., al-Kindī, *On First Philosophy* I.4 (ed. Abū Rīda, p. 161); Ibn Gabirol, *Fountain of Life* III.6, IV.6. Ibn Gabirol's own vacillations on the topic lead to two different accounts of creation in his works.

nothing (else), then in some sense he must *be* both its matter and its form.[7] David was promptly condemned for pantheism – as Saadiah Gaon had already pointed out, God's creating the world *ex se* could not very well be taken so literally (*Beliefs and Convictions* I.3)[8] – but a more acceptable formulation was hit upon by the tenth-century Jewish Neoplatonist Isaac Israeli, who contended that God's first creative act consisted precisely in the innovation of first matter and first form.[9] This would be followed by numerous authors as an answer to the question, "out of what did creation occur?"[10] Slowly but surely, the ages-old interpretation of a Platonic, demiurgic divinity shaping the world out of preexistent matter was edged out.[11] Moses Maimonides still put it forward as a putative account of creation, and a compromise position of sorts between the demands of reason and Scripture. Yet, in the same text (*Guide of the Perplexed* II.13), Plato's philosophical authority is surpassed by Aristotle's, who is portrayed as a staunch eternalist, while Moses, on the authority of Genesis 1, is presented as holding the strictly opposing viewpoint of a creation out of nothing in a limited time. It is these two positions that came to dominate the landscape, with the former being associated with philosophical doctrine (thanks to the dominance of Aristotle) and the latter with scriptural orthodoxy.

CAUSES AND OCCASIONS

When viewed in terms of Aristotle's *Physics* – the principal handbook of all mature medieval natural philosophy – speculation about matter and form gives us only half the story regarding a thing's coming-to-be. The late ancient philosophers had labeled these two "immanent" causes, because they are contained in their effects, and pointed to *Physics* II as providing a much needed supplement. Efficient and final causes may be considered "transcendent," since they are separate from their effects.[12] Through Avicenna, the distinction passes on to

---

[7] This is in the lost *Quaternuli* (fragments ed. Kurdzialek, p. 71), and see Aquinas, *Summa theol.* 1a 3.8c. Albert the Great accuses the "early Peripatetics" Hermes Trismegistus and Asclepius of the same mistake (*De causis et proc. univ.* I.4.3).

[8] See also Aquinas, *Summa contra gentiles* I.17 and I.27.

[9] See *Chapter on the Elements* sec. 1, tr. Altmann and Stern, pp. 119–20, along with their discussion on pp. 151–64.

[10] See, e.g., Ibn Gabirol, *Fountain of Life* V.42; Robert Grosseteste, *Hexaëmeron* I.9.2.

[11] Among late medieval philosophers, Levi ben Gershom is practically unique in holding that such an account would be both philosophically demonstrable and faithful to scripture (*Wars of the Lord* VI.17).

[12] See Syrianus, *In Metaphys.* III (ed. Kroll, pp. 13–14); Proclus, *In Timaeum* (ed. Diehl, I: 239–40), *Elements of Theology*, prop 75.

medieval teaching all the way to William of Ockham and beyond:[13] it provides a basis for talking about the "how" of creation in Aristotelian terms, and is therefore of interest to us.

That God is an ultimate final cause, the end in perfection that everything strives to imitate, was a medieval commonplace. The question of God's efficient causality is trickier. Averroes in his *Metaphysics* commentary reproduces the central conflict with admirable clarity:

In this matter, the two parties ultimately opposed to each other are the champions of immanence (*ahl al-kumūn*) and, second, the people who uphold creation and invention (*ibdāʿ wa-ikhtirāʿ*). Those who maintain immanence claim that everything is in everything and that generation is merely the emergence of things from one another . . . Evidently, the efficient cause or agent (*al-fāʿil*) for such people is nothing more than a mover. As for those who maintain invention and creation, they claim that the agent creates the existent in its entirety and invents it: they deny that the agent's act is conditioned by the existence of matter on which to act, claiming instead that he is the inventor of the whole thing. This is the well-known view of the theologians both of our religion and of the Christians; accordingly, the Christian John the Grammarian [Philoponus] believes that there is no possibility except in the agent.

(*In Metaphys.* XII.18, ed. Bouyges, pp. 1497–8)

In short, the advocate of immanence denies that there is any generation outside the intermixture of the elements – an emergent materialism of sorts, with no space left for a special creation – whereas the creationist claims that all true generation is always out of nothing and that therefore the only true agent is God. One extreme denies agency to the Creator, the other to the creature, while between the two fall a number of intermediary positions forging a middle path. The question turns on the correct understanding of efficient causality, also dubbed 'agency.'

Wholly immanent accounts of generation are scarce during the medieval period: Averroes's own view arguably comes closest, as he tacitly acknowledges (ibid., p. 1499). This is because Averroes is virtually alone in believing that a Prime Mover such as Aristotle's is in fact sufficient to account for creation. Still, when Averroes says that the sixth-century commentator John Philoponus spearheaded the opposing movement of viewing God as sole creator both of matter and of form, this is both correct and informative. To say that "there is no possibility except in the agent" in this context is to claim that the world sets no restrictions whatsoever on God's creative act, whether from the point of view

---

[13] See Robert Wisnovsky, "Towards a History of Avicenna's Distinction between Immanent and Transcendent Causes," in D. Reisman and A. al-Rahīm (eds.) *Before and After Avicenna* (Leiden: Brill, 2003) 49–68.

of its matter or its eventual form.[14] After all, as Philoponus had put it, if God "produces in a way similar to nature, then he does not differ from nature." And if he does not differ from nature, how then is he superior to it?[15] The theologians consequently interpreted God's infinite power, itself an Aristotelian concept (*Phys.* VIII.10), as God's capacity to bring about any effect directly without the cooperation of secondary causes. The only thing delimiting divine omnipotence is logical compossibility. Such was, for instance, John Duns Scotus's view, and it became a commonplace both in mainstream Muslim theology and among the Latin scholastics starting in the late thirteenth century.[16]

Of course, insisting on the primacy of divine causality need not entail a denial of secondary causes. The scholastics habitually subscribed to a distinction between *potentia Dei absoluta* and *potentia Dei ordinata*, where the latter allowed for the operation of nature, too.[17] And al-Ghazālī, to name but one prominent Muslim theologian, appears not to care whether causes (*asbāb*) and intermediaries (*wasā'iṭ*) are cited, just so long as God's power to effect (what are commonly known as) miracles is respected.[18] That such a stance might nonetheless lead to causal skepticism is spelled out for the Islamic world by al-Ghazālī in his celebrated criticism of the purported necessity of the causal nexus (*Incoherence* 17),[19] and for the Latin world by Robert Holcot. Holcot starts from Ockham's observation that the notion of causality, which by definition is a relation, cannot be grasped as an intuitive cognition.[20] Then again, Holcot reasons, if it is inferred on the basis of regular observation, this can never reach the certainty of demonstration either, but at best be a probable induction. Furthermore, if divine omnipotence is a valid alternative explanation to anything occurring in the natural world, then anything our mind presents as having occurred through natural causes could just as well have been effected directly by divine power. There simply is no way of telling between the two. Consequently causality is something "said" of things – a nominal definition, not a real one.[21]

---

[14] See al-Juwaynī, *Al-Shāmil fī uṣūl al-dīn*, ed. Klopfer, p. 132.
[15] Quoted by Simplicius, *In Phys.* VIII, ed. Diels, p. 1150; cf. pp. 1141 and 1142.
[16] See, e.g., Scotus, *Quodlibet* VII.4 and VII.9; *Ordinatio* I.42 (ed. Vatican, VI: 343–4). For the Islamic tradition, see my "Possible Worlds in the *Tahāfut al-falāsifa*: Al-Ghazālī on Creation and Contingency," *Journal of the History of Philosophy* 38 (2000) 479–502.
[17] See Lawrence Moonan, *Divine Power: The Medieval Power Distinction up to its Adoption by Albert, Bonaventure, and Aquinas* (Oxford: Clarendon Press, 1994).
[18] In favor of attributing belief in secondary causality to al-Ghazālī see Richard Frank, *Creation and the Cosmic System: al-Ghazālī and Avicenna* (Heidelberg: Carl Winter Universitätsverlag, 1992).
[19] This criticism was anticipated a century earlier in al-Bāqillānī, *Introduction* (ed. McCarthy, p. 43).
[20] Ockham, *Ordinatio* I.3 (*Opera theol.* I: 418) and I.6 (I: 497).
[21] Holcot, *Determinationes* 3 (ed. 1518); see Reijo Työrinoja, "God, Causality, and Nature. Some Problems of Causality in Medieval Theology," in E. Martikainen (ed.) *Infinity, Causality and Determinism: Cosmological Enterprises and their Preconditions* (Frankfurt: Peter Lang, 2002) pp. 53–5.

In the *Incoherence of the Philosophers*, al-Ghazālī presents for the reader's consideration occasionalism as one alternative way of construing causal relations. Within speculative Islamic theology (*kalām*), this is the thesis that God creates the world anew from one moment to the next by adjoining accidents to substances. On this radical view, creatures do not exercise causality at all: all secondary causation vanishes as illusory, as does the whole Aristotelian metaphysics of perduring, powerful particulars.[22] To say that God is the sole true agent, as the occasionalists do, is to say that *everything* is in his hand. If God is the causator of causes (*musabbib al-asbāb*), the one who grants causative power to everything else, then he is the creator (*khāliq*) not only of the pen and the hand but also of human power and will (*Revivification* [ed. 2002, I: 35]). Certitude in religion then has to do precisely with acknowledging God's universal efficacy.[23] Yet the price is undeniably high. If God is responsible for absolutely everything that happens, whether directly or indirectly, then what sense is there anymore, for example, in attributing actions to human beings?[24] It is instructive to note that when in the fourteenth century Nicholas of Autrecourt tried to introduce an occasionalist system within the framework of Latin scholasticism, John Buridan accused him of destroying not only the natural but also the moral sciences (*Quaest. Metaphys.* II.1). The Muslim theologians, for their part, tied themselves in knots trying to come up with a satisfactory account of the human acquisition (*iktisāb*) of the actions ascribed to them (see Chapter 29). Averroes, Maimonides, and Thomas Aquinas all denounced occasionalism for making a mockery not only of science and wisdom, but of God's benevolence as well.[25]

FROM ETERNITY, OR *EX NIHILO*?

According to Averroes, when positing a God whose action consists in constantly recreating the world *ex nihilo*, the Muslim theologians "did not postulate an Agent resembling empirical agents. In the empirical world, after all, an agent's act consists in changing an existent's attribute to another, not in converting privation

---

[22] See Richard Frank, "The Ashʿarite Ontology I: Primary Entities," *Arabic Sciences and Philosophy* 9 (1999) 165–231; Dominik Perler and Ulrich Rudolph, *Occasionalismus: Theorien der Kausalität im arabisch-islamischen und im Europäischen Denken* (Göttingen: Vandenhoeck and Ruprecht, 2000).

[23] See *Revivification* I: 74; *Beautiful Names*, ed. Shehadi, pp. 98–105.

[24] See Thérèse-Anne Druart, "Al-Ghazali's Conception of the Agent in the *Tahāfut* and the *Iqtisad*: Are People Really Agents?," in J. E. Montgomery (ed.) *Arabic Theology, Arabic Philosophy: From the Many to the One* (Leuven: Peeters, 2006) 425–40.

[25] See Averroes, *Incoherence of the Incoherence* 17 (ed. Bouyges, pp. 519–24); Averroes, *In Metaphys.* IX.7; Maimonides, *Guide* I.73; Aquinas, *Summa contra gentiles* III.69. Averroes's critique is analyzed by Barry Kogan, *Averroes and the Metaphysics of Causation* (Albany: State University of New York Press, 1985) pp. 86–164.

(*ʿadam*) into existence (*wujūd*)." On the latter, Aristotelian view (which Averroes himself advocates), an agent's actions may indeed result in a thing's becoming different from what it was "in substance, name, and definition"; yet the ancient principle is preserved according to which "the existent in the absolute sense is never generated or corrupted."[26] This is to say that nothing ever comes to be from absolutely nothing. Aristotelian doctrine in its unadulterated form thus allows for no original act of creation – no coming-to-be of the cosmic system as a whole or its regulative component, the eternally rotating heavens: the concept of agency or efficient causality is so intimately tied in with the notion of a proximate substrate from which every generated substance proceeds, and an existent world order that acts as its backdrop, that an absolute beginning becomes inconceivable.[27]

This is, perhaps, why so many thinkers who were wedded to scriptural notions of creation found Aristotelian eternalism utterly unpalatable. As Averroes puts the matter, "it was difficult for Muslims to call both God and world eternal, since they had no other understanding of the eternal than that which has no cause."[28] To those who had taken to heart the lesson of the *Timaeus's* being–becoming distinction, only the generated unequivocally possesses an efficient cause (*ʿilla fāʿila*) for its coming-to-be; the eternal, by contrast, can – by definition – have no generative cause to its being (*ʿilla mukawwina*).[29] By insisting on the difference between generation, which is from privation, and creation, which is out of nothing, the creationists might further distinguish between empirical agents and divine agency.[30]

This answer would satisfy the creationists' need to place creation in a category separate from ordinary causality – compare Aquinas's dictum according to which creation is neither a motion nor a change (*Summa contra gentiles* II.17) – but it would hardly suffice to paper over the many eternalist presuppositions at work in Aristotle's philosophy. Proofs for and against the eternity of the world accordingly proliferate in the medieval period, often as a preliminary to arguments for the existence of God (see Chapter 53). Proofs of the world's eternity would either start from certain conceptual necessities related to motion, time, the *ex nihilo nihil* principle, and the aethereal (and hence ingenerable and incorruptible) constitution of the heavens (all traceable back to Aristotle), or they would argue for a necessary equivalence relation between the world's eternal

---

[26] Averroes, *Incoherence* 3 (ed. Bouyges, pp. 221–2).

[27] See Aristotle, *Phys.* VIII; *De caelo* I.10–12; *De gen. et cor.* II.9–10; *Metaphys.* XII.3, 1069b35–70a2.

[28] *Incoherence* 2 (ed. Bouyges, p. 124); cf. Saadiah, *Beliefs and Convictions* I.2 (ed. Landauer, p. 39).

[29] This formulation is from Galen's paraphrase, the *Compendium Timaei* (ed. Kraus and Walzer, p. 4).

[30] See Isaac Israeli's influential *Book of Definitions* (ed. Muckle) secs. 42–4, drawing on al-Kindī, *On the True, First, and Perfect Agent* (ed. Abū Rīda) I: 182–4.

and benevolent cause and God's eternal effect. Proofs of creation, conversely, argue that the world's very structure is such that it must have an origin – witness Philoponus's famous proofs for the impossibility of an infinite past – or else claim that God's very uniqueness precludes another eternal entity along-side him.[31] All these arguments received refutations, and most of these in turn received rejoinders, so that the discussions become very complex to trace.[32]

Amidst these debates, proofs, and counter-proofs, the notion crops up that the issue might not be decidable by rational means at all (see Chapter 51). Drawing on Aristotle's *Topics* I.11, this first becomes a popular theme in twelfth-century Andalusian thought: it is found in Judah Halevi's *Khazari* (I.62–7) and given decisive formulation in Maimonides's *Guide of the Perplexed* (I.71, II.18), whence it finds its way to the Latin world and eventually Aquinas (*Summa theol.* 1a 46.1–2). Some would utilize it to emphasize the importance of revelation in disclosing the facts of creation – already Saadiah had made the point that an original act of creation by all rights should be inconceivable to us (*Beliefs and Convictions*, ed. Landauer, pp. 30–1) – while for others it would justify a division of labor between the arts and the divinity faculties. To some, the idea that God *could* create an eternal world even though in fact he did not was a welcome reminder of God's absolute omnipotence, while at the other extreme a committed Aristotelian like Boethius of Dacia maintained that the world is demonstrably eternal based on principles derived from created reality, yet actually originated according to a power greater than nature.[33] For Ibn Ṭufayl, the central point is that whichever view one takes on the origin of the world, its need for a creator remains (*Ḥayy ibn Yaqẓān*, ed. Gauthier, pp. 80–2). But how, if the world had existed forever?

ETERNAL CREATION

Philosophical models of eternal creation had, in fact, been devised early on. The Arabs knew, for instance, of a treatise by Ammonius of Alexandria purporting to demonstrate how Aristotle's Prime Mover is not only a source of the heavens'

---

[31] For Philoponus's infinity arguments see Richard Sorabji, *Time, Creation, and the Continuum* (London: Duckworth, 1983) pp. 210–31; for their Arabic history, see Herbert Davidson, *Proofs for Eternity, Creation, and the Existence of God in Medieval Islamic and Jewish Philosophy* (Oxford: Oxford University Press, 1987) pp. 93–134; the scholastics received these through Averroes and Maimonides, but also had an apparently independent source in Bonaventure, *Sent.* II.1.1.2.

[32] Davidson, *Proofs for Eternity*, comprehensively tracks the Arabic story; for the scholastics, begin with Richard Dales, *Medieval Discussions of the Eternity of the World* (Leiden: Brill, 1990) and Richard Dales and Omar Argerami, *Medieval Latin Texts on the Eternity of the World* (Leiden: Brill, 1991).

[33] The fourteenth-century Averroist John of Jandun likewise distinguishes between creation and temporal making, claiming that to God many such things are possible that appear impossible to the human observer: see Dales and Argerami, *Texts*, pp. 182–93.

eternal motion, but also of the world's eternal existence. This in time came to influence the scholastics,[34] as did the so-called *Liber de causis*, proposition 4 of which states that the First Cause firstly gives rise to being itself. The Arabic Plotinus repeatedly refers to the One as Creator,[35] whereas al-Fārābī is representative of the Arabic Aristotelians when he avers that "The First Existent is the First Cause of the existence of all the other existents" (*On the Perfect State* I.1.1, ed. Walzer, p. 56), and this forever. Still, what might giving existence or granting being entail? Because these are described simply as an emanation (*fayḍ*), there is no apparent way to relate any of these descriptions to the recognized Aristotelian causal explanations.[36]

This all changes with Avicenna, whose peculiar genius was to appropriate elements from across the Hellenic tradition and beyond in a highly creative synthesis. Avicenna places emanation squarely in the column of efficient causality, when the latter is suitably interpreted:

> The metaphysical philosophers do not mean by "agent" only the principle of motion, as the naturalists do, but the principle and giver of existence (*mabda' al-wujūd wa-mufīdu-hu*), as in the case of the Creator's relation to the world (*al-bārī li-l-ʿālam*). As for the natural efficient cause, it does not bestow any existence other than motion in one of the forms of motion. Thus, in the natural sciences, that which bestows existence is a principle of motion.
>
> (*Metaphysics* [*al-Ilāhiyyāt*] VI.1, ed. Marmura, p. 195)

This new understanding of efficient causality provides a suitably technical account of emanation; it connects it with Avicenna's groundbreaking essence–existence distinction and fleshes out his famed metaphysical argument for God's existence (as Aquinas clearly sees in *De ente* 5); it also makes both of these appear to be logical outgrowths of Aristotle's natural philosophy.[37] As in the late ancient system, matter, form, and worldly motion become contributing causes (*synaitiai*) which, however, take a back seat to the more primal modes of truly efficient (existential and productive) as well as final (essential and paradigmatic) causation.[38] Through the preexistence of all essences in the divine wisdom, God may act not only as the efficient but also as the formal and the final cause of the

---

[34] See Richard Sorabji, *Matter, Space, and Motion* (London: Duckworth, 1988) pp. 249–85.
[35] See Peter Adamson, *The Arabic Plotinus* (London: Duckworth, 2002) pp. 137–49.
[36] Al-Fārābī's reticence may stem from an awareness that emanation does not belong in Aristotelianism: see Thérèse-Anne Druart, "Al-Farabi, Emanation, and Metaphysics," in P. Morewedge (ed.) *Neoplatonism and Islamic Thought* (Albany: State University of New York Press, 1992) 127–48.
[37] *Physics* I.10, ed. Madkur Zāyid, pp. 48–9. Michael Marmura, "The Metaphysics of Efficient Causality in Avicenna (Ibn Sina)," in M. Marmura (ed.) *Islamic Theology and Philosophy* (Albany: State University of New York Press, 1984) 172–87.
[38] Avicenna, *Metaphys.* VI.2 (ed. Marmura, p. 202), with Proclus, *In Timaeum*, ed. Diehl, I: 1–2 and I: 263.

world's assuming the shape that it does, seeing as such essences are but paths by which limited beings draw closer to the divine goodness. That this represents a mingling of Platonic motifs with Aristotelian causal language is attested to not only by various post-Avicennian thinkers in the wake of al-Ghazālī and Aquinas, but also by William of Conches, who quite independently of the Arabic tradition (and in fact relying on the *Timaeus*) identifies God as the efficient cause of all things as their creator and the formal cause of all things through the divine wisdom.[39]

What is more, by insisting on the simultaneity of cause and effect, Avicenna alleviates the perceived problem of emanation being a mediated form of influence.[40] Because the entire order of existence is continuously dependent on the First Cause, God as the primary agent may properly be thought to sustain the world through all time. The Sufis were fond of citing the Quran on this point, saying "everything perishes except His face" (28:88). By this they meant that if God ever turned his back on creation, everything would perish in an instant, since nothing has existence of itself.[41] Thus God's creative activity, irrespective of specific essences and circumstances, touches everything equally and directly. Avicenna furthermore distinguishes between temporal and causal priority, and maintains that only the latter is essential (since temporally successive causes are only instrumental). This has the additional benefit of securing the contingency even of eternal entities such as the heavens and the separate intelligences.[42] A similar view was transmitted to the Latin scholastics by Augustine, who had used the metaphor of the footprint in the dust to illustrate a unidirectional yet atemporal dependency relation (*De civitate Dei* X.31). Even though Augustine himself did not subscribe to this Neoplatonic picture, his distinction was seized upon by some Latin thinkers, who saw it as a useful tool in securing a place for eternal principles besides God. Eriugena, for instance, argued that the primordial causes are eternal, because they are all at once (*simul*) in God's Word, but that they are nevertheless not coeternal, because

---

[39] Al-Ghazālī, *Beautiful Names*, ed. Shehadi, pp. 79–82, 92–93; William of Conches, *Glosae super Platonem* XCI.

[40] See Avicenna, *Annotations* (ed. Badawī, p. 157); Mullā Ṣadrā, *Four Intellectual Journeys*, III.3.6 (ed. Lutfi *et al.*, VI: 216); see also Marmura, "Avicenna on Causal Priority," in P. Morewedge (ed.) *Islamic Philosophy and Mysticism* (Delmar: Caravan Books, 1981) 65–83.

[41] A similar view was transmitted to the Latin tradition by Cassiodorus in his *Secular Learning on the Soul* I.4, where he says that "no created substance can be a creator since it requires God to exist, and cannot give to another the being (*esse*) that it has only as a possession."

[42] See Robert Wisnovsky, "One Aspect of the Avicennian Turn in Sunnī Theology," *Arabic Sciences and Philosophy* 14 (2004) 65–100. Ibn Kammūna ventured as far as to argue for the pre-eternity of human souls: even these will be causally secondary to the First Existent, and subsequently contingent. See Reva Pourjavady and Sabine Schmidtke, *A Jewish Philosopher of Baghdad* (Leiden: Brill, 2006) p. 24.

"the [divine] art precedes what subsists in it, through it, and by it" (*Periphyseon* III.5). Bernard of Chartres upheld a similar distinction between eternity and coeternity.[43] In all this, the Latin world found an admirable affinity between Avicenna's teachings and what they had previously come to understand of the Greek heritage.

Other aspects of Avicenna's teaching proved harder to assimilate. Consider, for instance, Avicenna's thesis that God does not act for any external end. On the face of it, this seems equally acceptable to the theologian and the Aristotelian-trained philosopher,[44] yet the principle could be taken in two ways: either to indicate that God creates for *no* reason, or that his creation proceeds from him intrinsically, for instance flowing from the pure goodness of the divine.[45] The first option would make God's creative act seem quite arbitrary (Aquinas, *Summa contra gentiles* II.24); the second holds other dangers. When Aquinas says that God does not create because of any need or for the sake of profit, but only for the sake of his own goodness,[46] is this to say that God's goodness necessitates the world's creation? Avicenna was commonly accused of having made just this inference, in line with the mainstream of Neoplatonic teaching, and of having compromised divine autonomy as a consequence. Does creating belong to God's essence and nature? Al-Ghazālī suggests a broad dichotomy:

Actions divide into two: voluntary, like animal and human action, and natural, like the sun's action in shedding light, fire in heating, and water in cooling... According to you [philosophers], God enacted the world by way of necessity from his essence, by nature and compulsion, not by way of will and choice. Indeed, the whole [of the world] follows necessarily from his essence in the way that light follows necessarily from the sun. And just as the sun has no power to stop light or fire to stop heating, the First has no power to stop his acts.

(*Incoherence* 11, tr. Marmura, p. 128)[47]

This misrepresents Avicenna in various ways, however. First, Avicenna distinguishes between divine goodness and generosity, the first being a self-referential property, whereas the other is other-directed.[48] Second, the distinction between natural and willed acts that other thinkers make much of simply does not exist for him in this way. A willed act is no less willed for being perfectly formed

---

[43] Reported by John of Salisbury, *Metalogicon* IV.35.
[44] See al-Bāqillānī, *Introduction*, sec. 54; Avicenna, *Metaphysics* (*Shifāʾ*) IX.4 (ed. Marmura, p. 326).
[45] See, e.g., Avicenna, *Remarks and Admonitions* (ed. Forget, pp. 158–9).
[46] *Summa theol.* 1a 19.2 and 44.4 ad 1.
[47] See also al-Ghazālī, *Incoherence* 3, p. 56. Compare Basil of Caesarea, *Hexaëmeron* I.2–3, 5–6; Aquinas, *Summa contra gentiles* II.23. According to Maimonides (*Guide* I.69) the theologians were reluctant even to talk of causes (ʿilla, sabab) in association with God because of the necessity that attaches to the relationship between cause and effect: see, e.g., al-Qushayrī, *Reminder*, ed. Busyūnī, p. 56.
[48] Al-Ghazālī himself puts this best, at *Incoherence* 5 (ed. Marmura, pp. 93–4).

and hence not an arbitrary choice (*ikhtiyār*) in the sense of choosing between alternatives.[49] Third, Avicenna is careful to talk about eternal creation being a "concomitant" (*lāzim*) of divine generosity and hence following upon it, not constituting it (*Annotations* [ed. Badawī, p. 103]).[50] Finally, as Aquinas helpfully points out, the sun-and-its-light metaphor originally was meant to underline not the necessary nature of God's creative act but the fact that, as generous, it extends everywhere indiscriminately (*Quaest. de potentia* 3.15 ad 1).

The dual notions that God both enjoys free will (and is self-sufficient) and is supremely good (and therefore benevolent) are, of course, theological tenets too, and consequently their reconciliation posed an enduring challenge for Christians and Muslims alike.[51] Starting with Odo Rigaldus in the thirteenth century, Christian thinkers made reference to the Trinity as offering a possible way out. If this perfect manifestation of God's creative action exhausts the demands of God's essential goodness (as spelled out in the principle attributed to Dionysius according to which "the good is diffusive of itself"), then the further creation of an imperfect external world would be a free act.[52] However, as has been pointed out, as long as the Platonic maxim according to which the good diffuses itself *maximally* is followed, this does nothing to dispel the trouble.[53] After all, as Proclus had already said, if procession stopped at perfect entities, then first things would be last (*In Timaeum*, ed. Diehl, I: 372–3).

AVERROISTIC NATURALISM

In this thicket of contending strands of Neoplatonic and creationist argumentation, the curiously conservative Aristotelianism of Averroes stands apart. Although originally steeped in Neoplatonism, Averroes's deepening acquaintance with Aristotle's texts, coupled with the profound impression made on him by al-Ghazālī's critique of the philosophers, persuaded him of the deleterious

---

[49] See Plotinus, *Enneads* VI.8.16.

[50] See Rahim Acar, *Talking about God and Talking about Creation: Avicenna's and Thomas Aquinas' Positions* (Leiden: Brill, 2005) pp. 140–6. Avicenna's talk of "following" mirrors al-Fārābī, *On the Perfect State* I.2.5 (ed. Walzer, p. 100).

[51] See Norman Kretzmann, "A General Problem of Creation: Why Would God Create Anything at All?," in S. MacDonald (ed.) *Being and Goodness: The Concept of the Good in Metaphysics and Philosophical Theology* (Ithaca, NY: Cornell University Press, 1991) 208–28; Eric Ormsby, *Theodicy in Islamic Thought: The Dispute over al-Ghazālī's "Best of All Possible Worlds"* (Princeton, NJ: Princeton University Press, 1984).

[52] Odo Rigaldus, *De erroribus circa durationem rerum exeuntium* (in Dales and Argerami, *Texts*, pp. 48–53); see also Henry of Ghent, *Quodlibet* VI.2, and see Juan Carlos Flores, *Henry of Ghent: Metaphysics and the Trinity* (Leuven: Leuven University Press, 2006) pp. 119–47. See also Bonaventure, *Itinerarium* VI.2.

[53] *Timaeus* 29e–30a; see Kretzmann, "A General Problem," pp. 219–20, commenting on Aquinas, *Sent.* I.2.1.4sc.

effects of the adoption of the language of emanation by latter-day philosophers (*al-muʾ akhkhirūn*). Because of the numerous difficulties ferreted out by al-Ghazālī, Averroes ended up reverting to a strictly Aristotelian take on causation in which the four causes, plus the distinction between potentiality and actuality, are made to do all the work. According to a justly celebrated passage in the *Commentary on the Metaphysics*, efficient causality reduces to neither invention (*ikhtirāʿ*) nor emanation, nor does it require a separate Giver of Forms – rather, it consists in educing actuality from the potentiality of matter (XII.18, ed. Bouyges, p. 1499). This strictly immanent process is spurred by the heavenly rotations and is ultimately inspired by the perfection of the separate intelligences, which in turn find unity in the supreme good of the Prime Mover:

> And if this were not so, then neither order nor proportion would exist here in this world. With this, the claim is verified that God is the creator (*khāliq*), supporter, and preserver of everything, as he says: "God supports the heavens and the earth, lest they should fall." [Quran 35:39] . . . Therefore the term 'agent' is applied equivocally to what is not in matter and what exists in matter.
>
> (*Incoherence* 3, ed. Bouyges, p. 230)

In fact, all that agency amounts to in the case of immaterial principles is final causation.[54] Followers of this model are hard to come by, although Albert the Great, ever the eclectic, refuses to admit a discrepancy between this account and the Neoplatonic one. Educing a form in potentiality from its matter is, according to Albert, merely the way creation is spoken of in physics, whereas procession or flux describes the same process in metaphysical terms. The one tracks generation from the point of view of the patient, the latter from that of the ultimate agent.[55]

Elsewhere, Avicenna's depiction of God as both the first existence-granting agent and ultimate final cause generally won out over Averroes's more austere musings. From among prominent Muslim thinkers, both al-Ghazālī and Mullā Ṣadrā (1571–1640) reproduce these Avicennian tenets when expounding on the divine attributes "the First, the Last," confirming that God is that from which all originally proceeds and that toward which everything finally turns.[56] Bonaventure is a prime example of the same happening in Latin (*Sent.* I.45.2.1c), while Maimonides is a likely bridge between the two traditions, talking as he

---

[54] On the details of this view see my "Averroes and the Teleological Argument," *Religious Studies* 38 (2002) 405–28.

[55] *Super Ethica* VI.8 par. 522 (ed. Cologne, 14.2: 448) identifies Avicenna as the prime expositor for the metaphysical viewpoint; see Therese Bonin, *Creation as Emanation: The Origin of Diversity in Albert the Great's* On the Causes and the Procession of the Universe (Notre Dame, IN: University of Notre Dame Press, 2001) pp. 15–17.

[56] See Ghazālī, *Beautiful Names* (ed. Shehadi, pp. 146–7); Mullā Ṣadrā, *Kitāb al-mashāʿir*, secs. 108–10.

does of God as being the "causator of causes," "form of forms," and "end of ends" (*Guide* I.69). These three phrases neatly recount the Neoplatonic moments of procession, staying, and reversion (*prohodos, monē, epistrophē*), and thereby reveal how far the discussion had advanced beyond either a pre-reflective creationism or a blind acceptance of Aristotle's categories of change. That Maimonides can simultaneously acknowledge that talk of emanation nicely accentuates the operation of efficient causality over a distance (*Guide* II.12) and deny that it presents a credible technical account of the creative process (*Guide* II.22) tells us, however, that even the Neoplatonic heritage was subject to critical review.[57]

There was, in addition, a worry about how to make the metaphysical model of causation fit with Aristotelian naturalism, as is evidenced, for instance, in Aquinas's criticism of Solomon ibn Gabirol (*Summa contra gentiles* III.69). According to Aquinas, Ibn Gabirol had denied causal powers to corporeal substances: the criticism may be misplaced, but it shows a concern with preserving ordinary causal efficacy in a world populated by seemingly omnipresent transcendent agents.[58] Likewise, Buridan – after first emphasizing that God as the Giver of Forms is the "common, first, and in every way primary agent" (*Quaest. Phys.* II.5 [ed. 1509, f. 32va]) – says that if one wishes to account for the diversity in nature without reverting to bare divine omnipotence, "in the natural mode it would be impossible for the same simple and invariable thing to produce different and contrary effects, now these effects and tomorrow others, unless there were other, diverse causes contributing to them" (ibid., II.13, f. 39rb).[59]

At Buridan's disposal is, in fact, a technical vocabulary that allows him to retain the analysis of natural agents and patients, while at the same time making room for divine omnipotence and a potentially omnipresent divine causality. In terms that became standard in the late thirteenth century, omnipotence was said to attach directly to a special "obediential potentiality" in creatures – that is, a unique passive capacity introduced precisely to explain how God might operate on all creatures directly. It is in accordance with this obediential potentiality that Adam could be fashioned by God directly from earth (Genesis 2:7), even against Aristotle's express stipulation that it is only seed and not earth that is potentially a man (*Metaphys.* IX.7, 1048b37–49a2). By contrast, natural agents only ever work on proximate matter and only ever bring out proximate

---

[57] See Arthur Hyman, "Maimonides on Creation and Emanation", in J. F. Wippel (ed.) *Studies in Medieval Philosophy* (Washington: Catholic University of America Press, 1987) 45–61.

[58] See John Laumakis, "Aquinas' Misinterpretation of Avicebron on the Activity of Corporeal Substances: *Fons Vitae* II, 9 and 10," *Modern Schoolman* 81 (2004) 135–49.

[59] For discussion, see Joël Biard, "The Natural Order in John Buridan", in J. Thijssen and J. Zupko (eds.) *The Metaphysics and Natural Philosophy of John Buridan* (Leiden: Brill, 2001) 77–95.

form. Duns Scotus had already taught the Franciscans to apply the notion of obediential potentiality sparingly – in effect, only in those cases where the divine will is freely exercised in accordance with absolute power, as in the first act of creation and the production of miracles (*In Metaphys.* IX.12). In adopting such a distinction, scholastics in the post-Scotus period could maintain much of what the Muslim theologians had wanted to emphasize regarding God's free and unfettered agency, while also respecting what the Aristotelian philosophers had to say regarding the natural invariance with which change and coming-to-be regularly occur in this world. The distinction led to numerous interesting thought experiments being conducted in the natural philosophy of Buridan and Nicole Oresme, among others, concerning states of affairs that God could bring about *supernaturaliter* even if they would never come to obtain under the system of causes and effects in place in the actual world.[60] This is another example of how the distinction between *potentia Dei absoluta* and *potentia Dei ordinata* proved fruitful for late scholasticism.

[60] See my "The Impossible, insofar as It Is Possible: Ibn Rushd and Buridan on Logic and Natural Theology," in D. Perler and U. Rudolph (eds.) *Logik und Theologie: Das Organon im arabischen und im lateinischen Mittelalter* (Leiden: Brill, 2005) 447–67.

18

THE INFLUENCE OF ARABIC ARISTOTELIANISM ON SCHOLASTIC NATURAL PHILOSOPHY: PROJECTILE MOTION, THE PLACE OF THE UNIVERSE, AND ELEMENTAL COMPOSITION

REGA WOOD

Most popular accounts of the introduction of Aristotle's natural philosophy credit Arabic civilization with transmitting classical Greek works to the Latin West.[1] By contrast, a few contemporary authors, hostile to Islam, deny any contribution of the Islamic world to scholasticism. Neither claim is credible. As we shall see, although Arabic Aristotelianism did not provide the primary access to Aristotle's texts themselves, it did make a profound contribution to scholastic natural philosophy.

Confounding this dispute is a misunderstanding of the significance of Arabic-based Aristotle translations. Scholastic authors seldom commented on translations based on the Arabic Aristotle. Almost every major scholastic commentary on Greek philosophical works is based on a direct translation from Greek into Latin, with a few early exceptions. Scholastics evidently recognized that though they were often harder to follow and more obscure than translations from the Arabic Aristotle, Greek-based translations were closer to the original.

So let us look chiefly at the influence of the interpretative tradition of Arabic Aristotelianism on the Latin West, after saying a few words on translations of Arabic texts. We will suggest that though scholastics did not comment on Arabic-based translations of Aristotle, without these translations and more importantly without the interpretative tradition that accompanied them,[2] the

---

[1] Jane Smith, "Islam and Christendom," in J. Esposito (ed.) *Oxford History of Islam* (Oxford: Oxford University Press, 1999) pp. 332–3. This chapter is dedicated to Richard Rorty, who made me aware of the problem.

[2] Cristina d'Ancona, who thinks the role of Arabic Aristotelianism in shaping its Latin counterpart already evident, has provided a helpful explanation of the incorporation of Greek exegesis in the Arabic commentary tradition. See her "From Latin Antiquity to the Arab Middle Ages: The Commentaries and the Harmony between the Philosophies of Plato and Aristotle," in L. Honnefelder *et al.* (eds.) *Albertus Magnus und die Anfänge der Aristoteles-Rezeption im lateinischen Mittelalter* (Münster: Aschendorf, 2005) 45–69.

scholastic tradition would have been much poorer; indeed, it might never have arisen. After all, James of Venice's translations had been available since about 1150, but Aristotelian analytics, metaphysics, and natural philosophy began to influence major scholastic authors only when the Michael Scot translations became available around 1225.[3] In fact, before 1225, translations of sections of Avicenna's *Shifā'*, chiefly the *Philosophia prima* and the *Liber de anima*, were more influential than Aristotle's own metaphysics and natural philosophy. Michael Scot's greatest contributions are his translations of Averroes, which, however, also include translations of Aristotle. When he translated Averroes's commentaries Scot also translated Aristotle from the Arabic; these translations appeared as separate text blocks of Aristotle followed by the corresponding Averroes commentary. Thus though scholastic authors did not comment on Scot's translation of Aristotle, they had it at hand and often quoted it for difficult passages. Scot also enabled his contemporaries to consult other Arabic authors. For example, Scot translated al-Biṭrūjī's (Alpetragius) *De motibus coelorum (Kitāb al-hay'a)* to accompany his translation of Averroes's long commentary on *De caelo*.[4] Similarly, Scot translated not only Aristotle's and Averroes's *De animalibus*, but also the corresponding section from Avicenna's *Shifā'*.

What the Latin West received from Arabic Spain is best seen not as a series of isolated works by Greek authors, but as a tradition of Aristotelian natural philosophy. Many problems central to scholastic natural philosophy were framed in that tradition by Muslim authors. This is true for topics in metaphysics and epistemology and in psychology and biology. Here, however, we will consider only two authors, Avicenna and Averroes, and three problems in the physical sciences: (1) projectile motion, (2) the place of the universe, and (3) elemental composition.

PROJECTILE MOTION

We will look first at the problem of projectile motion, since interest in it as an instance of action-at-a-distance antedated the reintroduction of Aristotle's natural philosophy proper. Projectile motion is a problem for Aristotle's account of motion because a thrown ball, unlike a pushed ball, is not in constant contact

---

[3] René-Antoine Gauthier, "Notes sur les débuts (1225–1240) du premier 'averroïsme'," *Revue des sciences philosophique théologiques* 66 (1982) 321–73.

[4] See Lynn Thorndike, *Michael Scot* (London: Nelson, 1965) pp. 22–5. See, more generally, Charles Burnett, "Arabic into Latin: The Reception of Arabic Philosophy into Western Europe," in P. Adamson and R. Taylor (eds.) *The Cambridge Companion to Arabic Philosophy* (Cambridge: Cambridge University Press, 2005) p. 380. Doubt has been raised about the attribution of many of Scot's translations, as Burnett notes.

with a pusher. Aristotle, however, claims that mover and moved thing must be together; there can be nothing in between them. Indeed, all movement caused by an external mover can be reduced to pushing and pulling by a mover in physical contact with the thing being moved (*Phys.* VII.2).

Authors such as Philip the Chancellor, who had only superficial knowledge of Aristotle's *Physics*, but did know Avicenna, see projectile motion as unproblematic. Philip mentions projectile motion as an example of a mover's power being present in the absence of its essence.[5] Robert Grosseteste's early notes on Aristotle's *Physics* treat projectile motion as at least a potential counterexample to the basic tenet of Aristotelian physics that mover and moved thing must be together. Commenting on *Physics* VII, Grosseteste sought to save the claim by positing a disposition in a thrown object caused by a thrower's great impact (*magna pulsio*). On account of this disposition, even in projectile motion, there was no distance between mover and moved object (ed. Dales, p. 127).

Richard Rufus of Cornwall was less sanguine about Aristotle's account. Moreover, he considered inadequate Aristotle's further suggestion that contact is maintained because the immediate mover in projectile motion is the medium – air, for example – through which the projectile passed. Rufus held that Aristotle's account of the thrower's action on the medium must be supplemented by an account of its effect on the projectile. Specifically, Rufus claimed that the projector produced an impression on the projectile (*In Phys.* VIII.3.1).[6]

Now dispositions are a part of Aristotle's ontology, but he seldom refers to forces and impressions.[7] By contrast, impressions are basic to Avicenna's account of certain acts – especially of images reflected in water or in mirrors and things sensed or understood. These are cases where physical contact between mover and moved object cannot, does not, or need not occur.[8] In a passage from *Liber*

---

[5] That is, the power (*virtus*) originating with a thrower is in the rock she throws without the thrower's being there. For Philip the example of projectile motion shows that place need not be determined by circumscription; the virtual presence of the thrower in the projectile suggests that the soul need not be in the body circumscriptively. See *Summa de bono*, ed. Wicki, p. 293.

[6] Silvia Donati disputes the attribution of this work to Rufus, particularly this question. See her "The Anonymous Commentary on the Physics in Erfurt," *Recherches de théologie et philosophie médiévales* 72 (2005) 232–62. For a reply to Donati, see Rega Wood, "The Works of Richard Rufus: The State of the Question in 2008," *Recherches de théologie et philosophie médiévales*, 76 (2009) 1–73.

[7] Older translations of Aristotle from the Greek, such as those of James of Venice, do not employ the term "impressio." By contrast, William Moerbeke introduces the term sparingly in the translations he redacted in the 1260s, as at *Metaphysics* 1046a25 and *De caelo* 301b17–30, which includes a description of projectile motion.

[8] Forms of the Latin *imprimo* translate a variety of Arabic words (*athar, inṭabaʿa, istathbata, munṭabiʿ*), often describing cases in which something immaterial acts on matter. Alternative translations of these same words also play a role; *athar*, for example, was sometimes rendered *affectio*, the term used in *Primus naturalium* (*Shifāʾ*) II.8 to describe projectile motion (see below). Shlomo Pines stresses not *athar* but *mayl quasrī* or violent inclination in his general account, but *mayl* is generally translated

de anima III.7, a work that undoubtedly deeply influenced the early development of scholasticism, Avicenna boldly claimed that contact or striking is not required for acting and being acted on. Just as immaterial objects such as God or the intellect can act on bodies without striking them, so bodies themselves can act on each other without contact. No one can prove that this is not possible, or that distance can prevent one body from acting on another (ed. Van Riet, I: 260–1).

Although Avicenna discusses projectile motion only twice, and those passages do not seem to have influenced the Latin West,[9] scholastic discussions of the topic are nevertheless indebted to Avicenna for his general account of bodies acting by impressions. This account licenses claims for action-at-a-distance, the class to which early "impetus" or "imprint" theories of projectile motion belong. Moreover, there is ample evidence of the influence of Avicenna's claim that bodies can act by imprinting in the works of early scholastics indebted to Avicenna. William of Auvergne, for example, mentions impressions made on souls (male and female), on semen, and so on.[10] Albert the Great, too, describes the efficacy of impressions, even deep within the earth (*Meteora* II.2.4, ed. Cologne, VI.1: 68).

For Latin authors around 1225 encountering for the first time not Avicenna's natural philosophy but Aristotle's physics itself, the problem with such accounts was that impressions fit so poorly into Aristotelian ontology. What sort of qualities were impressions?[11] How could impressions account for local motion? Why should we believe that an imprint or virtual influx could substitute for

"inclination" or "disposition," and so does not clearly indicate Avicenna's influence. See Pines, "Les précurseurs musulmans de la theorie de l'impetus," *Archeion* 21 (1938) 298–306. For a discussion of translations of *athar* in translations of Aristotle's *Meteorology* see Danielle Jacquart, "De l'Arabe au Latin: l'influence de quelque choix lexicaux (*impressio, ingenium, intuitio*)," in J. Hamesse (ed.) *Aux origines du lexique philosophique Europeen* (Louvain-la-Neuve: Fédération internationale des instituts d'études médiévales, 1997) pp. 167–9.

[9] Pines argues for Avicenna's influence in "Les Précurseurs musulmans," pp. 298–306. For the contrary view, see Anneliese Maier, *Zwei Grundprobleme der Scholastischen Naturphilosophie* (Rome: Edizioni di Storia e Letteratura, 1968) pp. 129–34. Of the two passages, only one was even available in Latin translation (*Liber primus naturalium* [*Shifā'*] II.8, ed. Van Riet et al., II: 267–70).

[10] For a more complete discussion of Avicenna's influence on Auvergne, see Roland Teske, "William of Auvergne's Debt to Avicenna," in J. Janssens and D. De Smet (eds.) *Avicenna and his Heritage* (Leuven: Leuven University Press, 2002) 153–70. Probably for William the most important role of impressions is in the production of virtues or habits and in perception or apprehension based on impressed similitudes or species. See Auvergne, "De virtutibus," "De moribus," "De vitiis et peccatis," "De retributionibus sanctorum," "De universo," 1.1, 2.2, 2.3, *Opera omnia* I: 105aD and 107bC–D (apprehensions), 117bC (celestial bodies); 250aG (sins); 268aF (semen); 318aH (vision in the eye); 615aC (basilisk), 682aE (sight), 922aE–G (human and angelic cognition); 1066bH (men's and women's souls).

[11] See the anonymous *Lectura in librum de anima* I.8, ed. Gauthier, p. 102.

substantial contact?[12] For those who considered these merely rhetorical questions, because they rejected such accounts of motion, Averroes provided an alternative account. According to Averroes, projectile motion does not depend on the thrower's continuing to act on the projectile after contact is lost. Instead, the nature of the media through which projectiles move explains how projectile motion can occur. In some respects Averroes is just restating Aristotle: after contact between thrower and thrown object is lost, the medium moves the projectile along. In Aristotelian layer theory,[13] the first layer of a medium moves the second, which moves the third, and so on. Each layer acts on the next after it has been acted on. The problem is to explain why media such as air and water should have the ability to propagate or convey motion from layer to layer, so that all the layers do not stop moving at once when the thrower stops moving (*Phys.* VIII.10, 267a3–4).

Averroes answers first by stating the problem as an Aristotelian puzzle: we can explain projectile motion only if we either (1) suppose that the projectile is a self-moved mover; (2) allow that bodies can move each other without contact; or (3) admit that projectile motion is not continuous. Aristotle opts for the last alternative, an explanation that relies on the fact that projectile motion occurs only in air or water or something of the kind, as Averroes points out. Averroes explains that it occurs only in humid bodies such as air and water, since they lack self-defined boundaries. Accordingly, the parts of such humid bodies do not all move at once; instead, waves travel outwards successively, as is evident when a rock falls into a pool. The motion of a projectile is much like that of a boat carried along on a wave. Since the density of water or air is not fixed, instead of moving as a whole when pushed, their parts move closer together or farther apart and thereby convey motion. Also, fluid bodies can penetrate each other, so that one motion in a fluid does not interfere with another. Fluidity, which the Latin Averroes describes as a quasi-spiritual quality, akin to matter in its receptivity, allows air and water once moved to become *per se* movers themselves. Thus motion in liquids is propagated in much the same way that wave motion propagates itself longitudinally (*In Phys.* VIII.82; cf. *In De caelo* III.28).

As Averroes himself points out, this is a novel interpretation, and it did not go unappreciated by the scholastics. Albert the Great's *Physica* VIII.4.4 is a close paraphrase of Averroes, including examples and adding allusions to such

---

[12] See Roger Bacon, *Quaest. Phys.* VII, ed. Steele *et al.*, XIII: 338–40.

[13] See Jürgen Sarnowsky, *Die Aristotelish-scholastische Theorie der Bewegung* (Münster: Aschendorff, 1989) p. 384, and also Abel Franco, "Avempace, Projectile Motion, and Impetus Theory," *Journal of the History of Ideas* 64 (2004) 521–46.

medieval military devices as the crossbow, the catapult, and the siege engine. For Albert the characteristics that make air and water capable of sustaining the force and vigor (*vim et robur*) of the initial mover are three: (1) they have no determinate shape; (2) their parts can move independently, one without the other; and (3) they resemble matter in their receptive capacity. Fluids yield to bodies thrown into them, moving in waves, each of which successively expels the next until the violence dissipates.

In a significant departure from Averroes, Albert frequently uses the term 'impetus.' Unlike Averroes, who refers once here to the *virtus movendi* but mostly to motors and motion, Albert speaks of the impetus of the violence of the first mover: the thrower. And, indeed, at this time 'impetus' was a term used not by proponents but by opponents of accounts of projectile motion as a consequence of impressions or virtual influx.[14]

Thomas Aquinas, too, adopts Averroes's explanation of projectile motion, though his presentation is less thorough than his teacher's. Thomas agrees that projectile motion is successive and not continuous despite appearances and that a humid body like air is necessary for projectile motion. He denies that violent motion without contact is possible. Of Albert's three reasons why air and water can continue projectile motion, Thomas considers only one: such media are more susceptible because they are lighter and more subtle than other bodies (*In De caelo* III.7.6; *In Phys.* VIII.22.4). Thomas uses both the terms 'impetus' and 'impression' in his discussion: 'impetus' and more commonly 'impulse' or '*virtus movendi*' describes the thrower's act (*In Phys.* VII.3.11–12; VIII.8.7; VIII.22.3); 'impression' describes its effect in the medium and in the projectile. The impression in the projectile ceases, however, when contact is lost (*In De caelo* III.7.6; *In Phys.* VIII.22.3–4).[15]

On this topic, Aquinas is more influential as a critic. He points out that motion arising from an internal form counts as natural not violent, so we cannot account for projectile motion, which is violent, by positing an intrinsic form.[16]

For those who explained projectile motion as an effect that continues without contact with the thrower it was always a problem to describe the ontological

---

[14] See also Bacon, *Quaest. Phys.* VII, ed. Steele *et al.*, XIII: 343.

[15] Some have suggested that Aquinas advocated impetus theory, but this seems mistaken. With the exception of a short phrase cited in defense of this suggestion from *Quaest. de anima* 11 ad 2, which is contradicted in his *De caelo* commentary, all the passages cited for this claim are susceptible of an alternate interpretation. For a more sympathetic evaluation of the suggestion see Maier, *Zwei Grundprobleme*, pp. 134–40.

[16] Like Bacon, Aquinas notes that impressions are posited to explain alteration, not local motion; moreover, Aquinas also observes that stones do not alter – by, for example, changing their color or shape – when thrown (*In De caelo* III.7.6).

status of its cause in such a way as to distinguish violent motion from natural motion. It was easy to adduce experiences incompatible with the Aristotelian explanation, but hard to answer the question: what is the nature of its cause? Richard Rufus, for example, describes projectiles moving at different speeds and in different directions in the same medium; he notices that very light objects are difficult to throw. But when it comes to describing the impression he posits, he says only that it is "some quality or form" (*In Phys.* VIII.3.1). What probably seemed to him a minor, peripheral anomaly did not prompt him to undertake a major reexamination of his ontology.

By contrast, Francis of Marchia did undertake such a reexamination.[17] He distinguishes subsistent from insistent or formally inhering movers, among which he includes the force left behind by the thrower in projectile motion. This *virtus derelicta* is a special kind of form, intermediate between successive and permanent forms. The motion this intermediate form causes is violent, absolutely speaking, since it is contrary to the natural inclination of the thrown object. It is also in a qualified sense natural, however, since it is in accordance with the accidental form imprinted by the initial force (ed. in Schabel, "*Virtus derelicta*," pp. 68–73, 77). Terminology appears to be a problem for Marchia, who starts by employing descriptions that make minimal ontological commitment: a *virtus derelicta* or *recepta* produces a semi-permanent effect, called an influence or impression. Discussion of imprinting and impressions is a sign of Avicenna's continuing influence. Marchia first deploys the concept in describing the effect of a magnet on iron, where its use is uncontroversial. It reappears when projectile motion is likened to the movement of the heavens.

Like Albert the Great, Marchia pays careful attention to Averroes's account. He carefully describes the example of the circular waves produced when a rock is dropped into water. Unlike Albert, however, Marchia is not convinced. He believes his own account is superior precisely because it better accounts for the appearance of continuous motion rather than the successive kind that invisible waves in the medium would produce. Projectiles are not carried along in the air like sailors in a boat. Given that projectile motion can be circular as well as straight, compound, not simple, bodies must play the primary role (ibid., pp. 66–7). Like Rufus, Marchia points to the fact that very light objects are difficult to throw, which is not what you would expect if only the medium moved the projectile (p. 67). And though Marchia, like Rufus, agrees that the

---

[17] *Sent.* IV.1.1, ed. Chris Schabel, "Francis of Marchia's *Virtus derelicta* and the Context of its Development," *Vivarium* 44 (2006) 60–80. See also Maier, *Zwei Grundprobleme*, pp. 168–80, and Fabio Zanin, "Francis of Marchia, *Virtus derelicta*, and Modifications of the Basic Principles of Aristotelian Physics," *Vivarium* 44 (2006) 81–95.

medium as well as the force in the projectile plays a role in projectile motion (pp. 70–1), he argues that the force imprinted on the projectile is much more important to the explanation than the action of the medium, and he defends this view regardless of what Aristotle and Averroes held (p. 69).

John Buridan, the most famous proponent of medieval impetus theory, holds views that are similar in many respects to Marchia's. His account of what makes projectile motion violent – its being contrary to the natural inclination of the projectile – might have been borrowed from Marchia, as could the central analogy with magnetic motion (ed. Maier, *Zwei Grundprobleme* pp. 212–14; *Quaest. Phys.* VIII.12, f. 120ra–b).[18] Some of Buridan's objections against Aristotle, including the difficulty of hurling a feather, are found already in Rufus. But Marchia's more distinctive argument, based on the fact that projectile motion can occur in every direction, also appears (pp. 210–11; ff. 120va–b). Like Marchia, Buridan is preoccupied with the problem of the ontological status of the impressed impetus, calling it a great and a difficult doubt. His solution is closely related to Marchia's. Unlike Marchia, however, Buridan does not claim the imprints are intermediates, neither successive nor permanent. Instead, he holds that an impetus is something permanent, though corrupted by the resistance it encounters (pp. 213–14; f. 121ra–b). Buridan states that Aristotle's explanation is impossible. He compromises little with Averroes, whose position he reduces to the claim that projectile motion works by impressing the disposition of lightness on the medium. Gone is the suggestion that the medium plays a role in augmenting projectile motion, and with it the implied acceptance of Averroes's claims about the significance of air's capacity for rarefaction and condensation (pp. 210–11; f. 120va–b).[19]

The use of the term 'impetus' by Buridan, a proponent rather than an opponent of imprint theory, is a new departure.[20] Just where this usage comes from is not clear. It seems to come neither from Avicenna, nor from early Aristotle translations. Still, both Averroes's and Avicenna's influence remains: Buridan defines the newly named quality of impetus as an Avicennian impression: it is a quality designed to move the body on which it is impressed (ibid., pp. 211, 214; ff. 120vb, 121ra–b). And though Buridan rejects Averroes's account of

---

[18] Maier prints a revised version of the 1509 edition in *Zwei Grundprobleme*, pp. 207–14. She also prints the text of Buridan's *Reportatio Phys.* VII.5, where many of the same claims are made, see particularly p. 374. Compare Marchia, *Sent.* IV.1.1, ed. in Schabel, "*Virtus derelicta*," pp. 72–3.

[19] Here Buridan quotes not only from the classic passage from Bk. VIII, but also from Bk. IV. See Averroes, *In Phys.* IV.68 (*Aristotelis opera* vol. IV).

[20] The use of the term by opponents of imprint theory may come from Averroes, who after explaining that there are only two species of motion, natural and violent, describes violent motion in air as an effect of impetus. The impetus (or vigor) the air sustains eventually passes away according to Averroes, *In De caelo Aristotelis paraphrasis resolutissima* III.28 (*Aristotelis opera* vol. V).

projectile motion, he accepts Averroes's description of compressibility and uses it to account for reflex motion.

Although in the fourteenth century Buridan's views had comparatively few adherents – none among the Mertonians at Oxford, for example – by 1600 the common scholastic position was that impressed impetus explains projectile motion.[21] Buridan's bold rejection of Aristotle was less popular. Fourteenth- and fifteenth-century proponents of impetus theory, such as Francisco Suárez, attributed their position to Aristotle. Moreover, they agreed with Rufus and Marchia that the medium as well as impressed impetus caused projectile motion. Galileo was in the minority when in *De motu*, an early work, he claimed that Aristotle rejected impetus theory.[22]

So ultimately the problem that Averroes posed for the scholastics was decided against him by fifteenth-century scholastics. Even Averroists such as Augustino Nifo,[23] unlike most great thirteenth- and fourteenth-century philosophers, espoused impetus theory. And to the extent that the scholastics developed a unique solution to the problem, it was in terms of concepts owed at least initially to Avicenna. So although the fortunes of Avicenna and Averroes varied greatly over time, their influence was never absent.

HEAVEN'S IMMOBILE PLACE

By contrast to the problem of projectile motion, the debate on heaven's place was central to medieval natural philosophy. Indeed, it was the most frequently discussed aspect of Aristotle's doctrine of place in the Aristotelian tradition (see Chapter 19). For Aristotle, place is the inner limit of an immobile, containing body. This account encounters difficulty in the case of the outermost sphere, since by definition that sphere has no container.

On this topic, Averroes offers a rich mine of information about the tradition of interpretation, and once more he states the problem as a puzzle: since it is manifest that the celestial spheres rotate, and everything that moves is in a place, they must be in a place. Since there is nothing outside the outermost sphere, (1) the place of the outermost sphere must be an empty dimension or vacuum, something that cannot exist according to Aristotle. Or if we reject that conclusion, then (2) something moves without being in a place, which is contrary to another basic principle of Aristotelian physics.

---

[21] See Maier, *Zwei Grundprobleme*, pp. 228, 304–5.
[22] See ibid., pp. 298–305. Maier also lists as later proponents of impetus theory such influential authors as Antonio Rubio, Domingo de Soto, and John Capreolus.
[23] See Maier, *Zwei Grundprobleme*, pp. 295–6.

Though Averroes considered both these alternatives unacceptable, he reports proponents of both views (*In Phys.* IV.43, 45). Indeed, he names adherents of most of the possible alternative views, including Themistius, Alexander of Aphrodisias, Philoponus, al-Fārābī, Avicenna, and Ibn Bājja. Averroes first reports Philoponus's view that (1) place is not the limit of a body, but an empty dimension. Embracing the other horn of the dilemma are Alexander of Aphrodisias and Avicenna, according to whom (2) the heavens are not in a place, either *per se* or *per accidens*.

Other views suggest that the heavens are in a place in virtue of the location of a part or parts. Not reported by Averroes, but sometimes ascribed to Aristotle, is the view that (3) the parts in question are the continuous parts of the last sphere – circle segments, as it were, which locate each other horizontally.[24] Also sometimes described as Aristotle's is the view that (4) the outermost sphere is in a place, not on account of the location of a particular part, but because all its parts are in a place. This view was mistakenly attributed to Themistius on the basis of Averroes's report and subsequently advocated by Aquinas, who held that rotating bodies did not require a containing place, since only their parts and not the entire sphere change places as a whole.[25]

Proponents of the remaining views ascribe the place of the outermost sphere to the location of a particular part. The first two refer to the limits of the outermost sphere itself or the sphere of Saturn which it immediately bounds. Not reported by Averroes is the claim that (5) the heavens are in a place in virtue of the outer limit of the outermost sphere itself. Themistius's actual position, which might have been teased out of Averroes's report, suggests that (6) the part in question is the convex outer limit of the sphere of Saturn around which the outermost sphere revolves. Though this position is now usually ascribed to Themistius, Averroes reports it as Ibn Bājja's, adding that it was also held by al-Fārābī.[26] Averroes's own position is that (7) the outermost sphere is in a place accidentally by virtue of the earth at its center, which has a fixed position *per se* (*In Phys.* IV.43).

---

[24] See Jon McGinnis, "Positioning Heaven: The Infidelity of a Faithful Aristotelian," *Phronesis* 51 (2006) p. 145. See also Cecilia Trifogli, *Oxford Physics in the Thirteenth Century (ca. 1250–1270): Motion, Infinity, Place and Time* (Leiden: Brill, 2000) p. 189; Richard Rufus, *In Phys.* IV.1.6, ed. Wood, pp. 154–5.

[25] See Trifogli, *Oxford Physics*, p. 191; Aquinas, *In Phys.* IV.7; Cecilia Trifogli, "Il luogo dell'ultima sfera nei commenti tardo-antichi e medievali a Phyica IV.5," *Giornale critico della filosofia italiana* 68 (1989) pp. 147–52.

[26] Edward Grant, "The Medieval Doctrine of Place: Some Fundamental Problems and Solutions," in A. Maierù and A. Bagliani (eds.) *Studi sul XIV seculo in memoria di Anneliese Maier* (Rome: Edizione di Storia e Letteratura, 1981) pp. 75–9. Cf. Trifogli, "Il luogo," pp. 150–5.

With the one exception of (5), every subsequent view espoused by a Latin medieval philosopher is included in Averroes's list of possible views, and scholastics generally referenced Averroes in stating their own views. Views not reported by Averroes generally did not get a hearing. Thus view (3), though now commonly attributed to Aristotle, was espoused by no well-known medieval philosopher. Similarly (4), which Averroes stated very briefly and refuted at length, always remained a minority opinion despite its espousal by Aquinas.

Thus Averroes's report of the tradition was deeply influential, as was his own opinion and Avicenna's. Avicenna's (2) was espoused by Robert Grosseteste,[27] Albert of Saxony, Buridan, and John the Canon; Averroes's (7), by Roger Bacon, Albert the Great, Giles of Rome, Walter Burley, William of Ockham, and John of Jandun. Let us look briefly at an Averroist and an Avicennian: Albert the Great and Buridan. It is easy to see why Albert found Averroes's very original solution to the problem attractive, since it provides a fixed location for the universe. It was based on Ibn Bājja's distinction between the places required for rectilinear and spherical motion: things that move up and down have a bounding place, but things that rotate are fixed in place by the core around which they rotate. Since the center of the outermost sphere, the earth, is fixed in place, Averroes indicates that the part that gives the universe its place is the core around which the outermost sphere rotates.[28] Here he parts company with Ibn Bājja, who pointed to the outer limit of the first sphere around which the outermost sphere rotates, the sphere of Saturn.

Albert the Great's discussion of the place of the heavens is an intelligent paraphrase of Averroes – intelligent because Albert states the view more crisply than the original; he makes clearer a distinction between being in a place *per accidens* and moving *per accidens*. Though it is in a place *per accidens*, the outermost sphere moves *per se*. This is important because otherwise, as Albert points out, opponents of the view could claim that it implied that the motion of the first mover that causes all other motions is itself only accidentally in motion – moved in virtue of the body it rotates around (*Phys.* IV.1.13).[29]

Buridan attacks Averroes's view (7) with a hostile thought experiment in which God moves the outmost sphere in a straight line, in which case even the point at the center of the earth would no longer be fixed. Buridan instead defends Avicenna's view (2) – namely, that the outermost sphere moves

[27] Grosseteste can also be considered a proponent of (5); see his *In Phys.* VII, ed. Dales, pp. 82–3. More generally here, see Grant, "The Medieval Doctrine," pp. 74–5; Trifogli, "Il luogo," p. 152.

[28] Averroes distinguishes not just between rectilinear bodies and spherical bodies, but between the outermost sphere and the whole universe, composed of the five simple bodies (*In Phys.* IV.43).

[29] This criticism was mounted by Averroes's Oxford critics; see Trifogli, *Oxford Physics*, pp. 196–7.

not by changing place, but in virtue of the changing position of its parts. The orientation of its parts changes on an imaginary axis as they rotate.[30] Since everyone agrees that the rotating outermost sphere does not as a whole occupy a spatially distinct place as it moves, the advantages of this position are obvious.

Since Averroes describes Avicenna's views in only two sentences, it is not entirely clear how much influence his views and particularly the relational aspects of his account exercised.[31] Even so, Buridan describes the ambiguity of the term 'place' in Avicenna's terms. Place properly speaking contains; place in a broad sense can be specified relationally or, as Buridan describes it, by attribution. In this broad sense of 'place,' a thing is said to have changed place if its parts are successively differently related to each other in position, or if over time the whole is differently related to itself in orientation. Buridan holds that if this extended sense of 'place' is admitted, it is easy to solve the problem of the place of the heavens. His view is stated in five conclusions about the outermost sphere (OS):

(1) Taking 'place' properly, the OS is not in a place.
(2) Having no place, the OS does not, properly speaking, move.
(3) Taking place as that in respect of which a body appears to move, OS has a place. Any arbitrarily chosen object will do – the earth, a rock, or Buridan himself.
(4) Averroes is right that OS is in a place *per accidens* as defined in (3), but wrong to hold it is fixed permanently by the earth at its center.
(5) Avicenna is right that OS moves in position as its parts assume successively different relations to the fixed parts of those bodies.

Buridan marvels at how Averroes and Aquinas could possibly disagree with Avicenna that the outermost sphere neither has nor changes place. The only arguments they can mount against considering the broad sense of 'place' are based on Aristotle's authority. But, according to Buridan, in denying motion outside the categories of place, quantity, and quality, Aristotle was referring only to the strict sense of place, and he often also speaks of place in the broader sense as position. As to Aquinas's objection that this would put place in the category of relation, Buridan holds that place, too, is positional since motion by place, like motion by position, signifies the relationship of one body to another. Moreover,

---

[30] See McGinnis, "Positioning Heaven," pp. 156–7.

[31] Compare Rega Wood, "Richard Rufus: Physics at Paris before 1240," *Documenti e studi sulla tradizione filosofica medievale* 5 (1994) pp. 112, 117; Trifogli, *Oxford Physics*, pp. 175–80. See also Georges Anawati's article on Avicenna in C. C. Gillispie (ed.) *Dictionary of Scientific Biography* (New York: Scribner, 1970–80) suppl. I: 496. Whatever the reason, relational accounts began gaining influence in the first half of the thirteenth century and reached their apogee in the works of John Duns Scotus. See Trifogli, *Oxford Physics*, pp. 184–6.

unlike other motions, motion by position can occur without a change in the relation of the whole to an extrinsic body or bodies (*Quaest. Phys.* IV.6, f. 72r–v).

Buridan thus accounts for the place of the heavens by appealing to relational concepts of place, concepts that may ultimately derive from Avicenna. So once again Avicenna's influence, like that of Averroes who frames the debate, is lasting and important. On this topic no one would suggest that Latin scholastic responses were entirely original. Equally, however, scholastic philosophers contributed to a debate that went far beyond what Aristotle, Averroes, or Avicenna said.

ELEMENTAL COMPOSITION

Elemental composition was a problem that became more pressing in the course of the Middle Ages. Almost no other topic in natural philosophy awakened so much interest in the fourteenth century. Indeed, focus on the problem eventually led in the sixteenth and seventeenth centuries to a reaction against scholasticism and formal and qualitative accounts of physical interactions.[32]

For scholastics the problem originates with a puzzle formulated by Aristotle himself. According to Aristotle, ordinary animate and inanimate bodies are heteromerous, made up of different kinds of parts, but those body parts are themselves like-parted or homoeomerous. An animal, for example, is made up of skin and bones, hair and teeth, and so on. But an animal's parts (its skin and bones, for example) are themselves like-parted, though composed of elements. The elements of earth, water, air, and fire are so combined in skin, for example, that they cannot be distinguished no matter how sharply we perceive skin. Nonetheless, the elements are present in such homoeomeries, which we will call "mixts" to distinguish them from the compounds that result from elemental combination in modern chemical theories.[33] Moreover, the ingredients from which mixts are generated reemerge in the process of decomposition. So the question is whether and how the elements are present in intact, homoeomerous bodily parts.

Aristotle himself posed the dilemma: if one or more of the ingredients were lost in the process of being combined, then the resulting mixt would not be

---

[32] See Maier, *An der Grenze von Scholastik und Naturwissenschaft*, 2nd edn (Rome: Edizioni di Storia e Letteratura, 1952) pp. 3–5.

[33] Paul Needham, following a clue in Duhem, introduced this practice in "Duhem's Theory of Mixture in the Light of the Stoic Challenge to the Aristotelian Conception," *Studies in History and Philosophy of Science* 33 (2002) 685–708, especially 687.

composed of them; if the process of mixture left them intact, then the mixt would not be homoeomerous (*De gen. et cor.* I.10, 327a35–b6). Aristotle solves the problem by claiming that the elements are present potentially.[34]

For medieval natural philosophers, the problem was to explain just what this means and how it is possible, since obviously neither the wetness of water nor the heat of fire is perceptible in such mixts as skin, for example. And, yet, presumably, if all four elements are present in skin, it should have the heat and dryness of fire, the heat and wetness of air, the wetness and frigidity of water, and the dryness and frigidity of earth. Avicenna solves this problem by claiming that elemental forms can be present even when their qualities are muted. Since there is some latitude in the heat required for elemental fire, the fire that is an ingredient of a mixt can be cooler than a flame. However, if its heat is reduced beyond a certain degree, fire will be transformed into another element and disappear. That limit is not reached, however, when the elements are combined in homoeomerous parts, such as skin, according to Avicenna.[35] By contrast, Averroes held that combining elements in a mixt diminished not just elemental qualities, but elemental forms themselves. Since the substance of fire, for example, was present only when there was heat in the highest degree, the fire in a mixt such as skin must be muted, blunted, or fractured.

Because Avicenna believed that elemental forms retained their identity in a mixt, his is called a theory of fixed forms (*formae fixae*); by contrast Averroes's is a theory of fractured forms (*formae fractae*), since he believed that they did not maintain their integrity (*In De caelo* III.67). Though Avicenna's claim that elemental forms retained their integrity in mixts was not generally accepted, his introduction of the concept of latitude into discussions of substantial change played a crucial role in subsequent discussions of alteration.[36]

---

[34] According to some distinguished Aristotle scholars, including Dorothea Frede, and according to Maier herself, this is a distinctively medieval problem. Aristotle himself escapes the dilemma in part by identifying elements with their qualities. Thus as long as the elemental qualities are present in the mixture, there is no need to explain separately the persistence of elements themselves as substances. See Maier, *An der Grenze,* p. 10; D. Frede, "On Mixture and Mixables," in J. Mansfeld and F. de Haas (eds.) *Aristotle: On Generation and Corruption, Book I* (Oxford: Clarendon Press, 2004) pp. 303–5.

[35] *Liber quartus naturalium* [*Shifā'*] II.1, II.2 (ed. Van Riet, pp. 79–81, 89); *Liber tertius naturalium* [*Shifā'*] 14, ed. Van Riet, pp. 138–41.

[36] In medicine, the idea of a latitude in health had been important since Galen's time, and Avicenna's discussions of the differences in the degree of heat between young and old animals (*De animalibus* XII, in *Opera phil.*) was not novel. However, introducing such concepts into discussions of chemical change was an important and influential innovation. On the background since Galen, see Per-Gunnar Ottosson, *Scholastic Medicine and Philosophy* (Naples: Bibliopolis, 1984) pp. 178–9; Timo Joutsivuo, *Scholastic Tradition and Humanist Innovation: The Concept of Neutrum in Renaissance Medicine* (Helsinki: Academia Scientiarum Fennica: 1999) pp. 111–16.

Anneliese Maier indicates that Avicenna's views were as invariably rejected by scholastics as they were universally cited.[37] But this is misleading, since it is only Avicenna's claims about the integrity of elemental forms that were rejected; the remainder of the account was generally accepted:

(1) qualitative latitude in elemental forms;
(2) matter disposed by the appropriate qualities prior to mixture;
(3) mixt forms introduced by a separated substance (giver of forms).[38]

Most importantly, Aquinas accepted these claims, and his briefly stated views were at the core of the third standard opinion, called the modern view.[39] Basic to the modern view is that when the disposition of matter by elemental qualities leads to the introduction of the mixt form, the elements themselves disappear. As Maier herself notes, a key to Aquinas's account is Avicenna's description of the disposition of matter by the mutual interaction of elemental qualities that results in intermediate qualities; the intermediate qualities so produced dispose matter to receive the form of the mixt.[40]

The three basic positions are distinguished, however, by the status of the elemental forms in the mixt composed of them. If Averroes's view posits fractured forms, and Avicenna's fixed forms, Aquinas's might be said to posit lost forms (*formae deperditae*), since he supposes that elemental forms disappear in the course of producing the mixt. His explanation of how the elements nonetheless remain potentially in the mixt depends on the persistence of intermediate qualities derived from mixing extreme elemental qualities. Since qualities act in virtue of the substances from which they originate, Thomas concludes that the elemental substances from which they derive are there virtually.

Most scholastics followed either Averroes or Aquinas. Authors such as Henry of Ghent accepted Averroes without much modification: because elemental forms are less perfect than other substantial forms, they can be diminished like accidental forms, and their partly corrupted substantial forms can be mixed (*Quodlibet* IV.15, ed. 1518, I: 128rM). Others who accepted Averroes's claim that elemental forms were in some respects like accidents include Albert the Great, Peter of John Olivi, Richard of Middleton, and John of Jandun.[41]

---

[37] Maier, *An der Grenze*, p. 36.   [38] Ibid., pp. 13–14.

[39] *De mixtione elementorum* (ed. Leonine, XLIII: 155–7). See Joseph Bobik, *Aquinas on Matter and Form and the Elements* (Notre Dame, IN: University of Notre Dame Press, 1998). For Aquinas's commitment to (3), see *De operationibus occultis naturae* (ed. Leonine, XLIII: 184–5) and *In De caelo* III.4.5.

[40] See Maier, *An der Grenze*, pp. 32–3.   [41] Ibid., pp. 38–43.

By contrast, some Averroists rejected his claim that elemental forms are like accidents that can be fractured. They held that elemental forms are subject to intension and remission only in the sense that they can be prevented from achieving full actuality, and their diminished actuality results in correspondingly less intense qualities. This modal interpretation of Averroes's account was first advanced by Richard Rufus. The elemental forms in a mixt are neither merely potentially there, nor fully actual, but rather in proximate or accidental potential, such that only an external impediment prevents their fully realizing their natures. Each of the elemental forms constituting a mixt prevents the others from emerging into full actuality, and that is what Aristotle means by saying that the elements in a mixt are there potentially.[42] Because elements in a mixt are not fully united like other substantial forms, but only fused together – confused to use the technical term – numerically the same elements can reemerge from the mixt when the mixt breaks down and the elements cease to interfere with each other's full actualization. Exciting variations on this modal theory of elemental composition were espoused by Roger Bacon, Henry Bate, Dietrich of Freiberg, Peter Auriol, John Baconthorpe, Francis of Marchia, and John the Canon.[43]

By the fourteenth century, not Averroes but Aquinas had more followers on the subject of mixture, and those followers included not only Dominicans, but Franciscans, such as John Duns Scotus and Ockham, and prominent secular philosophers, such as Walter Burley and Buridan. Duns Scotus's treatment of the problem is particularly clear. He starts by restating the positions of Avicenna and Averroes, claiming that Averroes did not refute Avicenna. Ultimately, however, Scotus rejects not just the positions of Avicenna and Averroes, but also of Aristotle: strictly speaking air, fire, water, and earth are not components of mixts. It is only prime matter itself that really is an element persisting in the mixt. That leaves Scotus with two problems: to provide an acceptable interpretation of Aristotle's words and to explain why certain transformations are possible and others are not: why can wine become vinegar, but the reverse is not possible?

A sign that Scotus takes Avicenna's medical authority very seriously is that before answering the question of why substantial changes occur in a certain order, Scotus offers an explanation of disease not based on conflicting elemental

---

[42] Rega Wood and Michael Weisberg, "Interpreting Aristotle on Mixture: Problems about Elemental Composition from Philoponus to Cooper," *Studies in the History and Philosophy of Science* 35 (2004) 698–704.
[43] Maier, *An der Grenze*, pp. 46–88.

qualities. Disease and death are caused not by the incompatibility of fire and water in the heart, but by organic parts with incompatible complexions. Having eliminated the dynamics of the interaction of elemental qualities as an explanation of internal changes, Scotus has to explain how it is that matter is disposed for one transformation but not another. He answers by distinguishing between the immediacy of perfection and the immediacy of transmutation. Though the form of the mixt immediately perfects prime matter, not just any arbitrary form can shape any matter. Rather a particular mixt form can only be infused in matter that has previously been informed by a series of other forms in a particular order. Any given mixt requires that the matter involved previously be prepared by a succession of substantial forms in a determinate order. Mixt forms immediately perfect prime matter, but they cannot perfect prime matter that has not previously been perfected by elemental forms.[44]

Scotus's interpretation of Aristotle follows Aquinas: the elements are only virtually contained in the mixt. But Aquinas had left unexplained whether the elemental qualities are virtually contained because they caused the mixt, or because qualities equivalent to the qualities obtained by mixing elements are found in the mixt. Some authors, such as Ockham (*Quodlibet* III.5), affirm both options, which are after all not incompatible. But Scotus clearly opts for resemblance rather than causation (*Reportatio* II.15, ed. Wadding XI.1: 343–5). This allows him a cleaner response to one objection than might otherwise be offered. How can qualities of the elements migrate from one subject to the next? Qualities are supposed to act in virtue of substances and not vice versa, so when matter is informed by a different substantial form, the qualities associated with the original substance should perish. And they do, according to Scotus, but they are replaced by similar qualities.

Burley's account of virtual containment mirrors Scotus's.[45] Mixts virtually contain elemental qualities not because elemental qualities cause the qualities found in a mixt, but because they resemble such qualities; the operation of mixed qualities is specifically similar to the operation of elemental qualities. In other respects, however, Burley is more radical. He subscribes neither to the claim that accidents act only in virtue of substances nor to the claim that agents must be as perfect as the effects they cause. Such considerations had

---

[44] Scotus's claims about the necessary succession of forms should not be confused with the theory of the plurality of forms, which claims that more than one substantial form is simultaneously present in physical substances (see Chapters 21 and 46). In fact, in *Opus Oxoniensis* II.15, Scotus begins by rejecting the suggestion that we need posit a plurality of elemental forms in a mixt (ed. Wadding VI.2: 753–7).

[45] Burley, *Tractatus de formis*, pars prior, difficultas 4 (ed. Scott, pp. 42–3).

motivated Scotus to posit a universal agent that acts at the instant the mixt form is induced, loosely modeled on Avicenna's *dator formarum*.[46] By contrast, Burley asserts that qualities can themselves cause a substance, and therefore there is no need to postulate a super-agent, a separated substance or a celestial body, to account for the production of the substantial form of the mixt. Recourse to the celestial to explain the production of more noble mixt forms from the less noble elements is unnecessary;[47] even non-self-subsisting, elemental qualities will suffice as agents.

By contrast, Buridan, like Scotus, supposes that the principal agents in substantial change are celestial forces. However, unlike Scotus, Buridan offers a causal account of the presence of elements in a mixt. A mixt is composite since it retains the powers of the elements (*virtutes elementorum*) that were corrupted when it was generated. Buridan agrees with Scotus that strictly speaking only matter is an element in the composite, and, like Scotus, Buridan distinguishes two kinds of immediacy, but there the agreement ends. Buridan contrasts the absence of a substantial intermediate with the absence of an accidental intermediate. Matter receives the mixt form immediately, but though it is not disposed by the elemental bodies, it is disposed by the qualities they leave behind as they are mixed. The matter that receives the mixt form has no other substantial forms, but it retains the accidents produced by their interaction. And since prime matter is the proper subject of elemental or primary qualities, for Buridan there is a sense in which elemental qualities can migrate from one substance to another. Though these qualities are attributed to composites of matter and form, their real subject is prime matter, and hence they can persist in matter even as the new substantial form is introduced (*In De gen. et cor.* I.22, II.7).

Buridan's is a radical account of the disposition of matter by elemental qualities prior to the introduction of the mixt form. It was a reasonable response, however, to a general problem for proponents of the third way: these philosophers accepted Avicenna's claim that the elements dispose matter for the induction of the mixt form, but since they held that the elements themselves are lost, persisting neither as fixed nor as fractured forms, they were awkwardly placed. Scotus accounted for the disposition by positing a necessary order of forms, with elemental forms necessarily preceding mixt forms. Burley allows elemental qualities to act on their own, and Buridan allows qualities to migrate from substance to substance, since they can persist in the matter without form.

---

[46] Scotus, *Additiones magnae* II.15.7 (ed. Wadding, VI.2: 755).
[47] Burley, *Tractatus primus: De comparatione specierum* (also known as the *Tractatus de activitate, De formis accidentalibus*, pars prima), as quoted by Maier, *An der Grenze*, pp. 116–18.

So we can see how strongly proponents of the third way are influenced by Avicenna's initial position. Averroes similarly influenced defenders of the second way, and also defined the problem. And though there were many important, original, and innovative scholastic responses, the influence of both Islamic authors persisted to the end of the scholastic period.

CONCLUSION

Each of the topics we have considered suggests a different narrative line, but in every case there is a story to tell about the influence of Avicenna and Averroes. Similar cases, often featuring other important philosophers in the Arabic tradition, such as Ibn Bājja, al-Fārābī, and al-Ghazālī, can be made for many other topics in natural philosophy. To name just a few, there is the controversy over the estimative faculty, over whether a vacuum is possible, and over the nature of an Aristotelian science. In some respects this is utterly unsurprising. Averroes and Avicenna came from the greatest scientific and scholarly tradition of the early Middle Ages, one that offered at the outset of the Latin university tradition the systematic interpretation of Aristotle provided by the peripatetic tradition. These thinkers grounded their Aristotelianism in logic and accompanied it with expertise in mathematics, astronomy, and medicine. Moreover, Avicenna and Averroes were great philosophers in their own right. Avicenna rethought much of the Aristotelian system of philosophy and offered a new theory of science. By contrast, Averroes criticized the new developments characteristic of Avicenna's Aristotelianism and emphasized the search for apodictic truth. His clear explanations of Aristotle's views and the introduction he provided to the interpretative tradition played a role that cannot be overstated. Without these contributions, comprehensive scientific views of the cosmos focused on significant physical problems might not have arisen in the Latin West.

The tradition of Arabic Aristotelianism achieved its greatest influence after the fundamental institution of Western learning, the self-governing university, had emerged, and after the development of the characteristic methods of scholasticism: disputation and the deliberate confrontation of opposed arguments and authorities. But the sciences of metaphysics and meteorology, physics and chemistry, biology and psychology were introduced together with Arabic Aristotelianism, and it is difficult to imagine what shape they would have taken without that foundation. Scholars recognise this influence in many particular areas, but specialists in scholasticism seldom acknowledge the general debt; hence this attempt to confirm the impact.

The acknowledgment of this debt is not intended to minimize other influences, and here one thinks particularly of great Jewish scholars such as Maimonides and of the Greek commentary tradition. Neither should this debt be understood as diminishing the accomplishments of Latin scholars; indeed, they clearly developed Averroes's views more imaginatively than his Islamic successors. Rather, the influence of Arabic Aristotelianism at the beginnings of distinctively Western science and scholarship is something to celebrate. The fruitful connections between Islamic and Christian Aristotelianism offer reason to hope that future contacts between the two traditions can also contribute to their flourishing.

19

CHANGE, TIME, AND PLACE

CECILIA TRIFOGLI

For Aristotle, the natural world is the world of things subject to change. Accordingly, Aristotle's natural philosophy essentially consists in a philosophical investigation of change. Aristotle deals with the most fundamental philosophical issues about change in the *Physics*. Here he determines the intrinsic constituents of a thing that make it possible for it to be subject to change (matter and form), he classifies the types of explanatory factor at work in the natural world (the distinction of the four causes), and in particular he argues for the claim that nature acts for an end (teleological explanation). He also gives a general definition of change, which relates the notion of change to the more basic notions of act and potency, he shows that every change is continuous, and he proves the existence of an eternal motion and an unmoved mover. In addition, he provides a philosophical treatment of the notions of time, place, the void, and the infinite, which are thought to be necessary parts of a complete discussion of change. Because of its extremely rich philosophical content, the *Physics* was intensely studied by medieval philosophers and became the focal text for the assimilation of Aristotle's natural philosophy.

The *Physics* was first made available to the Latin world in the second quarter of the twelfth century, when it was translated into Latin (from the Greek) by James of Venice. It circulated quite slowly, however, and so it was only around the middle of the thirteenth century that the *Physics* started to be widely studied. This is shown by the high number of extant works devoted specifically to the *Physics* – that is, commentaries on it – from the 1250s onward.[1] A clear sign of this great philosophical interest is that most of the major medieval philosophers wrote *Physics* commentaries: for example, in the thirteenth century, Robert Grosseteste, Roger Bacon, Albert the Great, Thomas Aquinas, Giles of

---

[1] On the Latin translations of the *Physics*, of the other works of Aristotle, and of Greek and Arabic commentaries see Appendix B. For further discussion, see Bernard Dod, "Aristoteles Latinus," in N. Kretzmann *et al.* (eds.) *The Cambridge History of Later Medieval Philosophy* (Cambridge: Cambridge University Press, 1982) 45–79.

Rome; and, in the fourteenth century, William of Ockham, Walter Burley, John Buridan, and John of Jandun.

The commentaries on the *Physics* from the thirteenth and fourteenth centuries are the main sources for the study of the Latin assimilation of Aristotle's natural philosophy. Some of these commentaries mainly reflect an exegetical activity aimed at providing an explanation of the literal meaning of the text of Aristotle, which is even more obscure in the Latin translation than in the original Greek. Many others, however, in addition to or as an alternative to the exegetical aspect, show a more philosophical approach, consisting in assessing the cogency of Aristotle's arguments, pointing out problems left open by Aristotle, and providing a solution to them. This chapter will consider three fundamental topics from medieval Latin philosophical discussions of Aristotle's natural philosophy: change, time, and place.

THE ONTOLOGICAL STATUS OF CHANGE

The problem raised in the medieval debate over the ontological status of change can be presented in very abstract terms as follows. Consider a body M (the "mobile") that changes from being non-F to being F, as for example when a body becomes hot – that is, changes from being cold to being hot. A crucial question for medieval authors is one of ontology: how many things and which types of thing are needed in order to account for M's becoming hot? There was common agreement that this requires:

 (i) The body (M) subject to the change of becoming hot (in medieval terms, the mobile substance).
 (ii) The degree of heat at each step of the way – that is, the coolness from which the change starts (the *terminus a quo*), the heat at the end of the change (the *terminus ad quem*), and all the intermediate degrees of coolness and heat that the body takes on while it is in the process of becoming hot. Each such degree is an accident in the category of Quality.
 (iii) The agent that makes the body hot – that is, the efficient cause.

What was controversial was whether or not (i)–(iii) are sufficient to account for the body's becoming hot, or whether one needs to posit a further entity, *the change itself*. Or, to take another formulation, if (as it is commonly agreed) one needs to posit the existence of a quality, heat, to account for the fact that a body *is* hot, should one not also posit the existence of a change, becoming hot, to account for the fact that the body *becomes* hot?

Medieval commentators were much concerned with this question. Indeed, it is distinctively medieval, inasmuch as Aristotle does not even explicitly consider it; nor do Greek commentaries on the *Physics*. The main philosophical motivation for postulating change as a distinct entity is that it seems to have quite distinct properties from the things listed in (i)–(iii). Compare, for example, the body that becomes hot and the becoming hot of this body. The body has extension and physical parts, and these parts are such that they can all exist at the same time. Medieval authors call a thing with this property a "permanent thing." All the things in (i)–(iii) are permanent. The body's becoming hot also has parts (that is, phases), but these parts are such that they cannot exist simultaneously. Instead, they can exist only one after the other: when the body is changing from heat of degree 1 to heat of degree 2, it is not also at the same time changing from heat of degree 2 to heat of degree 3. In medieval terms, the becoming hot of a body is successive rather than permanent. Now if the things in (i)–(iii) are all permanent and the becoming hot is successive, then it is legitimate to ask whether the becoming hot is a thing distinct from the things in (i)–(iii). This is essentially how Ockham in the fourteenth century formulated his question concerning the ontological status of change: are there successive things distinct from permanent things? (*Expositio in Phys.* III.2)

Medieval philosophers were divided on this issue. Some of them claimed that in order to account for the succession of phases in the change of a body it is not necessary to posit the change itself as a thing distinct from the relevant permanent things. They thus took a reductive position on the ontological status of change, in the sense that they posited that a change can be explained completely in terms of permanent things. Others argued that it is not possible to explain the successive nature of a change in terms of permanent things and held a realist view, positing change as a thing distinct from and irreducible to permanent things. The following provides more details about the early phase of the medieval debate in the second half of the thirteenth century.[2] (For fourteenth-century developments, see Chapter 20.)

Historically, Latin medieval philosophers were inspired to debate the ontological status of change by Averroes, whose commentary on the *Physics* was translated into Latin in the first half of the thirteenth century (see Chapter 18). Averroes introduces a distinction between two ways of regarding change. Change can be regarded either as differing only in degree (*secundum magis et minus*) from the form that is its *terminus ad quem*, or as a way towards the form (*via ad formam*). Change regarded as differing only in degree from its final form is nothing other than the form acquired by the mobile body through a change

---

[2] The most comprehensive account of this debate in both the thirteenth and fourteenth centuries is in Anneliese Maier, *Zwischen Philosophie und Mechanik* (Rome: Edizioni di Storia e Letteratura, 1958) pp. 59–143.

when this form is still in an incomplete state, namely, in the state of being generated and not in the actual state in which it exists as *terminus ad quem*. So, for instance, a body's becoming hot is nothing other than heat in an incomplete state – one of the intermediary qualities in (ii) above. Change regarded as a way towards the form, however, is really distinct from the final form and is an entity in its own right. Thus, becoming hot is a thing in itself distinct from heat. Averroes maintains that only the first way of regarding change, namely, as the final form in an incomplete state, is true, even if the second way can also be found in Aristotle (*In Phys.* III.4) (see also Chapter 20).

This distinction, which Averroes presents as between two ways of "regarding" change, in fact reflects two irreducible ontologies: reductive and realist. Treated in the first way, becoming hot requires only (i)–(iii) above, and these are all permanent things. If becoming hot is treated in the second way, however, then it is necessary to posit an additional thing, since that change, or way towards heat, is not really the same as heat nor as any other of the relevant permanent things. The ontological commitments of Averroes's distinction were clearly perceived by thirteenth- and fourteenth-century Aristotelian commentators, and the passage of his commentary on Book III of the *Physics* in which Averroes introduces that distinction becomes the *locus classicus* for questioning the ontological status of change.

The early phase of the Latin reception of Aristotle's *Physics* (that is, from around 1250 until 1270, when Aquinas wrote his commentary) is mainly represented by commentaries of English origin, written by arts masters in Oxford.[3] Around ten commentaries from the Oxford arts faculty are extant from this period. Some of the authors are known, such as Geoffrey of Aspall and William of Clifford, but the majority remain unknown.[4] This significant group of early English commentators heavily relies on Averroes for the exegesis of Aristotle's text. They strongly criticize Averroes's reductive view of change, however, and reject Averroes's assumption of a real identity between the change and the form that is its *terminus ad quem*.[5] They argue that since the successive character of

---

[3] For a list of the English and Parisian commentaries of these years and basic information concerning the contents, structure, and interrelations of the English commentaries, see Silvia Donati, "Per lo studio dei commenti alla Fisica del XIII secolo. I: Commenti di probabile origine inglese degli anni 1250–1270 ca.," *Documenti e studi sulla tradizione filosofica medievale* 2 (1991) 361–441, 4 (1993) 25–133.

[4] An edition of the questions on Books III and IV of the *Physics* in this group of commentaries is now available on a computer disk distributed with my second volume of repertory of these commentaries: *Liber Quartus Physicorum Aristotelis: Repertorio delle Questioni: Commenti Inglesi, ca. 1250–1270* (SISMEL: Florence, 2007).

[5] See Cecilia Trifogli, *Oxford Physics in the Thirteenth Century (ca. 1250–1270)* (Leiden: Brill, 2000) pp. 51–66.

change cannot be explained by something permanent, it is necessary to postulate the existence of a thing that is in its nature successive. They also argue that change cannot be a form because it is that through which or in virtue of which a form is generated in a substance. In making this assumption, they tend to conceive of change as a sort of formal cause of the coming into being of a form. For example, on this view, the body's becoming hot requires two distinct types of cause: an efficient cause (that is, something that actually produces heat in that body), and a formal cause (that is, something in virtue of which heat is produced in that body). The idea is that in the same way that a body *is* hot in virtue of heat as a formal cause, similarly a body *becomes* hot in virtue of a thing that is distinct both from the heat itself and from the efficient cause of this change.

Even some of those commentators who are not willing to adhere to a strongly realist view about change find Averroes's version of the reductive view unsatisfactory. This is the case, for example, with Thomas Aquinas. He makes the very plausible assumption that any ontology of change must be such that it accounts for the distinction between the change and the *terminus ad quem* of the change. After all, there would seem to be more to becoming hot than just the heat that is its *terminus ad quem*. In Averroes's theory of change this distinction can be maintained, since becoming hot is identified with heat in an incomplete state rather than with heat in its complete state as the *terminus ad quem*. Aquinas, however, shows that an incomplete form – for instance, heat in an incomplete state – fares no better as a candidate for the change. He makes this point very clearly with the example of water becoming hot:

For when water is hot only in potentiality, it is not yet moved; when it has already been heated the heating motion has been completed; but when it shares in heat to some degree, but incompletely, it is being moved toward heat, for what becomes hot shares in heat gradually by degrees. Therefore, the incomplete actuality of heat existing in the heatable thing is itself motion, not, indeed, insofar as it is in actuality alone, but insofar as what already exists in actuality is *ordered toward further actuality*. For if one were to take away its being ordered toward further actuality, the actuality itself, however imperfect, would be the terminus of motion and not motion, as happens when something heats partially.

(*In Phys.* III.2, ed. Maggiòlo, n. 285)

Aquinas's point is that, as long as water undergoes the process of being heated, it is not completely hot, but has only some intermediate and incomplete degree of heat; it is, for example, temperate. It would be wrong, however, to infer from this that the process itself of being heated is nothing other than the incomplete actuality of heat. Indeed, if the process of being heated were simply identified with the temperate, then being heated could not be distinguished from its *terminus ad quem*. Aquinas makes this point at the very end of the passage with a very illuminating example: if water starts being heated but the process stops abruptly before the water is completely hot, then the *terminus ad quem* of this interrupted change is the temperate form.

More generally, for Aquinas, any incomplete form is such that it can be acquired through a change and so be the *terminus ad quem* of a change. Therefore, identifying the change with an incomplete form always threatens to collapse back into the view on which the change is the *terminus ad quem*. On his view, what needs to be added is an "order toward a further actuality." For example, becoming hot is not simply a temperate form, but it is the temperate in the state of being "ordered" to the further actuality of heat. Here the notion of "order" gives the formal or distinctive condition of change because it adds to the incomplete form of Averroes a dynamical element, which is thought to be typical of change but that an incomplete form as such does not have.[6]

Aquinas's modified Averroism was very influential in the last quarter of the thirteenth century among supporters of a reductive ontology of change, since it avoids some obvious problems with Averroes's original formulation while reflecting the same type of reductive ontology. For both Averroes and Aquinas, change is not a thing distinct from the relevant permanent things involved in the change of a body because it is, in fact, essentially the same as one of those permanent things – namely, the final form. Aquinas's order toward further actuality does not add some new ontological entity to the final form; rather, it merely represents a mode of existence of this form.

THE ONTOLOGICAL STATUS OF TIME

In Aristotle's natural philosophy, time is not something that exists over and above temporal events as a separate entity in which temporal events take place and by means of which we measure their duration. Time rather is an attribute of change. An issue of major controversy among medieval commentators is what kind of attribute of change time is. Is time a real – that is, extramental – attribute or a mind-dependent attribute resulting from our activity of measuring the duration of a change? On another formulation, the question is whether there is a real distinction between time and change, so that time and change are two distinct extramental things, or rather only a conceptual distinction between the

---

[6] For a more detailed analysis of the ontological aspects of Aquinas's position, see Cecilia Trifogli, "Thomas Wylton on Motion," *Archiv für Geschichte der Philosophie* 77 (1995) pp. 147–51.

two, so that they are essentially one and the same extramental thing viewed in different ways.[7]

This medieval debate has an Aristotelian origin. Having defined time as some kind of number of change, Aristotle raises the question of whether the existence of time depends on the human soul. He argues that time does not exist without the soul because time is a number and the existence of number depends on the soul, because it depends on the mental operation of counting (*Phys.* IV.14, 223a16–29). Aristotle's dependence claim was accepted and expanded by Averroes. As in the case of change, Averroes's position on the ontological status of time was extremely influential and formed the standard starting point of debates on this issue, especially in the thirteenth century. Its influence stems from the fact that it gives explicit indications about how the dependence of number on the soul applies to the case of time conceived of as some kind of number of change. On Averroes's view, a collection of two stones, for example, and the number two of this collection have a different ontological status. The collection of two stones exists in extramental reality, whereas the number two of this collection exists in the soul and by means of the soul. Accordingly, the number two is not an extramental accident of the collection of two stones, but rather the result of our mental process of counting the stones belonging to that collection.

Averroes then maintains that the same ontological distinction holds for change and time as number of change: change exists outside the soul, in extramental reality, whereas time exists only in the soul (*In Phys.* IV.109, IV.131).[8] He specifies that the relevant collection of which time is a number is that of "the before and after in a change" – a technical medieval expression (arising from Aristotle [*Phys.* IV.11]) for the succession involved in change. Time therefore exists only as a result of the soul's act of numbering the before and after in a change.

In the preceding section, we saw that for Averroes one does not need to posit change as a successive thing distinct from permanent things in order to account for the succession involved in change. This does not imply, however, that the succession in a change is mind-dependent. On the contrary, for Averroes, this

---

[7] On this debate and other medieval debates about Aristotle's doctrine of time, see especially Anneliese Maier, *Metaphysische Hintergründe der Spätscholastischen Naturphilosophie* (Rome: Edizioni di Storia e Letteratura, 1955) pp. 47–137.

[8] Averroes's own formulation of this view is more complex. He qualifies the claim that number and time exist in the soul by saying that they exist in the soul in act but in extramental reality in potency. On the details of Averroes's formulation and some obvious problems in it discussed by fourteenth-century commentators (e.g., Thomas Wylton and John of Jandun), see Cecilia Trifogli, "Averroes's Doctrine of Time and its Reception in the Scholastic Debate," in P. Porro (ed.) *The Medieval Concept of Time* (Leiden: Brill, 2001) 57–82.

succession exists also in the absence of the soul. What does not exist without the soul is the "numbering" of the succession or of the before and after in a change, which defines time. Averroes does not clarify what the soul's numbering the before and after in a change is. He obviously does not mean that this is counting the before and after in a change, that is, determining how many such stages there are. He seems rather to mean our discernment and awareness of the succession in a change – for instance, our awareness that in becoming hot a body possesses first heat of degree 1 and later heat of degree 2, but without counting how many intervening stages there are.

Averroes's basic idea that time exists in the soul expresses a reductive view of time that posits that in extramental reality there are not two really distinct things corresponding to time and change, respectively. For Averroes, what distinguishes time from change is a mental operation. Many thirteenth- and fourteenth-century commentators share Averroes's reductive view. An eminent example is Ockham. He claims that "time is not an extramental thing distinct from motion. But every imaginable extramental thing signified by the name 'time' is also signified by the name 'first motion'" (*Expositio in Phys.* IV.27.4 [*Opera phil.* V: 291]). Ockham specifies, however, that the names 'change' and 'time' are not synonymous, inasmuch as they have different nominal definitions. In addition to the extramental things signified by the name 'change,' the name 'time' consignifies "the soul that numbers – that is, the soul saying that the mobile is first here and later there and that these are distinct; that is, that the mobile cannot be simultaneously here and there" (ibid., IV.21.6 [V: 225–6]).[9] Accordingly, for Ockham as for Averroes, what makes the difference between the notions of change and time is the reference to mental activity.

There was, however, also strong opposition to Averroes's reductive view. Many thirteenth-century commentators, including Roger Bacon, Albert the Great, William of Clifford and many anonymous English commentators, think that the claim that the existence of time depends on the soul is basically wrong.[10] They argue that this claim derives from mistaken assumptions about the ontological status of number and that it conflicts with other basic properties that Aristotle ascribes to time – for example, that there exists only one time and that time is a quantity. Yet these thirteenth-century realists, while advocating that time is an extramental thing distinct from change, do not provide very good arguments for this real distinction. Some fourteenth-century realists are more

---

[9] On Ockham's view on time, see Marilyn McCord Adams, *William Ockham* (Notre Dame, IN: University of Notre Dame Press) II: 853–99.
[10] See Trifogli, *Oxford Physics*, pp. 219–30.

successful in this respect. For example, Walter Burley, Ockham's most influential opponent, argues that one needs to posit time as an extramental thing distinct from change in order to account for the succession of past and future phases of a change. His idea is that being past and being future – in general, temporal succession – are found both in time and in every change, but that they belong to time primarily, and to change only secondarily, in virtue of time. So he claims that

> motion is said to be past only because it was in past time, and one of its parts is before and another after only because one part was in past time and another in future time . . . From these remarks it is evident that the before and after in duration primarily and essentially are in time and they are in motion only in virtue of time, since, that is, motion is conjoined to time. Hence it follows that time is really different from motion.
>
> (*In Phys.* IV, ed. 1501, f. 127rb–va)

THE IMMOBILITY OF PLACE

Aristotle defines the place of a body A as the surface or limit of the body B that contains A and is in contact with it. The example that Aristotle uses to illustrate his definition is that of the water contained in a vessel: the place of water is the internal surface of the vessel in contact with the water. The essential idea is to define the place of a body in terms of its surroundings, in terms of something containing it. He thinks that this idea reflects our ordinary intuition concerning how we locate things. In arguing for his container view of place, Aristotle also considers an alternative account of place as something coextensive with the located body. According to this alternative account, the place of the water contained in a vessel would be the extension between the sides of the vessel that the water occupies. Aristotle strongly rejects the coextensive view, however, primarily because it is committed to positing a three-dimensional incorporeal extension that is not the extension of a natural body – that is, it is committed to space. Aristotle, however, strongly denies the existence of any such incorporeal extension. Thus his container theory of place rests on the ontological assumptions that there is no space and that all we have to work with, in building a theory of place, are natural bodies (*Phys.* IV.4).

Medieval commentators generally agree with Aristotle that place must be defined without positing the existence of an incorporeal space and that being a container is an essential property of place. Many of them also think, however, that this cannot be the only essential property of place. Instead, they maintain that an adequate definition of the place of a body must also take into account the position of this body in the "cosmological" frame of reference, as given by the immobile central earth and the immobile celestial poles, the so-called "fixed

points of the universe." Place, on this account, depends on a body's distance
from these cosmological fixed points.

Medieval commentators appeal to these fixed points of the universe as an
attempt to solve an open problem in Aristotle's theory. Aristotle posits that
place is not just any container, but an immobile container. For example, the
water carried around in a vessel is not strictly speaking in the vessel as its place
because the vessel, although it is the immediate container of water, is subject to
motion, whereas place must be immobile (ibid., 212a14–24). The problem is
that this immobility requirement seems to be incompatible with the ontological
status of place. For Aristotle, place is a part of the containing body. (Since it is
merely a limit of that body, however, it is conceived of not as an integral part
but as an accidental form.) But the containing body, being a natural body, is
subject to motion; therefore its limit, namely, the place of the contained body,
should also be subject to motion. Thus it seems that the immobility of place
cannot be reconciled with its ontological status.[11]

In attempting to find a solution to this standard objection, thirteenth-century
commentators raise the preliminary question of why place should be immobile.
Aristotle gives no explicit reason for this, and neither does his authoritative
commentator, Averroes. Thirteenth-century commentators, however, point out
quite a good reason for the immobility requirement: that the admission of a
mobile place would create difficulties for the definition of local motion and
rest. They take it to be true, by definition, that something moves locally when
it changes place and is at rest when it is in the same place. But if place is taken
simply as the limit of the containing body without securing its immobility, then
the definitions of locomotion and rest would be inconsistent with our ordinary
intuitions. Consider the case of a ship anchored in a river. It is commonly
assumed that this ship is at rest, but if the place of this ship is the surface of
the water in contact with it, then the ship is never in the same place, because
it is constantly surrounded by different surfaces of water. Thirteenth-century
authors conclude from such examples that we judge rest and local motion with
respect to the cosmological frame of reference given by the fixed points of the
universe. We judge that the ship anchored in a river is at rest because its distance
from the fixed points of the universe does not vary, and we judge that a ship
carried downstream is in motion because its distance from the fixed points of
the universe varies. For both thirteenth- and fourteenth-century commentators,

---

[11] On the medieval debate over the immobility of place and other issues about place, see Edward
Grant, "The Medieval Doctrine of Place: Some Fundamental Problems and Solutions," in
A. Maierù and A. Paravicini-Bagliani (eds.) *Studi sul XIV secolo in memoria di Anneliese Maier*
(Rome: Edizioni di Storia e Letteratura, 1981) 57–79.

the universe with its fixed points is the privileged frame of reference that we implicitly assume in order to judge whether a body is at rest or in motion. Thirteenth-century authors commonly qualify Aristotle's claim that place is the limit of the containing body by adding this cosmological element. Aquinas, for example, maintains that "the limit of the containing body is place not insofar as it is this surface of this mobile body, but according to the order or position that this surface has in the immobile whole" (*In Phys.* IV.6 n. 469). Place is therefore the surface of the containing body considered as having a position in the cosmological frame of reference. Similarly, in interpreting Aquinas's view, Giles of Rome tends to think of place as a composite of the surface of the containing body and the distance of this surface from the fixed points of the universe: the surface of the containing body is the material component of place (or place taken materially), whereas the distance of this surface from the fixed points of the universe is the formal component (or place taken formally), which is what makes the surface of the containing body a place – that is, relevant for the location of bodies (*In Phys.* IV.7). These and many other thirteenth-century commentators contend that this formal component solves the problem of immobility. In the case of the ship at anchor in a river, the ship remains in the same place, because although the surfaces of water in contact with it always change, the distance of these surfaces from the fixed points of the universe stays the same.[12] Aquinas offers the analogy of a fire, which remains the same with respect to its form, even when new combustible matter is added to it (ibid., IV.6, n. 468).

This common thirteenth-century strategy to save the immobility of place is not successful. The problem is that the original ontological objection against the immobility of Aristotle's place remains valid against the "cosmologically" qualified notion of place. In our example, if the surface of the water in contact with a ship anchored in a river changes when the water flows, then there is no way to maintain that the formal component – distance from the fixed points of the universe – remains the same. The reason for this is that such distance is an accident of the surface of water, and accidents of numerically distinct subjects are numerically distinct. So if the surfaces successively in contact with the ship are numerically distinct (because of the flow of water), then the distance – the formal component – must undergo change as well.

Many fourteenth-century commentators (for example, Thomas Wylton, Scotus, Burley, Ockham, and John of Jandun) point out this fundamental problem.[13]

---

[12] On this attempted solution, see Cecilia Trifogli, "La dottrina del luogo in Egidio Romano," *Medioevo* 14 (1988) 260–90; *Oxford Physics*, pp. 175–86.

[13] See Trifogli, "La dottrina del luogo," pp. 275–81.

Most often, they give up the idea of an immobile place and acknowledge that place is to some extent mobile. The new strategy then consists in modifying the definition of locomotion and rest in such a way that the ship anchored in a river does not move locally even when its place changes. On this new approach, however, the notion of distance from the fixed points of the universe continues to play an important role. The most influential attempts, like that of Scotus,[14] to define the conditions that two numerically distinct places (two containing surfaces) must satisfy in order to be the initial and final places of some local motion rely on the notion of specific rather than numerical sameness and difference. For example, two numerically distinct surfaces of water successively in contact with a ship anchored in a river cannot be the *terminus a quo* and the *terminus ad quem* of a local motion – that is, no local motion can take place between them – because these two surfaces have specifically (even if not numerically) the same distance from the fixed points of the universe. Although the two surfaces are numerically distinct places with numerically distinct distances, they are, in Scotus's words, the same place "by equivalence with respect to local motion"; that is, they are as indistinct with respect to local motion as if they were numerically the same place.

In conclusion, medieval Latin commentators raise fundamental ontological questions about Aristotle's treatment of change, time, and place. In the case of change, the main issue is whether change is a successive thing distinct from the relevant permanent things involved in a change. A similar ontological issue arises in the case of time: namely, whether time is a thing distinct from motion or whether there is only a conceptual distinction between the two. As for place, a major open problem in Aristotle's theory is the immobility of place. Thirteenth-century commentators assume that immobility is necessary to save our ordinary intuitions about local motion and rest, but they point out that this requirement is not satisfied if place is given the ontological status of the limit of the containing body, as in Aristotle's definition.

---

[14] *Ordinatio* II.2.2.1, ed. Vatican, VII: 255–9. On Scotus's position and its fortune, see Grant, "The Medieval Doctrine," pp. 65–72. See also Cecilia Trifogli, "Thomas Wylton on the Immobility of Place," *Recherches de théologie et philosophie médiévales* 65 (1998) pp. 12–22.

20

THE NATURE OF CHANGE

JOHANNES M. M. H. THIJSSEN

In the *Rules for the Direction of the Mind* (Rule 12), René Descartes pokes fun at the Aristotelian definition of motion. "Who doesn't know what motion is?," he asks rhetorically; he then contends that motion has no need of an explanation, because each and every one of us knows what it is. In *The World* ch. 7, started around the same time, Descartes even claims that he finds the scholastic definition of motion so obscure that he is forced to leave it in "their language" – that is, *motus est actus entis in potentia prout in potentia est* ("motion is the actuality of a thing in potentiality insofar as it is in potentiality").[1] For Aristotle, however, and the medievals in his wake, motion was not merely an event familiar from everyday experience, but a phenomenon whose nature needed closer investigation. The central place that motion occupied in medieval thought can be understood only in the context of Aristotelian natural philosophy, particularly as it was set out in Book III of Aristotle's *Physics* and developed by medieval thinkers.

This chapter will restrict itself to the medieval discussion of the *nature* of motion – that is, it will restrict itself to the question 'What is motion?' or, more generally, 'What is change?' Other significant problem areas which medieval thinkers addressed include the dynamic and kinematic aspects of motion – that is, motion's relations to distance and time, and the causes of motion. In medieval terminology, these aspects concerned the study of motion "with respect to effect" (*penes effectum*) and "with respect to cause" (*penes causam*). In the latter case, some consideration was given also to the forces acting on bodies to produce motions. Phenomena that fourteenth-century thinkers discussed under these headings – and toward which they often took a quantitative, mathematical approach – were gravity, accelerated free fall, projectile motion, and also qualitative changes in a given subject, such as heating. Because the accomplishments of fourteenth-century scholars such as Thomas Bradwardine, Richard

---

[1] For further discussion of Descartes's criticism of the Aristotelian account of motion, see Daniel Garber, *Descartes' Metaphysical Physics* (Chicago: University of Chicago Press 1992) pp. 157–9.

Kilvington, Richard Swineshead, William Heytesbury, and John Dumbleton
(all at Oxford University's Merton College) and John Buridan, Nicole Oresme,
and Albert of Saxony (all at the University of Paris) on these topics have already
received considerable attention in histories of science,[2] however, this chapter
focuses instead on what one might call the "ontological" aspects of motion.[3]

THE ROLE OF CHANGE IN ARISTOTLE'S NATURAL PHILOSOPHY

The *Physics* was only one of Aristotle's works on natural philosophy, but from
the medieval perspective it was the most important one. It was understood to
provide a characterization of the most general principles and properties of the
"things that are by nature."[4] Examples of natural things are animals and their
parts, plants, and the four basic elements: earth, air, fire, and water. They are
natural in a way that other objects, such as artifacts and things that are due
to chance, are not. Why are plants natural objects, though, and beds not?
According to Aristotle, "things that are by nature" are distinguished from non-
natural things in virtue of having a special sort of cause – namely, an inner
source of moving and being at rest.[5] In contrast to human-made objects, a
natural object's specific nature disposes it to certain kinds of behavior, most
notably to all kinds of natural change. Fire, for instance, has an inner impulse to
communicate warmth. Acorns naturally develop into oak trees. Artifacts lack
such an inner source (although they too contain such an inner principle insofar
as they are made out of natural things). A coat, for instance, considered as a
coat, does not have an inner impulse to change.

---

[2] See, for instance, Marshall Clagett, *The Science of Mechanics in the Middle Ages* (Madison: University
of Wisconsin Press, 1959); Peter Damerow *et al.* (eds.) *Exploring the Limits of Preclassical Mechanics*
(Dordrecht: Springer, 1992); Edward Grant, *The Foundations of Modern Science in the Middle Ages.
Their Religious, Institutional and Intellectual Contexts* (Cambridge: Cambridge University Press, 1996);
John Murdoch and Edith Sylla, "The Science of Motion," in D. Lindberg (ed.) *Science in the Middle
Ages* (Chicago: University of Chicago Press, 1978) 206–65; Edith Sylla, *The Oxford Calculators*, in N.
Kretzmann *et al.* (eds.) *The Cambridge History of Later Medieval Philosophy* (Cambridge: Cambridge
University Press, 1982) 540–64; John North, "Natural Philosophy in Late Medieval Oxford," in
J. Catto and R. Evans (eds.) *The History of the University of Oxford*, vol. II: *Late Medieval Oxford*
(Oxford: Oxford University Press, 1992) 76–95.

[3] The following works have proved to be especially helpful in providing the background to this
chapter: Anneliese Maier, *Zwischen Philosophie und Mechanik* (Rome: Edizioni di Storia e Letteratura,
1958) esp. pp. 1–143; Cecilia Trifogli, *Oxford Physics in the Thirteenth Century (ca. 1250–1270). Motion,
Infinity, Place and Time* (Leiden: Brill, 2000) esp. pp. 37–86.

[4] For what follows, see Aristotle, *Physics* 192b9–193a30. The Presocratic and Platonic background
to Aristotle's views is explained in Friedrich Solmsen, *Aristotle's System of the Physical World: A
Comparison with his Predecessors* (Ithaca, NY: Cornell University Press, 1960) esp. chs. 4, 5, and 9.

[5] Aristotle, *Phys.* 192b9 (the opening line of Book II). For a modern discussion of what Aristotle
may have meant by "things that are by nature," see, for instance, Helen Lang, *The Order of Nature in
Aristotle's Physics: Place and the Elements* (Cambridge: Cambridge University Press, 1998) pp. 40–50.

Aristotle's account of nature and natural objects is couched in the terminology that was primarily reserved for local motion (*kinēsis*). But how does it relate to change in general? In an influential passage in Book III of the *Physics*, Aristotle maintains that motion does not constitute a separate category of its own over and above the things that are moving, but is placed in several categories of entities that are capable of change: Substance, Quantity, Quality, and Place (200b32–201a10). Thus "motion" in this broad Aristotelian sense includes (1) change of quantity (growth and decline); (2) change of quality (alteration, such as white into non-white); (3) locomotion; and (4) substantial change (generation and corruption). In the first three types of change, the substance remains the same and its properties change, whereas in the latter, the substance itself changes. Medieval thinkers did not consider generation and corruption as a type of motion (*motus*), but rather as mutation, or instantaneous change, whereas the other types of changes were viewed as gradual and successive processes.

Among the different types of change, Aristotle considered local motion as primary, in the sense that these other changes were all caused by an antecedent local motion. In a well-known cosmological argument, Aristotle even asserts that *generation* depends on local motion – namely, on the movements of the sun, which are caused by the rotation of the heavens. The sun, as generating body, approaches to and retreats from certain parts of the sublunary world, and thus produces generation and corruption, respectively.[6] 'Motion' (*kinēsis*; *motus*) is used either to cover change of all kinds, or specifically to mean 'local motion.' Since in contemporary contexts it is very hard not to read 'motion' as 'local motion,' this chapter will henceforth use 'change' for 'motion' in this broad sense.

The study of nature (*physis*) is central to Aristotle's physics. Its study determines the topics he chooses for discussion and defines the problems he sets out to solve. Intimately connected with the study of nature is the concept of local motion and, more generally, change: "Nature is a principle of motion and change (*kinēseōs kai metabolēs*), and it is the subject of our inquiry. We must therefore see that we understand what change is; for if it were unknown, nature too would be unknown" (*Phys.* III.1, 200b10–15). Thus, the question "What is change?," considered obsolete by Descartes, is crucial in Aristotle's project to clarify nature – an endeavor undertaken in Aristotle's *Physics*, particularly in the first three chapters of Book III. When late medieval thinkers came to discuss Aristotle's views on the nature of change, either in commentaries on the *Physics* or in other works, they concentrate on two main problems. The first concerns

---

[6] See Aristotle, *De generatione et corruptione* II.10, 336a14–b25. Another argument to vindicate the primacy of local motion is provided in *Phys.* VIII.7, 260b29–61a12.

the adequacy of Aristotle's definition of change – the *quid nominis*, so to speak. The second problem concerns the question of what change really is – that is, the *quid rei* or ontological status of change.

THE ARISTOTELIAN DEFINITION

As we saw above, late medieval texts usually render Aristotle's definition of change as "the actuality of a thing in potentiality insofar as it is in potentiality." A question typically raised at the beginning of Book III in fourteenth-century *Physics* commentaries is whether this definition is "good" (*bona*)[7] for, even on its face, it looks problematic. The definition appeals to the notions of actuality and potentiality, which Aristotle considered basic metaphysical factors,[8] but it seems to associate both at once with motion, even though they are contradictories.[9] The examination of these two concepts and their relation is what makes the medieval discussion of the definition of change philosophically interesting: although medieval thinkers always agree in the end that Aristotle's definition of change is, indeed, a good one, they take it in many different directions. Initially shaped by Avicenna and Averroes, the subsequent contributions of Thomas Aquinas, John Buridan, and William of Ockham illustrate something of the many different dimensions that were projected onto Aristotle's definition.

Avicenna introduces an important clarification of Aristotle's definition by observing that an object capable of movement possesses a double potentiality: first, to pass from rest to movement; second, to continue its motion up to the point where there is no potentiality left because the motion has reached its terminus (*Sufficientia* II.1, in *Opera phil.* f. 23rb). When seen from this perspective, the motion itself can be considered the first actuality of the mobile object, whereas the terminus of the motion is the second actuality. For instance, when a mobile has moved from A to B, its first actuality (in retrospect) would have been the transition from rest to movement in A; this would have been the actualization of the potentiality to move. The second actuality would have been the arrival of the mobile at B, when all potentiality to move further has expired. Avicenna's distinction led subsequent medieval authors to debate whether the

---

[7] The question harks back to the opening lines of *Phys.* III.2, 201b16–19: "The soundness of this definition is evident both when we consider the accounts of motion that the others have given and also from the difficulty of defining it otherwise." An excellent analysis of this discussion still is Maier, *Zwischen Philosophie und Mechanik*, pp. 1–59.

[8] 'Actuality' translates the medieval *actus*. For a modern discussion about the correct translation and interpretation of the Greek *entelecheia* (*actuality* or *actualization*) and about the cogency of Aristotle's definition, see, e.g., L. A. Kosman, "Aristotle's Definition of Motion," *Phronesis* 14 (1969) 40–62.

[9] Descartes found the definition absurd for this reason. In the discussion of John Buridan, *Quaest. Phys.* III.10, this same objection appears as the first argument to the contrary.

potentiality referred to in Aristotle's definition concerns a body's general disposition to move, or whether it concerns a moving body's potentiality to reach a specific terminus. In general, they concluded that Aristotle had meant the potentiality towards the motion's terminus, although Avicenna himself did not make a clear choice in this matter. He was merely drawing attention to the multiple dimensions of "potentiality" in Aristotle's definition.

Averroes's main contribution to the discussion of Aristotle's definition is his interpretation of "the thing in potentiality." Averroes takes the "potential being" of the changing object to be a successive passage from potentiality to actuality (*exitus de potentia ad actum*). In other words, on Averroes's view, a changing body does not *exist* in potentiality; it passes from potential being to actual being, and it is already partly in actuality. However, insofar as the change has not yet reached its terminus, it is also in potentiality (*In Phys.* III.9, ed. 1562, f. 89ra).

Aquinas's discussion of Aristotle's definition shows the influence of these Islamic treatments. Focusing on the basic notions of potentiality and actuality, Aquinas's *Physics* commentary (III.2) contends that something can be merely in actuality, merely in potentiality, or in a middle position between the two. Change occurs only with respect to things in this middle category between pure potentiality and actuality: things that are only potential do not change, whereas things that are only in actuality do not change either, because they have already completed their change. The conclusion seems to be that things that are changing are actual, in an imperfect way. In this way, Aquinas adds an important new element to Averroes's analysis: an object in the process of change is not merely incompletely actual; this incomplete actuality is ordered towards a further actuality that is still lacking. This order with respect to a higher actuality (*ordo ad ulteriorem actum*) is an important qualification. If it were taken away, Aquinas maintains, the imperfect actuality itself would become the terminus of the change and, hence, change would cease. Lukewarm water, for instance, is in actuality when compared to its previous cold state, but its actuality is imperfect. Were it not ordered toward further actuality that it does not have, that is, toward further heat, then lukewarm, rather than hot, would be the terminus of change. (See Chapter 19 for a more extensive discussion of Aquinas's account.)

Aquinas's notion of an order of actualities, which is rather obscure as he presents it, is later developed more clearly and extensively by John Buridan. Buridan, too, focuses on the relation between potentiality and actuality (*Quaest. Phys.* III.10, ed. 1509, f. 53v).[10] Like Aquinas (and Avicenna), Buridan maintains that things in motion have not yet fully acquired the perfection or disposition

---

[10] For a corrected version of this text (as well as other texts below), see Maier, *Zwischen Philosophie und Mechanik*, pp. 53–5.

they are in the process of acquiring. Hence, they are in actuality insofar as they have partially actualized this disposition or perfection, and they are in potentiality insofar as they still have to fulfill part of this disposition. The decisive feature of Buridan's view is that this potentiality is oriented towards its proper actuality. Without this actual tendency (*actualis tendentia*) or process (*processus*) towards what still has to be fulfilled, nothing would be changing. According to both Aquinas and Buridan, then, Aristotle's phrase "actuality of a thing in potentiality *insofar as it is in potentiality*" precisely captures the dynamic aspect of change: what is characteristic of beings in change is that they are oriented towards an ulterior goal, namely the actualization of what still is potential.

Ockham, earlier in the fourteenth century, had taken a completely different line. His understanding of "thing in potentiality" does not imply an ordering or tendency towards a higher actuality. According to Ockham, Aristotle's definition means that a changing body is in actuality with respect to one thing (be it a quantity, a quality, or a place), and that it is in potentiality with respect to something else (of the same genus), which it now lacks but will obtain immediately afterwards (*Expositio in Phys.* III.3.1).[11] So, for example, a white object that is changing into black is in actuality with respect to whiteness (a quality), and in potentiality with respect to the blackness (also a quality) which it will acquire immediately afterwards.

In their explanation of Aristotle's definition, Aquinas, Buridan, and Ockham were implicitly addressing the question of 'potentiality for what?' in the nature of change. They wish to emphasize that the potentiality of a thing in the process of change, is not a potentiality with respect to being (potential existence), but rather a transition from potentiality into an actuality that is currently lacking. Thus, Aquinas, and even more explicitly Buridan, read into Aristotle's definition that change is a process that strives at fulfillment in that it is ordered toward an ulterior actuality. Ockham, in a way, takes the same lead, but he interprets it in purely temporal terms: an object in change has already acquired something that it did not have before, and it will acquire something else immediately afterwards that it yet lacks.

WHAT KIND OF ENTITY IS CHANGE?

The second main problem associated with the nature of change concerns its ontological status: is change a separate entity, or is it nothing besides the thing changed? In a passage from *Physics* III cited earlier, Aristotle maintains that

---

[11] See ibid., pp. 40–5, and Marilyn McCord Adams, *William Ockham* (Notre Dame, IN: University of Notre Dame Press, 1987) II: 799–827.

change is not something over and above the things in change; it does not itself constitute a separate category, but it is placed in several categories, just like potentiality and actuality (200b32–201a3). More specifically, change pertains to the category of the entity that is changing. In the case of a change in color, this would be the category of Quality, but change could also belong to the categories of Substance, Quantity, or Place. Elsewhere, however, Aristotle had made other statements regarding the kinds of change and the category to which they belonged. In the *Categories,* in particular, he had claimed that change falls into one category only, namely that of *Passio* or Affection (11b1–8). In the medieval period, this claim especially came to be juxtaposed with the views expressed in *Physics* III.

Averroes's discussion and reconciliation of this apparent incompatibility also enters into almost all later discussions of this issue. He reconciled the *Physics* with the *Categories* by claiming that, in the former, Aristotle had set forth the more correct view, whereas in the *Categories*, as was his practice in that work, he had spoken according to the more common view. According to the truer view, change appears as a part-by-part generation of its terminus and, as a consequence, belongs itself to the category of this terminus – that is, to Substance, Quality, Quantity, or Place. Change differs from the terminus towards which it tends only in its degree of actuality or perfection, not according to category. But Averroes introduced a further alternative account, according to which change is a process (*via*) towards actuality or perfection. This view implies that change cannot coincide with its actuality. It belongs to a category of its own, different from the form it attains (*In Phys.* III.4). The same distinction recurs in Averroes's commentary on *Physics* V. There it is couched in the terminology of change "according to matter" and "according to form." According to matter, change and its terminus belong to the same category; according to its form, one must view change as a transmutation that takes place in time and constitutes a category of its own (ibid., V.9).

In the fourteenth century, these alternative opinions came to be classified under the formulas *forma fluens* and *fluxus formae*, a distinction that medieval authors usually attribute to Albert the Great (*Physica* III.1.3 [*Opera* IV.1: 151]).[12] According to the *forma fluens* theory, change is nothing but the successive impression of the form upon the changeable body. In the case of qualitative change, for instance, the *forma fluens* is the loss or acquisition of various degrees

---

[12] See Maier, *Zwischen Philosophie und Mechanik,* pp. 73–7 and E. J. McCullough, "St. Albert on Motion as Forma Fluens and Fluxus Formae," in J. Weisheipl (ed.) *Albertus Magnus and the Sciences: Commemorative Essays 1980* (Toronto: Pontifical Institute of Mediaeval Studies, 1980) 129–53, for a discussion of Albert's views and of Maier's interpretation thereof.

of a quality, such as blackness in the process of becoming black (*nigrescere*); in the case of local motion, it refers to the places successively acquired by the mobile body. In other words, change is the same as the perfection or form it attains, but it represents that form in a state of flux. How does this account of change relate to the common medieval view that forms are unchangeable? It should be noted that the flowing character of the flowing form is not *in* the form itself, but rather results from the degree of actualization of the form in the *subject*.[13] The *fluxus formae* theory, on the other hand, maintains that change is not the form acquired but is "the flux" of that form – that is, the flow, the process, or the road towards an actuality or perfection. Whether in fact the flow that constitutes change is different in essence from the acquired form became a subject of later debate.

The distinction between these two views provides a convenient framework for presenting the most prominent fourteenth-century views: those of Ockham, Buridan, Albert of Saxony, and Oresme. Ockham's discussion of the nature of change brings into focus the ontological implications of the debate. Although he does not use the terminology just described, his position in effect is that the only correct way to understand change is to see it as a *forma fluens*. According to Ockham, the *fluxus formae* theory implies that motion is a thing that differs from the starting point from which the motion proceeds, from the mobile object, and from the terminus to which it proceeds.[14] In other words, this position would make motion a thing (*res*) really distinct from the objects that move (or, in general, that change). Adhering to a *fluxus formae* theory of motion entails that, besides permanent things (*res permanentes*), the world is also inhabited by successive things (*res successivae*). Permanent things are those whose parts can exist all at once (see Chapter 19); Ockham's opponents had argued that motion could not be such a thing, but was essentially successive.

In contrast, Ockham argues extensively against the existence of successive things. His strongest argument, perhaps, is to invoke his famous Razor and to claim that it is superfluous to assume the existence of any successive things that are really distinct from permanent things. This position, however, leaves Ockham with the burden of explaining the phenomenon of motion (and change) without assuming such really distinct entities. In other words, he has to account for motion exclusively in terms of the individual mobile objects and the places (and forms) that they successively occupy. To this end he undertakes

---

[13] See Maier, *Zwischen Philosophie und Mechanik*, pp. 78–83.
[14] See *Expositio in Phys.* III.4.6 (*Opera phil.* IV: 473) and also *Quaest. Phys.* 18–19 (*Opera phil.* VI: 441–7), in which Ockham gives his explanation of Aristotle's and Averroes's position respectively. See also Adams, *William Ockham*, II: 804.

a semantic analysis of the terms 'motion' and 'change.' He concludes that they are not so-called "absolute" nouns referring to individual concrete things, but are really abstract nouns that abbreviate longer complex expressions.[15] Thus the phrase 'change is what goes from prior to posterior' is to be understood as meaning 'when something changes, it goes from prior to posterior'; and the proposition 'motion exists' really is an abbreviation for the proposition 'a moveable object now has something and immediately before did not have it but immediately afterwards will have something else.'[16] In similar fashion, each proposition that contains the term 'motion' can be expounded in such a way as to refer only to individual things. In response, Walter Burley would accuse Ockham of thereby denying the reality of change and, as a consequence, of destroying natural philosophy.[17]

A complication that runs through this debate is the distinction between several different kinds of change, especially between local motion and the others. In the case of local motion, there is no fulfillment of a perfection that inheres in the moving body, inasmuch as the change does not involve the acquisition of a form. Rather, local motion, or change of place, is directed toward an external goal. Despite this distinction, Ockham treated all types of change in the same way. This is not the case with Buridan, who distinguishes between several different kinds of change and qualifies his position accordingly. With respect to qualitative change (*alteration*), he follows the standard position, also defended by Ockham, that the change is not distinct from the subject and the quality that changes. When it comes to local motion, however, where there is no quality or other form to be changed, the flux theory of motion enters the picture. Although Buridan was usually in agreement with Ockham in his adherence to a sparse ontology and a predilection for a semantic approach towards natural science, he did not follow Ockham's more parsimonious account of local motion as a flowing form.

Buridan's defense of the position that motion is an additional flux is based at least partly on theological considerations. In particular, the condemnation of 1277 plays a crucial role in his argument.[18] The condemned proposition 49 denied that God could move the outermost heaven, and therefore the world itself, in a straight line, because such a motion would leave behind a void after the departure of the world from its present position. After the condemnation

---

[15] See Murdoch and Sylla, "The Science of Motion," pp. 216–17.
[16] See *Summula philosophiae naturalis* III.3 (*Opera phil.* VI: 252–5); *Quaest. Phys.* 36 (*Opera phil.* VI: 491–3), and also the anonymous Ockham-inspired *Tractatus de successivis* (ed. Boehner, pp. 45–9). See also Adams, *William Ockham*, pp. 822–4.
[17] See Maier, *Zwischen Philosophie und Mechanik*, pp. 46–7, which provides the quotation from Burley.
[18] See *Quaest. Phys.* III.7 concl. 1; see also Murdoch and Sylla, "The Science of Motion," pp. 217–18.

of this thesis, scholastics routinely conceded that God could indeed move the world rectilinearly (and circularly), if it pleased him to do so. But how should one imagine this movement of the entire cosmos as one body?

Aristotle had defined local motion as change relative to place, as "being one way earlier and another way later with respect to it" (*Phys.* V.1, 225a1–3). But on Aristotle's view there is no place outside the cosmos. So to what place should this type of motion be referred? Since there seem to be no places that are successively acquired by the cosmos, there seems to be no motion. But this conclusion is incompatible with Buridan's point of departure – namely, that God can indeed move the cosmos, if he wishes to do so. Therefore, if succession is to be preserved in this case, local motion must involve something else besides the mobile body and the places acquired. Buridan concludes that this something else is a purely successive thing, inhering in the mobile object and yet distinct from it. It is with respect to this flux that the cosmos in motion can be said to be in a relation of continuous change, "being one way earlier and another way later" (*Quaest. Phys.* III.7 concl. 6). Defined this way, 'the flux' designates something internal to the *mobile*.

From the hypothetical case of the cosmos's motion, Buridan applied his conclusions to all types of local motion, including those occurring in natural cases. The upshot of his discussion is that motion is a property or disposition intrinsic to the mobile body. As a quality or something that can be treated as a quality, it possesses a stable being. According to its nature, however, this quality is a purely successive being (ibid., III.12, ed. 1509, f. 54v).

Albert of Saxony, Buridan's colleague on the Paris arts faculty, subsequently defended essentially the same theory – and on the same grounds – but he made some interesting qualifications. Like Buridan and many others, Albert too rejects the view that qualitative changes require a flux that is additional to the attained quality (*Quaest. Phys.* III.5).[19] With respect to local motion, however, Albert distinguishes sharply between the natural and the supernatural cases; he devotes a separate question to each one of them (ibid., III.6–7). Albert's position is that, according to Aristotle and Averroes, motion is not an additional flux. Nevertheless, Albert holds that, according to both the Christian faith and the truth, local motion should be considered a flux inhering in the mobile body. His considerations are the same as those of Buridan. The possible movement

---

[19] Note that the older idea that Albert of Saxony and Nicole Oresme belonged to the "Buridan school" needs revision. It is more accurate to view these thinkers as belonging to an intellectual network, who interacted about their theories. See J. M. M. H. Thijssen, "The Buridan School Reassessed. John Buridan and Albert of Saxony," *Vivarium* 42 (2004) 18–42.

of the cosmos by divine omnipotence can only be explained by recourse to a conception of motion as a flux inhering in the mobile body. The conclusion that seems to arise from this discussion is that the *forma fluens* and the *fluxus formae* theories are equally valid, but the latter is preferred for theological reasons.[20]

A particularly nice example of fourteenth-century discussions of change is the first seven questions of Nicole Oresme's commentary on Book III of the *Physics*.[21] There, he discusses several different theories of change and examines arguments for and against them. Among the theories under consideration are both the view that change coincides with the changing object (III.3), and the view that change is itself a flux (III.6). In his overview of the different theories, Oresme ranks himself as an adherent of the *fluxus* theory. According to Oresme, however, if this flux is interpreted in the wrong way, it is the worst possible view. Unlike Buridan and Albert, Oresme does not take the flux as a thing (*res*) distinct from, and added to, the mobile body – instead, he introduces a distinct ontological entity, namely a *modus rei*, or a way of being. Oresme claims that motion, though not a separate successive thing, does have a successive character that is expressed by the mode or condition of the mobile object. These are the object's continuous internal changes, expressed in the now familiar definition of motion as "being in another way than before" (III.6).[22]

Oresme's stance in the fourteenth-century debate about the nature of motion illustrates that the dichotomy between *forma fluens* and *fluxus forma* is too crude. Oresme rejects the *forma fluens* theory. Yet, he sides with Ockham's position in that he, too, believes that motion is not a separate thing (*res*) inhering in the moving subject. Thus, the *fluxus* theory, which usually is a *res* theory, receives a distinctive twist in Oresme's hands. Although Oresme and Buridan disagree about the *res*-like character of motion, they both agree that motion requires an internal reference mark within the mobile body. It is with respect to this reference mark that motion or change can be said to be "in another way than before." In other words, their different positions can be expressed as follows: Oresme views motion as a successive being. The mobile body continuously changes its locations. Motion basically is a process, and it is the mind that

[20] See Jürgen Sarnowsky, *Die aristotelisch-scholastische Theorie der Bewegung: Studien zum Kommentar Alberts von Sachsen zur Physik des Aristoteles* (Münster: Aschendorff, 1989) pp. 144–9.
[21] The text and an analysis of Oresme's position in the debate about the nature of change is given in Stefano Caroti, "Oresme on Motion (*Questiones super Physicam* III, 2–7)," *Vivarium* 31 (1993) 8–36, and "La position de Nicole Oresme sur la nature du mouvement (*Quaestiones super Physicam* III, 1–8): Problèmes gnoséologiques, ontologiques et sémantiques," *Archives d'histoire littéraire et doctrinale du moyen âge* 61 (1994) 303–85. See also Stefan Kirschner, *Nicolaus Oresmes Kommentar zur Physik des Aristoteles* (Stuttgart: Steiner, 1997) pp. 52–78 and 206–34 for an edition of the Latin text.
[22] See also III.7 (ed. Kirschner, *Nicolaus Oresmes*, p. 234).

represents motion as a unity. Buridan, on the other hand, perceives local motion as a property, namely the property of being at a certain location now, and at another location immediately afterwards. The property of being in motion is such that the moving body continuously changes. As a property, however, motion inheres in a subject, namely the moving body.

In all of this, fourteenth-century theories of change typify the diversity and sophistication of medieval natural philosophy.

IV

SOUL AND KNOWLEDGE

21

SOUL AND BODY

JOHN HALDANE

BACKGROUND AND SOURCES

Most religions and pre-modern philosophies advance some idea of the soul. In ancient Hebrew thought the notion of *nephesh* refers to living things, but is most often used in connection with human beings, particularly in relation to characteristically human activities. Abstracting from these uses one gets the idea of soul as that which makes a living thing to be alive, and that is present in a body as a result of God's having breathed this life principle (*neshama*) into it. Correspondingly, death is associated with the departure of this animating force. So conceived, soul is not as such a uniquely psychological concept, nor is its referent necessarily a personal entity, and there is no sense that it could exist as a separate substance. Later Jewish thought, both that contemporaneous with the first centuries of Christianity, but more so that of the Middle Ages, does speculate about an immaterial part or element of human beings, but as with Christian doctrines of the immortal soul this is the result of encounters with Greek metaphysics.

The principal philosophical sources of medieval speculation about the existence, nature, and possible immortality of the soul derive from the works of Plato and Aristotle, mediated through later Neoplatonic and Islamic interpreters and commentators. In the *Meno* and the *Phaedo*, Plato explores the idea of the soul as an immaterial substance that animates a body, but that is itself an independently existing intellectual subject. The latter status raises the possibility of the soul's survival of its bodily partner's death, and indeed of its intrinsic immortality (as well as of its possible pre-existence). Plato rehearses a number of arguments that involve the idea that intellectual knowledge is of non-material 'objects' and hence is itself an immaterial power, of an immaterial agent.

These two dialogues were translated from the Greek into Latin in the mid-twelfth century by Henry Aristippus of Sicily, and they served to reinforce the idea, already familiar through Neoplatonic sources and through the translations and commentaries on Aristotle, that a primary function of the soul, from which its immateriality might be inferred, is the power of abstract thought or intellection.

More than any other source or work from the ancient world, Aristotle's *De anima* influences medieval thought about the nature of soul and its relation to body. The Latin title renders the Greek *Peri psuchēs*, and both expressions point towards a broader understanding of the idea of soul than is associated with later religious and philosophical dualisms of self and body. Interestingly, in fact, Aristotle's approach echoes that of Hebrew Scripture inasmuch as he too is concerned with what makes living things alive, though his enquiry systematizes the phenomena of life, arranges them hierarchically, and gives special place to reason.

In defining *soul* Aristotle makes use of two pairs of concepts that would come to feature extensively in medieval metaphysics: first, *form* (L. *forma*, Gk. *morphē*) and *matter* (L. *materia*, Gk. *hulē*); second, *potentiality* (L. *potentia*, Gk. *dunamis*) and *actuality* (L. *actus*, Gk. *energeia*). In general, forms may be thought of as structuring or characterizing principles; thus, the form of cubidity gives three-dimensional cubed form to a sugar lump, whereas the forms of whiteness and of sweetness characterize its color and taste. Forms that determine the primary or essential nature of substances are called "substantial forms" (see Chapter 46). In the case of material substances these structure and unify matter, making a quantity of it to be a such and such: a cabbage, a rabbit, a human being, or in the case of artifacts, a box, a room, a house, and so on. Matter in general may be thought to be "in potential" to receiving a range of forms, but all particular matter is made actually this or that by being informed by one or another structure. This is the metaphysics of "hylomorphism."

In *De anima* II.1, Aristotle writes that the soul is "the form . . . and actuality of a natural body that has life potentially" (412a27; tr. Hamlyn), meaning by this that it is the body's substantial form. He then adds, however, that actuality can be distinguished at two levels: capacity (*hexis*) and activity (*energeia*). At the first level, to be actual is to be alive and organically structured so as to be *capable* of various animal activities; at the second level, it is to be *active* with respect to these potentialities or capacities – that is, to be actually exercising these powers. Accordingly, potentiality is also distinguishable at two levels: first, being structurally such as may be made alive; second, once that first possibility has been actualized, being such as may become active in some respect or another. Thus Aristotle writes: "If we are to speak of something common to every soul [that is, give a general formula applicable to all kinds of soul], we must describe it as the first actuality of a natural body that has organs [a naturally organized body]" (412b4–5).

Two further points from the *De anima* need to be noted, since they serve to shape subsequent medieval discussions. First, Aristotle speaks of "kinds of soul," which he distinguishes according to the different sets of capacities associated with basic categories of living things. So, broadly, he distinguishes nutrition, growth, reproduction; locomotion, appetite, sensation; and memory, will, and intellect. It subsequently becomes an issue among commentators whether this is the correct basic identification of powers and where the precise boundaries of groupings lie, but in one way or another a three-fold classification emerges of *vegetative*, *sensory*, and *rational* souls. These are also seen to be hierarchically arranged, inasmuch as anything that has a higher set of powers has the lower ones but not vice versa. Rabbits, for instance, take in nutrients, grow, and reproduce just as cabbages do, but unlike cabbages they can also move from one place to another (as contrasted with simply *being moved* by an external force), and they have bodily appetites and sensations. Similarly, human beings are like rabbits in having all of these vegetative and sentient powers, but in addition, and unlike the lower life forms, they also have a rational faculty.

Second, the question arises of whether a soul as Aristotle conceives it – that is, as the substantial form of a living organism – could exist apart from the body it has hitherto informed. The general relationship of form to matter would suggest not. Aristotle writes that the body plus the soul constitutes the animal; he then continues "that the soul or certain parts of it, if it is divisible, cannot be separated from the body is quite clear; for in some cases the actuality is of the parts themselves" (413a3–5). In such cases, the actuality of the powers is the actuality of the relevant organs: thus, the actuality of digesting is the operative actuality of the gut; the actuality of smelling that of the nose; the actuality of seeing that of the eye, and so on. Evidently these activities are impossible without a relevantly organized living body. But, Aristotle then adds, "Not that anything prevents at any rate *some* parts from being separable, because of their being actualities of no body" (413a6). He returns to this possibility in Book III, where he considers reasons for concluding that rational or intellectual activities operate apart from a corresponding bodily part or organ. If this conclusion is in reach, then it seems there may be a route back to the Platonic idea of the soul as a separate something, for we may reason that an immaterial activity presupposes an immaterial power, and that an immaterial power presupposes an immaterial agent or subject.

The proper interpretation of these texts remains controversial. But whatever Aristotle's own view of the issue, the *De anima* generated a range of quite different understandings of the nature of the rational soul and its relation to the body in the later Byzantine, Islamic, and Christian traditions. Syrian Christians, for instance, began to translate Aristotle's Greek into Syriac in the fourth century, and these texts remained in Byzantine hands until the Islamic conquests of the seventh and eighth centuries. Thereafter these Syriac editions were translated into Arabic along with various Neoplatonic writings – some of which were misattributed to Aristotle (including some of the *Enneads* of Plotinus and some of Proclus's work), while others were recognized as commentaries (see Chapter 1). These texts became the subject of intense study by Muslim philosophers, and they gave rise to Eastern and Western traditions of Islamic philosophy. The most influential representatives of these traditions for the Latin West were al-Fārābī and Avicenna in the East, and Averroes in the West. Averroes, in particular, developed a complex account of the rational part of the human soul, arguing that it is indeed immaterial, separable, and immortal, but on that account it is not something individual or personal but rather a single cosmic intellect. This striking view was to resurface in later debates between Aquinas and Latin Averroists (see Chapters 23, 34).

A further central figure for the medieval Latin tradition was Augustine, who in many respects was aligned with Plato and the Neoplatonists. In Augustine, as to an extent in Plotinus, one finds an approach to the idea of the human soul that connects it with interiority or subjectivity, in the sense of first-person awareness (see Chapter 7). This approach has generally been associated with early modern thought (and in particular, with Descartes), but already in books VIII to X of *De Trinitate*, Augustine observes that we know what a soul is in virtue of having one, and he argues further that this immediate apprehension of the soul's existence and nature is incompatible with its being something bodily. As with Plato and Aristotle, the idea emerges in Augustine that the activity of the higher powers of cognition is immaterial, with the consequent possibility of its operating apart from the body. This view was also shared by two influential Christian–Platonic figures of the following century – namely, Boethius and pseudo-Dionysius (the author long believed to be the Dionysius mentioned in Acts as a convert of St. Paul).

THE HIGH PERIOD OF MEDIEVAL CHRISTIAN PHILOSOPHY

This rich and complex history of sources and ideas provides the main backdrop against which the major figures of medieval Latin philosophy work out their own accounts of the relationship of body and soul in human beings. This section considers five thinkers whose views proved particularly influential (addressing the first, however, only in passing): the Dominicans Albert the Great and Thomas Aquinas, and the Franciscans Bonaventure, John Duns Scotus, and William of Ockham.

With a new wave of Aristotelian material having made its way into Western Christendom in the twelfth century – both through direct translation from the Greek and via Arabic editions and commentaries – the scene was set for intellectual development (see Chapter 4). As part of the very new Order of Preachers, Albert the Great was disposed to innovate intellectually, particularly in bringing Greek philosophy into contemporary inquiry. What he drew upon was a mix of the influences described earlier, and he struggles to articulate a metaphysics that links ultimate principles to an explanatory account of empirical nature. So far as the soul is concerned, he strives to avoid a materialist reduction of the rational powers to complex bodily operations, while also resisting the more extreme versions of Islamic interpretation according to which intellect is an entirely separate single principle that somehow touches, ignites, or illuminates the natural power of imagination in individual human beings.

While agreeing with Averroes that intellect "comes from without" rather than being materially generated from within the body, Albert also believes that each individual has a numerically distinct "acquired intellect" (*intellectus adeptus*) that is immaterial and hence potentially separable.[1] It is hard to resist the conclusion that Albert's obscure theories are the penalty of his own extensive syncretism; but in requiring that a theory of human nature take account of the best philosophy, as well as of Christian teaching, he set a compelling (and rewarding) challenge for his greatest student, Thomas Aquinas.

Bonaventure, following his order's tradition of Augustinian theology, was far less inclined than Albert to grant a major role to philosophy, seeing it primarily as an instrument for articulating and assisting the application of religious ideas.[2] On his account, the human soul is directly created by God and not, as Albert seems to suggest, a product of some intermediary cosmic cause (*Sent.* II.18.2).[3] For Bonaventure, this view is both a matter of religious faith and also a conclusion of the argument that, since the soul is incorruptible and hence immortal, it cannot be an effect of material factors but must rather have an external and supernatural cause. Furthermore, since the soul's activities are in part spiritual, its source must likewise be spiritual – and that source must have the power to bestow sanctifying grace. Hence, the soul's cause must not only be beyond nature but also be a source of supernatural life, which only God can be.

---

[1] See *Liber de natura et origine animae* II.6 and *De anima* III. Albert develops his view with reference, but in opposition to Averroistic doctrines in his *Libellus de unitate intellectus contra Averroem*. For discussion of Averroes's view and that of other Islamic thinkers see Herbert Davidson, *Alfarabi, Avicenna, and Averroes on Intellect: Their Cosmologies, Theories of the Active Intellect, and Theories of Human Intellect* (Oxford: Oxford University Press, 1992).

[2] See, e.g., his *De reductione artium ad theologiam*.

[3] See Ilia Delio, *Simply Bonaventure: An Introduction to his Life, Thought and Writings* (Hyde Park, NY: New City Press, 2001) which also contains translated extracts.

Interestingly, even while opposing the introduction of Aristotelianism, Bonaventure himself adopts a metaphysics of form and matter and applies it universally, arguing that every created substance (angels, as well as human beings and other physical substances) is a composite of these two principles. (On such universal hylomorphism, see Chapter 46.) So far as soul and body are concerned, Bonaventure's Aristotelianism involves the following: God creates the entire human soul, which possesses vegetative, sensory, and rational faculties; the human body that derives from sexual reproduction is disposed for the exercise of these various forms of life, but is itself incapable of giving rise to them. Since the soul is the form of the living body, human souls are many in number, corresponding to the population of individual humans. Finally, as the principle of life and action for the entire human being, the human soul is present throughout the whole body – not as a collection of distributed parts, but rather through its simultaneous and unitary causality (*Sent.* I.8.2).

Here there emerges in Bonaventure's view a tension that becomes familiar in subsequent discussions – namely, a tension between the Aristotelian idea that the soul is the form of the body, with which it establishes a substantial unity, and the Platonic–Augustinian conception, which Bonaventure also affirms, of the soul as itself a complete spiritual substance. If the soul is a complete substance, then it must have an individuality apart from that associated with numerically distinct bodies. This, in turn, raises two questions. First, how is such individuation achieved if not through the body – why, in other words, is there not a single immaterial intellectual soul? Second, if the human soul is a something (*hoc aliquid*) apart from its substantial integration with its body, why is it united to a body?

Bonaventure answers the first question by appeal to his universal hylomorphism. Every created entity is composed of matter and form. The human soul is a created entity; hence it, too, is a metaphysical composite of form and matter. But since the soul is also a spiritual substance, its matter must be immaterial – an apparent contradiction that Bonaventure avoids by disambiguating the notion of *matter*. First, we may think of matter generally as the correlate of form. Deploying the concepts of potentiality and actuality, we can then hold that matter *per se* is the metaphysical possibility for the reception of form, resulting in the creation of a substance. This is the sense in which the immaterial soul contains both form and matter. We can distinguish this, however, from a second, more particular version of this potentiality that is corporeal or, as we might now prefer to say, spatio-temporal. This is empirical matter, space-occupying body, or extension, and it is in this sense that the body stands as form to the soul. But the existence of this specific kind of matter does not exclude the possibility of a non-empirical potential for the reception of form, namely, non-extensive matter.

Supposing this solution is accepted, what of our second question regarding the soul's unification with a material body? Bonaventure points out that the human soul includes vegetative and sensory as well as rational powers. At least the first two of these could not be exercised in the absence of embodiment, inasmuch as nutrition, growth, and sensation are exercised through bodily organs. Also, although rational thought might not require a body, its characteristic expressions in speech and writing do. So the human soul is naturally inclined towards embodiment, and the union of body and soul naturally perfects both. Furthermore, while Bonaventure insists on the spiritual nature of the soul, implying its sanctified fulfillment in mystical contemplation of God, his insistence on the proper completion of the soul in union with the body suggests that the future life for which Christians (and others) hope will also involve bodily resurrection. Thus he is able to remain faithful to the closing words of the Nicene Creed: *et expecto resurrectionem mortuorum et vitam venturi saeculi* ("I look for the resurrection of the dead and the life of the world to come").[4]

In 1270, four years before he and Bonaventure both died, Thomas Aquinas wrote a commentary on the First Letter to the Corinthians in which he follows Paul in tying the prospect of future life to the possibility of bodily resurrection, as established by the example of Christ. In the course of his commentary, Aquinas writes that "the soul is not the whole human being, and my soul is not I" (15.2, ed. Cai, n. 924). So long as 'I' is understood as *the living human being I am*, Aquinas is in agreement with Bonaventure. In other respects, however, there are significant differences.

First, Aquinas's deployment of the metaphysics of hylomorphism is close to that of Aristotle and it eschews the idea of immaterial matter. Second, Aquinas approaches the issue of the human soul–body relationship by deploying the general notion of soul as "the first principle of life in living things" (*Summa theol.* 1a 75.1). Accordingly, he recognizes the tripartite hierarchical structure of the vegetative, sensory, and rational souls. Since soul stands to body as form to matter, the human soul is the organizing and animating principle of the living human body, making it a specific kind of organism and also serving as the intrinsic cause of that organism's self-originating activities.

---

[4] Bonaventure argues that the unity of body and soul in the human person is such that, if Mary was taken into heaven, then this must have been a bodily assumption. He writes: "The person is not the soul, it is a composite. Thus it is established that she must be there [heaven] as a composite, of soul and body" (*De assumptione B. Virginis Mariae* I.2.9).

Aquinas's more thoroughgoing Aristotelianism also leads him to insist upon a number of points that at various times have been subjects of controversy. First, he maintains in opposition to the Platonists that a living human being is not a conjunction of two substances – body and soul – but a single unitary subject. He observes, for instance, that it is one and the same individual that walks and sees and thinks, and that it is the human being, not the body or the soul, that does this (ibid., 76.1).

Second, deploying the same observation, he insists against Siger of Brabant and other contemporary Latin Averroists in the University of Paris that Aristotle did not hold that there is but a single active intellect of which individual human minds are but effects, or by which they are temporarily animated souls (ibid., 79.4–5). Nor, he further insists, is this the implication of the *De anima* theory of the rational.[5] If it is the same thing that thinks about abstract ideas as sees (and walks and talks), and if patently it is individual humans who do the latter, then there is a plurality of intellectual thinkers. Similarly, the agent who acts, having chosen to do so, is the same subject who previously considered various courses of action antecedent to choosing, where considering options is a matter of contemplating abstractly specified possibilities, and so is an intellectual activity. Hence it is one and the same agent who contemplates, deliberates, chooses, and acts (ibid., 76.2).[6] Here there is power in Aquinas's arguments against the idea that an Aristotelian approach must lead to the idea of a single intellect (although it is less clear who has the better case so far as Aristotle's own direction of speculation is concerned).

Third, even while arguing that there is a plurality of rational souls corresponding to the number of living human beings, Aquinas insists that there is no more than one soul per individual human being. Someone might suppose otherwise by reasoning as follows. The structure and life of a cabbage is due to a controlling form that organizes various processes so as to effect nutrition, growth, and reproduction. Specifying the form by its proper effects and abbreviating those as "vegetative," we can say that a cabbage has a vegetative form or soul. Now, since a rabbit also engages in those characteristic activities, it too must have a vegetative soul; furthermore, since it also exhibits sensation, appetite, and locomotion, it has a sensory soul besides. Finally, since a human

---

[5] For a detailed account of the terms of this debate and the background to it, see Martin Stone, "The Soul's Relation to the Body: Thomas Aquinas, Siger of Brabant and the Parisian Debate on Monopsychism," in T. Crane and S. Patterson (eds.) *History of the Mind–Body Problem* (London: Routledge, 2000) 34–69.

[6] See also *De unitate intellectus contra Averroistas*, and the translation and analysis in Ralph McInerny, *Aquinas against the Averroists: On There Being Only One Intellect* (West Lafayette, IN: Purdue University Press, 1993).

being has both sets of powers, plus the additional ones constitutive of rational life, the human being also has a rational soul. So, a cabbage has one soul; a rabbit has two; and a human being three. Aquinas rejects this conclusion by advancing what we might term the "principle of hierarchical subsumption": namely, that lower-level powers are subsumed under higher-level ones. This has several merits to which I shall return shortly. For the moment, however, I wish to return to the remaining representatives of the Franciscan order, Scotus and Ockham.

Like Aquinas, Scotus is troubled by the Averroistic position that all human beings share a common intellect. Scotus observes, for instance, that the ancient definition of human being as 'rational animal' has been standard among philosophers – indeed, that "No philosopher of any note can be found to deny this except that accursed Averroes in his commentary on *De anima* Book III" (*Ordinatio* IV.43.2c; tr. *Phil. Writings*, p. 138). That definition provided Aristotle with an illustration of how definitions may be essence-specifying, for it first locates human beings within the genus of animals (animate substances) but then differentiates them from other animals by identifying their possession of the faculty of reason. If, however, Averroes were correct in his claim that intellect is a separate substance, conjoined to a human being only *per accidens* through its effects on an intrinsic faculty such as the imagination, then rationality would not be essential to being human.

Of course, pointing to unwelcome consequences of a position does not show that it is false; so, like Aquinas, Scotus sets out to argue the case for the rational soul's being, properly speaking, the form of a human being, and so distinct for each human being. His argument is somewhat similar to Aquinas's, to the effect that it is part of the intrinsic nature of a human being to engage in reflection, and thereby to achieve understanding of abstract issues. Such understanding, however, is a proper effect of the intellectual soul. Therefore, that by which one reflects is an intellectual soul, and since the powers one exercises derive from one's formal nature, it follows that the intellect is part of the essence of a human being. Thus, a human being is a rational animal *per se*.

Involved in both Scotus's and Aquinas's reasoning is the idea that intellectual activity is a non-sensory process, due to the immaterial nature of its objects: universals, essences, and so on, according to one's particular theory. Therefore it is not located in a part of the human body but is attributable simply to human beings as rational animals. Again, like Aquinas, Scotus also argues for our possession of a rational/intellectual faculty through considering the nature of voluntary action. Scotus's argument, however, proceeds via the thought that if volition were simply the exercise of material causality then both it and its effects would be necessitated, whereas the human will is not determined to its effects (that is, it is not determined to its choices). Freedom of will implies a non-deterministic rational nature that is, in part at least, outside the ordinary causal order.

It is a general feature of Scotus that he inclines to complexity in his theories, whereas Aquinas inclines to simplicity. Thus, while Scotus agrees that there is a single unitary human *soul*, he also maintains that there is a further substantial form of corporeity (*forma corporeitatis*) belonging to the human body as such, apart from whatever nature it possesses in metaphysical consequence of its having a rational soul. An implication of this view is that the rational soul is not the exclusive source of the being of the body. Although the soul confers upon the body the kind of being that constitutes vegetative and sensory bodily life, the body also has corporeal existence as a quantitatively bounded entity, and it acquires this existence through the form of corporeity.[7] For Aquinas, by contrast, the human animal has its being exclusively by virtue of its unitary soul.

Ockham moves yet further, and consciously so, from Aquinas's unifying conception, adding at the same time a thoroughgoing skepticism regarding our grasp of the soul through either immediate experience (in the style of Augustine) or reasoning (in the manner of Aquinas and Scotus). Ockham's avowed point is not to deny that there is an immaterial soul inhering in us, or an immaterial aspect to our nature, but to say that if we believe this to be so, then it is through faith rather than observation or inference. He writes:

> If we understand by 'intellective soul' an immaterial and incorruptible form that exists in the entire body and entire in each part [as was maintained by Bonaventure, Aquinas, and Scotus], it cannot be evidently known by reason or experience that such a form exists in us, nor that the understanding proper to such a substance exists in us, nor that such a soul is a form of the body. Whatever the Philosopher [Aristotle] thought of this does not now concern me, because it seems that he remains doubtful about it wherever he speaks of it. These three things are only matters of belief.
>
> (*Quodlibet* I.10; tr. Boehner, p. 143)

Ockham offers less an alternative theory than a series of challenges. Even if we know from experience that we engage in abstract reflection, he says, how do we know that this reflection is not attributable to a corporeal and corruptible form? Furthermore, even if we were confident that our understanding presupposes the existence of an incorruptible substance, how would we know that this is attributable to our formal nature, rather than perhaps being (as the Averroists hold) an effect of something operating through us as a cause of our thoughts? Ockham goes on to maintain that if such a spiritual or immaterial form were present, it could not inform the body directly; but since the living body must

---

[7] See Scotus, *Ordinatio*, IV.2.3.

be structured by a form, the animating principle must therefore be a sensory one. Like Scotus, however, Ockham thinks that the body possesses the form of corporeity independently, on the grounds that a body that is first living, then dead, then perhaps miraculously reanimated would be one and the same body. Thus he finds himself moving back in the direction of a plurality of forms – corporeal, sensory, and intellectual – but without much confidence in the possibility of philosophy determining their relationship, or even their intrinsic natures (see also Chapter 46).

FROM SCHOLASTICISM TO SKEPTICISM, AND BEYOND

Almost more interesting than Ockham's views on the relation of body and soul are his anticipations of difficulties that would come to loom ever larger in subsequent scholastic and post-scholastic thought. In casting doubt on what can be known of the mind's metaphysical nature through attending to mental acts, for instance, he not only challenges Augustinians, Neoplatonists, and Platonists, but he also prefigures a line of objection to Descartes – namely, that the mind's nature is not transparent to itself. Likewise, in probing the traditional arguments from the abstractness of the contents of thought to the immateriality of mental acts, he might be viewed as opening a door to the possibility of theories of mental computation that seek to show how intentional content can be carried by materially realized operations. Again, his suggestion that an immaterial form could not operate upon the body directly points to difficulties about causal interaction and the inherence in the same substance of material and non-material attributes or forms – difficulties that have bedeviled both substance and attribute dualists from Descartes to the present day.

Subsequent centuries saw many developments of Aristotelian approaches and reassertions of broadly Platonic ones, but the general drift of medieval and scholastic thought was toward an increasing skepticism about what might be demonstrated, culminating in the modern rejection of the whole apparatus of substantial forms in favor of quantitative understandings of bodies and their natures. In 1513, the fifth Lateran Council approved the Bull *Apostolici regiminis*, according to which:

We condemn and reprove all those who assert that the intellective soul is mortal, or that there is only one in all human beings, or who make this question a doubtful one. This is because the intellective soul is not only in its own right and of its nature the form of the human body . . . but it is also immortal, and there can be, are, and must be as many intellective souls as there are bodies into which an intellective soul is infused.[8]

---

[8] See C. F. J. Martin, "On a Mistake Commonly Made in Accounts of Sixteenth-Century Discussions of the Immortality of the Soul," *American Catholic Philosophical Quarterly* 69 (1995) 29–37, to which I am indebted for the translation of the Bull.

Yet despite the confident, authoritative tone of this declaration, the very fact that it needed to be composed and promulgated suggests that the tide was turning against the views upheld there. Indeed, whatever the threats of condemnation and reproval, the question *had* become a doubtful one in the minds of increasing numbers of philosophers, and the succeeding centuries have hardly restored certainty to the Christian Aristotelian account of these matters.

That said, there is real merit in the position developed by Aquinas. Setting aside the question of whether there is any cogency in the traditional Thomistic proofs of the immateriality of intellect,[9] Aquinas's principle of hierarchical subsumption suggests an approach to the unification of levels within a substance that is relevant to present-day attempts to reconcile physical, biological, and psychological causality within human beings. It also has implications for the description and explanation of human behavior, since it suggests (in a manner later championed by Wittgenstein) that initial characterizations of human and non-human animals as being engaged in the same activity, as identified through behavioral routines, may fail for want of recognizing that what would be the same activity, absent higher-order subsumption and direction, may be different on account of it. Dogs and human beings may both eat the same food from the same dish, but a man's consuming it may be his dining, whereas a dog's will only be his eating.

The other side of the Aquinian/Aristotelian coin is an insistence upon the bodily aspect of our nature, reminding us that we are animals – be it, perhaps, of a unique sort – and that our life as persons consists largely in bodily activities. Even the intellectual and spiritual aspects that may transcend matter are, nevertheless, expressed in word and deed. Thus any hope of living again recognizably as persons of the same basic sort must rest on some such belief as Aquinas derived from Paul – namely, that we may be recreated as part of a divine plan. The emphasis on human bodiliness is a useful correction to the old but recurrent dualist tendency to identify persons with unobservable selves temporally housed inside visible frames. Seven centuries later, however, the main threat to the scholastic–Aristotelian understanding of human nature comes not from ancient dualism but from modern materialism.

---

[9] For contrasting assessments of the traditional Thomistic arguments see Robert Pasnau, "Aquinas and the Content Fallacy," *Modern Schoolman* 75 (1998) 293–314, and John Haldane, "The Metaphysics of Intellect(ion)," *Proceedings of the American Catholic Philosophical Association* 80 (2007) 39–55.

THE SOUL'S FACULTIES

DAG NIKOLAUS HASSE

Most medieval thinkers assume that the human soul has several faculties or powers: basic faculties such as digestion or growth, more elaborate faculties such as movement, vision, or imagination, and the characteristically human faculties of will and intellect. This was the mainstream position, but it was not left unquestioned in the later Middle Ages and in early modern philosophy. Several nominalists, for instance, argue that the powers of the soul are nothing but different names for the soul itself, as it is active in different ways. Later, in the seventeenth century, mechanistic philosophers such as René Descartes claim that there is no real distinction between power and act, nor between soul and powers. Descartes reserves the term 'soul' for the mind, and so reduces the number of powers drastically; he claims that all lower powers, such as sense perception or imagination, are equivalent either to the mind or certain powers of the body. Even Thomistic authors of the sixteenth and seventeenth centuries, who usually defend the theory of the faculties, at times question the traditional set of faculties and reduce their number. Francisco Suárez, for example, holds that common sense, imagination, estimation, and memory are in fact one power, because all these functions can be attributed to one faculty.[1]

Nevertheless, in spite of the criticisms voiced by nominalist and early modern philosophers, medieval faculty psychology itself was well supported by arguments that have their origin in Greek philosophy. In the *Republic*, for example, Plato proposes a threefold division of the soul into reason, spirit, and desire. He bases this theory on the fact that there are conflicts in the soul: we may desire an object and at the same time reject it, as when we desire to drink something but reject it because we think it is bad for us. This can be explained, he believes,

---

[1] John Buridan, *Quaest. de anima* II.4, ed. Sobol; René Descartes, *Traité de l'homme* (ed. Adam and Tannery, XI: 201–2); Francisco Suárez, *Commentaria in De anima* 8.1–2. See Dennis Des Chene, *Life's Form: Late Aristotelian Conceptions of the Soul* (Ithaca, NY: Cornell University Press, 2000) pp. 143–51.

only by assuming that the soul has distinct parts that can come into conflict with each other (435e–439d).

Aristotle is the true founding figure of faculty theory. In the *De anima*, he distinguishes many different powers of the soul. Unlike Plato, however, he rarely calls them "parts" of the soul, and his principal argument for the existence of such powers is different from Plato's. Not only are the soul's powers clearly distinct logically, he says, but we also observe that they are distributed variously in nature. They, in fact, form a hierarchy: the lowest plants have only one or two powers, whereas the more complex animals already have a fuller set, and the highest animal – the human being – has the fullest set, including thinking and deliberation in addition to the powers of the lower animals. The soul is both the principle of these powers and defined by them (*De anima* II.2–3).

The Greek medical tradition reinforced the trend of distinguishing faculties of the soul by localizing some of them in different parts of the brain.[2] Galen, for instance, argued that physical damage to the brain often does not affect the entire soul, but only one or two functions, such as phantasy or memory, while the others remain intact. Nemesius of Emesa, in his *De natura hominis* – an influential treatise in Greek, Arabic, and Latin culture – assigned various internal powers of the soul to the different ventricles of the brain (ch. 13).

The high point of medieval faculty theory was classical Arabic philosophy and later medieval Latin philosophy. In the early Middle Ages, faculty psychology was not yet dominant among Christian authors, who were deeply influenced by the Augustinian idea that the soul is an indivisible unity. Hence they widely accepted that the soul and its faculties are identical.[3] When Greek and Arabic texts on faculty psychology were translated into Latin in the twelfth and thirteenth centuries, however, the discussion changes. Albert the Great is an early witness to this change. Albert holds – against the earlier tradition – that the soul's faculties form a unity with the soul only in the sense that soul and faculties together form a *totum potestativum* ("a totality of powers"). Ontologically they are distinct. On this matter, Albert adopts Avicenna's thesis that the organic and non-organic faculties emanate from one substance, the soul, which exists independently of both its actions and its body.[4]

Avicenna is the single most influential source (apart from Aristotle) for medieval faculty theory, in both the Arabic and the Latin world. He strongly

---

[2] See also Plato, *Timaeus*, 69c–73d, where the three parts of the soul are located in brain, heart, and liver.

[3] See Pius Künzle, *Das Verhältnis der Seele zu ihren Potenzen: Problemgeschichtliche Untersuchungen von Augustin bis und mit Thomas von Aquin* (Fribourg: Universitätsverlag, 1956).

[4] Albert the Great, *Sent.* I.3.34c; Avicenna, *De anima* (*Shifāʾ*) V.1 (ed. Rahman, p. 208; Van Riet, p. 80).

influenced the general principles of medieval faculty psychology and its detailed treatment of individual faculties.[5] Thus, this chapter will present his system of faculties first, before turning to disputed issues.

AVICENNA'S THEORY OF THE FACULTIES

Avicenna bases his distinction between the faculties on systematic criteria and on observational evidence. His basic principle is that "each faculty – insofar as it is a faculty – is such because from it originates a primary action that belongs to it" (*De anima* [*Shifāʾ*] V.7, ed. Rahman, p. 252; Van Riet, pp. 157–8). A faculty is identifiable by being the cause of an action that it does not share with any other faculty. Hence, the faculty of vision is identified by its primary action, perceiving color, although it also has many secondary actions, such as the perception of black or white. Furthermore, the faculties, Avicenna says, may impede and distract each other from their proper actions (ibid.). This echoes Plato's argument that conflicts in the soul point to the existence of the soul's parts. Avicenna adduces observational evidence to justify the differentiation between powers: unripe fruits possess the nutritive but not the reproductive faculty; decrepit animals possess the nutritive faculty, but they lack that of growth.[6] Avicenna thus adopts the Aristotelian principle that the faculties form a hierarchy and exist independently of each other in nature.

Avicenna's hierarchy of faculties begins with a set that is characteristic of plants but that also exists in animals and human beings – namely, nutrition, growth, and reproduction. These faculties are served by the so-called "subservient faculties" of attraction, retention, digestion, and excretion, which are often discussed in medical texts and which are concerned with the nourishment pertaining to the bodily organs: they attract it, keep it, digest it, and finally remove it.[7]

The animal faculties are generally divided into motive and perceptive faculties. Avicenna distinguishes between two kinds of motive faculties: those that give the impulse and order to move, such as desire and anger, and the faculty that performs the movement, a power distributed in the nerves and muscles, which prompts the muscles and ligaments to contract and extend. Like the majority of ancient and medieval authors, Avicenna holds that there are five external senses:

---

[5] This influence continues in the Renaissance; see Katharine Park, "The Organic Soul," in C. Schmitt *et al.* (eds.) *The Cambridge History of Renaissance Philosophy* (Cambridge: Cambridge University Press, 1988) 464–84, especially the table on p. 466, which presents a division of faculties typical for Renaissance philosophical textbooks.

[6] Avicenna, *Psychology* (*Najāt*), tr. Rahman, p. 24.

[7] Avicenna, *De anima* (*Shifāʾ*) I.5, ed. Rahman, p. 51; Van Riet, p. 101; *Psychology* (*Najāt*), p. 37; *Canon*, I.1.6.3 (ed. 1877, p. 68; Latin tr. f. 23vb).

sight, hearing, smell, taste, and touch. He also mentions, without adopting it, the position that there are eight external senses, on the grounds that touch is a genus of four distinct faculties discerning hot and cold, dry and moist, hard and soft, rough and smooth respectively.[8]

In addition to these, Avicenna ascribes to animals and human beings five so-called "internal senses" (*al-ḥawāss al-bāṭina*; *sensus interiores*): common sense, imagination, the cogitative/imaginative faculty, estimation, and memory.[9] Although the term 'internal senses' was coined in Arabic philosophy and popularized in the Arabic and Latin worlds through the work of Avicenna, the ultimate source of the doctrine is Aristotle's discussion of the soul's higher perceptual activities (*De anima* III.1–3; *Parva naturalia*). Aristotle observed, for instance, that we perceive ourselves perceiving, that we distinguish between sense data from different senses (such as sweet and white), that images remain in the soul after the object has disappeared, and that post-sensory images (he calls them *phantasmata*) play a major role in memory, dreams, sensory illusions, and the choice of actions, especially among animals. Avicenna draws on Aristotle, the anonymous Arabic *On sense and sensibilia*, and other Graeco-Arabic material, and in his hands the various doctrines concerning the internal senses develop into a systematic and comprehensive theory – an achievement that counts among the most original contributions of medieval faculty theory.

Avicenna's distinction between the five internal senses is based on two particularly influential principles. First, the faculties differ in that some of them *receive* sensory forms, whereas others *preserve* them. Second, some faculties perceive the "form" (*ṣūra, forma*) of the sensed thing – that is, they deal with data transmitted to them by the external senses, such as the shape and color of the wolf. Other faculties perceive so-called "intentions" (*maʿānī, intentiones*) – that is, attributes of objects that have a connotation for the perceiver that the external senses cannot perceive, such as hostility or friendliness (*De anima* [*Shifāʾ*] I.5). These principles, which were subsequently adopted by Thomas Aquinas and others

---

[8] *De anima* (*Shifāʾ*) I.5, ed. Rahman, pp. 41–3, 73; Van Riet, pp. 83–5, 141; *Psychology* (*Najāt*), tr. Rahman, pp. 26–7.

[9] The fivefold distinction of internal senses appears in Avicenna's main philosophical works. In his medical *Canon*, Avicenna mentions that the physicians recognize only three internal senses because they assign one faculty to each of the three ventricles of the brain and do not distinguish between common sense and imagination (anterior ventricle), nor between the imaginative/cogitative faculty and estimation (middle ventricle). This is because they are concerned only with the possible areas of injury. In the *Canon*, Avicenna also mentions a discussion among philosophers about whether memory and recollection might in fact be two faculties (Avicenna, *Canon*, I.1.6.5 [ed. 1877, pp. 71–2, Latin tr. f. 24v–25r]). The fivefold distinction of internal senses is not yet established in Avicenna's very early *Compendium on the Soul* (ed. Landauer, pp. 358–61); see Harry A. Wolfson, "The Internal Senses in Latin, Arabic and Hebrew Philosophical Texts," *Harvard Theological Review* 28 (1935) pp. 95–100.

(*Summa theol.* 1a 78.4c), allow Avicenna to distinguish systematically between the internal senses.

The common sense is located in the front of the brain's front ventricle. It is the place where all sensory forms are received and where such judgments are formed as that this moving thing is black. This, rather than the external faculties, is the power that *truly* senses, inasmuch as it is the center of the senses. The faculty of imagination, the second internal sense, is the storage place of the sensory forms; it does not perceive, but retains. It is located in the rear part of the front ventricle of the brain. The third faculty is called the "imaginative faculty" in non-rational animals and the "cogitative faculty" in human beings. In contrast to all other internal senses, it neither receives nor preserves forms, but acts upon them, combining and separating forms and intentions. This faculty, which resides in the middle ventricle, is responsible for the production of unreal images; its existence explains the hallucinations of mad, sick, or dreaming people. The cogitative faculty has a further important function in human thought: whereas the intellect is able to think in terms of universal concepts, the cogitative faculty combines particular concepts and thus aids the intellect.[10] The fourth internal sense is estimation (*wahm, aestimatio*), located in the rear part of the middle ventricle: it perceives intentions and forms judgments on their basis, such as the sheep's judgment that this wolf is to be fled. Memory, the last internal sense, is mainly responsible for the storage of intentions; it resides in the rear ventricle of the brain.

The number of internal senses becomes a matter of dispute in later medieval philosophy, since, unlike Avicenna, Averroes and Aquinas recognize only four internal senses (common sense, imagination, cogitative faculty, and memory): Averroes rejects the concept of an estimative faculty, whereas Aquinas makes estimation the animal counterpart to the human cogitative faculty, as will be apparent below.[11]

Avicenna further distinguishes two non-organic faculties: the practical intellect, whose main function is to govern the bodily faculties, and the theoretical intellect, which is concerned with grasping universal forms. A well-known doctrine of Avicenna's is his distinction between four theoretical intellects; in some places he calls them "powers," but in his most detailed descriptions it is obvious that the four intellects are four different relations (*nisab*) of the

---

[10] Dimitri Gutas, "Intuition and Thinking: The Evolving Structure of Avicenna's Epistemology," in R. Wisnovsky (ed.) *Aspects of Avicenna* (Princeton, NJ: Princeton University Press, 2001) 1–38.

[11] Averroes, *Epitome of Parva naturalia*, ed. Blumberg, pp. 42–3, tr. Blumberg, p. 26 (Blumberg's translation of *quwwa mumayyiza* ("discriminative faculty") as "estimative faculty" is misleading); Averroes, *Commentarium magnum De anima* III.6 (ed. Crawford, pp. 415–16); Aquinas, *Summa theol.* 1a 78.4c. See also note 9 above.

theoretical faculty to its intelligible objects. They are therefore not faculties of the soul, but different states of the same intellect that represent different levels of actualization and of intellectual development (see also Chapter 23).[12]

THE ORGAN AND MEDIUM OF TOUCH

A question of great disagreement in faculty psychology up to the sixteenth century concerned the faculty of touch. The discussion was sparked by the fact that Aristotelian and Arabic theories of touch were based on different epochs of medicine, inasmuch as Aristotle did not yet know about nerves. (These were first distinguished from veins and arteries by physicians in Alexandria, who had carried out dissections in the third century BCE.) Aristotle had maintained that the organ of touch lies within the body, close to the heart, and that although we do not usually recognize a medium of touch, there exists one within us, our flesh (*De anima* II.11). In contrast, Avicenna and other Arabic philosophers, attempting to make Peripatetic philosophy compatible with the medical knowledge of their time, held that the organ of touch is the collection of nerves distributed throughout the body's flesh and skin, and that there is no medium at all. The arguments of the Arabic authors are partly anatomical, partly philosophical: if flesh is not accompanied by nerves, it does not have the sense of touch; there is touch not only in flesh, but also in bones and teeth; finally, objects of touch are dangerous or conducive to the life of the animal, which is why the entire body is the organ of touch and why the objects are in direct contact with the organ.[13]

Subsequent medieval philosophers were thus offered two rival theories. Among the scholastics, there were many who avoided the problem (or perhaps did not see it) and who simply quoted one of the two positions. Others argued for one side against the other, or else proposed a compromise, as did, for example, John Blund and the *Summa fratris Alexandri*.[14] In this discussion, Albert the Great stands out because he changed his mind on the issue. In his early *De homine*, he distinguishes between an ontological and an epistemological meaning of 'touch.' In the first sense, touch is what makes an animal soul an animal soul – it is its perfection; in the second sense, it is a faculty and a part of the soul (*De homine* 33.1 [ed. Cologne, XXVII.2: 246b]). When considered ontologically, as

[12] Avicenna, *De anima* (*Shifā'*) I.5 (ed. Rahman, pp. 45–50; Van Riet, pp. 90–99); *Psychology (Najāt)* (tr. Rahman, pp. 32–5); see Dag Nikolaus Hasse, *Avicenna's De anima in the Latin West: The Formation of a Peripatetic Philosophy of the Soul 1160–1300* (London: Warburg Institute, 2000) pp. 177–83.
[13] Avicenna, *De anima* (*Shifā'*) II.3; Albert the Great, *De anima* II.3.34.
[14] Blund, *Tractatus de anima* XVI, ed. Callus and Hunt pp. 58, 60; Alexander of Hales *et al.*, *Summa theologica* II, pars I, IV.1.2.2.1. See Hasse, *Avicenna's De anima*, pp. 98–106.

a *perfectio*, the organ of touch is the entire body (in particular, nerves, flesh, and skin), and there is no medium. When considered epistemologically, however, as a *potentia*, flesh and skin are the first recipients of an impression from outside, which is then passed on to the nerve – this is a faint echo of Aristotle's original theory that flesh is the medium (ibid., 33.3 [252b–254a]). This – Albert's early position – can be reconciled with the Arabic and medical tradition, but not with Aristotle. Hence, he has to counter Aristotle's principal argument for the existence of a medium, which is that without a medium the organ would be in direct contact with the object, with the result that perception would not occur (*De an.* II.11, 423b20–1). It is a fundamental principle for Aristotle that all perception is perception of form, not of matter, and hence that a direct contact between organ and material object does not result in perception. Albert's answer is that only the nerves of the brain require a medium; the nerves distributed through the rest of the body are able to be affected directly and in a very subtle way by the object. In this respect, then, touch differs from the other senses (*De homine* 33.3, p. 253b). However, in his later *De anima*, Albert changes his mind: "Wishing both to save the truth and to give reverence to the father of the philosophers, Aristotle, we say that flesh is the medium of touch" (II.3.34, ed. Cologne, VII.1: 147a). Albert is aware that he has to reconcile this position with medical theory, and therefore he adds the qualification that teeth and nerves are "flesh-like" insofar as they have the same complexion as flesh. Albert's change of mind testifies to two developments in the second half of the thirteenth century: the growing authority of Aristotle, and the growing tendency to sacrifice the physiological part of faculty theory if it appears in conflict with philosophical teaching.[15]

In later medieval faculty theory, several attempts were made to reconcile Aristotle's theory of touch with later theories. One solution was to save Aristotle's view that the organ lies close to the heart by distinguishing between a primary organ of touch, the heart, and a secondary organ, the nerve.[16] Another strategy was to acknowledge the empirical incompleteness of Aristotle's theory and explain it in terms of the developing history of anatomy. Averroes first took this approach, in commenting on Aristotle's statement that the organ of touch lies "within" the body (423b23): "This is in accordance with what came out later (after Aristotle's death) through anatomy, namely that the nerves play a part in touch and movement. Therefore, what Aristotle knew in theory, later

[15] See Mark Jordan, "The Disappearance of Galen in Thirteenth-Century Philosophy and Theology," in A. Zimmermann *et al.* (eds.) *Mensch und Natur im Mittelalter* (Berlin: De Gruyter, 1992) 703–17.
[16] D. N. Hasse, "Pietro d'Abano's 'Conciliator' and the Theory of the Soul in Paris," in J. Aertsen *et al.* (eds.) *Nach der Verurteilung von 1277* (Berlin: De Gruyter, 2001) 635–53, esp. pp. 641–5.

was apparent through experience" (*Comm. magnum de anima* II.108, p. 298). Averroes interprets the term "within" as referring not to something close to the heart, but to the as yet unknown nerves below the surface of the skin. Aristotle had "smelled" the right solution, even though "the science of dissection had not been perfected in his time," as Peter of Abano put it in the early fourteenth century (*Conciliator* diff. 42, ed. 1565, f. 64va). This historical solution to the doctrinal problem appears in a good number of *De anima* commentaries, whereas other authors, such as Thomas Aquinas, generally avoid discussion of physiological issues. In any event, the case of the nerves is a good indication of the willingness of medieval authors to consider medical and empirical arguments in the philosophy of the soul.

THE TRANSMISSION OF ODORS

The question of whether odors are transmitted materially or immaterially was discussed by many scholastic authors, from Albert the Great to Suárez. The origin of the discussion lies in a disagreement between Avicenna and Averroes, which in turn goes back to ancient disputes. Plato had maintained that all odor is vapor or mist (*Timaeus* 66e), which most likely is the position Aristotle was targeting when he refuted the theory that odor is smoky evaporation (*De sensu* 5, 443a21–b2).[17] The ancient commentary tradition paid considerable attention to the question and introduced empirical evidence, such as that vultures smell dead bodies in places too distant for material particles to have traveled to the perceiver.[18] In light of this ancient background, Avicenna distinguished between three different explanations of how odors reach the organ of smell: on the first account, small particles are issued from the odorous body and mix with the air; on the second, the medium is changed by the odorous body; on the third, there is transmission of effect without any change in the medium, the function of the medium being merely to make transmission possible.[19] The first two explanations are viable, he says, and are supported by evidence, such as that decaying apples shrink because they issue odorous particles, which suggests an evaporation theory. The third explanation is untenable, however, because smells may remain in the medium after the smelling object has disappeared. Avicenna acknowledges the objection that vultures fly to distant places for prey – for example, to a battlefield in a different country – and that material particles or

---

[17] Aristotle's own view is not entirely clear; in *De sensu* 2, 438b20–7, he seems to embrace the smoky evaporation theory.

[18] Richard Sorabji, *The Philosophy of the Commentators, 200–600 AD: A Sourcebook* (Ithaca, NY: Cornell University Press, 2005) I: 47–52, III: 108–9.

[19] Avicenna, *De anima (Shifāʾ)* II.4, ed. Rahman, pp. 77–8; Van Riet p. 148.

alterations of the air cannot bridge such a distance, but he replies that vultures probably see rather than smell the dead bodies, because they circle at extreme heights.[20]

A different position was taken by Ibn al-Ṭayyib, a contemporary of Avicenna, who favors a position similar to Avicenna's third alternative: he claims that forms are imprinted upon the air as an immaterial (*rūḥānī*) impression. This must be so, he argues, because the air receives contrary properties (as when the images of a white and a black man are transmitted through the same region of air), whereas the corporeal impression of contrary properties is impossible.[21] Averroes also disagrees with Avicenna, without naming his opponent. He repeats the vulture argument, extending it to bees and tigers, and he concludes that odors exist in their medium in the same way that colors exist in the transparent medium – namely, with immaterial existence (*wujūd rūḥānī; esse spirituale*) – whereas they exist materially in the odorous body. He concedes that winds have an impact on the transmission of odors that they do not have on colors, but he responds that there are degrees of immateriality: colors are more immaterial (*rūḥānī; spiritualis*) than odors (*Comm. magnum de anima* II.97, pp. 276–8). Averroes also uses the argument from the reception of contrary qualities to argue more generally against the material existence of sensible forms in the medium.[22]

The scholastic tradition generally preferred Averroes's over Avicenna's theory, and often cited the vultures' long-distance sense of smell. Albert the Great, for instance, pointed out that the material theory in effect dispenses with a medium altogether, inasmuch as odors hit the organ directly (*De an.* II.3.25 [ed. Cologne VII.1: 135b]). This again has the problematic consequence that perception would result from direct contact between organ and object. On the other hand, an immaterial theory of transmission was difficult to reconcile with several pieces of evidence: the influence of wind, the shrinking apple, the hand that smells after touching something odorous, the interference of odors in the medium, and the odor's remaining in the medium after the disappearance of the odorous body. As a solution to this problem, Aquinas, John Buridan, and others argue that there exists evaporation, but only in the immediate vicinity of the odorous object. The remaining distance is bridged by an immaterial medium, which is affected qualitatively by the perceptible object.[23]

[20] Avicenna, *De anima* (*Shifāʾ*) II.4, ed. Rahman, pp. 78–81; Van Riet, pp. 148–54.
[21] See Cleophea Ferrari, "Der Duft des Apfels: Abū l-Faraj ʿAbdallāh ibn aṭ-Ṭayyib und sein Kommentar zu den *Kategorien* des Aristoteles," in V. Celluprica and C. D'Ancona Costa (eds.) *Aristotele e i suoi esegeti neoplatonici* (Naples: Bibliopolis, 2004) 85–106, esp. pp. 98–100. The argument from the reception of contrary qualities is already in Alexander of Aphrodisias; see Sorabji, *Sourcebook* I: 47–8.
[22] Averroes, *Epitome of Parva naturalia*, ed. Blumberg, pp. 23–4; tr. Blumberg, pp. 15–16.
[23] Aquinas, *In De anima* II.20; Buridan, *Quaest. de anima* II.20, ed. Patar, pp. 390–1.

THE ESTIMATIVE FACULTY

The estimative faculty was the most successful addition to Aristotle's faculty theory;[24] it was adopted by numerous writers in Arabic, Hebrew, and Latin. Medieval Latin authors were divided over a number of issues concerning the estimative faculty and its object, intentions, including whether estimation exists in animals only or in human beings as well; whether the intentions are derived from the perceived thing or from the processing of sensible forms; and, finally, what kind of judgments are made by estimation.

As to the first issue, Avicenna's contention that estimation is a faculty shared by animals and human beings was challenged by both Averroes and Thomas Aquinas. According to Averroes, although human beings and animals pass judgments about the intention of a specific image, human beings do so through the intellect, whereas animals employ a faculty without name, "which Avicenna calls estimation."[25] In the *Incoherence of the Incoherence*, Averroes claims that the assumption of an estimative faculty in animals can be dispensed with altogether, since all of its functions are performed by the faculty of imagination (tr. Van den Bergh, p. 336). Non-rational animals lack the cogitative faculty of human beings (he also calls this the "discriminative faculty"), which "separates and abstracts" individual intentions from the perceived images, for instance the intention of this individual man and the intention of this individual horse (*Comm. magnum de anima* II.63, pp. 225–6).

Aquinas further develops Averroes's line, relegating the estimative faculty to the animal realm. When animals perceive individual intentions, they are able to flee the harmful and pursue the useful. The estimative faculty is a faculty of instinct directly tied to actions: intentions are apprehended only insofar as they are the end or starting point of an animal's acting or being acted on. Human beings also compare individual intentions and apprehend the individual as existing under a common nature. In virtue of this, they cognize this human being as it is this human being, or this piece of wood as it is this piece of wood. This human faculty must thus be different from the animal estimative power, and Aquinas calls it the "cogitative power" or "particular reason." Only human beings have this faculty, because it operates in the vicinity and under the guidance of the intellect.[26]

---

[24] See Deborah L. Black, "Estimation (*Wahm*) in Avicenna: The Logical and Psychological Dimensions," *Dialogue* 32 (1993) 219–58, and Hasse, *Avicenna's De anima*, pp. 127–53.

[25] Averroes, *Epitome of Parva naturalia*, ed. Blumberg, p. 39; tr. Blumberg, p. 24.

[26] *In De anima* II.13, *Summa theol.* 1a 81.3c. Robert Pasnau, *Thomas Aquinas on Human Nature* (Cambridge: Cambridge University Press, 2002) pp. 267–78.

Albert the Great, and like him many other writers of the thirteenth century, take the opposite, Avicennian standpoint. Estimation is a faculty shared by both animals and humans. The human faculty of estimation is sometimes helped and advised by reason to pursue this or to avoid that, but it is impossible for estimation to understand individual intentions as falling under a common notion. This is the work of reason. Estimation is a faculty intimately connected to imagination, since it grasps intentions in this and that image. In fact, it is the extension of imagination into the realm of action.[27]

A second issue involving the estimative faculty concerns the ontological status of intentions. Avicenna had maintained that "some faculties perceive the forms of the sense-perceptible object and some perceive the intentions of the sense-perceptible object."[28] The form of the wolf is exemplified by its shape and color, the intention of the wolf by its hostility. In Avicenna's theory, an intention is not a meaning assigned by the perceiver to a perceived form, nor something abstracted from a perceived form; it is itself an object of perception, an immaterial thing that accompanies a particular sense-perceptible form and that is always grasped in connection with such a form.[29]

Later writers advanced conflicting theories of intentions as objects of estimation. John Blund, for instance, around the start of the thirteenth century, takes Avicenna's position to one extreme, claiming that intentions are properties of an object of the world, such as the quality of the wolf that makes the sheep flee. What is received by estimation is not the intention – that is, the property itself (as in Avicenna's theory) – but rather an image or likeness of the intention (*Tractatus de anima*, ed. Callus and Hunt, pp. 68–71). This realist interpretation of intentions was not shared by other writers. For Averroes, intentions were intentions *of* images; that is, they were not objects of perception on the same level as images (or sensory forms), but something like the meaning that an image has for the perceiver. Human beings are able to separate and abstract the intentions from the images.[30] Albert the Great follows Averroes on this point, arguing that the estimative faculty extracts intentions from the apprehended

---

[27] *De anima* III.1.2, ed. Cologne VII.1: 168; *De homine* 39.3, ed. Cologne, XXVII.2: 295b: "extensio phantasiae in praxim." Examples of authors who adopt the Avicennian standpoint are John Blund, William of Auvergne, Robert Grosseteste, Hugh of St. Cher, Roland of Cremona, John of La Rochelle, the *Summa fratris Alexandri*, Vincent of Beauvais, and Peter of Spain. The most elaborate discussions are in Blund, *Tractatus* XIX; John of La Rochelle, *Summa de anima* ch. 101; Peter of Spain, *Scientia libri de anima* (*Obras fil.* I: 319–23 [ed. 1941]).

[28] Avicenna, *De anima* (*Shifāʾ*) I.5, ed. Rahman, p. 43; Van Riet, p. 85.

[29] Avicenna, *De anima* (*Shifāʾ*) II.2, ed. Rahman, pp. 60–1; Van Riet, pp. 118–19; *Psychology* (*Najāt*), tr. Rahman, p. 39.

[30] *Comm. magnum De anima* II.63, ed. Crawford, p. 225; *Epitome of Parva naturalia*, ed. Blumberg, p. 39; tr. Blumberg, p. 24.

form. That is, intentions are the result of the internal processing of sensory forms. They are a product of abstraction.[31] In the ensuing scholastic discussions, both languages are adopted: that of intentions as objects of perception, as in Aquinas (*In de anima* II.13; *Summa theol.* 1a 78.4c), and that of intentions as products of abstraction, as in John Buridan (*Quaest. de anima*, ed. Patar, II.22).

A third issue concerns the content of estimative judgments.[32] The stock example of such a judgment, which was coined by Avicenna, is the sheep's judgment that the wolf is harmful and to be avoided. Like many other Arabic and Latin writers, Avicenna uses the term "judgment" in a wide sense that also covers non-linguistic acts. On this view, human beings and animals share several faculties that pass judgments, such as the external senses, common sense (for instance, "this moving thing is black"),[33] and estimation. The examples of such judgments are usually described in sentences, with the consequence that some writers, such as John Blund, were tempted to analyze animal judgments as consisting of several terms *(termini)* – for instance, 'this wolf' and 'to be fled' – in spite of the fact that animals do not have language (*Tractatus de anima*, pp. 68–71). Aquinas avoids this difficulty by distinguishing between "intellectual judgments" and "natural judgments." A natural judgment is prompted by instinct, which is the source of uniform actions: all swallows, for instance, form the natural judgment that nests should be made in a certain way (*Quaest. de veritate* 24.1c). In contrast, intellectual judgment is based upon inquiry and comparison, and is the source of free choice.

There were authors, however, who objected to the idea of animal judgments altogether. The background to this critique is a different notion of judgment that excludes non-linguistic judgments. William of Ockham thus maintains that the senses cannot judge, since judging presupposes the formation of a complex sentence – that is, a sentence composed of several terms, which can be assented to or dissented from.[34] Adam Wodeham shares this notion of judgment and infers from it that animals do not truly judge; they only appear to judge and to act like humans. The only form of cognition animals have is the non-complex, simple apprehension of something harmful or beneficial, which is directly followed by a certain reaction. This kind of cognition does not presuppose linguistic abilities.[35]

---

[31] *De homine* 37.1, ed. Cologne, XXVII.2: 284b; *De anima* II.4.7, ed. Cologne, VII.1: 157.
[32] See Dominik Perler, "Intentionality and Action: Medieval Discussions on the Cognitive Capacities of Animals," in M. Pacheco and J. Meirinhos (eds.) *Intellect et imagination dans la philosophie médiévale* (Turnhout: Brepols, 2006) I: 73–98.
[33] Avicenna, *De anima (Shifāʾ)* IV.1, ed. Rahman, p. 165; Van Riet, p. 6.
[34] *Ordinatio* prol. 1.1 (*Opera theol.* I: 16); *Reportatio* III.2 (*Opera theol.* VI: 85–6).
[35] *Lectura secunda* prol. 4.2.8 (ed. Wood and Gál, I: 99–100).

PROPHETIC FACULTIES: IMAGINATION, POWER
OF THE WILL, AND INTUITION

Faculty theory served many explanatory purposes in medieval philosophy. This is particularly true for phantasms, the post-sensory images that were employed to explain memory, dreams, sensory illusions, and also the abstraction process, and that eventually lead to intellectual knowledge. With respect to these topics, medieval authors moved largely in step with Aristotle. They clearly departed when discussing prophecy, however, because Aristotle did not share the belief of many contemporaries in the possibility of divinely inspired dreams (*On Divination in Sleep* ch. 1). Several Arabic and Jewish authors give philosophical explanations of prophetic phenomena such as visions or the working of miracles as relying – partly or even entirely – on the extraordinary disposition of human faculties.

Al-Fārābī, for instance, followed by other philosophers such as Avicenna and Maimonides, maintains that an extremely powerful faculty of imagination is a necessary condition for prophetic visions. Some human beings are naturally predisposed to receive in their faculty of imagination either particular forms or sensory imitations of universal forms from the active intellect – that is, from the lowest of the celestial intelligences (*On the Perfect State* IV.14.8–9). Maimonides emphasizes that the cerebral organ of imagination needs to be in the best balance of humors for such reception, and that prophets are born with such a perfect material disposition (*Guide of the Perplexed* II.36). Avicenna, on the other hand, distinguishes between different kinds of prophecy that depend on different faculties of the soul: the imaginative faculty, will, and intellectual intuition (*hads*). The extraordinary disposition of these three faculties explains, respectively, visions, the working of miracles, and the complete knowledge of all universal forms that are in the active intellect. Avicenna thus uses faculty theory to develop a naturalistic explanation of prophecy. Neither the working of miracles nor intellectual prophecy (which consists in intuiting middle terms that automatically trigger the emanation of intelligible forms from the active intellect) involves divine assistance. Only visions require a contact between the imaginative faculty and the divine realm.[36] Maimonides's explanation is less naturalistic: God bestows prophetic knowledge on whom he chooses, with the exception that he cannot turn stupid people into prophets (ibid., II.32).

The contention that prophecy is dependent on the disposition of certain faculties of the soul would be criticized by Thomas Aquinas, although he does

---

[36] *De anima* (*Shifāʾ*) IV.2 (on the imaginative faculty), IV.4 (on the power of the will), and V.6 (on intuition).

concede that a person may acquire a disposition for prophecy through repeated inspirations, and that such a person will more easily receive further inspirations. He also concedes that there is the phenomenon of "natural prophecy," which occurs when the faculties of imagination and intellect are put into contact with the celestial bodies and angels. This kind of prophecy does presuppose a specific balance of humors. Nevertheless, Aquinas maintains that natural prophecy ought to be distinguished from "divine prophecy," which is given by God and which is entirely dependent upon the divine will and not upon any form of preparedness.[37]

HOW THE SENSORY FACULTIES ASSIST
THE THEORETICAL INTELLECT

Medieval authors inherited from Aristotle various statements about the relation between the sensory and rational faculties that are difficult to reconcile. On the one hand, Aristotle stresses the separability of the intellect from the body and from the rest of the soul;[38] on the other hand, he maintains that "the soul never thinks without an image" (*phantasma*).[39] Avicenna holds that not all activities of the theoretical intellect are in need of phantasms, claiming that the sensory faculties bring to the intellect particular forms, which the intellect uses to abstract universal concepts and to form simply constructed premises based on empirical or transmitted data. These are the principles for the intellect's own activities of conception and judgment, for which the lower faculties are not needed, unless an additional principle needs to be obtained or an image retrieved. This happens more often at the beginning stages of intellectual life, but seldom with experienced and strong souls. In fact, if the intellect does not isolate itself from the lower faculties, they tend to divert it from its proper activity. Avicenna compares the lower faculties to a riding animal that is used to reach a certain place and afterwards becomes a useless instrument and a hindrance.[40]

Albert the Great follows Avicenna on this issue. In his commentary on Aristotle's *De anima*, he holds that all knowledge initially arises from the senses, but that once the intellect has acquired complete knowledge via the external and internal senses, it can be called the "acquired intellect" *(intellectus adeptus)* (see Chapter 23) and has no further need for the sensory faculties – just as someone

---

[37] *Quaest. de veritate* 12.1 ad 1, 12.3c, 12.4c. See Hasse, *Avicenna's De anima*, pp. 154–74.

[38] *De an.* II.2, 413b25–7; III.4, 429a18–b6.

[39] *De an.* III.7, 431a16–17. Cf. III.10, 432a8–9.

[40] *De anima (Shifāʾ)* V.3, ed. Rahman, pp. 221–3; Van Riet, pp. 102–5; *Psychology (Najāt)*, tr. Rahman, pp. 54–6.

who has used a vehicle to arrive in his home country can then dispense with it. Moreover, he claims that only the acquired intellect is an intellect in the full sense, since it is fully devoid of matter, unchangeable, and immortal, because it is not changed or influenced by the lower faculties (III.2.19). The *intellectus adeptus* is the result of a conjunction between the possible intellect and the active intellect, which is a part of the soul whose light is not always connected with the possible intellect. This *intellectus adeptus* is the last stage of an intellectual ascension in this life, which results in God-like knowledge of all intelligible forms. Only in this universal mode of knowing does a human being reach perfect contemplative happiness (see Chapter 33).[41] In other works, Albert adds that phantasms are indispensable for knowing physical and mathematical objects, but are not necessary for knowing the immaterial objects of metaphysics, that is, the separate substances.[42]

Aquinas, in contrast, denies that knowledge of the essences of immaterial substances is possible in this life. He insists that our intellect always needs to turn toward phantasms (*convertere se ad phantasmata*), not only at the beginning of the thinking process, but also after the acquisition of knowledge. Evidence for this is that brain damage may impede all thinking processes, and that we are unable to conceive an intelligible form without phantasms representing examples of it. The human intellect differs from the angelic intellect in that it is joined to the body; its proper object, which is proportioned to its capacity, is the quiddities that exist in matter. Separate substances can only be known indirectly via a comparison with material substances (*Summa theol.* 1a 84.7; *In De anima* III.13).[43] To say that the intellect can dispense with the senses just as a traveler can dispense with a horse upon arrival is true only of the intellect in the afterlife, when the soul, being temporarily separated from the body, has a different mode of knowing (*Quaest. de veritate* 18.8 ad 4). But one reason Aquinas offers for insisting on the resurrection of the human body is that such intellectual activity apart from the senses is foreign to the soul's nature. The human intellect, being weaker than the angelic intellect, has complete and proper cognition only when working with the senses (*Summa theol.* 1a 89.1).

---

[41] *De anima* III.3.11 (ed. Cologne VII.1: 221–2) and III.3.12 (ed. 7.1: 224b).

[42] Albert, *Metaphysica* II.2 (ed. Cologne XVI: 92–3); *Summa theologiae* II (ed. Borgnet XXXII: 196a). See Carlos Steel, *Der Adler und die Nachteule: Thomas und Albert über die Möglichkeit der Metaphysik* (Münster: Aschendorff, 2001) pp. 22–4.

[43] See Pasnau, *Thomas Aquinas on Human Nature*, pp. 284–95.

23

THE NATURE OF INTELLECT

DEBORAH L. BLACK

The views of medieval philosophers on the nature of the intellect were framed around the interpretation of Book III of Aristotle's *De anima*, especially Chapters 4 and 5, in which Aristotle investigates the nature of the power he calls *nous* – "mind" or "intellect." Medieval philosophers were also influenced by Neoplatonic sources such as Plotinus, Proclus, and Porphyry, as well as by the late Greek commentators on Aristotle's *De anima*, many of whom read Aristotle's theories through a Neoplatonic lens.

Aristotle's method for determining the nature of the intellect and other psychological faculties is to analyze the operations for which the faculty is responsible. Thus Aristotle begins his examination of the nature of intellect in *De anima* III.4 by noting that, like sense perception, the intellect's proper operation of thinking is a kind of process that involves a change or alteration on the part of the knower. Aristotle argues that the intellect must therefore be divisible in some way into two parts or aspects – one that is passive and receptive of the change, and another that is active, inasmuch as it produces the change in the patient. Among medieval authors, the former intellect came to be known as the "potential," "possible," or "material" intellect, and the latter as the "agent" intellect. Further developing this account of intellection as a process, Aristotle argues that before actually thinking, the intellect is potentially like its object; in the act of thought it is altered in a non-physical way, so as to become actually identified with that object. Thought, then, involves the cognitive assimilation or identification of the knower with the object known – a characteristic that on Aristotle's view thinking shares with sense perception.

Aristotle's account of intellection so far is thus entirely parallel to the account of sensation he develops in *De anima* II. But Aristotle and his medieval interpreters held that intellectual thought constituted a form of cognition that is distinct from and superior to sense perception. In order to understand the nature of intellect fully, then, one must examine the properties of intellection that set it apart from sensation. In *De anima* III.4, Aristotle focuses on the fact that all modes of sensation are limited in scope. Whereas each of the five senses is able to perceive only one type of quality – color in the case of vision, sound in the case of hearing, and so on – the intellect is subject to no such restrictions. From this Aristotle concludes that, unlike the senses, the intellect cannot have a predetermined nature of its own, and thus cannot be mixed with the body or operate through any organ. (This includes the brain and the heart, both of which Aristotle and medieval authors associate with the activities of sensation and imagination, and not directly with thinking.) Intellect, then, must be separable from the body in order to perform its proper activity, and for this reason Aristotle likens the intellect's state prior to actual thought to that of a writing tablet on which nothing has yet been written.

These characteristics, which are analyzed in III.4, pertain to the potential or material intellect – the passive and receptive element in thinking. In III.5, Aristotle briefly discusses the active or productive part of the intellect, which he describes as the power that "*makes* all things" rather than "*becoming* all things." It too is said to be separable from the body, unmixed with matter, and not susceptible to physical change. Aristotle tends, however, to resort to analogies to describe this part of the intellect, likening it first to art, and secondly to light. For this reason, III.5 has traditionally been considered the most cryptic and contentious chapter in Aristotle's *De anima*. In the medieval period, however, it was Aristotle's account of the material intellect in chapter 4 that became the main focus of controversy. In the Arabic and Jewish philosophical traditions, it was almost universally accepted that the agent intellect is a separate immaterial substance apart from individual human souls, and one for all human beings. In the later Christian tradition the agent intellect was generally viewed as a faculty within the individual human soul. Yet even philosophers who uphold this view, such as Thomas Aquinas, regard the alternative position, that there is only one agent intellect for all human knowers, to be fairly innocuous, on the grounds that it poses no real danger to Christian belief.[1] By contrast, the view that not only the agent intellect, but also the material or potential intellect, is one for all human beings, caused great consternation in the Christian West during the thirteenth and fourteenth centuries. This position, which originated with Averroes, effectively deprives humans of any individual intellective powers. For this reason, it was seen as a threat to the religious doctrines of individual immortality and punishment or reward in the afterlife, and it was accordingly subject to vigorous attack by Aquinas and many others.

---

[1] Aquinas, *De unitate intellectus* 4 (tr. Zedler, n. 86); *Quaest. de anima* 5.

THE ISLAMIC TRADITION[2]

The Islamic philosophical tradition accepted the basic framework of Aristotle's agent and material intellects. But Islamic philosophers also recognized that in many of the Greek commentaries on the *De anima*, the term 'intellect' was often applied to the various developmental stages in the material or potential intellect's acquisition of knowledge. Al-Kindī and al-Fārābī each wrote a *Treatise on the Intellect*, translated into Latin in the twelfth century, which was devoted to explaining the different meanings that the term 'intellect' had in philosophical texts. An enumeration of the different senses of 'intellect' was also incorporated into the psychological writings of Avicenna and Averroes – both important sources for philosophical speculation in the Latin West. The basic scheme, which was adapted by individual philosophers to reflect their own theories of the intellect, recognized four meanings of the term 'intellect':[3]

1. The *agent intellect* discussed by Aristotle in *De anima* III.5. As noted above, this was universally understood in the late Greek, Islamic, and Jewish traditions to be a separate substance, not a faculty of the individual soul.
2. The *potential intellect*, discussed by Aristotle in *De anima* III.4. In the Islamic and Jewish traditions it was often labeled the *material intellect*, following the custom of the Greek commentator Alexander of Aphrodisias. Latin philosophers also used the term *possible intellect*. Occasionally this intellect is also called the *passive intellect*, but more often than not, especially in the Arabic tradition, the "passive intellect" is not an intellect at all, but rather an alternative label for the imaginative faculties: that is, the internal senses in general, and in particular the human manifestation of the imagination, known as the "cogitative power" (see Chapter 22).
3. The *habitual* or *speculative intellect* is the name given to the material intellect once it has acquired some basic knowledge and thereby developed a disposition or habit for thought.
4. The *acquired intellect* is generally the name given to the habitual intellect when it has perfected itself by acquiring all possible intelligibles. Many Islamic philosophers suggested that those few individuals who were able to attain this level of intellectual perfection would become akin to the separate celestial intelligences, and thereby be able to have direct knowledge of the closest such intellect to us – that is, the agent intellect. This direct acquaintance with the agent intellect was called "conjunction" (see Chapter 33).

---

[2] For a comprehensive overview see Herbert Davidson, *Alfarabi, Avicenna, Averroes on Intellect* (Oxford: Oxford University Press, 1992).

[3] In addition to the treatises by al-Fārābī and al-Kindī, see Avicenna, *De anima* (*Shifā'*) I.5 (ed. Rahman, pp. 48–50) and *Psychology* (*Najāt*) tr. Rahman, pp. 33–5.

Al-Fārābī on the intellect

According to al-Fārābī, the material intellect is a power in the individual human soul, and the agent intellect is a separate substance that enables individual human knowers to abstract universal intelligibles from the sensibles they have experienced. Although Fārābī discusses the nature of the intellect in a number of writings, it is difficult to distil a consistent theory from these works. It seems reasonably clear that Fārābī views the process of acquiring intelligibles as one of abstraction, and that he believes that individual human beings require the help of the agent intellect in order to carry out the abstractive process. Unlike many later philosophers, however, Fārābī appears to make the material intellect itself the abstractive power, treating the agent intellect as providing the conditions – analogous to light in the case of vision – that enable the material intellect to abstract intelligibles for itself.[4] By the same token, Fārābī's writings do not make it entirely clear whether the abstractive activities of the material intellect are required for the acquisition of all intelligibles. While some works uphold a strong doctrine of the empirical origins of all intelligibles, including first principles and primary concepts,[5] other texts seem to imply that first principles are received by the material intellect directly from the agent intellect.[6]

Although Fārābī is the first philosopher in the Islamic tradition to articulate the notion of the acquired intellect that was to form the core of later philosophical discussions of human perfection, his views on this topic are also ambiguous. In his extant writings, Fārābī elaborates a doctrine of human perfection in which the potential intellect gradually becomes actualized and perfected through its accumulation of knowledge. If it reaches the stage of the acquired intellect, the potential intellect becomes completely actual; in effect, it attains a higher stage of being in which it becomes wholly immaterial – like the agent intellect itself, with whom it is now able to conjoin in a cognitive union. Fārābī makes it clear that conjunction is the condition on which the soul's immortality depends, since it is the only state in which the intellectual part of the soul loses its dependence on the body and thereby becomes eternal. Since very few people – presumably only philosophers – are able to attain the acquired intellect, it is clear that most human beings fail on Fārābī's view to attain immortality. Yet Fārābī seems to have become skeptical even of this limited doctrine of immortality in his later writings. In a lost commentary on Aristotle's *Nicomachean Ethics*, Fārābī is

---

[4] *Treatise on Intellect*, ed. Bouyges, pp. 12–13; tr. J. McGinnis and D. C. Reisman, *Classical Arabic Philosophy: An Anthology of Sources* (Indianapolis, IN: Hackett, 2007), p. 71.
[5] *Harmony of Plato and Aristotle* secs. 49–50, tr. Butterworth, pp. 151–2.
[6] *On the Perfect State* IV.13.2–3.

reported to have rejected the possibility of conjunction with the agent intellect as described in his own earlier writings, on the grounds that it entails a contingent, perishable being – the human intellect – being transformed into one that is wholly immaterial, immortal, and eternal, something that he came to believe was a metaphysical impossibility.[7]

Avicenna: intellect as self-subsistent

While Avicenna's account of the nature of the intellect picks up the basic framework sketched by Fārābī, Avicenna's view of both the intellect's ontological status and its operations is unique within Arabic philosophy. Avicenna accepts the traditional distinction between the agent and material intellects, but he upholds a form of dualism that sees each individual material intellect as a subsistent substance in its own right, which, while dependent upon the body for its first *temporal* moment of origination, is from the outset *ontologically* independent of it. In a famous thought experiment that has come to be known as the "Flying Man," Avicenna attempts to highlight what he believes to be a basic, though often overlooked, intuition that each human intellect has: namely, that it is innately aware of itself as an individual entity, independently of all bodily experience and any awareness of things other than itself. In this experiment, Avicenna asks us to imagine ourselves born all at once but mature, so that our minds are fully functional but lack any past experience of the physical world. He also instructs us to imagine ourselves suspended in a void so that we cannot sense either our own bodies or the external world. Avicenna then asks whether a person who finds herself in such a state will nonetheless affirm the existence of her individual self, and he is confident that her answer to this question will be a resounding "Yes!" Although Avicenna recognizes that such an intuition does not fully demonstrate the intellect's immateriality, he believes it provides powerful evidence that the true nature of the individual is that of an intellect completely separable from matter.[8]

To provide more rigorous demonstrations of the intellect's immaterial nature, Avicenna focuses on a variety of different properties unique to intellectual thought, which in his view preclude the intellect's having a corporeal subject or instrument of any kind. Among the arguments that Avicenna advances to this effect are that intelligibles are by definition *abstract* – that is, that they prescind

---

[7] See the report in Averroes, *Commentarium magnum de anima* III.36; see also Davidson, *Alfarabi, Avicenna, Averroes*, pp. 70–3.

[8] Avicenna, *De anima* (*Shifā'*) I.1; see also Michael Marmura, "Avicenna's 'Flying Man' in Context," *Monist* 69 (1986) 383–95.

from the very features that individuate material beings in the external world – and that they are *infinite*, since, as universals, they apply to a potentially infinite number of individuals. Because such properties are incompatible with material bodies, which are concrete and finite, the intellect must therefore be immaterial. Avicenna also appeals to the intellect's capacity for complete reflexive knowledge of its own acts and operations – something that is prohibited to material cognitive powers such as the senses, in virtue of the limitations imposed on them by their employment of bodily organs.[9]

Although Avicenna holds that the intellect is essentially immaterial and self-subsistent, he nonetheless recognizes that it relies on the body as both the occasion and the co-cause of its initial origination. Once in existence, however, and hence individuated, the human intellect is able to continue in existence even after the body has perished.[10] This limited-dependence view of the intellect–body relation is also reflected in Avicenna's account of knowledge acquisition. Unlike Aristotle, Avicenna denies that the acquisition of intelligibles can be explained *causally* as a process of abstracting universal essences from the sensible information preserved in the imaginative faculties in the brain. Although sensation and imagination are, in most cases, necessary preconditions for the acquisition of new knowledge – serving to explain why at any given time I acquire one kind of concept rather than another (*horse*, say, rather than *monkey*) – the abstract intelligible itself is produced in me through a direct *emanation* from the agent intellect.[11]

This account of knowledge acquisition as emanation has repercussions in a number of other aspects of Avicenna's theory of the intellect. The most well known and controversial of these for Avicenna's readers in the Latin West was his denial that there is such a thing as memory in the intellect itself. To support his point, Avicenna argues that thinking is just the actual and active presence of an intelligible or idea in an individual mind. If the mind is not actively thinking some intelligible, then there is no "place" where it can be stored. The notion of a storehouse is thus essentially physical, and as such incompatible with the incorporeality of intellect. Human beings do have memory, of course, but Avicenna locates this faculty in the brain. Thus, memory as such is a sense power and in no way part of the intellect. What, then, in the case of

[9] *Psychology* (*Najāt*) chs. 9–10; *De anima* (*Shifā'*) V.2.
[10] *Psychology* (*Najāt*) chs. 12–13; *De anima* (*Shifā'*) V.3–4; see also Thérèse-Anne Druart, "The Human Soul's Individuation and its Survival after the Body's Death: Avicenna on the Causal Relation between Body and Soul," *Arabic Sciences and Philosophy* 10 (2000) 259–74.
[11] *De anima* (*Shifā'*) V.5 (ed. Rahman, p. 235). An alternative interpretation of the respective roles of emanation and abstraction in Avicenna is provided in Dag Hasse, "Avicenna on Abstraction," in R. Wisnovsky (ed.) *Aspects of Avicenna* (Princeton, NJ: Wiener, 2001) 39–72.

the intellect's operations, accounts for the phenomenon that we usually call memory? For Avicenna, intellectual memory is simply the habit through which individual minds become easily able to conjoin with the agent intellect and receive the emanation of intelligibles on demand. Conceived in this way, then, memory is a disposition to perform an activity – namely, thinking – at will, rather than a storehouse or sub-faculty within the intellect. To the extent that intellectual memory requires a storehouse of intelligibles, it is the agent intellect that performs that function in Avicenna's system, inasmuch as it is always actually engaged in intellectual contemplation.[12]

Averroes and the unicity of the material intellect

Averroes's account of the nature of the human intellect was among the most notorious and misunderstood philosophical doctrines to emerge in the medieval period. While Averroes himself strove to offer the most lucid and coherent account of the intellect that could be extracted from Aristotle's *De anima*, many later readers found the view that he put forward implausible, if not abhorrent.

It is somewhat misleading, however, to speak generally of Averroes's account of the nature of the intellect without reference to a particular period in his intellectual development. Averroes wrote a series of commentaries on the *De anima* over the course of his career, and his interpretation of the Aristotelian text evolved considerably over this period.[13] Like most of his Greek and Islamic

---

[12] *De anima* (*Shifā'*) V.6 (ed. Rahman, pp. 245–8).

[13] Averroes wrote three types of commentaries on Aristotle: short commentaries or epitomes; middle commentaries or paraphrases; and great or long commentaries. He wrote commentaries of all three types on some of the most important works in the Aristotelian corpus, among them the *De anima*, *Physics*, and *Metaphysics*; he wrote short and middle commentaries on most others. In some cases a single commentary also exists in more than one version, as is the case with the *Epitome of the De anima*, which was revised several times to reflect Averroes's changing interpretations of the text. Scholars have generally assumed that the short commentaries were products of Averroes's youth, with the middle and long commentaries belonging to later stages in his career, although recently this picture has been called into question, especially with reference to the *De anima* commentaries. For a general overview of the various versions of Averroes's *De anima* commentaries, see Davidson, *Alfarabi, Avicenna, Averroes*, 258–314. For the competing views on the relative dating of the commentaries, see Herbert Davidson, "The Relation between Averroes' Middle and Long Commentaries on the De Anima," *Arabic Sciences and Philosophy* 7 (1997) 139–51, and Alfred Ivry, "Averroes' Three Commentaries on De Anima," in J. A. Aertsen and G. Endress (eds.) *Averroes and the Aristotelian Tradition* (Leiden: Brill, 1999) 199–216.

Many of Averroes's commentaries were translated into Hebrew and Latin in the medieval period, and some of the original Arabic versions do not survive, so in these cases we must rely on the medieval translations for our knowledge of Averroes's text. As a general though by no means universal rule, Hebrew translations were available of the epitomes and middle commentaries (this was the case for the *De anima*), whereas Latin translations were made of most of the great commentaries, and of the epitomes and middle commentaries where no great commentary existed. For an overview of Averroes's commentaries and the medieval and Renaissance translations of them, see Harry

predecessors, he spent little time worrying about the nature of the agent intellect, as discussed in *De anima* III.5, since he took it as obvious that Aristotle's brief remarks there could point only to a single being entirely separate from the individual. What concerned Averroes most was how to understand both the nature of the potential or material intellect described in III.4 and its relation to individual human knowers. His difficulties were compounded by the commentaries of Alexander of Aphrodisias and Themistius, which represented the two main interpretations of the text between which Averroes had to choose. In his early writings on the topic – most notably the first version of his *Epitome of the De anima* – Averroes followed the lead of Alexander of Aphrodisias, according to whom the potential or material intellect is simply a higher-order disposition within the imaginative faculty of each individual human knower that permits her to receive intelligibles. The difficulty with this position is that it seems incapable of fulfilling Aristotle's demand that the material intellect must be entirely unmixed with matter. At this early stage, Averroes resolved this problem by taking refuge in the fact that the imagination and its contents are psychological rather than physical entities; thus, they enjoy what Averroes calls a "spiritual" or "intentional" existence. This, Averroes believed, is sufficient to ensure that the intellect so construed is not material "in the way that bodily corporeal forms are material" (*Epitome*, ed. al-Ahwānī, p. 86). But since the material intellect ultimately depends on a bodily faculty as its subject, it too perishes along with the body.

Averroes gradually became dissatisfied with this rather weak account of the intellect's immateriality, and he moved towards a view that is closer to that of Themistius, in that it recognizes that both the material and agent intellects must be incorporeal in every respect. Yet despite its affinities to Themistius's view, Averroes's final position on the status of the material intellect is entirely novel with respect to the consequences that it entails for the individuation of the intellect. Revisiting the problem in his *Great Commentary on the De anima*, Averroes concludes that the material intellect, like the agent intellect, could in no way be a "body nor a power in a body," even in an attenuated sense. It must be totally separate and unmixed with matter in every way. Yet this posed a problem for the individuality of the intellect, since Averroes, like most medieval Aristotelians, holds that it is matter that differentiates one individual from another within a physical species. If, then, the material intellect is to be

Wolfson, "Plan for the Publication of a *Corpus commentariorum Averrois in Aristotele*," *Speculum* 6 (1931) 412–27, and "Revised Plan for the Publication of a *Corpus commentariorum Averrois in Aristotelem*." *Speculum* 38 (1963) 88–104. See also Gerhard Endress, "*Averrois Opera*: A Bibliography of Editions and Contributions to the Text," in Aertsen and Endress (eds.) *Averroes and the Aristotelian Tradition*, 339–81.

entirely immaterial, it cannot be "numbered according to the enumeration of individuals." Hence, just as there is only one agent intellect on which all human knowers depend in order to abstract universal intelligibles from sense images, so too there can be only one material intellect into which those intelligibles are received. Individual human beings "conjoin" with this material intellect via their imaginative faculties when they think, and it is the close connection between the material intellect and the imagination that produces the individual experience of thinking and that accounts for variations in knowledge from one human being to the next. Strictly speaking, though, individuals do not have personal intellectual faculties unique to them alone (*Commentarium magnum* III.4–5). This position is the notorious doctrine of the unicity of the intellect (or, less correctly, monopsychism, a misleading label since each individual does have her own *soul*) for which Averroes was much maligned throughout the centuries in the Latin West. As we shall see, readers of the Latin Averroes were principally concerned with the consequences of this position for personal immortality and moral responsibility (see also Chapter 34).

THE IMPACT OF ISLAMIC PHILOSOPHY IN THE JEWISH TRADITION

The views of Jewish philosophers up to the twelfth century generally followed the course set forth by al-Fārābī and, less frequently, Avicenna. Moses Maimonides largely adopts the Farabian account of the nature of the material intellect, treating it as "a faculty subsisting in a body and not separable from it," and thereby implicitly rejecting the Avicennian thesis that individual human intellects are self-subsistent (*Guide of the Perplexed* I.72). Maimonides also echoes al-Fārābī in his descriptions of how the intellect acquires knowledge and gradually perfects itself so as to attain the level of the acquired intellect. There are a few passages where Maimonides seems to espouse the Avicennian doctrine that intelligibles are acquired by us not through abstraction, but rather by a direct emanation from the agent intellect (ibid., II.4). Overall, however, Maimonides appears to be primarily a Farabian in his account of the intellect.

   Jewish philosophers after the twelfth century were most influenced by Averroes's earlier reading of the *De anima*, as transmitted in the *Epitome* and *Middle Commentary*, in which the doctrine of the unicity of the material intellect is not yet present. The most detailed account of the nature of the intellect among later Jewish philosophers is found in Levi ben Gershom's (Gersonides) magnum opus, the *Wars of the Lord* – the entire first book of which is devoted to theories of the intellect and their implications for the immortality of the soul. Levi ben Gershom generally upholds the Alexandrian view that the material intellect is a disposition whose subject is the imaginative faculty in the soul (*Wars* I.5). He rejects the views of Themistius, Avicenna, and many of his own contemporaries in the Christian tradition, who hold that the material intellect is both an incorporeal substance in its own right and a part of each individual human soul. Levi ben Gershom claims that this flies in the face of our empirical evidence that the human material intellect is subject to generation and corruption – physical characteristics that cannot be attributed to a substance that is immaterial, and hence eternal and incorruptible (*Wars* I.4).

MEDIEVAL CHRISTIAN PHILOSOPHY

The encounter with Avicenna

Although a direct translation from the Greek of Aristotle's *De anima* was available in the West, Christian authors up to the late twelfth and early thirteenth centuries generally preferred to follow the *De anima* portion of Avicenna's *Healing* (*Shifāʾ*).[14] One reason for this appears to have been the perceived compatibility between Avicenna's emanationist account of knowledge acquisition and the Augustinian doctrine of divine illumination, which led some thinkers to identify Avicenna's agent intellect with God himself (see Chapter 27). Others, however, were more critical in their appropriation of Avicennian and Aristotelian psychology into a traditional Augustinian framework. In particular, William of Auvergne raised a number of objections to the very notion of an agent intellect conceived along Avicennian lines (*De anima* V.6, in *Opera*, p. 122a). William argues that the doctrine of an agent intellect accords to individual human minds an utterly passive role in the acquisition of new knowledge, and he claims that passivity is a property that belongs exclusively to physical things (ibid., V.6, p. 121b). Although William appears to allow some role for divine illumination of an Augustinian sort in the intellect's acquisition of first principles, he is adamantly opposed to extending any such passivity into the intellect's subsequent operations (ibid., VII.4–6). Instead, William argues that the human intellect is an active and creative force capable of generating intelligibles for itself on the occasion of sensible encounters with the physical world (ibid., V.7, VII.8).[15]

---

[14] For an overview of the reception of Avicenna, see Dag Hasse, *Avicenna's* De anima *in the Latin West: The Formation of a Peripatetic Philosophy of the Soul 1160–1300* (London: Warburg Institute, 2000).

[15] See John Marenbon, *Later Medieval Philosophy (1150–1350): An Introduction* (London: Routledge, 1987) pp. 110–15. William's *De anima* has been translated by R. J. Teske (Milwaukee, WI: Marquette University Press, 2000).

Latin Averroism

With the translation of Averroes's *Great Commentary on the De anima* in the early
thirteenth century, Latin philosophers now had a comprehensive interpretation
of Aristotle's entire *De anima*, and they thus began to turn their attention to the
Philosopher's own text. While Averroes's aid in interpreting the difficult chapters
on the intellect was initially welcomed by readers struggling to understand
Aristotle, the implications of Averroes's teachings on the unicity of both the
agent and material intellects soon stirred up controversy. A number of arts
masters at the University of Paris – often referred to as "Latin Averroists" or
"radical Aristotelians" – began to promulgate Averroes's interpretation of the
De anima. This in turn provoked reactions from concerned theologians, who
responded both by criticizing Averroes and his interpreters and by offering their
own alternative accounts of Aristotle's theory of the intellect.[16]

The best-known Averroist of the thirteenth century was Siger of Brabant, the
Parisian arts master who wrote a series of works on the nature of the intellective
soul. Over time, Siger's views evolve from a strict and unapologetic Averroism
to a position similar in many respects to that of his staunch contemporary critic,
Aquinas. In his early *Questions on De anima III*, Siger describes the possible
intellect as one for all human beings, though it enters the individual soul from
outside and forms a unity with it. The union of intellect and individual is not
a substantial union, however, since the intellectual soul functions merely as the
mover of the body, performing the operation of thinking within the body by
making use of its sense images. Siger's radical views were soon subjected to a
virulent attack by Aquinas in his *On the Unity of the Intellect against the Averroists*.
In response to Aquinas, Siger begins to develop a more nuanced position, and
in later works he makes an explicit attempt to address the criticisms of both
Aquinas and Albert the Great. In *De anima intellectiva*, Siger continues to defend
Averroism as a legitimate interpretation of Aristotle's *De anima*, but he now
declares his personal allegiance to Christian beliefs where they conflict with
Aristotelian philosophy.[17] Siger accepts that the intellective soul is indeed the
form and perfection of the body, and, as such, the principle through which all
of a person's actions – including intellectual understanding – are performed.
But he denies that the intellective soul is united to the body by constituting its
substantial form. Instead, the union of the intellect with the body is a purely

[16] For a brief overview see Fernand van Steenberghen, *St. Thomas Aquinas and Radical Aristotelianism*
(Washington: Catholic University of America Press, 1980).
[17] *De anima intellectiva* 3, ed. Bazán, p. 87. For the response to Aquinas and Albert, see ibid., pp. 81–4.
Portions of this treatise are translated in John Wippel and Allan Wolter, *Medieval Philosophy* (New
York: Free Press, 1969).

operational one: the intellect and the body form a sort of team inasmuch as they "cooperate in a single task" of understanding. Siger refers to the intellect in this text as an "intrinsic agent" rather than an external mover (*De anima intellectiva* 3, pp. 84–5), but he remains unable to offer a philosophical account of how such an intellect could be "multiplied with the multiplication of human bodies," so as to avoid Averroism (ibid., ch. 7).

Later still, however, Siger distances himself entirely from his earlier Averroism and moves very close to Aquinas's account of the intellect, holding that each human being has only one substantial form, through which she is able to perform all her operations, including intellectual understanding. Siger now rejects the unicity of the intellect as both heretical and irrational, and he declares that it makes no difference what either Averroes or Aristotle held, since they were only human and thus subject to error.[18]

The Thomistic alternative

Aquinas was a fierce critic of Averroes's reading of the *De anima*, which he believed was unable to account for the basic fact that "this individual human being understands."[19] In a favorite example, Aquinas likens the individual on Averroes's scheme to a wall whose color is seen by the eye. Just as we would not say that the wall itself "sees" because its color is seen, neither can we say that the human being "understands" because she provides images to the material intellect. At best she is a passive and inert *object* of understanding, not a dynamic, knowing *subject*.[20]

Aquinas's alternative is to treat both the material and agent intellects as faculties within the human soul.[21] The material (or, as Aquinas prefers, "possible") intellect receives and understands the intelligibles which the agent intellect has abstracted from the individual's sense images. Intellection itself, however, is an entirely self-contained and autonomous process. While this solves the problems that Aquinas believes are associated with Averroism, it is still necessary to explain how these two intellectual faculties can be individuated while still remaining immaterial. For Aquinas, the fact that the intellect is able to perform its proper operations of abstraction and thinking without making use of a bodily organ is sufficient to meet Aristotle's immateriality condition. That the intellect needs no organ to think is, in turn, explicable because the human intellective soul is

[18] *Quaest. super librum de causis* qq. 26–7.
[19] *Summa theol.* 1a 76.1; *In De anima* III.7 n. 690; *De unitate* 3, tr. Zedler, nn. 63, 65, 66.
[20] *Summa theol.* 1a 76.1; *De unitate* 3 n. 66; *Quaest. de anima* 2c; *In De anima* III.1 n. 694; cf. *Summa contra gentiles* II.59.
[21] *Summa theol.* 1a 76.1–2, 79.1–5; *Quaest. de anima* 3–5.

a "form of matter" while not being merely a "material form" (*De unitate* 3, nn. 83–4). That is, the human intellectual soul is subsistent in itself (as it was for Avicenna) and capable of existence independently of the body, and so it is not entirely immersed in matter.[22] Nothing, however, prevents the intellective soul from also functioning as a "form of matter" both insofar as it gives being to the body and insofar as it is dependent on the body to individuate it and to aid it in the operations of sensation and imagination on which intellection also depends.[23] Without the body, then, the operations of the intellective soul and human nature itself are imperfect and incomplete. Thus, while the human soul can exist separately from the body, Aquinas makes it clear that its cognitive operations in such a state will be diminished (*Summa theol.* 1a 89).

The decline of the Aristotelian framework

After Aquinas, most medieval philosophers continue to view both the agent and potential intellects as faculties within the individual soul. John Duns Scotus, for instance, accepts the traditional arguments for the incorporeality and immateriality of the intellect, but he notes that the claim that the intellective soul is "immaterial" is ambiguous, and in some of his writings he suggests that ambiguity may block our ability to infer that the intellect has a natural capacity to exist without the body.[24] Questions increasingly arise during this period, moreover, concerning whether these two intellects are in fact separate faculties. New models of the nature of intellectual cognition and the operations that comprise it suggest that the intellect might be simple, rather than comprised of distinct active and receptive faculties. Although Scotus preserves the Aristotelian framework of the two intellects, others, such as Peter of John Olivi and William of Ockham, question the distinction. In particular, they question the traditional rationale for positing an agent intellect: namely, the view of knowledge acquisition as a form of abstraction.[25] Olivi takes issue with this picture because he questions the very capacity of physical bodies to affect an

---

[22] *Summa theol.* 1a. 75.2; *Quaest. de anima* 1–2; see also Bernardo C. Bazán, "The Human Soul: Form *and* Substance? Thomas Aquinas's Critique of Eclectic Aristotelianism," *Archives d'histoire doctrinale et littéraire du Moyen âge* 64 (1997) 95–126.

[23] For the dependence of the intellect on the operations of the bodily faculties of sense and imagination, see *Summa theol.* 1a 84.6–7.

[24] See *Ordinatio* IV.43.2 (*Philosophical Writings*, pp. 133–62) and *Quodlibet* 9; see also Richard Cross, "Philosophy of Mind," in T. Williams (ed.) *The Cambridge Companion to Duns Scotus* (Cambridge: Cambridge University Press, 2003) pp. 263–7.

[25] See Robert Pasnau, *Theories of Cognition in the Later Middle Ages* (Cambridge: Cambridge University Press, 1997) pp. 150–1, 176–7.

immaterial mind.[26] Ockham's nominalist rejection of the reality of shared essences or common natures (see Chapter 48), on the other hand, entails that there is nothing in particular for an agent intellect to abstract from. When we speak of that intellect's role as an abstractive agent, then, we must understand this not as a transformative or extracting operation, but rather merely as the act of forming universal concepts on the basis of prior intuitive acts of cognition in which the intellect directly apprehends the individual existent.[27]

Since Ockham has less invested in the traditional roles assigned to the agent and material intellects than his predecessors, it is not surprising that he takes a more dispassionate stance towards Averroism than they did. In a short question devoted to the topic of Averroes's views on the possible intellect, Ockham plays devil's advocate by offering a series of what he regards as plausible (although not demonstrative) arguments to show how the Averroist claim that the intellect is related to the body as its *mover* rather than as its *form* can be "salvaged."[28] Ockham continues to deny Averroism from the perspective of the faith, and he also rejects on rational and empirical grounds Averroes's claim that if the intellect is only the mover of the body, then there can be only *one* intellect for all human beings. This, Ockham says, is impossible, since it would entail a single subject, the separate intellect, experiencing contrary states such as knowing and ignorance simultaneously, in virtue of its multiple relations to individual human knowers (*Quodlibet* I.11). So for Ockham too the individuality of the intellect ultimately remains intact, even though the traditional Aristotelian structure of the mind is now deemed superfluous.

---

[26] Olivi, *Summa* II.72, ed. Jansen, III: 27–30.
[27] *Reportatio* II.13 (*Opera theol.* V: 304–10); see also *Quaest. variae* 5.
[28] *Quaest. variae* 6 art. 7; see also *Quodlibet* I.10.

24

PERCEPTION

A. MARK SMITH

The psychological ruminations of Plato and Aristotle gave rise to two interpretative streams that together shaped the course of later medieval theories of perception. The most important of these was the Arabic tradition, which profoundly influenced scholastic thought. Less significant, but still influential, were early Latin accounts of perception. Out of this legacy, scholastic Latin authors developed rich and varied accounts of the physiological and psychological mechanisms of perception.

THE GRECO-LATIN INTERPRETIVE STREAM

Early Latin accounts of classical Greek theories of perception were channeled through such encyclopedic thinkers as Pliny, Macrobius, and Martianus Capella, as well as Augustine and Boethius. Perhaps the most important among these channeling agents was Calcidius, whose fourth-century Latin translation of the first half of Plato's *Timaeus* – complete with commentary – proved enormously influential on the study of natural philosophy from the late Carolingian period to at least the mid-twelfth century.

Hugh of St. Victor's *Didascalicon* offers a good example of how this interpretive stream had developed by the early twelfth century to combine elements from Plato's account of perception with second-hand knowledge of Aristotle's theory. Hugh follows Aristotle's threefold division of the soul according to its fundamental capacities, beginning with nutrition, passing through sensation, and culminating with reason in humankind (I.3). The link between sense and reason, Hugh explains, is the imagination, which "is sensuous memory made up of the traces of corporeal objects inhering in the mind" (II.5, tr. Taylor, p. 66). Sensation, for its part, "is what the soul undergoes in the body as a result of qualities that come to it from without" (II.5, p. 67). In order to get the "traces of corporeal objects" necessary for cognition, the soul "rushes out toward the visible forms of bodies, and . . . draws them into itself through imagination." This notion – that the soul somehow "rushes out" to apprehend sensible

334

objects – is consonant with a standard Greco-Roman assumption, one of whose most significant proponents was Plato, that vision is accomplished by the emission of visual flux from the eye. That such extramission theories were in fact current even before the writing of Hugh's *Didascalicon* is clear from Anselm's account of vision in chapter 6 of the *De veritate*, where he explains how sight is deceived about the color of something it sees behind colored glass because it takes on the color of the glass as it passes outward through it.

In drawing visible forms into itself, according to Hugh, the soul is "penetrated by . . . hostile sense experience" and thus the soul is "cut away from its simplicity" (II.3, p. 64). Only by removing itself from the distractions of sense experience and "mounting from such distraction toward pure understanding" can the soul gather itself "into one," thereby becoming "more blessed through participating in intelligible substance" (ibid.). This ambivalence toward sense perception displays Hugh's Platonist leanings: on the one hand, sense perception is an aid to understanding; on the other, it is a snare that can divert the intellect from its proper upward gaze toward the ideal.[1]

THE GRECO-ARABIC INTERPRETIVE STREAM

In contrast to the Greco-Latin tradition, the Greco-Arabic stream was primarily Aristotelian in emphasis, with particular attention paid to the *De anima* and *De sensu et sensato*. Passing through Alexander of Aphrodisias, Porphyry, Themistius, and various other late antique Greek commentators, this interpretative stream culminated in a host of Arabic thinkers, among whom Ibn al-Haytham (Alhacen), Avicenna, and Averroes loom especially large.

Over the course of this transmission, several key suppositions came to the fore – most harking directly back to Aristotle. First, following *De anima* II.6, each of the five senses was associated (at least in principle) with a unique, proper sensible: sound with hearing, color with sight, savor with taste, and so on. (As in Aristotle, touch presented something of a problem insofar as it is susceptible to apparently unrelated data, such as hotness, smoothness, and hardness [see Chapter 22].) Second, certain ancillary sensibles, such as size, shape, and location, were understood to be grasped in an accidental way by more than one sense. These sensibles are therefore "common" in being shared (see *De an.* 418a18–19). Third, primitive, psychologically unmediated sensation was

[1] For another example of perception analysis within the Greco-Latin interpretive stream, see William of Conches, *Dragmaticon philosophiae*, tr. Ronca and Curr, pp. 150–73. Although both Hugh's and William's accounts allude to Aristotelian ideas (gotten at second-hand), both show clear Platonist leanings. For an overview of the Greco-Latin interpretive stream slanted toward vision, see David Lindberg, *Theories of Vision from Alkindi to Kepler* (Chicago: University of Chicago Press, 1976).

understood to be veridical; error in sense induction was blamed on perceptual
or intellectual misjudgments of the relevant sense data (see *De an.* 428b18–24).
Finally, all sensation was seen to be mediated both by a material substrate – air
in the case of sight and hearing, flesh in the case of touch, and water in the
case of taste – and by a qualitative representation of the sensible attribute that
existed in the medium independently of the corporeal object (*De an.* 419a12–
b2). According to the Greco-Arabic tradition, it was not the corporeal object
but rather this representation that brings about the appropriate sense impression
in a perceiver.[2]

The Arabic tradition also accommodated Aristotle's account of sense perception to Galenic anatomy and physiology by abandoning the perceptual role
Aristotle had given to the heart, and identifying the brain as the main locus for
the perceptual process. The sensory soul, on this account, is constituted from
the brain's three-fold ventricular structure and the animal spirit (Galen's *pneuma
psychikon*) that infuses it. Out of this accommodation of Galen and Aristotle
emerged a perceptual and cognitive model based on a series of "internal senses"
laid out according to specific psychological faculties, the *sensus communis* being
located with the faculty of imagination (Aristotle's *phantasia*) in the frontmost
cerebral ventricle, the estimative faculty and reasoning faculty in the middle
ventricle, and the faculty of intellectual memory in the occipital ventricle.[3] (See
Chapter 22 for further details.)

There was also an effort in this tradition to explain the mechanism by which
such 'objective' qualities as the color, hardness, and sweetness inhering in physical bodies could be transformed into 'subjective' qualities appropriate for apprehension by the perceptual system. Averroes, for instance, posited a change from
"material existence" in the object to "spiritual existence" in the medium so as
to accommodate the sensible data to the sensing subject. Avicenna, on the other
hand, had introduced a distinction between "form" (*sūra; forma*) and "intention"
(*maʿnā; intentio*) to explain how sense data convey information to the sensing
subject. On Avicenna's usage, the sensible qualities of a thing – its color, odor,
shape, and so on – are the forms of an object and are grasped by the five external senses. On the basis of these sense data, the internal senses are able to grasp
further features of an object, "intentions" that are not immediately perceptible.
In this way, a sheep not only sees a grey patch of color, but sees a threatening

[2] The notion that sensation involves an "impression" of sorts underlies Aristotle's seal-and-wax
analogy in *De anima* III.12, 434b29–35a10.
[3] For the classic account of the Arabic model of internal senses, see Harry Wolfson, "The Internal
Senses in Latin, Arabic, and Hebrew Philosophical Texts," *Harvard Theological Review* 28 (1935)
69–133. For the source of this model in Aristotle, see *De anima* III.1–7.

wolf (see Chapter 22). This philosophically powerful distinction would later be widely invoked in both the Arabic and Latin traditions.

The resulting model of sense perception and cognition emphasizes the empirical rather than the innatist nature of both processes and takes form roughly as follows. First, the object sends its form through the medium to the perceiver – a form that would come to be known in the Latin tradition as a "species." (The Latin word is generally left untranslated in modern discussions, and should be distinguished from the sense of "species" as a taxonomic kind.) Each sense organ is, in turn, affected by that species according to a particular intentional aspect, such as color, texture, or taste. The ensuing sense impressions are conveyed from each organ through the nerves to the *sensus communis* at the forefront of the brain, where they are combined into a composite intentional representation of the object. This representation comprises all of that object's perceptible attributes, including not only the proper sensibles (color, taste, feel [including hot, smooth, hard], odor, and sound) but also the common sensibles (such as size, shape, and motion). Remanded to the imagination for short-term memory, this composite form – which later comes to be known as the "sensible species" – constitutes an intentional representation of the object in all its physical and spatial particularity. As such, it stands proxy for the object itself and, bearing a host of ulterior intentions at the intelligible level, provides the wherewithal for a cognitive evaluation of what kind of object it is.

Underlying this model are three cardinal notions, the first of which is that sense perception is a complex process, not a singular event. As such, it unfolds in stages, each one at a higher level of abstraction and immateriality than its predecessor. During the initial stage, an object's species is received by the medium and conveyed through it to the sense organs. The second level, less material and accordingly more spiritual, involves the reception of that species by a given sense organ and the particular impression it makes on that organ. An object's color, for instance, is transformed in this stage from a wholly physical color effect in the aerial medium to a visible color effect in the eye itself. Finally, at the third and most spiritual level, the particular sense impressions aroused in each of the sense organs are passed neurally to the *sensus communis*, where they are combined with the common sensibles into a composite representation of the original object. Although the analysis depends critically on the process's becoming progressively more spiritual and less material, it is difficult to say just what those terms mean in this context, since the whole process takes place in the physical sense organs and the brain.[4]

---

[4] This analysis of sense perception depends on the process becoming progressively more spiritual and less material, but it is worth noting that the whole process takes place in the physical sense organs

The second cardinal notion that underlies this model is that species represent their objects to the senses and to the soul by being somehow like their objects, in the way that images are somehow like what they represent (see Chapter 25).[5] The third cardinal notion is that, *pace* Plato and Hugh of St. Victor, sense perception is not inherently deceptive. Properly regulated by reason, it is veridical. In fact, without the data of sense perception, reason has little or nothing to reason about and, therefore, no meaningful path to understanding.

SCHOLASTIC PERCEPTUAL THEORY

The flood of Aristotelian texts and corresponding Arabic commentaries that inundated Western Europe in the twelfth century (see Chapter 4) carried with it the Greco-Arabic interpretive stream just discussed, and within a matter of a few decades that stream had all but overwhelmed its Greco-Latin counterpart. By the second half of the thirteenth century, in fact, the internal-sense model of faculty psychology had taken such firm root within the scholastic community that it became the canonical framework for the analysis of perception. Accordingly, most subsequent analyses were cast in the language of proper and common sensibles, external and internal senses, abstraction, forms or species, material and spiritual existence, intentions, and psychological powers.

So much, at least, is true at a general level. At the level of specific application, however, disagreements about the details of analysis abounded. Rather than dwell on such disagreements, let us take as a more or less representative example Roger Bacon's analysis of visual perception in the *Perspectiva*.[6] Composed in the 1260s and originally appearing as Part 5 of the *Opus maius*, this work is based upon a remarkably wide variety of classical and Arabic sources, including Euclid's and Ptolemy's *Optics*, al-Kindī's *Optics* and *De radiis stellarum*, Aristotle's *De anima* and *De sensu*, and Avicenna's *De anima*. But the cardinal source for Bacon's analysis is Ibn al-Haytham's *De aspectibus*, the late twelfth-century Latin version of his *Kitāb al-Manāẓir* (*Book of Optics*), which was composed in Arabic around 1030. So influential was this treatise that it inspired not only Bacon but also a train of subsequent thinkers, Witelo and John Pecham in particular, whose works put special emphasis on the geometrical analysis of light and sight, and

---

and the brain. For discussion (focused on the Latin tradition), see, e.g., Robert Pasnau, *Theories of Cognition in the Later Middle Ages* (Cambridge: Cambridge University Press, 1997), and Myles Burnyeat, "Aquinas on 'Spiritual Change' in Perception," in D. Perler (ed.) *Ancient and Medieval Theories of Intentionality* (Leiden: Brill, 2001) 129–53.

[5] As Aristotle himself asserts, we never think without images (*De anima* III.7).

[6] For a study of this work that includes the critical Latin text and an English translation, see David Lindberg, *Roger Bacon and the Origins of* Perspectiva *in the Middle Ages* (Oxford: Clarendon Press, 1996).

formed the core of the Perspectivist tradition that held sway within scholastic circles from the late thirteenth century to the end of the sixteenth.[7]

Bacon opens the *Perspectiva* with a chapter extolling sight above all the other senses because it reveals the most about the world and, therefore, about God's providential order (I.1.1, 3). Having thus justified his focus on vision, Bacon turns in the next few chapters to a description of the perceptual system in the brain, both with respect to the internal senses seated in its ventricles and with respect to the basic sensibles appropriate to them. Altogether, he writes, there are twenty-nine of these sensibles, nine of which are proper to the individual senses: "vision concerning light and color; touch . . . hot, cold, wet, and dry; hearing . . . sound; smell . . . odor; and taste . . . flavor" (I.1.3, 9). The remaining twenty sensibles comprise such things as shape, size, distance, and spatial orientation, as well as corporeity, beauty, and ugliness – all of which are grasped by the *sensus communis* at the front of the brain.

According to Bacon, the mediating entities in this process are the forms or species that represent external sensibles. Take, for instance, a luminous or illuminated object surrounded by a continuous transparent medium, such as air. The surface of that object can be resolved into an indefinite number of infinitesimally small spots of light (*lux minima*). Each such spot is the minimum quantity capable of transmitting its species (*lumen*)[8] through the medium in a train of replications that starts with the spot-thick shell of the medium immediately surrounding the spot of *lux minima* and continues outward through a series of successive, ever-expanding shells. During this process, which Bacon calls "multiplication," the *lumen* at any point of the medium replicates itself in the spots immediately surrounding it as if it were *lux*, and the same holds for every other spot in the train of replications. The medium as a whole thus undergoes a qualitative change from "transparent" to "luminous" without thereby undergoing the physical effect of illumination appropriate to opaque bodies.

Bacon is adamant that these mediating species cannot exist without a material substrate of some kind, because he vehemently opposes the notion that species assume spiritual existence in media. On the contrary, he holds that such species have corporeal existence (*esse corporeale*) insofar as they require a material medium within which to subsist. According to Bacon's model, then, the light from any luminous or illuminated object is physically propagated through the medium in the form of a sphere, each of whose radii constitutes a rectilinear

---

[7] For an overview of the Perspectivist optical tradition and its development, see Lindberg, *Theories of Vision*.

[8] Following Arabic usage (that of Avicenna in particular), Bacon draws a clear distinction between the light that is inherent in luminous sources (*lux*) and the physical effect of that light in transparent media (*lumen*).

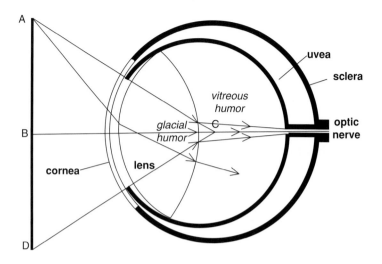

Figure 24.1

trajectory or ray. The same holds for every other attribute of the object, including not just sensible qualities like color but even the substantial nature itself of
the object: in each case, the species of that attribute is radiated in all possible
directions through the surrounding medium. It seems, therefore, that the species
of the object as a whole – the entire extended visual image – is apprehended
according to the aggregate of species emanating spot by spot from it.

How the physical impressions of light and color radiated to the eye through
the air are transformed into visual impressions is a matter of the eye's anatomical
and physiological structure, as illustrated in Figure 24.1. Bacon follows Ibn al-
Haytham in supposing that the eye as a whole forms a perfect sphere contained
by the scleral tunic, all of which is opaque except for the transparent cornea
at its front. Nested within this sphere is the opaque uveal sphere, which is
perforated in front by the pupil, and whose center is anterior to that of the eye
as a whole. Enclosed within the uveal sphere is the lens, which is filled with
glacial humor. Its anterior surface is flattened so as to be perfectly concentric
with the cornea. A thin membrane at the rear of the lens and ahead of the
eyeball's center differentiates it and the glacial humor filling it from the more
optically dense vitreous humor occupying the posterior portion of the uveal
sphere. At the very rear of the eyeball, finally, lies the opening of the hollow
optic nerve. From its juncture with the eyeball, this nerve winds back toward
the brain to meet its counterpart from the other eye at the optic chiasma. The
two nerves then bifurcate to join the brain on separate sides, where they open

into the first cerebral ventricle, whose anterior part has two branches. Being hollow, the optic nerves allow the animal spirit infusing the cerebral ventricles to flow into the eye in the form of visual spirit. Reaching the lens at the front of the eye, this spirit endows the lens with a special sensitivity to light and color (*Perspectiva* I.2.1–I.4.4).[9]

When the eye faces a luminous or illuminated object, it is bombarded from all sides by the light and color reaching it from every point on that object's surface. Because light and color are naturally apt to mingle, what actually reaches the eye is luminous color rather than light and color distinct from one another. If the eye were to sense all of that incoming radiation, the result would be a sheer chaos of overlapping color impressions. But the eye is providentially designed to make sense of that chaos, inasmuch as the anterior surface of the lens selects only those species of luminous color radiating to it along the perpendicular. This happens in virtue of both its optical and its sensory properties. First, because of its optical structure, only that radiation passes through the lens's surface without being refracted, and only that radiation continues in a direct line toward the center of the eye – all other radiation is diverted from that point by refraction. Thus, if line ABD facing the eye in Figure 24.1 represents a visible object, the rays originating at points A, B, and D that strike the lens orthogonally will pass straight toward centerpoint C of the eyeball, whereas any ray that strikes the surface of the lens obliquely will be refracted out of the way. In addition, the eye's special sensitivity permits the lens to be sensibly affected only by those species of luminous color that strike it directly along the perpendicular, because they make the most forceful impression. The rest, impinging at a slant, are too weak to be sensed (ibid., I.6.1–2).[10]

On the basis of this selection process, the lens abstracts a point-by-point representation of the object from all the species of luminous color reaching it from the object's surface. This representation (which constitutes what we might call the "visible species") continues in punctiform order toward the center of the eyeball, where all the individual species comprising it would, if unimpeded, converge to form a cone of radiation with its base on the visible object. Such convergence never occurs, though, because the rays along which the individual species pass are refracted at the interface between the glacial and vitreous humors, and thereby funneled into the hollow optic nerve in proper upright and punctiform order. Upon entering the nerve, this punctiform

---

[9] Much the same account is found not just in Ibn al-Haytham (Alhacen), *De aspectibus* I.6 (ed. Smith, pp. 348–55), but also in Witelo, *Perspectiva* III prop. 4 (ed. Unguru, pp. 105–11) and Pecham, *Perspectiva communis* I prop. 31 (ed. Lindberg, pp. 113–17).

[10] Again, compare Ibn al-Haytham (Alhacen), *De aspectibus* I.7 (ed. Smith, pp. 355–87), Witelo, *Perspectiva* III props. 6–18, and Pecham, *Perspectiva communis* I props. 33–8.

representation continues in proper order through the spirit pervading the nerve's hollow until it reaches the optic chiasma. There the representations from each eye merge to form a single, fused representation, which is then apprehended by the final sensor (*ultimum sentiens*). Constituting "perception by sense alone" (*comprehensio solo sensu*), this apprehension completes the act of sensation proper, which involves no cognitive mediation.

The visual representation thus abstracted by the lens and passed to the optic chiasma consists of nothing more than luminous color rendered visible. As such, it is like a mosaic; yet, like a mosaic, it also implies things that are not really in it, such as corporeity, shape, and so forth. Together, these implied things comprise the twenty sensibles mentioned earlier and referred to as "visible intentions" (*al-maʿānī al-mubṣara; intentiones visibiles*) by Ibn al-Haytham and his Latin disciples Bacon, Witelo, and Pecham. These intentions are discerned by the power of discrimination (*virtus distinctiva*) at the forefront of the brain – a power presumably exercised by the *sensus communis*. When presented with the visual representation apprehended by the final sensor, the common sense scrutinizes this representation by means of a scanning process called intuition (*intuitio*). Through this process, the power of discrimination apprehends the object represented according to its full array of visible attributes, including its inherent light and color. It also judges the quantity and quality of those attributes, determining, for instance, that the object is continuous and integral, small, red, bright, round, smooth, and so forth. The more intense the scrutiny, the clearer and more comprehensive the determination. After being apprehended and thus perceptually "realized" in this way, the compendium of sensible intentions is then sent to the imagination for short-term mnemonic storage. From there, this information can be recalled for subsequent scrutiny, either individually or as a whole that represents the object in all its physical particularity.

Repeated perception of such sensible intentions yields general impressions, which Bacon refers to as "vague particulars" (*particularia vaga*), each of which "is as common as its universal and is convertible with it." By means of such general impressions, we are able "to distinguish universals from one another and from particulars, and particulars from each other by comparison of the thing seen with the same thing previously seen, recollecting that it was previously seen and known to the observer" (*Perspectiva* I.10.3). That, of course, is how we recognize that the thing perceived is red, rather than green or blue, or that it is a horse, rather than a mule or a giraffe. Such recognition, however, is an intellectual rather than a perceptual act, and so it and everything that follows from it lies beyond the scope of this essay (see Chapter 26).

As both an exemplification of and elaboration on the species theory of sense perception, Bacon's account of vision rests on certain key assumptions that apply in one way or another to virtually every scholastic account of sensation based on species. First, the sensory soul is essentially a *tabula rasa* that, from infancy onward, is increasingly scrawled over with sense data in the form of intentional species. Second, those species constitute virtual images of physical particulars and their objective, defining characteristics. As such, they somehow resemble those particulars, which means that our overall internal impression of physical reality faithfully depicts (or at least *can* depict) that reality, albeit in a virtual way. From this it follows, third, that sense perception in general – and vision in particular – is veridical under certain normative conditions. If the object perceived is large enough, the ambient light bright enough, the intervening medium transparent enough, the sensing organ healthy enough, and so forth, that object will be apprehended as it actually presents itself to the perceptual system. Only when those normative conditions are transgressed does misperception arise, and misperception can be rectified by reason. Fourth, sense perception is not merely passive; rather, sensory intentions are realized according to the innate capacity of the sense organs and the faculties of the sensory soul to apprehend the information conveyed by the sense data. Finally, properly modulated sense perception leads directly to cognition. Indeed, taken to the extreme, this assumption implies the famous Aristotelian maxim that there is "nothing in intellect that was not previously in sense" (see, for instance, Thomas Aquinas, *Quaest. de veritate* 2.3 ad 19).

STRENGTHS AND WEAKNESSES OF THE SCHOLASTIC THEORY

Several features made the species theory of perception compelling to high medieval scholastic thinkers. For one thing, the theory makes intuitive sense. Then, as now, much common discourse about perception and cognition is governed by visual metaphor. Even some of the technical terminology of the species theory is rooted in sight words, two obvious instances being 'species' itself (which literally means *image* or *appearance*) and 'imagination' (*imaginatio*). In addition, the species theory was based on the best scientific evidence and principles of the time.[11] Finally, it offers, or at least *seems* to offer, the comforting assurance that sense perception leads to a true and certain understanding of physical reality according to its taxonomic and causal structure.

Yet, for all its apparent strengths, the species theory poses problems at both the specific and general level. The scholastic account of sound is a good case in

---

[11] This is especially the case with the Perspectivist account of vision, which draws heavily not only on Galenic anatomy and physiology, but also on Euclidean and Apollonian geometry for the basic principles of ray analysis.

point. For the most part, scholastic thinkers followed Aristotle (*De anima* III.8) in explaining sound as the result of an impact or percussion that is transmitted as movement through the air between what emits the sound and the ear. The problem here is that the movement generated in the air is not a replica of something formal in the object emitting it. In other words, according to this model, sound is not an inherent quality of external objects. Moreover, to suppose that actual sound consists not of the air's movement but of a species conveyed along with that movement is to beg the question, because it fails to explain what the species represents.[12]

In the context of the species theory, the case of distance and size is also problematic in at least two respects. First, distance and apparent size are relational and, as such, not actually in the object to which they are attributed. So how can there be an intention of such things in the sensible species? Ibn al-Haytham's answer, which is echoed by all the Perspectivists, is that we learn to visually estimate the size of objects and their distance from us on the basis of bodily experience, through which we acquire such notions as "one pace away" or "an arm's length away." Repeated experiences of these immediate distances carried incrementally outward, pace by pace, arm's length by arm's length, provide us with notions of longer and longer distances. Having fixed these notions in memory, we can then correlate them to the remembered notion of what a given object looks like at such distances. This, finally, enables us to estimate size and distance jointly according to the size–distance invariance principle, to which Ibn al-Haytham and his Perspectivist followers subscribed. Furthermore, if the space between viewer and object is punctuated by a succession of familiar objects (trees, people, houses, and so on) at familiar distances, we are able to extend our judgment of distance and an object's actual size to fairly long ranges. There are limits beyond which such judgment becomes so inaccurate as to cause misperception, however, as is the case with the "moon illusion," according to which we perceive the moon and sun as larger at the horizon than at the zenith.[13]

Second, as we saw earlier, both distance and size are assumed to belong to the set of twenty visible intentions that fall within the category of common sensibles by Bacon's account. Yet they are not apprehended in the same way

---

[12] For further analysis of medieval sound theory and its problems, see Robert Pasnau, "Sensible Qualities: The Case of Sound," *Journal of the History of Philosophy* 38 (2000) 27–40.
[13] For a more detailed analysis of this theory of distance and size perception, see A. Mark Smith, "The Alhacenian Account of Spatial Perception and its Epistemological Implications," *Arabic Sciences and Philosophy* 15 (2005) 219–40. On the moon illusion, see A. I. Sabra, "Psychology Versus Mathematics: Ptolemy and Alhazen on the Moon Illusion," in E. Grant and J. Murdoch (eds.) *Mathematics and its Applications in Science and Natural Philosophy in the Middle Ages* (Cambridge: Cambridge University Press, 1987) 217–47.

as, say, corporeity (that is, spatial extension) or shape, which can be inferred directly from the color-determined boundaries of the visible representations impressed on the anterior surface of the lens. Accordingly, the perception of distance and size seems to occur at a more abstract inferential level than that of shape or corporeity; this, in turn, implies that size and distance are not grasped in the same way as shape and corporeity and are therefore not "common" in the same way.

Even more acute than these specific problems, moreover, is the general problem posed by species themselves. After all, if we perceive the physical world by means of species, does it not follow that those species, rather than that which they supposedly represent, are the actual objects of perception? Might we not then be deceived in thinking that species faithfully picture their objects? Perhaps, in fact, our internal, perception-based impression of physical reality does not resemble that reality at all. These sorts of issues exercised a number of scholastic thinkers toward the very end of the thirteenth century and led to increasing skepticism during the first half of the fourteenth century (see Chapter 28). Indeed, a handful of fourteenth-century thinkers, William of Ockham foremost among them, rejected species entirely in favor of direct, intuitive apprehension of physical particulars (see Chapter 25).[14] Few were willing to go that far, however, and so the species theory of perception hung on, *faute de mieux*, until the turn of the seventeenth century. Among the developments that finally put paid to it, Johannes Kepler's theory of retinal imaging was of crucial importance insofar as it transformed the lens from a sensory selector of visual information to a mere focusing device, projecting a real, inverted image of the visual field onto the back of the eye. Such an image is nothing like a species, and indeed species played absolutely no functional role in Kepler's model of vision. Kepler thus set the stage for a radical transformation of visual theory (and perceptual theory in general) during the seventeenth century.

---

[14] See Katherine Tachau, *Vision and Certitude in the Age of Ockham: Optics, Epistemology and the Foundations of Semantics 1250–1340* (Leiden: Brill, 1988); Pasnau, *Theories of Cognition*; and Dallas Denery, *Seeing and Being Seen in the Later Medieval World: Optics, Theology and Religious Life* (Cambridge: Cambridge University Press, 2005).

25

MENTAL REPRESENTATION

CLAUDE PANACCIO

Medieval philosophers routinely distinguish between what is within the mind (*in anima*) and what is outside the mind (*extra animam*). Material substances and their qualities are taken to be paradigmatic cases of the latter, while emotions, acts of will, imaginations, and intellectual processes are salient examples of the former. An important array of problems these thinkers have to face, then, arise from the need to account for the various connections that can link the two realms. The most central of these problems is that some of the intramental stuff sometimes correctly represents the extramental: many of the philosophical preoccupations of the period, as it turns out, have to do with how *knowledge* comes about within the mind and how it is preserved.

The ultimate stake here is the human capacity for reaching *truth*. Following Aristotle, truth and falsity are thought of as features of *propositions*; and propositions, in Aristotelian logic, are taken to be complex units. Insofar, then, as the mental realm is the primary locus for knowledge, belief, and the like, there have to be propositions in it, and those have to be composed of simpler units: "for truth and falsity" Aristotle wrote, "involve a combination of thoughts" (*De anima* III.8, 432a10). Those subpropositional items, capable of serving as the basic representational units for the construction of mental propositions, will be the focus of the present chapter.

These items do not coincide, it must be said, with the whole range of what we might want to call "mental representations."[1] The medievals themselves, for one thing, would normally distinguish between the sensory and intellectual parts of the soul and, accordingly, between the sensible images, such as we use in imagining, and those *intellectual* representations that they took to be the basic

---

[1] I take 'mental representation' here as it is used in recent philosophy for any mental item that represents something. For the specifically medieval use of *repraesentatio*, see Henrik Lagerlund, "The Terminological and Conceptual Roots of Representation," in H. Lagerlund (ed.) *Representation and Objects of Thought in Medieval Philosophy* (Aldershot: Ashgate, 2007) 11–34.

components of scientific knowledge (*scientia*) (see Chapter 26). While both should be counted as mental representations, our focus here will be on the latter.

Two sorts of problems will be reviewed. First, how are such intellectual representations present in the mind? This question came to be subdivided into two distinct aspects in late medieval discussions: (a) How are they stored? (b) How do they occur in actual episodes of thinking? Second, in virtue of what do such intellectual representations represent whatever they represent – which is what we call today the "problem of intentionality"? The accent all along will be on what was by far the most fruitful period for these discussions: the hundred-year span that runs from the middle of the thirteenth century to the middle of the fourteenth, with such figures in the foreground as Thomas Aquinas, John Duns Scotus, William of Ockham, and John Buridan.

THE THEORY OF SPECIES

The main approach to the storing of intellectual representation during this period was the species theory. It flourished in the second half of the thirteenth century, but the inspiration for it came from as far away as Augustine and Arabic optical science. Augustine, drawing upon the Greek scientific tradition, explained in his *De Trinitate* that from the form of an external body to its representation in thought, "four species are found . . . born, as it were, step by step, one from the other " (XI.16). There is, first, the species of the body itself, its own bodily form; then, when perception occurs, a new form arises in the sense – the *species in sensu*; this in turn gives rise to a form in memory, the *species in memoria*, which, finally, produces a form in the gaze of thought, the *species in acie cogitantis*. In the Islamic world, on the other hand, a sophisticated account of vision, based on a mathematical model for optical radiations, was elaborated in the eleventh century by the mathematician and philosopher Ibn al-Haytham (Alhacen), whose treatise *De aspectibus*, once translated into Latin in the twelfth century, became the main source for the so-called 'perspectivist' theory of the thirteenth century, in which 'species' was the key term, meaning something like *representative form*.[2] (See Chapter 24 for further details.)

Robert Grosseteste and Albert the Great played significant roles in this integration of the optical model within the Augustinian and Aristotelian

---

[2] See, e.g., David Lindberg, *Theories of Vision from Al-Kindi to Kepler* (Chicago: University of Chicago Press, 1976).

frameworks, but its main proponent was the Franciscan Roger Bacon with his unified theory of the multiplication of species.[3] Bacon's idea was that every existing object continuously irradiates likenesses of itself into the surrounding parts of the universe, and that these emanations – called "species" – ultimately account for "every action in the world" (*Opus maius* IV.2.1). With respect to human cognition, when the species of material things propagated through the surrounding medium hit upon sensible organs, they produce new sorts of species within the sensory and eventually the rational parts of the soul. Mental representation, on this view, comes out as just a special case of the universal multiplication of species.

Bacon's interest in cognitional species focused more on perception than on intellection. It was his contemporary Thomas Aquinas, under the influence of Albert the Great, who most systematically applied the species scheme to the realm of intellectual representation and fused it into a general theory of abstraction. Aquinas, like Bacon, holds that human perception depends upon likenesses of the material things being propagated through the medium (the *species in medio*), leading to new likenesses being produced in the sensible part of the soul (the *species in sensu*). This process, which he sees as a progressive dematerialization, is brought to its full completion when the sensible species is transposed in turn into an even more purely spiritual sort of likeness, an intelligible species.[4]

Aquinas's theory has a number of salient features. First, it stresses the connection of the intelligible species with their prior sensible counterparts: "the whole of the intellect's cognition," Aquinas insists, "is derived from the senses" (*In De interpretatione* 1.3). On the other hand, the intelligible species, in his view, are *abstract* compared to sensible species. While the latter are singular representations of particular material things, the intelligible species are inherently general and refer the mind to the common natures – or quiddities – of things.

Intellectual representation is abstract in this way, according to Aquinas, because the intelligible species are produced within the mind as the result of the specialized action of what he calls, following Aristotle, the "agent intellect." Against Averroes and his Latin followers (such as Siger of Brabant), Aquinas thought of this agent intellect as a functional part of each individual human soul rather than as a separate transcendent power (see Chapter 23). He saw it,

[3] See Katherine Tachau, *Vision and Certitude in the Age of Ockham: Optics, Epistemology and the Foundations of Semantics 1250–1340* (Leiden: Brill, 1988).

[4] See (among many others) Leen Spruit, *Species Intelligibilis: From Perception to Knowledge* (Leiden: Brill, 1994–5); Robert Pasnau, *Theories of Cognition in the Later Middle Ages* (Cambridge: Cambridge University Press, 1997), and *Thomas Aquinas on Human Nature* (Cambridge: Cambridge University Press, 2002).

however, as largely independent of the will: the agent intellect, on his doctrine, operates as a continuously working spiritual transducer taking as inputs the particular sensible images stored in the human memory and yielding as outputs abstract general representations stored in the "possible intellect." That such abstraction routinely takes place within the human mind is for Aquinas the basic condition on the possibility of scientific knowledge. The process does not introduce any "veil of ideas" between the knowing mind and the external things, because Aquinas insistently describes the intelligible species stored in the possible intellect as the *means* of intellectual cognition (the "*quo*") rather than its objects (the "*quod*").[5]

Although the theory of intelligible species is further elaborated – to some extent on independent grounds – by Scotus,[6] Aquinas's version would remain the standard target for the critical discussion that soon developed around it. Various criticisms would be voiced in the last decades of the thirteenth century, by Henry of Ghent and Peter of John Olivi in particular,[7] but the most sustained attack comes from William of Ockham in the early fourteenth century. Ockham rejects altogether the *species in medio*, the sensible species, and the intelligible species as superfluous posits.[8] His point against postulating such species in the intellect, in particular, is that whatever theoretical job they are expected to do can be accomplished as well by the intellectual acts and *habitus* that everybody admitted anyway. This is a striking case of Ockham using the famous Razor principle that came to be associated with his name: it is vain to do with more what can be done with less. Presupposed by this discussion is the Aristotelian psychological vocabulary, in which actual episodes of thinking are called "acts" (*actus*) of the intellect. Like all other human acts (virtuous acts of the will, for example), those were thought to imprint on the mind, whenever they occurred, a certain disposition (*habitus*) that facilitates the reoccurrence of similar acts. Aquinas, like everybody else, had all of this. But he thought intelligible species were needed in addition as *preconditions* for intellectual acts to occur. This is where Ockham disagrees.[9] The most basic intellectual acts, he holds, are directly caused by external things, and these original "intuitive acts" in

[5] For one of Aquinas's typical statements about this, see *In De anima* III.2.
[6] Good presentations of Scotus's theory are found in Spruit, *Species Intelligibilis*, and Dominik Perler, "Things in the Mind. Fourteenth-Century Controversies over 'Intelligible Species'," *Vivarium* 34 (1996) 231–53.
[7] See Tachau, *Vision and Certitude*, ch. 2; Spruit, *Species Intelligibilis*, ch. 3; Pasnau, *Theories of Cognition*, chs. 5 and 7.
[8] Ockham's discusses the theory of species in *Reportatio* II.12–13 (for the intelligible species) and *Reportatio* III.2–3 (for the other two).
[9] That this is the gist of Ockham's critique of intelligible species is argued for in Claude Panaccio, *Ockham on Concepts* (Aldershot: Ashgate, 2004) ch. 2.

turn leave traces in the mind (*habitus*), which will sufficiently account for all subsequent intellectual acts. Much of the complicated apparatus of Thomistic intellectual cognition can thus be dispensed with.

It is often held that Ockham's critique of the theory of species did not receive much support after him and that even Buridan and other later fourteenth-century nominalists reverted to the doctrine Ockham had wanted to get rid of. This is true with respect to the *species in medio* and the *species in sensu*, which Buridan and his colleagues do make use of in their theory of sensible perception. The diagnosis is misleading, however, as regards intelligible species, for although Buridan, Nicole Oresme, and others active in Paris at this time revive the terminology of 'species' to refer to intellectual representations, what they mean in so doing is nothing Ockham could not have accepted. They clearly reject, in particular, the Thomistic idea that intelligible species are needed *prior* to the intellectual acts for them to occur: "such a species," Oresme writes, "does not precede the act of intellection, since it is acquired by such an act" (*In De anima* III.10). So although Oresme uses the terminology of an 'intelligible species,' he means it to describe what Ockham had described as a disposition. For both authors, consequently, the storing of intellectual representations is conceived as a matter of acquired dispositions (*habitus*), subsequent to the occurrence of intellectual acts caused in the mind by external things.

CONCEPTS AND INTELLECTUAL ACTS

The problem of what happens in actual episodes of thinking is not independent, of course, from that of storing mental representations. Even so, the two must be carefully distinguished, inasmuch as they give rise in medieval philosophy to distinct rounds of discussion. The new question here is whether a special mental object is produced by the intellectual act when a human being is engaged in the process of thinking. Peter Abaelard in the first half of the twelfth century suggested so:

> an understanding is a certain *action* of the soul on the basis of which the soul is said to be in a state of understanding. But the form to which it is directed is a kind of imaginary and made-up thing (*fictum*), which the mind contrives for itself wherever it wants and however it wants . . . We cannot call this either a substance or an accident.
> (*Logica "Ingredientibus"* [*In Porphyrium*], ed. Geyer, p. 96)

The act of thought, on this view, engenders its own objects as internal representations or likenesses for external things. Abaelard's remark about these made-up objects being neither substances nor accidents amounts to the idea that they should not be counted among the natural things of the world, but should be attributed a special, purely ideal, mode of existence as mere objects of thought. This is what later came to be called 'concepts.'

The most salient medieval doctrine of concepts developed along these lines is Thomas Aquinas's. Although this doctrine is distinct from his theory of intelligible species, he carefully combines the two. Thus, once a species is stored in the mind (through the previously described process), the *possible intellect* can use it in actual thinking by producing through it a new mental representation. This is what Aquinas calls a concept or mental word (*verbum*): it subsists only as long as the mind entertains it, and its mode of existence is purely *intentional* rather than natural.[10]

Aquinas deems such special objects of thought necessary in order to account for the possibility of thinking about things in their absence, and for our capacity to assemble mental propositions and to perform inferences. The theory, as a bonus, also has some theological appeal, since, in the spirit of Augustine's *De Trinitate*, Aquinas sees this internal engendering of concepts by the human mind as the best worldly model available for God's engendering of his Word.

For all its virtues, however, the doctrine would come under heavy attack in the last decades of the thirteenth century, especially from Franciscans. Olivi, William of Ware, and Walter Burley reproach it on two main grounds. First, concepts thus understood threaten to constitute an unwelcome array of cognitive intermediates between the mind and those external things that science is supposed to be about. If Aquinas had skillfully avoided the 'veil of ideas' problem in his theory of intelligible species by taking them to be the "*quo*" of cognition rather than the "*quod*," he did not seem to be nearly as successful with it in his theory of concepts, which he posited at times as the primary objects of thought.[11] Second, such internal ideal products, the critics insist, are superfluous: all the cognitive jobs they are supposed to fulfill can be attributed to the intellectual acts themselves. Duplicating these acts with such ghostly entities as these Thomistic concepts comes out in the end as both epistemologically harmful and psychologically useless. Still, for all that, these authors do not drop concepts from their cognitive picture: they simply *identify* them with intellectual acts.[12]

Mainstream philosophy of mind after Aquinas is characterized by this move from postulating special intentional objects to taking the intellectual acts

---

[10] This doctrine is frequently expounded by Aquinas. See, e.g., *Quaest. de veritate* 4, *Summa contra gentiles* I.53 and IV.11, and *Quaest. de potentia* 8–9.

[11] See, e.g., *Quaest. de potentia* 9.5: "What is intellected by itself is not the thing . . . What is intellected primarily and by itself, is what the intellect conceives in itself about the thing."

[12] More on this in Claude Panaccio, "From Mental Word to Mental Language," *Philosophical Topics* 20 (1992) 125–47.

themselves as the basic units of mental representation in actual thought. Ockham's own development in the 1310s and 1320s summarizes this passage.[13] In order to avoid positing universals and common natures outside the mind as the proper objects of intellectual activity, Ockham first subscribed to an Aquinas-like theory of concepts as mentally made-up units with a special mode of existence: this was his so-called *fictum* theory (see also Chapter 12). He changed his mind, however, when he realized that what is needed from concepts is that they can be used by the mind as general *signs* for things. This, he comes to think, can perfectly be accomplished by the intellectual acts alone: "all the advantages that derive from postulating entities distinct from acts of understanding can be had without making such a distinction, for an act of understanding can *signify* something and can *supposit for* [that is, stand for] something just as well as any sign" (*Summa logicae* I.12). Most later medieval philosophers eventually adopted this *actus*-theory of concepts.

INTENTIONALITY, LIKENESS, AND CONFORMALITY

A second important range of issues that medieval philosophers had to face with respect to intellectual representations revolved around what we now call the problem of *intentionality*: in virtue of what should any particular mental unit represent whatever it is that it represents? What is it about my mental concept *horse* that makes it a concept *of* horses? Aristotle's *De anima* provided medieval readers with a number of authoritative passages where the cognitive connection was described as a kind of *identity*, by sayings like: "the soul *is* in a way all existent things" (*De an.* III.8, 431b20), "intellect *becomes* each thing" (*De an.* III.4, 429b6), and so on. This suggested what has been called by recent commentators the *conformality thesis*: the reduction of intentionality to some *identity of form* between the knower and the known. Avicenna's and Averroes's highly respected comments on the Aristotelian psychology strongly supported this approach.[14]

Later medieval philosophy, however, progressively moved away from the con-formality thesis, as its drawbacks became more and more apparent. A first salient problem was to make it fit with a sound Aristotelian ontology: how can the sub-stantial form of a material body be identical with something accidental within the mind (as species and intellectual acts were taken to be)? One way out of this that was well known in the Latin Middle Ages was Avicenna's thesis of the

---

[13] See Panaccio, *Ockham on Concepts*, ch. 2.
[14] For good accounts of how the conformality thesis emerged out of the Aristotelian tradition, see Pasnau, *Theories of Cognition*, ch. 3; Peter King, "Rethinking Representation in the Middle Ages," and Martin Tweedale, "Representation in Scholastic Epistemology," both in Lagerlund, *Representation and Objects of Thought*, 87–108, 68–86.

indifference of essences: common natures, on this view, are in themselves indifferent to existing within material bodies or within the intellect; those are just two possible modes of existence of the *same* essences.[15] But it was hard to see how this gambit in the end could avoid Platonism, inasmuch as it seemed to require admitting Ideal Forms subsisting in themselves independently of their instantiations, a position that most of the Latin scholastics considered successfully refuted by Aristotle. Second, there were problems with harmonizing the conformality thesis with the accepted cognitive psychology: should the form of the thing as it exists in the intellect be identified with the intelligible species, with a mental *fictum*, with the intellectual act itself, or should it be added somehow to the furniture of the mind? All of these options led to serious difficulties.

Even Aquinas, to whom the conformality thesis is often attributed, can plausibly be interpreted as having kept away from it. It is true that Aquinas sometimes asserts that "natures have two kinds of being: one in the singulars and the other in the soul" (*De ente et essentia* 3.3). But he is usually very careful to qualify this Aristotelian way of speaking by explaining it, ultimately, in terms of 'likeness' and 'representation,' rather than the other way around: "what is intellected is not in the intellect through itself but through its likeness" (*Summa theol.* 1a 76.2 ad 4). Saying that the nature of the external thing comes to be within the mind is but a way of saying that this nature is *represented* within the mind by some *likeness* of it. Far from reducing intentional representation to the identity of form, Aquinas in the end does exactly the reverse, taking 'likeness' and 'representation' as more basic.[16]

It has been argued that 'likeness' in Aquinas's vocabulary is itself ultimately explainable in terms of identity, the main reference for this being to Aquinas's definition of 'likeness' (*similitudo*) as "an agreement or a communication in form" (*Summa theol.* 1a 4.3c).[17] But Aquinas in fact did not mean this definition to apply to the special case of *mental* likeness. When he gets specifically interested in the latter, he is eager, on the contrary, to distinguish it sharply from any "agreement in nature":

a likeness between two things can be understood in one of two senses. In one sense, according to an agreement in their very nature, and *such a likeness is not needed between the cognizer and the cognized thing*... The other sense has to do with *likeness by representation*, and this likeness is required between the cognizer and the cognized thing.

(*Quaest. de veritate* 2.3c)

[15] See Avicenna, *Metaphysics* V.1–2.
[16] See Claude Panaccio, "Aquinas on Intellectual Representation," in D. Perler (ed.) *Ancient and Medieval Theories of Intentionality* (Leiden: Brill, 2001) 185–201.
[17] See Dominik Perler, "Essentialism and Direct Realism: Some Late Medieval Perspectives," *Topoi* 19 (2000) 111–22.

Mental representation, as a result, is left unreduced with respect to any sort of identity.

Another medieval idea that is sometimes connected with the conformality thesis is that of "objective being" (*esse objectivum*), as it is found, saliently, in the work of Scotus.[18] Scotus's writings on this topic are notoriously difficult, yet on one plausible reading – suggested, for instance, by Scotus's close disciple William of Alnwick – the idea of objective being neither depends upon nor favors the conformality thesis.[19] An object x, on this terminology, is said to be objectively in a mind y if and only if x is the object of a cognitive state of y – if and only if, in other words, x is represented in y somehow. Think of a book about Julius Caesar. It could correctly be said, in the relevant sense, that Caesar is objectively in the book, not because he is hidden in the pages in some ghostly way, but simply because he is referred to in the book. Thus understood, the idea of 'objective being' presupposes that of being an object for a cognitive state, and can hardly serve, consequently, as the basis for a satisfactory account of intentionality.

The conformality thesis, in short, was not a preeminent contender in later medieval thought as a theoretical approach to mental representation. Neither Aquinas nor Scotus, with whom it is often associated, provided in the end a worked-out account of intentionality in terms of identity of form, and it is doubtful that they ever intended to.

SIGNIFICATION AND CAUSALITY

The early decades of the fourteenth century are often credited with a major revolution in philosophy of mind and language, and rightly so.[20] With respect to the intentionality of concepts, two major developments are of special relevance: a general semiotical turn in philosophy, and a strong intensification of the Aristotelian naturalistic drive.

Medieval logicians, from the twelfth century on, had progressively worked out a highly original body of semantic theory around what they called the "properties of terms," with the idea of *signification* at its core. In Walter Burley, Ockham, Buridan, and their contemporaries, this "terminist logic" reached a high degree of sophistication and became the main analytical tool for discussing all sorts of problems in philosophy and theology (see Chapters 11–12). There

---

[18] See in particular Perler, "Things in the Mind."

[19] The first of Alnwick's *Quaestiones de esse intelligibile* is translated in R. Pasnau, *Cambridge Translations of Medieval Philosophical Texts*, vol. III (Cambridge: Cambridge University Press, 2002) 152–77.

[20] See, e.g., King, "Rethinking Representation in the Middle Ages."

were many disagreements over the particulars of the theory, but on the whole the terminist apparatus for semantic analysis was found to be quite illuminating over a wide range of issues.

To Ockham in particular, the clarifying virtues of the approach suggested that the terminist grid, if suitably adapted, might be used for the description and assessment of discursive thought itself, rather than of external linguistic utterances only. From William of Auvergne to Roger Bacon, the basic units of intellectual representation had been counted as 'signs' by many in the thirteenth century. What Ockham did was to take them as signs in the precise sense that was relevant for terminist logic to apply: a mental 'term,' accordingly, was to be seen as a mental unit independently endowed with a signification and capable of various referential functions (called "*suppositio*") when combined with other similar units in syntactically well-formed sentences or propositions. It is one of Ockham's most influential contributions that he systematically brought the technical terminology of grammar and that of *significatio* and *suppositio* to bear upon the study of *concepts*: concepts, for him, are natural signs within the mind, interconnectable with each other as the basic elements of a semiotic system with a precise syntax and semantics.[21] Ockham thus resolutely defended a strong version of what is called today the "language of thought hypothesis," and the approach, after him, remained popular among scholastic thinkers until far into the fifteenth and sixteenth centuries.[22] The intentionality of thought, on this picture, was taken to rest, fundamentally, upon the *natural signification* of certain simple mental items syntactically combinable with each other.

This is where the naturalistic drive comes in. By the time of Ockham and Buridan, the main outcome of the debates summarized above over intelligible species and mental concepts was, as we saw, that intellectual acts and *habitus* themselves could serve as the basic units of cognition, with no need for postulating special extra representations in the mind either before the intellectual acts or as purely ideal products of them. But acts and *habitus*, by contrast with Aquinas's concepts, for example, were thought of as *natural* beings: they were taken to be *qualities* of singular minds, like colors are qualities of material substances, and to be unproblematically inserted, as such, in the network of *causal* connections that characterizes the realm of what is natural. From Scotus onward, much of the interest in epistemology revolves around the various causal links naturally involved in cognitive processes. Insofar as intentionality in general is

[21] See Claude Panaccio, "Semantics and Mental Language," in P. V. Spade (ed.) *The Cambridge Companion to Ockham* (Cambridge: Cambridge University Press, 1999) 53–75.
[22] See E. J. Ashworth, *Language and Logic in the Post-Medieval Period* (Boston: Reidel, 1974), and Gabriel Nuchelmans, *Late-Scholastic and Humanist Theories of the Proposition* (Amsterdam: North-Holland, 1980).

made to rest upon the natural signification of certain mental items, as Ockham proposes, it becomes very tempting to reduce natural signification in turn to some combination or other of causal connections. Ockham indeed explicitly defends this naturalistic program, with respect at least to the *singular* terms of our mental language: such a representation, he explains, "brings the mind to the cognition of this object by which it was (partially) caused" (*Reportatio* II, 12–13, 289). And he is strongly committed to taking natural causal connections as, at least partially, determining the signification of our basic general concepts such as *man*, *flower*, or *animal*, including, most probably, some relational ones such as *similar to* or *larger than*.[23]

Ockham never completely renounces the traditional idea that intellectual representations are *likenesses* of what they represent, but this, for him, is not to say much. His main point in following tradition here is to stress that the internal form of a concept is relevant somehow for its cognitive role to be correctly played: a concept, after all, should help us to recognize a new individual as falling under it, when it does, and for this, its own form must resemble in some way that of the external thing. But this is a secondary role for Ockham. What he wants concepts to do, primarily, is to stand – in his terms, to *supposit* – for certain things within mental propositions in such a way as to decisively affect the truth conditions of these propositions. Which things exactly they will stand for depends to a very large extent on which causal transactions a given mind is – or was – engaged in: the natural signification of our simple concepts thus turns out to be, basically, a matter of causality. Many fourteenth-century philosophers after Ockham, from Adam Wodeham and John Buridan to Nicole Oresme and Peter of Ailly, go along this semiotico-naturalistic path with him, producing in the process a rich literature of precise discussions over both the syntax and semantics of our mental language, and the causal connections that are required for cognition to take place. The so-called *via moderna* of the fourteenth century thus crucially tends to account for intellectual representation in terms of natural processes. Much research remains to be done as to how this program was carried on in the later Middle Ages, and how it was eventually superseded in the seventeenth and eighteenth centuries, but there is no doubt that the episode constitutes a high point in the history of epistemology and philosophy of mind.

[23] This is argued for at some length in Panaccio, *Ockham on Concepts*, esp. chs. 6–7.

26

SCIENCE AND CERTAINTY

ROBERT PASNAU

When James of Venice translated the *Posterior Analytics* from Greek into Latin, in the second quarter of the twelfth century, European philosophy got one of the great shocks of its long history. John of Salisbury famously remarked that "it has nearly as many obstacles as it has chapters, if indeed there are not more obstacles than chapters" (*Metalogicon* IV.6). Latin philosophers had taken themselves to have a grip on Aristotle's logic, but what they were discovering in the twelfth century was that their grasp extended only to what would be called the Old Logic, the *ars vetus*, leaving untouched the New Logic of the *Topics*, the *Sophistical Refutations* and, most importantly, the *Prior* and *Posterior Analytics*. Moreover, as the Latin philosophical canon swelled in the later twelfth century to include not just the full Aristotelian corpus but also the riches of Arabic philosophy, European authors realized just what a central role the *Posterior Analytics* in particular played in all this work. Although we now tend to focus on the recovery of Aristotle's natural philosophy, metaphysics, and ethics, it is arguably the *Posterior Analytics* – not the *Ethics*, the *Metaphysics*, the *Physics*, or the *De anima* – that had the most pervasive influence on scholastic thought. For it is here that Aristotle sets out the methodological principles that are to be followed in the pursuit of systematic, scientific knowledge: what the Latin tradition would call *scientia*. Inasmuch as scholastic philosophers take the goal of all their inquiries to be the achievement of such *scientia*, the strictures of the *Posterior Analytics* had an influence on virtually every area of scholastic thought, from theology (see Chapter 50) to metaphysics (Chapter 44), and from grammar (Chapter 15) to optics (Chapter 24).

The *Posterior Analytics* was important early in Islamic thought, and below I will suggest one respect in which this tradition had a significant influence on Latin scholasticism. But the focus of this chapter will be on how Aristotle's conception of science was developed in Christian Europe in the thirteenth and fourteenth centuries. The focus will not, however, be on science in our modern sense, inasmuch as that conception of science as something distinct from systematic inquiry in philosophy or theology is a strictly post-medieval development. The chapter's focus will be on science in Aristotle's sense: roughly, an intellectual grasp of a true proposition grounded in an understanding of why that proposition is true. Since there is no word in English that refers to this, I will often retain the terminology of the authors in question, and so speak of *epistēmē*, *scientia*, and *ʿilm*.

KNOWLEDGE AND SCIENCE

There were, of course, systematic attempts at knowledge among Latin authors prior to the recovery of the *Posterior Analytics* (see Chapter 16), and there were extensive discussions of what knowledge is. But once medieval philosophy fell under the domination of Aristotle in the thirteenth century, theoretical discussions of knowledge tend to presuppose the apodeictic framework set out in the *Posterior Analytics*. For a proposition to be the object of *scientia* in this sense, it must be necessary and universal, known on the basis of an affirmative demonstration in the first syllogistic figure, the premises of which are necessary and explanatory of the conclusion.

Plainly, there is not much that we know in this way. Accordingly, it was never tempting to treat the *Posterior Analytics* as a treatise of epistemology in our modern sense. Instead, scholastic discussions of *scientia* would typically begin by bracketing off Aristotle's conception of *scientia* from the more casual conception employed – then as now – in ordinary use. Thus, in the first Latin commentary on the *Posterior Analytics*, from the 1220s, Robert Grosseteste distinguishes four ways in which we might speak of *scientia*:

> It does not escape us, however, that having *scientia* is spoken of broadly, strictly, more strictly, and most strictly. [1] *Scientia* commonly so-called is [merely] comprehension of truth. Unstable contingent things are objects of *scientia* in this way. [2] *Scientia* strictly so-called is comprehension of the truth of things that are always or most of the time in one way. Natural things – namely, natural contingencies – are objects of *scientia* in this way. Of these things there is demonstration broadly so-called. [3] *Scientia* more strictly so-called is comprehension of the truth of things that are always in one way. Both the principles and the conclusions in mathematics are objects of *scientia* in this way . . . [4] *Scientia* most strictly so-called is comprehension of what exists immutably by means of the comprehension of that from which it has immutable being. This is by means of the comprehension of a cause that is immutable in its being and its causing.
>
> (*In Post. an.* I.2, ed. Rossi, p. 99)

The most familiar, and so in a way the most striking, of Grosseteste's four kinds of knowledge is the first: common *scientia*. It is not obvious that Aristotle did want to allow *epistēmē* of unstable (and so not even for the most part) contingent truths – at any rate, this takes us quite far from the *Posterior Analytics* framework.

Still, the need for something like this broad conception of knowledge seems to have been widely felt, judging from how pervasive the notion would become among later scholastic authors, who very often cite Grosseteste as their source.[1]

Scientia in this broad sense is very much like what we now call knowledge. Rather surprisingly – at least from a modern perspective – such a conception of "ordinary" knowledge received little more than passing, desultory attention in the Middle Ages. It was instead the strict requirements of the *Posterior Analytics* that benefited from exhaustive scholarly inquiry, both in textual commentaries and in independent logical treatises. One might conclude, on this basis, that Aristotle had a negative impact on scholastic thinking about knowledge, leading authors to concentrate on one quite narrow and idiosyncratic conception to the exclusion of anything like a generally adequate epistemology. One response to this charge would be the sort of move often associated with Platonism – namely, to dismiss everyday perceptual knowledge as not worthy of the name at all, or, in a phrase that al-Ghazālī ascribes to the theologians, that such knowledge "is a kind of ignorance."[2] This was never the common attitude of the scholastics, however, given their empirical, Aristotelian orientation. One might say instead that, in place of epistemology, later medieval Latin authors focused on cognitive theory (see Chapter 25). Yet this, too, would be somewhat misleading, inasmuch as it suggests that Aristotle's rigorous framework is unacceptable as an epistemic theory. On the contrary, a plausible case can be made for that framework as, if anything, a more attractive paradigm for what epistemology ought to be.

After all, as has become increasingly apparent in recent years, it is doubtful that there is *a* common conception of knowledge in the "ordinary" sense – even limiting ourselves to speakers of English – that can be given a satisfactory analysis. Moreover, even if such an analysis could be given, the effect would be to set up a rigid bar that beliefs must pass over in order to count as knowledge, yielding a crude binary account on which beliefs either succeed or fail to count as knowledge. So analyzed, all knowledge has the same epistemic credentials, meaning that there is no room to talk about having a more or less satisfactory knowledge of some proposition. By the same token, on this binary approach, questions of skepticism naturally loom large, because it might well be that when

---

[1] See, e.g., Albert the Great (*In Post. an.* I.2.1); Henry of Ghent (*Summa quaest. ord.* 1.1c); William of Ockham (*Summa logicae* III-2.1); John Buridan (*Summulae* 8.4.3–4). The distinction between a broad and strict sense goes back at least to Themistius's paraphrase of *Post. An.* (I.2), which was translated into Latin from Arabic by Gerard of Cremona before 1187, and which we know Grosseteste to have used. See Pietro Rossi, "Robert Grosseteste and the Object of Scientific Knowledge," in J. McEvoy (ed.) *Robert Grosseteste: New Perspectives on his Thought and Scholarship* (Turnhout: Brepols, 1995) 53–76.

[2] *Miʿyār al-ʿilm*, ed. Shams ad-Dīn, p. 244; tr. J. McGinnis and D. C. Reisman, *Classical Arabic Philosophy* (Indianapolis: Hackett, 2007) p. 239.

we alight upon just the correct height at which to set the bar of knowledge, none of our beliefs will manage to clear it, in which case we will have arrived at the result that no one knows anything.

This is not to say that the precise scheme of the *Posterior Analytics* can be defended today. That discussion is too wedded to the syllogism, and too obscure in many of its details to serve as an attractive model. Still, the *Posterior Analytics* offers a perspective worth taking seriously, in virtue of its overarching ambition to conceive of knowledge in terms of an epistemic ideal: what the perfect cognitive state is for beings such as us. This is how Thomas Aquinas, for instance, begins his gloss on Aristotle's definition of *epistēmē*: "When Aristotle says 'We think we have *scientia*,' etc. [*Post. An.* 71b10], he offers a definition of having *scientia simpliciter*. With respect to this we should consider that to have *scientia* of something is to cognize it perfectly" (*In Post. an.* I.4.5).[3] John Duns Scotus invokes the same idea, in discussing the same passage: "The first condition, that *scientia* be a certain cognition, excluding all deception, opinion, and doubt, applies to every intellectual virtue, because an intellectual virtue is a perfection of intellect, disposing it for perfect operation" (*Additiones magnae* prol. 1.1 [ed. Wadding, XI: 2]).[4] These passages reflect the standard scholastic conception of what it is to have *scientia*; as we will see, the subsequent details of their account follow directly from this starting point.

The above passage from Grosseteste illustrates how the Aristotelian approach puts knowledge on a sliding scale. The theory aims to identify an epistemic ideal – what would be the best epistemic state we could hope to achieve, given our cognitive abilities. This is the notion from which our modern usage of 'science' stems, via the seventeenth century, inasmuch as the scientist aims not just to acquire knowledge, but to achieve an ideally trustworthy and rigorous understanding of a given fact. When epistemology is so conceived, methodological principles immediately suggest themselves: thus, according to Aristotle, to achieve the ideal of *epistēmē*, we must formulate our conclusions in syllogistic form, aiming at necessary truths inferred ultimately on the basis of self-evident first principles. Yet, of course, when one begins with ideal theory, one must be prepared to relax those strictures as necessary, and so a good deal of medieval theorizing over *scientia* concerns what to do in cases where one or more of these

[3] See also *Summa theol.* 1a2ae 67.3c; *Sent.* III.31.2.1.1 obj. 4; *Quaest. de veritate* 11.1 sc 5; *Quaest. de virtutibus in communi* 7c: "someone is said to be understanding or knowing inasmuch as his intellect is perfected for cognizing what is true."

[4] See also *Ordinatio* prol. 3 n. 26; *Ordinatio* III.24 q. un. (ed. Wadding, VII.1: 482–3). Scotus's views are discussed in some detail in Eileen Serene, "Demonstrative Science," in N. Kretzmann *et al.* (eds.) *The Cambridge History of Later Medieval Philosophy* (Cambridge: Cambridge University Press, 1982) 496–517. This remains a useful summary of its topic.

desiderata cannot be achieved – as, for example, in biology, where conclusions tend to hold only for the most part rather than necessarily, or in theology, where first principles often are not self-evident but must be embraced on faith alone.[5] Given this picture, in fact, there is something absurd about singling out one point along the scale and engaging in a pitched battle over whether our beliefs pass that test. Accordingly, medieval authors are rarely very interested in the problem of skepticism (see Chapter 28).

THE OBJECTS OF KNOWLEDGE

Scholastic authors disagreed in various ways over what *scientia* had as its object. One disagreement, especially prominent in the early fourteenth century, concerned whether knowledge concerns things, linguistic–conceptual entities, or something else altogether. Walter Chatton argues for the first thesis: when one knows something about God, for instance, the object of knowledge is not a sentence or a thought but is, instead, God (*Sent.* prol. 1.1). Robert Holcot argues against this view. When one knows that man is not a donkey, is the object of knowledge man or donkey? Moreover, the object of knowledge is a truth, but things are not truths (*Quodlibet* I.6 in Courtenay, *Revised Text*). According to Holcot, the objects of knowledge must be thoughts and sentences. Ockham had thought this as well, but Holcot insists on something that was not quite clear in Ockham – namely, that the objects in question are particular tokens of a thought or sentence, so that what one knows is the sentence one is hearing right now, or the thought one is thinking (ibid.).[6] This is a plainly counterintuitive view: it does not seem that one comes to know more things by listening to people repeat themselves. If one thinks the objects of knowledge are neither things nor sentence tokens, though, then it seems that one needs to appeal to some more abstract sort of entity. This is the approach championed by Adam Wodeham, who contends that when one knows that man is an animal, the object is an abstract sentence type, man-being-an-animal (*hominem esse animal*). As for what that thing is, Wodeham seems to think that no good answer can be given (*Lectura secunda* I.1). Gregory of Rimini would later take much

---

[5] On for-the-most-part conclusions, see Aristotle, *Post. An.* I.30 and II.12, 96a8–18. On theology as a science, see the classic study of Marie-Dominique Chenu, *La théologie comme science au XIII* siècle (Paris: Vrin, 1957).

[6] There is an insightful discussion of Holcot's view in E. A. Moody, "A Quodlibetal Question of Robert Holcot, O.P. on the Problem of the Objects of Knowledge and of Belief," *Speculum* 39 (1964) 53–74. For the larger debate over the objects of knowledge, see the groundbreaking studies of Gabriel Nuchelmans: *Theories of the Proposition: Ancient and Medieval Conceptions of the Bearers of Truth and Falsity* (Amsterdam: North-Holland, 1973), and *Late-Scholastic and Humanist Theories of the Proposition* (Amsterdam: North-Holland, 1980).

the same approach and famously describe such an abstract entity as a *complexe significabile* – a signifiable complex (see esp. *Sent.* I prol. q. 1).[7]

One of Rimini's arguments in favor of abstract entities as the objects of *scientia* is that the theory of *scientia* requires its objects to be *necessary*, thereby excluding contingent entities such as token thoughts or utterances, or things in the world (ibid., art. 1 [ed. Trapp *et al.*, I: 6]). The necessity argument was part of Aristotle's official definition of *scientia*, which runs as follows: "We think we have *scientia* of a given thing *simpliciter*, and not in a sophistical way (which is by accident), when [a] we think we cognize the cause on account of which the thing is, and [b] that it is its cause, and [c] that it is not possible for it to stand otherwise" (*Post. An.* I.2, 71b10–12, translating from James of Venice's Latin version). The passage is hardly clear regarding what sorts of entities one has knowledge of, but clause (c) is at least clear that *scientia* concerns things that are somehow necessary. As noted above, this constraint is problematic in many areas of knowledge, such as biology – or indeed in any field where we seek *scientia* regarding particular individuals, or contingent states of affairs. What Aristotle seems to have had in mind in such cases is that *epistēmē*, even when concerned with the particular and the contingent, is nevertheless always concerned with necessary connections (or, minimally, with "for the most part" connections). And what the *Posterior Analytics* stresses as the key to grasping such connections is knowing "what a thing is" – or, in more medieval terms, knowing its essence.[8]

This is the ultimate foundation of the medieval preoccupation with essences. A scientific understanding of the natural world, on this view, is not simply a comprehensive listing of true sentences about that world; instead, it is a grasp of the essential features of the world, which brings with it an understanding of how things necessarily are, and how they necessarily relate to other things (for further discussion of essences, see Chapter 46). Here the methodological precepts of the *Posterior Analytics* interact with both the *De anima*'s theory of soul and the broader cognitive story in which that theory is embedded. It was clear to the earliest Latin commentators that one of the central cruxes of the whole account was how to square the generally empiricist Aristotelian approach with the need to arrive at a grasp of the inner natures or essences of things.

[7] See, most recently, Susan Brower-Toland, "Facts vs. Things: Adam Wodeham and the Later Medieval Debate over Objects of Judgment," *Review of Metaphysics* 60 (2006) 597–642, and Pascale Bermon, *L'assentiment et son objet chez Grégoire de Rimini* (Paris: Vrin, 2007). Both Holcot's and Wodeham's discussions are translated in Robert Pasnau, *Cambridge Translations of Medieval Philosophical Texts*, vol. III: *Mind and Knowledge* (Cambridge: Cambridge University Press, 2002) 302–51.

[8] The need to grasp what a thing is, and to make that the middle term in a demonstration, is the main theme of *Post. An.* Bk. II. On the connection between this and necessity, see the useful remarks in Jonathan Barnes's translation and commentary on *Post. An.* 71b10 (pp. 92–3).

Grosseteste, drawing on the *Posterior Analytics'* notoriously brief concluding remarks about how "perception instills universals" (100b5), offers this account:

> And so when, over time, the senses act through their many encounters with sensible things, reason, which is mixed up with the senses and in the senses as if it were carried toward sensible things in a ship, is awakened. Once awakened, reason begins to draw distinctions and to consider separately things that had been confused in the senses. Sight, for instance, confuses color, size, shape, and body, and in its judgment all these things are taken as a single thing. Awakened reason, however, distinguishes color from size and shape from body and then shape and size from the substance of body, and so by drawing distinctions and abstracting, it arrives at a grasp of the substance of body, which supports size, shape, and color.
>
> (*In Post. an.* I.14, ed. Rossi, p. 214)

Scholastic authors generally agree that something like this must happen, as the intellect takes a superficial sensory grasp of perceptual qualities and attempts to arrive at an understanding of the underlying substance or nature or essence of the thing. But the only common ground among authors with respect to the details of this process is their inability to supply persuasive details.

The main divide, in this domain, was over whether a naturalistic story could account for our grasp of essences. Grosseteste himself offers a kind of mixed verdict: in this life, we ordinarily rely on the senses for our intellectual grasp of the universal natures of things. But, sounding more Platonic and Augustinian than Aristotelian, he indicates that this orientation is not inevitable:

> If the highest part of the human soul, the so-called intellective part, which is not the actuality of any body and needs no corporeal instrument for its proper operation, were not clouded over and burdened by the weight of the corrupt body, it would have complete knowledge without the aid of sense perception, through an irradiation received from a higher light.
>
> (ibid., p. 213)[9]

Subsequent proponents of divine illumination (see Chapter 27) often argued for its necessity on the grounds that a strictly naturalistic account of concept formation through sense perception would not be adequate to explain our grasp of the natures of things.[10] And although scholastic authors from John

---

[9] This and the previous passage are based on an unpublished translation by Scott MacDonald. For a discussion of Grosseteste's views in this area, see Steven P. Marrone, *The Light of Thy Countenance: Science and Knowledge of God in the Thirteenth Century* (Leiden: Brill, 2001), and Christina Van Dyke, "An Aristotelian Theory of Divine Illumination: Robert Grosseteste's Commentary on the Posterior Analytics," *British Journal for the History of Philosophy* (forthcoming).

[10] This was, for instance, one of the main grounds of Henry of Ghent's protracted defense of divine illumination in the 1270s; see Robert Pasnau, "Henry of Ghent and the Twilight of Divine Illumination," *Review of Metaphysics* 49 (1995) 49–75.

Duns Scotus forward almost always rejected this sort of Augustinian appeal to the supernatural, there remained in their alternative accounts little by way of details regarding how one gets from sensory impressions to a grasp of essences, as well as widespread pessimism regarding the extent to which we in fact do manage to succeed in this.[11]

SCIENCE AND CAUSES

The first two clauses in Aristotle's definition of *epistēmē* require that we grasp "the cause on account of which the thing is." This idea gets expressed in scholastic texts as a distinction between a demonstration that merely establishes the fact of something's being so (demonstration *quia*), and a demonstration that establishes the reason why something is so (demonstration *propter quid*). In its original, pre-Kantian sense, an *a priori* demonstration is one that proceeds from principles that are causally prior, whereas an *a posteriori* demonstration reasons from effects back to causes. For this reason, only *propter quid* or *a priori* demonstrations yield *scientia* in the strict sense (see also Chapter 44).

When the Aristotelian program is understood as the characterization of an ideal cognitive goal, the causal requirement cannot really be very controversial. Even before Aristotle, Plato speaks of the need to grasp the "legitimate cause and reason" of natural phenomena (*Timaeus* 28a), and even before the recovery of the *Posterior Analytics*, Peter Abaelard quotes from Virgil's *Georgics* – "Happy the man who has been able to discover the causes of things" (ii.490) – in support of the claim that "the man of understanding is he who has the ability to grasp and ponder the hidden causes of things" (*Logica "Nostrorum,"* ed. Geyer, pp. 505–6). Although historians have sometimes found a rejection of this doctrine in the seventeenth century, in fact this is one part of the scholastic program that would be generally embraced by later thinkers. Even the great atomist Pierre

---

[11] Roger Bacon, *Opus maius* I.10 remarks that "no one is so wise regarding the natural world as to know with certainty all the truths that concern the nature and properties of a single fly, or to know the proper causes of its color and why it has so many feet, neither more nor less." Aquinas says almost exactly the same thing: "our cognition is so weak that no philosopher could have ever completely investigated the nature of a single fly" (*In Symbolum Apostolorum* prol. [*Opuscula theol.* II, n. 864]). For a discussion of Aquinas's views, see Philip Reynolds, "Properties, Causality, and Epistemic Optimism in Thomas Aquinas," *Recherches de théologie et philosophie médiévale* 68 (2001) 270–309. In the next century, William of Ockham would express great skepticism regarding our ability to distinguish differences in species (*Quodlibet* III.6), as would Francis of Marchia (*Sent.* I.3.1), among many others. For a general and pessimistic discussion of the gap between sense and intellect in scholastic accounts, see Peter King, "Scholasticism and the Philosophy of Mind: The Failure of Aristotelian Psychology," in T. Horowitz and A. Janis (eds.) *Scientific Failure* (Lanham, MD: Rowman and Littlefield, 1994) 109–38.

Gassendi can quote with approval the very same passage from Virgil (*Syntagma* II.1.4.1, ed. 1658, p. 283a).

The Aristotelian causal requirement might better be described as an explanatory requirement, where the kinds of explanations are the famous four causes: material, formal, efficient, and final. One way or another, virtually every scholastic author accepts this list, and also accepts that *scientia* requires a grasp of them all. This is not to say that scholastic authors were always optimistic about our ability to achieve this ideal. John Buridan, for instance, considers the question of whether "perfectly knowing some effect requires knowing all of its causes," and answers in the affirmative – but he then admits that this is impossible for us. This does not lead him to reject the causal requirement, however, but only to formulate a less demanding standard for *scientia* that we can meet. Nevertheless, that requirement still has a causal component; indeed, Buridan rather surprisingly denies that mathematics should be regarded as the most certain of sciences precisely because its demonstrations do not contain an account of the reason why the theorems of math are true (*Quaest. Phys.* I.5). Subsequent critics of scholasticism were not, in general, any more pessimistic than medieval authors regarding our ability to grasp the underlying explanations of things. Where they differed is in what sorts of explanations they recognized. Although Gassendi, for instance, accepts that a grasp of causes is a prime desideratum in physics, he insists that "only the efficient is properly called a cause" (*Syntagma* II.1.4.1, p. 284a). The rejection of forms, prime matter, and final causes lies at the very heart of what is supposed to be modern in seventeenth-century philosophy.

CERTAINTY AND EVIDENCE

Surprisingly, Aristotle says nothing at all about certainty in the *Posterior Analytics*. By the later Middle Ages, however, the link between *scientia* and certainty becomes taken for granted, and the certainty of perfect, demonstrative *scientia* is contrasted with the merely plausible arguments of dialectic. The idea of certainty is hardly present in Grosseteste's commentary on the *Posterior Analytics*, but it appears very prominently a generation later, at the start of Albert the Great's commentary:

A human being ought to fill his soul not with what is [merely] plausible (*probabile*) and credible (*opinabile*), because they do not yield a stable (*stantem*) disposition in the soul, but with things that are demonstrable and certain, which render the intellect certain and stable, because such things are themselves certain and eternally stable. And from this it is clear that this alone . . . is the end and most perfect and is unconditionally desirable among the logical sciences.

(I.1.1, ed. Jammy, I: 514a)

Albert invokes the preface to Ptolemy's *Almagest* in defense of this claim, but it
seems likely that his true inspiration is not Greek but Arabic authors, for whom
certainty (*yaqīn*) was a crucial desideratum in knowledge (*ʿilm*) from the start of
their discussions.

This association between knowledge and certainty was virtually inevitable
within the Arabic tradition, because the standard Arabic translation of the *Posterior Analytics*, by Abū Bishr Mattā, employs *yaqīn* quite liberally throughout the
text in places where Aristotle speaks simply of knowledge or demonstration.[12]
Al-Fārābī puts particular weight on certainty as a characteristic of science,
describing "certain philosophy" as the culmination of a process that first proceeds through sophistical and dialectical reasoning (*Kitāb al-ḥurūf*, ed. Mahdī,
nn. 108–42). He defines certainty in terms of a kind of meta-conviction about
one's beliefs:

> Certainty means that we are convinced, with respect to what we assent to, that it
> cannot possibly be different from our conviction. Moreover, we are convinced that this
> conviction about it also cannot be otherwise, to the point that when one reaches a
> given conviction concerning his initial conviction, he maintains that it, too, cannot be
> otherwise, and so on indefinitely.
>
> (*Kitāb al-burhān*, ed. Fakhry, p. 20)[13]

The interesting idea here is that to be certain is to have something more than
a mere conviction. One might be convinced of certain political beliefs, for
instance, and yet know that if one had been born in a different time or place,
one's political views would most likely be different. Certainty, then, is to be
convinced in such a way that one is further convinced that such conviction itself
cannot be otherwise, and that this further conviction also cannot be otherwise,
and so on, as far upward into higher-order beliefs as one cares to go.

When authors invoke certainty as a requirement on knowledge (*ʿilm* or *scientia*), however, it is often difficult to know whether they mean it in a subjective

---

[12] See Deborah L. Black, "Knowledge (*ʿilm*) and Certitude (*yaqīn*) in al-Fārābī's Epistemology," *Arabic Sciences and Philosophy* 16 (2006) 11–45.

[13] The translation is that of McGinnis and Reisman, *Classical Arabic Philosophy*, p. 64 (slightly revised). The relevant parts of the *Kitāb al-ḥurūf* are translated in Muhammad Ali Khalidi, *Medieval Islamic Philosophical Writings* (Cambridge: Cambridge University Press, 2005) pp. 1–18. See also Avicenna: "certitude is to know that you know, and to know that you know that you know, *ad infinitum*" (as quoted in Black, "Knowledge and Certitude," n. 68). Al-Ghazālī similarly takes for granted the link between demonstrative knowledge and certainty: "know that true demonstration is what provides necessary, perpetual and eternal certainty that cannot change" (as translated in McGinnis and Reisman, *Classical Arabic Philosophy*, p. 239). See also Farid Jabre, *La notion de certitude selon Ghazali dans ses origines psychologiques et historiques* (Paris: Vrin, 1958). For a broader discussion of Islamic scientific methodology, see Jon McGinnis, "Scientific Methodologies in Medieval Islam," *Journal of the History of Philosophy* 41 (2003) 307–27.

or objective sense. Al-Fārābī's definition focuses on the subjective sense, but of course mere subjective certainty can hardly be sufficient for perfect knowledge. The difference between the subjective and objective senses is brought out clearly in the Latin tradition by Buridan, who insists that both are required, and who then goes on to distinguish between two sorts of objective certainty:

In the genus of human cognition there are several kinds of certainty and evidentness. On our part, certainty should not be called that of *scientia* or assent unless it is firm – that is, without fear [of the opposite]. On the part of the proposition, one sort of certainty is that which pertains to a proposition so firmly true that there is no power by which it (or any like it) can be made false . . . Another human certainty on the part of the proposition obtains because the proposition is true and cannot be made false by any natural power and natural manner of action, although it can be made false by a supernatural power and in a miraculous manner.

(*Summulae de dialectica* VIII.4.4, tr. Klima, p. 709)

Subjective certainty consists in the subject's confidence. Buridan takes for granted here the standard scholastic characterization of opinion as a less perfect cognitive state in which we assent to a proposition, but with some concern that the opposite might in fact be true. A minimal condition on *scientia* is that it be distinguished from mere opinion by a sufficient degree of confidence in the proposition believed. A further condition on *scientia*, according to Buridan, is objective certainty, which concerns the truth of the object believed – a proposition that will be certain insofar as it is necessarily true. Here he distinguishes two kinds of necessity, which are plainly versions of what are now called logical and natural necessity.

In the elided parts of the quoted passage, Buridan uses this distinction between two kinds of necessity to respond to Nicholas of Autrecourt's notorious arguments for a nearly global skepticism (see Chapter 28). If propositions must be certain in the first, stronger sense, then there is almost nothing of which we have certain knowledge. Yet, as he points out: "This sort of certainty is not required for *scientiae* that are natural or metaphysical, let alone in the arts or in practical matters" (ibid.). In the natural sciences, the second sort of certainty is sufficient. And in practical matters, we do not require even that much. Here Buridan describes a third and still weaker form of certainty:

Yet there is still another weaker evidentness that suffices for acting well morally. This goes as follows: if someone, having seen and investigated all the attendant circumstances that one can investigate with diligence, judges in accord with the demands of such circumstances, then that judgment will be evident with an evidentness sufficient for acting well morally – even if that judgment were false on account of invincible ignorance concerning some circumstance. For instance, it would be possible for a judge to act well and meritoriously by hanging a righteous man because through testimony and other documents it sufficiently appeared to him in accord with his duty that that good man was a bad murderer.

(*Quaest. Metaph.* II.1, ed. 1518, ff. 8vb–9ra)

This notion of moral certainty would become extremely influential in the seventeenth century, as a strategy for replying to skepticism.[14]

What makes Buridan's moral certainty particularly interesting, however, is not that it weakens the notion of certainty to a point where it is applicable to our practical lives, but that it adds something crucial to any workable systematic account of objective certainty – namely, the notion of a thing's being certain relative to a body of evidence. If we follow the *Posterior Analytics* and focus only on necessary truths (logical or metaphysical), then this notion of relative certainty has no application. The propositions in question will be necessarily *simpliciter*, and our only task will be to produce a syllogism showing why they are necessary. But if we attempt to apply the theory to the contingent truths of everyday life, then we need to consider whether a proposition is certain relative to the evidence that we have for it: is it, for instance, certain that a man is guilty, given the testimony we have heard? Such considerations blur the distinction between demonstrative and dialectical reasoning, and open the door to a wide range of new questions that would emerge in the modern era regarding probability and reasoning in light of probabilistic evidence.

---

[14] On the later history of moral certainty, see Henry van Leeuwen, *The Problem of Certainty in English Thought: 1630–1690* (The Hague: Nijhoff, 1970). For further discussion of Buridan's views on certainty, see Jack Zupko, "On Certitude," in J. Thijssen and J. Zupko (eds.) *The Metaphysics and Natural Philosophy of John Buridan* (Leiden: Brill, 2001) 165–82. More generally, see Peter King, "Jean Buridan's Philosophy of Science," *Studies in History and Philosophy of Science* 18 (1987) 109–32.

27

DIVINE ILLUMINATION

TIMOTHY NOONE

Illumination has an intriguingly complex history, which could be approached in many different ways. One could trace the philosophical evolution of the theme of light as a metaphor for understanding intellectual cognition, in which case our treatment would have to commence with the discussion of intellectual cognition among the major figures in Greek philosophy, especially Plato and Aristotle, both of whom regularly employed the metaphor of light in their efforts at grappling with the mysterious nature of intellectual cognition.[1] Alternatively, one could focus on theories of human intellectual cognition that appeal to intellects higher than ours but still not divine to account for how human intellectual activities are possible. But the object of the present chapter, more narrowly still, is to trace out the theory of *divine* illumination – that is, the theory of how God's light is required to account fully for how humans are capable of attaining the truth that they manage to attain through their intellectual activities. Considered in this way, the philosophical story we shall trace begins with Augustine, though the figures we shall be focused upon mainly are thirteenth-century philosophers. The reason for targeting thirteenth-century figures is that, although the texts of Augustine that inspire the theory were well known throughout the Middle Ages, it was only in the late twelfth and early thirteenth centuries that philosophers writing in Latin began to perceive, largely through their acquaintance with the recently translated Arabic sources and translations of Aristotle, that an alternative approach to that of Augustine was a genuinely viable option. Hence, prior to the thirteenth century, one might speak of the theme of divine illumination, but not a theory of divine illumination. The theory of divine illumination is something that occupies Latin philosophers' attention for about a century, eventually yielding to accounts of intellectual cognition in which no or little appeal is made to the divine light.

---

[1] R. E. Houser, "Philosophical Development through Metaphor: Light among the Greeks," *Proceedings of the American Catholic Philosophical Association* 64 (1990) 75–85.

AUGUSTINE

Augustine advances his view of divine illumination in various texts throughout his literary career. A handy text for seeing one of the considerations that lead him to do so is his famous discussion of language in the dialogue *De magistro*. There Augustine and his son, Adeodatus, eventually reach a conclusion opposed to the one that seemed so clear at the outset of their discussion: they conclude that words do not ultimately teach us anything unless we are acquainted previously and directly with the items to which they refer. Applied to the order of items of intellectual acquaintance, this outlook on language requires that there must be universal types that we "see" in the light of truth, inasmuch as we are not necessarily acquainted with the same individuals and do not "see" the truth of such universals in each others' minds. We might, accordingly, label this the argument from the identity and permanence of the intelligible object. The unchanging commonality and universality of the types seem to warrant their being available in a light superior to our minds or to the minds of any other creatures.

This argument, though prominent in other texts as well, competes with two others in Augustine's outlook. One of these arises from the historical context that influences so much of Augustine's thinking – namely, the thought of Plato and the Neoplatonism of Plotinus and Porphyry. Plato argued for the claim that number is a basic notion not able to be gotten out of the objects of experience, since any example of a given number of things or of a sensible whole possessing parts presupposes a prior acquaintance with the concept of *unit* or *whole*. These concepts are a necessary condition for grasping that there is a number of things, or that there is one whole thing composed of parts.[2] In Augustine's presentations of this claim, the range of objects underivable from ordinary sense experience is expanded to include moral virtues and moral principles, but in both cases the point is the same: such objects inform our thinking and are true of the sensible examples to which we apply them in judgments, but they cannot be items epistemically available to us simply through sense experience. They must instead be prior to the items of sense experience and made available to us in a light present both to our minds and to those of all other intellectual creatures.[3]

The final consideration to which Augustine appeals is the eternity of truth, a version of the same kind of incommensurability between sensory experience and intellect that Plato invokes, but now occurring at the level of judgment and not only simple apprehension. Certain truths, such as *Every whole is greater than*

---

[2] Plato, *Republic* 524e–525a; *Philebus* 14e–15c. Cf. Plotinus, *Enneads* IV.4, VII.3, VIII.9.
[3] See for example Augustine, *De libero arbitrio* II.9.27.

its parts or *Seven and three equal ten* or *Justice is to be sought and injustice opposed*, seem to be such that they would hold in the absence of any sensible items or situations answering to their descriptions; indeed, they would hold even if no creatures existed. Yet this observation seems incompatible with the idea that what makes them true – their truthmakers, if you will – are just created items of a certain type; their truth is unchangeable and eternal, and yet all creatures are changeable and temporal. Hence Augustine concludes that neither the creatures to which such notions apply nor the finite minds that understand such truths are the ultimate source of such truths. Rather, the source lies in something prior both to the creatures known and to the creatures knowing – namely, it lies in God, who is the Eternal Truth enlightening the mind.[4]

Augustine's view of divine illumination is rich in its suggestiveness, but not very well developed in terms of details. For example, another feature of his epistemology is the claim that the types with which we are acquainted through the divine light are the divine ideas through which God makes and forms creatures. But exactly how the considerations described above are to be understood in reference to the divine ideas as models of creatures is left underdeveloped by Augustine, something that explains both the subsequent appeal of Augustine's philosophy of knowledge and its perennial currency in various later theories of knowledge, inasmuch as practically all later thinkers, illuminationists and non-illuminationists alike, seem to find something in Augustine's views worthy of preservation and adaptation.

ANSELM

The most important continuator of Augustine prior to the entry of the Aristotelian tradition into the Latin West at the end of the twelfth century was undoubtedly St. Anselm. Anselm certainly thought of himself as a faithful disciple of Augustine and explored in much finer detail many of Augustine's ways of thought. Prominent among the latter were Augustine's ideas on truth, studied by Anselm at length in his dialogue *De veritate*. According to Anselm's teaching in this dialogue, truth is an uprightness that is perceptible to the mind alone; it is an awareness that things are as they ought to be, and that they conform to their ultimate measure in the divine mind. What this means is that the truth found in creatures consists in their conformity to their eternal divine models. It cannot be adequately explained simply by appealing to the conformity of finite minds with the objects of their immediate awareness. This kind of "horizontal" approach was favored, seemingly, by the notion of logical truth expressed by

---

[4] Ibid., II.12.33–15.39.

Aristotle in the saying that theoretical truth consists in thinking of and saying something that is that it is and of something that is not that it is not.[5] The horizontal approach overlooks a crucial feature of creatures, namely, their being expressions of the eternal truth of God, which suggests in turn that we can speak of their essences as true when they conform to their divine models. Hence to know the truth of creatures involves not simply being aware of them, but also, however slightly, being aware of their "vertical" relation to the divine mind. The eternality of truth, as that theme is found in both Augustine and Anselm, points to there being one eternal truth behind all expressions of truth, both in the created objects and in our thoughts about them, mental, spoken, and written. Although we may say there are many truths, this is the case only in a manner of speaking, just as we may say there are many times because there are many objects in time, when actually there still would be time even if those particular objects did not exist (see, for instance, Anselm, *De veritate* 13).

AVICENNA

Resources in Latin for philosophical psychology were limited up until the late twelfth and early thirteenth centuries; here, as in epistemology, the main source for most authors was Augustine, and in particular the *De Trinitate*. This picture began to change rapidly after 1170, when the writings of Avicenna appeared in Latin translation, many of them done by the Spaniard Dominicus Gundisalvi. For our purposes, the most influential passage is the following:

We shall first remark that the human soul is something that first understands potentially and then understands actually. Every thing, however, that passes from potency to act does so only through a cause that is actual and draws the potential principle to actuality. There must exist, therefore, a cause through which our souls pass, in regard to intelligible realities, from potency to act. But the cause that gives the intelligible form can only be an Intelligence in act and in which the principles of intelligible, abstract forms abide.

The comparison of this Intelligence to our souls is akin to the relation of the sun to our faculties of sight. For just as the sun is an object of sight in its own right and actually, and things are seen by its light actually that were not formerly visible, so too for the disposition of this Intelligence to our souls. For when the rational power considers individual items that are found in the imagination and is enlightened (*illuminatur*) by the light within us of the Agent Intelligence (of which we have spoken previously), the objects cognized become abstracted from matter and its concomitants, and are impressed on the rational soul. It is not that the objects of the imagination are changed into our intellect, or that the notion (*intentio*) found in many makes something like itself in the

---

[5] Aristotle, *Metaphysics* IV.7, 1011b25–30. Cf. *De interpretatione* 9, 18a36–b5.

intellect (for the notion is abstract, insofar as it is considered in itself) – rather, from the consideration of these things in the imagination, the soul is rendered apt to receive the abstraction emanating into it from the Agent Intelligence.

(*Liber de anima* [*Shifā'*] V.3)

What Avicenna is describing is clearly the process whereby intelligible contents come to be possessed by our minds. Yet, despite the dematerialization or "abstraction" to which he adverts, which seems akin to a process of eliciting the actual intelligible from the potentially intelligible found in the imagination, it is clear that the actual intelligible as such comes from the Agent Intelligence upon the occasion of the human mind's considering the items found in the imagination. Hence, the intelligible results not so much from the mind's abstraction as from an emanation from above. Latin readers from Gundisalvi to Roger Marston in the last quarter of the thirteenth century could not resist seeing in this Agent Intelligence the Divine Mind, although the Agent Intelligence to which Avicenna himself refers is actually the tenth of a series of intelligences emanating from the one Necessary Being and is thus, in Christian terms, a creature. The thirteenth-century Latin tendency to combine elements taken from Avicenna with the more traditional psychology and epistemology of Augustine and Anselm has been called by Étienne Gilson *Augustinisme avicennisant*, and it is certainly one recurring pattern in the Latin illuminationist tradition.[6]

GROSSETESTE, RUFUS, AND BONAVENTURE

Prior to Robert Grosseteste in the Latin West, several lesser figures invoked the sort of illumination we have been discussing,[7] but Grosseteste is the first to treat these issues in detail. In his *De veritate*, a work dating in all probability to the period of his theological teaching at the Franciscan house in Oxford (*ca.* 1229–36), Grosseteste treats the central issue that emerged at the end of Anselm's own *De veritate* – namely, the unity and multiplicity of truth. According to Grosseteste, the conformity of created things to the speech (*sermo / verbum*) of the Father is their truth, for that is what they ought to be and is the rightness perceptible to the mind that Anselm describes as the truth of the essences of

---

[6] Étienne Gilson, "Les sources gréco-arabes de l'augustinisme-avicennisant," *Archives d'histoire doctrinale et littéraire du moyen-âge* 4 (1929) 5–149; "Avicenne en occident au moyen-âge," *Archives d'histoire doctrinale et littéraire du moyen-âge* 36 (1969) 89–121; "Pourquoi saint Thomas a critiqué saint Augustin," *Archives d'histoire doctrinale et littéraire du moyen âge* 1 (1926–7) 5–127. See also Roland de Vaux, *Notes et textes sur l'avicennisme latin aux confins des XIIe et XIIIe siècles* (Paris: Vrin, 1934).

[7] Chief among them is John Blund. See his *Tractatus de anima* ch. 25 sec. 23 (ed. Callus and Hunt, nn. 372–5).

things. In fact, according to Grosseteste, the Anselmian definition embraces both the highest truth and the truth of things, though it expresses the former as the rightness that rectifies all others and the latter as a rightness that is made right (ed. Baur, p. 135). Falsity is just the failure to conform to the speech of the Father, whereas, conversely, truth is lack of defect or, more accurately stated, the fullness of being (*plenitudo essendi*). Yet there is a twofold being of things, Grosseteste tells us: their *primum esse*, which is their metaphysical or ontological constitution, such as the union of soul and body in a human being; and their *secundum esse*, which is the activities or functions that an entity should have, such as honesty in a human being. If we utter a proposition such as 'A human is an ass,' we utter something that has a kind of truth as *primum esse* – it is, after all, a meaningful statement or proposition – but it entirely lacks *secundum esse* because it fails to state what is the case (ibid., pp. 135–6).

Grosseteste's position on truth, as one can readily see, is quite heavily indebted to Anselm. Regarding the issue of whether truth is one or many, however, he takes a different position, arguing that truth must be many and not one. His reason is that the term 'truth' would not be capable of distribution (that is, being said of many things) if there were not many truths, for the comparison of one thing to many things does not produce a genuine plurality. So, by implication, what stands against Anselm's view that all truth is one and the Highest Truth is just that we do speak of many truths, and that our doing so cannot be rendered plausible without there being many truths and not simply many true things (ibid., pp. 138–9).

The strong commitment that Grosseteste makes to a multiplicity of truths dominates his consideration of two issues bearing upon illumination: first, whether other lights of truth besides that of the Highest Truth are rendered superfluous if the Highest Truth is sufficient for showing all truth; second, whether we can make any sense of the truth of a created thing understood as a conformity to the eternal reason (the *ratio aeterna*) in the divine mind without our being aware of the divine mind as such. (On the eternal reasons as divine exemplars, see Chapter 6.) Grosseteste's reply to both of these doubts hinges on an analogy he proposes for how the human mind grasps truths. The human mind's way of understanding may be aptly compared to our seeing a colored body. In the absence of light, a person may not see anything at all in a colored body, yet light is not color; color may be called "embodied light" but it nonetheless is distinct from light in the sun and the medium. Likewise, the human mind cannot grasp the concrete essence (*id quod est*) of creatures without the light of the eternal reason shining upon the object and the mind; the created truth discloses the created essence, but only under the light of the Highest Truth (ibid., pp. 137–8). That is precisely why the light of the Highest

Truth does not render another light superfluous and that is why, too, we do need to be in contact with the eternal reason somehow to surmise a conformity to the eternal exemplar. The light of the Highest Truth cannot substitute for the light of the created essence (or that of the mind, presumably), any more than the light of the medium or the source can substitute for the color of the colored body. In a word, although we do not see the divine mind or its eternal *ratio*, we perceive truth through that eternal reason, just as we see through light and things in light, yet scarcely notice the light. The eternal reason is present to our minds, but in a manner so self-effacing as to be readily overlooked. Hence, those who are unclean of heart never notice what it is that allows them to know (ibid., p. 139).[8]

Grosseteste's case for postulating divine illumination rests largely on the immutability of the truths we know. This is most clearly seen, perhaps, in the case of first principles, but nearly any intelligible truth will do. The simple fact of the matter, for Grosseteste, is that the fixity and stability of the truths we know about creatures could not arise solely from creatures, even if the content of what we know does. The basic reasoning for this claim is that things cannot give what they do not have. If there is no absolute fixity in created things, created things cannot generate constancy of meaning even if they in some way express that meaning.

If Grosseteste's theory is largely a continuation of Anselm, with agonizingly few details regarding how human psychological faculties relate to the divine light, the same cannot be said of the views of Richard Rufus of Cornwall, Bonaventure, or most of the other later figures in the illuminationist tradition.[9] On the contrary, they felt the need to clarify precisely what the human faculties could and could not attain through their activities so as to articulate precisely how and why divine illumination is needed.

Rufus's texts on illumination, although few in number, are extremely interesting. Regarding the role of the agent intellect, he suggests that it is a part of the soul just as much as the possible intellect is. However, he also treats it as analogous to memory in Augustine's Trinitarian anthropology, and he makes it the source of actual awareness – indeed, he treats it as aware in its own right of

---

[8] For a study of Grosseteste's doctrine of truth, see Steven Marrone, *William of Auvergne and Robert Grosseteste: New Ideas of Truth in the Early Thirteenth Century* (Princeton, NJ: Princeton University Press, 1983).

[9] For information on how Grosseteste's thinking impacted Parisian authors, see Camille Bérubé and Servus Gieben, "Guibert de Tournai et Robert Grosseteste: sources inconnues de la doctrine de l'illumination suivi de l'édition critique de trois chapitres du *Rudimentum doctrinae* de Guibert de Tournai," in *Sanctus Bonaventura: 1274–1974* (Grottaferrata: Collegium Sancti Bonaventurae, 1973) 627–54.

things that the individual human being is not aware of.[10] The precise role of God's light, according to one of the few texts that deals with the matter, is to render more fully intelligible the items not made fully intelligible by the human agent intellect.[11] What this may mean historically is that Rufus is one of the very first authors to suggest the subsequently commonplace hypothesis of two agent intellects, one divine and the other human.[12]

Although Bonaventure's theory relies on many of the same sources as Grosseteste's, his appreciation of the role of the human intellectual faculties in the process of ideogenesis and his own metaphysical views on creation cause him to have a unique view in the history of illuminationism. To start with the former point, Bonaventure offers an account of how the agent and the possible intellects can be said to be two distinct powers and yet still belong to the soul. He rejects any suggestion that these intellects are distinct entities in the category of substance, whether that effort identifies the separate agent intellect with an Intelligence (as in Avicenna) or even with God (a view some were trying to read into Augustine, and that would soon be reworked in theorists such as Roger Marston). Instead, Bonaventure insists that the two intellects, agent and possible, are parts of the human soul that function as coordinated but interdependent causes in the activity of knowing. Each is, in a way, both active and passive, inasmuch as the agent intellect is passive with respect to the phantasm that it requires for abstraction, and the possible intellect exercises the activity of knowledge once it is prompted by the agent intellect (*Sent.* II.24.1.2.4c). The process of abstraction and consequent intellection are normal and natural for the human soul in all of its conditions: prior to the fall, after the fall, and in the perfected resurrected state. Hence there is no room in Bonaventure's theory for the view proposed by Rufus – namely, that the agent intellect is the only permanent and essential part of the mind, and that it knows things that the individual human being does not (*Sent.* II.24.1.4 ad 5–6).

---

[10] Rufus, *Scriptum super Metaphysicam* XI d. 2 lect. q. 3 V (ed. Timothy Noone, *An Edition and Study of the Scriptum super Metaphysicam, bk. 12, dist. 2* [Ph.D. dissertation: University of Toronto, 1987], p. 216). Note that before William of Moerbeke's translation of *ca.* 1265, Bk. XI = Lambda (the modern Bk. XII).

[11] Rufus, *De ideis* (Prague ms. 1437, ff. 35va–36ra; Erfurt ms. Q. 312, fol. 84ra). For Rufus's explanation of physical light, see Timothy Noone and R. James Long, "Fishacre and Rufus on the Metaphysics of Light," in J. Hamesse (ed.) *Roma, magister mundi: Mélanges offerts au Père L.E. Boyle* (Louvain-la-Neuve: Féderation internationale des instituts médiévales, 1998) I: 517–48.

[12] See Leonard Bowman, "The Development of the Doctrine of the Agent Intellect in the Franciscan School of the Thirteenth Century," *Modern Schoolman* 50 (1973) 251–79; Jean Rohmer, "La théorie de l'abstraction dans l'école franciscaine de Alexandre de Hales à Jean Peckham," *Archives d'histoire doctrinale et littéraire du moyen âge* 3 (1928) 105–84. On Bacon's and Rufus's views of the agent intellect, see Timothy Noone, "Roger Bacon and Richard Rufus on Aristotle's *Metaphysics*: A Search for the Ground of Disagreement," *Vivarium* 25 (1997) 251–65, esp. pp. 256–7.

Bonaventure argues for illumination by examining the transcendental framework within which human knowledge transpires – its foundation in the transcendental concepts of being and true – and by insisting on the incommensurability between human (or angelic) knowers and the eternal truths that are the foundation for their knowledge. What makes Bonaventure's case for the transcendental framework so closely connected with his doctrine of abstraction is that, in his metaphysics, each creature is a natural sign of its respective divine idea. Consequently, the more the human mind delves into the particular item it knows through sense experience, the more it is redirected toward the exemplar that is the eternal source of intelligibility for the item known.

Bonaventure exploits the transcendental framework within which the human mind functions by beginning with the commonplace view, derived from Avicenna, that being is the first object known. According to the doctrine of Bonaventure's *Itinerarium*, continued reflection upon the notion of *being* will cause the mind to understand being in its fullness: pure being that lacks no perfection (ch. 5). In a word, implicit in the notion of *being* that is the first object of the human mind is the notion of *Being* that belongs exclusively to God. Hence, God and his light are the precondition for knowing whatever it is that we do know. We should, however, be leery of identifying this notion of the divine being's intentional presence in our most fundamental notion with an innate idea of God, even though there appears some surface resemblance to René Descartes's later views. Bonaventure is aware of teaching of this sort – in his time it is found in Thomas of York and, at a certain stage of his career, Roger Bacon[13] – but he explicitly rejects it (*Sent.* II.24.1.2.4c). Instead, the notion of *being* functions like a sign pointing to the eternal source of all knowledge, and so there is a kind of reflection or abstraction involved in reasoning that reaches God.

When Bonaventure argues explicitly and directly for the thesis of divine illumination in his *Disputed Questions on the Knowledge of Christ*, he focuses upon the issue of eternal truths and their incommensurability with the human mind and the created things in which those truths are expressed. Taking up examples found in Augustine, Bonaventure argues that the fact that we know mathematical, moral, and metaphysical truths that cannot fail – truths that would be true whether or not creatures exist – is a sure indication of the presence of the divine light to the human mind in its knowledge. Alternative explanations that try to locate the source of such truths in the world or in the human

---

[13] See Thomas of York, *Sapientiale* VI.26, as cited in Matthew of Aquasparta, *Quaestiones disputatae de fide et de cognitione* (Quaracchi: Collegii S. Bonaventurae, 1957) p. 257; and Roger Bacon, *De multiplicatione specierum* 1.3 (ed. Bridges, *Opus maius* II: 433).

mind undercut themselves immediately, for neither the object known nor the human knower has the characteristics of the truths known and hence neither can be the total source of human intellectual knowledge. Bonaventure does not, however, deny a role to sense knowledge or abstraction (as we have already seen) in intellectual knowledge; the senses and the intellect are partial causes in the production of the act of knowledge, cooperating with the divine light. The latter is described by Bonaventure as a "regulating and moving cause," combining with the human soul's causality to produce the act of knowledge. Though the point remains somewhat disputed, the most plausible reading of Bonaventure's theory of illumination is that he takes the divine light to guide our intellectual acts of judgments, both simple and complex, and that he thus holds that the divine light is present in all our acts of intellectual knowledge.[14]

MATTHEW OF AQUASPARTA, JOHN PECHAM, AND ROGER MARSTON

Of all Bonaventure's disciples, the most faithful in many ways was Matthew of Aquasparta, who taught at Paris in the late 1270s. Yet, when we read his *Disputed Questions on Cognition* from that period, we are immediately alerted to a change since the time of Bonaventure's teaching in the 1250s: the doctrine of Thomas Aquinas has now impacted the way in which defenders of divine illumination present their views. In Matthew's case, we see this in his references to "philosophically minded authors" who follow Aristotle's teaching in such a way that God's light is only a general cause of human cognition and that the light referred to by Augustine is a designation for the human agent intellect and its connatural light. Aquinas's proposal, as early as his own *Disputed Questions on Truth*, was that human intellectual cognition is explicable naturally by reference to natural causes, presupposing only the intelligibility of the world and the creation of the human intellect with its natural dispositions. Matthew tries to counteract Aquinas's teaching by arguing, in the fashion of Bonaventure, that the very immutable and eternal character of the truths known means that there must be an eternal and immutable principle directly involved in our knowing.[15] Matthew also adverts to several of the considerations found in Bonaventure and earlier thinkers: that the truth of the creature just is its conformity to the divine exemplar; that the being of anything cannot be analyzed fully without ultimate

---

[14] Bonaventure, *Quaest. de scientia Christi* 4 ad 12 s.c. For a discussion of this point, see Steven Marrone, *The Light of Thy Countenance: Science and Knowledge of God in the Thirteenth Century* (Leiden: Brill, 2001) ch. 5; Bernard Gendreau, "The Quest for Certainty in Bonaventure," *Franciscan Studies* 21 (1961) 104–227; Christopher M. Cullen, *Bonaventure* (Oxford: Oxford University Press, 2006).

[15] *Quaest. de cognitione* 2c (ed. Quaracchi, pp. 238–9).

reference to being in its fullness found in God; and that creatures are signs that point to God. Matthew conceives of the divine light as working only as a means (*quo*) for our knowing, a means not merely as an efficient cause in the act of knowledge but also as a formal cause, allowing us to see in and through it.[16]

We find quite a different response to Thomism and Neo-Aristotelianism in the writings of John Pecham and Roger Marston. Pecham's teaching as the Franciscan regent master of theology at Paris (beginning in 1269) overlapped with Aquinas's second regency in the Dominican chair of theology, so he was quite familiar both with Aquinas's naturalistic account of intellectual cognition and with similar views proposed by contemporary arts masters. One of Pecham's strategies is to argue, following the line of interpretation advanced earlier by Roger Bacon,[17] that Aquinas and the arts masters have not correctly understood Aristotle, their favored authority. What Pecham proposes in this regard, drawing perhaps on Rufus's suggestions, is a clear doctrine of two agent intellects: one uncreated or divine, to which certain texts in Aristotle's *De anima* III refer, and another created human agent intellect (*Tractatus de anima* 5). The function of the uncreated agent intellect is, in part, to render the human agent intellect actual so that the latter can engage in acts of abstraction. There is also a second function for the divine agent intellect: it provides the means of knowing whereby the human intellect knows immutable truths, especially the truths of first principles such as *Every whole is greater than its parts.*

Pecham exploits the putatively episodic nature of human intellection to argue that, given the Aristotelian tenet that all our understanding occurs in time, and given that no two objects can be simultaneously understood, it follows that there must be a "place" wherein the entire proposition *Every whole is greater than its parts* may be grasped. Otherwise, Pecham argues, the proposition could never be grasped as such and thus its truth could never be known. The "place" where the truth of such a self-evident proposition is known is the divine light ever present to the human mind in its acts of knowing.

Apart from this curious psychological argument, Pecham also advances the by now commonplace arguments regarding immutable and eternal truths and their incommensurability with the nature of the human mind and the created things of the world (*Quaest. disputatae, De anima* q. 6 n. 55). In explaining how the divine light is present to the human mind, moreover, Pecham emphasizes that it is never known directly, but functions as a completely self-effacing means of knowing (*ratio cognoscendi*), after the fashion of the sensible species of color. If pressed to identify its mode of causality, Pecham thinks of the divine

---

[16] Ibid., pp. 234–5.   [17] Roger Bacon, *Opus maius* II.5 (ed. Bridges, suppl. vol., pp. 44–9).

light as a quasi-efficient cause. As an analogy, he invokes the manner in which the sensible species coming in through both eyes form a single species in the optic nerve. In like fashion, the single composite act of knowledge comes to be in the human possible intellect from the diverse causalities of the divine light and the agent intellect (ibid., nn. 75–6).

Roger Marston, a disciple of John Pecham, follows his master's teaching on many points, including the positing of two agent intellects, divine and human. The philosophical argumentation advanced by Marston, however, leans heavily upon an element that was somewhat neglected by earlier authors: the identity of the intelligible object. According to Marston, the way Aquinas and others understand Aristotle would, by making the intelligible light interior to a given individual human soul, also make the objects seen in that light private and hence not commonly available to all. Returning to the texts of Augustine, Marston challenges anyone to understand what Augustine means by the claim that we all see in a common light, if the light in question is identical to a power of any individual human soul (*Quaest. de anima* 3c, ed. Quaracchi, p. 253). He thereupon sketches out his own understanding of how the divine light relates to the light that, he acknowledges, arises from the human agent intellect: they are related as something that fully renders things intelligible and illuminates is related to what only partially illuminates (ibid., p. 258). The light of the agent intellect may be sufficient to abstract something of the intelligible content of the phantasms, but if the possible intellect is to perceive eternal truths, the human agent intellect must receive an impression from the divine agent intellect. This impression remains in the human mind as a created effect and, after the fashion of a signet ring impression, reflects the image of its maker, thereby allowing the human mind to attain to the immutable truths that would otherwise be beyond its reach (ibid., p. 267).

HENRY OF GHENT, VITAL DU FOUR, AND THE END OF ILLUMINATION

By the time the illuminationist tradition reaches the thought of Henry of Ghent, beginning in the mid-1270s, many of the difficulties implicit in the various attempts to explain how the divine light interacts with ordinary powers of human understanding were well known. The extent to which this is so may be readily gathered from the objections listed by the contemporary Franciscan Peter of John Olivi. Olivi puzzled in particular over both how to characterize the type of causality exercised by the divine light and how its activity, as an uncreated cause, could be coordinated with the created causality of the human mind.

At the same time Olivi acknowledged that admitting the human mind knows eternal truth seems to pose its own problems.[18] Henry of Ghent approaches the problem anew, questioning at least in part the value of our powers of sense and intellect, absent the divine light.

Henry's account of the need for divine illumination begins with his observation that, on the part of the intelligible object, the first of the transcendentals – namely, being – is logically prior to and thus intelligible apart from unity, truth, and goodness. In principle, the intellect can know the being of the thing without grasping its truth, since the latter has to do with the conformity of the thing to its exemplar and not simply the being of the thing. Henry dubs the intellect's awareness of the thing according to its being "knowing what is true within it" (*id quod verum est in ea*), as opposed to the intellect's judgment of the thing's truth (*veritas*). He proposes that the intellect can know what is true without illumination, but that it cannot know the truth of the thing without illumination. Here, unsurprisingly, Henry appeals to the authority of Augustine and Anselm, pointing to the latter's texts regarding truth as conformity to the divine mind. In terms of arguments for illumination, Henry develops three independent lines of analysis, the first two having to do with mutability and the last with epistemic reliability. Regarding mutability, Henry notes that both the created exemplar in the mind (here he means the intelligible species[19]) and the mind itself are inherently mutable. Hence neither the created exemplar nor the mind can on its own produce the stability needed for certain cognition. The epistemic reliability of the exemplar is called into question, moreover, in Henry's third argument for illumination. Since the sensible species and the intelligible species arising from it both originate in the senses, they both share in the nature of the false as well as the true; indeed, as Henry observes, we rely on the same sense images to adjudge things rightly that we use to "judge" things in our sleep or in fits of madness. Pure truth (*veritas sincera*) requires, however, that we be able to distinguish the true from the false – and it is just such a standard or criterion of judgment that the sense-based exemplar does not provide of itself. The only recourse, therefore, for the soul to attain certain and scientific knowledge is the divine light (*Summa quaest. ordinarium* 1.2 [*Opera* XXI: 43–5]).

Henry emphasizes that the divine exemplar or divine light is not attained as an object known distinctly in itself but simply as means of cognition (ibid., XXI:

---

[18] Olivi, *Summa* (ed. Jansen [appendix q. 2], III: 502, 511–13).
[19] Henry later denies intelligible species: see *Quodlibet* V.14. For a discussion of this shift, see Robert Pasnau, *Theories of Cognition in the Middle Ages* (Cambridge: Cambridge University Press, 1997) appendix B.

50). This tactic was, as we have seen, a commonplace feature of illuminationist epistemologies and allowed the proponents of illumination to forestall objections about our being unaware of the divine mind. Regarding the precise mode of the divine light's influence upon us, Henry maintains that it transforms the created exemplar or intelligible species derived from the process of abstraction into the character that the divine art has given things in creation. Although in certain texts he talks as if the divine light and the human exemplar work as coordinated causes, on balance he is committed to the divine light's standing to the intelligible object present in the human mind as form stands to matter (*Summa* 1.3 [*Opera* XXI: 84–7]). It is on just this point that Henry accuses Aquinas's teaching of falling short. Aquinas has the first principles come, in a sense, from the divine light, which impresses its light upon the human agent intellect – an event that Aquinas locates at the creation of the human soul and the natural endowment of the agent intellect. Aquinas denies any further need for the divine light to interact with the human intellect beyond this initial orientation. Henry, in contrast, holds that such a theory overestimates the power of the human intellect and does not distinguish critically enough between the truths that can be obtained from sense-based images and the eternal truth.

Practically every thinker of the last decade of the thirteenth century was indebted to Henry's illuminationism. A good example of someone who defended and restated Henry's theory is Vital du Four, whose disputed questions on cognition end with a question on divine illumination.[20] Vital follows Henry in rejecting Marston's account of God as the agent intellect. Again like Henry, and contrary to what Aquinas held in his mature writings, Vital argues that the two exemplars, created and uncreated, are required for the human mind to attain pure truth (*Quaest. de cognitione*, ed. Delorme, pp. 333–7).

Although the tradition of divine illumination dominated the discussion of epistemology in the second half of the thirteenth century, by the second decade of the fourteenth illumination was no longer considered a viable option. Both modern scholars and their Renaissance predecessors have questioned whether this ought to have occurred, but historically speaking there can be no doubt that the non–illuminationist account of mind, first advanced by Aquinas and then developed into a thoroughgoing theory by Scotus, displaced illumi-nationism. The focus of epistemology shifted from the problem of eternal truth and certainty to the topic of universal knowledge analyzed through competing versions of intuitive and abstractive cognition. When the problem of eternal truths was later revived in the generation of Francisco Suárez and Descartes, the

---

[20] See John Lynch, *The Theory of Knowledge of Vital du Four* (St. Bonaventure, NY: Franciscan Institute, 1972).

illuminationist tradition was all but forgotten.[21] Whether this judgment of the centuries is final remains to be seen, for the problem of eternal truth seems to have a surprising resiliency.

[21] Armand Maurer, "St. Thomas and Eternal Truths," in *Being and Knowing: Studies in St. Thomas and Later Medieval Philosophers* (Toronto: Pontifical Institute of Mediaeval Studies, 1990) 43–58; also "St. Thomas and Historicity," ibid., 95–116. For an analysis of the transition from illuminationist to non-illuminationist epistemologies, see Timothy Noone, "The Franciscans and Epistemology: Reflections on the Roles of Bonaventure and Scotus," in R. Houser (ed.) *Medieval Masters: Essays in Memory of Msgr. E.A. Synan* (Houston, TX: Center for Thomistic Studies, 1999) 63–90.

28

SKEPTICISM

DOMINIK PERLER

Searching for skepticism in medieval philosophy seems to be a vain enterprise, because no philosopher in the Christian tradition radically doubted or even denied the possibility that human beings can have knowledge. Nor did thinkers in the Jewish or Islamic tradition categorically refute the claim that human knowledge is possible, despite their criticisms of the incompleteness and fallibility of our cognitive faculties. All of them agreed that our faculties enable us to acquire a wide range of knowledge – of material things as well as of mental, mathematical, and other intelligible objects. Their main concern was not to establish *that* we can have knowledge but to explain *how*, that is, by what kind of cognitive mechanism, we are able to acquire it. There is no evidence that they were interested in Pyrrhonism, one of the main forms of ancient skepticism that aimed to show how one can reach "mental tranquility" and a happy life by suspending all beliefs. Although a Latin translation of Sextus Empiricus's *Outlines of Pyrrhonism* was available before 1300, this key text had no visible impact on debates in Western Europe.[1] All philosophers in the Latin tradition subscribed to the thesis that we are entitled to have beliefs; they even claimed that we need beliefs to choose specific actions and to pursue a happy life. Thanks to Cicero's *Academica* and Augustine's *Contra academicos,* Academic skepticism, the second major form of ancient skepticism, was to some extent known during the Middle Ages. But it did not spark an extensive debate or a "skeptical crisis."[2] Medieval authors in the Latin West occasionally referred to skeptical arguments and examples presented in these texts (such as cases of sensory illusions and dream experiences), but without drawing radical skeptical conclusions.

---

[1] See Roland Wittwer, *Sextus Latinus: Die erste lateinische Übersetzung von Sextus Empiricus' Pyrrhoneioi Hypotyposeis* (Leiden: Brill, forthcoming). Only a later translation of Sextus Empiricus's text (printed 1562) created a new interest in Pyrrhonism.

[2] Only Renaissance authors discussed these texts in detail, as Charles Schmitt, *Cicero Scepticus. A Study of the Influence of the Academica in the Renaissance* (The Hague: Nijhoff, 1972) has pointed out.

How can we legitimately speak about skepticism in medieval philosophy when no author denied that belief and knowledge are possible? To answer this question we need to distinguish between different attitudes toward skepticism. A philosopher can take a skeptical *position* by straightforwardly rejecting the thesis that knowledge is possible and by systematically destroying knowledge claims. But one can also choose a skeptical *method* by presenting arguments that refute a certain conception of knowledge and attempt to introduce a new one – a conception that is supposed to give a better explanation of what knowledge is and how it can be acquired. A number of medieval authors made methodological use of skepticism in this sense: they appealed to skeptical arguments in order to work out a satisfying account of knowledge, to defend it against rival accounts, and to test its explanatory force. This chapter illustrates that use by focusing on some key scholastic philosophers in the Latin tradition.

HENRY OF GHENT, SCOTUS, AND THE POSSIBILITY OF ESSENTIAL KNOWLEDGE

One of the first medieval authors in the Latin tradition who made explicit methodological use of skeptical arguments was Henry of Ghent. In the opening questions of his *Summa quaestionum ordinariarum* (*ca.* 1276), he claims that one cannot reasonably defend the view that knowledge is possible unless one has a clear concept of what knowledge is. Accordingly, he carefully distinguishes two understandings of knowledge that give rise to two different types of knowledge claims. Understood in a broad sense, knowledge is "every certain cognition by which a thing is known as it is, without any error and deception" (1.1, *Opera* XXI: 10). This kind of knowledge is possible, Henry states without hesitation, because our sensory capacities enable us to cognize individual items with respect to their perceptible features. Thus, when I am looking at a blossoming tree, I am perfectly capable of cognizing that there is something brown with green and pink spots in front of me. Of course, I may be deceived under special circumstances, for instance when I am seeing the tree on a foggy day or when my vision is blurred. But under normal circumstances, I successfully see it as it is, and I am even able to correct an earlier misperception. Following the Aristotelian tradition, Henry claims that the senses assimilate the sensory forms of a material thing, thus providing the basis for a correct cognition of its perceptible features (see Chapter 24).

Yet this first basic form of cognition does not exhaust all the epistemic possibilities, for one might also want to know the essence of a thing. I might, for instance, wish to know what makes the thing in front of me a tree – that is, what is responsible for its metaphysical makeup. In order to gain this kind of knowledge, I need to have some model (*exemplar*) that indicates the typical, non-accidental features of a tree. But how can I acquire such a model? The standard scholastic answer, and the one that Henry first considers, is that I might simply abstract it from the sensory images I have received when looking at a particular tree, thus forming an "acquired model" (*exemplar acquisitum*) that can be applied in future cases.

Henry adduces three skeptical arguments against this empiricist line of reasoning (*Summa* 1.2, *Opera* XXI: 43–4). All of them were inspired by ancient sources (Cicero's *Academica* and Augustine's *Contra academicos*) that were well known to him. First, individual things that are accessible in sense perception are mutable and therefore display a variety of changing features. Grasping these accidental features does not enable us to abstract a model that presents the unchanging essential features of that thing. Second, our cognitive capacities are mutable as well. We focus on different aspects at different moments, sometimes under unreliable conditions, and therefore grasp a great variety of features. Nothing in our changing perceptual activities guarantees that we successfully abstract a stable model that indicates just the essence of a thing. Third, even if we happen to abstract such a model, there is no veracity built into it. It could be the product of a dream or a hallucination, and we would have no criterion to distinguish a veridical model that presents the real essence from a non-veridical one. Given this lack of a criterion, we can never trust an "acquired model." From this, Henry concludes that we need a second model, a stable and infallible one, that unfailingly presents the real essence. This is the "eternal model" (*exemplar aeternum*), existing in the divine mind and made accessible to us by divine illumination.[3] Only with this model can we go beyond a mere cognition of the perceptible features and know what makes each thing the very thing that it is.

Henry's appeal to an "eternal model" announces his commitment to the Platonic–Augustinian tradition of explaining human knowledge with reference to ideal entities that are neither created nor abstracted by human beings (see Chapters 6 and 27).[4] What is of interest here, however, is less the account Henry gives of this tradition than the purpose of the three skeptical arguments. Henry uses them in order to show the limits of a purely empiricist theory and to pave the way for an alternative theory that emphasizes the crucial function of a non-empirical element in human knowledge. On his view, the skeptical

---

[3] See *Summa* 1.2 (*Opera* XXI: 45) and 1.3 (*Opera* XXI: 71–5).

[4] On Henry's use of this tradition, see Steven Marrone, *The Light of Thy Countenance: Science and Knowledge of God in the Thirteenth Century* (Leiden: Brill, 2001), and Robert Pasnau, "Henry of Ghent and the Twilight of Divine Illumination," *Review of Metaphysics* 49 (1995) 49–75.

arguments make clear that essential knowledge is impossible on purely sensory grounds. Although the perception of individual things suffices for knowledge in the broad sense, it cannot yield knowledge in the proper sense, because it does not provide a stable and infallible model of the essence of perceptible things. Skeptical arguments serve, as it were, as a methodological weapon to defeat the empiricists who fail to notice this crucial point. This anti-empiricist attitude motivated later authors, among them Gianfrancesco Pico della Mirandola, to repeat and endorse Henry's arguments.[5]

But is empiricism inevitably doomed to failure? And do we really need to appeal to divine illumination in order to explain the possibility of essential knowledge? John Duns Scotus, Henry's first critic, answered these questions in the negative. On his view, we can have a rich variety of knowledge, notably knowledge of analytic principles and of our own acts, without needing divine assistance (*Ordinatio* I.3.1.4). And even if we aim at essential knowledge, we do not need to have access to ideal entities. It suffices to abstract cognitive devices, so-called "intelligible species," from sensory images. Intelligible species have a specific content that is distinct from the content of the changing sensory images, and they unfailingly present the essence of material things. No matter how unstable the perceptible features of a thing may be, the intellect is, at least in principle, always capable of abstracting intelligible species that present the essential features in a stable and infallible way: the essence "shines" perfectly in the species.[6]

This reply shows that skeptical arguments gave rise to a fundamental debate about the status of human knowledge. Whereas Henry of Ghent firmly believed that knowledge in the proper sense is impossible without a foundation in ideal entities that cannot be extracted from sense experience, Scotus defended a somewhat naturalist view that explains the acquisition of essential knowledge on purely natural grounds. Both took a non-skeptical position, but both spelled it out by examining skeptical arguments.

OCKHAM, CHATTON, PETER OF AILLY, AND THE HYPOTHESIS OF DIVINE INTERVENTION

Medieval philosophers did not just discuss arguments that were already prominent in ancient debates, especially in the tradition of Academic skepticism. They also developed new arguments that grew out of their specifically Christian

---

[5] See Pico's *Examen vanitatis doctrinae gentium*, ed. 1557, II: 1091–105.
[6] See *Ordinatio* I.3.3.1 (ed. Vatican, III: 235), and a detailed analysis in Dominik Perler, *Theorien der Intentionalität im Mittelalter* (Frankfurt: Klostermann, 2002) pp. 207–30.

context. One of these arguments appealed to God's omnipotence. Theological doctrine, reaffirmed in the influential Parisian condemnation of 1277, claimed that God's omnipotence is not only to be understood in an "ordinary sense," according to which God respects the natural laws in his actions, but also in an "absolute sense," according to which he is free to do whatever he likes as long as he does not violate the law of non-contradiction. Thus, God could cause a mental state in me that presents a blossoming tree, even though there is no tree in front of me. This possibility gives rise to a serious worry: how can I ever be certain that my mental states present *real* things and that I have knowledge of a *real* world if God can manipulate me at any time? To be sure, medieval theologians did not intend to invoke a capricious tyrant by referring to God's absolute omnipotence. They rather used the doctrine of omnipotence as an analytical tool in order to point out what is not only physically but also logically possible. Their aim was to test out the metaphysical realm of possibilities.[7] Nevertheless, if it is logically possible that God intervenes in our cognitive process at any time, then we seem to have no certitude that our mental states are causally linked to real things. Consequently, external world skepticism seems inevitable.

William of Ockham was well aware of the impact the doctrine of divine omnipotence has on epistemology. In his *Commentary on the Sentences* (1317–19) he explicitly mentions it and concedes that God could indeed intervene at any time and cause an "intuitive cognition" of a non-existent or non-present object. But Ockham hastens to add that this involves no deception, because in this case a person correctly judges that no object is actually existing or even present (*Ordinatio* prol. 1.1 [*Opera theol.* I: 38–9]). Only if an intuitive cognition is caused in a natural way by an actually present object does one judge that it is in fact present. Thus, there is some kind of cognitive mechanism that guarantees successful cognition and rules out deception.

This explanation clearly avoids skeptical consequences, but it has a serious drawback, as Walter Chatton, Ockham's contemporary and colleague in Oxford, was quick to point out. Why should a supernaturally caused intuitive cognition give rise only to a negative judgment? Suppose that God is causing an intuitive cognition in me of a star and that he is doing it so perfectly that I have a vivid impression of a bright celestial body that in no way differs from the impression that I would have if I were really seeing a star. Why should I then come up with the judgment that no star is actually present? The phenomenological basis is, after all, the same as in the case of a natural causation. Chatton accordingly

[7] See William Courtenay, "The Dialectic of Omnipotence in the High and Late Middle Ages," in T. Rudavsky (ed.) *Divine Omniscience and Omnipotence in Medieval Philosophy* (Boston: Reidel, 1985) 243–69.

draws the conclusion that an intuitive cognition inevitably leads to a positive existential judgment, whether there really is an existing and present thing or not (*Sent.* prol. 2.3, ed. Wey, p. 102).

In response to this objection, Ockham acknowledges that God could bring about an act by which we erroneously judge that a non-existing thing exists. But he does not adopt Chatton's solution, which clearly has skeptical consequences. Instead, he revises his early position, claiming in his later *Quodlibet* V.5 that in the case of divine intervention a person has a mere act of believing, which is not an intuitive cognition. When having such an act, which God directly implants in the intellect, one makes a false judgment and therefore falsely believes that a non-existing thing exists. However, God does not tamper with the cognitive mechanisms that lead to an intuitive cognition, leaving the natural processes that provide correct judgments untouched.

This solution has the advantage of allowing for false judgments while preserving the reliability of our natural cognitive processes. It does not, however, exhaust all skeptical questions. How can someone who falsely believes that a non-existing thing exists distinguish this belief from a correct judgment based on an intuitive cognition? Ockham does not provide any criteria that would enable a person to identify a mere act of believing; nor does he indicate any phenomenological features that would characterize such an act. This means, of course, that he acknowledges the possibility that a person could mistake a false act of believing for a correct judgment: there is no absolute certainty. Does he thereby open the door to radical external-world skepticism? This suggestion may be tempting, but on a closer look at Ockham's entire epistemological program, it is hardly convincing.

First, one should take into account the fact that Ockham (unlike René Descartes) never introduces radical doubts. He does not use the hypothesis that God or an evil demon could deceive us in *all* our cognitive acts, but confines himself to pondering the possibility that God could intervene in *some* special cases. He never doubts that we are, in principle, in contact with a real world and that things in this world cause most of our beliefs. Global skepticism is not an issue for him.

Second, following the Aristotelian tradition, Ockham commits himself to the thesis that we have reliable cognitive capacities that provide, in principle, correct information about the real world. That the cognitive mechanisms may be disturbed or manipulated by God in some cases does not show that they are never to be trusted. And that we may not always be able to distinguish a false belief from a correct judgment does not prove that all our judgments are to be suspended. False beliefs caused by God are to be seen as exceptional cases, comparable to the equally exceptional cases of sensory illusion.

Moreover, they can be corrected if they are linked to other beliefs and evaluated in a broader context. Ockham simply never discusses the possibility that God could manipulate all cognitive acts and create an all-embracing net of false beliefs.

Third, Ockham develops his epistemology in a metaphysical framework that emphasizes the contingency of all events. There is no absolute necessity in the world, neither in cognitive nor in simple physical processes. Should someone ask whether we can be certain that the sun will rise tomorrow, Ockham's response would be: given the natural course of nature, we can indeed be certain, but there is no guarantee that this course will continue without exception. Likewise, there is no absolute guarantee in the realm of cognitive processes. All we can say is that if the natural course determined by natural laws continues, our mental states are reliably caused by material things and present them as they are. All we can strive for is this kind of hypothetical certainty and a high degree of reliability. A dogmatic philosopher who tries to rule out every possible error ignores this basic fact.

This line of reasoning, aimed at a rejection of exceedingly high epistemic standards, was adopted by a number of later medieval philosophers. John Rodington, Robert Holcot, Gregory of Rimini, and many other fourteenth-century authors conceded that supernaturally caused deception could occur in exceptional cases without thereby giving up the general thesis that natural knowledge is possible.[8] In his *Commentary on the Sentences (ca.* 1376), Peter of Ailly explicitly claims that we need to distinguish between two types of certainty when dealing with skeptical arguments. In the case of self-evident principles and our own mental acts, we have *absolute* evidence that allows us to have infallible knowledge. For instance, my judgment that a whole is greater than each of its parts is simply based on an understanding of the terms 'whole' and 'parts,' regardless of the existence of wholes and parts in the material world. And the judgment that I am thinking right now is equally independent of the actual existence of material things. For all other judgments, we only have *conditional* evidence, because

in the unconditional and absolute sense, nothing sensible outside us can evidently be known to exist, for instance that whiteness is, that blackness is, that a human being is, that a human being differs from a donkey, etc. . . . If, however, one speaks about relative and conditional evidence, that is, if one assumes that God's general influence is maintained

---

[8] See the classical study by Anneliese Maier, "Das Problem der Evidenz in der Philosophie des 14. Jahrhunderts," in *Ausgehendes Mittelalter: Gesammelte Aufsätze zur Geistesgeschichte des 14. Jahrhunderts* (Rome: Edizioni di Storia e Letteratura, 1967) II: 367–418; Dominik Perler, "Does God Deceive Us? Skeptical Hypotheses in Late Medieval Epistemology," in H. Lagerlund (ed.) *Skepticism in Medieval Philosophy* (Leiden: Brill, forthcoming).

and that the normal course of nature continues without a miracle, then we can know such things sufficiently with evidence, in such a way that we cannot reasonably doubt them.

(Sent. 1.1)

The crucial point is that Peter of Ailly does not give up all knowledge claims; rather, he specifies that different evidential bases justify different types of knowledge claims.

Here, again, we see that skeptical arguments did not motivate medieval philosophers to take a radical skeptical position. The argument of divine omnipotence inspired Ockham and his successors to differentiate between various types of knowledge and to spell out the certainty that is possible in each case. Therefore, it would hardly be adequate to consider their discussions as mere anticipations of the Cartesian argument of radical deception.

OLIVI, CRATHORN, AND THE THREAT OF REPRESENTATIONALISM

Deeply influenced by the cognitive theory outlined in Aristotle's *De anima*, later medieval philosophers typically claimed that one cannot have an epistemic access to material things unless one assimilates their sensory and intelligible forms. But how is this possible? Beginning in the mid-thirteenth century, many authors tried to answer this question by invoking "sensible" and "intelligible species" as devices that make the forms cognitively present (see Chapter 25).[9] Most Aristotelians agreed that the species are not cognitive objects, but mere instruments that one needs to make the forms accessible. Thus, Thomas Aquinas claims that the intellect primarily cognizes the forms presented by the species and cognizes the species only secondarily, namely when it reflects upon how the forms are cognized (*Summa theol.* 1a 85.2c).

Yet not all philosophers shared this interpretation. In his *Summa of Questions on the Sentences* (*ca.* 1280), Peter of John Olivi notes that one cannot cognize anything by means of a species unless one first pays attention to it and grasps it as an inner object. That is why the species has "the character of a first object" (*Summa* II.58, ed. Jansen, II: 469). A person can turn her attention to the form present in a material thing only secondarily – when thinking about the cause of this inner object. With this interpretation, Olivi obviously turns the species into an inner representation that is set apart from the external thing. It is therefore

---

[9] See Leen Spruit, *Species Intelligibilis: From Perception to Knowledge* (Leiden: Brill, 1994) vol. I, and Katherine Tachau, *Vision and Certitude in the Age of Ockham: Optics, Epistemology and the Foundations of Semantics 1250–1340* (Leiden, Brill, 1988).

hardly surprising that he thinks a species "would veil the thing and impede its being attended to in itself, rather than aid in its being attended to" (ibid.).[10] This talk about an inner veil is, of course, characteristic of a representationalist theory that denies the possibility of an immediate access to external things. Yet it does not necessarily have skeptical consequences, for one may always say that even if the species is the primary object we cognize, we can immediately grasp the external thing (or its form) as a secondary object, because we can make an inference from the inner effect to the outer cause.

It is precisely at this point that Olivi makes use of a skeptical hypothesis. "Let us suppose," he writes, "that God presents such a species to our [intellectual] gaze without there existing a thing or without there being a thing actually present. In that case, something would appear as well as in the case in which a thing exists or is actually present. In fact, no more or less would something appear in that case" (ibid., II: 470). Since the supernaturally caused species could be as vividly present as the naturally caused one, a person could never tell whether or not there is a corresponding thing in the material world. He or she would be somehow imprisoned in the inner world of species.

To be sure, Olivi does not commit himself to this position. He uses the skeptical scenario to attack the species theory. On his view, anyone who adopts this theory will inevitably end up with representationalism and skepticism. To avoid this consequence, he argues that one should reject the introduction of species right from the start and defend the thesis that a person *directly* perceives and thinks about external things, without needing inner cognitive objects. Therefore, his use of a skeptical hypothesis is motivated by a methodological goal: to overcome the devastating species theory and reintroduce a robust form of direct realism.

A similar motivation was the driving force behind William Crathorn's appeal to skeptical arguments. In his *Questions on the Sentences* (*ca.* 1330) he extensively discusses not only the theory of intelligible species, but also the theory of sensible species that are supposed to exist in the inner senses, making the sensory forms cognitively accessible. According to Crathorn, if there really are such entities, then they must be grasped by the inner senses so that they can have a cognitive function. But if they are grasped, they are equally well cognized as the sensory forms of external things, because they are immediately and infallibly present. No obstacle could prevent a person from cognizing them. This immediately leads to a skeptical question: how can a person ever tell whether she is cognizing the inner sensible species or the outer sensory form? Both are present to her,

---

[10] A detailed analysis of this passage is provided by Robert Pasnau, *Theories of Cognition in the Later Middle Ages* (Cambridge: Cambridge University Press, 1997) pp. 236–7.

and there is no inner sign that would enable her to distinguish them (*Sent.* I.1, ed. Hoffmann, p. 123).

Now one may respond that this does not present a serious problem, for even if a person cognizes the species, she can be certain that she also cognizes the sensory form, because the form is the cause of the species and fixes its cognitive content. If, for instance, I cognize the sensible species presenting whiteness, I grasp *eo ipso* the form of whiteness existing in a material object, because it is this form that brought about the species and endowed it with a certain content. But how can I be certain that there really is an external cause? This is a second skeptical question, which Crathorn illustrated with the following hypothetical example:

God could maintain a species, which was caused by a color, and at the same time destroy the external thing that was originally seen, without letting the person who has the species know this. If God were doing this, the seeing person would judge that he sees the previously seen whiteness and that this whiteness exists, and he would err exactly in this judgment.

(ibid., p. 124)

There is no guarantee that there really is a causal link between outer form and inner species. It could always happen that the natural causal chain is interrupted so that the person grasps nothing but the species. Consequently, one can never know with certainty that there is a real color corresponding to a sensible species.

Like Olivi, Crathorn presents this argument not to support a skeptical position, but to illustrate the devastating consequences of the species theory. Invoking God's veracity and benevolence, he concludes that we should not be afraid of divine intervention (ibid., pp. 126–7), but we should be aware that God *could* intervene if inner representational species are set apart from outer objects. Here again, a skeptical strategy is introduced for methodological purposes – namely, to spell out the implications of a representationalist theory of perception.

AUTRECOURT, BURIDAN, AND THE QUEST FOR A FOUNDATION OF KNOWLEDGE

The hypothesis of a possible divine intervention in cognitive processes, popular among many fourteenth- and fifteenth-century authors, provoked a general debate about the foundation of knowledge. How can our knowledge ever have a secure foundation if God is free to manipulate all cognitive processes? Could he not manipulate mental acts that directly refer to external things as well? In addition, cases of sensory illusions were cited to show that our thoughts about external things can be mistaken even if the natural course of nature is not interrupted.[11] For instance, when I am looking at a stick partly submerged in water, it looks bent to me, and I inevitably think that it is really bent. So, what justification do I have for assuming that my thoughts correspond to things as they are? Should I not concede that even the naturally caused thoughts could be false and that I am not able to distinguish the false from the true ones?

This line of questioning sparked a controversy between two Parisian philosophers, Nicholas of Autrecourt and Bernard of Arezzo.[12] In his first letter to Bernard (prob. *ca.* 1335–6) Nicholas harshly criticizes his colleague's view that "in the natural light we cannot be certain when our awareness of the existence of external objects is true or false" (ed. de Rijk, p. 47). This view paves the way for a disastrous skepticism, as Nicholas points out with colorful examples. For if there were no certainty, Bernard could never know if the chancellor or the pope really exists. Nor could he know if he himself has a head and a beard – all thoughts could be false. To avoid these absurdities, Nicholas claims that he is evidently certain of the objects of the five senses and of his own acts, at least when these objects are present to him "in full light," that is, under normal perceptual circumstances (ibid., p. 57).[13]

This last claim makes it clear that Nicholas rejects a skeptical position by appealing to the reliability of sense perception and to an empirical foundation of knowledge. But did he thereby validate all knowledge based on sensory experience – for instance, knowledge of a causal relation between perceived objects? Not at all. On his view, knowledge needs to be certain, and certainty has to be reducible to the first principle, that is, the principle of non-contradiction. But this principle does not justify causal claims. Nicholas illustrates this point with the following example. When I am seeing a burning piece of linen "in full light," I am entitled to say only that I know that there is something burning in front of me and that the contradictory statement is false. I am not entitled to claim that the fire has caused the burning, because the causal relation is not an immediate sensory object, nor is the statement about such a relation reducible to the first principle. This principle justifies only statements of the type 'If it is true that *a* (the burning linen) exists, then the contradictory statement is not true.' The principle does not justify statements like 'If it is true that *a* exists, then it is also true that *b* (the fire) exists and that *a* exists because of *b*.' This

[11] Debates about sensory illusions were mostly inspired by Peter Auriol, who discussed eight cases (*Scriptum* I.3.14 art. 1). See Tachau, *Vision and Certitude*, 85–104, and Dallas Denery, *Seeing and Being Seen in the Later Medieval World: Optics, Theology and Religious Life* (Cambridge: Cambridge University Press, 2005).
[12] On the historical context of the controversy, see Zénon Kaluza, *Nicolas d'Autrécourt: ami de la vérité* (Paris: Académie des inscriptions et belles-lettres, 1995).
[13] See also *Exigit ordo*, ed. O'Donnell, pp. 228, 234.

would go far beyond the certitude guaranteed by the sensory experience and the first principle. Likewise, I am not entitled to say 'If an accident exists, then a substance exists,' because this statement is not reducible to the first principle, and no substance (or inherence of an accident in a substance) is immediately perceivable. Only perceptible accidents are objects of the five senses.

These observations lead Nicholas to radical, anti-Aristotelian conclusions. He claims, for instance, that "Aristotle never possessed evident knowledge about any substance other than his own soul" (ibid., p. 73) and "that we do not evidently know that anything other than God can be the cause of some effect" (p. 175). These theses, shocking in the ears of orthodox Aristotelians, were condemned in 1346 by a papal commission, and Nicholas had to recant them. Even modern commentators have judged them to be destructive and thought that they manifested Nicholas's radical skepticism.[14] Yet, one should note that Nicholas does not defend a skeptical point of view. He rather adopts a foundationalist position by looking for an infallible foundation for all knowledge – a foundation he locates in the first principle and in immediate sense perception. Consequently, Nicholas rejects all knowledge claims that are not firmly based on this foundation. This does not, however, amount to a denial of the possibility of knowledge. On the contrary, Nicholas's purpose is to guarantee this possibility by establishing a secure foundation and by carefully distinguishing knowledge from mere belief.

But should all knowledge be reducible to the first principle? John Buridan, Nicholas's colleague at the University of Paris, critically discusses this question and argues that Nicholas's requirement is too austere. According to Buridan, "there is not a single first and indemonstrable complex principle to which everything is to be reduced, but there are as many principles as demonstrated conclusions."[15] Therefore, one should not look for a single foundation but for different foundations that secure different types of knowledge, including the knowledge of causal relations. Moreover, these foundations do not simply consist in analytical principles, but in a variety of principles that are acquired through sense perception, memory, and inductive reasoning. Admittedly, sense perception may be fallacious in *some* cases, but it is not completely deceptive in *all* cases. That is why fallacious perceptions can be corrected and frequent sensory experience can provide true principles – for instance, the principle that linen burns when in contact with fire. It would be pointless to aim at a reduction of this principle to a more basic one that is not grounded in experience.

---

[14] A critical evaluation of these interpretations is provided by Christophe Grellard, *Croire et savoir: les principes de la connaissance selon Nicolas d'Autrécourt* (Paris: Vrin, 2005).

[15] *Summulae de demonstrationibus* 8.3.6, ed. de Rijk, p. 83; see also p. 122.

Buridan's reaction to Nicholas of Autrecourt's position shows that two different conceptions of knowledge were at stake in the fourteenth-century Parisian debates. Whereas Nicholas thought that skeptical arguments cannot be refuted unless one adopts a foundationalist conception that restricts knowledge to a small number of beliefs that can be justified with reference to a single principle, Buridan defended a pluralist conception that accepts a variety of principles and, consequently, a variety of justifications for beliefs. And whereas Nicholas held that an appeal to sense perception is admissible only if an object is immediately present to one of the five senses, Buridan accepted any sensory or intellectual process, including memory, that repeatedly occurred and proved to be reliable. Neither of them took a skeptical position, but both discussed skeptical objections to delineate their conceptions of knowledge.

It is in fact this methodological use of skepticism that characterizes many scholastic debates and distinguishes them from true skepticism, which aims at a radical denial of the possibility of knowledge. As employed by these medieval authors, skeptical arguments serve as a key to better understanding the nature and scope of knowledge.[16]

---

[16] For a detailed analysis of this general goal, see Perler, *Zweifel und Gewissheit: skeptische Debatten im Mittelalter* (Frankfurt: Klostermann, 2006).

V

WILL AND DESIRE

29

FREEDOM AND DETERMINISM

PETER ADAMSON

Nowadays philosophers who worry about determinism are usually worrying about determination by physical causes. A prominent question is thus whether physical causes[1] might necessitate my performing a given action, and yet leave me free to choose with respect to that action. But this is not a central question in medieval discussions of freedom, which tend rather to center on God. There are two features of God's nature that might seem to imply determinism. First, God is the creator of all things. How, then, does his creative act relate to human acts? If he is the real agent of these acts, it would seem that it is God, and not us, who is morally responsible for them. Second, God is omniscient, which seems to mean that God knows in advance what I will do. How, then, can I be free with respect to what I do?

Why were the medievals not particularly worried about physical determinism? In part the explanation, as is so often the case, goes back to Aristotle. Aristotle and philosophers in the Aristotelian tradition make a fundamental distinction between what is necessary, essential, and always the case, and what is possible, accidental, and only sometimes the case. For example, human beings are necessarily, essentially, and always rational, whereas human beings are merely possibly, accidentally, and sometimes bald. Already in the late ancient tradition, most particular events and properties in the physical world were normally consigned to the realm of chance and the accidental.[2] By the medieval period, Aristotelianism so dominates natural philosophy that philosophers rarely take seriously the idea that physical causes could necessitate everything, including human actions.[3]

---

[1] Or more rigorously, physical laws plus the condition of the physical world at some past time.

[2] For instance, the Aristotelian commentator Alexander of Aphrodisias rejected Stoic determinism by claiming that necessity within the physical world is found only at the level of species, not at the level of the individual. See R. W. Sharples, *Alexander of Aphrodisias on Fate* (London: Duckworth, 1983).

[3] One exception to the rule is astrology, which in both the ancient and medieval period is often yoked to a deterministic conception of astral causation. Most medieval authors opposed astrology, especially in its determinist form. But for deterministic astrology early in the Muslim tradition, see

Furthermore, medieval thinkers accept the reality of immaterial causes: God, the angels, and the human rational soul itself. This prevents it from being the case that everything is necessitated by physical causes. In particular, our actions will not be so necessitated, assuming our souls play some causal role in action. And this returns us to what most concerns the medievals: that an immaterial cause other than our souls, namely God, might determine human actions instead. In order to fend off this kind of determinism, the medievals need to show both that God is not the real *agent* or *cause* of all human actions – especially the evil ones – and that God's *foreknowledge* has no deterministic implications. The first order of business must be to clarify this very distinction between necessitation by divine causation and necessitation by divine knowledge. Accordingly, this chapter will examine texts from the earlier centuries of the medieval period in which philosophers disentangle these two sorts of putative necessitation. We will consider both the Arabic and Latin traditions, which develop in parallel ways but in response to rather different initial debates.

THE ARABIC TRADITION

In Arabic, the initial debate is one within Islamic *kalām* (roughly, "speculative theology"). This debate is normally summarized as one between the Muʿtazilite and Ashʿarite schools. Indeed, this is one of the chief points of dispute between the two schools.[4] The Muʿtazilites believe that human actions are free, and that determination (even by our own motivations) would be incompatible with this freedom.[5] They sometimes defend this view by appealing to our strong intuition that we do possess free will. At least as important, though, is another theological commitment, namely divine justice: if I am not free with respect to an action, then it will not be just for God to punish me for that action. The rival school, founded in the early tenth century by the lapsed Muʿtazilite al-Ashʿarī, seeks instead to safeguard divine power. Ashʿarites object to the Muʿtazilite claim that humans are the authors or even "creators" of their actions. The Ashʿarites instead say that God creates my action, and that I "acquire" the action by

---

Peter Adamson, "Abū Maʿshar, al-Kindī and the Philosophical Defense of Astrology," *Recherches de philosophie et théologie médiévales* 69 (2002) 245–70.

[4] The most significant other point of disagreement is over divine attributes: the Muʿtazilites adopt an austere view according to which God has no distinct attributes, but is identical with his own knowledge, power, etc. The Ashʿarites deny that the possession of such attributes would compromise divine simplicity.

[5] As shown by Richard M. Frank, "The Autonomy of the Human Agent in the Teaching of ʿAbd al-Jabbār," *Le Muséon* 95 (1982) 323–55.

performing it. This "acquisition" (*kasb* or *iktisāb*) makes me morally responsible for my actions and, thus, subject to just punishment.[6]

In the early period at least, the *falāsifa* (scholars primarily engaged with the Greek philosophical tradition, rather than with theology) tend to sympathize with the Muʿtazilites.[7] This is in part because Aristotle was so clearly opposed to determinism. One central text is chapter 9 of *De interpretatione*, where Aristotle presents the famous sea battle argument for determinism: if it is true today that there will be a sea battle tomorrow, then it is inevitable or necessary that the sea battle occur. This provokes a discussion of determinism in the tenth-century commentary of al-Fārābī.[8] Al-Fārābī follows ancient commentators in thinking that Aristotle meant to rebut the deterministic argument by saying that statements about future contingents, such as 'there will be a sea battle tomorrow,' have only an "indeterminate" truth value. This seems to mean that such statements are either true or false, but not yet one or the other. Al-Fārābī then digresses from his commentary to consider the implications of divine foreknowledge. After all, such statements must have a truth value if God knows them to be true. Al-Fārābī does not explicitly distinguish the idea that God *causes* things to happen from the idea that God's *knowing* about them in advance shows that they are necessary. But he does make a distinction that would help solve the latter problem: "a thing may follow from something else necessarily, but not be necessary in itself" (ed. Kutsch and Marrow, p. 99). In other words, it is true that:

Necessarily: if God knows that P, P is true.

But this should not be confused with:

If God knows that P, P is necessarily true.

---

[6] In fact, a stark opposition between Muʿtazilite and Ashʿarite schools is too simple. For one thing, the Muʿtazilite position itself responds to earlier deterministic positions, for example that of Jahm ibn Ṣafwān (who said that God truly acts, whereas we act only in an extended or metaphorical sense) and that of Ḍirār ibn ʿAmr (who already uses the language of *kasb*). Also, there is extensive debate within both schools. Early libertarian thinkers before the time of al-Ashʿarī, who are in retrospect grouped together under the heading of 'Muʿtazilism,' have every reason to see fellow libertarians as their main opponents in the debate, and think of finer points as the ones worth debating. One such fine point, which we will meet again below, is whether or not the "capacity" to perform a free action already exists before the performance of the action.

[7] The boundaries of what counts as *falsafa* are contentious, but for the early period discussed here it is characterized by a direct engagement with Aristotle and other Greek philosophical works (see Chapter 1). Matters become more complex with the coming of Avicenna (d. 1037), because after him the *falāsifa* tend to respond to Avicenna as much as to Aristotle, while Avicennian ideas are also integrated into the *kalām* tradition.

[8] See my "The Arabic Sea Battle: al-Fārābī on the Problem of Future Contingents," *Archiv für Geschichte der Philosophie* 88 (2006) 163–88; Robert Wisnovsky, *Avicenna's Metaphysics in Context* (Ithaca, NY: Cornell University Press, 2003) pp. 219–25.

Al-Fārābī stresses that, with his distinction in hand, we can admit, for instance, that Zayd will travel tomorrow, while maintaining that there is a "power" in Zayd not to travel; he is *qādir*, "capable," with respect to both traveling and not traveling (ibid.).

At around the same time, we find Jewish and Christian authors writing in Arabic about the same issues. Saadiah Gaon, one of the earliest Jewish medieval philosophers, is often said to have followed the Muʿtazilite school of Muslim *kalām*, especially on the problems of divine attributes and freedom. His discussion of freedom in the *Book of Beliefs and Convictions* is much briefer than his discussion of divine attributes, but it is at least as clear in adopting the Muʿtazilite view. Like the Muʿtazilites, Saadiah begins from the premise of divine justice. It is out of justice that God "gives [a human being] power (*al-qudra*) and capacity (*al-istiṭāʿa*) to do what [God] commands him to do, and avoid what he forbids him to do" (ed. Landauer, pp. 150–1). For God would not command a person to do something that was not in that person's power.[9]

Saadiah had said earlier that every agent must be possessed of choice (*mukhtār* [ibid., p. 58]), and he repeats the point here: "it must be explained that man performs no *action* unless he *chooses* his action, since it is impossible that someone without choice acts, or that someone acts if he is not possessed of choice" (pp. 151–2). And we are immediately aware that we do possess choice (p. 152). Furthermore, a single action cannot proceed from two agents – in other words, from both God and a human being. What Saadiah seems to mean here is that an action must not be *overdetermined*, in other words brought about by two distinct sufficient causes. The true cause is either God or the human agent. But if all human actions proceed from God, then it would be unjust of him to punish evil actions (here the act in question is disbelief in God [pp. 152–3]). So they must proceed from us alone. At this point Saadiah considers an objection. Perhaps someone will say that God "has already known (*fa-qad ʿalima*) that the man will be disobedient; so it is inevitable (*lā budda*) that the man is disobedient" (p. 154). In response, Saadiah argues that God's knowledge of an action is not the cause (*sabab*) of the action. If it were, then actions would be eternal, just like God's knowledge itself. Instead, God knows things "as they really come to be (*ʿalā mithl ḥaqīqa kawnihā*)." Unfortunately, Saadiah does not explain his solution in detail. He seems to mean that, just as God has eternal knowledge of things

---

[9] Saadiah also responds to a Muʿtazilite problematic when he argues that "capacity" must already be present prior to our action *and* at the moment of action (see above, n. 6). In the Latin tradition, Anselm, in a text discussed below (*On the Fall of the Devil* 12), also discusses the issue of what needs to be present in the agent prior to his or her action. For further discussion of Saadiah's views, see Israel Efros, *Studies in Medieval Jewish Philosophy* (New York: Columbia University Press, 1974) ch. 6.

that are not eternal, so God inevitably has knowledge of things that are not inevitable. (Interestingly, in his commentary on the *De interpretatione*, al-Fārābī considers, but rejects as mere verbiage, a solution along these lines [ed. Kutsch and Marrow, p. 98].) Still, Saadiah sees what is needed, namely a way that God can know what we will do without thereby causing us to do it.

This point is developed much more explicitly by the Christian philosopher Yaḥyā ibn ʿAdī, a student of al-Fārābī and, like him, a member of the Aristotelian school at Baghdad which produced translations of and commentaries on Aristotle. Ibn ʿAdī's treatise *On the Possible* is arguably the most sophisticated discussion of possibility and human action in Arabic philosophy prior to Avicenna. The treatise has an unusual format, consisting of a lengthy independent section followed by a line-by-line commentary on chapter 9 of the *De interpretatione*.[10] In the independent section, Ibn ʿAdī addresses an argument to the effect that divine omniscience entails determinism. The argument turns on the claim that the "state of a knower" must be the same as the "state of the object known." In the case of God we have a knower who is "stable in existence, unchanging and unable to change." Therefore "the state of the things he knows is necessarily unchanging, and cannot change" (ed. Ehrig-Eggert, p. 66). But the possible is precisely that which can change from not-existing to existing, or vice versa. So if God knows everything, and everything God knows must be, like him, unchanging, then there is no such thing as possibility. Notice that 'possibility' here must mean two-sided possibility or contingency (that is, that which is neither necessary nor impossible) rather than one-sided possibility (that is, whatever is not impossible, including what is necessary).

Ibn ʿAdī responds to this deterministic argument by contending that God's foreknowledge is not a cause (*sabab*) for the existence of the things he knows. He proceeds by distinguishing six types of cause, and showing that God's foreknowledge does not fall under any of the six types.[11] The most interesting possibility seems to be that God's knowledge might be the efficient or agent cause (*sabab fāʿil*) of all things (ibid., pp. 68–9). There are, says Ibn ʿAdī, two types of efficient cause: those that act by nature and those that act by choice (*bi-ikhtiyār*). Causes that act by nature produce their effect whenever they exist, so that cause and effect co-occur. But God's foreknowledge *precedes* what he

---

[10] Part of the treatise is translated into English in J. McGinnis and D. C. Reisman (ed. and tr.), *Classical Arabic Philosophy: An Anthology of Sources* (Indianapolis, IN: Hackett, 2007) pp. 128–39. There is a German translation and commentary in Carl Ehrig-Eggert, *Die Abhandlung über den Nachweis der Natur des Möglichen von Yaḥyā ibn ʿAdī (gest. 974 A.D.)* (Frankfurt: Institut für Geschichte der Arabisch-Islamischen Wissenschaften an der Johann Wolfgang Goethe-Universität, 1990).

[11] He follows the Neoplatonists in expanding Aristotle's list of four causes (formal, material, efficient, and final) to include paradigmatic and instrumental causes.

knows. Thus God does not cause the objects of his knowledge by acting through his nature. That leaves God's acting by choice. But the assumption that God *voluntarily* causes all things to exist already implies that those things are possible, since voluntary choices are between multiple possibilities.[12] This assumption already undermines the opponent's conclusion, which is precisely that nothing is possible.

Thus far, Ibn ʿAdī has responded to the determinist in an indirect way. His aim has been to persuade us that there is no causal link between God's knowledge and what he knows. The point seems to be that, in the absence of such a link, there is no reason to think that the status of God's knowledge could in any way affect the status of the things he knows. Next, Ibn ʿAdī turns to a more direct refutation of the claim that the properties of a knower automatically transfer to what it knows. This is false, as Saadiah also pointed out, since God is eternally existent and yet it is patently the case that some objects of his knowledge are not eternally existent. There are, then, some properties of a knower that are not shared with what is known. Ibn ʿAdī explains how, in particular, it could be the case that God is unchanging even though what he knows is changing:

> The knower, insofar as it is a knower, changes its relation to the object of knowledge, along with the changing of the states of the object of knowledge. Even though the essence of the knower remains unchanged, it is not right to say that the knower is unchanged *insofar as it is a knower*, as it is taken in this argument.
>
> (ibid., p. 75)

Suppose (to take Ibn ʿAdī's own example) that Zayd dies, and thus goes from existing to not-existing. In this case God will go from knowing that Zayd exists to knowing that Zayd does not exist.[13] But this does not imply that God *himself* changes, because his knowledge is relational – that is, extrinsic to his own essence. It is only *qua* knower that God changes, not *qua* God.

So far, Ibn ʿAdī has argued negatively: there is no causal link between God and creatures sufficient to underwrite determinism, and the determinist's crucial premise is false. But he also supplies a positive reason for affirming the reality of the possible (ibid., p. 79). As we have seen, Aristotle identified the necessary with what always exists, and the impossible with what never exists. The possible must then be what exists sometimes but not always. Ibn ʿAdī accepts these

---

[12] "[Voluntary agency] applies only to agents who are able to do or refrain from one and the same thing. But this requires something that possibly exists (*imkān al-wujūd*), for which there exists the power (*qudra*) to make it exist or make it not exist. But this conflicts with the necessity of things, because it is obvious that whenever something necessarily exists, there can only be a power to make it exist, not one to make it not exist" (ibid., 68).

[13] He does not seem to envision the possibility that God *timelessly* knows that Zayd exists at such and such a time, and also *timelessly* knows that Zayd does not exist at some other time.

identifications. Therefore, to prove the existence of the possible, we need only give a single example of something that exists sometimes but not always: for instance, a man's walking. While this might seem a bit glib, it is important to remember that Ibn ʿAdī takes himself already to have eliminated any support for determinism. At this point, he need only reaffirm what we all intuitively believe in the first place, namely that some things are possible or contingent.

But there are grounds for unease. Go back to Ibn ʿAdī's discussion of whether God is an efficient cause. There, he seemed to leave it open that God might be a "voluntary" cause of what he knows. For Ibn ʿAdī this presented no difficulty, because if God voluntarily chooses (say) that Zayd will go on a journey, it immediately follows that it was possible that Zayd will *not* go on the journey: "voluntarily choosing" a thing makes sense only when that thing is two-sided-possible (neither necessary nor impossible). But this is really no comfort. What we want is for at least some things to be chosen by *us* and not God. Ibn ʿAdī has shown only that God's foreknowledge is consistent with two-sided possibility, not that there are possibilities whose realization lies in our power rather than God's. Though it is clear that Ibn ʿAdī does think there are such possibilities, his argument rather skirts the issue, because he is concerned only to prove that possibility does really exist. To put it another way, Ibn ʿAdī is here satisfied with showing that nothing in the created world is in itself necessary; he is not worried about whether created things might be (voluntarily) necessitated by God.

But further light is shed by another work by Ibn ʿAdī, a rebuttal of the afore-mentioned Ashʿarite theory of *kasb* (acquisition).[14] (This is a rather surprising topic for Ibn ʿAdī to have taken up, given that he is a Christian and that *kasb* is a notion originating in Islamic *kalām*. Indeed, Ibn ʿAdī says at the outset that he bothers with the question only at the request of the recipient of the treatise.) Again, the discussion takes the form of refuting a deterministic argument, this time one with a distinctively *kalām* ring. The opponent claims that humans cannot cause their own actions, since this would be to "create" something or "bring it into existence," while creation is proper only to God. Furthermore, the actions clearly do not bring themselves into existence. That leaves God as the only possible cause. Ibn ʿAdī responds with a closer inspection of the key terms 'fiʿl' and 'khalq' (action and creation). He claims that, although in Arabic these two terms are normally synonymous, creation is sometimes used in the narrow sense of bringing into existence a matter–form composite without a

---

[14] For an edition and translation see S. Pines and M. Schwarz, "Yaḥyā ibn ʿAdī's Refutation of the Doctrine of Acquisition (*Iktisāb*)," in J. Blau *et al.* (eds.) *Studia Orientalia Memoriae D.H. Baneth Dedicata* (Jerusalem: Magnes Press, 1979) 49–94.

preexisting material substrate. Though it is true that this sort of causation – creation *ex nihilo* – is exercised only by God, it does not follow that only God ever brings anything into existence. In particular, humans are able to "create" their actions, which are accidents rather than matter–form composites. (For instance, if I walk, the walking is an accident that belongs to me, not a matter–form composite in its own right.) To assume that this is impossible is simply to beg the question in favor of determinism.

THE LATIN TRADITION

For authors writing early in the Latin medieval tradition, the crucial context for these questions is provided by a different debate – namely, that between Augustine and the Pelagians. Pelagius held that it is within the power of human beings to be good and to merit salvation. Augustine disagreed, arguing that in our state of original sin, God's grace is a necessary condition for good human actions (see Chapter 32). It was Augustine who prevailed, and Christian medieval authors therefore write in a context where Pelagianism is a heresy. But this is not to say that Christian medieval philosophers must reject the reality of human freedom. Far from it: Augustine himself insisted that the need for divine grace is compatible with human freedom. Indeed, although Augustine could agree with the Ashʿarites that God must act in order for us to do good, he would nonetheless agree with the Muʿtazilites that we must be the sole agents when we do wrong, if God is to be just in punishing us.

Thus, philosophers in the Augustinian tradition must preserve what I will call the *asymmetry thesis*: that the human capacity to do evil does not imply an equal capacity to do good. There are good theological reasons within Christianity to uphold the asymmetry thesis (in particular, the absolute need for divine grace helps us to make sense of the Incarnation), but it seems to cause problems in the case of both good and evil actions. Why should I be rewarded for good actions, if it is God's grace that brings them about? And in what sense am I free when I do evil? If, with Saadiah and Ibn ʿAdī, we assume that my doing something freely requires the possibility to refrain from doing that thing, it looks as though I can be free with respect to sin only if it is possible for me to refrain from sinning. But this is precisely what Augustine seems to deny. Of course one might be free in the sense that one could choose from among a range of possible sins; but this would not be morally significant freedom, since any exercise of such freedom would be evil. Nor is this the only worry about freedom bequeathed to the medievals by Augustine. He also took up the problem of divine foreknowledge in his early work *On Freedom of Choice* and elsewhere (such as *The City of God* Book V).

Although the Latin medievals were also deeply influenced by Boethius's treatment of this problem in his *Consolation of Philosophy*, it was Augustine who was the central authority in a particularly important early dispute about freedom and determinism that took place in Carolingian France. The dispute was triggered by the theological position adopted *ca.* 840 by a monk named Gottschalk.[15] Gottschalk believed that human beings are subject to a double or "twin" predestination: there is one predestination for the elect, another for the damned. He saw this doctrine as Augustinian; it guarantees that those given divine grace are certainly saved, whereas those from whom God withholds grace are certainly damned. Other theologians were unwilling to accept that God predestines sin, however, on the grounds that this comes too close to placing the blame for evils with God, and could encourage the faithful to believe that it is pointless to expend effort in attempting to be good (because it is up to God, not me, whether I am saved). Gottschalk did have supporters, and some rejected double predestination yet pled for tolerance of his view. But Hincmar of Rheims and other opponents had Gottschalk condemned at Querzy in 849. Ordered to be silent, Gottschalk nevertheless continued to defend his controversial thesis, provoking a series of works against double predestination by Hincmar and others. Hincmar then turned to the Irish scholar John Scottus Eriugena for a demonstration of the falsity of Gottschalk's position, grounded in the liberal arts.[16] The resulting treatise *On Predestination* turned out to be an embarrassment to Hincmar. Eriugena displeased his own allies with some of the audacious positions he adopted, not least regarding eschatology, and he himself became the target of condemnatory refutations.

Eriugena begins his attack on Gottschalk by emphasizing a theme that will be prominent in his later *Periphyseon* – namely, God's simplicity. He argues (sec. 2) that since God's predestination is identical with God himself, a double predestination would imply duality in God, which is absurd. Eriugena also appeals to divine will and divine justice. Divine will would be vitiated if God were *necessarily* to predestine both the saved and the damned, for "where there is inevitability there is no will" (2.1). We must instead say that God

---

[15] For overviews of the dispute see, for instance, Maïeul Cappuyns, *Jean Scot Érigène: sa vie, son œuvre, sa pensée* (Paris: De Brouwer, 1933) pp. 102–27; David Ganz, "The Debate on Predestination," in M. T. Gibson and J. L. Nelson (eds.) *Charles the Bald: Court and Kingdom* (Aldershot: Variorum, 1990) 283–302; and, focusing on Eriugena's role in the debate, J. J. O'Meara, *Eriugena* (Oxford: Clarendon Press, 1988) ch. 3.

[16] On the methodology of Eriugena's treatise see Gangolf Schrimpf, *Das Werk des Johannes Scottus Eriugena im Rahmen des Wissenschaftsverständnisses seiner Zeit* (Münster: Aschendorff, 1982) pp. 72–131. For an illuminating philosophical study of the treatise which connects it to themes from the *Periphyseon*, see John Marenbon, "John Scottus and Carolingian Theology: from the *De praedestinatione*, its Background and its Critics, to the *Periphyseon*," in Gibson and Nelson, *Charles the Bald*, 303–25.

predestines voluntarily, which excludes all necessity. Divine justice would be vitiated were God to punish sinners, having himself predestined those sinners to sin. This point, already familiar to us from the Muʿtazilites, is emphasized repeatedly by Eriugena (see, e.g., 4.3, 5.8–9). Nevertheless, an omniscient God must know in advance what sinners will do. Eriugena thus follows Hincmar and other opponents of Gottschalk by repeating a distinction they find in Augustine: God foreknows both good and evil, but he predestines only good.[17]

This solution raises several questions. First let us consider good actions. Are humans still free with respect to such actions, even though they are predestined? Eriugena replies by distinguishing between having a will and having a *free* will. Adam, prior to original sin, had a free will, which means that his will had sufficient "strength" or "power" to choose good as well as evil (4.6). In the Fall, humans lose this strength to do good, but retain their will. Indeed, argues Eriugena, they must retain this, because will is a "natural" or "essential" capacity of humankind. In other words, human beings can lose freedom while remaining human, while to lose the will is to cease being human. For Eriugena, even Adam had the freedom to choose good only by God's grace – because by nature Adam possessed only will, not free will. In original sin, this grace was spurned. It is offered to us again in the Incarnation, but always remains a gift from God, and God predestines only some to receive it. Thus when a fallen human being manages to do good, there are in fact two causes of the good action: the willing human and God, who facilitates the action by bestowing grace (8.7).

Does this imply that God is after all a cause of human actions? At one point Eriugena seems to imply so: he says that God is a "voluntary" rather than a "necessary" or "compelling" cause (5.5). But as other examples of "voluntary causes" Eriugena names "wisdom for the wise man" and "sight for the seeing man." The point would seem to be that if I will to see, this project will succeed only if there is sight in addition to the willing. Similarly, if I will to do good, this will be possible only if grace is added. God's grace is thus only a cause in the sense of a necessary condition. The claim that God's grace is a necessary condition allows Eriugena to steer clear of Pelagianism. The claim that God's grace is not a sufficient condition allows him to avoid overdetermination, which is the absurdity criticized by Saadiah.

Regarding evil actions, Eriugena has already secured what he thinks he needs to preserve God's justice. For God to be just in punishing me, it is enough that

[17] For this claim in Ratramnus, Hrabanus, and Hincmar see, e.g., Ganz, "The Debate," p. 291; Marenbon, "John Scottus," p. 306.

I will my sin. God's justice does not, however, require my willing freely. So he can justly punish those who do not receive grace and who thus remain unable to avoid sin. On the other hand, Eriugena insists that God in no sense compels or causes my sin. This leads to another problem. God is the cause of all that is. So if he is not the cause of sin, how can there be sin? As we saw, the Ashʿarites admit that God creates even evil actions, since only he can create – though they tried to preserve human responsibility through their doctrine of acquisition. But Eriugena has a different solution, which goes back to Greek Neoplatonism by way of Augustine: God does not cause evils to exist, because evil is nothing at all. It is privation or a lack of being. This enables Eriugena to add yet another argument against Gottschalk: God can hardly predestine sin if sin is nothing. But surely this means that God cannot foreknow sin either? Eriugena concedes the point, saying that statements about God's foreknowledge of sin need to be understood in a rather special, extended sense (sec. 10). Some of the notions he uses here were to be developed further in the *Periphyseon*, which extensively explores problems of speaking about God and about non-being. In the present treatise, though, the doctrine that evil is non-being leads Eriugena to some of his most controversial claims. He needs, for example, to say that the suffering caused by divine retribution is not itself created by God. This is at the root of the eschatology that would embarrass Hincmar and inspire several refutations of *On Predestination*.

In this work Eriugena offers no comprehensive solution to the problem of divine foreknowledge. He claims that God foreknows – but does not predestine – some actions, without stopping to ask whether foreknowledge might have the same deterministic consequences as predestination. The best Eriugena can offer is the thought that evil actions are not even foreknown in the strict sense, because they are nothing. With respect to good actions, he simply accepts that they are inevitable, because they are predestined. Two centuries later, however, we find Anselm thinking in a more systematic fashion about both divine foreknowledge and predestination in such key texts as the *De concordia* (1107–8) and an earlier trilogy of philosophical dialogues, *On Truth*, *On Freedom of Choice*, and *On the Fall of the Devil* (1080s).

In *On Truth*, Anselm discusses how truth applies to a wide range of things, including the will. He defines truth in both will and action as uprightness (*rectitudo*, chs. 4–5), and defines justice as uprightness of the will preserved for its own sake (ch. 12). The implications of this for the notion of freedom are explored in *On Freedom of Choice*. Anselm defines freedom of choice as "the power to keep uprightness of will for the sake of this uprightness itself" (ch. 3). Unlike most modern-day definitions of freedom, this definition tells us that freedom is directed specifically at goodness, rather than being an ethically neutral capacity to make any choice whatever.[18] One advantage of this definition is that it allows for the freedom of beings who cannot sin, namely God and the good angels who are now confirmed in rectitude.[19] But it seems to have the awkward consequence that sin will not be a manifestation of free choice. Anselm's answer to this difficulty is that the power of choice need not be used for its intended purpose (ch. 2). As long as the sinner sins "without being compelled by anything else and out of no necessity, but on his own," we can say that the sin was an exercise of this power. Still, such a sin falls short of being a "free choice" in the full-blooded sense required by the definition, because it does not realize a capacity to preserve rectitude.[20]

Consider the choice of Adam or Satan to defy God. In *On the Fall of the Devil*,[21] Anselm argues that Satan must not have been compelled to sin. As we have just seen, this is a necessary condition for Satan's genuinely *choosing* his sin. But it is also required to preserve divine justice: everything about Satan before his fall is given by God, so if his fall is necessary then God, not Satan, is to blame. Anselm therefore argues that Satan must be choosing between two wills, both given to him by God and directed to two different goals, namely happiness and justice (chs. 12–13) (see Chapter 35). If Satan had only one goal, he would choose it of necessity.[22] His sin, then, lies in choosing his own happiness over justice – a choice that, ironically, leads to unhappiness, while the good angels who choose justice receive happiness anyway in recompense. We should not be misled here into thinking that Anselm is saying that one needs to have multiple

---

[18] This "teleological" aspect of the definition is well treated in Sandra Visser and Thomas Williams, "Anselm's Account of Freedom," in B. Davies and B. Leftow (eds.) *The Cambridge Companion to Anselm* (Cambridge: Cambridge University Press, 2005) 179–203.

[19] Anselm insists at *Freedom of Choice* 1 that the definition must apply to God, angels, and human beings, and therefore rejects the definition of freedom as the ability to sin or avoid sin. The point is emphasized by G. R. Evans, "Why the Fall of Satan?," *Recherches de théologie ancienne et médiévale* 45 (1978) p. 143.

[20] One might compare the use of medical knowledge to poison someone, or (to adapt an example used by Anselm, on which see further below) the use of sight to perceive darkness. On this argument see further Visser and Williams, "Anselm's Account of Freedom," pp. 183–4.

[21] As Evans, "Why the Fall of Satan?" points out, the focus on Satan is presumably for the sake of conceptual clarity. Anselm's concern is likely to be at least as much with Adam as with Satan.

[22] Furthermore, Satan must not know what will befall him if he sins, because if he did he would of course not sin. Nonetheless, he must know in advance that his sin is wrong, because otherwise he would not be blameworthy (chs. 21–2). With these two additional conditions Anselm is walking a careful line between asserting the utter perversity of Satan's choice – because he wants to ensure that Satan does not deliberately choose his own downfall – and asserting that Satan acts in complete ignorance. It seems then that Anselm concedes the possibility of *akrasia*, the deliberate choice of what one knows to be wrong, but does not concede the possibility of knowingly acting against one's self-interest. I offer this point as a supplement to the excellent discussion of the primary requirement for two wills in Calvin Normore, "Picking and Choosing: Anselm and Ockham on Choice," *Vivarium* 36 (1998) 23–39.

possibilities open to one in order to be free. After all, God and (once they are confirmed in rectitude) the good angels have a single will for the single goal of justice. The problem is rather that a single will for justice would itself come from God, so that Satan would be *compelled* to be just.[23]

What about postlapsarian humans? It might seem that we are compelled to sin, because without grace we cannot choose justice. But Anselm disagrees: after the Fall humans do have this ability; it is just that they cannot *use* the ability without God's help. Anselm compares this to someone who can see, but is blindfolded or in the dark (*Freedom of Choice* 3). This is Anselm's way of defending the asymmetry thesis: I can sin and can preserve rectitude, but 'can' means something different in the two cases. Anselm emphasizes that the power of free choice is inalienable, even if we are not always able to use it. It cannot be removed by temptation, nor even by God – not only because God is good and would not do so,[24] but because the power is "essential to rational nature."

In the trilogy, Anselm is concerned primarily with whether God's gifts (or lack thereof) to his creatures compel them to be good or evil. He does raise the divine foreknowledge problem (*Fall of the Devil* 21), only to defer it to another occasion. That occasion is the *De concordia*, whose title refers to the "harmony" between divine foreknowledge and freedom. Anselm is more explicit than any philosopher we have yet discussed in separating God's *knowing* a future action from his *causing* that action. Indeed what God foreknows in the case of voluntary action is just that: an action that is voluntary, and hence uncaused.[25] But does not foreknowledge alone show that the action is necessary? Anselm argues that it does not, by distinguishing "subsequent necessity" from "preceding necessity" (1.3). Something has preceding necessity if it is caused or compelled; it has merely subsequent necessity if it follows from some presupposition. For instance if we presuppose that a sea battle will occur tomorrow, then from this it necessarily follows that there will be a sea battle, but not that the sea battle is itself necessary.[26] And divine foreknowledge, according to Anselm, involves only subsequent necessity, since it is not a cause of what is foreknown.[27]

---

[23] Here I follow Visser and Williams, "Anselm's Account of Freedom," pp. 186–94.

[24] On this and, in general, the question of whether God can do evil, see William Courtenay, "Necessity and Freedom in Anselm's Conception of God," *Analecta Anselmiana* 4 (1975) 39–64.

[25] See *De concordia* 2: "God foreknows the very fact that the will (*voluntas*) is neither compelled nor prevented by anything, and thus that what is done voluntarily (*voluntate*) is done freely (*libertate*)."

[26] This is the same distinction drawn by al-Fārābī, as we saw above. It is described by some Latin authors using the language of *de dicto* versus *de re* modality (see Chapter 13).

[27] Here numerous complications arise. For instance, in *De concordia* 1.5 Anselm follows Boethius in holding that God's knowledge does not in fact temporally precede that which he knows. Rather his knowledge is timelessly eternal. Anselm thinks this helps us see how God could "immutably" know something mutable.

The *De concordia* also discusses divine predestination. Anselm argues that God need not actually create evils, because they are quite literally nothing insofar as they are evil (1.7, 2.2). His only direct causal role regarding evil action is creating the will and the action, not creating the evilness of the action (which is nothing but a lack of justice). By contrast, in the case of good actions God creates both the action and its goodness (1.7). So, like Eriugena, Anselm depends on the Augustinian claim that evil is non-being. Apart from that, says Anselm (2.3), the problem of divine predestination adds no threat of determinism over and above the problem of divine foreknowledge, which has already been solved.[28]

CONCLUSION

Obviously, this has been a rather incomplete survey of a central issue in medieval philosophy, focusing only on early figures from the Arabic and Latin traditions. But these early discussions set the agenda for later thinkers. For instance, there is the question of what necessity is and how it relates to divine knowledge. Is the necessary, following Aristotle, that which is always the case, and the (two-sided) possible what is sometimes but not always the case? As we saw, Ibn ʿAdī endorses this assimilation, even though he wants to define choice in terms of selecting from multiple possibilities. At the same time, his teacher, al-Fārābī, hesitantly discusses the view that some things that are never realized might nonetheless be possible.[29] A generation later, the new modal theory of Avicenna will give the Arabic tradition new tools for thinking about the relation between time and modality. Avicenna will also influence ongoing Latin debates about modality, a foretaste of which can be found in Anselm. Briefly, Avicenna denies Aristotle's identification of the eternal with the necessary. For him, something's necessity or (two-sided) possibility is determined by its own essence: God is necessary-in-himself, whereas created things are merely possible-in-themselves.

---

[28] Obviously this requires that the doctrine of grace has no deterministic consequences of its own, since what God predestines is precisely who receives grace and who does not. This issue is addressed in the third *Quaestio* of the *De concordia*, where Anselm refers back to the distinctions made in the trilogy, especially *On Freedom of Choice* (see, e.g., 3.4).

[29] On this see Adamson, "The Arabic Sea Battle." Al-Fārābī gives the example of whether it is possible for God to do evil, which is a worry for Anselm as well (see n. 24 above). See also Josef van Ess, "Wrongdoing and Divine Omnipotence in the Theology of Abū Isḥāq an-Naẓẓām," in T. Rudavsky (ed.) *Divine Omniscience and Omnipotence in Medieval Philosophy: Islamic, Jewish, and Christian Perspectives* (Dordrecht: Reidel, 1985) 53–67; in the same volume, see Richard M. Frank, "Can God Do What Is Wrong?," 69–79.

Some created things (the world, the heavens) are eternal, however, because their possible existence is realized eternally, through God's creative act.

Another important issue is the place of will in human psychology. We have seen that both Eriugena and Anselm associate the will strongly with rationality, and hold that humans possess a will essentially. This means modifying traditional Aristotelian psychology to accommodate a *sui generis* power to choose. As we have seen, in the Christian tradition this capacity is retained in defective fashion even after the Fall. Like their predecessors, the later medievals need to explain how even this defective will can account for moral responsibility, without obviating the need for divine grace. Alongside the problem of divine foreknowledge, it is thus the metaphysical nature of the will, and the theological ramifications of this special power, that most occupy the attentions of later Latin philosophers when they think about freedom.[30]

---

[30] See further David Burrell, *Faith and Freedom: An Interfaith Perspective* (Oxford: Blackwell, 2004); William Lane Craig, *The Problem of Divine Foreknowledge and Future Contingents from Aristotle to Suarez* (Leiden: Brill, 1988); Hester Gelber, *It Could Have Been Otherwise: Contingency and Necessity in Dominican Theology at Oxford 1300–1350* (Leiden: Brill, 2004); Harm Goris, *Free Creatures of an Eternal God. Thomas Aquinas on God's Infallible Foreknowledge and Irresistible Will* (Leuven: Peeters, 1996); Anthony Kenny, "Divine Foreknowledge and Human Freedom," in A. Kenny (ed.) *Aquinas: A Collection of Critical Essays* (Notre Dame, IN: University of Notre Dame Press, 1969) 255–70; Rudavsky, *Divine Omniscience and Omnipotence*; Eleonore Stump, "Aquinas' Account of Freedom: Intellect and Will," in B. Davies (ed.) *Thomas Aquinas: Contemporary Philosophical Perspectives* (Oxford: Oxford University Press, 2002) 275–94; Linda Zagzebski, *The Dilemma of Freedom and Foreknowledge* (Oxford: Oxford University Press, 1991).

30

INTELLECTUALISM AND VOLUNTARISM

TOBIAS HOFFMANN

The terms 'intellectualism' and 'voluntarism' classify theories of moral psychology and of ethics according to whether primary importance is placed on the intellect or the will in human agency. Though classical and early medieval moral theories have a notion of willing as an act of desire (whether rational or not), they lack a concept of the will as a power of the soul distinct from the intellect and from the sense appetite. Only in the later Middle Ages, when the will is thus conceived as a distinct power of the soul, do the classifications of intellectualism and voluntarism properly apply.

Although intellectualism and voluntarism are apt terms for describing the extreme viewpoints, not every writer fits neatly into one of the two main camps, since there are considerable differences among them when it comes to the details of their moral psychology and ethics. An author may, for instance, have both intellectualist and voluntarist tendencies in different respects, or may consider the activities of intellect and will as so intertwined that these classifications become useless.

Historically, this split originated from specific innovative questions which were made a litmus test for a successful defense of human freedom; the fundamental issue was not whether human beings are free, but whether intellect or will is ultimately responsible for their freedom. This chapter focuses on the period in which these discussions among Latin authors were most heated and philosophically most fruitful – namely, from the late 1260s until the early 1300s – a time when ecclesiastical interventions were exacerbating the division. It concludes with some reflections on the wider implications of these rival accounts of human freedom for alternative views of human psychology and ethics.[1]

---

[1] The most valuable studies are Bonnie Kent, *Virtues of the Will: The Transformation of Ethics in the Late Thirteenth Century* (Washington, DC: Catholic University of America Press, 1995); Peter S. Eardley, "The Foundations of Freedom in Later Medieval Philosophy: Giles of Rome and his Contemporaries," *Journal of the History of Philosophy* 44 (2006) 353–76; François-Xavier Putallaz, *Insolente liberté: controverses et condamnations au XIIIᵉ siècle* (Paris: Cerf, 1995); Ernst Stadter, *Psychologie und Metaphysik der menschlichen Freiheit: Die ideengeschichtliche Entwicklung zwischen Bonaventura und*

BONAVENTURE AND AQUINAS

Until the 1270s, explicit mention of "free will" (*voluntas libera*) was rare in medieval discussions of human freedom. The common term was rather *liberum arbitrium* (free decision, literally free adjudication). Thirteenth-century authors generally agreed with Peter Lombard's formula that free decision is a "faculty of reason and will," which they thought he had received from Augustine (*Sentences* II.24.3).

Bonaventure, in line with this tradition, holds that free decision encompasses both reason and will. Freedom – that is, acting or refraining from acting as one wants – requires the self-movement of the will and the cognitive capacity for reflecting upon one's own act (*Sent.* II.25.1.1.3). The will depends on reason for its act, for without prior knowledge it cannot elicit its act. Yet, freedom consists principally in the will: reason's control of the lower powers of the soul depends on the "command" (that is, the control) of the will, and the will is not bound to follow the dictate of reason unless it is a "definitive judgment." Moreover, the will influences practical reason's definitive judgment of what is to be done. Thus, "the will does not principally follow a foreign act [that is, the act of reason], but it rather pulls the foreign act towards its own act." Even if reason judges an act of the will to be evil, the will has the option of desisting from this act or not (*Sent.* II.25.1.1.6). Important themes foreshadowing later voluntarist accounts of free decision are already present here: the self-movement of the will, "command" as an act of the will, and the will's dominance vis-à-vis the judgment of reason. Conspicuously absent is the mention of practical deliberation in the generation of an act of free decision.

Thomas Aquinas emphasizes much more than Bonaventure the will's dependence on reason. His position is neatly summarized in a passage from the *Summa theologiae*:

> The root of freedom is the will as its subject, but reason as its cause. The will is, in fact, free with regard to alternatives, because reason can have different conceptions of the good. Accordingly, the philosophers defined free decision (*liberum arbitrium*) as free judgment owing to reason, implying that reason is the cause of freedom.
>
> (*Summa theol.* 1a2ae 17.1 ad 2)

For Aquinas, the will is a moved mover, a passive potency that is actualized by the object presented to it by the intellect.[2] As a rational appetite, the will's

---

Duns Scotus (Paderborn: Schöningh, 1971); and Odon Lottin, *Psychologie et morale aux XIIe et XIIIe siècles* (Gembloux: Duculot, 1948–60) I: 11–389. A further, though not always reliable, resource is Antonio San Cristóbal-Sebastián, *Controversias acerca de la voluntad desde 1270 a 1300: estudio histórico-doctrinal* (Madrid: Editorial y librería co., 1958).

[2] See, e.g., *Summa theol.* 1a 80.2c. In the late *Quaest. de malo* 6.1, Thomas emphasizes more than in previous texts the active character of the will.

proper object is the good apprehended as suitable. Thus one can desire something, whether in truth it be good or evil, only under the appearance of the good (*sub ratione boni*).[3] For Thomas, this implies that the will cannot desire or choose contrary to what the practical intellect judges in a particular instance to be best and most suitable.[4] Hence the will acts freely to the extent that reason judges freely (*Quaest. de veritate* 24.1–2). A faulty will presupposes some defect of knowledge or of judgment (ibid., 24.8c; *Summa theol.* 1a2ae 77.2c).

The free judgment of reason and the free inclination of the will are codependent for Aquinas: reason moves the will, and the will moves reason, yet in different respects. Reason moves the will by formal causality, "determining" or "specifying" the will's act (desiring to study, choosing to take a walk). Yet reason does not move the will by necessity, except when it proposes an object that is good and suitable from every point of view, such as happiness. Conversely, the will moves reason by efficient causality to exercise its act (to think or not, to dwell on a consideration or not). The will also moves itself to exercise its act. In virtue of desiring an end (such as health), it moves itself to desire a means, and it moves the intellect to deliberate about which means to choose (taking medicine, observing a diet). Thus the choice of the will is informed by the judgment of reason resulting from deliberation. Even the decision to deliberate depends on a previous deliberation. To avoid an infinite regress, Thomas posits that the first movement of the will is due to an impulse from God, who moves the will without imposing any necessity on it.[5] Besides initiating deliberation, the will also governs the complexity and duration of deliberation. Whether a judgment resulting from deliberation is definitive or only provisional depends on whether the will adheres to it or moves reason to reconsider the options (cf. *Quaest. de malo* 6.1 ad 15).

In his account of free decision, Thomas distinguishes, but does not separate, the acts of intellect and will. Every act of the will is informed by an act of the intellect, and the way in which one uses the intellect depends on the will. The activities of intellect and will penetrate each other, and ultimately it is the human person who moves him or herself to a choice by means of reason and will.[6] Because Thomas considers acts of intellect and will to be blended in

---

[3] See, e.g., *Summa theol.* 1a2ae 8.1, 1a2ae 9.1–2, *Quaest. de malo* 6.1c.

[4] See, e.g., *Summa theol.* 1a2ae 77.1c, 3a 18.4 ad 2, *Quaest. de veritate* 24.2c. Thomas does not, of course, deny that one can act contrary to conscience. A judgment of conscience (*iudicium conscientiae*) is merely theoretical, whereas the practical judgment that informs a choice (*iudicium electionis*) is constituted by thought and desire. Thus it may happen that the judgment of conscience remains intact, while the practical judgment is perverted. See *Quaest. de veritate* 17.1 ad 4.

[5] *Quaest. de malo* 6.1c; see also *Summa theol.* 1a2ae 9.1, 1a2ae 9.3, 1a2ae 10.2.

[6] See, e.g., *Summa theol.* 1a 82.4 ad 1, 1a2ae 17.1c, 1a2ae 17.5 ad 2.

this way, his doctrine does not neatly fit into the categories of intellectualism and voluntarism.[7]

INTELLECTUALISM BEFORE 1277

The most prominent intellectualist in the years prior to the condemnations of 1277 is Siger of Brabant. His concern is to reconcile necessity and free decision. Acts of free decision are caused by necessity, Siger believes, for, according to Avicenna, every cause causes its effect by necessity. Moreover, according to Aristotle, when something that moves draws near to a movable thing, if both are properly disposed, then it is necessary that the one cause motion and the other be moved.[8] Accordingly, the will is necessarily moved by its object when the object is present and the will is disposed to be moved by it; thus the will is neither the first cause nor first mover of its own acts.[9]

Against those who denied free decision on such grounds, Siger argues that the necessity involved in the will's act does not impair the will's freedom. The will is moved not by "absolute necessity" but "by conditional necessity" or "necessarily contingently,"[10] which belongs to a cause that can be impeded. Sensory appetites are determined in the first way, because the "judgment of the sense" is determined: the senses cannot judge something white not to be white, for example, or something pleasurable not to be pleasurable. The causality of the will's object, in contrast, may be impeded by practical deliberation. The judgment of reason regarding good and evil is not determined by the intellect's natural constitution, but remains open to contraries, and consequently the act

---

[7] The interpretation of Thomas's account of free decision is debated with no less liveliness today than it was in the decades after his death. Odon Lottin argued long ago that voluntarism and intellectualism are not fit categories to describe Thomas's theory, see *Psychologie et morale* III.2: 651–66. For a summary of the more recent debate and for a case in favor of an intellectualist interpretation, see Jeffrey Hause, "Thomas Aquinas and the Voluntarists," *Medieval Philosophy and Theology* 6 (1997) 167–82. Robert Pasnau considers Aquinas a compatibilist (freedom coexists with determinism). See *Thomas Aquinas on Human Nature: A Philosophical Study of* Summa theologiae *1a 75–89* (Cambridge: Cambridge University Press, 2002) pp. 221–33. Cases against ascribing intellectual determinism to Thomas's explanation of free decision are made by David M. Gallagher, "Free Choice and Free Judgment in Thomas Aquinas," *Archiv für Geschichte der Philosophie* 76 (1994) 247–77, and Tobias Hoffmann, "Aquinas and Intellectual Determinism: The Test Case of Angelic Sin," *Archiv für Geschichte der Philosophie* 89 (2007) 122–56.

[8] Avicenna, *Liber de philosophia prima* 1.6 (ed. Van Riet, pp. 45–6); Aristotle, *Physics* VIII.1, 251b1–5. See Siger of Brabant, *De necessitate et contingentia causarum* (ed. J. J. Duin, *La doctrine de la providence dans les écrits de Siger de Brabant* [Leuven: Institut Supérieur de Philosophie, 1954], p. 32); *Quaest. in Metaphys.* [Paris] VI.9 (ed. Maurer, pp. 317 and 320); *Quaest. in Metaphys.* [Vienna] VII.1 (ed. Dunphy, p. 378).

[9] *Quaest. in Metaphys.* [Paris] VI.9, p. 325; *Quaest. in Metaphys.* [Vienna] VII.1, p. 386.

[10] For this distinction, see *Quaest. in Metaphys.* [Paris] VI.9, p. 321; *Quaest. in Metaphys.* [Vienna] VII.1, p. 380.

of the will is not predetermined.[11] Thus Siger can say that people become good or bad on account of their good or bad judgments. Still, there is a conditional necessity, because after a particular practical judgment has identified a particular course of action as the best, the will is not able to choose a contrary act (*Quaest. in Metaphys.* [Vienna] V.8, pp. 330–1). In this way, Siger seeks to uphold necessity while denying external determinism.

VOLUNTARIST WORRIES

Was Siger's defense of free decision successful? Not according to Stephen Tempier, the bishop of Paris. In 1270, even before Siger's lectures on the *Metaphysics* (from the mid-1270s), Tempier had condemned the views that the will chooses necessarily and that free decision is a passive power whose act is necessitated by the desired object. This condemnation did not stop Siger from professing his theory, however, and so it is hardly surprising that these claims appeared again in Tempier's more famous condemnation of 1277 (see Chapter 8). Among the 219 propositions solemnly condemned were the view that volitions are moved externally by necessity, together with assertions expressing a strict dependence of the will on the intellect, such as the view that the will cannot depart from the particular judgment of reason.[12]

Though these condemnations were targeted at arts masters and not at Thomas Aquinas, several of Thomas's critics argued that they affected some of his positions as well. Among the critics was William de la Mare, whose *Correctorium fratris Thomae* was highly influential because in 1282 it became obligatory reading for Franciscans who read Thomas's works. William interprets Thomas as holding that the judgment of reason necessitates the will's adherence, a view he saw articulated in three of the condemned articles.[13]

What was the rationale behind Tempier's condemnation of intellectualist propositions? The bishop did not provide any explanations himself, but Henry of Ghent's first *Quodlibet* of 1276 offers some hints. Henry, a secular master (unaffiliated with any religious order), was part of the sixteen-member commission

---

[11] *Quaest. in Metaphys.* [Vienna] VII.1, p. 380; *Quaest. in Metaphys.* [Paris] VI.9, pp. 325–6; *De necessitate*, p. 35. For a thorough discussion, see Christopher J. Ryan, "Man's Free Will in the Works of Siger of Brabant," *Mediaeval Studies* 45 (1983) 155–99.

[12] Articles concerning the will that have a direct connection with Siger's writings are 131, 134, 194, and to some extent 158. See Roland Hissette, *Enquête sur les 219 articles condamnés à Paris le 7 mars 1277* (Leuven: Publications universitaires, 1977) pp. 230–63. For a useful collection of articles, see Jan Aertsen *et al.* (eds.) *Nach der Verurteilung von 1277: Philosophie und Theologie an der Universität von Paris im letzten Viertel des 13. Jahrhunderts* (Berlin: De Gruyter, 2001).

[13] William quotes articles 158, 159, and 164 (*Correctorium*, ed. Glorieux, p. 232).

of theologians who investigated the works of the arts masters at Tempier's behest and who compiled the list of propositions that the bishop condemned. Some of the condemned intellectualist articles uphold the very views that Henry opposed. In particular, he may well have been the motivating force behind the censure of the propositions that deny the will's freedom to accept or reject the practical judgment (articles 129, 130, 158, and 163) or to choose a lesser of two goods (article 208).[14]

This latter issue, the problem of the will's freedom to choose the lesser of two goods presented to it, was posed to Henry in his first quodlibetal disputation. For Henry, this problem turns on the question of whether freedom is principally rooted in the intellect or in the will. Against Aquinas, who traces freedom in the will to freedom of judgment, Henry argues that in order to avoid cognitive determinism one must posit something more than reason's freedom of judgment (*libertas arbitrandi*): one must further posit the will's "freedom to choose what is judged" (*libertas eligendi arbitratum*). Cognitive reason by itself is in fact not free, because the intellect has no control over its own cognition. Rather, it assents to a truth in proportion to that truth's evidence. If the will's acts depended exclusively on reason, they would not be free either. Far from causing the will's acts, the knowledge proposed by reason provides only the occasion for willing or, as Henry will say in later *Quodlibets*, its necessary condition (*causa sine qua non*). Knowledge does not move the will, but the will itself is a "first mover."[15] Denying that the Aristotelian axiom "whatever is moved is moved by another" applies to non-material things such as the will, Henry considers the will to be an active rather than passive power.[16] Later he will explain in detail why freedom presupposes self-movement of the will and how this is metaphysically possible.[17]

A consideration about sin confirms, for Henry, that freedom originates in the will rather than in reason. If the will were bound to follow reason, then a

---

[14] The following provide a representative picture of what were the most debated articles. 129: "While passion and particular knowledge are in act, the will cannot act contrary to them." 130: "If reason is right, then the will is right. – Error, because it is contrary to a gloss by Augustine . . . and because according to this statement, grace would not be necessary for the rectitude of the will, but only knowledge, which is the error of Pelagius." 163: "That the will necessarily pursues what is firmly believed by reason, and that it cannot abstain from that which reason dictates. Yet this necessitation is not a coercion, but natural for the will." For the Latin text in a critical edition, see David Piché, *La condamnation parisienne de 1277* (Paris: Vrin, 1999) pp. 118, 126, 128.

[15] *Quodlibet* I.16, *Opera* vol. V, esp. pp. 98, 102, 107–8, 112. For the intellect as *causa sine qua non* of the will's act, see *Quodlibet* IX.5, X.9, XI.6, XII.26, XIII.10–11, and XIV.5.

[16] *Quodlibet* X.9. The Aristotelian axiom applies to natural but not spiritual powers (ibid., *Opera* XIV: 234 and *Quodlibet* XIII.11, *Opera* XVIII: 131–3).

[17] *Quodlibet* IX.5, XII.26, XI.6, XIII.11.

defective – that is, sinful – will must be traced to a cognitive defect. Yet, unless this cognitive defect is itself the fruit of a depraved will, the first occurrence of sin remains unexplained (*Quodlibet* I.16, *Opera* V: 112). On these presuppositions, Henry explains that incontinence (acting against one's better knowledge), occurs because this knowledge gets clouded due to passion. If passion clouded reason without the will's consent, however, and if the ensuing practical misjudgment necessarily entailed a disordered will, then it would not be up to free will whether one sins or not, but sin would follow in the natural course of events. Accordingly, throughout his entire career Henry holds the opposite view: a disorder of reason results from a disorder of the will, not vice versa.[18]

Since reason cannot compel the consent of the will – whereas the will can constrain reason to abandon its judgment – the will rather than reason is the highest power of the soul. Accordingly, Henry rejects Aquinas's view that "command" is an act of reason presupposing an act of the will (*Summa theol.* 1a2ae 17.1). Rather, for Henry it is the will that commands all the powers of the soul (*Quodlibet* IX.6, *Opera* XIII: 142–3). Henry calls the will the "first mover in the kingdom of the soul." Although it is true that the intellect directs the will, it does so not as the master directs the servant, but rather "as the servant ministers to the master by carrying before him the lantern at night so that the master does not stumble" (*Quodlibet* I.14, *Opera* V: 85, 90).[19]

An example of someone who abandoned an intellectualist view, presumably as a result of the condemnation, is Giles of Rome, who belonged to the order of the Augustinian Hermits and was probably a disciple of Aquinas. Giles came under pressure from Tempier for his views and had to leave Paris until his rehabilitation in 1285, several years after Tempier's death. In the same year, the Parisian masters of theology conceded a statement by Giles that Tempier had censured in 1277: "There is no evil in the will without error in reason." This came to be known as the "Magisterial Proposition" (*propositio magistralis*). At face value, this proposition seems to conflict with Tempier's condemnation of the intellectualist articles 129 and 130. Yet there was room for disagreement. Henry of Ghent distended the meaning of the *propositio magistralis* to make it fit the condemnation, while Godfrey of Fontaines argued conversely that the

---

[18] Henry makes this point throughout *Quodlibet* I.17. He attributes his own view to Aristotle, giving a detailed commentary of *Nicomachean Ethics* VII; see *Quodlibet* I.17 ad 1.

[19] For the broad outline of his theory, Henry was indebted to Walter of Bruges, a Franciscan and a student of Bonaventure, whose writings on freedom date from the late 1260s. Walter had already argued that the intellect is not free, and that the root of freedom is therefore to be found in the will, which as an active power moves itself and is capable of acting contrary to the practical judgment. Walter also developed the image of the soul as a miniature world with the will as its king (*Quaest. disputatae* 4–5, ed. *Phil. Belges* X: 34–55).

Magisterial Proposition should be the criterion for interpreting the condemned articles.[20]

After his rehabilitation, Giles developed an account of free decision that, although somewhat inspired by Aquinas, contained a strong voluntarist bent. Contrary to Henry, Giles holds that the will does not move without being moved. It needs to be "actuated" by the intellect's presentation of something good. If that object is not good from every point of view, then the will does not desire it necessarily. As long as one continues to engage in a "split consideration" (*consideratio bifurcata*) of the object's good and bad aspects, the will is not yet "determined" to pursue it or not. It must first determine itself to desire further consideration of the object. Then it can freely determine the intellect to focus on one aspect above another: for example, on the pleasure of committing adultery rather than its disorder. The practical judgment resulting from the consideration commanded by the will then informs the will's choice. It is thus that the will determines its own actions (*Quodlibet* III.15, ed. 1646, pp. 178–80). The intellect, which is indeterminate with regard to alternate possibilities, lacks the ability for self-determination. Thus it must be determined by the will, which is by nature capable of self-determination (*Quodlibet* IV.21, pp. 258–9). This is importantly different from Aquinas's account of the relationship between will and intellect. For Thomas, the will's activity is guided by reason from beginning to end, whereas, for Giles, the will directs the attention of reason according to its own liking. For Giles, the will's freedom presupposes the indetermination of the intellect, but it is not derived from the freedom of the intellect (ibid.).

INTELLECTUALIST REPLIES

Giles of Rome and, to an even greater extent, Henry of Ghent were severely criticized by Godfrey of Fontaines, a prominent secular master who was influenced by Siger of Brabant and Thomas Aquinas. Godfrey vigorously argues that any self-movement, including that of the will, is metaphysically impossible. For Godfrey, the Aristotelian principle that whatever is moved is moved by another holds true for the entire realm of being, including intellect and will. A reduction from potency to act requires not only that something already be in act, but also that the thing in act be really distinct from the thing in potency, for one and the same thing cannot be both in act and in potency with respect to itself.

---

[20] Giles of Rome, *Sent.* I.17.1.1 (ed. 1521, f. 89vM), I.47.2.1 (f. 237rG); Henry of Ghent, *Quodlibet* X.9, X.10, X.13 (*Opera* XIV: 243–8, 258–71, 287–9); Godfrey of Fontaines, *Quodlibet* VIII.16 (ed. *Phil. Belges* IV: 165–6). See also Peter S. Eardley, "The Problem of Moral Weakness, the *Propositio Magistralis*, and the Condemnation of 1277," *Mediaeval Studies* 68 (2006) 161–203.

In this context, Godfrey's main adversary is Henry, who held that the will can move itself entirely on its own. To refute this view, Godfrey argues that even the more moderate view of the Franciscan Master John of Murro faces the same metaphysical obstacles as Henry's. For John, the will is capable of self-movement because the desired object causes in it inclinations (*affectiones*) that play a role analogous to that played by intelligible species in intellection.[21] For Godfrey, in contrast, "the will does not move itself, but is moved by the apprehended good according to the mode and form of the apprehension" (*Quodlibet* VI.7, ed. *Phil. Belges* III: 163). By itself, the will is indifferent with respect to specific volitions; since it cannot determine itself, the will needs to be determined by another. What determines the will is the object as evaluated in a practical judgment. The object thus apprehended moves the will as an efficient cause.[22]

In addition to the metaphysical problems that Godfrey finds in Henry's account of free choice, Godfrey attacks the theory as an unreasonable account of human agency. If the will moves itself, even contrary to practical judgment, its willing would be without any object and the practical intellect would be useless (*Quodlibet* VI.10, pp. 202–5; *Quodlibet* VI.11, p. 219). For Godfrey, the will can seek or shun only what practical judgment presents as desirable or undesirable. Since the will controls the exercise of the intellect only in virtue of a previous intellectual judgment, it has no autonomous power over the intellect (*Quodlibet* VIII.16, pp. 169, 176; *Quodlibet* X.13, pp. 375–6). The content of the practical judgment depends only indirectly and incidentally on the will, to the extent that previous actions cause a virtuous or vicious disposition that influences one's practical deliberation (*Quodlibet* VI.11, pp. 220–4). Not surprisingly, Godfrey rejects Henry's claim that the will is a higher power than the intellect (*Quodlibet* VI.10).

For Henry, the activity of reason is deterministic. This makes it necessary to accord to the will the freedom to depart from reason, in order to safeguard free decision. Giles, in contrast, considers the intellect to be indeterminate and in need of determination by the will, which alone is formally free. In contrast to both, Godfrey takes the intellect itself, no less than the will, to be formally free,

---

[21] Godfrey, *Quodlibet* VI.7 (ed. *Phil. Belges* III: 150–8); *Quodlibet* VIII.2 (ed. *Phil. Belges* IV: 20–30). For the text of John of Murro's disputed question, see Éphrem Longpré, "L'œuvre scolastique du cardinal Jean de Murro, O.F.M. (†1312)," in *Mélanges Pelzer* (Leuven: Bibliothèque de l'Université, 1947) pp. 488–92. Godfrey's critique of Henry is directed against his *Quodlibet* XIII.11, where Henry opposes John of Murro's theory that *affectiones* are required for the will's self-movement and reiterates his own arguments for the will's ability to move itself, even without *affectiones*.

[22] *Quodlibet* VI.7 (pp. 158–64). For the efficient causality of the object on the will's act, see also *Quodlibet* VI.11 (p. 221); *Quodlibet* VIII.16 (ed. *Phil. Belges* IV: 173–4); *Quodlibet* XV.4 (ed. *Phil. Belges* XIV: 25).

because both are rooted in the immaterial soul.[23] In response to Giles's claim that the intellect is indeterminate with regard to alternate possibilities and needs to be determined by the will, Godfrey asks how the will can determine the intellect without being itself determined by some prior cognition motivating the will to determine the intellect in a specific way. Again, when Giles says that the will is naturally constituted so as to determine itself freely, Godfrey asks why he does not grant that ability to the intellect as well, since the two powers are equally immaterial. Godfrey assumes that the intellect no less than the will is free, but that neither can reduce itself from potency to act.[24] What resolves the initial indeterminacy with regard to an object of choice is practical deliberation, which is put into motion by an object that causes someone to know and desire it. When deliberation is completed, the will cannot will contrary to the determination of the practical judgment. Yet the deliberation itself is free, because it could have arrived at a different conclusion. Accordingly, following Siger of Brabant, Godfrey says that it is not by absolute but by conditional necessity that the will chooses the course of action that is determined by the practical judgment (*Quodlibet* VIII.16, pp. 159–61, 168–73). Godfrey considers his own account of free decision to be not only metaphysically more sound, but also more effective in safeguarding free decision (*Quodlibet* XV.4).

The difference between Godfrey's and Aquinas's accounts of free decision is subtle but important. First, Thomas admits that the will moves itself. When it desires an end (such as health), it moves itself to desire the means to the end (some medicine). Precisely in virtue of this self-movement, Thomas attributes to the will control over its act (*Summa theol.* 1a2ae 9.3). Godfrey, in contrast, denies that there is any self-movement of the will. The will does not move itself to desire the means to the end, but it is the apprehended object that causes the will to desire the end and the means (*Quodlibet* VIII.2, pp. 24–5). Second, for Thomas, what the will desires or chooses depends on the intellect as its formal cause, but not as its efficient cause. Though a formal cause has an influence on its effect, it does not move anything to a specific action. This means that although every act of the will is informed by the intellect, the intellect does not move the will to do one thing rather than another without the consent of the will. Whether or not the will actually wills something or not depends as its efficient cause on the will, not on the intellect. For Godfrey, however, both *what* the will desires and *whether or not* it desires depend on the apprehended object as the efficient cause. This means that, in his view, the intellect alone determines the will to

---

[23] *Quodlibet* VIII.16 (pp. 149–50, 155–6, 175); see also VI.10 (pp. 206–9).
[24] *Quodlibet* VI.16 (p. 151); see also *Quodlibet* X.13 (ed. *Phil. Belges* IV: 373–6). Henry of Ghent critiques Giles's theory for the opposite reason: he thinks it still grants too great a role to the intellect and thus endangers free decision, *Quodlibet* XII.26–7.

desire or choose something in a particular instance. Last, contrary to Godfrey, Thomas denies that the intellect necessitates the will's adhesion to particular goods, unless they have a necessary connection to happiness (*Summa theol.* 1a 82.2c). In sum, for Godfrey, the activity of the will is entirely accounted for by the activity of the intellect apprehending and evaluating an object. For Thomas, conversely, although the will's activity is always informed by the intellect, it cannot be fully traced to the intellect's activity. The will never chooses without a reason, yet no full account can be given why it chooses for one reason rather than another.

VOLUNTARIST INNOVATIONS

Godfrey provoked strong reactions from the Franciscans. John Duns Scotus, drawing on the work of earlier Franciscans, formulates the objections against Godfrey and other intellectualists in a way that is both lucid and sharpens the contours of a voluntarist account of free decision. Scotus objects that to construe the will as completely dependent on the intellect for all its volitions would mean that human actions could be traced entirely to external things that are not under the person's control (*Lectura* II.25 nn. 28, 31). The heart of the matter for him is whether the will is the kind of thing that produces a given result in a given set of conditions. This is what characterizes "natural agents": when they are unimpeded and in proximity to the things they act upon, they produce in them determinate effects. The causality of the apprehended object is that of a natural agent; under like circumstances, it produces like results. Accordingly, the object itself cannot cause the acts either of willing or of not willing in a given situation, for to make the will dependent upon the causality of the object would undermine its freedom (ibid. n. 36). It is true that natural agents can cause opposite effects in different things, depending on what they are acting on. For example, the sun can cause ice to melt and mud to dry. Only the will, however, is such that it can determine itself to opposite acts: to will or not to will something. In this, the will differs from everything else in the universe (ibid. nn. 92–3).

Self-determination is what most fundamentally characterizes the will in comparison to the intellect, for the will elicits its act freely, whereas the intellect does not. Since the intellect does not have the power to understand or not, it is a natural power. Scotus pushes this idea even further: the will is most properly a rational power and the intellect an irrational power, if by 'rational' one means (with Aristotle) the capacity for contrary effects, and by 'irrational' the fact of being fixed to a specific effect.[25]

---

[25] *Quaest. Metaphys.* IX.15 nn. 21–2, 35–41; cf. Aristotle, *Metaphys.* IX.2.

Scotus grants that the will itself can be considered a nature. As a nature, it has a natural inclination toward perfection, which Scotus identifies with Anselm's "inclination for benefit" (*affectio commodi*) (see Chapter 35). If the will were considered merely a rational or intellectual appetite, it would have only this inclination for benefit: it would not be in its power to will something other than that which the intellect presents as conducive to happiness. As a free power, however, the will has an additional "inclination for justice" (*affectio iustitiae*), which is precisely the innate freedom of the will with respect to opposite acts. Thanks to the will's inclination for justice, one can desire – or fail to desire – an intrinsic good, even when it conflicts with one's personal benefit (*Ordinatio* II.6.2 nn. 49–56).

Scotus stresses that the will's freedom with respect to opposite acts implies that it has alternate possibilities in the present and with respect to the same moment – not merely successively. (This doctrine has come to be known as "synchronic contingency.") The will obviously cannot *realize* alternate possibilities simultaneously, for it cannot will and not-will at the same time and in the same respect. But when the will wills x, it remains possible at that moment for it not to will x. So if there were a will that existed for just a single instant, it would be free then to choose between alternatives, and yet it could not choose them successively.

Scotus owes this account largely to Peter of John Olivi, a Franciscan from the generation before Scotus. If alternate possibilities were not open to the will in the present moment in which it chooses, its acts would be not contingent but necessary, as Olivi emphasizes. It does not suffice to say that the will acts freely because *prior* to its act, the opposite act was possible. This prior moment lies in the past, but the act in question is in the present. If every act of will is traced to an event that precedes its act, then it is never free. Thus to preserve the will's freedom, one must grant that in the present the will chooses contingently rather than necessarily, that is, that it chooses with respect to synchronic alternate possibilities.[26] With this novel theory, Olivi and Scotus shift the focus from the freedom of the will in relation to intellect towards the freedom of the will considered in itself.

Scotus offers a rigorous account of what characterizes the will: it is distinguished from all natural agents, including the intellect, in that it elicits its own act freely. He goes on to draw the ultimate consequence from this account: that one can never fully explain the will's acts by tracing them to antecedent factors. The ultimate reason why the will wills x lies in the will itself (*Quaest.*

---

[26] *Lectura* 1.39 nn. 45–60; *Quaest. Metaphys.* IX.15 nn. 59–60, 64–6. See also Olivi, *Summa* II.42 (ed. Jansen, I: 705–6) and II.57 ad 10 (II: 348–53). For a lucid discussion, see Stephen D. Dumont, "The Origin of Scotus's Theory of Synchronic Contingency," *Modern Schoolman* 72 (1995) 149–67.

Metaphys. IX.15 n. 29). The causality of the desired object must be subordinate to the causality of the will — either as a partial cause, as Scotus teaches early in his career, or as a necessary condition (*causa sine qua non*).[27]

COROLLARIES

In accordance with their different explanations of free decision, intellectualist and voluntarist thinkers tend to have opposing views on central ethical themes. They generally agree that moral perfection involves not only acting according to right reason, but also having proper emotional responses. It is thanks to the moral virtues that the emotions are disposed in accordance with right reason. Contention arose, however, over where to place the moral virtues, that is, whether temperance, courage, and justice and their affiliated virtues should be placed in the sense appetite or in the will. The question thus concerned the role of the will with respect to moral virtues. Aquinas takes a middle position: for him, the moral virtues are located in the will or in a power moved by the will. He places temperance and courage in the sense appetite, and justice in the will (*Summa theol.* 1a2ae 56.3–4, 56.6). After Aquinas, the debate centers on the question of whether the will infallibly follows practical judgment. For instance, Henry of Ghent reports a view that all the moral virtues are located in the sensory appetite, for virtues are required in those powers that are indeterminate with respect to the judgment of reason. Such is the case, according to this view, only for the sense appetite, and not for the will, which is bound to follow practical judgment (*Quodlibet* IV.22, ed. 1518, ff. 138rP–138vP). Godfrey of Fontaines later defended this same opinion, arguing explicitly that not only temperance and courage, but also justice are located in the sense appetite (*Quodlibet* XIV.3, ed. *Phil. Belges* V: 341–3). For the opposite reason, Henry of Ghent placed all the moral virtues in the will, for unless the moral virtues incline the will to follow the practical judgment, the will does not command the sensory appetite in accordance with right reason. As a result of his voluntarism, therefore, he argued that the moral virtues are essentially in the will, and only derivatively in the sense appetite.[28]

Henry did not yet acknowledge the full implications of his account of free decision for virtue theory. If the will can act contrary to practical judgment, could there not be prudence on account of correct practical judgments, yet

---

[27] *Lectura* II.25 nn. 69–73; *Reportatio* IIA.25 (cod. Turin, Biblioteca Nazionale Universitaria, K, ii, 26, f. 150ra). Cf. Stephen D. Dumont, "Did Duns Scotus Change His Mind on the Will?," in Aertsen et al., *Nach der Verurteilung von 1277*, 719–94.

[28] *Quodlibet* IV.22, ff. 138vQ–140vA. For an excellent discussion, see Kent, *Virtues of the Will*, pp. 199–245.

without the moral virtues ensuing, in the event that the will does not choose accordingly? This would contradict the Aristotelian theory of the connection of the virtues, which was generally accepted at the time. According to Aristotle, prudence and the moral virtues presuppose each other, and when prudence is had, all the moral virtues are obtained as well (*Nicomachean Ethics* VI.12–13). Henry upholds the connection of the virtues, not because prudence entails moral virtue, but because vice entails imprudence (*Quodlibet* XII.14). Only Duns Scotus will draw the full consequence of the voluntarist account of free decision for virtue theory and deny that the virtues are connected (*Ordinatio* III.36 n. 72).

Intellectualist and voluntarist accounts of free decision have reverse strengths and weaknesses. Intellectualists emphasize that free acts must be rational and must intentionally refer to an object apprehended and evaluated by the intellect. Yet does the intellect do the whole work in free actions, even in sinful ones? Is moral deficiency ultimately due to defective reasoning? Voluntarists more easily account for the contingency of human actions, including the possibility of radical sin. But why would the will abandon what here and now is judged as the best option? Aquinas's theory seems to avoid the extremes: the practical intellect and the will so interpenetrate each other that they cannot be disentangled. Yet he does not offer answers to all the questions that the later debate would raise. The later debates thus provide valuable philosophical insights that can enrich earlier accounts.

31

EMOTION

SIMO KNUUTTILA

This chapter deals with the basic tenets of ancient philosophical theories of emotions, the reception and transformation of these in the Middle Ages, and some late medieval innovations, concentrating on how emotions were understood as psychological phenomena rather than on an analysis of particular emotions or their role in ethics. Although various theories of the soul influenced the general analysis of emotions, ancient thinkers usually accepted similar descriptions of paradigmatic emotions, such as desire, fear, or anger. This is also typical of later philosophical discussions. In the light of philosophical sources, some emotions look pretty much the same from the days of Plato and Aristotle to our time, while others have changed and still others have become unusual or disappeared (for example, some monastic feelings).[1]

ANCIENT THEORIES

The philosophical analysis of emotions was introduced by Plato and Aristotle, both of whom distinguished between various elements in occurrent emotions as follows. First, the *cognitive* element is an unpremeditated evaluation that states that something positive or negative is happening, either to the subject or to someone else in a way that is relevant to the subject. Second, the *affective* element is the pleasant or unpleasant feeling about the content of the evaluation. Third, the *dynamic* element is the spontaneous behavioral impulse towards a typical action. Fourth, associated with the affective element are *bodily* reactions which, as distinct from emotional feelings, may occur in other occasions as well.[2]

[1] The Greek term for emotions is *pathos* and the usual medieval Latin terms are *passio* or *affectio*. The English word 'emotion' began to replace a variety of other terms in the nineteenth century. Although this is argued to be associated with creating a special category of "emotion" that essentially differed from "passion" (see, e.g., Thomas Dixon, *From Passions to Emotions: The Creation of a Secular Psychological Category* [Cambridge: Cambridge University Press, 2003]), dictionary definitions hardly suggest the rendering 'passion' rather than 'emotion' for Greek and Latin terms.

[2] See Plato, *Republic* IV, 435a–441c; *Timaeus* 69c–d; *Philebus* 33d–e, 43a–c, 47d–50d; Aristotle, *Rhetoric* I.10–11, II.1–11. For recent studies of emotions in ancient philosophy, see Martha Nussbaum, *The*

Table 31.1

		Time	
		Present	*Future*
Value	*Good*	Pleasure	Desire
	Evil	Distress	Fear

Historically, this compositional approach has been the most influential paradigm for thinking about emotions; it is often employed in philosophical psychology today as well. All ancient and medieval theories were cognitive – that is, they associated some kind of evaluation with an emotion. Even the Stoics, who did not accept the general scheme, endorsed this first stage. As for the affective component, Plato and Aristotle taught that emotions involved a pleasant or unpleasant awareness of oneself in a situation, and many ancient and medieval authors continued to be interested in the subjective aspect of emotion. In most ancient theories, moreover, emotions involved bodily changes in the heartbeat, vital spirits, humors, or facial expressions. While this was the prevailing medieval view as well, fourteenth-century voluntarists also introduced the conception of passions in the will, which had been traditionally regarded as an immaterial intellectual faculty.

Plato and Aristotle taught that human beings were naturally emotional, emotions being the reactions of an emotional part in the soul. The Stoics denied this. In accordance with their rational conception of the unity of the soul, the Stoics argued that emotions are essentially self-regarding judgments – false value judgments, by which people mistakenly evaluate things from their subjective perspectives, thus deviating from the rational view of reality codified in Stoic philosophy. The Stoics divided emotions into four basic types (as shown in Table 31.1), depending on whether the object is evaluated as a present or future good or a present or future evil. This is one of the most repeated classifications in the history of emotions, another being the Platonic division into concupiscible

Therapy of Desire: Theory and Practice in Hellenistic Ethics (Princeton, NJ: Princeton University Press, 1994); Juha Sihvola and Troels Engberg-Pedersen (eds.) *The Emotions in Hellenistic Philosophy* (Dordrecht: Kluwer, 1998); John Cooper, *Reason and Emotion: Essays on Ancient Moral Psychology and Ethical Theory* (Princeton, NJ: Princeton University Press, 1999); Richard Sorabji, *Emotion and Peace of Mind: From Stoic Agitation to Christian Temptation* (Oxford: Oxford University Press, 2000); William Fortenbaugh, *Aristotle on Emotion*, 2nd edn (London: Duckworth, 2003); Simo Knuuttila, *Emotions in Ancient and Medieval Philosophy* (Oxford: Clarendon Press, 2004); David Konstan, *The Emotions of the Ancient Greeks: Studies in Aristotle and Classical Literature* (Toronto: University of Toronto Press, 2006). A. A. Long and D. N. Sedley, *The Hellenistic Philosophers* (Cambridge: Cambridge University Press, 1987) includes a collection of Hellenistic texts on emotion with translation and commentary.

and irascible emotions.[3] Perhaps the best-known part of Stoic philosophy is the philosophical therapy of emotions (*therapeia*) described in works by Cicero, Seneca, and Epictetus. Stoic therapy aimed at *apatheia*, the extirpation of emotions, because emotions were regarded as false judgments. Other philosophical schools followed Plato and Aristotle, arguing instead for the moderation of emotions (*metriopatheia*). *Apatheia* was regarded as impossible and inhuman. Plotinus also argued for *apatheia*, though this did not involve the disappearance of the emotional part of the soul; earthly emotions simply become useless in higher Neoplatonic spheres.[4]

Early Christian thinkers were strongly influenced by Hellenistic discussions of emotions. The Alexandrian theologians Clemens and Origen, for example, combined Stoic and Platonist ideas, arguing that freedom from emotion was part of Christian perfectibility and the precondition of divinization through participation in divine love (*agape*). This mystical union was described in highly emotional language, although supernaturally caused spiritual feelings – as experiences of the apathetic soul – were not called emotions. Through John Cassian, this combination of supranatural love with freedom from earthly emotions ("purity of heart") became part of Western monasticism. The Cappadocian fathers and Augustine, in contrast, were more inclined to *metriopatheia*.[5]

In addition to relying on ancient therapy models, introspective monastic psychology took up two far-reaching topics related to emotions. The first was the Stoic doctrine of first movements, which Origen, followed by Augustine and many others, applied to the Christian conception of sin. The Stoic idea, described by Seneca in *On Anger* (2.1–4), was that even apathetic persons may react quasi-emotionally on an exceptional occasion; this is a brief reaction, however, and not really emotion because it does not involve judgmental assent. Augustine taught that the permanent inherited weakness of the soul

---

[3] Pseudo-Andronicus, *Peri pathōn* 1.1 (Long and Sedley 65B); Stobaeus II.88.16–21 (Long and Sedley 65A). For more detailed lists of emotions classified in accordance with this typology, see pseudo-Andronicus, *Peri pathōn* 1.2–5; Diogenes Laertius, *Vitae philosophorum* VII.110–14; Stobaeus II.90.7–92.17 (Long and Sedley 65E); Cicero, *Tusculan Disputations* IV.11–22.

[4] There are extensive studies of the analysis and therapy of emotions in Stoic, Epicurean, and Platonist philosophy in Pierre Hadot, *Exercises spirituels et philosophie antique*, 2nd edn (Paris: Études Augustiniennes, 1987); Nussbaum, *Therapy of Desire*; Sihvola and Engberg-Pedersen, *The Emotions in Hellenistic Philosophy*; and Sorabji, *Emotion and Peace of Mind*.

[5] Knuuttila, *Emotions in Ancient and Medieval Philosophy*, pp. 113–76. The monastic therapy of sinful emotions is presented in John Cassian's *De institutis*; contemplative exercises described in the *Conlationes* show similarities to Origenist mystical theology as it was developed by Evagrius of Pontus. John Climacus's *Scala paradisi* (*The Ladder of Divine Ascent*) was the most influential treatise on *apatheia* and divine love in Byzantine theology. Augustine discusses the philosophical theories of emotions in Books IX and XIV of the *City of God*; see also Johannes Brachtendorf, "Cicero and Augustine on the Passions," *Revue des Études Augustiniennes* 43 (1997) 289–308.

(a consequence of original sin) inclines people to sinful things by producing sinful thoughts that become sins through consent: "We do not sin in having an evil desire but in consenting to it."[6] This was later developed into a detailed theory of the degrees of venial and mortal sin, depending on how much acceptance was involved.[7] Peter of Capua describes one development of these ideas at the start of the thirteenth century:

> Sometimes a movement of the sensual part towards forbidden things, such as anger or fornication, arises without a thought or decision to realize or not to realize it, and this is always a sin, though a venial one. Some people draw a distinction here. They say that some of these movements are primarily first movements, namely those to which we do not offer any opportunity and that occur involuntarily, and they think that these are not sinful. Movements to which we offer an opportunity are secondary first movements, for example when someone goes to a party for recreation and something seen there gives rise to a first movement without a thought, and these are venial sins. We call both venial sins, but the latter are more serious.[8]

So when we expose ourselves to possible sensual influences – for instance, by going to a party – the fault is more serious. He goes on to say that one might think about the realization of a forbidden thing without a decision. If this consideration is of short duration, the act is a venial sin, but if it is longer, it is a mortal sin involving some sort of consent to pleasure, and so on.

The second influential monastic theme was mystical ascent (see Chapter 52). While the language continued to be affective, the mystical experiences described in emotional language were not regarded as standard emotions. In dealing with divinization, for example, Bernard of Clairvaux tries to find various metaphors for describing the experience of being affected by divine action (*sentire intra se actitari*).[9] This introspective analysis of subjective feeling is one of the philosophically interesting parts of medieval spiritual literature.

---

6   *Expositio quarumdum propositionum ex Epistola Romanos* (ed. Migne, *Patr. Lat.* 35: 2065–6); see also *De Trinitate* XII.12. For Origen's account of sins and first movements, see *De principiis* III.1.3–4. First movements were also called pre-passions (*propatheia, propassio*); see Knuuttila, *Emotions in Ancient and Medieval Philosophy*, pp. 64, 122, 143, 179–84, 186, 193–94.
7   When Augustine said that a sinful thought leads to action through suggestion, pleasure, and consent (*suggestio, delectatio, consentio*), "suggestion" means a thought that can arouse an actual desire, "pleasure" its initial stage, and "consent" the acceptance of thinking about action with pleasure or the decision to act (*De sermone Domini in monte* 12.34–5). Most twelfth-century theologians dealt with the doctrine of sin and first motions. For medieval texts on this matter, see Peter Lombard, *Sententiae* II.24.6–12, II.33.5.5 and Odon Lottin, *Psychologie et morale aux XIIe et XIIIe siècles* (Gembloux: Duculot, 1948–60) II: 496–520 and V: 73–4, 222.
8   Text quoted in Lottin, *Psychologie et morale* II: 499.
9   *Opera* II: 10.28–9; III: 143.12–24; V: 205.17–19; see also Ulrich Köpf, *Religiöse Erfahrung in der Theologie Bernhards von Clairvaux* (Tübingen: Mohr, 1980) pp. 136–74.

EARLIER MEDIEVAL DISCUSSIONS

Most detailed twelfth-century Latin treatments of the emotions are found in the-ological and spiritual treatises influenced by the monastic traditions. An impulse to new approaches was supplied by new Latin translations of various Greek and Arabic philosophical and medical works. Among the authoritative medical works was Constantine of Africa's late eleventh-century partial translation of the Arabic medical encyclopedia of 'Alī ibn al-'Abbās al-Majūsī, the *Pantegni*, which contains various remarks on the emotions based on Galen's medical philosophy. Some elements of ancient medical and philosophical theories of emotions were also included in Nemesius of Emesa's fourth-century *De natura hominis*, a work translated by Alphanus of Salerno (*ca.* 1080) and again by Burgundio of Pisa (*ca.* 1165). Parts of Nemesius's accounts of emotions were also copied in John of Damascus's *De fide orthodoxa*, which was translated into Latin by Burgundio of Pisa (*ca.* 1153). An important sourcebook for medieval philosophical psychol-ogy until the middle of the thirteenth century was the translation of the sixth book of Avicenna's *Shifā'* (*ca.* 1150) by Dominicus Gundisalvi and Avendauth, often called Avicenna's *De anima*. Aristotle's *De anima* was translated *ca.* 1150 by James of Venice. Its Latin reception was slow, the first commentaries being written in the 1240s. Avicenna made use of Aristotle's *De anima* as well as various Neoplatonic and medical sources.

The medical theory of the emotions concentrated on the Galenic ideas of the humors and the system of the spirits: the vitalizing spirits in the heart and the psychic spirits in the nerves and the brain. In the *Pantegni*, the physical aspects of the emotions were dealt with as movements of the vital spirits towards the heart or away from it. Using 'distress' instead of 'anxiety,' as later authors usually did, the classification is shown in Table 31.2. This was a well-known model until early modern times.[10]

Avicenna's treatises on the soul analyze and systematize psychological phe-nomena as activities of special powers or faculties. The faculties of the sensory soul are divided into apprehensive powers and moving powers. The apprehen-sive powers involve the five external senses and five internal senses, namely common sense, imagination, the imaginative power, the estimative power, and

---

[10] *Pantegni*, Theorica VI.110–14; see Pedro Gil-Sotres, "Modelo teórico y observación clínica: las pasiones del alma en la psicología medica medieval," in *Comprendre et maîtriser la nature au Moyen Age: mélanges d'histoire des sciences offerts à Guy Beaujouan* (Geneva: Droz, 1994) 181–204. The elements of the Galenic physiology of emotions were also known through Nemesius's *De natura hominis*, as well as Avicenna's *De anima* and *Canon of Medicine*, among various other sources (see E. Ruth Harvey, *The Inward Wits: Psychological Theory in the Middle Ages and the Renaissance* [London: Warburg Institute, 1975]). For discussions of emotions in the medical school of Salerno (*ca.* 1200), see the anonymous texts edited by Brian Lawn in *The Prose Salernitan Questions* (London: Oxford University Press for the British Academy, 1979).

Table 31.2

		Direction	
		Centrifugal	*Centripetal*
Intensity	*Slow*	Joy	Distress
	Quick	Anger	Fear

memory. The moving powers are, in turn, divided into commanding moving powers and executive moving powers. Emotions are treated as acts of the sensory commanding moving power – reactions to evaluations of the sensory part of the soul that are accompanied by bodily affections and behavioral changes. The moving power of the intellectual soul is the will which, together with practical intellect, should control the emotions (*De anima* I.5; *Kitāb-al-najāt* II.6.2–4). The sensory commanding faculty is divided into the concupiscible and the irascible. The reactions of the concupiscible power are desires for things taken to be pleasurable, and the reactions of the irascible power are desires to defeat adversaries and repel things regarded as harmful.[11]

Avicenna also analyzed feelings as pleasant or unpleasant perceptions associated with estimative and moving acts, and he dealt with the physiological changes following the medical spirits.[12] An influential part of Avicenna's theory was that the estimative power moves the commanding power by noticing the helpful and harmful aspects of things, which are called 'intentions' (see Chapter 22). As an occurrent emotion involves acts of two separate powers, there must be a governing awareness that combines these two acts:

Again, we say 'When I perceived such and such thing, I became angry,' and this is a true statement, too. So it is one and the same thing that perceives and becomes angry . . . This is then due to its being in possession of a faculty by which it is capable of combining both these things.[13]

EARLY THIRTEENTH-CENTURY THEORIES

Dominicus Gundisalvi combined Avicennian themes with traditional Augustinian psychology in his treatise *De anima*, which consists to a great extent

---

[11] *De anima* I.5 (ed. Van Riet, p. 83); IV.4 (pp. 56–7).
[12] For concupiscible and irascible acts, see *De anima* IV.4 (pp. 57–9), and, for cardiac and spiritual affects, ibid. (pp. 61–2). Pleasure and distress are characterized as apprehensions (ibid., pp. 57, 59) and *De medicinis cordialibus* (ed. Van Riet [in the same volume], pp. 192–4). Pleasant or unpleasant apprehensions may be about either bodily conditions or other states; see also *De anima* I.3 (pp. 65–6).
[13] *Kitāb-al-najāt* II.6.15 (tr. Rahman, pp. 65–6); see also *De anima* V.7.

of long quotations from the translation of Avicenna's *De anima*.[14] The central ideas of Avicenna's faculty psychology were also discussed in many thirteenth-century treatises before the turn to Aristotle's *De anima* in the 1240s.[15] David of Dinant suggested that emotions as psychic phenomena are caused by cardiac and spiritual changes, but this deviated from the standard view which John of La Rochelle put forward in his interpretation of Avicenna – namely, that commanding motive acts are reactions to evaluative acts and give impulses to behavioral changes and immediate physiological affections.[16] Avicenna's division of emotions into acts of concupiscible and irascible powers was repeated by John Blund, who also tried to combine it with Aristotle's view that these powers may have contrary acts.[17] An influential new classificatory idea for solving this problem was put forward in the anonymous *De potentiis animae et obiectis*. The objects of the contrary concupiscible acts were simply pleasurable or painful, whereas the objects of the irascible acts were in addition arduous – that is, difficult to obtain or to avoid (ed. Callus, pp. 159, 164).[18]

The most detailed early thirteenth-century classification of emotions is John of La Rochelle's taxonomy in his *Summa de anima*. Following Avicenna, he regarded emotions as the acts of two moving powers, the concupiscible and irascible, both of which have several reaction types, which are divided into contrary pairs. The concupiscible pairs are associated with contrary dispositions of liking (*placentia*) or disliking (*displicentia*) and irascible emotions with strength (*corroboratio*) and weakness (*debilitas*). The new systematic idea was to use these contraries as classificatory principles. John does not explain what he means by these "dispositions," but he probably had in mind the different ways of actualization, depending on the nature of representations and the state of the subject, and perhaps also various subjective feelings.

According to John of La Rochelle, the contrary emotions of the concupiscible are: (1) appetite (*concupiscentia*) and distaste (*fastidium*), which are the orientating

[14] Excerpts from the passages on the emotions in Avicenna's *De anima* are quoted at pp. 80–2 (ed. Muckle).

[15] John Blund, *Tractatus de anima* (*ca.* 1210); the anonymous *De anima et de potentiis eius* (*ca.* 1225) and *De potentiis animae et obiectis* (*ca.* 1230); John of La Rochelle, *Tractatus de divisione multiplici potentiarum animae* (*ca.* 1233) and *Summa de anima* (*ca.* 1235).

[16] David of Dinant, *Fragmenta*, 36–9, 67–8 (cf. John Blund, *Tractatus de anima* ch. 25.4 n. 380); E. Maccagnolo, "David of Dinant and the Beginning of Aristotelianism in Paris," in P. Dronke (ed.) *A History of Twelfth-Century Western Philosophy* (Cambridge: Cambridge University Press, 1988) 429–42; John of La Rochelle, *Summa de anima* II.101, 104–10.

[17] *Tractatus de anima* ch. 6 n. 55, ch. 7.

[18] This became the standard thirteenth-century view. Various earlier divisions are discussed in Knuuttila, *Emotions in Ancient and Medieval Philosophy*, pp. 227–33, including those in William of St. Thierry's *On the Nature of the Body and the Soul*, Isaac of Stella's *Letter on the Soul*, and the anonymous *On the Spirit and the Soul*, all translated in B. McGinn (ed.) *Three Treatises on Man: A Cistercian Anthropology* (Kalamazoo, MI: Cistercian Publications, 1977), as well as the division in Hugh and Richard of St. Victor.

reactions toward something attractive or unattractive at the sensory level; (2) desire (*desiderium*) and aversion (*abhominatio*), the stronger forms of the basic reactions; (3) joy (*gaudium*) and pain (*dolor*), which are felt when the desire is fulfilled or when that which one seeks to avoid happens; (4) delight (*laetitia*) and distress (*tristitia*), which are caused by the thought that the actualized pleasant or unpleasant state of affairs will be of longer duration; (5) love (*amor*) and hatred (*odium*), the acts of desiring something good or something evil to somebody else; and (6) envy (*invidia*) and pity (*misericordia*), of which the former is an act of disliking with respect to another person's prosperity and the latter one with respect to another person's troubles.

Of the emotions of the irascible power and its "arduous and difficult objects," (1) ambition (*ambitio*) and (2) hope (*spes*) pertain to future honor and excellence, hope involving the belief that they will be achieved. The opposite of ambition is poverty of spirit (*paupertas spiritus*) and the opposite of hope is despair (*desperatio*). Three emotions are associated with attempts to strengthen one's social ranking and power: (3) pride (*superbia*), (4) lust for power (*dominatio*), and (5) contempt (*contemptus*). The opposite of pride and lust for power is humility (*humiliatio*), and the opposite of contempt is reverence (*reverentia*). Of the acts directed towards evil things, (6) courage (*audacia*) is a desire to meet the enemy with the confidence that one is going to win, (7) anger (*ira*) is a desire for revenge, and (8) magnanimity (*magnanimitas*) is rising up against evil. John mentions three further emotions that represent various forms of the flight from evil and are somehow opposites of courage: penitence (*paenitentia*) toward past evil things, impatience (*impaciencia*) with present evil things, and fear (*timor*) of future evil things (*Summa de anima* II.107).[19]

ALBERT THE GREAT AND THOMAS AQUINAS

Also following Avicenna's faculty psychology, Albert the Great and Thomas Aquinas treated emotions as acts of the sensory moving powers caused by external objects by means of the evaluations of the estimative power, and necessarily accompanied by changes in the movements of the heart and the spirits. While Albert employed the classifications of Nemesius of Emesa and John of Damascus, Thomas Aquinas put forward a new taxonomy (which was probably influenced by John of La Rochelle). Albert was interested in the question of why emotions were called movements; in his opinion they should be regarded as qualities, as Aristotle described them in *Categories* 8. Aquinas deviated from his teacher here, contending that emotions are indeed movements of the soul,

---

[19] There is a longer list of concupiscible and irascible emotions in William of Auvergne's roughly contemporary *De virtutibus*, chs. 16–18.

and finding the basic classificatory principles of emotions in Aristotle's doctrine of contrary movements in *Physics* V.5.[20]

Aquinas's discussion of emotions in *Summa theologiae* 1a2ae 22–48 is the most extensive medieval treatise on the subject. Emotions are first divided on the basis of their generic objects, so that the concupiscible emotions react to what seems good or evil at the sensory level (for short, *sense-good* and *sense-evil*), whereas the irascible emotions react to arduous sense-good and sense-evil. Although the sensory moving faculties are activated by these objects through cognition, the modes of the resulting emotional movements serve as further qualifications in defining particular emotions (ibid., 23.1, 4). The Aristotelian contraries of movements are of two types: approach to something and retreat from it, as in coming to be something and ceasing to be it, or movements associated with contrary endpoints: thus bleaching, the movement from black to white, is the contrary of blackening, the movement from white to black. The contrary movements of the concupiscible power are of the second type, since there are no sensory motive acts away from the sense-good or towards the sense-evil except accidentally. Irascible emotions – with the exception of anger – are contrary movements of the irascible power with respect to objects of the same kind. The arduous future sense-good may give rise to (1) hope or (2) despair, the arduous future sense-evil to (3) fear or (4) courage, and the arduous present sense-evil to (5) anger (ibid., 23.2–3). The movements of the concupiscible power are of three types:

> It is clear that everything which tends to an end first has an aptitude or proportion to the goal, for nothing tends to a disproportionate end; second, it moves towards the end; third, it comes to rest in the end once it has been attained. The aptitude or proportion of the appetite to a good thing is love, for love is precisely the liking of some good, the movement towards the good is desire or concupiscence, and resting in it is joy or pleasure.
>
> (ibid., 25.2)

So (6) love, (7) desire, and (8) pleasure or joy are the three concupiscible emotions with respect to the sense-good; the contrary movements with respect to sense-evil are (9) hatred, (10) aversion, and (11) pain or distress (ibid., 23.4).[21]

---

[20] For Albert the Great, see *De homine* (*Summae de creaturis secunda pars*) qq. 66–7; *De bono* 3.5.2, 3.5.3; *Commentarius super Librum de sex principiis* 2.1, 2.5, 3.1–2. For the estimative power in Avicenna and Aquinas, see Deborah L. Black, "Imagination and Estimation: Arabic Paradigms and Western Transformations," *Topoi* 19 (2000) 59–75.

[21] For Aquinas's taxonomy, see also Peter King, "Aquinas on the Passions," in S. MacDonald and E. Stump (eds.) *Aquinas's Moral Theory: Essays in Honor of Norman Kretzmann* (Ithaca, NY: Cornell University Press, 1999) 101–32. Aquinas also arranges emotions on the basis of the order of occurrence. Love and hatred are preconditions of any further affective involvement (1a2ae 25.3).

Aquinas is impressed by the possibility of dealing with emotions with the help of the general theory of motion derived from Aristotelian natural philosophy. He sometimes distinguishes between love, desire, and pleasure as the incipient movement, actual movement, and rest of a subject with respect to an object. This, however, seems to imply a confusing identification of the emotions with the behavioral changes they are supposed to cause (ibid., 25.2, as quoted above). Sometimes emotions are characterized as movements of the moving power, but it remains unclear how the differences between these movements should be understood (ibid., 30.2; see also 23.4). While these movements constitute the formal part of an emotion, physiological changes – such as the movements of the heart, the spirits, and the humors – are the material part (ibid., 28.5, 44.1). A further problem in applying the general theory of natural movements to emotions is how to describe pleasure and distress. Aquinas explains that even though one can speak about a stone as loving its natural place and desiring to be there, it does not make sense to speak about the pleasure or pain of a stone, since these involve an awareness of one's state (ibid., 41.3). He seems to think, like Aristotle and Avicenna, that pleasure or distress is a pleasant or unpleasant awareness of oneself.

In addition to these matters of classification and general analysis, Aquinas's main discussions of emotions in the *Summa theologiae* involve detailed terminological, psychological, and ethical remarks on each particular emotion type. Like all medieval authors, Aquinas argues that the intellectual soul should keep emotions under strict control, but he also criticizes the Stoic ideal of *apatheia*, partially following Augustine, and he remains aloof from Plotinus's version of the freedom from emotion, which was known to him through Macrobius's *Commentary on the Dream of Scipio* (ibid., 24.3, 59.2, 61.5).[22] Aquinas's theory was very influential until the seventeenth century.[23]

For some problems in this theory and in Aquinas's conception of emotions as contrary movements, see Knuuttila, *Emotions in Ancient and Medieval Philosophy*, pp. 242–53.

[22] For various interpretations of the role of emotions in Aquinas's ethics, see Mark Jordan, "Aquinas's Construction of a Moral Account for the Passions," *Freiburger Zeitschrift für Philosophie und Theologie* 33 (1986) 71–97; Judith Barad, "Aquinas on the Role of Emotion in Moral Judgement and Activity," in B. C. Bazán et al. (eds.) *Les philosophies morales et politiques au Moyen Âge* (New York: Legas, 1995) II: 642–53; Eileen Sweeney, "Restructuring Desire: Aquinas, Hobbes, and Descartes on the Passions," in S. F. Brown (ed.) *Meeting of the Minds: The Relations between Medieval and Classical Modern European Philosophy* (Turnhout: Brepols, 1998) 215–33; Claudia Eisen Murphy, "Aquinas on our Responsibility for our Emotions," *Medieval Philosophy and Theology* 8 (1999) 163–205; Andrea Robiglio, *L'impossibile volere: Tommaso d'Aquino, i tomisti e la volontà* (Milan: Vita e Pensiero, 2002).

[23] Giles of Rome added an opposite of anger to Aquinas's list and was followed by John of Jandun; see Costantino Marmo, "Hoc autem etsi potest tollerari . . . Egidio Romano e Tommaso d'Aquino sulle passione dell' anima," *Documenti e studi sulla tradizione filosofica medievale* 2 (1991) 281–315; "Retorica e motti di spirito. Una 'quaestio' inedita di Giovanni di Jandun," in P. Magli et al. (eds.) *Semiotica: storia, teoria, interpretazione* (Milan: Bompiani, 1992) 23–41. Aquinas's taxonomy is found in Peter

SCOTUS AND LATE MEDIEVAL DISCUSSIONS

John Duns Scotus gives up the idea of appealing to arduousness to distinguish between concupiscible and irascible emotions, regarding irascible emotions instead as aggressions.[24] Furthermore, Scotus argues against the influential Avicennian idea that there are "intentions" in things that can be grasped by an estimative power; instead, he claims that representations of a certain kind simply cause behavioral changes in certain animals and others in others (*Ordinatio* III.15 nn. 34–42; see also *Ordinatio* I.3.1.1–2 n. 62).

The most original part of Scotus's approach to emotions is to question the sharp divide between the passions of the sensory soul and the analogous phenomena in the will. According to Scotus, grasping the things that are called helpful or harmful necessarily moves the sensory emotional part. Being helpful or harmful with respect to voluntary acts is something else because the will is a free cause. This is an important part of Scotus's voluntarism (see Chapter 30). When a person voluntarily desires something and achieves it, the next step is the apprehension of the actuality of what was desired. Regarding this stage, Scotus says, "there follows a passion of the will, joy or distress, which is caused by the object present in this way." These passions are not caused by the will as a free cause:

> Distress, properly speaking, is a passion of the will, as is seen from the fact that it is not any of its actions or operations . . . This passion is not in the will through the will's being its efficient cause, because then it would be immediately under the power of the will, as volitions or nolitions are. But this is not the case, for when one wills against something and it happens, it is seen that the subject does not have distress under one's immediate power.
>
> (*Ordinatio* III.15 n. 48)

According to Scotus, there are in the will immediate acts of liking and disliking, *complacentia* and *displicentia*, which are not yet efficacious acts; second, there are efficacious acts, which Scotus calls elections; third, there is pleasure and distress. That these are not free acts is clearly seen in the fact that people cannot restore pleasure or expel distress by simply willing it. While extending the traditional

---

of Ailly's influential *Tractatus de anima* (ed. Pluta, pp. 30–1, 90–2), and as a classificatory framework in John Gerson's *Enumeratio peccatorum ab Alberto posita* (*Œuvres* IX: 158–61), which involves the longest medieval list of emotions, with some 100 items. While Cardinal Cajetan defended Aquinas's classification against Scotus's criticism, Suárez did not find convincing reasons for it. See Peter King, "Late Scholastic Theories of the Passions: Controversies in the Thomist Tradition," in H. Lagerlund and M. Yrjönsuuri (eds.) *Emotions and Choice from Boethius to Descartes* (Dordrecht: Kluwer, 2002) 229–58.

[24] *Ordinatio* III.34 (*Will and Morality*, pp. 358–9). Peter of John Olivi had earlier criticized the assumption of two sensory moving powers; see *Summa* II.69 (ed. Jansen, II: 626–28).

terminology of emotions as the passions of the sensory soul to include pleasure and distress as the passions of the will, Scotus also treats liking and disliking, the unpremeditated first reactions and necessary concomitants of other acts, as analogous to sensory emotional reactions, except that they are free acts (*Lectura* II.6.1, n. 13; II.2, n. 26; *Ordinatio* III.33, n. 55). William of Ockham's theory of emotions is largely based on Scotus's ideas.[25] John Buridan, who otherwise follows Scotus and Ockham in this area, states that the first orientations of the will (*complacentia, displicentia*) are not free and are in this respect similar to pleasure and distress (*Quaest. Ethic.* X.2).

Scotus presents a detailed list of the factors that are sufficient to cause distress as a passion of the will. These involve apprehensions that (1) something takes place contrary to one's actual will against it, (2) what is willed takes place when it is willed in circumstances in which the opposite is preferred but cannot be achieved, for example, throwing cargo away in order to save the ship, (3) something happens contrary to one's natural inclination to happiness (*affectio commodi*) even though no particular act of will is actual, and (4) something happens contrary to the emotional dispositions of the sensory soul. There are also corresponding factors sufficient to cause pleasure in the intellectual part of the soul (*Ordinatio* III.15 nn. 50–60).

This analysis shows that the intellectual soul is very emotional. Its feelings change not merely on the basis of actual volitions or nolitions, but also on the basis of the inclinations of the will and the sensory part of the soul. Because these states greatly influence the activities of people, Scotus tends to shift the discussion of moral virtues from the sensory passions to the intellectual soul, seeing the practical goal of moral education as giving strength to the inclination for justice (see Chapter 35) and other good habits. This is possible through our indirect control over psychic pleasure and distress – if the habits of willing are changed, the occasions for feeling pleasure or distress are also changed.[26]

Scotus's discussions of the emotions of the soul are associated with the theological question of whether love and pleasure (*dilectio* and *delectatio*) are really distinct in eternal enjoyment (*fruitio*). His view is that they are, because love is a free act of the will and pleasure is not. One theological argument for this distinction is that the devil loves things and has experiences of the fulfillment of his will, but no pleasure (*Reportatio* I.1.3, ed. Wadding XI: 26–7). While Ockham follows Scotus here, some others, including Walter Chatton, Adam Wodeham,

---

[25] See Vesa Hirvonen, *Passions in William Ockham's Philosophical Psychology* (Dordrecht: Kluwer, 2004).
[26] See also Olivier Boulnois, "Duns Scot: existe-t-il des passions de la volonté?" in B. Besnier *et al.* (eds.) *Les passions antiques et médiévales: théories et critiques des passions* (Paris: Presses Universitaires de France, 2003) I: 281–95.

and Gregory of Rimini, found it problematic that there could be eternal vision and love of God without pleasure, which Scotus considered logically possible.[27]

Influenced by Scotus's idea of emotional will, but turning in another direction, Adam Wodeham argues that volitions and nolitions are evaluations, to which all human emotions can be reduced because of the unity of the soul.[28] This assimilation of emotions to evaluative thoughts is to some extent similar to the Stoic theory, although Wodeham does not refer to Stoic authors or share their criticism of emotions.[29]

Medieval theories of emotion would be discussed in such influential Renaissance works as Gabriel Biel's *Collectorium* on Lombard's *Sentences* (III.26) and the commentaries on Aquinas's *Summa theologiae* by Cardinal Cajetan, Bartolomé de Medina, and Francisco Suárez. Many sixteenth-century theologians comment on the differences between the theories of Scotus and Aquinas, whose writings themselves continue to influence later discussions.[30] It is of some interest to notice that in his popular early sixteenth-century encyclopedia *Margarita philosophica*, Gregor Reisch puts forward John of La Rochelle's taxonomy of emotions, though without mentioning his name (12.4–5).[31] Through these and other routes not yet systematically studied, medieval views pass on into early modern philosophy.

---

[27] See A.S. McGrade, "Enjoyment at Oxford after Ockham: Philosophy, Psychology and the Love of God," in A. Hudson and M. Wilks (eds.) *From Ockham to Wyclif* (Oxford: Blackwell, 1987) 63–88; Severin Kitanov, "Beatific Enjoyment in Scholastic Philosophy and Theology 1240–1335" (Ph.D. dissertation: University of Helsinki, 2006).

[28] *Lectura secunda*, prol. q. 1 secs. 2, 5–6; d. 1 q. 5, secs. 4–5, 11. For Wodeham and other late medieval thinkers, see Knuuttila, *Emotions in Ancient and Medieval Philosophy*, pp. 275–86.

[29] For late medieval interest in Seneca's view of emotions, see Jill Kraye, "Moral Philosophy," in C. B. Schmitt and Q. Skinner (eds.) *The Cambridge History of Renaissance Philosophy* (Cambridge: Cambridge University Press, 1988) pp. 360–70; Letizia Panizza, "Stoic Psychotherapy in the Middle Ages and Renaissance: Petrarch's *De remediis*," in M. J. Osler (ed.) *Atoms, Pneuma, and Tranquility: Epicurean and Stoic Themes in European Thought* (Cambridge: Cambridge University Press, 1991) 39–65.

[30] See King, "Late Scholastic Theories of the Passions"; Robiglio, *L'impossibile volere*, pp. 35–42, 115–19; Amy M. Schmitter, "17th and 18th Century Theories of Emotions," in E. Zalta (ed.) *The Stanford Encyclopedia of Philosophy* (http://plato.stanford.edu).

[31] For ancient and medieval themes in Juan Luis Vives's influential *De anima et vita*, see Lorenzo Casini, "Cognitive and Moral Psychology in Renaissance Philosophy: A Study of Juan Luis Vives' *De anima et vita*" (Ph.D. dissertation: University of Uppsala, 2006) pp. 131–59.

32

WEAKNESS AND GRACE

RICHARD CROSS

That human beings sometimes act wrongly – be it through ignorance, weakness, or malice (deliberate wrongdoing) – is a commonplace of human experience; that divine grace can help them avoid such wrongdoing is a central feature of Christian doctrine, and thus accepted by all the Christian philosophers whose work is the principal focus of this chapter. These philosophers also accepted that the possibility of weakness – sometimes, but not always, characterized as weakness of will – results from a decisive sin of the first human beings. This "original sin" introduced the kind of disorder into human psychology that is, according to the medieval philosophers, the major component of moral weakness. Grace begins, among other things, the process of reordering this defective psychology. Two very disparate figures inform the presentation of these various issues in the high Middle Ages: Augustine and Aristotle. From Augustine, the medievals derived accounts of original sin, of grace, and – most importantly of all – the beginnings of a theory of consent somehow distinct from both reason and emotion; from Aristotle, they derived an account of moral weakness that they sometimes struggled to integrate with Augustinian teachings on the will, a view of the virtues that informed their account of grace, and a theory of motion that they used to talk about God's activity in the soul.

WEAKNESS AND WILL

Technically, weakness of will (usually *akrasia* in Greek, the technical translation of which term in Latin is *incontinentia*) is exhibited in those cases of action in which an agent acts against what he or she believes to be good. The phenomenon presents a particular problem for those who believe that human action is in principle always rational – a belief that was commonplace in traditions deriving from Socrates, who held that all wrongdoing is explained by ignorance (see Aristotle, *Nic. Ethics* VII.2, 1145b27–31). On this account, there is no room for *akrasia* at all, and our impression that some of our acts are akratic is itself simply mistaken. This conclusion is felt by most people to be counterintuitive;

one way of allowing for *akrasia* is to maintain, with Plato, that human decisions are affected not merely by rational beliefs about the good, but also by irrational desires (emotions or passions) that can cause people to act against reason, causing them either to avoid goods or to desire evils (by means respectively of what the later tradition would call "irascible" and "concupiscible" appetites) (Plato, *Republic* IV, 439c–41c).

Aristotle held that this Platonic view, unmitigated, entails that we are coerced by emotion, and thus that we are not responsible for akratic actions (*Nic. Ethics* VII.2, 1145b23–4). Aristotle agreed, however, that the soul should be thought of as possessing different parts (deliberative and appetitive or emotional), and he maintained too that emotion, even while leaving choice (for the good) unaffected, can have some effect on human action – sometimes, in fact, causing people to act against their choices (ibid., VII.10, 1152a15–17). Specifically, it can lead people to prefer a lesser good to the one that they choose by means of their deliberative processes. It does this by causing some kind of temporary ignorance of the application of a good general principle to the particular case at hand, such that the *akratēs*, whether or not he believes his action to be good, certainly fails to realize that the proposed action should not be done.[1] Postulating this sort of ignorance allowed Aristotle to avoid the undesirable conclusion that reason is simply overcome by emotion, and thus it allowed him to accept that akratic actions are blameworthy. But it has the curious consequence that, at the moment of action, we do not seem to know that what we are doing is wrong; in this sense, it is difficult to maintain that the action, at the time of the action itself, is against our (rational) choice. The settled intellectual error proposed by Socrates is in these cases simply replaced by temporary forgetfulness. So it is hard to see that Aristotle has really got an account of *akrasia* at all. Whatever we make of this assessment of Aristotle's account, however, he held that *akrasia* or incontinence can be avoided in two ways: by continence, leaving the emotions disordered but allowing the agent to control them (ibid., VII.2, 1146a12–16), and by temperance, bringing order to the emotions themselves (ibid., 1146a11–12; VII.9, 1152a1–2).

Clearly, then, talk of weakness of *will* is an odd way of talking about *akrasia* in this classical philosophical context, though as we shall see it is singularly appropriate for some of the Christian writers who are the main focus of this chapter. For Christian writers developed an account of the will as a faculty distinct both from reason and emotion. The will intervenes between deliberation and action, such that the mere combination of belief about what should be done and the influence of passion is not sufficient for action. What is required,

---

[1] *Nic. Eth.* VII.3, 1147b1–5, 9–18. See also VII.2, 1146b22–24 and VII.8, 1151a11–14.

minimally, is a capacity for *consenting* to one or other of two conflicting desires. The beginnings of such an account, in the context of the performance of actions that are somehow against the agent's considered judgment, can be found in Augustine. Augustine adapted from the Stoics the notion of consent: specifically, in Augustine's account, the notion of consenting to the stronger of two conflicting desires (*De civ. Dei* IX.4; *De sermone domini in monte* I.12.34). This application of the notion of consent is rather different from the Stoics', who spoke of rational consent in the context of a denial of different parts of the soul, to explain the overcoming of emotion: refusing consent to an emotional pull is a way of securing good activity in accord with reason. Like Aristotle, and unlike the Stoics, Augustine did not believe that all emotions are bad. He did believe, however, that as a result of the sin of Adam, all human beings have an inclination to seek the satisfaction of their (bad) emotional longings – longings that he identified as concupiscence (*concupiscentia*) – that is in conflict with humans' beliefs about what they should do (*Confessions* VI.11.20). A human being consents to whichever "pull" is stronger – concupiscence or reason – and in the case that concupiscence is stronger, sins (*Conf.* VIII.9.21, VIII.10.24). To this extent it is possible both to act and to choose against better judgment, and even reluctantly so, in the sense that it is possible to consent to the stronger pull of emotion against the influence of reason (*De spiritu et littera* 31.53). Indeed, Augustine's considered view is that human beings without the benefit of additional divine aid – that is, without grace – cannot avoid consenting in this way, and thus cannot avoid choosing badly (see, for example, *Contra duas epistolas Pelagianorum* III.8.24).

The crucial difference between this account of sinful action and Aristotle's account of akratic action is that on Augustine's theory the sinful action is consented to, and thus *chosen*; this insight ultimately requires the development of a fuller doctrine of the will to provide the relevant explanation of weakness. (It is tempting to think that, with the inclusion of this additional factor, the problem of *akrasia* simply disappears, since on the face of it akratic actions can be explained straightforwardly by appeal to a defective will. But this, as we shall see, oversimplifies a much more complex picture.) Historically, Augustine's account influenced the medieval West before Aristotle's did, since the relevant Aristotelian discussions were not available in Latin until Robert Grosseteste's translation of the complete *Nicomachean Ethics* in 1246–7. So voluntaristic accounts of weakness dominated the earlier Middle Ages, with Aristotelian ones reappearing rapidly from the 1250s onwards.

The Augustinian claim that choice is not always in accord with reason, and that it can sometimes instead be in accordance with the pull of emotion, found important support and development in Bernard of Clairvaux, who was the first writer to talk of the problem specifically in terms of weakness of will. When agents find themselves in cases where reason and emotion are in conflict, he claims, they can consent to one or the other of two options; weakness of will (*infirmitas voluntatis*) is exhibited in those cases where they consent to the emotional drive rather than the rational one (*De gratia et libero arbitrio* 12.38). Advancing from Augustine's view, Bernard explicitly holds that neither reason nor passion can necessitate this consent (*De gratia et libero arbitrio* 2.4–5).

There is no doubt of the importance of Bernard's teaching for the later tradition. Putting the matter very simply, what the thirteenth-century masters added was a conception of the will as a *faculty* distinct from both reason and emotion. The impetus for this distinction came from two different thinkers, both themselves influenced by sources in antiquity. The first is John of Damascus, whose *De fide orthodoxa* (translated into Latin in 1153) distinguished between *rational* appetite, or will, and two *irrational* appetites, the irascible and concupiscible (*De fide orthodoxa* 2.12 n. 15). The second is Avicenna, whose so-called *De anima* (the sixth book of his *Shifā'*) was translated into Latin in 1152–66. Avicenna holds that human beings possess both animal and rational souls, and that each type of soul includes both apprehensive and motive powers (*Liber de anima* I.5). This psychology thus allows for sense apprehension and appetite in addition to intellectual apprehension and appetite – that is, reason and will. This refinement of the Platonic division of the soul further allows for the Stoic notion of *consent* to be located in the will, and thus it allowed for a notion of choice or consent that does not reduce the appetitive component of human activity merely to the level of emotional pull.

A third important influence on some theories of the fourteenth century was Anselm's account of two affections or inclinations that each human being possesses (see Chapter 35). As Anselm sees it, human beings – and created rational beings in general – are inclined to act both in accordance with what is just and in accordance with what is beneficial (see *De casu diaboli* 4). Anselm refers to these inclinations as "wills," and later thinkers would identify these inclinations as belonging to a specific faculty or causal power, namely the will; thus, the will itself was seen as having inclinations to sometimes very different actions.

With these basic distinctions in place, we can begin to classify the positions of various philosophers by considering the following pair of questions. First, is weakness of will the result (loosely speaking) of something internal to the will, or not? Second, is the opposite of weakness (continence or temperance) the result of something internal to the will, or not? The response to the first question offered by someone broadly sympathetic to Aristotelian explanations of action would be that incontinence is caused by emotions (of the sense appetite). But someone more minded to develop some of the suggestions from the Augustinian tradition might be more likely to answer in terms of (Anselm-style) inclinations, or of involuntary reactions (emotions) *intrinsic* to the will, or even in terms of the will's liberty of indifference (such that a person could, in exactly the same circumstances and with exactly the same set of antecedent beliefs, choose either to act or to refrain from acting). In line with this, thinkers inclined more in the direction of an Aristotelian-style action theory would very likely locate some moral virtues in the sense appetite, ordering the emotions so as not to be negative influences on intellectual deliberation. A more voluntaristic thinker might be more inclined to locate all moral virtues in the will, allowing it to control emotions and the sense appetite in the right way. The fundamental impetus for these differences is the presence of different theories of the will, respectively more or less dependent on deliberation and reason.

SCHOLASTIC TREATMENTS OF WEAKNESS

The recovery of Aristotle's discussions in the middle of the thirteenth century immediately provoked a wide range of responses.[2] Very few thinkers claimed that Aristotle was wrong, though in fact many of them disagreed with him on fundamental issues. A good example of a strongly Aristotelian approach can be found in the very first medieval commentator on the relevant parts of the *Nicomachean Ethics*: Albert the Great. Albert persistently claimed that both the akratic person and the wicked or malicious person are in some sense ignorant. The wicked person acts from choice, however – that is, from a settled (bad) moral disposition – and for this reason is culpable of any ignorance about moral matters (*Ethica* III.1.10). The ignorance of the akratic person, on the other hand, is explained by emotion (in the Augustinian guise of concupiscence),

---

[2] There are an increasing number of useful resources on the question of weakness of will in scholasticism. See, for example, the following two helpful collections: Henrik Lagerlund and Mikko Yrjönsuuri (eds.) *Emotions and Choice from Boethius to Descartes* (Dordrecht: Kluwer, 2002), and Tobias Hoffmann *et al.* (eds.) *Das Problem der Willensschwäche in der mittelalterlichen Philosophie* (Leuven: Peeters, 2006). Risto Saarinen, *Weakness of the Will in Medieval Thought from Augustine to Buridan* (Leiden: Brill, 1994) is an excellent introduction to the whole topic, as, in a more restricted way, is chapter 4 of Bonnie Kent, *Virtues of the Will: The Transformation of Ethics in the Late Thirteenth Century* (Washington, DC: Catholic University of America Press, 1995). See, too, Bonnie Kent, "Evil in Later Medieval Philosophy," *Journal of the History of Philosophy* 45 (2007) 177–205, and "Aquinas and Weakness of Will," *Philosophy and Phenomenological Research* 75 (2007) 70–91. For a systematic treatment of the history of emotion in antiquity and the Middle Ages, see Simo Knuutilla, *Emotions in Ancient and Medieval Philosophy* (Oxford: Clarendon Press, 2004). Aspects of the issues are treated in Bernard Besnier *et al.* (eds.) *Les passions antiques et médiévales* (Paris: Presses universitaires de France, 2003). I found all of these to be invaluable in preparing the first two sections of this chapter; all of them contain useful bibliographies of further relevant material.

and acts against his settled moral judgments and choices in such a way that the choice, although not the ignorance, is culpable (*Ethica* III.1.14; *Super Ethica* VII.3 n. 623). These emotions belong to the sensory part of the soul (*De bono* III.5.1 and III.5.3). Continence allows the agent to avoid the pull of concupiscence without the emotions themselves being well ordered by the virtue of temperance (*Super Ethica* VII.1 n. 600).[3]

Albert's student, Thomas Aquinas, was similarly Aristotelian in his general trajectory, though his theory includes more identifiably non-Aristotelian components – in particular, the notion that akratic actions are somehow chosen. For Aquinas, contingency in human activity is the result of rational *deliberation*, not of any self-determination on the part of the will. The will is (automatically) responsive to goods determined by reason, and is in effect the executor of reason's determinations (for instance, *Summa theol.* 1a 82.4c and ad 3). In line with this, Aquinas understands weakness to be the consequence of disorder in the emotions of the sense appetite – Augustine's concupiscence (*Summa theol.* 1a2ae 77.2c).[4] The role of moral virtues is thus to reintegrate the emotions, and Aquinas is explicit that some of the acquired moral virtues belong to the sensory part of the soul and not to the rational will (ibid., 56.4). This means that the sensory part of the soul is able to cooperate fully in rational, moral, human activity (ibid., 59.5c): the rule of reason over the sense appetites is, as Aquinas puts it, following Aristotle, not despotic but *political* (ibid., 58.2).

In line with Aristotle's account, Aquinas sees the emotions as impacting on reason directly (rather than through the medium of some kind of prior impact on the will), the result of which is a failure to apply the good general rule to the particular circumstances (ibid., 77.1c). Aquinas worries, though, about the Aristotelian claim that *akratic* actions are not chosen – for if they are not chosen, they are not voluntary. Aquinas claims instead, sharing something of Augustine's line here, that the incontinent agent acts *eligens, non electione* ("electing, but not from election") (ibid., 78.4 ad 3). But while this solves one problem, it immediately raises a further problem. Only what is believed to be good can attract the will, so the incontinent person must judge that the proposed action is good – that it should be done. And this is a different and stronger judgment than one to the effect that the action is not such that it should not be done, since this latter judgment is consistent with the action being morally neutral. This Augustinian addition to Aristotle's account moves Aquinas's interpretation

---

[3] For this account, see Saarinen, *Weakness of the Will*, pp. 94–118.

[4] Aquinas holds that incontinence is thus a consequence of original sin: whatever may have been the origin of Adam's sin, it was not a case of *akrasia*. Adam sinned in full knowledge of what he should and should not do, and without bad emotions making a difference to his decision, since disordered emotions are a consequence of original sin, not its cause (*Summa theol.* 2a2ae 163.1c, 1a2ae 82.3c).

of Aristotle in a decidedly Socratic direction. Aquinas attempts to mitigate the counterintuitive aspect of this position by claiming that the akratic action is nevertheless not "from election": election (internal to the will) is not the *cause* of the action, because passion (external to the will) is the cause (*De malo* 3.12 ad 11); presumably, the election is not in accordance with the incontinent person's (good) settled moral principles.

One way of overcoming the evident problems with such an account is to give a more independent role to the will, along the lines inchoately suggested in Bernard of Clairvaux. On the face of it, such a role is itself problematic: if reasons do not determine how we act, then how can our acts avoid being (at best) irrational or (at worst) random? Many medieval thinkers – notably, many Franciscans – took exactly this line, however, claiming that the will is radically free in a way that avoids intellectual determinism but without making the will merely a randomly acting power. This in turn suggests answering both of the questions from the end of the previous section in terms of the will rather than the emotions or sense appetite: both weakness and virtues would thus be fundamentally located in the will. In contrast to the Aristotelian account of Aquinas, then, these thinkers proposed accounts on which no acquired moral virtue is physiological in character, inhering in the sensory appetite. Rather, such moral virtues are all purely immaterial properties of a purely immaterial substance – namely, the human soul. Indeed, it became commonplace among such voluntaristic thinkers to assign certain emotions to the will too. This is not to say that such thinkers necessarily denied that the emotions could be disordered, or that they could be made to be such that the intrinsic disorder is overcome. On the whole, however, any such intrinsic ordering was held to be the result not of naturally acquired virtues, but of other, generally supernaturally infused virtues (see Chapter 36).

The general view of such thinkers is that the will can simply will against the judgment of reason both in particular cases and in general principles, willing the lesser of two (or more) goods over greater ones.[5] This account can explain both *akrasia* and intemperate or malicious action. First, insofar as emotion has an impact on the intellect, it is not *direct*: emotion does not cloud the intellect other than with the consent of the will;[6] in such cases, presumably, reluctant action, rather than ignorance, distinguishes cases of *akrasia* from simple malice. A similar account is found in John Duns Scotus: incontinence as such is a disposition in the will that produces foolishness in the intellect (*Ordinatio* III.36

---

[5] See, for instance, Gonsalvo of Spain, *Quaest. disp.* 8; Walter of Bruges, *Quaest. disp.* 6 ad 14; and John Duns Scotus, *Ordinatio* II.43.2 nn. 5–6.

[6] See, for instance, Peter of John Olivi, *Summa* II.86 (ed. Jansen, III: 191).

q. un. nn. 72–5).[7] Second, Scotus explicitly holds that there are wrong actions
that are the result of the influence of passion on the will, without involving
any ignorance (*Ordinatio* II.43.2 nn. 5–6); but the will nevertheless is in any
case more inclined to follow intellect than some unmediated passion (*Reportatio*
II.39.2 n. 5). Malice, analogously, is the willing of some lesser good under the
influence neither of ignorance nor of passion (*Ordinatio* II.43.2 nn. 5–6).[8]

Thinkers who appeal to ignorance do so in this context only because it is
one way of avoiding the problem that it is not possible to will evil as such – a
position that was generally held until the introduction of William of Ockham's
more radical incompatibilist account of the will, according to which the will
can choose as it wants, with no teleological inclinations or constraints (*Ordinatio*
I.1.2 [*Opera theol.* I: 399]). Henry of Ghent, for example, while holding strongly
to the will's independence from reason, nevertheless holds that ignorance is
required in the case of akratic action. Even in such cases, however, he believes
both that ignorance requires the prior consent of the will (such that emotion
cannot cloud reason without the will's permission), and that this consent of the
will is not moved by the intellect (see, for example, *Quod.* 1.17 [*Opera* V: 128–9]).
This is in decided contrast to the more Aristotelian view of Aquinas, for example, according to whom emotion affects the reason directly, and according to
whom every voluntary consent is moved by the intellect.

There are other ways, too, of allowing for a voluntaristic account of *akrasia*
without contravening the Aristotelian principle that we cannot will evil as
such. Scotus borrows Anselm's two inclinations here: the will is inclined to
two different goods; even in the case that choosing one of them is sinful, the
object chosen is not chosen *as evil* (*Ordinatio* II.6.2 nn. 40–51). Anselm's two
inclinations also allow Scotus to deal with the question of the motivation for
sinful action: the beneficial motivates as much as the just does, to the extent
that the will has a natural inclination to it (*Ordinatio* III.26 q. un., nn. 110–11).

Positing emotions in the will – involuntary or automatic reactions, positive or
negative, to external stimuli – provides yet another kind of explanation for the
will's choice. Scotus, for example, holds that there are concupiscible and irascible
emotions in the will; temperance moderates the former, and fortitude the latter
(*Ordinatio* III.34 q. un., nn. 38–51). These involuntary affective reactions incline
the will to its natural goal, the beneficial; the affection or inclination for the
just "moderates" these reactions, such that they are "rectified" (*Ordinatio* III.33
q. un., nn. 34–6, 61). Nevertheless, it remains unclear just how these *emotions*
in the will relate to the two *affections* that Scotus adopts from Anselm. On the

---

[7] On all this, see Kent, *Virtues of the Will*, pp. 174–98.
[8] On this account of malice, see also Aquinas, *Summa theol.* 1a2ae 78.1c.

one hand, both seem to perform the same kind of explanatory function; on the other hand, emotions are clearly psychological kinds of explanation of choice, whereas inclinations seem to provide some sort of metaphysical explanation.

In line with all of this, there was an increasing tendency to locate *all* moral virtues in the will, for the general reason that virtues are supposed to have a causal role in good choice, and should thus inhere in the faculty responsible for choice.[9] The contrast, of course, is with thinkers more influenced by the Aristotelian insight that choice is fundamentally a matter of reason, such that the will is naturally disposed to follow reason in a way that sense appetites do not.[10] This teaching proved, for reasons seen, outrageous to the more voluntaristic thinkers just examined.

GRACE

The doctrine of grace plays a number of different roles in Christian theology.[11] It is by means of grace that human beings are forgiven both original and individual sin. Grace is often taken to be a principle of merit, allowing its possessor to merit further grace, or everlasting life. Of key philosophical significance in this chapter, however, is the role that grace plays in action theory and philosophy of mind. During the Middle Ages, a doctrine of grace developed that either identifies grace as a kind of virtue, or at least understands grace in a way highly analogous to virtue. Viewed in this way, grace is a kind of additional remedy for the various kinds of weakness introduced by original sin. Basically, grace performs the role assigned by Aristotle to continence, allowing the will to control rebellious sense appetites, and in this way avoid *akrasia*. It does not, however, of itself bring anything analogous to Aristotle's temperance – it does not remove the rebellious character of the sense appetites altogether. *Akrasia* thus remains a real possibility for the person who possesses grace.

9 See, for example, Bonaventure *Sent.* III.33 q. un, a. 3; Henry of Ghent, *Quod.* IV.22 (ed. 1518, I: 139v–rS); Olivi, *Quaest. de virt.* 4 (ed. Emmen and Stadter, p. 224); Scotus, *Ord.* III.33 q. un., nn. 44–5.
10 See, for instance, Godfrey of Fontaines, *Quod.* XIV.3 (*Phil. Belges* V: 342).
11 The philosophical aspects of the topic of grace are not as well served in the literature as the question of weakness is. The best general history is Alister McGrath, *Iustitia Dei: A History of the Christian Doctrine of Justification,* 3rd edn (Cambridge: Cambridge University Press, 2005). Chapter 1 of Joseph Warwykow, *God's Grace and Human Action: "Merit" in the Theology of Thomas Aquinas* (Notre Dame, IN: University of Notre Dame Press, 1995), provides a useful conspectus of much of the literature on Aquinas. For the question of the effects of grace, and its relation to original sin, see William van Roo, *Grace and Original Justice According to St Thomas* (Rome: Gregorian University, 1955). Perhaps unsurprisingly, this material focuses more on theological questions than on the precise relationship between justifying grace and the moral virtues of continence and temperance. For an account of the moral virtues relevant to this whole set of issues, see Kent, *Virtues of the Will.*

For Augustine, grace, although not obliterating the human inclination to seek the satisfaction of (bad) emotional longings – concupiscence[12] – was what allows humans freely to will the good (*De spiritu et littera* 30.52). Augustine often identified grace as the *operation* of the Holy Spirit in a human person, making him or her just (*Epist.* 98.2), though he sometimes talked as well of grace as an *effect* of the operation of the Holy Spirit. But Augustine provided little by way of technical clarification here: how precisely grace achieves its effect is left obscure.

Theologians of the late eleventh and early twelfth centuries made more progress on the theory of the virtues than they did on grace as such. Grace was largely seen in terms of God's bringing about good effects – such as the theological virtues – in the soul. Anselm, for example, repeats Augustine's account of grace as allowing humans to will the good, though Anselm adds the clarification that the fallen will always retains the power so to will, but that it is incapable of actualizing this power because of its lack of rectitude (*De libertate arbitrii* 3). Virtues themselves, in contrast, were viewed as habits, either as fixed dispositions, or (in more Aristotelian fashion) as susceptible of growth and confirmation by exercise.[13]

A considerably greater advance was made on these topics in the thirteenth century, when the influx of a cluster of relevant Aristotelian concepts allowed the development of a detailed account of the 'mechanics' of grace. In particular, theologians came to see a link between the nature of grace and the nature of virtue, categorizing grace, like the virtues, as habits and thus as some kind of *quality* of the soul. As early as the second half of the twelfth century, Alan of Lille sees baptismal grace as a kind of habit or disposition, analogous to a virtue (*Regulae caelestis iuris* 86). According to the Aristotelian physics introduced into the West in the thirteenth century, qualities are forms, all virtues are habits (*Nic. Ethics* II.5, 1106a10–13; *Cat.* 6, 8b29), and habits are a kind of quality (*Cat.* 6, 8b26–7). The purpose of such habits is to help human beings to act well (*Metaphys.* V.20, 1022b10–12). If we envisage grace along the lines of an Aristotelian virtue, we will think of it as a kind of form or formal cause: something inherent in the individual that explains her being such-and-such – in this case, having a certain resemblance to the divine nature that is found only in those who are saved. This link was first made explicitly by Philip the Chancellor in the early thirteenth century, who identified grace as a habit inhering in the soul's essence and the theological virtues as habits inhering in the soul's powers (*De bono gracie* 1.2 [*Summa de bono*, ed. Wicki, I: 360]).

---

[12] See *Enchiridion* 1.44; *Contra duas epistolas Pelagianorum* 1.13.26–7.
[13] See the discussion in Marcia Colish, *Peter Lombard* (Leiden: Brill, 1994) II: 476–7.

According to Aristotle, virtues are habits caused by our (good) actions (*Nic. Ethics* II.1, 1103a31–b2). Aquinas agrees with Aristotle that there are many such virtues: he calls them "acquired" virtues – that is, virtues that it is in our own power to gain (*Summa theol.* 1a2ae 51.2c, 55.1c, 63.2c). He argues that such acquired virtues are qualities (ibid., 49.1c) that must have as their subject the powers of the soul (ibid., 50.2c, 56.1c).[14] Aquinas also adds a new type of habit to those considered by Aristotle, arguing that some habits are given to us directly by God (rather than being caused by our own actions [ibid., 51.4c]). Aquinas calls these "infused" habits (as opposed to acquired habits) (see Chapter 36). The reason some habits have to be infused is that our supernatural goal – salvation and the beatific vision – is beyond our natural powers. If we are to be disposed to such a goal, we thus need supernatural habits or dispositions (ibid., 62.1c, 63.1c). These infused habits are the theological virtues of faith, hope, and charity, inhering in the various powers of the soul. (Faith inheres in the intellect [2a2ae 4.2c], and hope and charity in the will [2a2ae 18.1c, 24.1c].)

In addition to these infused habits, there is also an infused habit of grace. According to Aquinas, this habit is distinct from the theological virtues and is presupposed by them. Aquinas grounds this claim on Aristotle's principle that a virtue as such is a "disposition of a perfect thing" (*Phys.* VII.3, 246a13). So, in order to receive a virtue, a thing's nature must *already* be perfected. Thus, before it can receive a supernatural virtue, it must have some supernatural perfection. This is grace (*Summa theol.* 1a2ae 110.3c). From this it follows, Aquinas argues, that the subject of grace must be the *essence* of the soul, not the powers of the soul (ibid., 110.3c), and thus that grace must be both distinct from and prior to the theological virtues.

Aquinas's account of habitual grace is explicitly directed against that of Peter Lombard, who – referring to the dictum of 1 John 4.8 and 4.16 that "God is love" – identified the love by which we love God as the Holy Spirit (*Sent.* I.17.1 nn. 2–3). In Lombard's view, the Holy Spirit is something in us, identified as the love that we have for God and our neighbor. Aquinas rejects this view. Our act of love, he argues, must be something we in some sense do, and as an action of ours it must in some sense inhere in us. Equally, the principle or cause of this love must likewise be internal to us, in the sense of being something created and inhering in the soul.[15] Aquinas understands Lombard to be maintaining that

---

[14] Note that Aquinas, unlike Aristotle, distinguishes the essence of the soul from its powers: see *Summa theol.* 1a 77.1c.

[15] Aquinas is thus committed to the view that habitual grace is an inherent quality. Although he sometimes talks of such grace as created (see, e.g., *Summa theol.* 3a 7.11sc), strictly speaking he denies that any inherent accidents are created. Only substances are created. Accidents are said to be "concreated," in as much as they are that *through which* a substance exists in a certain way (whiteness

the Holy Spirit moves a person to act in certain ways – perhaps meritoriously – without the person's having any intrinsic capacity that might enable him or her to cooperate with the relevant divine action. The act, in short, is not an act of the human person's at all. Aquinas does not disagree that God moves the soul in all cases of meritorious activity. He merely disagrees with what he takes to be Lombard's claim that the soul contributes nothing itself (*Summa theol.* 2a2ae 23.2c).

Aquinas's account of God's causal activity in the soul also marks a considerable theoretical improvement on Lombard's, in the sense that Aquinas makes use of an analysis of motion from Aristotle's *Physics* in order to describe the relevant divine activity. Aquinas argues that the human soul is moved by God in all of its (internal) acts of knowledge and love, and thus that these internal acts count as things brought about in the soul by God: for "motion is an act of the mover in the thing moved" (1a2ae 110.2c).[16] Aquinas talks about this divine operation as *actual* grace, as opposed to *habitual* grace (ibid.). But such internal acts cannot be acts of the person's without the person's having an internal capacity or habit to ground participation in such acts.

Distinguishing grace from the theological virtue of charity (as Aquinas does) was unusual in the later medieval debates: thinkers were usually content to identify the two, perhaps on the simple grounds of parsimony. (Aquinas's additional layer of explanation, distinguishing grace from the theological virtues, does no obvious work, and seems in any case to be based on a curious reading of Aristotle.) In effect, the twelfth-century account of grace becomes Aquinas's *actual* grace, and the role played by the theological virtues in the twelfth century is played, in a more theoretically nuanced way, by both the theological virtues and habitual grace in Aquinas's account. Fourteenth-century theologians simply dispensed with habitual grace as something over and above the habitual virtue of charity. The notion that charity should be understood as a habit perfecting the rational part of the soul – in this case, the will – seems to have been accepted universally by later thinkers. What was not so readily accepted is the idea that there is any kind of *intrinsic* link between the habit of grace/charity and the state of being saved. Scotus develops a complex argument against the necessity of such habits for salvation – God could save someone without the habit of charity (*Ordinatio* I.17.1–2 n. 160) – and Ockham claims not only that such a habit is not necessary for salvation, but also that it is not sufficient (*Ordinatio*

is that through which a substance is white): see *Summa theol.* 1a 45.4c. Nevertheless, Aquinas's intention is plain: there is no sense in which he would want to assert that habitual grace belongs to the uncreated order. It is "concreated" as and when its subject receives it.

[16] Aquinas has in mind Aristotle, *Phys.* III.3, 202a13–21; see too, e.g., Albert, *Sent.* 4.17.A.15 (ed. Borgnet, 29: 684a).

I.17.1 [*Opera theol*. III: 470]): positions that some of his contemporaries believed to be heretical.[17] But this takes us into more specifically theological territory, and away from the philosophical topics under discussion here.

Clearly, in the complex context of an understanding of weakness that owes much to both Augustinian insights about the will and Aristotelian insights about the passions, theologians of the thirteenth century had many more options than their predecessors in considering the effects of grace. Aquinas, for example, holds that grace allows the sense appetites and passions to be subject to reason (*Summa theol*. 1a2ae 113.1c). In effect, this makes grace something like continence – it does not prevent the rebelliousness of the sense appetites, but it does allow reason to control it, and thus performs a role analogous to that assigned by Aristotle to continence, not temperance. (Unsurprisingly, Aquinas holds that temperance is a virtue [2a2ae 141.1–2], and that it is a higher virtue than continence [ibid., 155.4c]; he holds, too, that a supernatural gift corresponding to temperance is bestowed on a person as a result of the presence of grace, though not to be identified with grace itself [1a2ae 68.4 ad 2].) Aquinas holds that grace entails all other virtues (since it entails the theological virtues, and these cannot be had without all the acquired virtues too [ibid., 65.3c]). So a concomitant of grace, though not its immediate or proper effect, is that the sense appetites have their own virtues and supernatural gifts, and thus that they begin to be ordered in a less rebellious way.

Scotus also holds that grace gives a person the power to control rebellious sense appetites, though in line with his greater emphasis on the will he holds specifically that the will is the part of the soul that controls the sense appetites (rather than thinking of the sense appetites themselves as intrinsically disposed in a better way as the result of grace) (*Ordinatio* II.29 q. un. n. 9). So Scotus can affirm without qualification the Augustinian language about the strengthening of the will by grace. He does not believe, however, that the presence of the theological virtues entails all other virtues (*Ordinatio* III.36 q. un. n. 113), and so is not committed to the view that the sense appetites begin necessarily to be intrinsically more controllable once grace is present.

---

[17] On this, see Marilyn McCord Adams, *William Ockham* (Notre Dame, IN: University of Notre Dame Press, 1987) II: 1279–95.

VI

ETHICS

33

HAPPINESS

LENN E. GOODMAN

THE ARISTOTELIAN BACKGROUND

At the beginning of the *Nicomachean Ethics*, Aristotle claims that all arts and inquiries, acts and choices, aim at some good. Indeed, they presume an ultimate good. For if they sought no good at all they would not be chosen, and without an ultimate intrinsic good their rationality would collapse. Aristotle's title for that ultimate aim, a title meant to be uncontroversial, is *eudaimonia*, loosely translatable as happiness. Its nature is not a given: philosophy has its work cut out for it in clarifying just what this ultimate human goal must be. Some seek happiness in pleasure, wealth, or honor; others scramble for whatever sensation appeals at the moment or blindly pursue domination. Aristotle, however, maintains that (1) *eudaimonia* is something objective, not mere gratification, euphoria, or complacency; (2) it is not merely a passive state of well-being but an active life of doing well (*euprattein*); and (3) the virtues are dispositions that promote the good life that we seek. Aristotelian moral virtues such as courage, generosity, and self-control are dispositions, or habits of acting in accordance with a mean discerned by reason. *Phronesis*, strength in deliberation, is an intellectual virtue, but *sophia*, the queen of the intellectual virtues, finds our most godlike activity in contemplation. As Aristotle sees it, the virtues point the way to happiness, much as Plato sought the nature of reality through his conception of knowledge.

For medieval philosophers, as for Aristotle, contemplation is typically the consummate human goal, finding its highest object in the divine. Philosophers disagree, however, about the rapport of happiness with an active life. Horrified by the world's state, some seek withdrawal; others strive for engagement, integrating contemplation and inquiry with moral, social, and political responsibility.[1] Some reserve ultimate felicity to the hereafter, whereas others see windows opening on it in the here and now.

---

[1] For medieval versions of the ideal of the role of wisdom in politics, see for instance, Abraham Melamed, *The Philosopher King in Medieval and Renaissance Jewish Philosophical Thought* (Albany: State University of New York Press, 2003).

JUDAISM

From the Torah's standpoint, Aristotle's foils – pleasure, wealth, and honor – may seem a bit too hastily cut off from the good life's fullness; and the person who enjoys Aristotelian *eudaimonia* may look rather isolated, despite Aristotle's ideal of the *polis* and his trenchant charge that life outside an integrated community is either subhuman or superhuman. Biblical writers situate fulfillment in a community spanning the generations, responsive to a sacred trust with ancestors and heartened by God's promises of triumph over history's vicissitudes.[2] To medieval Jewish thinkers as well, the founders of Israel's law and eponyms of its ancestry remain a living presence. The Rabbinic tradition that grounds medieval Jewish theology and law makes them contemporaries, paragons of the piety proudly held aloft as Israel's moral and spiritual heritage. Nor are future generations ever far from view. Glossing God's reproach to Cain, "The voice of the bloods of thy brother cry to me from the earth" (Genesis 3:10), the Rabbis ask why the Hebrew has 'bloods' and not 'blood.' Their answer: Cain destroyed not just Abel but all his hope of posterity. Biblically, they infer, to take one life is to destroy a world (Mishnah Sanhedrin 4.5).[3] So Job, not an Israelite at all but an everyman of theodicy, finds solace in his progeny. His new offspring do not replace the lost children, but seeing his grandchildren's children assures Job of his futurity.

Saadiah Gaon, the first systematic Jewish philosopher, conceives of happiness in pluralistic terms – that is, as a blend of diverse goods. Surveying the putative goods mentioned in the Torah and the common notions they reflect, he identi-fied thirteen objects of interest that might be sought as goods: asceticism, food and drink, sexual gratification, romantic love, wealth, progeny, urban and agri-cultural development, longevity, political power, vengeance, knowledge, piety, and rest. Each of these names stands for a mode of activity that could frame a lifestyle. But such focusing, Saadiah argues, would be a badly mistaken strategy:

I find some people suppose, indeed are certain, that it is man's duty to order his entire life by a single trait of character, preferring the love of one thing above all other objects of desire, and hating one thing above all else. Examining this view, I find it utterly mistaken, in several ways. First, if the love of a single thing and preference of it to all else were best for us, the Creator would not have implanted in human nature the love of any other . . . [Second,] don't you see that even the most elementary actions cannot

---

[2] Two learned and thoughtful studies bear special mention here: Jonathan D. Levenson, *Resurrection and the Restoration of Israel: The Ultimate Victory of the God of Life* (New Haven, CT: Yale University Press, 2006), and Hava Tirosh-Samuelson, *Happiness in Premodern Judaism: Virtue, Knowledge, and Well-Being* (Cincinnati, OH: Hebrew Union College Press, 2003).

[3] The standard English translation of the Mishnah is Herbert Danby (tr.) *The Mishnah* (Oxford: Clarendon Press, 1933).

succeed with just one element? How then can the whole complex? If a builder built a house of stones, or teak, or thatch, or nails alone, it would not do at all – as it would if he built it of all these in combination. Likewise with cooking and food, drink and dress, service, and all our other needs. Doesn't it open one's eyes to see that none of these specific activities works with just one means, although all of them serve our comfort? How much less can the needs of our soul and character be met by a single object![4]

Saadiah argues, in practical terms that make full use of his powers as an observer of the human condition, that pursuing any one of the goods he has listed, to the exclusion of the rest, is inherently self-defeating. Each of these values may be a prima facie good. But other values plainly relevant to human fulfillment will be neglected in too single-minded a pursuit of just one such good alone. Moreover, even *that* aim will inevitably be frustrated: the good sought will prove unsatisfying, and unsatisfactory in isolation from the rest. The single-minded ascetic, for instance, will turn misanthropic and defeat the quest for piety (or even health) that might have motivated his choice. Even knowledge does not suffice as life's goal; if pursued exploitatively (as Aristotle seems to recommend), it leads to isolation – wisdom unshared and untransmitted. No single good, then, can constitute the good life. One needs a mix of goods – in proportions, Saadiah suggests, that the Torah can teach us.

Taking up the question where Saadiah left it, Moses Maimonides seeks the proper way of integrating our human purposes. Before turning to his answer, however, we need to consider Saadiah's thoughts as to happiness beyond this life, for he makes it very clear that even given the best mix of worldly goods, time and change will erode and ultimately frustrate every human appetite and desire.

Convinced by history and experience that worldly ills outweigh goods, Saadiah faces an acute version of the problem of evil, to which he responds by falling back on the promise of the hereafter. History will climax, in the messianic age, with the resurrection of the dead. Israel will be restored; her martyrs will witness vindication of her mission in the world. Beyond that, the accounts of justice will be rectified, as the Rabbis promised – the righteous will be rewarded and the wicked will be punished (*Beliefs and Convictions* VII, VIII, IX). Saadiah rejects the claim of his Muslim contemporary, al-Ashʿarī, that God may treat his creatures as he likes. Only fear, venality, or ignorance would lead a judge to an unjust judgment, but God's rule is founded on his justice, and that justice is vouched for by his grace, for the act of creation was a pure expression

---

4 Saadiah Gaon, *Kitāb al-Amānāt wa-al-iʿtiqādāt* (*The Book of Critically Chosen Beliefs and Convictions*, or *Sefer Emunot ve-Deot*) X.1 (ed. Kafih, pp. 288–9). Saadiah's vision of the good life is discussed in Lenn E. Goodman, *God of Abraham* (New York: Oxford University Press, 1996) pp. 141–52.

of grace, responding to no prior desert.[5] What then can one say of the suffering of innocents, of which Job's sufferings are emblematic? Clearly they must be requited in the hereafter: adherence to God's law lightens and brightens the souls of the righteous but darkens and scorches the souls of the wicked, blocking the light that the righteous enjoy, just as the clarity of righteous souls guards them from that heat (Psalms 97:11, glossed at *Beliefs and Convictions* V.1, VI.4, IX.5, 8). God's justice levies the consequences of human acts on the righteous and the wicked alike. Despite the losses every living being must suffer, then, for Saadiah life is neither tragic nor absurd. A good life is possible, as the Torah promises, and the course the Torah outlines guides one reliably toward life's pleasures and rewards (see also Chapter 56).

Maimonides rejects Saadiah's thesis that evils outweigh goods in this life; he maintains that good is preponderant and that many of our sufferings stem from our own acts or omissions. Needing no recompense for worldly ills, Maimonides rejects Saadiah's recourse to the rabbinic doctrine of the sufferings of love, which he calls unbiblical and untrue. For God to torment his creatures undeservedly, even in order to enhance their reward, would be utterly unjust. Saadiah, Maimonides argues, weighed happiness in the wrong coin, misled by an equation of good with pleasure and evils with pains. Pains are evils, to be sure; and wholesome, measured pleasures are goods. But hedonism affords no adequate gauge of value. The peak of happiness lies in knowledge of God and in emulation of his ways. Job's losses were indeed natural outcomes of human embodiment, as he himself might have seen had he been wise as well as upright. Job's requital came in his epiphany, not his progeny – what warrants every vulnerability is the chance of knowing God (*Guide of the Perplexed* III.12).

Knowledge of God's infinite perfection, of course, must be approached asymptotically. But it is by perfecting ourselves that we emulate God. The purpose of the Torah is to guide us to a way of life that fosters that emulation – in practical terms, as the Talmudic Rabbis taught, by promoting an ethos of love, charity, and justice; in spiritual/intellectual terms, through rituals and symbols that open up the mind to ever higher apprehensions of God's perfection. It is here that Maimonides finds the key to integrating the diverse goods that Saadiah had calendared:

A person should deploy all the powers of his soul under the guidance of reason . . . and focus his gaze on a single goal: apprehension of God, insofar as this is possible for a human being. That means knowing Him and directing every act, every movement and cessation, and every utterance toward this goal, leaving no act whatever vain or pointless, that is, undirected toward this end. In eating or drinking, for instance, in sexual relations,

---

[5] Commentary on Job 34 (tr. Goodman, pp. 359–60), and Introduction to Job (tr. Goodman, p. 127).

sleeping or waking, moving or stopping, one should aim solely for bodily health. And the purpose of bodily health is to enable the soul to find its tools in sound working order, for use in the sciences and in garnering the moral and intellectual virtues, so as to reach this ultimate goal.

(Eight Chapters 5)

Maimonides here fuses the biblical mandate to pursue God's holiness (Leviticus 19:2) with Plato's exhortation to become as like to God as humanly possible (*Timaeus* 176b). Through knowledge of God we realize our intellectual affinity to him, announced when Genesis declares that we humans were created in God's image. But it is in acts of kindness that we emulate God's grace in the governance of nature. In both the practical and the intellectual spheres reason leads the way: for it is reason that guides us to the mean that marks the path of moral virtue, and it is reason again that grasps the inner meaning of the Torah's symbols, raising us toward an ever less inadequate grasp of God's perfection.

Maimonides subordinates all human acts to the service of our highest goal, but without robbing them of their intrinsic worth. Even in pursuit of the ultimate, no human good is left behind:

[The Torah's] intent is only that a person should live naturally and follow the middle path, eating and drinking what is his to eat and drink, in moderation, enjoying sexual congress with whom it is permitted, again in moderation, living in society, in justice and equity, not in caves or mountains, not wearing hair shirts, or abusing and afflicting his body.

(Eight Chapters 4)[6]

Saintly persons, reacting against the decadence of their times, may seek surcease from society or lean somewhat toward the ascetic. But those who seek to emulate such abstemious figures through extreme renunciation are like fools who suppose that if small doses of medicine aid the ailing, larger doses will be all the better for the healthy.

God, the highest object of our awareness, is both manifest and hidden: plain as daylight in the broadest terms, but far beyond the reach of the most penetrating human mind in his ultimacy. Awareness of God's perfection is the ultimate object of the human quest. But that awareness does not compete with other human goals. Intellectual consummation spills over into holy acts of guidance and generosity. So Abraham will have followers, not only in his lifetime but in every generation. And Moses will experience no mere ecstasy but an all-encompassing vision of nature; he will transmit an articulate system of law and morals to guide his people in every generation. The traffic on Jacob's ladder

---

[6] Citing Nazir 19a, 22a; Ta'anit 11a; Baba Kamma 91b; Nedarim 10a.

moves downward as well as up, Maimonides writes: "How wisely is it written, 'ascending and descending,' ascent before descent. For after rising and reaching a given rung on the ladder comes the descent with what has been gained, to govern and teach the people on earth."[7] Reason, the source of every sound inspiration, will guide practice, supported by it and supportive of it. And the glittering sword does not just bar the way to Eden. Spinning (*mithapekhet*) swiftly on its axis, it casts rays of enlightenment that we can apprehend, in the measure of our capacity, lighting the path to immortality.

CHRISTIANITY

Christianity is born as Hellenism dies. When Jesus is hailed as the Answer and the Way (John 14:6), the Gospel audience already knows the question. The Hebrew for salvation (still echoed in the name Jesus) no longer means victory or vindication, as it once did, or even endurance, as a Stoic might expect, making Herakles his hero, and not Achilles or Odysseus.[8] Salvation now means escape from the world's toils – above all, from sin. Paul had blamed the Law for trapping men in sin (Romans 3:20, 5:13, 20, 7:7–13, 8:2). But the search for meaning in Christ's death, by an ironic twist, makes sin irredeemable without his sacrifice. And, again ironically, the very effort to make his way universal turns his teachings into a particularism: No salvation without him.

Augustine fought clear of his Manichean phase. His mother's love and the philosophy of Plotinus, accessible in the Latin of Marius Victorinus,[9] taught him to accept his body and ascribe his youthful, willful passions not to some inner evil but to a misguided spiritual hunger that mistook folly for joy, license for liberty, false pride for shame, and wild alliances for friendship. Reflecting on his youthful theft of pears from a neighbor's orchard, he wrote:

What then did wretched I so love in thee, thou theft of mine, in that sixteenth year of my age? . . . and wherein did I corruptly and pervertedly imitate my Lord? Did I wish even by stealth to do contrary to Thy law, because by power I could not do so – so that being confined I might mimic a stunted liberty by doing with impunity things unpermitted me, a darkened likeness of Thine omnipotence?

(*Confessions* II.12–14 [tr. Pusey, pp. 27–9])

---

[7] *Guide* I.15, glossing Genesis 28:13; and see *Guide* I.38 and 63, citing Genesis 12:5, and *Guide* II.35–8.

[8] See E. R. Dodds, *The Greeks and the Irrational* (Berkeley: University of California Press, 1964); *Pagan and Christian in an Age of Anxiety* (Cambridge: Cambridge University Press, 1965).

[9] See Peter Brown, *Augustine of Hippo* (London: Faber and Faber, 1967) p. 92.

As Augustine came to see, "Even in their sins souls seek a sort of likeness to God, in a proud, perverse, and, if you will, slavish freedom" (*De Trinitate* XI.5).

Yet, even as he sees a dark shadow of God's truth in vice itself, Augustine still finds a deep duality between the present world and God's kingdom – the best good life of worldling philosophers, Augustine argues, is misery alongside God's peace. Moral virtue is the best of this life's goods, since it does battle with the passions. But its hold is tenuous, the life it commends inchoate. Only life eternal offers consummation; only grace can steady faith enough to give it entrée to that life. The loss of friends and the all too human sense of anxiety are faith's allies in disguise, turning our gaze heavenward and allowing us, if not happiness itself, at least the chance to live in hope (*City of God* XIX.4–12).

Anselm, as a child in the Alpine town of Aosta, dreamed of climbing to God's manor in the mountains and warning the steward of the wayward women who reaped in God's fields. In maturity, Anselm would forge new ways of meditation, aiming to open up to others his contemplative access to the divine.[10] God's image, Anselm writes, lies within, but in a soul corroded by sin, leathered over by vice:

I acknowledge, Lord, and give thanks that you have created your image in me, so that I may remember you, think of you, love you. But this image is so effaced and worn away by vice, so darkened by the smoke of sin, that it cannot do what it was made to do unless you renew it and reform it. I do not try, Lord, to attain your lofty heights, because my understanding is in no way equal to it. But I do desire to understand your truth a little, that truth that my heart believes and loves. For I do not seek to understand so that I may believe; but I believe so that I may understand. For I believe this also, that "unless I believe I shall not understand" [Isaiah 7:9].

(*Proslogion* I.1; tr. Charlesworth)

Anselm's vision is dark. Convinced that he was fallen, convicted of a sin that no mortal could purge, he sought refuge in Christ's sacrifice, all the while taking life itself, and the powers of thought that he so treasured, to be God's precious gifts. Yet the question remained, how could that be, if our mortality stands embattled by sin and hopes for escape from a sinful world?

Thomas Aquinas resolves this conflict in classic scholastic form, with a distinction: true, happiness is the vision of God's essence, and that cannot be enjoyed here in this world; at the same time, this life of ours does afford a natural wealth. God's bounty does grant happiness in some measure, even though our bodies are weak, our appetites strong, our minds ignorant. Here in the world

---

[10] See Richard W. Southern, *Saint Anselm: Portrait in a Landscape* (Cambridge: Cambridge University Press, 1990) pp. 91–106.

the soul naturally and rightly rules the body, and Augustine erred in assuming that beatitude means shedding the body. But in the hereafter souls will receive a spiritual body, infused with incorruption by the joy of their new and clearer vision. Even the good of externals like friendship may be restored. So a man may be happy in this life and still pant after ultimate bliss, not ignorant of his goal, yet not knowing it as he will after death.

All actions, as Aristotle held, pursue some good. And, as Augustine learned when he probed his youthful wildness, even wrong choices pursue some simulacrum of the good. But the final good that warrants every sound pursuit is God:

> The particular good is directed to the common good as its end, for the being of the part is for the sake of the being of the whole [cf. Aristotle, *Politics* I.4]. So it is that "the good of the nation is more godlike than the good of one man" [*Nic. Ethics* I.2]. Now the supreme good, namely God, is the common good, since the good of all things depends on Him, and the good whereby each thing is good is the particular good of that thing, and of those that depend thereon. Therefore all things are directed to one good, namely God, as their end.
>
> (*Summa contra gentiles* III.17, tr. Pegis, II: 28)

What Thomas achieves here is to reconcile worldly with ultimate aims without sacrificing either to the other. Just as Aristotle and Maimonides had subordinated the aims of daily living to the ultimate goal of knowing God, so Aquinas sees in the hierarchy of means and ends a way of integrating the aims of human happiness and the good life in this world into a larger picture, where ultimate causes move proximate causes, and ultimate ends afford the warrant for proximate ends.

Surveying the same goods that Aristotle placed in service to *eudaimonia*, Thomas argues that the natural wealth of God's abundant care for creation, along with the more conventional wealth that allows us to procure natural goods, is quite properly sought – but as means to an end, never as a final end (*Summa theol.* 1a2ae 2.1c). Honor recognizes virtue, so it can accompany happiness, which the virtues promote. But honor, therefore, clearly cannot constitute happiness (ibid., 2.2c). Nor can any bodily good. Even a good of the soul cannot be our ultimate good, for we must distinguish the object of desire from its actual use and enjoyment. The soul, considered in itself, has only the potential, say, for the knowledge or virtue it seeks: its true goal is fulfillment of such quests. Happiness itself is "something outside the soul" (ibid., 2.7c). Three things must coincide for us to possess it: "vision, which is perfect knowledge of the intelligible end; comprehension, which implies presence of the end; and delight or enjoyment, which implies repose of the lover in the beloved" (ibid., 4.3c). Thus will, too, is requisite, as part of what makes one capable of enjoyment (ibid., 4.4c).

Rectitude of will, Aquinas argues, is necessary for happiness, just as well-disposed matter is needed for the reception of form. God might have made a will with just the right tendency. But divine wisdom forbids such mere puppetry: no pure creature fittingly gains happiness without striving. As Aristotle saw (*Nic. Ethics* I.9), happiness is the reward of works of virtue (*Summa theol.* 1a2ae 5.6c). As for the body, although it does not bring us the highest happiness, it does allow us happiness of a lesser sort (ibid., 4.5c). What virtue calls for, then, is not the body's rejection but its perfection. For "beauty of body" and keenness in its care are parts of human perfection. Here Thomas reproves Augustine and all who overly incline toward the ascetic: happiness in this life plainly needs a well-disposed body.

ISLAM

Muslim thinkers too hanker after otherworldliness while still seeking an accommodation to the world and a taste of its fruits. Al-Kindī, writing in the ninth century, for a prince, on how to banish sorrows, will diagnose all anxieties and sorrows as the results of losses or the fear of loss. His prescription: detachment from transitory things, prizing intellectual realities in their place, for Ideas – pure Ideas like those that Plato spoke of – are safe from change and decay. Easily won, unlike the elusive goods of the senses, they are never really lost. For as objects of the understanding they become the very substance of the mind. Friendships fade; loved ones are lost. Worldly bonds only tie us to the world, but Ideas endure and bear seeds of immortality, for the soul infused with them not only holds them secure but becomes like them and so shares in their deathlessness. Seeking philosophical and thus conceptually robust consolations, Kindī quietly renounces bodily resurrection. The houris and wine boys promised in the Quran balk at the barrier that only pure Ideas can traverse.

In an extended allegory from his essay "On How to Banish Sorrow," Kindī treats our lives here below like a journey in a ship that has made a stop:

When the captain calls the passengers for embarkation, some return loaded down with all they have gathered and collected . . . They can barely squeeze into the ship, and that only uncomfortably and unhealthily. Some have wandered so far and strayed so deep into the woods that the voice of the ship's master does not even reach them. The vessel departs, leaving them behind, cut off from their homeland in wild, hostile, deadly surroundings, horrible and ruinous. Some are carried off by wild beasts. Others fall into a pit or crevasse or sink into quicksand. Some are crushed by snakes. Their desolate and decaying bodies, limbs scattered, mangled and hideous, are an object of pity to strangers but a lesson to all who knew them, who see them exiled from the homeland they had set out for.

Those who board the ship with the heavy loads they have amassed of objects that deceived their minds and now rob them of their freedom, deprive them of rest, cramp their quarters, and weigh down their baggage, soon see their flowers fade, the stones lose their luster, deprived of the moisture that made them gleam and sparkle . . . Before they reach port they are sick with the putrid odors of all that they've brought on board. They've sapped their strength, exhausted by living in close and rough quarters and by their servile attendance on things that bring them only blight and ruin.

Some die before reaching port. Some arrive sickened and weak. Those who lagged behind to look and sniff but went no further may lack only comfort and space on the journey. Those who got back to the ship without becoming engrossed in any of the objects that accosted the senses, beyond noticing them as needful on first debarking, now in the most spacious and comfortable places, reach their homeland well rested.

Kindī makes no pretense to originality in writing out his prescription. Indeed all the exempla in his essay stem from Greek sources.[11] His byword, drawn from Aristotle, is that one should take truth where one can find it.[12]

Abū Bakr al-Rāzī too, despite his worldly, largely hedonic ethics, takes an Epicurean line, finding that we maximize pleasure by minimizing desire. Like Kindī, he finds his highest good through philosophy, saying that: "One who applies his mind to ideas, probes and thinks for himself is on his way to truth. For our souls are purged of the sludge of this world and freed for the next only by philosophical thinking. If an inquirer engages in philosophy and understands a bit, however little, his soul is cleansed and freed."[13] What then of a philosopher who adheres to a prophetically revealed religion? Rāzī answers: "How could he study philosophy while believing those old wives' tales, founded on contradictions, obdurate ignorance, and dogmatism?"[14] Every human being of normal capacity can think independently, for God's guidance is not confined to some elect elite. Prophetic claims to exclusive audience with God are demonically inspired at best, and their partisans wreak only bloodshed. The ingenuity of craftsmen in solving practical problems plainly shows that if they applied their minds to more speculative questions, they too, like Rāzī, would have gained the insights that would free them from the slough of ignorance. Their lives would

---

[11] Readers may recognize the ship, for instance, from the *Enchiridion* of Epictetus (sec. 7).

[12] See *On First Philosophy*, tr. Ivry, p. 57.

[13] *Munāẓarāt*, tr. L. E. Goodman, in "Rāzī vs Rāzī: Philosophy in the Majlis," in H. Lazarus-Yafeh et al. (eds.) *The Majlis: Interreligious Encounters in Medieval Islam* (Wiesbaden: Harrassowitz, 1999) pp. 90–1.

[14] Ibid., p. 92.

be calmer and more reasonable, and their measure of intellectual independence would win them their portion of immortality.

Rāzī is dismissive of religion – not of God, whom he hopes his soul will rejoin when reasoning has freed it of its earthly trammels, but rather of the pretensions of prophets and their marketers and enforcers. His contemporary al-Fārābī is far more irenic, seeking and finding a place for the rituals, laws, and symbols of scriptural religions. Paradise and Hell, he argues, like creation and resurrection, are poetic tropes. Felicity, as for the other philosophers in the Platonic tradition, is still the mind's linkage with the divine. The virtuous society fosters that end. For its laws, beliefs, symbols, and institutions reflect the lawgiver's wisdom, much as Plato hoped they would once poets pursued truth for its own sake and philosophers found voice for their insights in wise legislation.

Fārābī agrees with Aristotle's teaching that ethical virtues and vices are habits, "established in the soul by sheer repetition" (*Fuṣūl al-madanī* 8). We humans are not born vicious or virtuous – any more than we are born weavers or clerks – although our natural inclinations may predispose us to some particular vice or virtue (ibid., 9). A person wholly disposed toward the virtues, who actually attains them through steady practice, was called divine by the ancients and deemed a city's rightful ruler – in fact, Fārābī writes, the rightful ruler of any city (ibid., 11). Just as a physician guides patients to the proper mean through bodily regimens, the statesman finds a mean in actions, fostering a moderate and balanced character among the populace (ibid., 19; cf. sec. 24). The rightful ruler fosters genuine happiness among his people, pursuing not wealth or honor or sheer domination over others but the virtues of proper statesmanship: self-governance and the promotion of virtuous actions that will solidify as habits, balanced virtues of character (ibid., 27–9). Laws and institutions are critical tools in this regard. So is oratory. Poetry is even more vital to the political art, however, for while rhetoric may yield action through persuasion, poetry – linking a poet's vision with the imagination of his audience – yields a more direct response (ibid., 51).

Imagination can represent not only sensory objects and impressions but also inclinations and emotions, and even concepts (Fārābī, *Perfect State*, IV.14.2, 14.5), including ideas of the highest: "the First Cause, and non-physical things, the heavens, and the noblest and most perfect of sensory objects, such as things of great visible beauty" (ibid., IV.14.6). Receptive to the ideas that emanate from the Active Intellect – the divine hypostasis that informs all things in nature – imagination can clothe them in sensory forms drawn from the images it stores and constructs, yielding veridical dreams and visions, prophetic promptings, and premonitions (ibid., IV.14.7–9). It is this kind of vision that makes possible the kind of philosopher king that Fārābī sees as the ruler of the ideally virtuous

state. Such a man "can be ruled by no other" – at least not rightfully. He will
need to develop the virtues that make for excellence in the art of governance
(IV 15.7). Intellectually, he needs a perfect mind, fully transparent to itself and
informed by every pure idea showered on the mind by the Active Intellect.
Ideally, too, his imagination will work at the highest range of receptivity (ibid.,
IV.15.8), so that it, too, will catch fire, and both mind and imagination will be
invested by the Active Intellect and raised to a higher plane, intellectually and
practically (see Chapter 23). Farabi describes the situation as follows:

> In any man who perfects the passive intellect by grasping every rational idea and becom-
> ing in actuality both thought and thinker, so that what he thinks is the mind he thinks
> by, there arises a mind higher than the passive intellect, stronger and more perfect,
> divorced from matter. This is called the Acquired Intellect. It mediates, without further
> intermediary, between the passive and the Active Intellect... And when this natural
> disposition [our rational capacity] becomes matter for the passive intellect, making it a
> realized mind, and the passive becomes matter for the Acquired, and the Acquired, for
> the Active Intellect, and the whole unites as one, the Active Intellect is indwelling (*halla
> fī-hi*[15]) in that man.
>
> If that affects both parts of his rational faculty, the practical and the speculative,
> and spreads to his imagination, that man is a man inspired: God grants him Revelation
> through the Active Intellect... So, by dint of the emanation his passive intellect receives,
> he becomes wise, a philosopher, a consummate thinker; and by dint of the flow to his
> imagination, a prophet who warns of future events and informs of present facts. This
> man holds the highest rank of humanity and the supreme degree of happiness. His soul
> is united, as it were, with the Active Intellect.
>
> (ibid., V.15.8–11)

So divine an intellect, that of someone who is at once a philosopher and a
visionary, understands every act conducive to human happiness. That is "the
first requisite of a leader" (ibid., V.15.11). But "beyond that, he must have verbal
power, to image ably in words all that he knows and guide people to felicity and
to the actions conducive to it." These criteria set a standard that reaches beyond
the familiar Islamic tests of leadership, grounded in a sound bodily constitution,
fit for the work of war. Fārābī's rightful imam, ruled by no other man, is the
rightful "first head of the virtuous state, the virtuous nation, and indeed, the
entire world!" (ibid., V.15.11).

Not every state or nation will be blessed with a prophet king. So Fārābī
allows for a declension into joint rule and rule by individuals who possess
some but not all of the qualities he seeks in his ideal. Critical in his account,
though, is his founding of the ideal state on receptivity to the pure Ideas shed
by the Active Intellect on the mind of the philosopher and mediated to the

---

[15] The language is Shīʿite, glossed philosophically by Fārābī.

populace by the imagination. Fārābī sets out his ideal in generic terms, giving a cosmopolitan turn to his reading of the ideas of prophecy and statecraft and rendering his model appropriable by others, such as Maimonides. Still, his enthusiasm for the rule of virtue carries a taint of triumphalism when he calls his ideal imam the rightful ruler of the world. That taint is not diminished when Fārābī recasts Aristotle's own triumphalism about the civilizing effects of slavery for erstwhile barbarians, and applies it to the expansion of Islam, suggesting in *On the Attainment of Happiness* that aggressive wars are justified when they aim "to conquer nations and cities that do not submit to doing what will give them the happiness man is made to acquire . . . The warrior who pursues this purpose is the just warrior, and the warfare that pursues this purpose is just and virtuous warfare."[16] Yet despite this aggressive posture, Fārābī rejects mere conquest for the sake of self-aggrandizing aims, and he conceives of happiness in intellectual terms: reason affords the key to self-rule and self-transcendence. Happiness is intellectual fulfillment, and supreme happiness is the union with the Active Intellect that infuses the mind with the all-embracing wisdom that God himself vouchsafes.

Even Miskawayh, perhaps the most worldly of our philosophers – a courtier and minister of state, historian and lover of literature, who believes that *adab*, courtesy, manners, ethics, and refinement can be won through the study of literature and history – grafts a Platonizing pursuit of contemplative fulfillment onto his Aristotelian vision of the active life, guided by practical and social virtues. The fulfilled mind, he writes, at home in the intelligible world, becomes what it knows. Thus, without loss of worldly engagement it becomes a microcosm, repository of the Forms of all things, illuminated by the divine light that imparts bliss, a fountain of wisdom to others, proof against suffering, ready to rise yet higher to the God-like activity that finds its end within itself and is undisturbed by fear of death, which it now sees as the soul's liberation.[17]

Still, an immortality won by engulfing eternal Forms and letting them infuse the mind with their immutability might seem to come too dear. Matter was purged with the loss of the body and letting go of the world, as Plato's account of the soul's liberation seemed to promise (*Theaetetus* 176ab), but was individuality lost as well? Accountability in the hereafter was no longer the issue it had been for many a philosopher. Plato had claimed in the *Republic* that the just man's well-knit soul is more fit for immortality than the distracted, earthly, or scattered

---

[16] *Fī taḥṣīl al-saʿāda* (*On the Attainment of Happiness*), in al-Fārābī, *Philosophy of Plato and Aristotle* tr. M. Mahdī (Ithaca, NY: Cornell University Press, 1962) p. 37. Cf. al-Fārābī, "Le sommaire du livre des 'Lois' de Platon," ed. T. Druart, *Bulletin d'études orientales* 50 (1998) p. 126.

[17] See Majid Fakhry, *Ethical Theories in Islam* (Leiden: Brill, 1994) pp. 119–21.

souls of the tyrant, hedonist, or democrat. That morally grounded argument also bolstered the *Phaedo*'s appeal to the kinship of minds to the ideas they hold. Medieval intellectualists gave little thought to tales of retribution, however; the unmindful, they reasoned, would meet their fitting end in failure to escape the body's dissolution. Bound to the earth by their desires and appetites, they would naturally miss the sailing of their ship and lose the chance of reunion with their ultimate source. As for the philosopher, his rational soul would dissolve in the divine, from which it sprang. But was the rational soul that merged with the divine still in any sense the same person it once was? True, it was his highest, most divine self. But was it still he? This question is soft-pedaled in philosophers like Kindī and Rāzī; Fārābī does his best to finesse it, but his varied answers sound equivocal to later writers like Ibn Ṭufayl. Still the issue remained: if immortality is won by the realization of the soul's affinity to Forms that are, after all, universals, how could what survives be an individual?[18] (See Chapter 34.)

To Avicenna, the immortality worth wanting was personal. The challenge was to show how individuality survives the body. His answer lay in the idea of intensionality. Personal history, begun in our embodiment, could outlast the body, for consciousness did not imply physicality. One could readily conceive oneself aware while afloat, sensationless, in the cosmos. Thus, thoughts of thinking entailed no posit of a body (see Chapter 23).[19] The idea that individuation might depend on self-awareness, not embodiment, was taken up by Ghazālī, Ibn Bājja, Ibn Ṭufayl, Maimonides, and Levi ben Gershom. It proved invaluable even to Spinoza and Leibniz. But the immortality it promised would still look rather bloodless to many a Muslim, Christian, or Jew. Intellectualism, in the end, seemed to set happiness at too great a remove from the world.

Hence the reaction from literalists like the Zāhiriyya, the movement founded in the ninth century by Dāwūd ibn Khalaf and brought to fruition in the eleventh century by traditionalists like Ibn Ḥazm. They take the eschatological promises and threats of Scripture far more literally than did the Platonizing philosophers, even as they press for more worldly visions of romance, keen to sunder divine from earthly love and to purge piety of erotic antinomianism and pantheistic yearnings.[20] Theologians like Ash'arī expect the orthodox to "confess that the Garden is real and the Fire is real," that "the Hour is surely coming," that "God will raise the dead from their graves" – and that God has a

---

[18] See Philip Merlan, *Monopsychism, Mysticism, and Metaconsciousness* (The Hague: Nijhoff, 1963).

[19] See Lenn Goodman, *Avicenna* (Ithaca, NY: Cornell University Press, 2006) ch. 3.

[20] See Lois Giffen, *Theory of Profane Love among the Arabs* (New York: New York University Press, 1971); J. N. Bell, *Love Theory in Later Hanbalite Islam* (Albany: State University of New York Press, 1979); Lenn Goodman, *Islamic Humanism* (New York: Oxford University Press, 2003) pp. 61–6.

face, two hands, two eyes, and a throne on which He sits, "not asking how."[21] Authoritative creeds will insist on a real scale on which deeds are weighed, and they will not give up the dark-eyed maidens promised to the blessed in the Quran – or the interrogation in the grave by the angels Nakir and Munkar, the "torment in the tomb." Salvation, the creeds will say, rests on grace, for God guides or abandons whom he will.[22] Mystics will seek pathways of their own toward grace, seeking direct contact with God, and visions of the furniture and architecture of his kingdom, using ascetic, ecstatic, or antinomian exercises, not sheerly intellectual contemplation. An orthodox spirit like Ghazālī finds in intuition answers to the questions he still frames cognitively. Sufi praxis, he avows, affords a "taste" of divinity that dissolves all doubts.

Ḥasdai Crescas, the fourteenth-century Jewish philosopher, responds to the intellectualist tradition by locating human fulfillment not in knowledge but in fear and (reciprocated) love of God. Thus, fulfillment of God's commandments has intrinsic and not just instrumental value. Man is not the same as his mind, and the philosophers' coy promises of intellectual contact with the divine are deluded. The "Acquired Intellect" is an incoherent notion, riven between immanence in the soul and its purported free-standing hypostatic reality. Yet Crescas, too, pays tribute in a way to the intellectualism he spurns. For the love of God, and its counterpart in fear of God, like the prayer bouts and spiritual feats of fakirs and mendicants, were still meant as ways of bringing the transcendent into human lives. If the love and fear that Crescas commends were found in ethical and ritual adherence to God's commandments, were they not still, as the philosophers contended, ways of linking with God – putting the mind in touch with him, and thereby bearing one's soul upward, toward his transcendence? Who knows, perhaps even one's body is borne along with the soul – and if one's body, why not one's friends?

[21] See al-Ashʿarī, "Two Creeds," in *Kitāb al-Lumaʿ*, ed. McCarthy, pp. 236–7.
[22] The documents are translated in A. J. Wensinck, *The Muslim Creed: Its Genesis and Historical Development* (Cambridge: Cambridge University Press, 1932) pp. 129–31, 194–6.

34

IDENTITY AND MORAL AGENCY

MIKKO YRJÖNSUURI

As moral agents, people are disposed to act for the sake of what they judge to be morally good. Modern philosophers have often considered such a disposition to be in opposition to another disposition, called "self-interest." In the Middle Ages, however, moral action was often – or even usually – thought to agree with one's own genuine best interests. In effect, all medieval thinkers based their theory of action on the fundamentally Aristotelian principle that human beings are rational agents aiming at the fulfillment of their own nature, guided by judgments about what is good for them – a principle that had been generally accepted even in other ancient philosophical schools. In the medieval period, the most philosophically interesting debates concerned different understandings of this principle rather than its validity. Medieval philosophers fundamentally disagreed about what human persons are as moral agents, and thus they also disagreed concerning the nature of self-interest and its relation to morality.

In particular, medieval philosophers recognized that Aristotle's eudaimonistic principle is philosophically vague in at least two ways. First, the connection between this principle and ethical judgments is in need of an explanation. Does this principle describe the ultimate foundation of morality? Or does it describe individual self-interest as something that is fundamentally distinct from the moral perspective? In other words, is aiming at what is good *for oneself* the same as aiming at what is good *morally*, or is there some other (external) ground for moral goodness? Second, the principle looks vague from another direction because it needs to be grounded on a specific theory of the self. What is the self that acts as a moral agent? Is it the bodily human individual, a psychophysical being that needs food and shelter? Is it an incorporeal soul distinct from the body? Is it some kind of abstract immaterial universal principle that all humans share equally? Accordingly, should we seek our fulfillment in terms of individual or universal good? As we shall see, each of these viewpoints was taken by medieval philosophers, who thus ended up having very different understandings of the Aristotelian principle.

This chapter limits itself to three core issues. The first relates to the problem of our constitution as moral agents: *what are we?* According to the general picture shared by practically all the late ancient and medieval schools, human selves lie in between the corporeal and the intellectual realms, where the intellectual realm that lies above individuation is the ethically higher one. For this reason, classical Neoplatonic thought accounted for moral development as elevation towards the intelligible realm and away from corporeality. The Neoplatonic discovery of one's own real self was a turn away from the particularities of worldly life toward what is universal. In the Middle Ages, a heated discussion arose concerning whether moral development requires one to overcome one's own individual identity in such a manner, with philosophers in both the Arabic and Latin traditions generally holding to the negative. Intellectuality and individuality thus had to be brought to cohere in new theories of the human self, as this chapter will consider through the theories of Avicenna and Averroes.

Second, most medieval thinkers understood morality in terms of self-control, following the ancient tradition.[1] Acting morally was identified as governing oneself in the best way in a given situation. Often, but not always, this entailed suppressing the behavioral impulses of the emotions under rational command. In many cases, however, medieval authors recognized that good self-governance does not always go hand in hand with rationality. That is, they called into question the classical identification of the self-controlling moral agent with an ideally rational agent. As medieval authors often thought, even rationality has its limits, and it is not the case that the wisest human is always the morally best one. When authors like Boethius of Dacia suggested that wisdom is the highest goal of a happy human life, they were promptly rejected.

The limits of rationality become even more obvious in the third and last of the discussions to be considered here. By the late thirteenth century, Latin authors began to question the moral motivation for self-sacrifice. Many of them wanted to remain faithful to their ancient sources and show that, on the final analysis, even self-sacrifice must be motivated by what one believes to be one's own authentic best interests in the circumstances. Some authors, however – most prominently John Duns Scotus – defended what would become a distinctively modern view: that acting rationally means acting for one's own individual best interests, but that this may in some cases – as in the case of morally well-founded self-sacrifice – conflict with what one ought to do. Morality is, in the end, superior to rationality.

---

[1] See, e.g., Simo Knuuttila, *Emotions in Ancient and Medieval Philosophy* (Oxford: Clarendon Press, 2004) esp. pp. 111–76; Richard Sorabji, *Emotion and Peace of Mind* (Oxford: Oxford University Press, 2000) pp. 159–349.

WHAT ARE WE?

In *Alcibiades I*, a Platonic dialogue if not by Plato himself, Socrates argues that a human person ought to understand himself as a soul using the body as an instrument for acting in the world and for interacting with other people (see esp. 130a–31a). In the Neoplatonic tradition, the idea that the body is an *instrumentum* (in Latin) or an *organon* (in Greek) is described as the true Platonic position.[2] In his *De anima* (413a8–9), Aristotle mentions this position in a manner that has often been understood as approving of it – but, in fact, his main argument runs against central tenets of the Platonic position as it has been understood since the Neoplatonic era. Aristotle denies, for instance, that the soul is a thing separable from the rest of the human being in the way the heart is. In his view, the soul–body union ought to be understood in terms of the more general form–matter union; just as forms are not (independently existing particular) *things*, neither is the soul a *thing* in its own right (see Chapter 21). Thus, one should identify oneself with the soul–body composite – indeed, there is no other thing that one could identify oneself with. As a practical agent, then, one ought not to identify oneself as a soul, but as a full, embodied person.

In the medieval period, Avicenna (whose *Liber de anima* [from the *Shifāʾ*] was widely used in both East and West) gave the Platonic position its most influential formulation among both Arabic and Latin authors. The core of Avicenna's theory is that, as a moral agent, I ought to understand myself as an incorporeal, immortal thing that has a particular relation to one particular corporeal object – namely, the human body that is mine. For Avicenna, it is important to understand that the soul is a thing distinct from the body, a thing whose existence is not dependent on that of the body. He knows of theories where the soul is taken to be a separable bodily part of a human being, consisting of subtle matter of a different kind from the rest of the body,[3] but he rejects this model on the grounds that, as human persons, we are in a very special way present both to ourselves and to the whole intelligible world. Such self-presence is not to be found in the material world, however. Ultimately, we are things of a very special kind: immaterial individuals.[4]

---

[2] See, e.g., *Enneads* IV.7.1; for wider discussion see Simplicius, *In Epicteti Enchiridion* 8, comm. 14. To the late ancient Platonists it was, however, important to emphasize that the rational soul does not need the body for its proper operations: see, e.g., Simplicius (?), *In De anima,* ed. Hayduck, p. 96, commenting on *De an.* 413a8–9.

[3] The notion that the soul is a bodily particle of especial subtlety (*laṭīfa*) was prevalent among the *kalām* Muslim theologians: see al-Ashʿarī, *Maqālāt al-islāmiyyīn,* ed. Ritter, pp. 329–37.

[4] Avicenna presents his well-known "Flying Man" thought experiment (see Chapter 23) to exhibit if not prove the difference between the self and the body, and in this sense there clearly is some similarity to Descartes's *cogito* argument (see *Liber de anima* [*Shifāʾ*] I.1, ed. Rahman, p. 16; ed. Van Riet, pp. 36–7). For discussion and further references, see Michael Marmura, "Avicenna's

Despite this view, which emphasizes our distinction from other animals, Avicenna follows Aristotle in his general metaphysical theory, including the idea that matter is the principle of individuation for most things in the world.[5] Indeed, he thinks that no other animal is a soul in the same way that human beings are: for plants and non-human animals he seems to accept the Aristotelian position that the soul is merely the form of the living substance. The only way to distinguish between the soul and body in these cases is to distinguish between form and matter, where the form is a universal principle. Both plant and animal souls exist as separate from their bodies only as universal denizens of the intelligible world: only human souls can have individual existence even in a disembodied state.[6] Avicenna seems to think that even the sense in which non-human animals can be said to act as unified moral agents must be different from the human case. For us, it is the self-presence of the soul to itself that makes us unified agents capable of controlling different impulses coming from different directions. Since other animals have no such capacity and thus are merely bodily things, their self-conception is by necessity bodily, and thus also the nature of their individual agency is different.[7]

Avicenna's picture suffers from a deep metaphysical problem, however, given that he is working in a broadly Aristotelian framework. It is a fundamental principle of Aristotelian metaphysics that individuality and change stem from materiality.[8] Thus, if the soul is incorporeal, how can it be individual? That is, how could I myself be an individual moral agent if I am incorporeal and merely using a corporeal body? Would it not rather be the body that is the individual agent? Avicenna's general answer to these problems leans on admitting that even human individuality originates in corporeality, or having a body. However, when the soul is separated from the body at death, it continues to exist as an individual. As regards this time, further problems arise. Will the incorporeal soul be capable of *single* actions (even mental acts, understood as individuated events involving change), or will its actuality be limited to eternal and unchanging contemplation of intelligible things without any real agency? Avicenna does hold that separated souls are genuine individuals in virtue of

'Flying Man' in Context," *The Monist* 69 (1986) 383–95, and Jari Kaukua, *Avicenna on Subjectivity: A Philosophical Study* (Jyväskylä: University of Jyväskylä, 2007) pp. 71ff.

5 See Michael E. Marmura, "Avicenna's Chapter on Universals in the Isagoge of his Shifāʾ," in A. T. Welch and P. Cachia (eds.) *Islam: Past Influence and Present Challenge* (Edinburgh: Edinburgh University Press, 1979) 34–56.

6 For the distinction between the two types of soul, see *De anima* (*Shifāʾ*) I.1; for the incorporeality of the human soul, see ibid., V.2.

7 See ibid. V.7, ed. Rahman, pp. 253–4, 256–7; Van Riet, pp. 158–9, 164–5.

8 For individuation through matter see Aristotle, *Metaph.* VII.8, 1034a5–8, as well as Averroes's commentary (*In Metaph.* VII.28) and Alexander of Aphrodisias, *Quaestiones* I.3.

their own intellectual characteristics and that they even exist as agents capable of their own individual intellectual action, but the story is too complex to go into details here (see Chapter 23). Instead, let us turn to Averroes, who seems to have bitten the bullet and accepted that, even in the case of the human soul and its mental acts, individuality requires materiality.

Averroes does not deny that human beings are capable of reaching the incorporeal realm of intelligibility or that this is the highest capacity we have. He also holds that human beings are the only animals who possess the power for understanding the universal natures of things. Despite these views, however, he does not think that the human soul differs from that of other animals in being an incorporeal entity; he holds instead that we reach the intelligible realm as bodily beings. According to Averroes, the soul is not a *thing*, it is the *form* of the animal. In human beings this form somehow yields access to something even higher than the bodily functions – namely, the incorporeal power of understanding. This power, however, is not a part of the human soul.

With respect to Aristotle's distinction between two intellects, active and potential, Averroes agrees with Avicenna that active intellect lies above individuality and acts on the potential intellect to produce understanding. With respect to the potential intellect, however, they hold different views, because Avicenna allowed that the potential intellect is individualized in each person and that each person has his or her own individual power to understand. Averroes, in contrast, thinks that as individuals we are material, but that as intellectual beings we do not differ from each other. Rather, we all share the same power of understanding (see Chapter 23).

In the Latin tradition, Averroes's claim was often misunderstood to different degrees. Importantly, Averroes does not claim that the shared active and potential intellect amount to anything like a human soul: there is no single shared soul in such a sense, and the intellect we all share is not metaphysically an individual – it is not like being logged onto one and the same central computer with one CPU. Even Averroes thought we think our thoughts ourselves.[9] He seems to be claiming only that, as soul–body composites, we share intellectual powers and contents with other people, although we of course may happen to think different thoughts at any given time. Thinking about the number two, we think

---

[9] This is, however, a point that medieval Latin authors emphasize more than Averroes. Aquinas, for instance, refers to how we experience our thoughts to be our own and not anyone else's – that by which I think must, therefore, be my own individual intellect (*Summa theol.* 1a 76.1). Ockham, for his part, claims to refute the Averroistic theory of the intellect by referring to disagreements between people, which could not exist if all beliefs were contained in the same subject (*Quodlibet* I.11). Both of these arguments seem to assume that the shared intellect is an individual like us.

about the same content with the same power, but it may of course happen that my thought with its particular phantasms located in my brain (see Chapter 22) occurs at a time different from the time at which you think about the number. In some sense, Averroes may have thought that really understanding the number is something that happens in us rather than something we do. Nevertheless, there is no reason to suppose that Averroes believes I am being acted on by any special, intellectual thinking thing. Instead, he seems to have thought of the human soul on all of its levels as a form of the body. Thus, while Avicenna bound personal identity to the soul in its immortal incorporeality, Averroes bound it to embodiment: we are those things we are as bodily beings. The two authors thus have different views on how exactly to identify the moral agent that each of us is.

The view that the body contributes to our nature as persons has broad roots within medieval thought. In the Galenic medical tradition that dominated the whole medieval period, for instance, the character of a person was explained through different balances of the bodily fluids. Being melancholic, for example, was thought to consist of having black bile as the dominant fluid.[10] Biological sex was also thought to be fundamentally a bodily characteristic, and it deserves mention that central authors in the Christian tradition argued that sex is so crucial to human character that, even after the bodily resurrection, our new, perfect bodies will be sexed.[11]

Different medieval theories embrace to different degrees the idea that qualitative personality derives from the body and its history in the corporeal world. Despite his assertion that we are incorporeal souls, even Avicenna accepted to some degree that this is so. As separated souls we are by necessity very similar to each other; indeed, separated souls seem to differ on his theory only in terms of what they intellectually know. Thus, despite their numerical distinctness, there is little that qualitatively differentiates one soul from another. Knowledge is acquired during an embodied life, moreover, and thus differences between separated souls depend indirectly on differences between embodied souls. To go back to the Platonic example, captains of ships would not, on this theory, differ qualitatively at their origins. Rather, differences between the captains would build up from their having to steer a particular ship. Briefly put, they will learn different things during their careers. According to Avicenna, with respect

---

[10] See Noga Arikha, *Passions and Tempers: A History of the Humours* (New York: Ecco, 2007).

[11] The Origenists defended a stronger distinction between earthly and heavenly bodies and opposed this view. For discussion and references, see Caroline Walker Bynum, *The Resurrection of the Body in Western Christianity 200–1336* (New York: Columbia University Press, 1995) pp. 37–8, 67, 74–5, 90–1.

to our inner nature, we are all similar, but due to our individual histories of life, as well as to our particular psychological natures explained by our bodily constitutions, we develop intellectually in different degrees and directions, thus becoming distinct even as separated souls.

Within the Christian camp, the philosophical discussions of the thirteenth century led to the position that who a person is – and thereby also moral responsibility – is to be tied primarily to the soul rather than the body. It became generally accepted that after death God could make a new body for a person but not a new soul, as the soul is what the person is and its replacement would bring about a new person. Some sort of bodily continuity from earth to heaven was still seen as required for personal identity, however, and so the doctrine of bodily resurrection remained in place.[12] Interestingly enough, Augustine had already considered the bodily characteristics each of us would have at the resurrection. He thought that the body's qualitative distinguishing features should and would survive, like the look of the face, sexual organs reflecting sexual identity, scars reflecting martyrdom, and other such things, but that the physical body will, as a whole, be made better in heaven. Following in this tradition, mainstream Christian authors accepted the position that we are not mere souls but have bodies by necessity, and bodies of a very particular kind. Origen's idea that, after the resurrection, we have the perfect shape of a ball never reappeared in later discussions.[13] The opposition between Plato and Aristotle, concerning whether we are souls or ensouled bodies, was never really resolved, however; indeed, in modern conceptions of personal identity we still carry both the intuition that we are psychological selves and the intuition that we are bodily beings.

SELF-CONTROL

The condemnation of 1277 (see Chapter 8) addresses a large number of issues related to identity and moral agency: any reader of this document notices that the psychological constitution of a human being was one of the hottest topics of the time. The Platonic metaphor that the soul is in the body like the helmsman in his ship is forbidden (prop. 7), but so is the Aristotelian extreme, that the

[12] See Christina Van Dyke, "Metaphysical Amphibians: Aquinas on the Individuation and Identity of Human Beings" (Ph.D. dissertation: Cornell University, 2000); Robert Pasnau, *Thomas Aquinas on Human Nature* (Cambridge: Cambridge University Press, 2002) ch. 12.
[13] Origen's view is documented in Justinian's letter to the patriarch Menas and in Methodius, *De resurrectione* 3.7.1–7; it seems to take inspiration from the commentary tradition on Plato's *Timaeus* 41d–e, where the stars become the vehicles for the newly crafted rational souls. For discussion see, e.g., Henry Chadwick, "Origen, Celsus, and the Resurrection of the Body," *Harvard Theological Review* 41 (1948) esp. pp. 95ff. For wider historical perspectives, see Bynum, *Resurrection of the Body*.

soul is inseparable from the body (prop. 116). The same pattern can be seen in doctrines concerning moral responsibility – the condemnation prohibits a wide array of views that limit human freedom and a person's accountability for his or her own actions. The interest of the church in this document was to counter any philosophical teaching to the effect that mentally healthy, normal adult persons are not free and do not possess moral responsibility for the majority of their actions.

One ongoing discussion at the time concerned the loss of self-control in madness and in the face of strong emotions. It was generally agreed that mental disorder might interfere with moral responsibility: mad people are not to be held responsible for what they do, and such loss of responsibility has to be accepted.[14] But the condemnation draws a line and prohibits the view that emotions can be so strong as to amount to compulsion (prop. 136), or that right action would have to wait until the passion loses its grip (prop. 129). On the other hand, the authorities force everyone to admit that sexual pleasures may impede mental powers, although not excusing one from moral responsibility in the process (prop. 172). It is noteworthy that such propositions come on the list along with those prohibiting astrological explanations (props. 132, 161, and 162), which might give an excuse from one's own responsibility, and that they are complemented by others that prohibit deterministic accounts of nature. Even the view that reasoning may compel one to do something is forbidden. As the condemnation has it, the will is not necessitated by knowledge (prop. 159), nor is it bound to proceed to action after the conclusion in a practical syllogism has been reached (prop. 158).

The propositions listed in the condemnation provide a good overview of the philosophical topics that were taken to be of real importance by the end the thirteenth century, and to some extent in medieval philosophy more generally. One such topic was how to account for the psychological mechanisms behind human agency; perhaps the most distinctive feature of thirteenth-century discussions is the way in which they account for self-control. Classical authors had earlier grappled with the problem of bringing the emotions under rational control, and medieval authors leaned on this tradition (see Chapter 31). Many authors in the Arabic tradition appear to have been relatively satisfied with the idea that reason needs no further control, since it is the highest and best part of human nature – the part that should be in control rather than controlled.[15]

---

[14] See, e.g., Henry of Ghent's discussion of "lunatic fury" (*furia lunatica*) that necessitates a person to bad actions; moral responsibility is even here connected to the freedom of the will (*Quodlibet* III.26).

[15] On the side of the theologians see, e.g., al-Ghazālī, *Al-maqsad* (*On the Beautiful Names of God*), ed. Shehadi, pp. 74, 86.

The condemnation of 1277 shows that, even among thirteenth-century Latin authors, there were those who believed that the best life is gained through the intellectual virtues; Boethius of Dacia, for instance, takes this position in his *De summo bono*.[16] At the same time, many other thinkers insisted that the best sort of human life is not just a life of wisdom. Thus, people need to exercise self-control even in the realm of reason and rationality.

Many thirteenth-century authors claim that the faculty of will can – and should – control the intellect, thus casting the requirement that reason must be controlled in terms of a theory of the will. Peter of John Olivi, for example, makes it clear that the will is higher than reason in all relevant respects: the will can choose between different ultimate aims or even suggest new ones at any time, the will can opt for different means for achieving any given aim, and the will can simply choose to do a certain action without any rational support. To make the point even more clearly to his contemporaries, Olivi claims that when the mind has reached the conclusion of an Aristotelian practical syllogism, the will is still free to choose any other line of action – a choice that need not imply weakness of the will, but rather strength of will in the face of rationality (*Summa* II.85–6).[17]

Although the classical heritage behind medieval views on self-control seems to lie in Stoic thought, the major novelty in medieval philosophy is that self-control does not and should not necessarily rely on rationality. Among both Islamic and Christian philosophers, the primary aim in controlling oneself is to remain good and faithful to God; the aim is not directly that of remaining rational, as it was among the Stoics.

SELF-INTEREST AND RATIONALITY

Individuality, rationality, and morality were brought together in an especially interesting way in certain late thirteenth-century discussions concerning the question of what could motivate a person to die for his nation. Or, as the more exact formulation of the problem goes: what could be the motivation for such an act, and could there be any motivation at all for a person who has no hope for eternal salvation? Could the moral worth of an action be high enough to motivate one last good choice? Or could the good of the nation be an important enough consideration?

---

[16] The first set of seven condemned propositions concerns this issue. According to the first, for instance, "there is no more excellent state than to study philosophy" (ed. D. Piché, *La condamnation parisienne de 1277* [Paris: Vrin, 1999]).

[17] See also *Summa* II.57 ad 13 (ed. Jansen, II: 356): "Howsoever much the understanding both universally and particularly considers and actually knows . . . still the will can do whatever."

In general, this discussion assumes both that such an action is indubitably the morally correct choice and that it is fatally bad for the individual. Also, it is assumed that human agents are driven by the Aristotelian striving for happiness. However, in a case like this, referring to such motivations appears to amount to claiming that death could foster one's own happiness. How could that be? Three main solutions are put forward.

1. Godfrey of Fontaines claims that individual life has a lesser value than the common good for a rationally behaving person. The hero feels so strongly a part of the whole that he actually sees himself benefiting from the action that ends with his death; he sacrifices his individual good for the good of the whole because he is, very importantly, a part of the whole.[18] The discussion refers back to the ancient metaphor of society as an organic whole where individuals are like limbs. As Godfrey of Fontaines interprets the metaphor, the limb aims in a way at its own best interests when it tries to protect the whole at its own individual expense, because the best for the part is whatever is best for the whole. Godfrey does understand that most of the nation is outside the individual, and in this sense he accepts that in self-sacrifice the individual is aiming at something that must be seen as an extrinsic good in a sense. However, it is extrinsic only to the individual, not to the whole whose part he is. In this sense, Godfrey of Fontaines emphasizes, "his own best good results" (tr. McGrade, p. 306).

This suggestion can be labeled "collectivist." Self-interest can motivate self-sacrifice only if it is accompanied by a conception of the greater collective self whose interest is to be served. From the collectivist viewpoint, the self whose interest a rationally behaving person serves is the whole nation. (This also is the formulation given by Remigio de' Girolami some decades later when he says that in such a sacrifice the person takes the nation as his own self.[19])

2. Henry of Ghent objects to this way of looking at the situation by pointing out that if the limb in the mentioned metaphor had its own mind, it would not make the choice to sacrifice itself for the whole.[20] His approach is more individualistic; he thinks that every person with his or her own mind is a self for himself or herself. If we do all have our own minds, however, then it appears that no one will have a sufficiently strong collectivist self-understanding as to give his life for his nation. As Henry of Ghent sees it, such heroic acts must

---

[18] See *Quodlibet* X.6 and XIII.1, both translated in A. S. McGrade *et al.*, *Cambridge Translations of Medieval Philosophical Texts*, vol. II: Ethics and Political Philosophy (Cambridge: Cambridge University Press, 2001) pp. 271–84 and 301–6; see esp. pp. 305–6.

[19] See M. S. Kempshall, *The Common Good in Late Medieval Political Thought* (Oxford: Clarendon Press, 1999).

[20] *Quodlibet* XII.13, translated in McGrade *et al.*, *Cambridge Translations* II: 267.

arise from individualistic considerations. The person may think, for instance, that vice must be avoided at all costs. Thus, if he does not give his life, then the badness of the undone deed will follow him, and he will not be able to enjoy virtuous life anymore. Heroic death, in contrast, will make everyone remember him in an honorific way. In taking this approach, Henry of Ghent follows the Aristotelian (and even more generally ancient) thinking that morally good choices are always in one's own best interests.[21]

Despite their different conceptions of the self, these two approaches share the classical presumption that there are no motivational forces besides self-interest: the explanation for why a person sacrifices his life and everything he has must be self-interest, because there are no other psychological motivations. Even heroic virtue derives from self-interest, assuming the person has a correct self-understanding and can see what is best for himself.

3. Franciscan authors of the time think differently. On their view, human freedom is wide enough to allow the possibility of recognizing other ultimate ends besides one's own happiness, even when that happiness has been clearly identified. Some, most prominently John Duns Scotus, invoke the Anselmian distinction between affection for benefit and affection for justice (see Chapter 35). On this view, a person acting only for happiness does not rise to the moral level at all, for ethics depends on valuing the affection for justice. Other Franciscans, like Olivi, even hold that there are no restrictions on what one can posit to oneself as an ultimate end (*Summa* II.57 ad 28, ed. Jansen, II: 376). As a typical example of an ultimate end that is freely chosen, he mentions other people: in loving a person, one freely chooses to take that person and what is best for her as ends in themselves, and indeed without any other motivation whatsoever.

In general, the Franciscans agree that all human beings have a natural tendency to act for their own individual best interests. This is not, however, what morality consists in. Rather, human beings are free to strive for other ultimate ends, and moral ends are one such category. Although human beings have the capability to be moral, this would not necessarily be in their own individual best interests. This is the line of thought that Scotus, for instance, follows in his explanation of self-sacrifice (*Ordinatio* III.27). His idea is that a person chooses to put the welfare of society as an end in itself, and even a higher end than his own best interests. Thus, in his choice, he is knowingly and willingly acting against his own good.

---

[21] Aristotle considers the case in *Nic. Ethics* IX.8, 1169a18–20 and III.6, 1115a24–b7. Henry's remarks come very close to what Aristotle says in the latter text.

Scotus seems to have thought that such a choice is rationally motivated, but it is clear here that he does not understand practical rationality in a genuinely Aristotelian way. What we have is the contrast between rationality as leading one to act for one's own good, and morality as leading one to act as one should according to eternal or natural law. In extreme cases, morality may require one to act against what rationally would be one's individual best interests.

35

THE INCLINATION FOR JUSTICE

JOHN BOLER

Ancient philosophers had a well-equipped repertory of descriptions for human activity, but it was only after Augustine that thinkers, especially in the Latin West, adopted an explicit concept of the will. This allowed them, for better or for worse, to set out a good portion of their philosophical psychology in terms of the interaction of intellect and will (see Chapter 30). Toward the end of the eleventh century, Anselm proposed a distinction *within* the will between an "inclination for justice" and an "inclination for benefit." An agent's "every merit, whether good or evil," he says, derives from one of these two basic inclinations (*De concordia* III.12). Two centuries later, citing Anselm, John Duns Scotus adopts the labels but, as we shall see, develops a significantly distinctive account. Pairings of this general sort can be found in ancient philosophy (and will be discussed briefly below), but the developed idea of dual basic inclinations of the will is probably unique to Anselm and Scotus. But while explicit appeal to inclinations of the will is thus rare, the issues raised here by Anselm and Scotus are central even nowadays in the analysis of moral psychology (as in debates about the nature of the moral object or the status of free will) as well as in moral theology (on sin and grace).

ANSELM

Justice is a central concept in Anselm's moral theory, and it appears in all his writings. In several works – *De casu diaboli* (*The Fall of the Devil*) and *De concordia* – he considers justice in the context of the two basic inclinations of the will. In an earlier dialogue, *De veritate*, he takes up directly the more fundamental question with which we should begin, the question of what justice is.

Anselm's basic notion when dealing with normative issues is *rectitudo* or rightness.[1] At one point, Anselm says that truth, rightness, and justice are

---

[1] See *De veritate, passim.* As Jasper Hopkins remarks in his useful guide to Anselm's work in general: "Anselm will attempt to show that every instance of truth is an instance of rightness. He investigates

484

defined in terms of one another. The student objects that we do not speak of the justice of a stone. But Anselm replies only with a distinction: "I see you are asking for a definition of that justice that is praiseworthy, even as its opposite – that is, injustice – is blameworthy." The implication is that he does not object to speaking of the justice of the stone! But it is typical of Anselm to adapt ordinary words as technical terms: here, to situate the notion of justice he has in mind, he restricts the notion to that justice that is praiseworthy. Consequently, the teacher and student in the dialogue set about the analysis of "that justice," concluding that it is rightness of the will maintained for its own sake: that is, not willed out of ignorance or because of coercion, or for any other end (for instance, vainglory).[2]

Jasper Hopkins, presumably concerned that Anselm's definition might seem to locate moral value in the will to the exclusion of the action involved, glosses it as "willing what is right only because it is right (i.e., always willing it for no other reason than that it is right)."[3] And Anselm does say that "whoever does not will what he ought to will is not just" (*De veritate* 12).[4] That is, he is willing to describe actions as morally right or wrong, good or bad, and to figure that into the evaluation of the agent's rightness of will. But he is equally insistent that "Every rational nature, as well as any of its actions, is called just or unjust in accordance with a just or unjust will" (*De concordia* I.7). What this reflects, however, is not a suspicious voluntarism on Anselm's part, as if he were a forerunner of Peter Abaelard's exclusive focus on the will's consent as the locus of moral value (see Chapter 37). Instead, this is what one might call a "grammatical remark" that need start no moral hares. Nowadays we may think of justice primarily in connection with kinds of action. But Anselm would not be unusual in his time in thinking of a kind of justness that is a "virtue of the soul." That is, for Anselm, the proper subject of "is just" or "has justice," as he means it here, is a person, an agent with reason and will.

If justice is uprightness of will kept for its own sake, Anselm points out, then we are dealing not only with what a person ought to do – he seems to take pretty much for granted that his readers can make that judgment – but more importantly with the *reason* the agent performs the action (*De veritate* 12). The approach he takes here parallels the one in which we can repeatedly ask, "Why is the agent doing that?", eventually arriving at the allegedly basic motive: "Because (he thinks) it will be to his benefit" or alternately "Because it will

correct statements, right thoughts, upright willing, righteous action, correct perception, the straightness of a material object, and the rightness of all natures" (*A Companion to the Study of St. Anselm* [Minneapolis: University of Minnesota Press, 1972], p. 231 n. 5).

[2] *De veritate* 12. It is "the truth of the will": *De veritate* 4.

[3] Hopkins, *Companion*, p. 232 n. 8.   [4] See also *De veritate* 5.

make him happy." Anselm thinks that his analysis of justice shows that we need
to recognize another basic inclination. In sum, we can determine what an action
is – correctly describing it as, say, theft or almsgiving – and evaluate it as good or
bad, simply in terms of the kind of action it is, but we do not fully understand
the moral situation until we know ultimately why the action is done: that is,
is it done for benefit (to achieve one's perceived advantage), or is it done to
maintain rightness of the will for its own sake? As Anselm says, an agent's "every
merit, whether good or evil," derives from one of these two basic inclinations
(*De concordia* III.12).

One might expect that dual basic inclinations would have a similar structure,
but Anselm takes pains to show how radically different they are (ibid.). To have
the inclination for justice, he says, is to have justice (to be just). Since one can,
as the devil did, "desert" justice, it follows that one can lose the inclination
for justice; once lost, Anselm says, creatures cannot recover it on their own,
but require the grace of God.[5] By way of contrast, Anselm holds that the
inclination for benefit is "natural" for rational creatures and so cannot be lost.
It is an inclination to *seek* benefit, and Anselm maintains we always act on that
inclination (*De casu diaboli* 12). This is a matter of self-interest, of course, though
that is not the same as selfishness. For the most part, the inclination for benefit
will have to do with actions that are, in themselves, morally neutral; thus, there
is no necessary conflict between seeking benefit and acting justly. It is clear that
Anselm is thinking as well of the inclination for benefit in the broader sense
of a flourishing human life. Even here, however, the only source for conflict
Anselm sees between the two inclinations would be if we have an inadequate
idea of where our true or ultimate benefit lies.

We learn something more about the role of these basic inclinations of the
will in *De casu diaboli*, though Anselm assumes there that the reader is already
familiar with his account of justice and with the idea of basic inclinations. His
labels sometimes vary – he will speak of an inclination for rightness (*voluntas rec-
titudinis*) and more frequently an inclination for happiness (*voluntas beatitudinis*) –
but the doctrines are the same as with justice and benefit.[6] The central issue

---

[5] That the inclination for justice can be lost, see *De concordia* III.12. On the need for God's grace, see
note 9 below.

[6] *De casu diaboli* 12 and 13. In the *De casu diaboli*, he speaks of a "will" for justice and for benefit or
sometimes happiness (see especially chs. 12 and 13), but later in *De concordia* III.11 he recognizes
that his use of *voluntas* is equivocal: sometimes meaning the instrument for willing (i.e., the will),
sometimes the exercise of that instrument (individual acts of willing), and sometimes the inclinations
of the will (*affectiones*). Scotus follows the mature usage, referring to an *affectio iustitiae* and an *affectio
commode/beatitudine* (see note 12 below).

here is how good creatures can go bad.[7] The devil provides a pure case of doing evil because he is not given to intellectual mistakes nor swayed by passion. Something the same can be said of prelapsarian Adam and Eve, due to their preternatural properties – properties that were lost to the rest of us because of the Fall.

Anselm proposes a thought experiment in which God creates an angel step by step, first providing it with a will and then equipping it with one or the other basic inclination (*De casu diaboli* 13–14). This is a pure fiction, of course, and it is hard to imagine what such half-finished creatures would be like if they existed. Anselm's point is that such a partially equipped angel would not be an autonomous agent and so could not be held morally responsible for its actions. An agent with only one such inclination would necessarily seek the highest benefit or the highest justice available to it.[8] That principle is important for Anselm. But he wants the thought experiment to show in particular that the inclination for justice enables a "complete" rational agent to moderate what would be an otherwise unchecked desire for benefit.

The angels (as well as Adam and Eve) were created as complete, rational agents with both inclinations. Moreover, they were not created in some neutral state and then expected to attain justice; Anselm holds that no creature can attain justice on its own (that is, without the grace of God) (see Chapter 32).[9] When the evil angels and the first human beings "desert" justice, they are then necessarily limited to the pursuit of the highest attainable benefit; since they cannot attain the higher happiness that would go with acting justly (*De concordia* I.6), they will seek to satisfy lower – what Anselm calls "base" – desires in an intense and unjust (that is, a corrupt or distorted) way (*De casu diaboli* 13). That is to say, sinners who desert justice will have a false picture of true human flourishing. They will presumably be able to handle normal means–ends decisions about their benefit, but Anselm thinks those will be operative within a life orientation that is perverse.

It is important, however, not to confuse the condition of the human or angelic sinner with that of the incomplete angel. Lacking the inclination for justice, sinners will not be able to moderate their desire for benefit. But Anselm says that sinners (unlike the incomplete angel) are still responsible for

---

[7] See *De concordia* III.13, where this is likewise the central issue.
[8] Sandra Visser and Thomas Williams defend the interesting interpretation that Anselm is not arguing here from a need for alternate possibilities but rather a notion of autonomy: "Anselm's Account of Freedom," in B. Davies and B. Leftow (eds.) *The Cambridge Companion to Anselm* (Cambridge: Cambridge University Press, 2004) pp. 186–94.
[9] *De casu diaboli* 9; *De concordia* I.7, III.3–4; *De libertate arbitrii* 5–7.

their indulging these "base desires" because of the original desertion of justice (*De concordia* III.7). Presumably this goes along with the fact that rational creatures (again unlike the incomplete angel) have by nature the ability to retain justice. Interestingly, it is this latter ability rather than the inclination for justice that Anselm identifies with the "*power* of free choice." While the presence of the inclination for justice makes the agent capable of moderating the inclination for benefit, it is retaining justice, presumably in the face of temptation, that Anselm sees as the true exercise of free choice (*De libertate arbitrii* 3).[10] In holding that this power is natural to rational agents, Anselm can maintain that humans (and presumably the devil) never lose free choice – though without justice, of course, it is useless. But for humans, at least, when justice is restored by the grace of God, their full autonomy, including the exercise of freedom of choice, is again effective.

The loss of the inclination for justice leaves a rational being in the most grievous of circumstances, unable to act justly until that inclination is restored. Presumably, it is only the most serious sin that results in that loss. Even so, it is interesting to consider the resulting state of the sinner. Anselm insists that nothing essential to the agent is lost along with justice (*De libertate arbitrii* 2). And he is probably thinking that his special analysis allows him to claim that the sinner retains the "power of free choice." But elsewhere he holds that it is rational to choose happiness with justice over happiness without justice (*De concordia* I.6). If to fail to make that choice were acting irrationally, the devil's "misjudgment" would seem to be an intellectual error. It is likely, then, that Anselm thinks the loss of justice carries with it a certain "warping" of reason, such that even if simple means–ends reasoning is active, good sense about ends is still obscured.

Anselm does not develop what one might expect today as a moral theory. He gives very few examples of morally good and bad actions, generally avoiding problematic cases and offering no test for their discrimination. As we have seen, his concern in these discussions is how good creatures can go bad, and the context of his solution is a theological one of sin and grace. In the process, of course, he has opened up central issues in moral psychology. And, as might be expected, philosophical commentary – when it has dealt with these texts at all and not been distracted by the irresistible fascination of his "ontological argument" – has focused on that aspect of the dual inclinations.

---

[10] Anselm argues that the power of free choice cannot be an ability to choose good or evil. To choose evil, he claims, is a failing or weakness and not an exercise of the power of free choice (*De libertate arbitrii* 1) (see Chapter 29).

JOHN DUNS SCOTUS

Writing two centuries after Anselm in the intense atmosphere of the universities in the high scholastic period, Scotus has a much more fully developed moral theory, along with a sophisticated metaphysics that underlies his account of free agency.[11] Although it will not do justice to the details of Scotus's full treatment of the issues, it is possible to characterize the essentials of his notion of dual basic inclinations of will by playing it off against Anselm's account. When setting out his own idea of the inclinations, Scotus cites Anselm's thought experiment of the angel-in-progress in *De casu diaboli* and adopts the labels of *affectio commodi* and *affectio iustitiae*.[12] Moreover, he describes the inclination for justice as moderating the inclination for benefit.

Although these are not insignificant parallels, in fact the similarity pretty much ends there. In Scotus's account, even the two inclinations show important differences from Anselm's treatment. Scotus describes the inclination for benefit as a "natural will." More precisely, he sees it as the natural appetite of an intellectual agent, and he claims that, as such, it is no more free than any natural appetite, such as the sensory appetite.[13] What he has in mind here is an Aristotelian theme within medieval thought that has developed well after Anselm, where choosing what we take to be good means choosing something perfective of us, something that actualizes our potentialities. The moral outlook is then situated within this single human purpose now usually referred to as "human flourishing."[14] Scotus's view is that such a natural appetite does not attain to the moral order at all.[15] He allows that, because of that appetite, we cannot nill happiness or will to be miserable. But he maintains that in order to act as we ought, it may be necessary at times simply not to will either way on

---

[11] Allan B. Wolter, *Duns Scotus on the Will and Morality* (Washington, DC: Catholic University of American Press, 1966) is a convenient source for the references to Scotus made here, containing both an English translation and the Latin texts.

[12] *Ordinatio* III, suppl. dist. 26 (ed. Wolter, p. 179). As it happens, Scotus does not use the Anselmian labels at all frequently. However, in extended discussions of the sin of Lucifer (*Ordinatio* II.6.2 [ed. Wolter, pp. 462–77]) and of happiness (*Ordinatio* IV, suppl. dist. 49 [ed. Wolter, pp. 182–96]), it is clear that he has the two inclinations in mind and that he associates with the inclination for benefit such single-purpose systems as that of Aquinas (note 14, below).

[13] *Ordinatio* IV, suppl. dist. 49, qq. 9–10 (ed. Wolter, pp. 185, 191); *Ordinatio* II.6.2 (ed. Wolter, pp. 469, 471); *Ordinatio* III.17 (ed. Wolter, pp. 180–3). See also Thomas Williams, "From Metaethics to Action Theory," in T. Williams (ed.) *The Cambridge Companion to Duns Scotus* (Cambridge: Cambridge University Press, 2003) pp. 343–5.

[14] Williams, "From Metaethics," p. 334. One can see this in Aquinas (whom Scotus surely had in mind in his criticism): *Summa theol.* 1a2ae qq. 1–5 (on the ultimate end of humans) and q. 94 (where this is spelled out for virtue).

[15] *Ordinatio* II.6.2 (ed. Wolter, pp. 472–5). For a helpful discussion, see Williams, "From Metaethics," pp. 335–45.

the scale of benefit, but to override or set aside considerations of happiness or personal fulfillment.[16]

What allows us to operate within the moral order is, then, the inclination for justice. For Scotus, the freedom that this requires is not due to the interplay of the two inclinations but is the product solely of the inclination for justice. In fact, the character of that inclination for him derives less from an analysis of justice or rightness of action for its own sake and has to do more with the idea of freedom itself. The inclination for justice is the "innate freedom of the will."[17] As the locus of free choice, then – Scotus does not adopt Anselm's special definition of "free choice" – the inclination for justice cannot be lost. It follows that having a will for justice is not, as with Anselm, having justice or being just. If it were, then everyone would be just simply by dint of having the rational power that is the will.

For Scotus, moral responsibility requires that the will be a "rational power" – a power for opposites – and a good deal of recent commentary has understandably been directed to the radical notion of freedom (or autonomy) presented in Scotus's analysis of a rational power (see Chapter 30).[18] His predecessors allowed that, prior to choosing, a rational agent had the power to will and the power not to will (or to will this rather than that). But when the choice was made, and while the will to do *x* was actual, the agent did not have the power to will not-*x*. (Compare: It is not necessary that Socrates sits; but when he sits, he sits necessarily.) For Scotus, however, freedom of the will requires that the agent must have the power to do otherwise even while willing *x*.

Scotus's radical notion of freedom in the will is important in itself and for understanding the inclination for justice as the "innate freedom of the will." However, it should not distract attention from the role of the inclination for justice in Scotus, which lies precisely in its enabling the rational agent to respond (freely) to the values of a moral life.[19] That is to say, the inclination for justice provides not only "freedom from" necessity but "freedom for" a certain kind of life. The full story of Scotus's theory therefore requires an inquiry into the nature of the morality that the inclination for justice supports. By appealing to a distinct inclination for justice, Scotus offers a picture of the moral life as rising above the world of nature, including even the natural appetite of an intelligent

---

[16] *Ordinatio* IV suppl. dist. 49, qq. 9–10 (ed. Wolter, pp. 192–3).

[17] *Ordinatio* II.6.2 (ed. Wolter, pp. 468–9).

[18] *Quaest. in Metaphys.* IX.15 (ed. Wolter, pp. 144–73). See also Calvin Normore, "Duns Scotus's Modal Theory," in Williams, *The Cambridge Companion to Scotus*, 129–60; and also Simo Knuuttila, *Modalities in Medieval Philosophy* (London: Routledge, 1993).

[19] Williams, "From Metaethics," p. 348; Richard Cross, *Duns Scotus* (Oxford: Oxford University Press, 1999) p. 87.

creature. To say anything more about what that inclination consists in is just to spell out Scotus's substantive ethical theory. The major controversy here is whether Scotus defends a divine command theory or a more familiar scholastic theory dependent upon right reason.[20] It is a complex and controversial issue that, like the analysis of his notion of freedom itself, exceeds the limits of the present chapter.

EARLIER PAIRINGS

Before closing, a brief word may be in order on the tradition of "moral pairings" preceding Anselm. As early as Plato and Aristotle, one finds the pair *agathon* and *kalon*. *Agathon* is "good" broadly taken: that is, what one aims at or what satisfies one's aims. So understood, there are many "goods," and central to those is the notion of benefit or usefulness in achieving personal well-being (see, for instance, *Nic. Ethics* VIII.2, 1155b20). *Kalon*, in contrast, has the sense of excellence and beauty, or even style.[21] More important for present purposes, it has to do with ends pursued for their own sake, in contrast to the useful or beneficial as means to a happy or satisfying life.

Apparently the Cynics were unusual if not unique in finding a basic conflict between *kalon* and our natural aims. In part this stemmed from the fact that, for them, nature is primitive and opposed to culture and the rational, so "living according to nature" is brutish and in conflict with civilized society.[22] But for the Stoics – Seneca, and especially Cicero, who was a more direct influence on medieval Latin authors – a conflict could only arise if we had an inadequate understanding of our true happiness. The correct grasp of human happiness is "living according to nature"; and for them that meant living according to virtue in preference to any other aim.[23]

In any event, the Latin translation of *agathon* and *kalon* would be *bonum* and *honestum*, with the focus in the former on what is beneficial or useful (*commodus, utile*). The connotation of *honestum* is something sought or desired for its own sake.[24] This terminology was familiar throughout the Middle Ages. It seems

---

[20] Thomas Williams argues for the former (Williams, "From Metaethics," p. 346–7); Allan Wolter (introduction to *Duns Scotus on the Will and Morality*, pp. 3–5) and Richard Cross (*Duns Scotus*, pp. 90ff) defend the latter.

[21] Terence Irwin's translation of the *Nicomachean Ethics* renders it as "fine" (p. 401; cf. p. 406).

[22] See Frederick C. Copleston, *A History of Philosophy* (Westminster, MD: Newman Press, 1946–75) I: 395, 410, 417.

[23] Terence Irwin, "Stoic Naturalism and its Critics," in B. Inwood (ed.) *The Cambridge Companion to Stoicism* (Cambridge: Cambridge University Press, 2003) 345–64. The reference to Cicero is *De officiis* III.21–8.

[24] See Thomas Aquinas, *Summa theol.* 1a 5.6, 1a2ae 8.2 ad 2, and 8.3 ad 4.

doubtful that Anselm read widely in the ancient Greek sources. But it is likely he read both Seneca and Cicero and he could have got the general contrast, as well as the specific pair, from Ambrose (*De officiis* I.9). The usage was reinforced later on when the writings of Aristotle became influential.[25]

The history of the *honestum–commodus* pair is an interesting one that deserves more attention in the study of medieval moral theories than is usually given it. But it is worth repeating that it is in Anselm and Scotus that we find the developed idea of dual basic inclinations of the will.

[25] Aquinas cites Aristotle and Cicero, e.g., in *Summa theol.* 2a2ae 145.1c and ad 1.

36

VIRTUE THEORY

BONNIE KENT

BASIC ISSUES

From antiquity through the Hellenistic era, all the leading philosophers argued that people acquire virtues naturally, through their own learning and practice. As we are the sole or principal cause of our virtues, so too are we the sole or principal cause of our happiness. The theocentric ethics favored by later Jews, Christians, and Muslims left open to question what insights might be gleaned from these earlier anthropocentric theories. As a result, disputes about the various causal theses of ancient ethics run like a leitmotif through the medieval literature. Are virtues God-given, or can we acquire them just by exercising the natural human capacities of intellect and will? Are virtues sufficient, or even necessary, for obedience to God's law? Is happiness, whether now or in the afterlife, actually caused by our virtues, or is it a divine reward – perhaps even simply a divine gift?

On the whole, medieval thinkers concentrated less on criticizing earlier views than on developing alternative theories of virtue. In constructing such theories they argued as much with each other as they did with the teachings of ancient philosophers. As it was open to debate how philosophical works should be interpreted, so it was open to debate how Scripture and the "authoritative" works of one's own religious tradition should be interpreted. Much of what today is orthodox doctrine was still in the making. For instance, even Muslims who agreed that people attain complete happiness only in the afterlife disagreed about how this relates to virtue. Inspired by Neoplatonic teachings, Avicenna described the soul's fortunes after the death of the body as the effect of the individual's own conduct in this life. Eternal happiness is achieved by acquiring the moral dispositions necessary to purify one's soul; it is not some external reward meted out by God for good behavior.[1] Al-Ghazālī, on the other hand,

---

[1] Avicenna attributes this doctrine to the ancients in his short "Essay on the Secret of Destiny." He defends it as his own in the *Metaphysics* of *The Healing* IX.7, X.3. A helpful survey of medieval Muslim

strongly opposed the claim that human self-development brings happiness in
the afterlife. On his view, this naturalistic doctrine is doubly mistaken, for no
virtue can be acquired without God's assistance, and no virtues that we do
acquire bring eternal happiness. Such happiness comes always as a divine gift or
favor.[2]

Aristotelian ethics, especially as developed among Islamic interpreters, took
on a strong current of intellectual elitism: it suggested that only people with well-
developed intellects can achieve true happiness (see Chapter 33). This became
a major source of controversy among Jewish thinkers. Moses Maimonides was
among those who believed such elitism compatible with the true message of
the Torah. His *Guide of the Perplexed* claims that moral perfection is necessary
for intellectual perfection but should not be sought for its own sake. Few people
ever acquire true metaphysical opinions about God, but intellectual perfection
should still be our goal, for it alone enables the soul to survive the death of the
body and attain the greatest happiness possible for human beings (I.34, III.51–4).
Ḥasdai Crescas rejected this conclusion on both philosophical and religious
grounds. His *Light of the Lord* argues that happiness and immortality come from
the perfection of the soul, something attainable by all who love and fear God.
Not only are Aristotelians wrong in overvaluing intellectual achievement, they
are wrong in thinking that the human intellect could become an immortal
substance by acquiring true beliefs (II.6.1).[3]

At first, medieval Christians stayed largely within the theocentric framework
of the Church Fathers. They endorsed three basic theses, all of which had been
defended by Augustine:

(1) The ultimate end of happiness (*beatitudo*) lies in the afterlife, in the soul's union
with God.
(2) Nobody can attain happiness without charity, the root of merit and of all genuine
virtues.
(3) Charity is itself a gift of grace, not a reward for antecedent merit (see Chapter 32).

All of these theses enjoyed wide support up to the end of the Middle Ages,
except for the claim that charity is the root of all genuine virtues, which
Augustine himself seemed to endorse in some places but not in others.

---

accounts of virtue is given in George Hourani, *Reason and Tradition in Islamic Ethics* (Cambridge:
Cambridge University Press, 1985).

[2] See *Revival of the Religious Sciences* 32.3 (tr. Littlejohn). See also Mohamed Ahmed Sherif, *Ghazali's
Theory of Virtue* (Albany: State University of New York Press, 1975) ch. 3.

[3] W. Harvey translates this section of *The Light of the Lord* in A. Hyman and J. Walsh (eds.) *Philosophy
in the Middle Ages,* 2nd edn (Indianapolis, IN: Hackett, 1973) pp. 440–9. For a detailed study of
medieval Jewish debates about the virtues, see Hava Tirosh-Samuelson, *Happiness in Premodern
Judaism: Virtue, Knowledge, and Well-Being* (Cincinnati, OH: Hebrew Union College Press, 2003).

Until the mid-fourteenth century only a small percentage of Augustine's works was actually studied. Medieval scholars knew his vast body of writings mainly through collections of excerpts (*florilegia*), creating no small puzzlement about how his various *dicta* fit together.[4] In one work, for instance, Augustine defines virtue as the perfect love of God and presents each of the cardinal virtues as a form of love. In a second work, he distinguishes virtues, which cannot be "badly used," from powers of the soul, which can be. In a third work he says that virtue is the good use of free will, which comes from God.[5] With so many divergent passages about virtue to choose from, medieval authors typically highlighted those they favored and downplayed the ones that seemed wrong.

When authors combined non-Christian sources with specifically Christian ones, the task of theorizing became even more challenging. For example, the Church Fathers had endorsed the fourfold Stoic division of virtue, but they christened wisdom (or prudence), justice, temperance, and fortitude the "cardinal" virtues and recast them in Christian terms.[6] These four virtues accordingly joined faith, hope, and charity, the God-given virtues praised by Paul (esp. I Cor. 13) as staples of medieval virtue theory. Following Cicero's lead, twelfth-century authors introduced a good many other virtues as "parts" of the cardinals. And from Macrobius they learned of Plotinus's hierarchical scheme, with "political" virtues at the bottom and "exemplary" virtues at the top.[7] The notion of "political" virtues, however, ushered in a different conception of the cardinals: namely, as virtues that someone without God-given charity might acquire through her own natural resources. These conflicting conceptions of the cardinal virtues posed problems for medieval theorists. When the cardinal virtues are naturally acquired – and so are merely "political" or "civic" virtues – are they true virtues? If not, does God's gift of charity transform them into true virtues?[8]

[4] For example, scholars have established that Peter Lombard, whose *Sentences* comes packed with over 650 quotations from Augustine, had direct knowledge of only four works by Augustine: *On Christian Doctrine,* the *Enchiridion, On 83 Different Questions,* and the *Retractationes*. See Jacques Guy Bougerol, "The Church Fathers and the *Sentences* of Peter Lombard," in I. Backus (ed.) *The Reception of the Church Fathers in the West* (Leiden: Brill, 1997) I: 115. The "Augustinian revival" of the mid-fourteenth century is discussed in William Courtenay, *Schools and Scholars in Fourteenth-Century England* (Princeton, NJ: Princeton University Press, 1987) pp. 307–24.
[5] Augustine, *De moribus ecclesiae* XV.25; *De libero arbitrio* II.18; *Retractationes* I.9.
[6] For examples see Jerome, *Epist.* 66.3, which makes following Christ the supreme example of wisdom, and Ambrose, *De officiis* I.28, which explores the cardinal virtues only after arguing that nothing is virtuous unless it helps in attaining eternal life.
[7] Cicero, *De inventione* II.53–4; Macrobius, *In Somnium Scipionis* I.8; Plotinus, *Enneads* I.2.
[8] The first stage of debate on this topic is recounted in Odon Lottin, "Les vertus morales acquises sont-elles vraies vertus? La réponse de théologiens de Pierre Abelard à St. Thomas d'Aquin," *Recherches de théologie ancienne et médiévale* 20 (1953) 13–39. Augustine sometimes uses the term "civic" in describing the virtues of pagans.

Over the course of the twelfth century, as a growing number of authors began to classify virtue as a *habitus*, some were plainly influenced by ancient ethics.[9] One source for this classification was Cicero's definition of 'virtue' as "a *habitus* of the soul in agreement with the mode of nature and reason." Another was the *Categories*, where Aristotle describes a *habitus* as a quality more permanent and harder to change than a mere condition.[10] Since Aristotle's reference to knowledge and the virtues as examples of *habitus* seemed to resonate with Cicero's later usage, Peter Abaelard cited both as support for his own account of virtue as a *habitus* of the soul – that is, a quality produced by our own efforts and very difficult to dislodge.[11] Roughly the same account of virtue appears in the dialogue between a philosopher and a Christian in Abaelard's *Collationes*, though here it is the philosopher who presents virtue as a *habitus* of the soul acquired by practice and deliberation. The Christian claims that only charity should be called a virtue if "virtue" is properly understood as that which obtains merit with God.[12] Alas, the text of the dialogue ends without any explanation by Abaelard of how virtue "properly understood" might relate to virtue understood as a *habitus* acquired by our own efforts.

Other twelfth-century authors, probably influenced by Augustine, distinguished sharply between having a virtuous *habitus* and performing, or even being able to perform, related actions. Some proceeded to argue that babies receive virtuous *habitus* through the grace of baptism, although they cannot exercise these virtues until they mature.[13] In 1201 Pope Innocent III mentioned their opinion without accepting or rejecting it.[14] In the later thirteenth century, Peter of John Olivi accordingly felt safe in opposing this "modern" doctrine. Why should infants need supernaturally caused *habitus* in order to be acceptable to God? One need not posit a change in the child as a result of baptism, Olivi argues, but only a change in the child's relationship to God. Experience

---

[9] The Latin *habitus* appears in some English translations of medieval texts as "disposition"; in many more it appears as "habit." The first is a better translation than the second but still seems too narrow and naturalistic, because most medieval theologians from the late thirteenth century onward held that virtuous *habitus* are supernaturally infused into infants as a result of baptism. For this reason I have chosen to leave the word untranslated. (Note that the plural form of *habitus* is the same as the singular.)

[10] Cicero, *De inventione* II.53; Aristotle, *Cat.* 8b26–9a4.

[11] Abaelard, *Ethics* pt. II (ed. Luscombe, p. 128). The (unfinished) text of Abaelard's *Ethics* ends soon after this passage.

[12] *Collationes* II.100, 111. See also *Sic et non* q. 137, where Abaelard quotes various authorities both for and against the thesis that only charity should be called a virtue.

[13] The distinction between virtue *in habitu* and virtue *in usu* is found in Augustine, *De bono conjugali* 21.25–22.27. For the extension of this distinction to infant baptism see Simon of Tournai, *Institutiones in sacram paginam* 8.2.

[14] Innocent III, letter to Humbert, archbishop of Arles, in H. Denzinger (ed.) *Enchiridion symbolorum* (Freiburg: Herder, 1963) n. 780.

suggests that young Christian children have no special *habitus* that young Muslim children lack; indeed, people expose the Christian faith to ridicule in claiming otherwise (*Summa* III, ed. Emmen and Stadter, appendix to q. 2, p. 175). Olivi's critics worried that his line of reasoning might lead one to question whether even adults need God-given *habitus* of virtue. This brief excursion into sacramental theology should serve as a warning: medieval theorists often appropriate terms from ancient ethics, such as *habitus*, while extending them well beyond the naturalistic framework of ancient ethics.

Books II and III of the *Nicomachean Ethics* were translated into Latin in the twelfth century but remained little studied until the early thirteenth century, when a translation of Book I was added. When readers knew at most three books of the *Ethics*, they often drew erroneous conclusions about Aristotle's teachings. They assumed, for example, that he saw moral virtues as separable from one another, because they are acquired by different kinds of actions, and each moral virtue has a different mean lying between contrary vices. Only around 1246–8, when Robert Grosseteste's complete translation of the *Ethics* began to circulate, did readers learn Aristotle's argument that nobody can have any moral virtue without prudence, nor can someone have prudence without *all* the moral virtues.[15] Aristotle's action theory, which some scholastics thought deeply misguided, became another source of controversy. For although he has much to say about choice and even defines moral virtue as a *habitus* concerning choice, he says nothing about *free* choice, let alone about free will.[16]

From this rapid survey of issues we turn to the virtue theory articulated in part two of Aquinas's *Summa theologiae* (1268–72). A monument to system building, the theory still has many admirers today. As we will see, its reception among thinkers of the late thirteenth and fourteenth centuries was more mixed, in part because they focused on aspects now often overlooked.

AQUINAS'S THEORY

Part two of the *Summa theologiae* begins with a broad characterization of complete happiness (*beatitudo*) as the ultimate end of human life and builds gradually towards a highly specific discussion of the virtues. The first part of part two (the *Prima secundae* [1a2ae]) lays the foundations and provides an overview of the entire theory. Here Aquinas considers general questions about human acts,

---

[15] Early scholastic arguments about the connection of the virtues are detailed in Odon Lottin, *Psychologie et morale aux XIIe et XIIIe siècles* (Gembloux: Duculot, 1942–60) III: 195–252.

[16] Late thirteenth-century debates about freedom are discussed in Bonnie Kent, *Virtues of the Will: The Transformation of Ethics in the Late Thirteenth Century* (Washington, DC: Catholic University of America Press, 1995) ch. 3. (See also Chapter 30.)

passions, *habitus*, virtues, vices, and sins, as well as law and grace. The second part (the *Secunda secundae* [2a2ae]) opens with more specific questions about faith, hope, and charity – the theological virtues – before giving detailed accounts of the four cardinal virtues. Here Aquinas casts a dazzling variety of other virtues as "parts" of the cardinals. Only a small number of them figure as constitutive or "integral" parts. Most are either "subjective" parts (different species of a cardinal virtue, in the way that chastity and sobriety are different species of temperance), or merely "potential" parts (that is, secondary virtues "annexed to" but not essential for the cardinals).[17] Aquinas's leading authorities on the cardinal virtues and their parts are the Church Fathers and Cicero, not Aristotle.

A close reading of the *Prima secundae* reveals two reasons why Aristotle's teachings end up with a much smaller role than modern readers often assume. First, Aquinas defines a *habitus* as that through which one acts when one *wills*. Thanks to the power of will, humans can choose whether or not to act in accordance with their *habitus*. Non-rational animals, which lack the power of will, cannot do the same; thus, Aquinas denies that the dispositions acquired by these animals are properly called *habitus*.[18] Second, Aquinas posits a host of moral virtues that share the same names as Aristotelian virtues but that are infused by grace and hence radically different in kind.

As we will see, the second move was the more controversial. With respect to the first, most theorists of the period agreed that we can always act contrary to the *habitus* constituting our character as so far formed. Just as the most virtuous person on earth can still choose a morally bad act, so the most vicious person on earth can still choose a morally good act. But because Aristotle failed to defend this view – indeed, he even appeared to contradict it[19] – support had to be sought elsewhere. Aquinas finds it in *dicta* by Augustine and Averroes, one of those unlikely pairings so common in medieval works. Averroes describes a *habitus* as that whereby one acts when one wills; Augustine describes it as something by which one acts when there is a need. Aquinas enlists both in order to characterize a *habitus* as a disposition that may or may not be "used" (or exercised) by the will.[20] He diverges still farther from Aristotle's teachings

---

[17] A more detailed summary of *Summa theol.* 2a is given in Stephen Pope, "Overview of the Ethics of Thomas Aquinas," in S. J. Pope (ed.) *The Ethics of Aquinas* (Washington, DC: Georgetown University Press, 2002) 30–53.

[18] *Summa theol.* 1a2ae 50.3.

[19] For example, in *Nic. Ethics* III.5, 1114a13–21 Aristotle argues that vicious people cannot act out of character but that they still remain responsible for their actions. Helpful analysis of his views on this issue is given in Susan Suavé Meyer, *Aristotle on Moral Responsibility: Character and Cause* (Oxford: Blackwell, 1993) ch. 6.

[20] Averroes, *In De anima* III.18; Augustine, *De boni conjugali* 21, 25; Aquinas, *Summa theol.* 1a2ae 49.3, 50.5.

when he argues that only some *habitus* are acquired through the agent's own actions; others are infused by God (see below).[21] In this section of the *Prima secundae*, Aquinas works to make the concept of a *habitus* sufficiently wide and thin to support a theory comprehending both the naturally acquired virtues praised by Aristotle and the God-given virtues praised by the Church Fathers. Only when the task is complete does he turn to the definition of virtue.

The definition that Aquinas chooses to discuss comes not from Aristotle but from Peter Lombard's *Sentences*, the standard theological textbook of the period: "virtue is a good quality of the mind, by which we live rightly, of which no one makes bad use, which God works in us without us."[22] Aquinas suggests that *habitus* be substituted for 'quality' in order to make the definition more specific – a modest suggestion, given the revisions he has already made to the Aristotelian notion of a *habitus*. He accepts the thesis that nobody makes bad use of a virtue, because it does not entail that someone having a virtue is *determined* to act in accordance with it. If the agent chooses not to act in accordance with her virtue on a given occasion, then it is not that she is using the virtue badly, but that she is not using the virtue at all, and indeed may even be acting contrary to it.[23] As for the definition's last clause – "which God works in us without us" – this narrow conception of virtue as always divinely infused began losing its attractions in the late twelfth century and had already been rejected by thirteenth-century theorists before Aquinas. He himself suggests that the clause be dropped so that the definition can cover all virtues, both naturally acquired and supernaturally infused.

Aquinas's concern for a definition of 'virtue' broad enough to encompass naturally acquired virtues reveals his conviction that they can indeed be genuine virtues. At the same time, he demotes them to virtues in a relative sense, always imperfect by comparison with the perfect, unqualified virtues given by God. This brings us to the second (aforementioned) reason why Aristotle's teachings play a smaller role in Part II of the *Summa* than many modern readers assume. Aquinas includes among the God-given virtues not only theological virtues like charity but also God-given *moral* virtues infused together with charity and having the same names as Aristotelian moral virtues: infused prudence, infused justice, infused fortitude, and so on.

According to Aquinas, acquired moral virtues are directed to the imperfect happiness of this life. Infused moral virtues belong to a different

---

[21] *Summa theol.* 1a2ae 51.4. See also *Summa theol.* 3a 69.7, where Aquinas argues that infants receive infused *habitus* through the grace of baptism.

[22] The definition, attributed to Augustine in *Sent.* II.27.1.1, is discussed by Aquinas in *Summa theol.* 1a2ae 55.4.

[23] Aquinas defends this position explicitly in *Summa theol.* 1a2ae 71.4.

species – essentially connected to God-given charity but not to acquired moral virtues. Whereas acquired moral virtues observe a mean established by human reason, their infused counterparts observe a mean appointed by divine law. Also, because acquired moral virtues always work to eliminate contrary passions, the agent usually takes pleasure in acting virtuously. The moral virtues infused together with charity cannot be counted on to have the same effect right away. A new convert, for example, might well feel more internal conflict and less pleasure than a virtuous pagan, though his infused virtues will give him the strength to lead a good life. Furthermore, acquired moral virtues are both developed and lost little by little. Infused moral virtues are lost through a single act of mortal sin and can be increased only by God, not by human actions.[24]

Having cast naturally acquired virtues as virtues only in a relative sense, Aquinas's discussion in the *Secunda secundae* shifts from charity to the cardinal virtues that are infused together with charity. The focus on infused moral virtues explains why the principal act of fortitude becomes martyrdom – not enduring death in battle for the sake of one's country, as a good pagan might do (see Chapter 34), but enduring death from the love of God, through faith in Christ.[25] Aquinas echoes Augustine in referring to the virtue praised by ancient philosophers as merely "civic" fortitude. Since only God-given virtues are virtues *simpliciter*, the *Secunda secundae* has little to say about naturally acquired virtues. Aquinas mentions them now and then mainly to distinguish them from the perfect, unqualified virtues that Christians have as a gift of grace.

WHY POSIT VIRTUES?

After Aquinas's death in 1274, less than a decade passed before Parisian theologians began to challenge the most distinctive aspect of his theory. Is it necessary, or even helpful, to posit infused moral virtues? Around 1281–2, Henry of Ghent rehearsed the various arguments for positing such virtues and rejected all of them as unpersuasive. According to Henry, the infused theological virtue of charity suffices to redirect naturally acquired virtues to the ultimate end. When charity elevates the end of these virtues, their targeted means change, too. Hence

---

[24] For further discussion of the infused moral virtues see Bonnie Kent, "Habits and Virtues," in Pope, *The Ethics of Aquinas*, 116–30; John Inglis, "Aquinas's Replication of the Acquired Moral Virtues," *Journal of Religious Ethics* 27 (1999) 3–27; Angela McKay, "The Infused and Acquired Virtues in Aquinas' Moral Philosophy" (Ph.D. dissertation: University of Notre Dame, 2004); and Jeffery Hause, "Aquinas on the Function of Moral Virtue," *American Catholic Philosophical Quarterly* 81 (2007) 1–20.

[25] Aquinas, *Summa theol.* 2a2ae 124.2.

an action chosen by someone with the virtue of charity could look extreme to someone with only naturally acquired virtues.[26] Agreeing with Henry that infused moral virtues are superfluous, Godfrey of Fontaines raised a different objection to them. As Aristotle teaches, moral virtue moderates the passions. When one posits, as Aquinas did, infused moral virtues that do not moderate the passions, they can be called *moral* only in an improper, equivocal sense.[27]

Here we see the growing tendency to distinguish questions about moral goodness in earthly society from questions about "meriting" God's reward of eternal happiness. With accounts of moral goodness increasingly framed in naturalistic terms, and masters well schooled in Aristotle's works, virtue theory faced new challenges. For example, what should one make of Aristotle's argument that nobody can acquire prudence without all the moral virtues (*Nic. Ethics* VI.13, 1144b3–45a1)? How much of it rests on conceptual claims about necessary connections between virtues, how much on only empirical, psychological claims? Does prudence itself have an indivisible, organic unity? Or are there different prudences, each related to some specific moral virtue that might be acquired independently of others? If each moral virtue is essentially linked to the others, are they really different virtues or only different aspects of a single virtue?[28]

Soon masters started to wonder what work virtuous *habitus* actually do in ethical theory. What does a *habitus* explain that one could not explain without it? With the idea of infused moral virtues already spurned by all but the most loyal Thomists, disputes centered instead on infused theological virtues and naturally acquired moral virtues. Developing the line of argument about infant baptism suggested by Olivi, John Duns Scotus concludes that we believe only through faith that nobody attains eternal happiness without the infused *habitus* of charity. Since this virtue is itself a pure gift of grace and not a divine reward for good behavior, it cannot explain why God chooses to accept some people but not others. While Christians should believe God has ordained that nobody will be saved without charity, there is nothing about this or other infused virtues that makes them intrinsically necessary for salvation. They have the status of secondary causes that God could have, by his absolute power, chosen to dispense

---

[26] Henry of Ghent, *Quodlibet* VI.12.

[27] The text of this disputed question by Godfrey on infused moral virtues is published in Lottin, *Psychologie et morale aux XIIe et XIIIe siècles*, III: 497–500.

[28] Later medieval arguments about the connection of the virtues are discussed in Marilyn McCord Adams, "Scotus and Ockham on the Connection of the Virtues," in L. Honnefelder *et al.* (eds.) *John Duns Scotus: Metaphysics and Ethics* (Leiden: Brill, 1996) 499–522, and Rega Wood, *Ockham on the Virtues* (West Lafayette, IN: Purdue University Press, 1997) ch. 4.

with. Thus, the causal role they play in salvation arises strictly from the covenant that God generously made and faithfully keeps.[29]

A fellow Franciscan, Peter Auriol, insisted that the infused virtue of charity plays a more important role in salvation. In his view, infused charity is not simply the consequence of divine acceptance but necessary by its very nature in order to make the soul acceptable to God. William of Ockham, in turn, opposed Peter's teaching on this issue and sided with Scotus. Ockham argued that infused charity is *de facto* necessary because of God's covenant but neither intrinsically nor ontologically necessary for divine acceptance. As other masters joined the fray, it developed into a free-for-all that was by no means limited to Franciscans. Durand of St. Pourçain, for instance, angered fellow Dominicans with a scathing critique of Aquinas's teachings on virtue. Not only did Durand see no reason to posit infused moral virtues, but he argued that acquired virtuous *habitus* do much less to explain moral actions than Thomists think they do.[30]

Durand's arguments on this issue were not soon forgotten. In the mid-fifteenth century, when John Capreolus produced his ambitious defense of Aquinas's theology, he did his best to prove the importance of positing virtuous *habitus*, both acquired and infused. John's recitation of arguments to the contrary begins with a great many quotations from Durand (*Defensiones* III.23.2).[31] He clearly thinks that nobody can defend Aquinas's ethical theory without proving the need to posit virtuous *habitus*. At the same time, he evinces little interest in continuing debates about what God could have done by his absolute power, or whether "Whatever God wills, just because he wills it, is right." There is no evidence in Capreolus's *Defensiones* for the idea, so common in modern histories, that "divine command theory" posed a major threat to medieval virtue theory.[32] But the dispute about positing virtuous *habitus* lasted until the sixteenth century, when Martin Luther dismissed the very idea of virtuous *habitus*, whether infused or naturally acquired, as evidence of Aristotle's baneful influence on medieval theology.[33]

---

[29] *Ordinatio* I.17.1.1–2 nn.125–94, esp. 160–4.

[30] *Sent.* III.23.1–4; III.33.5. In arguing against infused moral virtues Durand repeats the charge of equivocation, but on different grounds. He suggests that virtues are called "moral" because they come from practice (*ex more*), so that virtues infused by grace can be called "moral" only in an equivocal sense.

[31] Although John treats Durand as his chief adversary on this issue, he also considers some arguments by Scotus and Peter Auriol. William of Ockham goes unmentioned.

[32] This historiographical observation is ably defended in Sigrid Müller, "The Ethics of John Capreolus and the *Nominales*," *Verbum: Analecta Neolatina* 6 (2004) 301–14.

[33] Peter Auriol, *Sent.* I.17.1.2; Ockham, *Sent.* I.17.1. The debate about positing an infused *habitus* of charity, from its origins through the works of Luther, is discussed in Alister McGrath, *Iustitia Dei: A History of the Christian Doctrine of Justification*, 3rd edn (Cambridge: Cambridge University Press, 1998) esp. pp. 59–72, 176–86.

VIRTUE AND ACTION

In the case of naturally acquired virtues, the issue is not whether one needs them to choose acts "meriting" reward in the afterlife, but whether they make one's action morally good in the earthly sense. Scotus questioned the need to posit such virtues by reflecting on the likeness principle that Aristotle appeared to endorse: moral virtues are developed by choosing like acts – temperance from choosing temperate acts, justice from choosing just acts, and so on (*Nic. Ethics* II.1).[34] If only someone with a virtuous *habitus* can choose a morally good act, Scotus argues, then how could she choose the kind of acts necessary in order to acquire the *habitus*? To avoid circularity we must grant that someone without virtue can choose a morally good act, so that virtue cannot be what makes an action good. An act is morally good because it conforms to what the agent's right reason dictates should be done, including the appropriate time and place and, above all, the end for the sake of which one should act.[35]

By "right reason" Scotus does not mean, as some of his contemporaries do, the intellectual *habitus* of prudence. "Right reason" denotes an occurrent mental state rather than a mental disposition. Most present-day virtue theorists instead favor the dispositional account of moral goodness. Supporters of the occurrent-state view protest that someone without any stable disposition to choose good actions might at times rise to the occasion, and if she does, her action is no less good than the action of someone who has such a disposition.[36] But if a virtuous *habitus* does not account for the moral goodness of the agent's action, what does it explain?

As a natural cause, Scotus argues, a virtuous *habitus* might figure in psychological explanations. It could explain why someone with such a *habitus* does morally good acts more promptly, easily, and with greater pleasure than he would otherwise. Considering two psychological roles that a *habitus* might play – as either an active but secondary cause of the will's actions or merely a non-causal inclination – Scotus argues that a *habitus* is not strictly necessary to explain the different way in which the virtuous agent acts; yet he himself opts for the first account, which assigns a larger role to the *habitus*.[37] Thus began

---

[34] See also *Nic. Ethics* II.4, where Aristotle highlights the differences between actions by persons who have virtuous dispositions and actions by persons who lack such dispositions.

[35] Scotus, *Ord.* I.17.1.1–2 nn. 6–100. Owing to limits of space, I present a radically abbreviated account of Scotus's arguments on this topic. For a more detailed summary see my "Rethinking Moral Dispositions: Scotus on the Virtues," in T. Williams (ed.) *The Cambridge Companion to Duns Scotus* (Cambridge: Cambridge University Press, 2003) 352–76; see also Mary Beth Ingham and Mechthild Dreyer, *The Philosophical Vision of John Duns Scotus* (Washington, DC: Catholic University Press, 2004) ch. 7.

[36] See, for example, Thomas Hurka, "Virtuous Act, Virtuous Dispositions," *Analysis* 66 (2006) 69–76.

[37] Scotus, *Ord.* I.17.1.1–2 nn. 47–52, 69–70.

an expanding controversy over how naturally acquired virtuous *habitus* help to explain morally good actions, if indeed they do.

Did Aristotle himself teach that a virtuous *habitus* makes one's action morally good? Fourteenth-century commentators on his *Ethics* disagreed. While all labored to interpret Aristotle's work with charity, some worried more than others about circularity. For instance, Gerald of Odo argues that a right choice is impossible without right reason; right reason cannot exist without prudence; and prudence cannot exist without good moral character. Therefore, a right choice is impossible without the good moral character inseparably related to prudence (*Expositio in Ethicam* II.8). There can be no doubt that this Franciscan master of theology awards the virtuous *habitus* constituting moral character a much greater role than Scotus did. In Gerald's view, one must distinguish between the kind of choices that *generate* virtue and the kind that are an *effect* of virtue. The latter involve a firm and unchanging desire for the good, which can come only from a virtuous *habitus*. Such a desire cannot come from the power of will because the will in its own right is unlimited, just as capable of bad choices as good ones (ibid., III.13).

John Buridan, a master of arts with no degree in theology, argued for a different reading of Aristotle; and Buridan's commentary enjoyed the kind of success that few ancient specialists today even dream of. Not only did it circulate widely in later medieval manuscripts, it went on to be published in five printed editions in the early modern period, the last produced at Oxford in 1637. Buridan knew Gerald's commentary on the *Ethics* well; indeed, his own commentary borrows freely from it.[38] Yet Buridan diverges sharply from Gerald on the relation between virtuous *habitus* and morally good actions. As he interprets Aristotle, a *habitus* of the will is generated by the will's choices. A virtue of the will is generated by those choices commensurate and consonant with right reason. Aristotle's theory appears circular only because some people equate right reason with the *habitus* of prudence. Buridan explains why this is a bad mistake:

Prudence is not formally right reason, that is, right judging, just as moral virtue is not formally right choice; rather, prudence is a *habitus* determining the intellect to judging promptly and firmly about possible actions. But I do not say that such a *habitus* is necessary for judging rightly, just as I do not affirm that moral virtue is necessary for choosing rightly. Rather, from freedom of choice we are able to judge correctly and choose rightly, even if we were badly brought up, although this is exceedingly difficult.

(*Quaest. Ethic.* II.4)

---

[38] Buridan's borrowings from Gerald's commentary are catalogued in James Walsh, "Some Relationships between Gerald Odo's and John Buridan's Commentaries on Aristotle's Ethics," *Franciscan Studies* 35 (1975) 237–75.

Like Scotus, Buridan defends the occurrent-state view of morally good actions, not the dispositional view. He elaborates on his position in discussing a second thesis: namely, that actions preceding and following the acquisition of a virtuous *habitus* are of the same kind (ibid., II.5). One objection to this thesis rests on the popular *dictum* that "virtue makes one's action good."[39] How, then, could acts performed before someone acquires virtue be of the same kind as those performed afterward? On the opposite side Buridan marshals arguments he considers more persuasive. One recites the likeness principle: we become just by doing just acts, temperate by doing temperate acts, and so on. Another claims that actions preceding and following the acquisition of a virtuous *habitus* differ only in "mode": someone with a virtuous *habitus* acts firmly and promptly and in other respects *well*, whereas someone without one does not.

Buridan's solution distinguishes between what good action strictly requires and what makes it easier. While a virtuous *habitus* makes good actions easier, it is not strictly necessary for them. Is it even strictly necessary in order to do good actions firmly, promptly, and in other respects *well*? It would be difficult for the will lacking a virtuous *habitus* to choose as well as the will that has one, says Buridan, and this hardly ever happens. But perhaps the will lacking a virtuous *habitus* could, through its freedom, choose as well as the will having a virtuous *habitus*, and if it did, its choice would have the same essential moral goodness. Hence Aristotle's claim that only someone with the *habitus* of justice acts justly should not be taken to mean that it is impossible for anyone else to act justly, only that this is difficult and exceedingly rare (ibid., II.5). So understood, the virtues continue to have a place in moral theory, albeit a smaller one than they did in ancient ethics.

[39] This common saying – *Virtus perficit habentem et opus eius bonum reddit* – is routinely attributed by scholastics to Aristotle. What Aristotle actually says is that virtue perfects the possessor and makes him function well (*Nic. Ethics* II.6, 1106a16–17). Both the original and the revised versions of Grosseteste's translation accordingly use the adverb *bene*, not the adjective *bonum*: "*et opus eius bene reddit.*" The popularity of the spurious *dictum* might be explained by the scholastics' tendency to rely on *florilegia*, by their use of some other translation of the *Ethics*, or both.

37

ACTION AND INTENTION

JEAN PORTER

Near the beginning of the second part of the *Summa theologiae*, Thomas Aquinas offers a detailed analysis of human action. This analysis presupposes that the human act has an objective, complex, and morally significant structure (see 1a2ae 18.4 ad 3), and that any adequate moral theory will give a central place to this structure. Today, even those most sympathetic to Aquinas's moral theory are likely to find these presuppositions unconvincing and the details of his analysis bewildering. Yet Aquinas was hardly alone, either in his presuppositions or in the attention he devoted to the analysis of human action. On the contrary, earlier Latin discussions contain a rich and complex debate over the moral and theological significance of the structure of the human act. The terms of this debate are complex and by no means identical to Aquinas's own. For that very reason it is worth examining in its own right, for its substantive interest and also for its continuing relevance to contemporary moral and legal philosophy. What follows represents an attempt to trace the main lines of this debate, without claiming an exhaustive treatment. Given its continuing importance, Aquinas's analysis will be given extended attention, but as will be apparent, that analysis is only fully comprehensible in the context of the preceding debate.

ACTION AND INTENTION IN EARLIER LATIN THOUGHT

The late eleventh and early twelfth centuries comprised a period of far-reaching institutional development and reform, both in the church and in civil society. In this context, long-standing questions about the meaning of sin or wrongdoing and the status of problematic actions took on new urgency.[1] Throughout the twelfth and thirteenth centuries, theologians and jurists devoted considerable attention to identifying the components of the human act in virtue of which

---

[1] As Richard Southern observes, in *Scholastic Humanism and the Unification of Europe* (Oxford: Blackwell, 1995–2001) I: 145–58.

it is sinful or praiseworthy, and drawing out the practical consequences of this analysis. At the same time, the twelfth and thirteenth centuries were also marked by intense attention to the inner life of the individual and to the value and appropriate expressions of inner freedom.[2] In many respects, these tendencies arose out of the same matrix of causes and were mutually reinforcing. With respect to the questions we are considering, however, these tendencies stood in tension with one another, in such a way as to shape what became the defining issue for debates over merit and sin – that is to say, what is the relation between the exterior act, so carefully defined in institutional and legal contexts, and the inner intention, so vitally important to the life of the individual?

Contrary to what is sometimes said, from the late eleventh century onwards everyone agreed that sin must stem from something within the person. The debate then focused on just what it is within the individual that constitutes sin. According to one widely influential view originating with Anselm of Laon at this time, the motion of the soul toward sin proceeds through a series of stages, each of which after the first is itself at least potentially sinful. Although the details vary, the different versions of this "stage theory" offer a remarkably broad and comprehensive account of sin, according to which not only bad acts and intentions but even bad desires and tendencies are at least potentially sinful.[3]

In contrast, Peter Abaelard argues that only consent to an illicit act "is properly called sin, that is, a guilt of the soul through which damnation is merited, or which constitutes one as guilty before God."[4] Thus, neither vice *per se* nor spontaneous desires for illicit pleasures should be regarded as sins. Rather, sin consists solely in actual consent – that is to say, in readiness to perform the act in question as soon as the opportunity arises. This line of argument leads him on to his best-known claim, namely that the external act is in itself neutral, neither increasing nor mitigating the guilt of a sinful consent. The performance of an external act is the normal *sign* of consent, but the external act itself, like the bad desires leading up to it, does not in itself constitute sin, nor even add to the sin inherent in the consent itself.

Contrary to what is commonly supposed, Abaelard is not advocating a kind of moral subjectivism, according to which moral good and evil are wholly

[2] As Giles Constable shows in *The Reformation of the Twelfth Century* (Cambridge: Cambridge University Press, 1996) pp. 257–93.

[3] For further details of the stage theory of sin, see Robert Blomme, *La doctrine du péché dans les écoles théologiques de la première moitié du XIIe siècle* (Louvain: Publications universitaires, 1958) pp. 3–99, and John Marenbon, *The Philosophy of Peter Abelard* (Cambridge: Cambridge University Press, 1997) pp. 253–5.

[4] *Ethics*, ed. Luscombe, pp. 4–6. For Abaelard's definition of consent, together with the claim that external acts add nothing to the guilt incurred by consent to sin, see pp. 14–15.

determined by the agent's good or bad intentions.[5] His concerns lie elsewhere; above all, he wants to safeguard the connection between sin and human freedom. Neither external acts nor bad desires count as sins, for just the same reason – that is, neither is under the agent's control.[6] On the one hand, bad desires arise spontaneously, without the agent's consent; on the other, the agent's consent to a particular act can be frustrated in all sorts of ways, including lack of opportunity and physical incapacity. Against those who would assert the moral significance of either a bad desire or a particular external act considered in itself, Abaelard insists that only the agent's consent to a particular action can count as a meritorious or sinful act. Nonetheless, it does not follow that the moral value of the act that is chosen, considered abstractly as a *kind* of performance, is determined by the agent's intent. On the contrary, the moral value of the kind of action envisioned in the agent's consent determines the moral value of the consent itself. Thus, when Abaelard distinguishes in the *Ethics* between grave and light sins, he does so in terms of distinguishing kinds of actions that are seriously wrong from those that are not. After referring to the practice of daily confession, which is meant to deal with light faults such as sins of negligence, he goes on to say that this is not an appropriate way of dealing with "damnable and more serious sins" such as murder and adultery – actions that are of such a kind as to render anyone who consents to them "execrable and very hateful" (*Ethics*, p. 70). To be sure, sin does not consist in a specific external act of murder, perjury, or adultery, but in the consent to the act in question. At the same time, the consent is gravely sinful because the act to which consent is being given is an act of a kind that is gravely wrong. Thus, even though a particular external act, considered in itself as a singular event, has no independent moral value, nonetheless, the abstract kind of action that it represents (for instance, as an act of murder) is morally significant, in a way that is not determined by the agent's consent. Abaelard's analysis of sin in terms of consent, so far from committing him to moral subjectivism, presupposes objective standards by reference to which consent is formulated and in terms of which it can be evaluated.

While the distinction between vicious tendencies and actual sin was persuasive to many, a number of theologians were troubled by the implication – whether fairly drawn or not – that external actions have no independent moral significance, apart from that bestowed by the agent's aim or motive. In order

[5] Marenbon argues that Abaelard's moral theory presupposes an objective moral law in *The Philosophy of Peter Abelard*, pp. 265–7, but this still seems to be the minority view.
[6] I argue for this claim in more detail in "Responsibility, Passion, and Sin: A Reassessment of Abelard's *Ethics*," *Journal of Religious Ethics* 28 (2000) 367–94.

to forestall this implication, Peter Lombard drew on Augustine in support of the view that "all acts are to be judged good or evil in accordance with intention and motive, except for those that are evil, in such a way that they never can be good, even if they seem to have a good motive."[7] Subsequently, Latin theologians develop and qualify this basic point in diverse ways. A number of them develop a claim that Lombard also notes but does not endorse: namely, that just as there are some actions that are evil in themselves, so some kinds of actions are intrinsically good, in such a way that they can never be performed in such a way as to render them bad. By this point, what began as a debate over the relation between the inner states of the agent, and the external acts through which those states are exhibited, was increasingly focused on an analysis of logical and definitional questions pertaining to the description of the act, and, more specifically, to the implications of describing an act as good or bad "in kind." This tendency becomes marked in the early thirteenth century, as we will see.

EARLY THIRTEENTH-CENTURY DISCUSSIONS

By the early decades of the thirteenth century, analyses of the description of the act had become quite complex. We see a good illustration of this in the work of William of Auxerre, who distinguishes two ways in which actions can be said to be good or bad "in kind" (*in genere*) – either intrinsically (*secundum se*) and of necessity (*ex necessitate*), or else generally but not necessarily (*in se*) (*Summa aurea* III.10.4.5.1). Actions of the former kind retain the same moral value whatever the circumstances, whereas the moral value of actions of the latter kind may be altered by circumstances. And so, for example, an act of charity is, as such, necessarily good, whatever the circumstances, whereas the act of giving alms, while generally a good kind of action, may be rendered bad if done in an inappropriate way. Similarly, the anonymous author of the *Summa Duacensis* claims: "we take three kinds of goodness that we posit with respect to actions, saying something is good in accordance with its kind, and it is good from circumstances, and it is good from grace."[8]

Subsequently, a number of theologians took up the question of what it means to attribute some quality to something "in kind," *in genere*. This question, in

---

[7] *Libri IV Sententiarum* II.40. Furthermore, as Lottin observes, he refers to this as a widely held view; see Odon Lottin, "Le problème de la moralité intrinsèque d'Abélard à saint Thomas d'Aquin," in *Psychologie et morale aux XIIe et XIIIe siècles* (Gembloux: Duculot, 1948–60) II: 422. In general, I rely on Lottin for the overall history and development of Latin views on the normative evaluation of the human act.

[8] As quoted in Lottin, "La moralité intrinsèque," II: 433.

turn, prompted an extended discussion of the different senses of "genus," which, as we might expect, quickly moved to a high level of abstraction. Finally, Albert the Great cut off this line of analysis, remarking that it had simply become too complicated to be helpful.[9]

It is hard not to sympathize with Albert here, but these discussions yielded at least one valuable insight (which Albert himself appropriates) – namely, that we are to understand an act that is good or bad "in kind" as an act joined to an appropriate or inappropriate matter. Of course, this way of formulating the point begs for further clarification – just what is "the act" that is joined to "due matter" in this context, and how does it relate to the act that we characterize *in genere*? Correlatively, what counts as "the matter" of the act? We do see attempts to clarify this distinction. According to an anonymous author drawing on the *Summa Duacensis*, a good act, such as feeding the poor, can only be regarded as good in light of the "conjunction of the matter to the act," since neither the matter nor the act, taken by itself, is necessarily good. It is not determined by the kind of act taken by itself – that is, feeding someone – since in that case feeding a madman would be a good act. Nor is it determined by the matter alone – that is, the poor – since in that case any treatment toward the poor would be good – for instance, it would be good to treat the poor with contempt. An appropriate conjunction of kind of action and matter is necessary if an act is to be regarded as good.[10] This helps, insofar as it clearly identifies the act with an operation, while the matter of the act is identified with whatever it is on which the operation is performed. Yet even here, the distinction between "the act" that is good in kind (feeding the hungry), and "the act" considered as an operation joined to due matter (feeding, or else showing contempt, as directed towards the poor) is unclear. Moving beyond this author, we find further unresolved issues: sometimes, the circumstances seem to be assimilated to the matter, and sometimes they are distinguished from it; similarly, the purpose or motive often seems to be incorporated into the identification of the kind of act that is in question.

I noted above that Albert sets out to simplify and clarify the issues pertaining to the moral evaluation of acts. When we turn to the *De bono*, we find that he does so by analyzing actions in terms of their appropriateness as expressions of virtues or vices; thus, for him, the conceptions of virtues and vices provide a framework for identifying kinds of acts. As he explains, the phrase "good in kind" identifies a kind of human action that "is ordered more to one contrary, that is to the good of virtue"; correspondingly, an act that is evil in kind "inclines more towards vice" (*De bono* I.2.4). Thus, as he explains in response

---

[9] As Lottin observes, ibid., II: 451.   [10] The relevant text is quoted ibid., II: 437.

to objections, "good in kind" does not stem from any circumstances whatever, but only from those that establish a kind of virtue, and correlatively the species of an act is determined by reference to the kind of virtue that it represents. He goes on to say that some kinds of acts are good only if they incorporate appropriate circumstances:

> [T]here are many voluntary acts that can in no way attain the due proportion to the matter in themselves, but only clothed in circumstances, such as to have sexual relations, to kill, and others of this kind . . . If we say, "to kill one who ought to be killed," or, "to have sexual relations with one's wife," the phrases 'ought to be killed' or 'one's wife' bring in circumstances through which the act itself is ascribed to a particular virtue — namely, to justice or to conjugal chastity.
>
> (*De bono* I.2.4 ad 7)

Albert thus simplifies the earlier discussion by tying the analysis and identification of kinds of actions explicitly to moral evaluations, more specifically to our conceptions of virtues and vices. This is an elegant move that allows him to cut through much of the confusion of earlier lines of analysis. At the same time, however, Albert's analysis does not fully resolve the ambiguities noted in earlier authors. He claims that one's sexual partner or victim cannot be said to be the matter of an act of sexual intercourse or killing, to which the act stands (or fails to stand) in due proportion (ibid.). But what then is the matter of these acts? He does not seem to say. What is more, the category of acts "prone to" moral good or evil — acts that are likely to be virtuous unless corrupted, or vicious unless redeemed – calls for further explication. What is it about these kinds of actions that inclines them to be good or evil, prior to their further specification by circumstances? Albert seems to assume that certain kinds of operations (such as sexual intercourse and killing) are at least problematic, if not always prohibited – but his views at this point are not entirely clear.

ACTION AND INTENTION IN AQUINAS

The ambiguities just described help to explain why Aquinas complicates what Albert simplified, even as he builds on Albert's key insight. Aquinas frames his analysis of the human act in terms of his metaphysics and his theory of the will, in such a way as to develop a set of criteria for distinguishing the different components of the act and explaining how they fit together in moral evaluation. At the same time, his analysis allows him to address a further set of issues that recede in Albert's account, but that are nonetheless central to discussions of the human act up to Albert's time – namely, the relation between the exterior act and the interior act of the will from which it stems.

Aquinas's analysis of the components of the human act in *Summa theologiae* 1a2ae 18–20 occurs within the context of a wider discussion of actions, including both distinctively human acts and those kinds of acts that we share with other animals. He begins by framing issues relating to the formation of human acts in terms of their most general characteristic, that is to say, their quality as voluntary or involuntary acts stemming (or failing to stem) from the distinctively human rational appetite (1a2ae 6). This leads him to consider circumstances that, as he explains, are relevant to theology because they qualify the overall evaluation of an act even though they remain external to its substance (1a2ae 7.1, 2). He goes on to consider acts of the will – both those acts immediately elicited by the will (1a2ae 8–16) and those acts commanded by the will, that is to say, carried out through the other faculties and organs of the body (1a2ae 17). At this point, Aquinas turns to the considerations in terms of which acts are judged to be morally good or evil. 1a2ae 18 is devoted to an analysis of the goodness and evil of human actions generally considered, after which Aquinas takes up the goodness or evil of interior and external acts (1a2ae 19–20). In 1a2ae 18, he identifies the relevant respects in which an action must be good if the act taken as a whole is to be morally good – namely, the object of the act (1a2ae 18.2), its circumstances (1a2ae 18.3), and the end towards which it is directed (1a2ae 18.4). Defect or deformity with respect to any of these vitiates the moral quality of the action; for example, an act that is bad in kind cannot be redeemed by the agent's good intention.

This analysis is recognizably an intervention in the ongoing debates over the proper analysis of human acts. At the same time, Aquinas's language is distinctive – particularly, his use of the terms "object" and "end" – and this distinctive usage reflects something more fundamental about his overall approach. More clearly than his predecessors had done, he considers the human action as an event, constituted by a causal operation through which the agent brings about a state of affairs (or at least, attempts to do so) regarded by him as being in some way good or desirable (see 1a2ae 1.3).[11] Although the complexity of his analysis can obscure this point, Aquinas consistently maintains that the human action is a unitary reality, which for that very reason can be described in both moral and non-moral terms (1a2ae 1.3 ad 3). The non-moral descriptions of the act may capture considerations in virtue of which that act is either desirable or repugnant, even apart from a final judgment on its moral value. This move enables him to capture the intuition, expressed in different ways by William of

Auxerre and Albert (among others), that some kinds of actions are especially morally salient, even though their moral value considered as such is indeterminate. An act of killing, for example, is always morally significant, but a particular act of killing may be either a praiseworthy act of justice or a sinful act of murder.

In this way, Aquinas's analysis represents an advance in analytic clarity. At the same time, however, his most distinctive contribution to the analysis of human actions depends on his metaphysics and philosophy of nature, rather than on free-standing conceptual or logical analysis. More specifically, the key to understanding what is distinctive about Aquinas's account lies in his analysis of the object of an act, understood in terms of whatever considerations define the act as a representative of a general kind (to give alms, to murder, and so on).[12] Hence, the goodness or evil deriving from the object of the act is equivalent to what Aquinas's interlocutors describe as goodness or evil *ex genere*, as he explicitly notes (1a2ae 18.4). This is not just a terminological change. Aquinas speaks in terms of the object of an action because, as he explains in his commentary on Aristotle's *De anima*, every act or operation derives its species – is defined as the kind of operation that it is – in terms of its characteristic object. The objects of the passive powers of the soul (such as sensation) are defined in terms of whatever it is that engages these powers (as, for example, the visible engages the power of sight). He continues, "The objects of the active powers are their operations. Moreover, it is plain that, with respect to any of these, besides the operations there are things done through the operations, which are the ends of the operations, as is said in the first book of the *Ethics* – as for example, the house that is built is the end of building" (II.6.305). The object of the act is thus an operation, rather than the target or terminus of the agent's activity. To return to the example mentioned above, the object of the act of feeding the poor is the act of feeding, considered (and chosen by the agent) as an act of feeding understood as a way of giving sustenance to someone in need.

We can now begin to see how the diverse elements of the human act fit together on Aquinas's account. The first point to keep in mind is that, for Aquinas, the human act is a unitary reality – that is, an event establishing a relation between the agent's exercise of causal efficacy and the terminus of that exercise.[13] The distinctions set forth in 1a2ae 18 provide the terms necessary to analyze an action as a unitary whole, taking account both of the operation that is the terminus of the agent's immediate choice – this is the object – and

---

[12] This is true generally speaking, at any rate, but Aquinas's position is complex and seems to have changed over time. For details, see Joseph Pilsner, *The Specification of Human Actions in St. Thomas Aquinas* (Oxford: Oxford University Press, 2006) pp. 70–140.

[13] On the individuation of actions thus understood, see Brock, *Action and Conduct*, pp. 49–93.

the state of affairs in view of which the agent chooses – namely, the end (1a2ae 18.2, 4). We must also take account of circumstances because these qualify the agent's overall choice, even though by definition they do not determine the rational structure of the act (1a2ae 18.3).

The role of circumstances should be underscored. Unlike his interlocutors, Aquinas distinguishes between those aspects of a particular act that constitute its object and those that are truly circumstantial (1a2ae 18.10, 11). The point is not that one set of considerations is morally relevant, whereas another is not – on the contrary, Aquinas insists that circumstances do affect the moral evaluation of particular acts (1a2ae 7.2, 18.3). Yet he distinguishes between these two sorts of considerations on the grounds that only some of them have a direct and independent bearing on the kind of action that one is performing, seen from a moral standpoint; others, circumstances properly so called, derive their normative significance from the overall context of a particular act (1a2ae 18.11). So, for example, although location generally has no distinctive moral significance taken by itself, the sinfulness of an act of fornication would be aggravated by being done out in the streets, since this circumstance would reflect a shameless disregard for the feelings of others and an indifference to scandal. Thus, the considerations determining the object and those considerations setting the circumstances work together to (partially) determine the goodness of the will choosing them – but in two distinct ways, following on their distinctive significance as discerned by reason.

In *Summa theologiae* 1a2ae 19, Aquinas adapts these distinctions in such a way as to account for the distinctive features of the inner act of the will, namely, its choice of a particular act. The discussion here is notoriously problematic. Aquinas begins with the claim that the goodness of the will depends entirely on its object (1a2ae 19.1, 2). As he explains, "the end is the object of the will, and not of the other powers. Thus with respect to the act of the will, there is no difference between the goodness deriving from the object and that deriving from the end, as there is with respect to the acts of the other powers" (1a2ae 19.2 ad 1). But in that case, what becomes of the distinction between object and end so carefully delineated at 1a2ae 18.7? Similarly, the circumstances are assimilated into the object of the interior act of the will – at least, insofar as the agent is aware of the relevant circumstances – in such a way that they qualify what he voluntarily does (1a2ae 19.2 ad 2). It appears that Aquinas is disregarding the carefully drawn distinctions between object, end, and circumstances set forth in 1a2ae 18.

This inconsistency, however, is only apparent. Aquinas's conception of the act as a unified event allows him to distinguish between the interior act of the will and the external act, while maintaining that these are in reality two components of one and the same action (1a2ae 20.3). For this very reason, the terms of analysis set forth in 1a2ae 18 can be applied in different ways to the descriptions of the act considered as an interior act of will and considered as an external performance. What is at stake are two different analytic descriptions of the same action, which track the relevant considerations from two different vantage points. Considered as an operation of the soul, the interior act of the soul is identified in terms of the object of the agent's choice, which is constituted by the concrete act proposed by reason as good and worth pursuing here and now (1a2ae 19.1 ad 3, 19.3). As such, the object of the interior act must be considered globally, as a concrete whole encompassing everything that the agent knowingly chooses – this particular act, chosen in these circumstances as a means to or constituent aspect of this further end. That is why Aquinas says that the goodness of the interior act of the will is determined by the object alone. The object in *this* context is nothing other than the particular, fully determinate action that is chosen; therefore, all the components of the act considered as a whole must be considered in this context as complex determinates of one specific choice (1a2ae 19.2, esp. ad 1). We see here an application of the general point that the operations of the active powers of the soul can be defined in reference to the end, as well as in terms of the operation itself. Nonetheless, these distinctions presuppose a more comprehensive analysis of human action, considered in its integral reality as an event (the external act) relating the agent who chooses to the chosen state of affairs.

The complex character of Aquinas's account becomes still more apparent when we turn to the next question (1a2ae 20), which considers the morality of the external act. In the first article of this question, Aquinas explicitly poses the question running through the whole debate over merit and sin: are good and evil in human actions constituted fundamentally by the inner act of the will, or by the external act? Aquinas replies that it depends. Insofar as the goodness or evil of a particular act stems from the end for which the agent acts, these do depend on the will, and in this respect the goodness of the external act is dependent on the goodness or evil of the interior act of the will. At the same time, "the goodness or evil that an external act has in itself, on account of due matter and due circumstances, is not derived from the will, but rather from reason" (1a2ae 20.1). Yet in another sense, the goodness of the external action adds to, and indeed partially determines, the good of the interior act of the will, precisely because it provides the will with its "terminus and end," and thus, "it adds to the goodness or badness of the will; because every inclination or motion is perfected in this, that it achieves its end or attains its terminus" (1a2ae 20.4). The external act thus stands in the same relation to the inner act as reason, generally considered, stands to the will – or, more precisely, the relation between external and inner act is one expression of the overall relation between reason and will. Considered as a kind of act with an intelligible structure, the external act has a moral significance of its own that determines the sinfulness or merit of the agent choosing it – that is to say, the agent's will in choosing is informed by her rational grasp that this (particular) act has the rational structure and significance it does as an act of a specific kind, with a determinate object. Thus, the external act, considered as a representative of a kind, can inform the inner act of the choosing will because it has a rational structure (of appropriateness or equity or their opposites) that can be discerned by reason.

It was suggested above that this is what Abaelard too was driving at. Yet it is difficult to imagine Abaelard saying point blank that the external act determines the goodness or evil of the agent's consent. The fact that Aquinas can say this, without denying that a particular act has moral significance only insofar as it is voluntary, reflects both the complexity of the intervening debates and the distinctive character of Aquinas's intervention in these debates.

38

THE CARE OF SOULS AND "PRACTICAL ETHICS"[1]

M. W. F. STONE

Despite the vast amount of attention that medieval ethics has received, there has been comparatively little scrutiny of what might be called "practical ethics." A significant proportion of medieval ideas about the scope and point of human conduct is not to be discovered in works of "moral philosophy" (at least as we may understand that term), but is more likely to be found in a treatise of canon law, or a work concerning the practice of confession, or a didactic moral treatise written for the instruction of the clergy or laity. The literary genre of "pastoral writings" to which these texts belong[2] also includes treatises on vices and virtues, as well as collections of popular sermons and discussions of the seven sins. Although this much larger body of literature might lack the abstract precision that we rightly associate with the efforts of medieval thinkers who commented on Aristotle's *Nicomachean Ethics*, it is replete with novel insights and sobering reflections about the care and guidance of the human soul. These materials can be combined with a further body of texts that includes quodlibetal disputes focused upon the topical moral issues of the day,[3] and also

---

[1] For Leonard E. Boyle O.P. (1923–99). *Ar dheis Dé go raibh a anam.*

[2] The work of Leonard Boyle did more than most to open up the field of *pastoralia* to generations of medievalists. See the papers collected in *Pastoral Care, Clerical Education and Canon Law, 1200–1400* (London: Variorum, 1981), as well as "*Summae confessorum*," in R. Bultot (ed.) *Les genres littéraires dans les sources théologiques et philosophiques médiévales: définition, critique et exploration* (Louvain-la-Neuve: Université catholique de Louvain, 1982) 227–37; "The Fourth Lateran Council and Manuals of Popular Theology," in T. J. Hefferman (ed.) *The Popular Literature of Medieval England* (Knoxville: University of Tennessee Press, 1985) 30–43; and "The Inter-Conciliar Period 1179–1215 and the Beginnings of Pastoral Manuals," in F. Liotta (ed.) *Miscellanea, Rolando Bandinelli, Papa Alessandro III* (Siena: Accademia senese degli intronati, 1986) 45–56. See also Joseph Goering, *William de Montibus (c. 1140–1213): The Schools and the Literature of Pastoral Care* (Toronto: Pontifical Institute of Medieval Studies, 1992) pp. 58–102.

[3] On the quodlibets see Palémon Glorieux, *La littérature quodlibétique de 1260 à 1320* (Paris: Vrin, 1925–35); Amedeus Teetaert, "La littérature quodlibetique," *Ephemerides theologiae Lovanienses* 14 (1937) 77–105. All earlier work has now been superseded by two state-of-the-art volumes edited by Christopher Schabel: *Theological Quodlibeta in the Middle Ages* (Leiden: Brill, 2006–7).

the lengthy discussions of social problems,[4] conscience,[5] usury,[6] economic life,[7] population,[8] suicide,[9] human sexuality,[10] contraception,[11] marriage,[12] lying and other sins of the tongue[13] that are present in literally hundreds of theological disputations and in commentaries on Lombard's *Sentences*. When we take all of this together, we can appreciate the extent to which the practical as well as the speculative scrutiny of ethical issues was a marked feature of medieval intellectual life.

This chapter offers a general description of the casuistical character of canon law, as well as the pastoral outlook of medieval preaching, the literature on vices and virtues, and confession. Although far from comprehensive as a survey, it attempts to demonstrate that medieval thought about moral practice was a much more synoptic phenomenon than is countenanced by current philosophical scholarship, and that interesting ideas about how ethical norms can be applied to human action are to be found in these diverse sources. Yet despite sharing a quite basic interest in the more concrete dimensions of ethical inquiry, medieval

---

[4] See Georges de Lagarde, *La naissance de l'espirit laïque au declin du moyen âge* (Louvain: Nauwelaerts, 1956–70) esp. vol. II; and Elsa Marmursztejn, *L'autorité des maîtres: scolastique, normes et société au xiie siècle* (Paris: Les Belles Lettres, 2007).

[5] The primary texts related to conscience are collected in Odon Lottin, *Psychologie et morale aux XIIe et XIIIe siècles* (Gembloux: Duculot, 1948–60), esp. vol. II.

[6] See John T. Noonan, *The Scholastic Analysis of Usury* (Cambridge, MA: Harvard University Press, 1957); and Odd Langholm, *The Aristotelian Analysis of Usury* (New York: Columbia University Press, 1984).

[7] On this subject see three important books by Odd Langholm: *Wealth and Money in the Aristotelian Tradition* (New York: Columbia University Press, 1983); *Economics in the Medieval Schools: Wealth, Exchange, Value, Money and Usury According to the Paris Theological Tradition 1200–1350* (Leiden: Brill, 1992); and *The Legacy of Scholasticism in Economic Thought: Antecedents of Choice and Power* (Cambridge: Cambridge University Press, 1998).

[8] See Peter Biller, *The Measure of Multitude: Population in Medieval Thought* (Oxford: Oxford University Press, 2000).

[9] On this see Alexander Murray, *Suicide in the Middle Ages* (Oxford: Oxford University Press, 1998–2002).

[10] For a sober and scholarly discussion of this most complicated of topics see James A. Brundage, *Law, Sex, and Christian Society in Medieval Europe* (Chicago: University of Chicago Press, 1987); and Pierre J. Payer, *The Bridling of Desire: Views of Sex in the Later Middle Ages* (Toronto: University of Toronto Press, 1993).

[11] See John T. Noonan, *Contraception: A History of its Treatment by the Catholic Theologians and Canonists* (Cambridge, MA: Harvard University Press, 1965).

[12] See Jean Gaudemet, *Le mariage en Occident: les mœurs et le droit* (Paris: Cerf, 1987); Christopher N. L. Brooke, *The Medieval Idea of Marriage* (Oxford: Oxford University Press, 1989); Philip L. Reynolds, *Marriage in the Western Church: The Christianization of Marriage during the Patristic and Early Medieval Periods* (Leiden: Brill, 1994); and D. L. d'Avray, *Medieval Marriage: Symbolism and Society* (Oxford: Oxford University Press, 2005).

[13] See Carla Casagrande and Silvana Vecchio, *I peccati della lingua: disciplina ed etica della parola nella cultura medievale* (Rome: Istituto della Enciclopedia Italiana, 1987); and my "In the Shadow of Augustine: The Scholastic Debate on Lying from Robert Grosseteste to Gabriel Biel," in J. A. Aertsen and M. Pickavé (eds.) *Herbst des Mittelalters? Fragen zur Bewertung des 14. und 15. Jahrhunderts* (Berlin: De Gruyter, 2004) 277–317.

thinkers were engaged in an intellectual enterprise that cannot be compared usefully to that of contemporary applied ethics. The care and guidance of souls was a quite different activity, predicated on a wholly different set of theological aims and objectives.

CANON LAW AND EQUITY

Among other tasks, canon law was concerned with the analysis of the views of "authorities" (*auctoritates*) regarding specific practical questions (*casus*), as derived from the decrees of ecumenical and local church councils, epistles of various popes and bishops, diocesan statutes and ordinances, as well as from the diverse pronouncements of the Church Fathers and other ecclesiastical texts. Since sources such as these could be highly specific both in their provenance and content, producing at times a wide variety of incompatible precedents, the task of the canonist was to pick out, in the midst of this welter of conflicting advice, what was salient to each particular case in accordance with the teaching of the church and the demands of natural justice. The chief collection of canon law during the later Middle Ages was the *Decretum*, a collection of canons of church councils and decrees of popes, put together at Bologna during the fourth decade of the twelfth century, primarily by an individual known as Gratian.[14] One example of a problem from the *Decretum* can suffice to illustrate the methods used by the canonists:

A certain bishop makes a statement on oath that turns out to be false, though he thought it true. When the apparent perjury is made known, his archdeacon swears he will never obey the bishop again. The bishop compels the archdeacon to obedience, and is accused of perjury on two counts: as a principal for his original false statement on oath; and as an accessory, for compelling the archdeacon to break his oath.

(II C. 22, ed. Richter and Friedberg, I: 860)

The question posed is this: "To what extent is the bishop guilty on either of these counts?" The solution proposed by the text (ibid., *quaest.* I–V) need not detain us, since what is more relevant to our argument is the method used in

---

[14] See Stefen Kuttner, "Graziano: L'uomo e l'opera," *Studia Gratiana* 1 (1953) 17–29; Andrea Lazzarini, "Gratianus de Urbeveteri," *Studia Gratiana*, 4 (1956) 1–15; John Noonan, "Gratian Slept Here: The Changing Identity of the Father of the Systematic Study of Canon Law," *Traditio* 35 (1979) 145–72; and Anders Winroth, *The Making of Gratian's Decretum* (Cambridge: Cambridge University Press, 2000) pp. 1–33. On the composition of canon law with reference to works both before and after the *Decretum*, see Gabriel Le Bras and Jean Gaudemet, *Histoire du droit et des institutions de l'Église en Occident* (Paris: Cujas, 1955–8) I: 22–159; Charles Duggan, *Twelfth Century Decretal Collections* (London: Athlone Press, 1963); and Gérard Fransen, *Décrétales et les collections de décrétales* (Turnhout: Brepols, 1972).

order to arrive at a resolution of the case – namely, a procedure that identifies all the known features of the case, together with the claims they make on the agent. In this manner, the *Decretum* deems that the business of canon law is to approximate, as far as possible, the verdicts of informed judgment, where these are understood as the pronouncements of reputable *auctoritates*. The way canonists like Gratian aimed to arrive at a solution to the problems raised by a case was by assembling all the divergent sources so that a just interpretation could be facilitated and the different recommendations of the *auctoritates* assessed and eventually harmonized.[15]

Instruction in medieval law faculties was conducted almost exclusively by means of a dialectical analysis of texts. This method followed the structure and organization of a particular work and aimed to explain the meaning and application of each sentence and paragraph of that text, commencing at the beginning and proceeding systematically to the end. Odofredus da Ponte (d. after 1337),[16] a teacher of civil law from around the start of the fourteenth century, described for his students the standard method of analyzing a legal text:

First, I shall give you the summaries of each title before I come to the text. Secondly, I shall advance well and distinctly and in the best terms available to me, the meaning of each law. Thirdly, I shall read the text in order to correct it. Fourthly, I shall briefly restate the meaning. Fifthly, I shall resolve any conflicts, adding general points of interest (which are commonly called *brocardica*) and subtle and useful distinctions and questions with the solution, so far as Divine Providence shall assist me. And if any law is deserving of a review by reason of its fame, or difficulty, I shall reserve it for an afternoon review session.[17]

The available evidence suggests that teachers of canon law followed a style of lecturing that was nearly identical to this.[18] The art of analyzing a case by first dissecting its evident features and hounding its minutiae, and then seeking to specify an existing precedent in the light of this careful consideration, was to have a lasting influence on medieval moral practice, and would foster the importance of detailed discernment in later forms of casuistical reasoning.

The formal requirement that any student in the theological faculty must comment on the four books of *Sentences* by Peter Lombard afforded those thinkers

---

[15] See Richard Southern, *Scholastic Humanism and the Unification of Europe: Foundations* (Oxford: Blackwell, 1995) pp. 305–10, and Winroth, *Making of Gratian's Decretum*, pp. 9–11.
[16] For a discussion of Odofredus see Johann Friedrich von Schulte, *Geschichte der Quellen und Literatur des canonischen Rechts* (Stuttgart: Enke, 1875–80; repr. Graz: Akademische Druck, 1956) II: 232–33; and Friedrich Carl von Savigny, *Geschichte des römischen Rechts im Mittelalter* 2nd edn (Heidelberg: Mohr, 1834–51) III: 236–48, 393–9, V: 323–44.
[17] The text containing Odofredus's statement can be found in von Savigny, *Geschichte des römischen Rechts* III: 511 n. 29.
[18] See for instance Hostiensius, *Summa aurea* 5; *De magistris* sec. 6.

with a prior expertise in canon law an opportunity to consider a wide range of practical issues. Book IV of Lombard's great work of synthesis concerns the sacraments (baptism, penance, communion, confirmation, marriage, extreme unction, and holy orders),[19] a subject to which canon lawyers had much to contribute. In many thirteenth-century commentaries on Book IV, we find pertinent discussions of the sacraments that are not only informed by canon law, but also guided by a concern to make canonical precepts applicable to the needs of human life.[20]

By the fourteenth century, the study of canon law had established itself as one of the main disciplines in which substantive moral debates took place. This last claim can be illustrated by consulting the work of Peter of Palude, a Dominican friar of aristocratic birth who distinguished himself through his formidable prowess as a legal theorist. In the prologue to his *Sentences* commentary (3.5.1), he compares the value of canon law to theology with that of naval astronomy to pure astronomy. Unlike the divine science of theology, which is based on divine revelation, canon law – the product of human reason – is nevertheless a worthwhile ancillary subject in much the same way that naval astronomy is a practical application of pure astronomy.[21]

In his comments on Book IV, Peter goes on to discuss a wide range of moral subjects so as to prove his claim that canon law is a practically efficacious discipline. One such is his treatment of the rather daunting question of whether heretics should be "exterminated" (13.3 [ed. 1514, ff. 56v–57r]). For Peter, this is an issue that can be settled by canon law. He reaffirms the standard canonical doctrine that recidivist heretics are to be handed over to the secular authorities as soon as it is possible to do so, lest they continue to proselytize their heresy. If heretics are not caught actively preaching their "poison," they can nevertheless be convicted by the testimony of reliable witnesses or else by their own confessions. Significantly, Peter adds that confessions extracted through torture or fear of torture do not always inspire confidence or secure convictions, and should be avoided where possible. In addition, he was adamant that the punishment of any convicted heretic should always be commensurate with the gravity of their offense (ibid., f. 57r).

A further indication of the extent to which medieval moral thought was shaped by the methods of canon law can be illustrated by examining the notion

---

[19] For a detailed discussion of Lombard's position on the individual sacraments see Marcia Colish, *Peter Lombard* (Leiden: Brill, 1994) II: 517–697.

[20] See G. R. Evans (ed.) *Mediaeval Commentaries on the Sentences of Peter Lombard* (Leiden: Brill, 2002).

[21] Cited by Guiseppe Groppo, "La teologia e il suo 'subiectum' secundo il prologo del commento alle sentenze di Pietro de Palude, O.P. († 1342)," *Salesianum* 23 (1961) p. 261.

of *aequitas canonica*.[22] This idea was fashioned from two different sources by which the notion of equity had come down to medieval Europe: the doctrine of *aequitas* as it had been set out in the tradition of Roman law, and the Aristotelian virtue of *epieikeia* (equity or fairness), both of which were altered by coming into contact with the Christian concept of mercy (*misericordia*). The union of these ideas would provide later medieval writers with a coherent framework in which they could explain how and why the law should, in certain circumstances, be corrected due to its inherent deficiencies, and when it ought to pay heed to the requirements of natural justice and compassion.

A notable storehouse of canonical thinking on *aequitas* can be found in the thirteenth-century *Summa aurea* of Hostiensis. According to Hostiensis, justice must always be tempered by compassion and administered in a humane manner. While a judge is not free to alter at will statutory penalties clearly enacted by the law, he does have greater freedom where no such legal limitations exist, and in these cases, Hostiensis urges him always to observe equity and adopt the course that will prove to be more kindhearted in the circumstances.[23] Thus the judge should exercise compassion, even when he has to inflict punishment.[24] The need to temper justice with compassion is a theme that runs throughout the *Summa aurea*.[25]

The other main source from which medieval writers fashioned their notion of *aequitas canonica* was Aristotle's virtue of *epieikeia*, discussed in *Nicomachean Ethics* V.10 – a concept that they believed resembled *aequitas* in its stress on humaneness.[26] Robert Grosseteste, the first Latin translator of the *Nicomachean Ethics*, was foremost among those in the thirteenth century who appreciated the importance of Aristotle's concept of *epieikeia*, even to the extent of bringing it to the attention of the papal curia at Lyons in 1250.[27] Other important sources

---

[22] A detailed discussion of this concept, with full references to primary sources, can be found in Eugen Wohlhaupter, *Aequitas Canonica: eine studie aus dem kanonischen Recht* (Paderborn: Schöningh, 1931); Charles Lefebvre, *Les pouvoirs du juge en droit canonique* (Paris: Sirey, 1938); and Pio Fedele, "Aequitas Canonica," *Apollinaris* 51 (1978) 415–38.

[23] *Summa aurea* I; *De officio ordinarii*, n. 4.

[24] Compare Hostiensis, *In I–VI Decretalium libros commentaria* D. 45 c. 15.

[25] For further discussion of this point see Charles Lefebvre, "'Aequitas canonica' et 'periculum animae' dans la doctrine de l'Hostiensis," *Ephemerides Iuris Canonici* 8 (1952) 305–21.

[26] For more details on the concept of *epieikeia* see Charles Lefebvre, "Épikie," in R. Naz (ed.) *Dictionnaire du droit canonique* (Paris: Letouzey et Ané, 1935–65) V: 364–75; R. A. Coutre, "The Use of Epikeia in Natural Law: Its Early Developments," *Église et Théologie* 4 (1973) 71–93.

[27] See Richard Southern, *Robert Grosseteste: The Growth of an English Mind in Medieval Europe*, 2nd edn (Oxford: Clarendon Press, 1992) pp. 279–91; and Joseph Goering, "Robert Grosseteste at the Papal Curia," in J. Brown and W. Stoneman (eds.) *A Distinct Voice: Medieval Studies in Honor of Leonard E. Boyle O.P.* (Notre Dame, IN: University of Notre Dame Press, 1997) 253–76. See also S. Harrison Thomson, "The 'Notule' of Grosseteste on the Nicomachean Ethics," *Proceedings of the British Academy* 19 (1934) 3–26.

for thirteenth-century reflections about equity[28] include the work of Albert the Great and Thomas Aquinas.[29] For Thomas, equity or *aequitas* is both a formal mechanism that supplements and corrects the letter of the law (*correctio legis*), and a virtue that addresses the needs and circumstances of hard-pressed agents from the perspective of natural justice and compassion. Seen thus, *aequitas* is a *mitigatio juris*.[30]

PREACHING

In societies where large numbers of people were illiterate, sermons were an important means by which both laity and clergy received moral and spiritual instruction.[31] The duties of any priest included preaching, which meant not only exhorting those in his pastoral care to steady moral improvement but also involved instructing his charges in the rudimentary tenets of the Christian faith. At the parochial level this would often express itself in the preaching of catechetical formulas like the Creed, the seven works of Corporal Mercy, the Seven Sins, and behind them all, the Christian Scriptures. The significance of such preaching was recognized by all levels of the clergy: from the semi-literate priests who ministered to rural parishes to the intellectually capable friars and seculars who inhabited the universities, towns, and cities, preaching was understood as an indispensable part of the practice and promotion of the Christian religion.[32]

---

[28] For further discussion of the role of equity in thirteenth-century thought see Pier Giovanni Caron, "Aequitas romana, 'Misericordia' patristica e 'Epicheia' aristotelica nella dottrina decretalistica del Duecento e Trecento," *Studia Gratiana* 14 (1967) 309–47, and "Aequitas et interpretatio dans la doctrine canonique aux XIIIe et XIVe siècles," in S. Kuttner (ed.) *Proceedings of the Third International Congress of Medieval Canon Law* (Vatican: Biblioteca Apostolica Vaticana, 1971) 131–41. For a corrective to Caron's interpretation see my "Equity and Moderation: The Reception and Uses of Aristotle's Doctrine of *ΕΠΙΕΙΚΕΙΑ* in Thirteenth-Century Ethics," *Documenti e studi sulla tradizione filosofica medievale* 17 (2006) 121–56.

[29] For discussion of Albert's and Thomas's doctrine of equity see Stone, "Equity and Moderation," with references to other commentators.

[30] Thomas's moral views influenced a whole generation of canonists, such as Guido de Baysio, who used the Angelic Doctor's work in his *Rosarium super decreto*. See, e.g., Guido's use of *aequitas* (ad dist. 45 c. 9, as cited by Alphonse Van Hove, *Commentarium Lovaniense in codicem iuris canonici*, 2nd edn [Mechelen: Dessain, 1930] I.ii: 280 n. 2).

[31] The importance of preaching for the study of medieval life in general, and for medieval moral thought in particular, is clearly spelt out by John W. O'Malley, "Medieval Preaching," in T. L. Amos *et al.* (eds.) *De Ore Domini: Preacher and Word in the Middle Ages* (Kalamazoo, MI: Medieval Institute, 1989) 1–13.

[32] For a general history of preaching in the Christian tradition see Johannes Baptist Schneyer, *Geschichte der katholischen Predigt* (Freiburg: Seelsorge, 1969); Werner Schütz, *Geschichte der christliche Predigt* (Berlin: De Gruyter, 1972).

A work that advanced the case for popular preaching during this period was the *Ars praedicandi* of Alan of Lille.[33] He was of the view that preaching could be "most dangerous" (*periculosissimum*) if left to the auspices of an uneducated clergy, since such persons would not know what should be preached, nor to whom, nor how and when and where preaching should be done.[34] That is why ignorant clergy and their poorly educated flocks were in need of sound moral guidance. Alan compares the work of the preacher to Jacob's ladder.[35] There are seven steps one must follow to learn the art of preaching, the first three of which concern prayer. One begins with confession, advances to supplication, and ends in thanksgiving. That preaching is the fruit of prayer is to be observed in this remark:

> It is in turning away from sin that man ought first to put his foot on the ladder of confessing sin; then to ascend to the second rung of the ladder he prays to the Lord that grace be conferred on him, then to the third rung he continues by giving thanks for the grace that he has been given.
>
> (*Summa contra haereticos* [*Patr. Lat.* 210: 111])

The fourth rung of the ladder is an intensive study of the Scriptures. Such study is to be prayerful and yet genuinely critical. Problems of interpretation should be addressed, and one requires the fifth step – grace – to tackle such problems in a spirit of intellectual charity and openness. Grace is assuredly given, Alan thinks, for resolving those difficulties that are germane to any faithful analysis of Scripture. Divine grace finds further expression in the many guides to Scripture that the preacher can utilize in his studies. These aids include biblical commentaries, lexicons of different sorts, mathematical and etymological works, geographical treatises that explain the terrain of the Holy Land, and also works of the natural sciences that classify and explain the exotic plants and animals that are mentioned in the Scriptures.[36] The sixth rung in

---

[33] For a discussion of the *Ars praedicandi* and other related issues see Marie-Thérèse d'Alverny's introduction to Alan of Lille's *Textes inédits* (Paris: Vrin, 1965) pp. 109–19; Michel Zink, "La rhétorique honteuse et la convention du sermon *ad status* à travers la *summa de arte praedicatoria* d'Alan de Lille," in H. Roussel and F. Suard (eds.) *Alain de Lille, Gautier de Châtillon, Jakemart Giélée et leur temps* (Lille: Presses universitaires de Lille, 1978) 133–70; and G. R. Evans, *Alan of Lille: The Frontiers of Theology in the Later Twelfth Century* (Cambridge: Cambridge University Press, 1983) pp. 87–101.

[34] See *Summa contra haereticos* (*Patr. Lat.* 210: 379c–d).

[35] The biblical reference here is to Genesis 28:12ff. The motif of a ladder was commonly used by monastic authors as a way of detailing the incremental pursuit of spiritual perfection; see Benedict's *Regula monachorum* 7, and Hugh of St. Victor, *Didascalicon* V.9–10.

[36] For a short but synoptic portrait of his writings which contains an analysis of his scientific, theological and moral thought see Evans, *Alan of Lille*.

the homiletical ladder is the exposition of Scripture with the aid of others. Here Alan has in mind the specific activities and literature that were used in the formal study of Scripture in the schools of his day.[37] The last step is to preach openly to a congregation on the many subjects one has learned about from Scripture (ibid.).

The importance attached to popular preaching is further evident in several measures taken by the church in the last years of the twelfth and the early part of the thirteenth centuries. Pope Innocent III (1161–1216) employed carefully written sermons as a means of promoting his plans of reform,[38] and prominent *magistri* in the cathedral schools at Paris (such as Peter the Chanter,[39] Stephen Langton,[40] and Robert of Courson[41]) responded enthusiastically to the pope's call for moral improvement. These individuals were interested in the renewal of Christian teaching, and for this reason they attached great importance to popular preaching. The process begun by Innocent III and continued by the Parisian masters was consolidated at the Fourth Lateran Council (1215), whose tenth canon, *De praedicatoribus instituendis* (On Appointing Preachers), recognized the responsibility of every bishop to name priests suited to fulfill the important task of instructing the faithful by deed and word (*opere et sermone*).[42]

A further consequence of the Council was its establishment of both a close connection between preaching and confession and the role of preaching in the pastoral war against sin.[43] In this connection, it is important to understand that in medieval Latin *predicare* (preaching) was a broad term. While in the first instance it signified preaching and delivering sermons – which increased in number and status as the thirteenth century developed – it also conveyed, more generally,

---

[37] See Beryl Smalley, *The Study of the Bible in the Middle Ages*, 3rd edn (Oxford: Blackwell, 1983) pp. 196–263; and G. R. Evans, *The Language and Logic of the Bible: The Earlier Middle Ages* (Cambridge: Cambridge University Press, 1984) pp. 80–120.

[38] See Jane Sayers, *Innocent III: Leader of Europe, 1198–1216* (London: Longman, 1994) pp. 49–162, and Brenda Bolton, *Innocent III: Studies on Papal Authority and Pastoral Care* (Aldershot: Variorum, 1995) pp. 40–65.

[39] See John W. Baldwin, *Masters, Princes and Merchants: The Social Views of Peter the Chanter and his Circle* (Princeton, NJ: Princeton University Press, 1970) I: 107–17.

[40] See Phyllis B. Roberts, *Stephanus de Lingua Tonante: Studies on the Sermons of Stephen Langton* (Toronto: Pontifical Institute of Mediaeval Studies, 1968) pp. 30–87.

[41] See Marcel Dickson and Christiane Dickson, "Le Cardinal Robert de Courson, sa vie," *Archives d'histoire doctrinale et littéraire du moyen âge* 9 (1934) 53–142. Robert's *Summa theologica*, a work incomplete at his death, deals with a host of moral problems, among them usury.

[42] See Norman Tanner (ed.) *Decrees of the Ecumenical Councils* (London: Sheed and Ward, 1990) I: 239–40.

[43] On the connection between preaching and confession in the conciliar documents see Richard Rouse and Mary Rouse, *Preachers, Florilegia and Sermons: Studies on the "Manipulus florum" of Thomas of Ireland* (Toronto: Pontifical Institute of Medieval Studies, 1979) pp. 56–8.

teaching others how to live a Christian life, being a form of *catechesis* directly related to confessional practice.[44] In this way, preaching was the principal means used to move the laity (and indeed other priests) to contrition, and then to confession.[45] After the Fourth Lateran Council had required annual confession of all Christians, English diocesan statutes (to cite one example among countless others) established a clear connection between confession and preaching about sin in the vernacular. A statute from Worcester in 1240 states, for instance, that since "the Decalogue and fleeing the Seven Sins are necessary for salvation," they must assume an important role in confession, and they must be preached frequently to the people.[46]

The new orders of friars – Franciscans, Dominicans, Carmelites, and Augustinian Hermits – further assisted the cause of popular preaching and provided a more sophisticated penitential rationale. Their rapid growth and establishment in cities, towns, and universities throughout the first half of the thirteenth century may be seen as a continuation and extension of a theologically renewed church's mission to educate, encourage, and exhort its members. In the friars' hands, moreover, the production of sermons reached new levels of accomplishment.[47] To help the preacher perform his task, they produced a vast body of didactic literature, which includes not only theoretical treatises such as *Liber de eruditione praedicatorum* (1263) by the Dominican Humbert of Romans, but also technical works such as the *Forma praedicandi* (1322) by Robert of Basevorn and the *De modo componendi sermones* (*ca.* 1340) by the Dominican Thomas Waleys, which acted as detailed guides to sermon construction.[48]

---

[44] See Roy Martin Haines, *"Ecclesia Anglicana": Studies in the English Church of the Later Middle Ages* (Toronto: University of Toronto Press, 1989) pp. 135–7; Vincent Gillespie, *"Doctrina* and *Predicacio*: The Design and Function of Some Pastoral Manuals," *Leeds Studies in English* n.s. 11 (1980) pp. 40–6.

[45] See Lester Little, "Les techniques de la confession et la confession comme technique," in *Faire croire: modalités de la diffusion et de la réception des messages religieux du XIIe au XVe siècle* (Rome: École française de Rome, 1981) pp. 88–92.

[46] Roberto Rusconi, "De la prédication à la confession: transmission et contrôle de modèles de comportement au XIIIe siècle," in *Faire croire*, pp. 72–3.

[47] For discussion of all aspects of Franciscan and Dominican preaching see Anscar Zawart, *The History of Franciscan Preaching and of Franciscan Preachers (1290–1927): A Bio-bibliographical Study* (New York: Wagner, 1928); Bert Roest, *A History of Franciscan Education (c. 1210–1517)* (Leiden: Brill, 2000) pp. 272–324; H. C. Scheben, "Prediger und Generalprediger im Dominikanorden des 13. Jahrhunderts," *Archivum Fratrum Praedicatorum* 21 (1961) 112–41; Mary E. O'Carroll, *A Thirteenth-Century Preacher's Handbook: Studies in MS Laud misc. 511* (Toronto: Pontifical Institute of Medieval Studies, 1997) pp. 35–57; David d'Avray, *The Preaching of the Friars: Sermons Diffused from Paris before 1300* (Oxford: Clarendon Press, 1985).

[48] For a discussion of Robert's *Forma praedicandi* see Thomas-Marie Charland, *Artes praedicandi: contribution à l'histoire de la rhétorique au moyen âge* (Paris: Vrin, 1936) pp. 9–12, 73–81, 110–28, 132–54, 167–78, and 211–30. The work of Thomas Waleys is discussed by Beryl Smalley, *The English Friars and Antiquity in the Early XIVth Century* (Oxford: Blackwell, 1960) pp. 75–108.

Specific sermons were also written for specific groups of people. Known as *ad status* homilies, these were directed to the particular pastoral needs of different social groups in medieval society, ranging from merchants, artisans, and clerical students to knights and kings.[49]

The moral ideas of three well-known late medieval preachers and moralists – John Gerson,[50] the Franciscan Bernardino of Siena,[51] and the Dominican Antoninus of Florence[52] – provide constructive examples of the connection between medieval moral thought and preaching. What is initially striking about their work is the way in which they used the established techniques of popular preaching to persuade their varied audiences of the need to bring about the moral amelioration of their lives. In the course of encouraging small and large congregations to higher things, these preachers also expended considerable effort on understanding the challenges presented to Christian morals by cases of conscience (*casus conscientiae*) or moral dilemmas. The moral thought of Gerson, Bernardino, and Antoninus is irreducibly practical;[53] in their work, any systematic or more speculative reflection on the problems and issues of human life is always indexed to an overriding concern to guide and change moral behavior. Hence the importance of preaching: through its office, the pastor could offer concrete guidance to individuals in their daily lives. For Gerson, Bernardino, and Antoninus, the preacher's words, whether they be in Latin or in the vernacular, were never abstract formulas that were then to be applied to hypothetical cases. Rather, the preacher's utterances were based upon a sure

---

[49] On this see Odd Langholm, *The Merchant in the Confessional: Trade and Price in Pre-Reformation Penitential Handbooks* (Leiden: Brill, 2003).

[50] On Gerson's moral thought see Brian Patrick McGuire, *Jean Gerson and the Last Medieval Reformation* (University Park, PA: Pennsylvania State University Press, 2005); and D. Catherine Brown, *Pastor and Laity in the Theology of Jean Gerson* (Cambridge: Cambridge University Press, 1987). On his preaching see Louis Mourin, *Jean Gerson prédicateur français* (Bruges: De Tempel, 1952).

[51] For detailed analysis of Bernardino's preaching, see Paul Thureau-Dangin, *Un prédicateur populaire dans l'Italie de la Renaissance: Saint Bernardin de Sienne, 1380–1444* (Paris: Bloud et Gay, 1926); Loman McAodha, "The Nature and Efficacy of Preaching According to St. Bernandine of Siena," *Franciscan Studies* 27 (1967) 221–247; Renzo Lo Cascio, "La predica del predicare di San Bernardino," in F. d'Episcopo (ed.) *San Bernardino da Siena predicatore e pellegrino* (Galatinna: Congedo, 1985) 63–73; Franco Mormando, *The Preacher's Demons: Bernardino of Siena and the Social Underworld of Early Renaissance Italy* (Chicago: University of Chicago Press, 1999).

[52] For a helpful discussion of Antoninus's thoughts on preaching and their general relation to his moral thought, see Stefano Orlandi, *Antonino, arcivescovo di Firenze, dottore della chiesa: studi* (Florence: Il Rosario, 1959); and Peter F. Howard, *Beyond the Written Word: Preaching and Theology in the Florence of Archbishop Antoninus 1427–1459* (Florence: Olschki, 1995).

[53] This is so even in the case of Gerson who is an advocate of so-called "mystical theology": see my " '*Initium omnis peccati est superbia*': Jean Gerson's Account of Pride in his Mystical Theology, Pastoral Thought, and Hamartiology," in R. Newhauser (ed.) *In the Garden of Evil: The Vices and their Culture in the Middle Ages* (Toronto: Pontifical Institute of Mediaeval Studies, 2005) 293–323.

knowledge of the actual circumstances in which men and women lived out their moral lives. In many respects, their work provides a window on late medieval pastoral thought in action.[54]

VIRTUE, DEADLY SINS, AND CONFESSION

The plural sources from which medieval ethicists drew their ideas about virtue can also be said to have conditioned their approach to practical questions. When classical moral philosophy was revived in the twelfth century, the texts of Cicero helped to disseminate certain Stoic ideas, while the writings of Macrobius (*fl.* 395–423) made Neoplatonic notions distilled from Plotinus available to a new generation of ethicists.[55] Although these authors were known in the Latin West, their works had been largely ignored by earlier generations of moral theologians, who tended to look for pastoral guidance to monastic writers such as Gregory the Great (*ca.* 540–604) and John Cassian (360–435), or else to Augustine. This, however, was to change. With the inclusion of a more extensive repertoire of ancient sources, which from the mid-thirteenth century onwards included not only the ethics of Aristotle but also a deeper understanding of the Stoics, medieval moralists had before them a wider set of ideas about virtue with which to tackle a host of pressing moral problems.[56]

Alongside virtue, medieval thinkers mused at great length on sin and vice. The seven deadly sins of pride (*superbia*), avarice (*avaritia*), lust (*luxuria*), anger (*ira*), gluttony (*gula*), envy (*invidia*), and sloth (*acedia*) provided a general matrix for the moral assessment of acts and character. When combined with detailed theological schemes for the classification of sins,[57] the topics of vice and virtue played a vital component in medieval pastoral thought and literary culture.[58] Loosely corresponding to the order of the seven "bad thoughts" originally

---

[54] See specifically John Gerson, *Œuvres complètes* VII: 399, 482; VIII: 10–12, 73; IX: 70; X: 314–15. For Bernardino see the *Opera omnia* I: 178, 206; II: 188–293; V: 68–170, as well as the vernacular sermons *Le prediche volgari (Firenze 1424)* (*Opera* II: 282–311); and Antoninus of Florence, *Summa theol.* III.18.3 par. 2 (ed. 1740, col. 1018a), par. 3 (col. 1018b–c), par. 1 (col. 1014c).

[55] On this revival see István Bejczy and Richard Newhauser (eds.) *Virtue and Ethics in the Twelfth Century* (Leiden: Brill, 2005).

[56] See Lottin, *Psychologie et morale* IV.2, and Bonnie Kent, *The Virtues of the Will: The Transformation of Ethics in the Late Thirteenth Century* (Washington, DC: Catholic University of America Press, 1995).

[57] See for instance, Thomas Aquinas, *Sent.* Bk. II, dist. 35–7, 39, 41–3; *Summa contra gentiles* III.9; *Summa theol.* 1a2ae qq. 72 and 81.1; and John Duns Scotus, *Ordinatio* Bk. II, dist. 37–40 and Bk. IV, dist. 15 q. 1 n. 12, and *Quodlibet* 18 nn. 1–12. For other texts and commentary see Lottin, *Psychologie et morale* IV.1.

[58] See Carla Casagrande and Silvana Vecchio, *I sette vizi capitali: storia dei peccati nel medioevo* (Turin: Einaudi, 2000).

set down by Evagrias of Pontus (346–99), the seven deadly sins were first systematized in the West by monastic writers such as John Cassian and Gregory the Great.[59] By the fourteenth century, the teaching on these seven capital vices had become widespread in Latin Christendom. Although the list of seven sins had definite limitations and was later displaced by the Decalogue as the most authoritative scheme of moral taxonomy,[60] the astonishing resilience of this series of moral entities was such that it enjoyed a high profile in medieval literary culture[61] and was further responsible for a genre of didactic treatises that aimed to explain the causes and origin of each vice and its remedy in virtue. Due to the profusion of these works,[62] the German Dominican Henry Suso was moved to remark sometime between 1331 and 1334 that "there are so many books that treat the vices and virtues . . . that this short life would come to an end before one could study all of them" (*Horologium sapientiae* II.3, ed. Künzle, pp. 540–1).

One notable work in this genre was the mid-thirteenth century *Summa de vitiis et virtutibus* of William Peraldus, a book that enjoyed considerable influence due to its use and promotion by Peraldus's fellow Dominicans.[63] Its subject matter particularly commended it to confessors, since its stated aim was the identification of sin and the exhortation of virtue. The moral tract further suggested themes for sermons, and it offered *exempla* that the preacher could use to illustrate various moral points. There are over two

[59] For discussions of the history and development of the seven deadly sins see Morton W. Bloomfield, *The Seven Deadly Sins: An Introduction to the History of a Religious Concept* (East Lansing: Michigan State College Press, 1952) pp. 69–104; Rosamond Tuve, "Notes on Virtues and Vices," *Journal of the Warburg and Courtauld Institutes* 26 (1963) 264–303; 27 (1964) 42–72; Siegfried Wenzel, "The Seven Deadly Sins: Some Problems of Research," *Speculum* 43 (1968) 1–22; Aimé Solignac, "Péchés capitaux," in M. Viller *et al.* (eds.) *Dictionnaire de spiritualité* (Paris: Beauchesne, 1937–95) XII.1: 853–62; Richard Newhauser, *The Treatise on Vices and Virtues in Latin and the Vernacular* (Turnhout: Brepols, 1993) pp. 97–152; Newhauser, *The Early History of Greed: The Sin of Avarice in Early Medieval Thought and Literature* (Cambridge: Cambridge University Press, 2000); Newhauser (ed.) *In the Garden of Evil*; and Newhauser (ed.) *The Seven Deadly Sins: From Communities to Individuals* (Leiden: Brill, 2007).
[60] Carla Casagrande and Silvana Vecchio, "La classificazione dei peccati tra settenario e decalogo (secoli XIII–XV)," *Documenti e studi sulla tradizione filosofica medievale* 5 (1994) 331–95; and John Bossy, "Moral Arithmetic: Seven Sins into Ten Commandments," in E. Leites (ed.) *Conscience and Casuistry in Early Modern Europe* (Cambridge: Cambridge University Press, 1988) 214–34.
[61] Newhauser, *In the Garden of Evil*, pp. vii–x.
[62] See Richard Newhauser and István Bejczy, *Towards a Revised Incipitarium: Corrections, Supplements, Deletions, and Additions to Update Morton Bloomfield et al., Incipits of Latin Works on the Virtues and Vices* (Turnhout: Brepols, 2007).
[63] See Antoine Dondaine, "Guillaume Peyraut, vie et œuvres," *Archivum Fratrum Praedicatorum* 18 (1948) 162–236, and Siegfried Wenzel, "The Continuing Life of William Peraldus's *Summa vitiorum*," in M. D. Jordan and K. Emery (eds.) *Ad Litteram: Authoritative Texts and Medieval Readers* (Notre Dame, IN: University of Notre Dame Press, 1992) 135–64.

hundred *exempla* in the *Summa de vitiis et virtutibus*,[64] supplemented with long lists of *auctoritates* and stock arguments that preachers could also employ in their sermons.

The ultimate remedy for vice was the sacrament of confession, which up to the end of the twelfth century was widely administered in the form of private confession by a priest to a penitent.[65] This practice was fully standardized in the Western church when Innocent III convoked the Fourth Lateran Council in 1215. As mentioned above, one of the famous decrees of this council, *Omnis utriusque sexus fidelis* ("All the faithful of either sex"), declared that every Christian was required to go to confession once a year. As a result of this injunction the clergy, who at this time were not educated to a uniform standard, were in need of instruction as to how to hear confessions responsibly, given that they had to assign particular penances to the various *casus* presented to them by their penitents. In order to meet this pastoral need, a new mode of writing was developed, and the books that eventually emanated from this genre were known as *Summe confessorum* or confessional manuals.[66]

Such penitential writing was a distinctive part of medieval literary culture, encompassing academic tracts as well as works of popular devotion written in vernacular languages. At their least distinguished, the *summe confessorum* that poured forth from the universities and religious houses imposed nothing more than a tariff on human failing by assigning particular penances to particular sins; at their best they provided concrete yet sagacious instruction to individual priests in the hearing of confessions, in accordance with the guidelines set out by the Fourth Lateran Council. These guidelines, which can be found in the second part of *Omnis utriusque sexus fidelis* require that:

the priest be discerning and prudent (*discretus et cautus*), so that like a skilled doctor he can apply wine and oil [cf. Luke 10:34] to the wounds of an injured person, diligently inquiring about the circumstances of the sinner and the sin, through which he can

---

[64] On the *exempla* see Jean Thiébaut Welter, *L'exemplum dans la littérature religieuse et didactique du moyen âge* (Paris: Occitania, 1927) p. 165, and Jacques Berlioz and Marie Anne Polo de Beaulieu, *Les exempla médiévaux: nouvelles perspectives* (Paris: Champion, 1998).

[65] Alexander Murray, "Confession before 1215," *Transactions of the Royal Historical Society*, 6th series, 3 (1993) 51–81. See also Henry Charles Lea, *A History of Auricular Confession and Indulgences in the Latin Church* (London: Swan Sonnenschein, 1896); Jean Delumeau, *L'aveu et le pardon: les difficultés de la confession xiiie–xviiie siècle* (Paris: Fayard, 1990); and Peter Biller and A. J. Minnis, *Handling Sin: Confession in the Middle Ages* (Woodbridge [Suffolk]: York Medieval Press, 1998).

[66] An extensive history of the *Summe confessorum* is related in the classic series of studies by Johann Dietterle, "Die *Summae confessorum (sive de casibus conscientiae)* von inhren Anfängen an bis zu Silvester Prierias (unter besonderer Berücksichtigung über den Ablass)," *Zeitschrift für Kirchengeschichte* 24 (1903) 353–74, 520–48; 25 (1904) 248–72; 26 (1905) 59–81, 350–62; 27 (1906) 70–83, 166–88; 296–310, 431–42; 28 (1907) 401–31. A more recent account of this genre of writing can be found in Boyle, "*Summae confessorum.*"

prudently understand what counsel he ought to give, and what sort of remedy to apply, trying various things to heal the sick person.[67]

The analogy of priest as physician of the body was an ancient one.[68] It had been applied to Christ by the early Fathers of the church,[69] and the images of both doctor and the healing powers of medicine were commonplace in the early penitentials.[70] By using this image, the Fathers of the Fourth Lateran Council never had it in mind to institute the sacrament of penance as a verdictive instrument for the chastisement of individual sinners, but rather intended that penance would "heal" or "cleanse away" the defects or impediments in an individual's soul that had been brought about by the deleterious influence of sin. As medieval thinkers understood it, penance was a necessary remedy for moral turpitude, a "cure" that had been granted to fallen individuals by the benign and compassionate offices of a loving deity.

An important influence on the *Omnis utriusque sexus fidelis* were theological developments that had taken place in the schools of northern France in the twelfth century. In the writings of Peter Abaelard[71] and Peter Lombard,[72] close attention was paid to the relative importance of various parts of penance, in particular an interior act of contrition.[73] A circle of talented theologians in late twelfth-century Paris extended the purview of these theological discussions of penance in two significant ways. First, they advocated that the actual rite of confession, that is, of confessing one's sins to an appropriately qualified priest,

---

[67] Tanner, *Decrees of the Ecumenical Councils*, I: 245.

[68] For a very full discussion of this idea see Jean-Claude Larchet, *Thérapeutique des maladies spirituelles: une introduction à la tradition ascétique de l'Eglise orthodoxe* (Paris: Cerf, 1997).

[69] For a discussion of this concept in relation to the work of the Fathers see Rudolph Arbesmann, "The Concept of '*Christus medicus*' in St. Augustine," *Traditio* 10 (1954) 1–28.

[70] John T. McNeill, "Medicine for Sin as Prescribed in the Penitentials," *Church History* 1 (1932) 14–26.

[71] On inner acts in Abaelard's ethics, see Chapter 37. For general studies of Abaelard's views on penance see Polykarp Schmoll, *Die Busslehre der Frühscholastik: Eine dogmengeschichte Untersuchung* (Munich: Lentner, 1909) pp. 28–35; Amédée de Zedelghem, "L'attritionisme d'Abélard," *Estudis Franciscans* 35 (1925) 178–84; 333–45; J. G. Sikes, *Peter Abailard* (Cambridge: Cambridge University Press, 1932) pp. 196–200; and Paul Anciaux, *La théologie du sacrament de pénitence au XIIe siècle* (Louvain: Nauwelaerts, 1949) pp. 64–70, 165–75, and 286–94.

[72] Peter's views on penance are discussed by Schmoll in *Die Busslehre der Frühscholastik*, pp. 67–74; Joseph Spitzig, *Sacramental Penance in the Twelfth and Thirteenth Centuries* (Washington: Catholic University of America Press, 1947) pp. 67–85; Anciaux, *La théologie du sacrament de pénitence*, pp. 223–31, 329–35; and Colish, *Peter Lombard*, II: 583–608.

[73] For a helpful discussion of the development of this view see Baldwin, *Masters, Princes and Merchants*, I: 50–110. A more recent study of this issue can be found in Jean Charles Payen, "La penitence dans le contexte culturel des XIIe et XIIIe siècles: des doctrines contritionnistes aux pénitentiels vernaculaires," *Revue des sciences philosophiques et théologiques* 61 (1977) 399–428. For further discussion of 'contritionism' see Joseph Goering, "The Internal Forum and the Literature of Penance and Confession," *Traditio* 59 (2004) 175–227.

was just as important as the inner act of contrition; second, they argued for the importance of an understanding of the "circumstances" of sin and the sinner in any account of penance.[74] Among these theologians, Peter the Chanter's *Summa de sacramentis et animae consiliis (ca.* 1191) brought a circumstantial awareness to bear on a number of moral issues that would have been presented to any medieval confessor: theft, simony, incest, usury, vows, and oaths. Other authors who wrote *Summe confessorum* were Alan of Lille, whose *Liber penitentialis* was written around 1200; Robert of Flamborough, who composed his *Liber penitentialis* sometime between 1208 and 1213; Peter of Poitiers, who wrote the *Summa de confessione*; Thomas of Chobham, whose *Summa confessorum* was written around or just after 1216; and William of Auvergne, who wrote two works on penance: the *Tractatus novus de penitentia*, and a much longer discussion that forms part of his treatise on the seven sacraments, *De sacramentis.*[75]

From the mid-thirteenth century onwards, the writings of the friars helped to develop the *summe confessorum* even further. Among the Dominicans, Raymond of Pennafort wrote the widely admired *Summa de paenitentia* (sometimes referred to as the *Raymundina*) (*ca.* 1221). One of the interesting features of the writings of the Dominicans was the extent to which their efforts in academic theology informed their penitential outlook, especially with regard to the study of thorny cases of conscience, many of which were broached in the *quodlibeta* of late thirteenth-century Paris. For example, the early *quodlibeta* of Thomas Aquinas (1256/9)[76] abound with problems that arise from the vicissitudes of priestly life or else attend the hearing of confessions.[77] Many of the pastoral views expressed by Thomas would prove influential for later manualists. John of Freiburg, for instance, copied and adapted a large part of Thomas's moral thought into his *Summa confessorum* of 1298. Parisian moral theology from the second half of the thirteenth century was further circulated either directly, through the large

---

[74] See D. W. Robertson, "A Note on the Classical Origins of 'Circumstances' in the Medieval Confessional," *Studies in Philology* 43 (1946) 6–14.

[75] Both these treatises are edited in William's 1674 *Opera omnia.* For a general discussion of William and all the other writers listed above see Josef G. Ziegler, *Die Ehelehre der Pönitentialsummen von 1200–1350* (Regensburg: Pustet, 1956); Spitzig, *Sacramental Penance*, pp. 38–106; Alfred Vanneste, "La théologie de la pénitence chez quelques maîtres parisiens de la première moitié du xiiie siècle," *Ephemerides Theologicae Lovanienses* 28 (1952) 24–58; Pierre Michaud-Quantin, "A propos des premières *summae confessorum*," *Recherches de théologie ancienne et médiévale* 26 (1959) 264–306; Herbert Vorgrimler, *Busse und Krankensalbung (Handbuch der Dogmengeschichte* IV.3) (Freiburg: Herder, 1978) pp. 114–53; Pierre Adnès, "Pénitence," in Viller *et al.*, *Dictionnaire de spiritualité* XII.1: sec. 5.

[76] See Kevin White, "The Quodlibeta of Thomas Aquinas in the Context of his Work," in Schabel, *Theological Quodlibeta*, I: 49–134.

[77] See Leonard Boyle, "The *Quodlibets* of St. Thomas and Pastoral Care," *Thomist* 38 (1974) 232–56; reprinted in Boyle, *Pastoral Care*.

numbers of copies of John's *Summa confessorum* that found their way to most parts of medieval Europe, or else indirectly, through the various works that plundered John's *Summa* for its quotations of Parisian theologians.[78]

The central place of confession in Franciscan pastoral care explains that order's contribution to the production of confessional manuals, both to teach their own incumbent preachers and to supply the secular clergy with additional materials. Several of these confessional manuals – such as the *Summa de casibus conscientiae* (*ca.* 1317) (sometimes known as the *Astesana*) by Astesanus of Asti and the *Summa confessorum* by John of Erfurt – found their way all over Europe. Other important Franciscan authors who wrote manuals were John Rigaud, John of Wales, Marchesinus de Reggio, Nicholas Byard, and Servasanto of Faenza.

No discussion of the confessional literature of the later Middle Ages would be complete without consideration of the work of John Gerson. Despite his wide intellectual interests and the prominent role he played in public life as chancellor of the University of Paris, Gerson saw himself as above all a working pastor, and his overt concern for the spiritual welfare of his flock lies at the heart of his writing and other public activities. Even his university lectures reveal a preoccupation and concern for the spiritual and moral plight of *les simples gens*. Gerson was also a very popular preacher, both in court circles and in parish churches in and around Paris.[79] Among his works on confession, the so-called *Opus tripartitum* or *Doctrinale* was certainly the most influential and remarkable. Its three parts – an exposition of the Ten Commandments (*Le livre des dix commandements*), a treatise on confession (*L'examen de conscience*), and a preparation for death (*La science de bien morir*) – were all written separately, but they were soon put together to make a book that was celebrated throughout late medieval Europe.

Gerson also developed various techniques to aid the confessor in extracting a complete and candid confession from the penitent. These are explained in his treatise *De arte audiendi confessiones*.[80] The confessor, he writes, should be affable at first to gain the confidence of the penitent and impress upon him or her the necessity of hiding nothing. If he suspects anyone of duplicity he should give

---

[78] See Leonard Boyle, "The *Summa confessorum* of John of Freiburg and the Popularization of the Moral Teaching of St. Thomas and Some of his Contemporaries," in A. Maurer (ed.) *St. Thomas Aquinas, 1274–1974: Commemorative Studies* (Toronto: Pontifical Institute of Mediaeval Studies, 1974) II: 245–68; reprinted in Boyle, *Pastoral Care.*

[79] On Gerson's status as a preacher see McGuire, *Jean Gerson*, pp. 184, 308; and Gilbert Ouy, "Discovering Gerson the Humanist: Fifty Years of Serendipity," in B. P. McGuire (ed.) *A Companion to Jean Gerson* (Leiden: Brill, 2006) 79–132.

[80] A good discussion of this work and its relationship to Gerson's general views on penance can be found in Brown, *Pastor and Laity*, pp. 56–72 and McGuire, *Jean Gerson*, pp. 172–7.

the impression that he thinks it is being done out of inadvertence rather than with prior intention, so that a confrontational atmosphere is not created. It is advisable, Gerson thinks, for the confessor to begin by asking questions about sins which almost all people commit and which are therefore easy to admit. From there he should move on to rarer and more serious sins. Throughout the whole process, the penitent must not feel that the confessor is disposed to think badly of him. Gerson is adamant that the experience of confession must be an affirming religious ritual that will reconcile the penitent to the ways of God and the requirements of probity. Gerson's *De arte audiendi confessiones*, like so many of its thirteenth-century predecessors, is marked by a sensitivity and gentleness, as well as an urbane psychological acumen, that manifests the very best features of the *summe confessorum*.

Another giant of late medieval penitential thought was Antoninus of Florence. One of his manuals to enjoy great popularity was the *Confessionale defecerunt*, first published in 1472. Even more influential was the *Summa theologica*, which went through no fewer than twenty complete editions in four large folio volumes. This work might more properly be thought of as *Summa moralis* rather than a *Summa confessorum*: its opening part treats the soul and its faculties, the passions, sin and law; the second and third deal with the different states and professions of life (social, ecclesiastical, and religious), together with a treatise on the pope, councils, and censures. The fourth part of the work is devoted to the cardinal and theological virtues. Antoninus's *Summa* is among the first of the manuals to treat all the matters that relate to the spiritual and moral life from a purely practical point of view. The work contains many insights and reflections that would now belong within the purview of the social sciences, and reveals its author to be one of the foremost ethicists of his age.[81]

Medieval thinkers like Gerson and Antoninus – who so fervently pursued the art of moral exhortation, aimed to diagnose the extent and ill-effects of human sinfulness, and proposed practicable resolutions to the recalcitrant quandaries of conscience – were concerned foremost with the care and salvation of souls. Such a pastoral commitment expressed itself in a distinctive outlook on moral practice which, while not wholly 'philosophical,' was characterized nevertheless by a casuistical sensitivity to the circumstances in which a person acts, the dispositions of that agent, and the kinds of precepts that ought or ought not to ground action. By means of the assorted methods of canon law, the art of preaching, reflection on vice and virtue, and the *summe confessorum*, medieval thinkers constructed

---

[81] For one of the very few studies on Antoninus's moral thought see William Gaughan, *The Social Theories of Saint Antoninus from the Summa Theologica* (Washington, DC: Catholic University of America Press, 1951).

for themselves a complex description and analysis of the causes, nature, and circumstances of practical conduct that proved indispensable to the guidance of souls (*regimen animarum*). Since the path to salvation was thought to be facilitated by humane and holy guidance, medieval ethicists embraced the challenge to make moral inquiry responsive to a clear and detailed understanding of the foibles, exigencies, and vicissitudes of human life.